And Nothing is Said

Wartime Letters,
August 5, 1943-April 21, 1945

And Nothing is Said

Wartime Letters,
August 5, 1943-April 21, 1945

by
Michael N. Ingrisano, Jr.

SUNFLOWER UNIVERSITY PRESS

1531 Yuma • P.O. Box 1009 • Manhattan, Kansas 66505-1009 USA

Printed in the United States of America on acid-free paper.

ISBN 0-89745-263-1

Sunflower University Press is a wholly-owned subsidiary
of the non-profit 501(c)3 Journal of the West, Inc.

To Bettyjeane Louise Hill Ingrisano,
whose unselfish love guided me through
the hell of combat,
the struggles for an education and economic survival,
the joys of an unblemished marriage, and
the sorrows of an untimely death.
Where all was said and remembered in
"I love you!"

Michael N. Ingrisano, Jr.
McLean, Virginia
May 2002

Contents

Introduction

$\mathcal{T}$HE TITLE FOR these wartime letters is derived from a Valentine card given to me on February 14, 1985, by my wife, Bettyjeane Louise Hill Ingrisano. "It is that moment of exquisite tenderness between two people when everything is felt and understood, *and nothing is said* . . . I love you!"

Bette died from cancer five months later on July 9, 1985.

Soon after her death, after more than 40 years of marriage, among other memorials, I found the letters that I had written to Bette shortly after I left for overseas duty — as a radio operator in the 37th Troop Carrier Squadron — until I returned home 21 months later. I also found the bouquet of flowers which she had carried on our wedding day, May 30, 1945. The flowers had lost their aroma, but the memories lingered.

Although nothing could be said, everything that had to be said is in almost 350 letters I had written from August 5, 1943, to April 21, 1945.

I did not realize that Bette had saved every letter. Unfortunately, I had none of hers because the first batch had floated out of my tent in Borizzo, Sicily, during a raging storm. The rest of her writings, which fed my hunger for conversation through Sicily and England from February 1944 to May 1945, had to be discarded because of the limitation on weight when we prepared to go home. Although I was with the United States Army Air Forces, I had flown in my plane for its last flight in April 1945, when we left our aircraft for the next users. We came home aboard a Liberty ship, the USS *General J. R. Brooke.*

The first letter, dated August 5, 1943, was written somewhere between Baer Field in Fort Wayne, Indiana, and probably Goose Bay, Labrador. The last letter was written on April 21, 1945, from my bunk at Cottesmore Royal Air Force Base, England.

I make no apology for the grammatical clumsiness of my writings, and have done little editing, except where the errors are so glaring that they are embarrassing to read. The contents, however, are reflective of the times, the places, and the circumstances that drove me to survive. All is not said in these letters. That was impossible, given the strict censorship and security imposed upon us because of the "ears of the enemy." But not much is left unsaid in regard to our personal relationships, or my personal experiences when after-action trauma set in from the fear felt in combat, or the emptiness of loneliness, or of the impatience with the men, the times, and the frequent lapses in mail that separated us and wasted some of our most cherished years.

Yet who were we? Certainly no different from the millions of men and women who lived through the same experiences from the 1920s to the 1940s. Some of us were from immigrant parents, and many were lucky to get high school educations because the Depression forced us into the labor market at a time when it was more important to eat than to think. Then as we assumed fairly stable existences, and were feeling self-satisfied with our lives, we were thrown into the maelstrom that became World War II. And I do believe that Bette and I were typical of that generation.

So we left our homes. Mine was in Brooklyn, New York, where I was born to Italian immigrants in March 1921. Bette was born in St. George, Kansas, in March 1922. Her parentage was mixed — part immigrant, part American stock — but tillers of the soil. Our experiences, though, were somewhat similar. She managed to get a year of college in Kansas City, Missouri, before having to go to work. I finished high school and worked until I enlisted in September 1942.

After basic training in Miami, Florida, and radio/mechanic training in Chicago, Illinois, I was sent to the 72nd Troop Carrier Squadron stationed in Alliance, Nebraska. As part of the new cadre, I found no planes and little else but menial duties. Fortunately, I was sent to Kansas City for advanced radio training conducted by TWA (TransWorld Airlines).

Like the song says, "I left my heart at the stage door canteen." Not really. But one Saturday night, I was on my way to the Playmor ballroom where one of the big bands of the era was playing (I believe it was Glen Gray and his Casa Loma Orchestra). I never made it. I first stopped at the USO, which was nearby. There I saw this lovely person dancing with a GI who was a foot shorter than she. I had no choice but to put her out of her misery. I cut in. That was in March 1943.

When duty would permit, Bette and I saw each other more than frequently. Then I had to return to Alliance in June. By then, the 72nd Troop Carrier Squadron had planes, and I was assigned as a flight crew member. I earned my wings, and my stateside experience. One of my favorite pilots was ordered to go overseas, and he asked me to join his crew as radio operator. I agreed. We were sent to Baer Field in Fort Wayne, Indiana, to pick up a new aircraft and the remainder of a crew. The highlight of my stay at Baer Field was Bette's visit. We spent five days together. I left for overseas duty on August 3, 1943. We would not see each other again for 21 months.

My first intention was to use our correspondence as a base for a history of my unit, the 316th Troop Carrier Group. But as I researched that history, I found that those records would provide substance to some of my letters, enabling me to match my writings with the facts of troop carrier life. Therefore, I reversed fields and wrote a group history, adding those letters that fit into specific events or time periods. That combination resulted in the book entitled *Valor Without Arms: A History of the 316th Troop Carrier Group, 1942-1945* (Bennington, VT: Merriam Press, 2001).

To bridge the gaps between that history and the letters, I have used excerpts from the War Diaries of my squadron, the 37th Troop Carrier Squadron, the 316th Troop Carrier Group, and the 52nd Troop Carrier Wing, our parent organization. The War Diaries did not become standard reporting procedure until October 1943, however. Therefore, many of my letters from August to October 1943 are lacking that operational information. But I have added explanatory comments, where necessary.

So that is what these letters are all about, two people separated for 21 months by thousands of miles. It's all here — the joys, the sorrows, the fears, the frustrations, the loneliness, the companionship, the emptiness, the love, and the fulfillment.

Chapter 1

Middle East-North Africa
(August 5 to November 29, 1943)

TWO YEARS AFTER Nazi Germany signed an August 1939 non-aggression pact with Russia — then attacked Poland that September, starting World War II — Imperial Japan bombed Pearl Harbor on December 7, 1941, drawing the United States into the war against Japan, Nazi Germany, and Fascist Italy (the Axis).

Most Americans were vaguely aware of the German aggression against Belgium, Holland, and Northern France, the bombings of England proper and the Axis invasion of Russia in June 1941. They may have also been aware of the Japanese invasion of Indochina (September 1940), Thailand (December 1941), and of the Philippines, Hong Kong, and Malaysia on the same day that Japan bombed Pearl Harbor. But "Remember Pearl Harbor" remains imbedded in the memories of those who lived during this period.

I was on a date with a young lady friend. We were going to a matinee in Radio City Music Hall in New York. While waiting for her to complete dressing, I was listening to a pro football game when the announcement came over the wire. President Franklin D. Roosevelt's "Day of Infamy" was followed with a declaration of war on December 8 against the Axis.

In June 1942, the U.S. defeated the Japanese in the Battle of Midway, and then followed with the island campaigns in the Pacific (Guadalcanal and New Guinea), August 1942 to January 1943.

In November 1942, the Allies invaded North Africa (OPERATION TORCH); Axis resistance ended in May 1943. U.S. and British troop carrier aircraft dropped and towed American and British airborne and glider forces in the invasion of Sicily (OPERATION HUSKY) July 9-11, 1943. Twenty-three of the U.S. aircraft were downed by "friendly fire." Italy surrendered September 8, 1943, but German forces in Italy resisted the Allied advance. The Allies invaded Italy (AIRBORNE OPERATIONS GIANT) when the U.S. 5th Army landed at Salerno September 9, and took Naples October 1, but the Germans seized Rome and other Italian cities.

August 5, 1943 [*Thursday*]
[*En route Middle East-North Africa*]

Dearest Bette,

It seems strange to be sitting where I am and realize that only a short while ago you were in my arms. To satisfy your concern the only thing that I can say is that I am healthy and extremely happy.

We finally decided on a name of our ship. It is "Jippa." It is the first letter of each of our last names. J. Johnson (Crew Chief), I. Ingrisano (?), P. Pappaeliou (Navigator), P. Parker (Co-Pilot), A. Agle (Pilot). Rather original, isn't it? I had to paint the name on the ship and under each position I put nicknames, "Pappy," "Ace," "Nick," "Ax," & "Mike." I may not be Rembrandt but it will suffice until someone tries to do better. "Jippa" is quite a gal, she has had some bad luck but she has been up to it.

The whole crew has gotten crew cuts and Gad, we look like the Georgia road gang. Not to mention the mustaches that each of us is growing and later perhaps the beards.

It has been strange not to receive your daily letters. When they do catch up to me, I shall spend endless hours reading and rereading every word. I was looking through my clothes and I found a handkerchief that had some of your lipstick on it. It's funny how those little things can induce so many memories. Your pictures are a great comfort to me. God! You are a lovely creature.

Well, Darling, I cannot write much more. I'll try to keep you well-informed, Don't worry about me. I'll be OK. Are you still saving that bottle of Seagram's for me?

So long. May God Bless You. Give my love to your Mother. It will be swell to see you again. Love, Mike.

We left Baer Field on August 3, 1943, flying a brand new C-47 which was eventually destined for a squadron overseas. Our route took us to Presque Isle, Maine; Goose Bay, Labrador; Bluie West 1, Greenland; Meeks Field, Reykjavik, Iceland; Nutts Corner, Belfast, Ireland; St. Mawgan, southern England; Marrakech, Morocco; Algiers; Castel

Benito, Tripoli; El Adem; Tobruk, Libya; and Heliopolis, Cairo, and El Kabrit, Egypt. There, on August 16, 1943, we joined the 37th Troop Carrier Squadron (TCS), 316th Troop Carrier Group (TCG).

The 316th TCG A-2 Section Consolidated Mission reports for HUSKY 1 and HUSKY 2, dated August 5, 1943, describe the group's first two combat missions — during the invasion of Sicily. In the Sicily invasion, only the 36th, 44th, and 45th Squadrons of the 316th participated, dropping the 82nd Airborne Division into Sicily on July 9-11, 1943. The 37th TCS was flying supply missions out of El Kabrit, Egypt.

August 17, 1943 [*Tuesday*]
Middle East, N. Africa [*El Kabrit, Egypt*]

Dearest Bette,

Hello! You big, gorgeous, lovely, lovable blonde. It has been such a long time since I have heard or even written to you that I feel like I have come thru another world.

Your pictures are an endless source of comfort to me. Your best is hanging directly over my cot. During the trip over, you were in my thoughts quite often, I can't help but admit my thoughts are split between you and Stretch [*Mary L., a friend in New York*]. That, as you understand, is normal because of my long relationship with her. But, as I have often said, you leave me little chance of alternative.

Well, Darling, our trip was easy and not too dangerous. It's too bad that you couldn't come along, it would have been as educational and interesting as it was for me.

You were a good dancer but I am afraid that the girls of Belfast [*Ireland*] outshine most of the girls in the States. Gad! They jitterbugged me right off my feet. Fortunately, I was ½ potted from drinking Irish whiskey and Guinness' Stout that it didn't make much difference to me what happened. It was great!

I was quite proud of myself when we reached Tripoli because I acted as interpreter. The city is infested with Italians and naturally I had to use my Brooklynese-Italo lingo on them. We managed to do fairly well. That city was one of the most beautiful I ever saw. Unfortunately, the war changed it a bit.

I wish I could go into detailed descriptions but I think the censor wouldn't like it so much. Nevertheless, this will suffice until I really spiel when this mess is over. You asked me to get you some dogs. Well, Honey, it has been a rather difficult situation. First of all, we didn't stay in one place long enough and I didn't have a chance to see much of these cities. Secondly, the rate of exchange changed in every place we visited. The only thing I have is a fairly good collection of queer coins and no pictures. Damn it!

Our mail hasn't reached us yet. We are all anxiously waiting. It certainly will provide loads of enjoyment. We have a cinema which provides some entertainment. I don't have to worry about a suntan because in a short while I'll be as black as the natives.

Well, Darling, I must close. I miss you. Give my regards to your Mother. May God Bless You and take care of you. Really things aren't so tough. Pray for me. I'll be seeing you. Love, Mike.

August 18, 1943 [*Wednesday*]
Middle East, No. Africa

Good Morning, Darling,

I am writing this letter during working hours but since I have nothing more to do, I am sure no one will mind.

A friend of mine who is with me here, wrote to one of his gals yesterday and both our letters went to the same city, Kansas City. He met this girl when he was going to T.W.A. We are both from the same city. It sounds like a trade treaty.

Bette, the more of these B-25s I see, the more I'd give my right arm to hop in one of them. Gosh, they are beautiful ships. You remember how we used to sit and gaze, well, I still do it and yearn but now I do it alone. The spirit is there but the body is missing. (And a lovely body at that.)

Darling, I know this is going to seem like a strange question but I know that you will understand! Do you feel that our friendship was built up on the physical attraction only? Here I am thousands of miles away, and yet I think about something I have never wondered about when we were together. Do people just live, the way we did? You and I existed, just as 2 people — we love life! Do you believe that is advantageous or not? I don't want to feel that I am being skeptical. It is merely that my thoughts have been rather strange these days.

I relive every moment. I can see no cross paths or cross words! I see no domination nor unequal thoughts. I feel no fear nor distrust in you. I am grateful for your kindness and consideration and above all your fine love for me and the fact that you are not afraid to admit it. You and I are playing a long shot but the odds are getting smaller. You have proved yourself to me.

On the other hand, the years I spent with Stretch. She has never proved herself. She said she loved me but how could I know! It is funny how tortured I feel yet I know what I want.

Dearest Bette, you have never doubted me. Please don't! You always said that I could guide you blindly and that you would follow. I am not blind! I need the time for the realization of the wealth of life and love I hold in my hands. You know what I am saying, do not feel hurt because this is not meant to hurt you but to reassure you that I am the same person. We were both lost and confused. We won't be for long. Dawn is coming and I can see your beautiful smile. Keep that chin up, Honey!

So long, for now, Bette. Give my best regards to your Mother. May God Bless you and take care of my beautiful blonde. Love, Mike.

P.S.: Still saving that bottle of Seagram's?
Gosh, you are swell. I'll be back! M.

August 19, 1943 [*Thursday*]

Good Morning, Darling,

You must forgive me for writing you in pencil, yesterday, but ink gets rather messy under certain circumstances.

I feel like saying something witty and unintelligent but I can't seem to. I feel good but I feel too sensible. I am afraid that my age is catching up to me and I "can no longer" be too carefree. (Is that possible?) Nevertheless, I want to tell you a few things about "Ace" Parker — my Co-Pilot. "Ole Ace" is a Texan and as usual a quiet one at that. He is about a year older than I am but he is one Hell of a swell guy. It is not difficult to confide in him, and above all, he is sure, steady, and sensible. One night back in Ft. Wayne, we [*were*] both high and we were sitting on the steps of his barracks. We got rather chummy. You know the way friends are. Naturally, we talked about our women and our ideas about life. Once again, during our trip, we scaled a large mountain, so that we could survey the country-side. Naturally, again [*in*] those circumstances life offers quiet, peace of mind and freedom of thought. We agreed to spend a few days at my home and then go down to his home in Texas. All this was to be part of our honeymoon. Sounds like a bunch of lovers, doesn't it! But, you understand what I mean. What I am trying to say, is that he is one Hell of a nice guy and above all well worth knowing. Enough! Isn't it?

Well, Darling, I am still taking life easy. Have a day off to-day but I go back to work to-morrow. Your picture (The good one I took in KC) is sitting right in front of me. Gad, You are beautiful. I found some of your old letters and I damn near know them by heart. Gosh, it would feel good to run my fingers thru' your long, blonde hair. I'll never forget that night in the Drum Room [*Hotel President, Kansas City, Missouri*] when I paid you those $4. And when I turned around, you were leaning on the bar and barking at the money. I guess you remember that was the night I got pretty damn drunk. I wonder what could have caused it! Ha! Ha! (Next time we'll know better.)

Well, Honey, I must close. Have a few personal things to straighten out. Give my regards to your Mother. May God Bless You and take care of you — You're swell. Love, Mike.

P.S.: That Seagram's is going to taste good! M.

[*V-Mail — microfilmed letters, airmailed, reproduced, and delivered*]
August 21, 1943 [*Saturday*]

Hello Darling,

I could think of a million things to say but I don't have a million hours nor enough pages to put it all on. So, to save you a lifetime of boredom and to save my right arm, it is best that I just spill a few words of simplicity and join the rest of this simple world. In one of your past letters, you asked why I was drinking beer. At that time, my finances were low, so I discovered that I could get drunk [*just as easy*] on ten glasses of beer than on ten

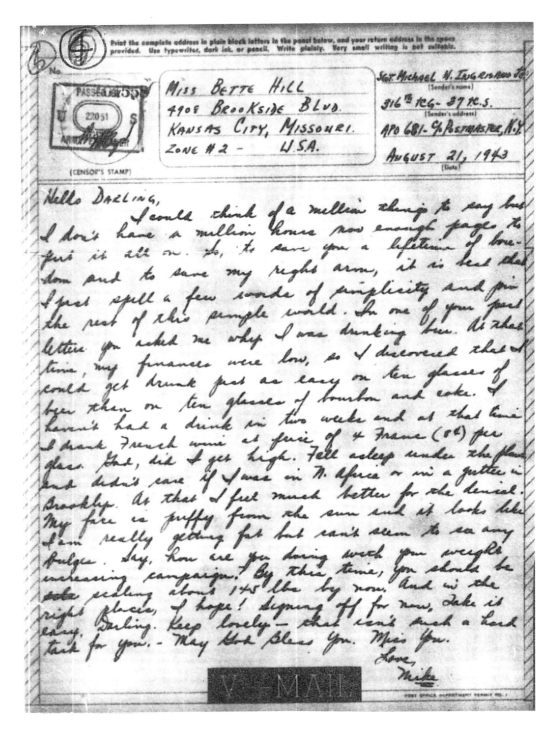

glasses of bourbon and coke. I haven't had a drink in two weeks and at that time I drank French wine at 4 Francs (8 cents) per glass. Gad, did I get high. Fell asleep under the plane and didn't care if I was in No. Africa or in a gutter in Brooklyn. At that I feel much better for the denial. My face is puffy from the sun and it looks like I am really getting fat but can't seem to see any bulges. Say, how are you doing with your weight increasing campaign? By this time you should be scaling about 145 lbs. And in the right places, I hope! Signing off for now. Take it easy, Darling. Keep lovely — that isn't such a hard task for you. — May God Bless You. Miss you. Love, Mike.

August 24, 1943 [*Tuesday*]

Hello Darling,

Sorry I haven't written for the last few days but I have been rather busy and consequently I have been caught short.

However, I have been able to catch up on my reading and I must have devoured innumerable copies of *Reader's Digest*. They are always interesting regardless of how old they are. I had the opportunity to read *Queens Die Proudly* again. As in the first time, I enjoyed this last reading.

Often have I regretted because I didn't listen to you when you told me that I should sign up to be a Cadet. You said that I would be a good pilot because I didn't give a good damn about so many things. Especially my own life. If I get back to the States, and this mess is still on I shan't waste a minute to sign. I told you that I didn't want to waste all my previous service, that I wanted to peek at this show before it was over. Well, here I am. Now, I want to start all over again, so that if it is still on, I can really get my teeth into it. I was speaking to a fighter pilot the other day, and the more he spoke, the more anxious I got. My biggest desire is to sit in one of those North American jobs [*B-25*]. I had some stick time on the way over, the more I had, the more I loved it. Hell, aren't I ever satisfied?

But, Darling, before I do that there are a few personal things that I am going to accomplish first. Things that . . . have always been a concern to me. Things, that I know I have wanted all my life. They have never been so exaggerated as they are now — now that I can't just reach out and see or feel the persons I want. Yep! Bette, ole gal, my mind is running in a very smooth channel.

Say, you big, ugly blonde, I'll thank you to keep out of my dreams. Gad, 3 hours last night before I succumbed to Morpheus. All I could think about was you and us. It's not fair. You mustn't take unfair advantage of me from such a distance. You have undoubtedly noticed my strong reluctance to saying so many things. You must bear with me, Darling, because the formulation of ideas and strength is becoming a great counterpart of this new life. Silly and hard to understand, isn't it? But, someday, you'll know all the answers. I can't frighten you because you know me too well. Oh Yes! To continue my scolding — to top it all, I couldn't sleep and I had to get up extremely early this AM. I guess I can't do anything but excuse you. I should kick, I'm not tired, yet!

I had intended to go on almost indefinitely but quite unlike me, I have developed a terrible headache. I haven't had a drink since I was in Marrakech, quite a while back. Gad! Didn't think I'd be able to stand it.

Well, Darling, I must close. So sorry that my letters are so short. Hell! If it isn't enough, they will have to start the mills rolling for more paper. So long, Honey — give my regards to your Mother. I am still waiting patiently for my mail to arrive.

Keep your chin up, Baby, things aren't too tough. May God Bless You. Love, Mike. [*This letter was written on Presque Isle stationery.*]

August 27, 1943 [*Friday*]

Dearest Bette,

I have spent a good part of the morning reading some mail that I had carried over from the states. Since, I haven't received any mail yet. It is the only source of correspondence for us. It is like draining the sap from an old tree, as little as we may get, it is still life sustaining. In the same manner, it has become a question of to whom to write. I could think of countless people but you are my best listener and severest critic. (That is, if you ever criticized!)

These letters help to capture a lot of spare thought. Thought lost thru' time. "Doc" [*My brother, Captain Dr. Lou Ingrisano, who was with the 116th Medical Detachment, 41st Infantry Division in the Pacific Theater*] telling me to be careful and to limit my flying. Urging me to keep up the family ties and to assure them that no harm will come to him in that faraway land. He asks that I drop him a line occasionally and tells me to be a good soldier.

Tony [*my brother, Captain Tony Ingrisano, the commanding officer of Childress Air Force Base in Texas*] writes and goes thru' some morbid ideas that if anything should ever happen to Sheila [*Tony's wife*] or to himself, I would be the "Rebel's" [*my godchild, Lillian Teresa's*] guardian. He's so damn proud of me that it hurts. He goes thru' a philosophy on people and their differences from the animal. People who are honest and have no fear of the truth and are able to discuss things sensibly. It's great!

"Stretch" thanks me for my honesty. She is grateful that we parted as friends and appreciates the fact that I will still correspond with her. She understands all that I tried to tell her and admits that she has missed a lot of life thru' our friendship (or at least the obligation caused by it). A chance to live freely, at least without me in the background.

Tommy, the priest, my brother [*Fr. Thomas Ingrisano, a Carmelite*], begs that I take care of myself. Believing and trusting the things that I was taught to love. Apologizing because he can't be with me but realizing (and rightfully so) that God has chosen him for a task greater that I could ever dare to try. He is preparing to remodel the world that we are trying to salvage. He is so firm and strong. God made no mistakes when He chose Tom.

Jesse [*Staff Sergeant Jesse Calvert*] a buddy of mine from the old 72nd [*Troop Carrier Squadron*] sends his home address and knows that we will meet again. He's a Hell of a fine fellow.

Then looking thru' a few letters, I find postmarks — July 23, 24, 26, 27, 29, and 30 — What happened to the 25th and 28th? And I realize that Bette [*is*] always apologizing for the boredom she is reaping on my head. Asking me to take care. Wondering if her patience will be in vain. How can a guy forget a person like you? Since the day you left Ft. Wayne, I haven't shared a moment with anyone. Darling! Slowly I have pushed away the physical and have seen you as I should have seen you a long time ago. I keep a diary (Not Cows!) [*but*] make very few entries. This AM I put in one — "Wonder how I will support Bette. — But I guess it won't be too difficult." Again, I am casting aside the material world and wanting only the spiritual world. The world which you & I have always lived in! The other will take care of itself. . . . Sounds flimsy for practical people like ourselves but I know it's that easy because we are practical.

Well, Darling, thanks for the soft shoulder. That long, blonde hair kind of tickled my nose but Hell it felt good.

So long for now. Give my regards to your Mother. May God Bless You. Love, Mike.

The Group Historical Report for August 1943, dated September 24, 1943, stated: "Under General Orders 78, Ninth Air Force, 26 August 1943, the 316th Troop Carrier Group was formally transferred to the 12th USAAF, thus ending a long period of operations over the African desert country."

September 1, 1943 [*Wednesday*]

Hello Torturer,

Don't worry about that name, Darling, thousands of miles apart, one does not need to wonder why!

I have felt, in the last few weeks, that there are so many things I want to know about you and yet I don't know where to start. Honestly, I don't care to start because I feel that I know what I want to know and the only things that are uncovered about both of us are unimportant and they will come out in time.

However, I believe I know your personality quite well. You told me that you were domineering. I have never found that too extreme and if so, I shall stampede it even if I have to drag you around by that lovely, blonde hair. You spoke about a temper which I have never seen and which I hope never to see. If so, you will be placed across my knee and I shall proceed to paddle you in the most unethical manner. Aside from those two meager failings, our personalities are parallel. We like to drink, smoke, dance, laugh, love. All in all, one might say, we like life. I have no fears nor worries. Our patterns of life are swell and to some people strange.

What the Hell am I being so firm about? Darling, you are great! Wait for me; the time will pass.

Well, we fixed up our home. It is not that little nest in Brooklyn but it will suffice for the environment. As a matter of fact, . . . after a long trip, it feels like a palace in the sand. Comfortable, cozy, cool, and above all, it is home. They have been keeping me fairly busy and it has been hard to keep up my correspondence. You must excuse me, Darling. We haven't received any mail yet and I don't know whether you are calling me names or telling me that you still love me. Hope it's the last.

Well, Honey, must close. Times awasting and I have things to do. Give my regards to your Mother. May God Bless You and take care of you. Love, Mike.

The 37th Troop Carrier Squadron, still in Egypt, did not begin to write its War Diary until November 1943, when the squadron moved to Tunisia. As a result, it is impossible to know the reasons for the days which are skipped because no letter was written for the week between my letters of September 1 and 8.

In the meantime, the 316th Group War Diary for September 1943 records that the group (Headquarters, 36th, 44th, and 45th) moved from Enfidaville, Tunisia, to Mazara del Vallo, Sicily. On September 14, 36 planes flew to Borizzo, Sicily, where the 82nd Airborne and its equipment were loaded for a mission called GIANT 3 — a paradrop in the vicinity of Agropoli to reinforce the U.S. 5th Army. The mission was successfully accomplished, despite the failure of three planes to find the Drop Zone (DZ). There were no losses of personnel or equipment.

September 8, 1943 [*Wednesday*]

Dearest, Darling, Lovable Bette,

That is for every day that I have missed writing to you. I know it has been almost a week but Hell you can't expect a guy to use paper just for a salutation. I have been rather busy and it has been difficult to write.

To-day, is truly a red letter day for me. I received my first letter from home. A small V-letter with perhaps 20 lines, if that many and yet, I was able to answer with a four-page letter. I was the first fellow in our gang to get a letter, and they are all anxiously looking forward to receiving some mail. As it was, it took 7 days for my letter to reach home, and it took 14 days for the letter to reach me. I don't care how long it took as long as it got here.

My brother, Tony, the fellow in Texas, is sending his wife and child back home to New York. I guess he doesn't want the baby to be raised as a rebel. Those damn Yankees.

I saw the Pyramids the other day. It wasn't a particularly close-up view — nevertheless I saw them. That's something to tell our children about.

Clark Gable — step aside — Bette, you ought to see my mustache — it really is blooming out to a height where it is something to be proud of. It doesn't look so bad either. It is not entirely black. There are some red spots here and there. It looks — oh! so attractive. I wonder if it tickles. (Or should you ask that question?)

I am sorry, Darling, if my letter sounds rather sketchy. There are a lot of personal things I want to say but I am waiting for your answers to my other letters first.

I have a celluloid cigarette case. It protects the cigarettes from the sweat. On each side of it, I have a picture of you. Those pictures that we took in KC. One of them is a cute shot, where you have your lips puckered, ready to be kissed. The other is that honey of a shot that was spoiled because one side of your collar was tucked in. The only bad effects of that, is that not only do I smoke more (to gaze at your ugly face) but every time I reach for a cigarette, some nosy guy wants to see the pictures, and consequently, helps himself to a cigarette. It's great though, it helps me to be able to think about you. It helps to build beautiful castles in the air. Occasionally, I'll probably write, "let's know each other better" letter. There are a few things that I'd like to question you about. Not 3rd degree, merely questions which we would ordinarily discuss if we were together. Hope you don't mind.

Well, Gorgeous, think I'll sign off for a while. You will have to excuse me, if I don't write too often, can't help myself. Please write to me as often as you can. Miss you a Hell of a lot. Can't stop thinking about you. Don't want to stop.

Give my regards to your Mother. May God Bless You. Are you putting on any weight? You know, in the proper places. You promised, remember? Miss you terribly. Pray for me. Yours in Everlasting Happiness — Love, Mike.

September 12, 1943 [*Sunday*]
[*The proposal*]

Dearest Bette,

I received your letter written on the 26th of August. I couldn't answer immediately because I was very busy. As a matter of fact, it came while I was away. It will probably be a Hell of a long time before I receive your other letter written to the other APO [*Army and Air Force Post Office*] 12260 because that was a traveling # assigned to us while we were coming across. Gross inefficiency or we would have received our mail thru' them. Nevertheless, I shall wait and in the meantime, your mail will start coming thru' this #.

Bette, Darling Bette, I have often regretted my lack of pure understanding. Your letter worried me because I had left you in such an unnecessary quandary. I left doubt in your mind and questions. I didn't want to do that. I was trying to tell you that before I met you. I was dreaming a beautiful obsession — beautiful because it kept me ignorant and mystified as to my true course. This bubble has burst. I can see that life isn't built on dreams but on realities. The first part of your letter was beautifully executed, but then (and only thru' my stupid blundering) you ask if you should wait for me or to just forget the whole thing and chalk it up to experience. Never in all my life have I been so serious. My dreams were shattered because I am now faced with (that word again) realities. Only once did I tell you that I loved you. Once in Ft. Wayne, just before you left and then in my telegram of apologies. You trust me. You must go on trusting me for our lifetime because I am coming back and there is one person I want — it is you.

I didn't fall asleep until 3 AM this morning because there were so many things I wanted to say to you. I don't want to be melodramatic. It's too childish. I want to be honest. I have relived every moment with you and in your letter you claim that you want me to be happy. Bette, Darling, I love you — you have given me a responsibility that no one has ever placed on me before. You trust me implicitly, so strictly that I have become your guiding star. Do not doubt this — and never fear, I shan't let you down. You'll never be haunted by the ghost of another person because that person was my obsession. Gone like the rest of my impossible dream.

Oh! Bette, I want to say so much and like a fool, I let it wait until we were thousands of miles apart. But someday we will be together. That is the day we are living for. In one of my previous letters, I said that there were 2 things I wanted to do when I got back — one of them was cadet training. The other, the more important and the first thing I am going to think about is marriage — will you? Yes, it's a proposal but we won't broaden on it until more time has passed and the waiting won't be too long. Believe me, Darling, you want me to be happy — isn't it fitting that you share it with me ?

There you are — these are just a few of the things that I wanted to tell you in all my other letters. I waited for your letter so that I could be sure of myself. So I am offering you a fool, a drunkard, no future, but a guy who will try to bring you all the happiness in the world.

I am going to close. I have tried to make myself plain. I know now that there will be no doubt in your mind. There mustn't be — if there is, let me know so that I can rectify it. Write to me, Darling, write to me often, very often. If I seem lax, it will because I can't help it! I can't tell you why — you know that there is a war going on!

Before I close, there are a few questions. Did you receive my radiogram? Hell, I can't think any more! Too happy — I haven't told the folks of my ideas but they can suspect because I write about you often enough.

I visited Scordia (Sicily) the other day. It is truly a beautiful country. Some what like our Southern California. Orchards, vineyards, green, beautiful green country, quite unlike our desert here. That's about all I can write about it. I have no urge to be picturesque.

That bottle of Seagram's has more significance to me than the sun and the moon.

Say — if you ever get a vacation, why don't you visit Brooklyn. I am sure that they would love to have you. (Am I getting to be typically "fogey"?) Just a thought. I can't welcome you but they really are a great bunch.

So long, Honey. Give my regards to your Mother — take care of yourself. Gotta go to church — have some special requests to make. May God Bless You. Love, Mike.

September 18, 1943 [*Saturday*]

Good Morning, Darling,

I don't know where to start because there are so many things that I can say. You see your mail finally caught up to me. First of all, you're marvelous. Secondly, if you ever send any more of those "abbreviated hunks of stenographic short hand" letters (V-mail), I shall be forced to spank your lower extremities.

You mustn't worry too much about time, Darling. I have accepted another one of my usual philosophies and I am letting it (time) take care of itself. It will; it always has. Patience is normal; let's accept it as such. I have been trying to avoid any mention of time and hopes of seeing you because it makes it easier for both of us. Let's pretend that I am still in the States and that we are just "sweating out" a furlough. Ooo-kay!

I am so glad that [*my sister*] Lucy answered your letter. You see, she has been very apologetic to me for being so lax. I was rather muddled about this "Bette called and said she was sorry that she couldn't come over" — I was wondering what the Hell was going on! Glad that you straightened that out for me. Now, did (Inter-office correspondence: Avoid Verbal Orders. Just stealing a line from you.) you call from KC or didn't you call at all? I don't know any other Bettes — at least I don't think so.

I am glad that you are taking a night course. Not because my reasons are the same as yours (to keep out of trouble. Shame on you!) (That is the least of <u>our</u> troubles.) but because it will keep you occupied. Again — time will pass quickly. I know. I'm as busy as a rooster in a hen house. (Not in the same manner.)

You know it will be comforting on those long, cold winter nights to sit and listen to you play "Elegy" and "The Beguine." I knew that you would learn it and for them — I am most grateful to you for your compliments. Your influence is so great that I really feel honest and good. I love you. Those times that you speak of will all be forgotten and repaid a hundredfold when I get back to you.

You mention the money angle. Well, it might be a good idea to save some of that filthy stuff — when Mike Comes Marching Home. It might come in rather handy. I am doing my damnest to save as much as I can. We can at least get off to a fairly good start. When we drain our resources, then we can start fighting or I can stand on the corner of 42nd and Broadway [*New York*] or 12th and McGee [*Kansas City*] and sell pencils. I'll have enough old uniforms and service ribbons.

Gosh, Bette, it was good hearing from you. I got a letter from my buddy, Joe Huss, (He stopped in KC for about an hour; I told you about him) — He is with a bomber group, somewhere in the So. Pacific. He [*apologizes*] for not being able to keep our date in No. Africa. He sent the letter to Alliance [*Nebraska*]. He doesn't know that I am keeping ½ of our promise. You'll like him. He's so damn unlike Gene [*Bagnoli, another Army buddy*] and he's honest and a good skate.

Whenever you have anything to say, please do. It will be a Hell of a while before I can hear it personally, and besides if you wait that long, we will spend all our time just talking — that ain't good. I want to hear you say anything as long as I hear it from you. You are the first person who sincerely confessed anything for me without an outlook for yourself. I can never forget your kindness and above all your admissions, so honestly made.

Darling, I must answer some of my other letters. My letters to you will be sporadic because it isn't often that I get much time for myself.

In my last letter I told you a few things which I have honestly never told to another person. I have vowed myself to you. I shall never let you down. If ever I do, you will be the first to know about it. I have accepted my religious duties more faithfully than I ever have. All my prayers are being answered and morally I am stronger than I have ever been. You have helped me to do all this. I would never dare to hurt you. In most of your letters, you speak of my strength and faith in God. If ever you had reason to believe otherwise, you would lose every precious thought that you have ever had of me or Him. Could I let both of you down? Darling, these are not just words. All work and no play may make some

Jacks dull boys but I know that I am well on the way to disprove that. I might pitch a drunk once in a while but the thing that I am talking about cannot be conquered by alcohol. In love songs, it's "Saving Myself for You."

So long for now. Give my regards to your Mother. I know that Seagram's is still waiting. I'll never doubt that it won't be. May God Bless You — someday you may care to share the same faith with me, Darling. It is most comforting. Take care of yourself. Please write often. Send me some more pictures, if you can. Would like to have a large one to liven up my tent. So long. Pappy [*Addison Agle*] and the boys send their love. Love, Mike.

P.S.: I have written to Lucy and Mom and told them of my intentions — if you accept me. It will be a great day when I present you to my family as my wife. Your Lover (Sounds good. Doesn't it?)

[*At the end of my letter I wrote "over." And there, our navigator, Nick Pappaeliou, wrote to Bette:*] Mike's a swell chap and you won't go wrong — if you ever hitch up with him. Hell! I navigated him across the ocean and all he was talking and thinking about — was his gal in KC. Please forgive this initiative of mine to write this. Post Script. I'm Mike's censor and I wish you two — the best of luck — in anything you two venture upon. *Buenos dias, senorita —*

September 23, 1943 [*Thursday*]

Dearest Darling, Lovable Bette,

Had a good breakfast; have written to Mother, and Tony and now I can devote some time to us. They have decided to give me a day of rest and to top it all most of my mail reached me. All I received from you was a mere 21 letters. You are marvelous. Can't help myself just have to love you — you don't know what your letters mean to me. You speak of things that are so vivid. Simple things like playing the piano, sitting on the porch, having a drink at the Plaza Royale, seeing a show — all these things, Darling, put me right next to you. Before I write any more, I'll try to answer a few of your questions. You're marvelous!

I haven't received the film yet because it usually takes a little longer for packages to arrive. It is great that you are so attentive to me. I hardly expected so much. Have always been used to giving — not receiving.

You asked me if I needed anything from the States. You know that I need the film. The only thing that I need is you. Outside of that I am quite adjusted and satisfied with my surroundings.

In my last letter, I believe I exploited the fine points of your newly thought of education. I don't think there is any further necessity for me to add anything else. Someone in our family has to know how to do something, don't they?

I did get quite a kick out of a few things. Twelve bottles, that cartoon (which is almost typical of our outfit) and lastly your suggestion that I try to see some picture. (*Stormy*

Weather). I am not laughing at you, Darling, but it seems rather hard to just try to see something like that. Just can't go round the corner to the local show house. We have to take what we get and that is usually a few years old. Thanks for the suggestions, I might try.

I did receive a card from Gene [*Bagnoli*]. He has been disqualified from flying due to an ear conformity or infection. And I was slightly jealous of him. . . . He did send me some bad news. Little George Kurchak, he went to school with us in KC and he was in the 74th at Alliance, was killed in a crash! He had just returned from furlough; he had just gotten married, and they were so much in love. I saw him just before I left Alliance. Then I heard that they had had a series of bad luck but I didn't know who was involved. Tough break.

I am glad that you like "Ace." He is all that I said he was. Great, I couldn't find a better pal and confidante. You'll like him when you meet him.

[*The next one-fourth of the page was cut out by the censor.*]

That little idea that you thought about those song titles was quaint. You aren't crazy, Bette, songs are as expressive as we can be because the words that the writers used are the same words that we get from Webster's. I love you is the same whether it is written that way or in quotes. "I love you." Thanks, it was swell and I know that you mean every word of it.

That question about information that girl wants. She can write to the Commanding Officer, 434 TCG [*Troop Carrier Group*], Alliance, Nebraska. I think that ought to do the trick. If she hasn't already gotten the info'.

Darling, if I miss any of your questions, it is because they just slipped my mind and that there are so many things I want to say. I am so sorry that I can't write more often. It isn't so very often that I get the chance to set my fanny down very comfortably. But when I do, I try to make it worthwhile to receive a letter from me. I write small and cover as many pages as I can. I am anxiously awaiting your answer to my proposal.

You must forgive me if I don't get very mushy, but it would tend to hurt us. I have lost many nights of good sleep thinking about our future, but it is best that we wait to make it our present before we build little castles in the air. I don't have to tell you that I have already told you that you are beautiful! I am concerned about your weight, and I have told you that. So far you have gained 4 lbs. You need as much as you can add. First to help yourself — your physical resistance, and 2ndly because you'll need a Hell of a lot to handle me or am I being too bold?

Every time that you write and you mention that bottle of Seagram's it makes me feel as good because it is so significant. Maybe when I get home, we won't ever drink it but we will save it for one of our fondest memories.

You are proud of me. You write during your spare moments. You write twice a day — what more can a guy ask. I am not doing a Hell of a lot except to sacrifice a few of our best years. We can always make up for it. Two people like ourselves very rarely waste any time on words. Thank God for that.

I had occasion to read a condensation of *Song of Bernadette* in *Omnibook*. It was truly a great story. I suggest that you read it. Try to get the full novel, and save it for our library. I might like to do <u>some</u> reading when I get home. It was written by a Jew and his descriptions of the Blessed Mother are beautiful. My church at home is "Our Lady of Lourdes."

In our Grotto we have a replica of the Shrine in Lourdes, France. So you see, it holds special significance for me.

Darling, I am so proud of you. You speak of my God as if you too had a strong faith in Him. You speak of Him as a person we both know and understand. You don't know how happy it makes me because I realize that you have changed from the girl I knew who had no faith nor could gain any courage from one she didn't know. Believe me, Darling, He will play a most important part in our lives. You may not yet fully realize it but someday you will.

Darling, you speak of a vacation. I have hinted to you that it would be a swell idea to go to NY. That will be a great opportunity to not only see our city but to meet my folks. You could stay at my home and Lucy can act as a sort of guide for you. Don't be terrified. They are really swell people. They are expecting you anyhow so that would be the most opportune time. Try it!

Well, Bette, I must close. Starting to develop a blister. Wish I could write more often. Circumstances — Give my regards to your Mother. I'd like to take shot at that kid you were talking about. Wonder if I could set him straight. Sounds like he lacks a little intestinal fortitude. Would be a great experiment. So long for now, Darling. May God Bless You. Pray for you and as always — Love, Mike.

September 23, 1943 [*Thursday*]

Good Evening, Darling,

It isn't really early evening but I felt as if I had to write a few lines before I retire. I just received your letter of the 6th. Although my finger is slightly blistered from so much letter writing to-day, I had to spill out a few lines. Just scraps of nothing.

As far as I know, Darling, we have no cable address. So, I don't think you need to worry about receiving one. You must excuse my "fairy" nice paper. It was the only stuff I could get and the guys have been kidding my neck about it. Calling me such sweet names.

Since the gang of us all received our mail last night, it was quite a gala affair. Each guy would take his turn at reading little excerpts from his gal. One of them said his gal was planning 4 children when he got home. So "Ax" [*Chalmers Johnson, my crew chief on the trip to El Kabrit*] very cleverly added, "I guess she'll have the 4 ready and waiting for you when you get home." It struck us all very funny, except the guy who it was said to. My contribution to this festive mood was ejaculations of — "I'm in love." "She's great" and "That blonde son of a gun has some nerve writing V-mail." You are well-known in my tent, Darling, I talk about you enough.

You have a funny idea that your letters aren't interesting and that you wish you could write the way I do. Shame on you, Darling, you are marvelous. Or did I say that before?

You mentioned in one of your epistles that you knew that I was having fun. I am. My joy has been in my work and in my associations. We are damn near always laughing and our rarely intelligent moments are extremely interesting.

I don't think I told you about the squadron party that we had a little while back. They had an extremely large amount of port and sherry wine and a punch made of rum, brandy, gin and mule kick (I guess?). Well! I was rather tight. Into the wee hours of the morning you could hear us singing a song. I didn't get to bed until 4 AM. I was awakened at 5:00 AM because I had to fly. As a matter of fact, "Mac" [*Ray McGuire, one of the crew chiefs that was in our two-plane flight from the States*] said that I got up, put on one stocking, and then fell back to sleep with the other one in my hand. It was the first good drunk I pitched since Marrakech, Fr. Morocco.

Darling, I am sending this letter mail instead of Air Mail. Let me know how long it takes.

Although I spoke to you earlier in the day, I feel as if I could go on like this throughout the night.

I wrote to my brother, Tom, to-day and I gave him my spiritual report. I was so proud of myself that I know he will be proud of me. I attributed a great deal of my attentiveness to you and it is true and I told him so. I expressed the wish to him that I hope you and I can be present for his ordination next May [*1944*]. I have asked him to pray for our happiness. There I go again talking about "My Lovable Gang" again. Can't help it, they are truly great.

"Ax" said that I should send money to you so that you can buy the ring but I feel as if it is best if we do that together. Shall we say, it is more romantic. Almost typically Latin, isn't it? Do you enjoy being wooed by this Latin Cuss? Supposition — suppose she says — "no" — you can't.

We ought to make a pretty good couple. We can drink like fishes, and Hell there aren't many times when we are very solemn. Somehow I feel as if we will never grow old. Or should we let nature take its course, the way we always have?

Honestly, Darling, I'm not getting "mushy." I am just trying to say a lot of things I am really thinking about and which I feel deeply.

For the second time in your letters you said, "Thank God for memories." For the short time that we had, we really did create a wealth of them, didn't we? I don't think that KC will forget our wanderings, we were pretty nice people when we got lit. "Begin the Beguine" and "Elegy," those cute gals in that place in the Plaza, "El Caminado" (or something [*El Camino*], I believe). Those H.S. kids on their way home from their prom. That fight in Mary's, phone calls from Alliance, KC, and Ft. Wayne. Telegrams any time anywhere. "Arrive from Tulsa at 1 PM. Meet me" "Sorry for my phone call last night, am I forgiven? I love you." "Bette, I'm as drunk as a lord but I had to talk to you. When are you coming to Ft. Wayne again?" Your train hours late, waiting and hoping — finally, you came. Beautiful and lovely even with the dirt of 3 states on your face. Sliding your bag down the ramp and rushing into my arms [*Fort Wayne*]. Gad! I'd give a million bucks to duplicate that. The weary people in that station saw 2 happy, jabbering monkeys walk out. We didn't know what to say nor how to say it. Memories, Darling — We've only started.

Sorry I rambled on like that but it was so fine that my arm moved like it was driven by electricity. I just can't help myself when I start to write like that. It is as if the years, months, days, hours, minutes and seconds just roll before my eyes and I don't want to waste them. If I am not just putting them on paper, I am telling them to you—the person who shared all that with me.

Darling, you must forgive me but I must get some sleep. I have to get up early and it is imperative that I have my beauty nap. I shaved my mustache, but again I started not only to raise one but to add a beard. I began to look too much like the local natives. Mustache and face are doing fine. Beard is down the drain. At least I could do it. Just wanted to prove to myself that I was man enough.

Good night, Darling. Give my regards to your Mother. Take care of yourself. May God Bless You. Love, Mike.

P.S.: Sorry about that French wine. Perhaps the only stuff like that that I'll bring home will be in my stomach. I'll try — though — if it's at all possible — M.

September 26, 1943 [*Sunday*]

Hello Darling,

You must excuse the fancy ink and the paper but under the circumstances there is nothing else I can do. Since you wrote to me while you were at work, there is no reason why I can't duplicate that. I must admit that I don't have the comforts of home nor of a writing table but I guess the cockpit of a plane will suffice. For the second Sunday in a row, I have been unable to attend Mass, but then again, there isn't a Hell of a lot I can say about that. Before I go any further, I must admit that my mood is far from pleasant. Perhaps, it is a bit nasty. Nevertheless, I won't bother to involve you but merely to use you as an outlet. The best way to do that is to talk to you about anything and everything.

Yes, Darling, I received the film. They were in good shape and I was as pleased as punch to receive them. I haven't used them as yet because I haven't found any decent subject matter. I certainly am not going to waste them on myself.

The fellows are helping me to "sweat it out" — waiting for your answer concerning my proposal. Every time, I receive a letter from you, they group around and ask me "Is that it?" So far I can only answer in the negative. I have forgotten when I sent the letter, naturally, I can't judge, approximately, when the answer will come. We'll wait.

"Ax" wrote to his gal for some pictures of her hidden charms. She sent some excellent "leg" shots. Hell! We all looked at then, and ejaculated with approving "Oohs" and "Ahs." I don't think that he'll be showing us those for a while. It was a good idea of him to ask.

You will remember in one of my letters, I explained the meaningless of the ghost of my near last life. I received a letter from her and she asked if I would like a picture of her for Christmas. My retort was rather a long one because I explained the whole situation. I told her about you and me, and advised her that she was about a year too late to send me the picture that I was asking for — for that length of time. For once and for all, I dismissed any thought for any sort of reconciliation. I was very stern, fatherly, and sorry but the situation warranted as much tact as I could muster. Thank you, Darling, for saving me from something I may some day tell you about. In the meantime, our interest is us and not shadows.

The news these days has been rather encouraging, but then what else could one expect now that we are here.

Say, Bette, has much of my stuff been cut out? Tell me so that I can modify some of my writings. I daresay that I blame you for being fascinated by a description of Marrakech, since you heard it on the radio. But, believe me, if you had seen the dump, I mean place, your fascination would have to be realized visually, and not by smell. No incense or sweet flowers. Need I say more.

Sorry, Darling, I will continue to-morrow, if it is possible. If not, I'll just close and add more if possible. (Repetitious, aren't I?) Give my love to your Mother. May God Bless You. So long for now. Take care of yourself. Love, Mike.

9/27 [*Monday*] — Sorry I can't add any more — want to get this mailed so that you can get the info' you wanted. So long for now, Darling. Love, Mike.

჻჻჻჻

[*Written on paper from the American Red Cross Club, Karachi, India.*]
October 5, 1943 [*Tuesday*]

Good Morning, Darling.

Again I must apologize for not being able to write as usual I have been rather busy.

I can add three more countries to the list I have already visited, Iran, Persia, and India. I can't say too much about the first 2 because I really didn't see enough of them. At any rate they are nothing but desert and well what else is there in this part of the world. India is not worth the price of admission. Karachi, India, is in the northwestern part of the country. It is one of the largest cities and reported to be one of the best. If that is so, I think the states must be heaven, even Brooklyn. I tried my damnest to get you a dog but it seems that the Indians specialize in camels, bulls, and rabbits — there isn't a dog to be found. The streets are cluttered with beggars, and nude kids that shout, "Hello, Yank, what's cooking?" (Part of the civilization that the American soldier has brought to this part of the world, no doubt.) And that well-known Sacred Bull. They practically own the city. Eat better than the populace.

These professional beggars of India really tend to tear down the little beauty that there may be. Most of the sights were so pitiful and disgusting that I dare not waste film on them. It was as far from civilization as the pre-historic man. I shan't go through any long discourse because I want to wait until I have more time so that I can paint a more minute picture for you.

Darling, I haven't been able to get my mail because I have been busy. Naturally, I don't miss it for that reason but believe me I am anxious to slip my peepers on your handwriting. I cabled birthday greetings to my Mom. She will be 50, I believe, on Oct. 16. I wish I could send more.

Well, Darling, I am going to close this short note. There are thousands of words I can add and will as soon as I can get comfortable enough. You have examples of my book-length epistles.

So long for now, Bette. May God Bless You. Give my regards to your Mother. Take care of yourself. Love, Mike.

October 6, 1943 [*Wednesday*]

Good Morning, Darling,

You can imagine my surprise when I came home to find a load of mail and a new home. Believe me, it left me in a state of complete loss and mystery. First, because it has been such awhile since I have been able to receive mail and secondly because everything has been so confused, it wasn't funny.

I have been extremely anxious to answer your mail. As a matter of fact, I have been quite upset because I couldn't write. As I write you will understand why. Darling, in all the letters I didn't receive the answer to my proposal. Gad! I don't know what to say nor how to say it. Very confusing, isn't it?

There are three more countries I can add to my list. Persia, Iran, and India. I shan't bother to go through much description of any of them but India. In a previous letter I described things. (That pen stinks!) (So does India.) Some of the sights of those professional beggars is really beyond comprehension, unless you can see it yourself. It was the picture of lost civilizations. I don't know whether I felt pity, disgust, or just indifference. I didn't take any pictures of these scenes because it just wasn't the sort of stuff you take. Tried every place along the main drag to buy you something. I didn't succeed because there was nothing that I liked. The handiwork was beautiful but — I had a couple of sailors who helped me on my tour. They were swell fellows and they promised to visit my folks as soon as they got to the States.

I am afraid that I can't be very descriptive this AM because there were a few things that confused me. You speak about a job. A job that would take you from KC. Damned if I know what you are talking about, Darling. And then you say that if I get home and you aren't in KC that I can find you thru' your Mother. Darling, are you going some where? I am hoping to come back to you and live happily ever after.

I reread all your letters and I still can't find anything about a job unless your are referring to NAA [*North American Aviation*].

Let me paint a picture for you. Maybe then you can realize how confused I was. First off, I was slightly inebriated (stewed, plastered, etc.); secondly, I had been so busy that I didn't sleep on my own bed since the last letter I wrote to you [*September 26-27, but I had written a short note on October 5*]. Which was a long time ago. I felt dirty and tired. All my things had been moved to another barrack. My clothes were disorderly and my bags just thrown in. My new OD [*olive drab*] blouse which I had just paid $15 for looked like it had survived a run thru' a pig-sty. I was worried because I hadn't written to you or to Mom for such a Hell of a long time. All that, I couldn't even think straight. Your letters and letters from Tony (picture of the baby included) and letters from Lucy were my only source of grace and your picture was manna from heaven; yet, I was in a fog. I threw all my clothes off my cot and said, "Be damned, I'm tired." I slept and when I awakened I was ready to face my problems. I am slightly straightened out but I hope that these words could reach you on wings. I love you, Darling and I care for nothing else. I am looking forward to the day when we can say "to Hell" with the whole world and just live, you and I. Castle in the air. — Gad! I must be building skyscrapers.

Darling, I am going to close now but I'll write again today. I must answer my sister's letters so you must be patient. I miss you and there are a few things that have happened that can prove that I am on the ball — Faithfully and honestly.

Give my regards to your Mother. May God Bless You. Love, Mike

P.S.: Cabled my Mother — Birthday Greetings — Oct. 16th.

October 6, 1943 [*Wednesday*]

Hello Darling,

Here I am back again. There was a line in my last letter that I think will leave some doubt in your mind. Something about things happening and my proud boasting about my proud actions and stuff. Well this is what happened. When I visited Tel-A-Viv [*sic*] recently I had a funny experience happen to me. You see there are quite a few women there. I have spent most of my time at the Ice Cream Bar and the Red Cross and a few other places where a guy can get a drink. I was walking down near the boardwalk and this old dame came up to me and tried an old hustling game. She wasn't the biggest bag in the world. She tried the best sales talk that she could muster and then she walked away quite disappointed because she couldn't make a touch. You see, Darling, I am changing. At one time, I might have reconsidered. No more, when a guy's in love, it isn't hard to stay on the ball. Can I expect a pat on the back?

No kidding, Bette, I am confused a bit about that job you were talking about. I don't care but I just want to know where you are when I get back. Maybe I didn't read your letter right but I do hope that those castles in the air concern the two of us. Honestly, Bette, I miss you very much. My happiness is broadened because I know that you will be waiting for me. I do remember that your last words before you left Ft. Wayne were that you would wait for me. But I left you with such an uncertain answer. Now I am trying to make it all up to you.

I spent the whole morning writing letters. I received a picture of my brother's baby — the Rebel — She hasn't got a stitch of clothes on. Someday when I am old and gray, and she is young and beautiful, I can make my favorite niece cringe with shame when I show it to her. Tony and his family are very happy.

Darling, you apologize for 2 things. One, because you should use some decent paper when you write to me. Bette, you could use old wrapping paper if you wish. As long as you write to me as often as you have. It really is swell to receive so much mail from you. Secondly, you said that you wish you could tell me ½ the things you want to say. Something about "cold pen and cold paper." The Hell with that — you aren't writing to these things but you are writing to me. Woman, remember that — It's me — say what you want to say, whenever you want to say it.

That really was a keen picture you sent me. Darling, you are a very beautiful woman. Or, have I said that before? You mustn't apologize. You needn't be vain because of me.

I hope you had a good time in Salina [*Kansas*]. I must admit that I was a bit jealous of your description of a quiet Sunday afternoon. "We are sitting here drinking bourbon and ginger ale. There is a zippy breeze blowing and I only wish that you were here to make it complete." Dearest, Darling, Lovable Bette, I'd give a million *paistres* to be sitting right next to you. I admit it made me a bit jealous. Especially after the heat of Persia and India. Gad! I damn near suffocated. Tell Marguerite [*Bette's aunt, Mrs. M. Busboom*] that I am looking forward to meeting her. If she is, as you say, like you, I know that I like her. We'll try to hurry home as soon as this mess is over.

Everyone that wrote to me made it a point to mention that the Surrender of Italy [*September 8, 1943*] was celebrated very jubilantly. However, I had to disappoint all of them when I told them that we were very quiet about it. It just happened and it was accepted as part of the war. [*Though Italy had surrendered, German forces — particularly in northern Italy — maintained fierce resistance to the Allies.*] Our celebrating will be done when we get home. Right now, the World Series is more important to us. Hope to hell the Yanks beat the devil out of the Cards.

I must say you speak about doing a lot of things together. It certainly does make a guy feel good to hear that. It helps to take away a lot of the loneliness because I can always look forward to the day when we will be together.

Well, Darling, I must close for awhile. Tell your Mother that I am sorry because I can't write to her. I hardly have time to write to you. I guess you have noticed that. I try to make it up to you whenever I get the chance.

So long, Darling, take care of yourself. May God Bless You. Pray for us. I know that all my prayers are not wasted. See you later. — Love, Mike.

October 7, 1943 [*Thursday*]

Good Morning, Bette,

Here's that man again just trying to make up for lost time and lack of words and stuff.

Right at this moment, I am resting on my fanny, puffing a big, black cigar and feeling quite at ease with the world. As a matter of fact, I haven't a wish in the world other than to sit across from you at our breakfast table. By the way, can you cook anything besides a mess of ham and eggs? Or do we eat out all the time? Kind of like to slip into a cozy chair after a hard day and let the rest of the world hurry by. A couple of more years of this life and you will never be able to get me off my "sack."

Say, Bette, what about this shorthand business? Don't tell me that you have resigned yourself to giving up a small thing like that! But, then again, I am not going to lecture about it. Just beat the smaller things and the world is an easier place to live in.

Your quotation about prayer is both vivid and accurate because it has worked that way for myself and the members of my family. I am not trying to sell you anything but I am merely trying to point out a few things. Bear with me for a while and think about the things I say. — I'll start down the list.

When Mom's first baby was born — Tony — he was very ill. Since Mom was still a new hand at it, and medicine was still a superstition — she took it upon herself to care for her child. The effects were almost disastrous — She vowed to the Blessed Mother that if her child was saved, she would seek Her advice forever. Tony grew up to be a normal, intelligent, good-looking, good skate. My Mother has never forgotten this favor that was granted to her. Her faith is boundless.

Tony spent a lot of his life just roaming the world. At the age of 30, he found a woman whom he loved. Sheila and Tony were married Oct. 2, 1942. The time came when they were to be gifted with a child. You know some of that story. I told it to you when I saw you in KC on that Sunday after I visited my brother in Childress [*Texas*]. They were to lose the child. If not, when the baby was born, it would be deformed. Tony prayed and hoped. He asked God, Why? If there was a grudge why not take it out on Tony, not on the girl and the baby. I admit that I prayed for the first time in a long while. The baby was born on June 22, 1943. The "Rebel" is adorable and she's my favorite niece. Tony tells me that I am her favorite uncle. The picture I have of her certifies everything that I have heard about "La Belle Rebel."

During my lifetime, I have felt the need for prayer only for my own selfish reasons. Since I have been over here, I have learned the power of prayer. Nothing has happened to better my physical self. But when a guy can feel a new spring, his will power or should I say the strength of it is not a phrase but a fact, then something must be up. I am sure of myself and you are forever included in my feelings. I am not talking of a young man's fancy but of a man's dream. My resolution of body and soul to you is not a word; it, too, is a fact, and I am proud of my strength. I know you feel some of it with me, Darling, because if you didn't you wouldn't speak of prayer and patience. Believe me, my task has been easy and the time is passing. With the help of God, we may say, "I am here." Not "I wish you were here." This time no matter how long, will be just an iota of our time.

Gad! Was that me talking? Do you see, darling, that guy that said that he wanted to sit across the breakfast table from you, is going to be an awfully windy bloke.

Funny thing, I meant to keep this letter in a very light view and just spill nothing into your lovely ears and I end up being a Socrates or such.

You know, Bette, I won't ask any questions. The future that you and I wish to seek, will be sought not thru' letters but thru' actualities. I am not going to ask how many children you want. — We'll let nature take its course. All those castles — feel and believe them but save them in your heart until we can talk about them together.

Well, my luscious blonde, I think I'll hand the microphone over to you. My words are spent — at least for a while. Hope to Hell I can write to you as often as I have in these last two days or isn't that often enough.

Give my love to your Mother, Marguerite and Alice and the rest of the people you mention. Well, the cigar is finished — so is the letter.

So long, Bette, May God Bless You and take care of you, I love you. Mike.

October 7, 1943 [*Thursday*]
Later in the Day

Hello —

Don't look now but it's that man again. Egad! The creature doesn't know when to stop and why should I — who says we don't get news quickly — the Yanks won the first game and St. Louis won the second game. They are re-broadcasting the games from Cairo and luckily we can pick up the station.

You know, Darling, those are some of the things I miss. I didn't see Brooklyn play one game this season. I see the football season has started. Wouldn't mind sitting in on a few of those games. But at any rate, we can get back to all that sooner or later. <u>Circumstantially</u>, (Gad, isn't that a long word). Later.

Someone just remarked that we ought to put some mustard on our barracks — and then add us — the sardines. Hell! You ought to hear some of the remarks that pass thru' these halls. Of course, a great part of them are unprintable.

You know, I didn't realize how much I had said this AM until I started to think about some of the things I had said. Some times I wonder who I inherited all my taciturnity (?) from — My Dad and Mom are both quiet. I guess their kids have to make up for their misgivings.

Here we go again — the weather has been rather cool these days. I doubt very much if there is anything but 2 seasons — hot and cold. One of the natives told me that they have snow once every five or six years and then it is only an inch or two deep.

I don't know if I mentioned anything about the women of India. Most of them are typically native. Some of them want to learn western civilization and consequently their best source of education is the American Red Cross. When I was there, they had a tea dance, and there were American, Dutch, and Indian women. The A. gals weren't bad to look at. The Dutch were solid and . . . well-built, and they could swing a mean Lindy Hop. Their dress is not native but just the same as our style, perhaps a few years late. I must admit that their skirts were a bit short, at that, their legs weren't bad to look at — ahem!

I danced with one of the American girls. She was from New York City. From one of the more exclusive parts of town. She flattered me by tossing a bunch of compliments at me. I told her I was sorry but I didn't belong to the Indo-China command and that I wasn't staying in that neighborhood very long. Pardon my conceit, but she did sound a bit eager. Ain't interested.

Damn — I almost forgot. Look Honey, I don't care if its 5 crown or 7 crown — as long as the two of us are together. I love you.

You said something in one of your letters about my catching up with my reading. The tragic thing, — one day I started to read a story in *American* magazine. Nearing the end of it, I realized that it was to be continued. A few weeks later, I came upon another copy of the same magazine and sure enough, there was the story, but I am only ⅔'s finished. I am waiting to run across the next and last chapter. I don't know the name of the story but I could easily recognize it. Something about one of those cold women who cares more about her home than about her husband. Naturally, the man makes a play for the kid sister. Can't blame him; it's tough to sleep with a person and just sleep. Some day I'll run across the last chapter. His wife is trying to do her best to get him back. They haven't any children and yet they have been married at least five years. She is trying to regain his love by an over show of allure and stuff. She was doing OK until she said the wrong thing. Gad! I hope they get together — I know she will change and make a good wife.

Now you can imagine the things I worry about in the leisure time when I am not thinking about you.

In most of your letters you tell me to enjoy myself. I have told you that the extent of my joy is the thought of you, an occasional drunk, and my work. I'm doing OK. I guess neither of us are looking for trouble, are we? We can look for it (trouble) together. And Hell, no one can say that we can't find it. Have you been giving any 2nd Lts. any hot-seats these days?

Darling, in one of your previous letters, you said that you hadn't had a drink for a while. Of course, after that, you said you had — naturally. But your question was — "Maybe I'll break the habit, is that bad?" Well, it ain't good. Look, Baby, when I get back that is another one of the things I have to make up. I don't intend to do anything alone. If I could speak to you, I would add a few things that might sound uncouth and bold in my letters but if I spoke them to you, we would just be kidding. We were never bashful about a Hell of a lot of things except one and that is attributable to our decent environment.

Gad! You big blonde, you have me writing and writing. Hell! I must have written at least 25 pages in the last 2 days. I am going to close. I am sending this letter "free" mail so that in case I can't write one week, this will reach you unexpectedly. I love you.

So long for now, Bette, take care of yourself. May God Bless You. Glad to hear that your clothes are getting tighter. Are the bumps in the right place? Eek! How crude of me — but I think I should be of some concern — if you say: "Yes, Darling, I will." — Love, Mike.

October 7, 1943 [*Thursday*]

Hello Darling,

This is the 3rd letter for to-day and yet this is the most important of all because I just received your letter concerning your new job.

I am not going to scold you because I know that this is the opportunity you have been waiting for. It will enable you to do a lot of the things that you have always wanted to do. Your letters got mixed up and I didn't know what you were referring to. Now, I realize that you got such a break.

I know that your first concern was that I'd think that you'd change. Darling, live in the present but think in the future. I told you to stay in KC because I believe that you were set there. Since so many things have happened there is no reason why you should be subjected to so much bunk. Independent people don't have to take rot. (P.S. Let me know all about your job!) (DEEPLY INTERESTED!)

Again concerning your changing. I am fully aware, Darling, that my love for you is unwavering. The changes that are brought about will be caused only by yourself. Since you have told me that you were sure of yourself concerning me why should there be a change in you, if only your environment changes. The money difference should do no more than to get you a lot of things you have always desired. Don't let that astounding figure change you so that I'll not be able to come up to your expectations, I'd be in a hell of a fix. You can't say that I am marrying you for your money because I asked you before I knew about all this. I love you (and I am not kidding) regardless of change.

You say that you promise to go home when it comes time to change to get along — Buck up — Darling, you are too fine a person to have to change to get along. Quit when things become disgustingly unbearable, but in this wise world you are wiser yet and capable enough to handle these stupid, simple situations brought about by the stupid, simple people in this world.

I am sure that your love for me is strong enough to be able to face meager problems. When I told you to stay put, it was because your weren't quite ready. Do not accept my words as boasts or conceit but merely as advice, forwarded only after the keenness of observation. When I first met you, you were physically and mentally upset. I hope that I have supplied the spark to enable you to settle your human failings. I do sound like the guy who thinks that he has brought the world to your feet. "Opened your eyes" as they say in the Bible. Maybe I have. Not because I'm exceptional but because I got there first with, I hope, the strength you desired.

Have I answered all you want? Or have I accepted too much and made you feel as if I am a God? I don't mean it that way. I am merely trying to furnish the words to help you along on your new venture. I am behind you all the way, Darling. If you are wrong, I shan't say — "I told you so." You are an independent soul, backed by a shadow — me! May God Help and Bless You. If you ever feel the need for any help — I am always near you. And my family will be there when you want a little companionship. Darling, I trust your judgment as implicitly as you have trusted me. Have I failed you? Then you shan't fail me.

Must close. Must rise early. Busy. I'll write as soon as possible. May God Bless you. I'll pray for you. Say a prayer for me. I love you. You have supplied a spark for me. I hope I am doing the same for you — REMEMBER — "Live in the present, but think in the future!" Love, Mike.

October 8, 1943 [*Friday*]

Dearest Darling,

It seems that I am emitting an endless chain of words. But my letter last night was written rather hurriedly because I felt that the faster I wrote it, the faster it would get to you.

Last night's letter was rather hastily written because (My God! I said that already, didn't I?) What I meant to say was that my thoughts were conceived as fast as my pen could write. I may have left a few things out but I do hope that I said the words you wanted to hear. It is not easy to be a "spur-of-the-moment John," so I hope that I didn't sound too sketchy.

I received your letter of the 20th a few days after the letter of the 21st. Naturally, I reread both so that I could get the full idea of your words. The only thing that made me fret, Darling, was the fact that you said that if I ever got back to the States, I could always find you thru' your mother. Bette, I don't intend to lose contact with you. After my primary touch on those shores, I want to hurry to you. There is no reason to take back alleys and crossroads. Wherever the Hell you are, I'll be there to get you. Or don't I make myself clear. Hell! Bette, let's stop playing games. You and I know what we want. The one thing we are seeking is happiness. We found it and it only lasted for a short while. Some day, and the time will pass, we are going to find it and find it together.

In your letter of the 20th you almost speak of me as a foster father not as a lover. I am to understand everything and I do. My love for you is not to be shown by dominance and blood and thunder, but by understanding and tenderness. The only time I'll apply the whip is when I feel that you really need it. And believe me, you will know when. But not now, just because you are doing something different from the sheltered life you are used to. Is there anything wrong with progressiveness?

I understood all that you were saying. You admit that your feet are on the ground. Then there is no fear of anything. If you must admit defeat, don't be afraid to — but in your defeat take away the victory that, at least, you tried.

"Darling, if you don't like the idea, don't scold me too severely because I know that you told me not to do it. Anyway I can always quit." You admit that at the time I said that you were a bit confused. My advice was centered on that and I felt that your Mother & friends could supply some of the companionship you so badly needed. "But now it seems as though I have my feet so well on the ground it won't matter. Darling, I know you understand what I am trying to say." Let me go thru' a series of suppositions so that I may be blunt. Your greatest fear was yourself because (and may I be to the point?) of your human urges brought about by a condition of nature. . . . That one condition caused all that fear in your soul. Now, you feel that most of that has been overcome by your companionship and the deepness and full meaning of it and the moral strength it has supplied for both of us. I am not being too presumptuous, Darling, because that is what you have done to me. I am no different from you on that score. Consequently, on the face of that you should have nothing to fear in your physical self. You won't change. I left my environment in the States and believe me I haven't changed. I am being virtuous because of you and what you mean to me. Stick that chin out, Darling, and beat the Hell out of the world.

Let me quote so that I can show you what I mean. This is from one of my brother's, Tony's, letters. It is a magnifying glass for what I mean. "No matter what happens or how often we are separated, Sheila and I know that we belong completely to each other and there is room for no one else. It is so complete that we never use the word 'faithful.' It is unnecessary. There is just no room for anyone else, Mike." May I in turn say that to you, Bette? Never in my life have I felt so sure of it.

OK now, let's forget the changes in scene. Write to me and tell me all about your job. Continue to tell me about little happenings. Get enthusiastic and excited and let me share it with you. Live as normally as you have always done so. My letters won't change. Why should they? Let's continue to dream. We love each other, no one can change that. I miss you, Darling, and I will miss you even if you were in KC, NC, NY, or China. It's you that I love. It can't be dampened by where you are.

I sent $60 home yesterday. At any rate, that filthy stuff will keep piling up. Gad! We'll be rich. We can take a nice vacation when I get back.

Oh Yes! Bette, if you get near Washington, D.C. look up my brother Tom. — His address:

Frater George Maria Ingrisano
Whitefriar's Hall
1600 Webster Street, NE
Washington, DC
You see, you won't be lacking friends if [*you*] get near the eastern shoreline.

So long for now, Bette. I'll write later. Shall we consider the discussion terminated? If there is anything else, let me know. Always willing to talk. — You know me.

May God Bless You. Take care of yourself. I am praying for you. Love, Mike.

October 11, 1943 [*Monday*]

Hello Darling,

I am in the midst of a "bull" session and it might be a rather rough deal to get thru' this epistle. I can't guarantee a very good letter because I'm afraid I've got a bit of a headache from overindulgence. Or do I sound too stiff? That's what was wrong with me.

Before I go any further I want you to notice my APO. It is APO 760. The rest is the same. Here, also, are a few pictures I had taken around and about. Please don't be too disgusted, Darling, pictures don't always tell the truth. I may look motley but there is nothing there that a little civilian life wouldn't hurt. I have been rather lucky these last few days. I have been able to do a little extra "sack" detail. ("Sack" meaning sleep.)

I visited Ismailia [*Egypt*] recently. It is a typical canal town. I can't very readily suggest it for a tourist tour but it has been the first city that made me realize that I am on this side of the world. It would be very embarrassing if I had to show you the place. You see, there's a canal that runs right thru' the town. Naturally, they use the canal for everything. (Hell! There are a bunch of jokes being told and it is rather difficult to keep right on writing but I'll try!) They use the canal for watering their bulls, and a few other things. I don't believe that they know what a latrine is. You can imagine what I mean. At least the sky is beautiful. Aside from the soldiers, the town is rather picturesque. It's hard as hell to try to describe it because it really must be seen. There was one that really caught my sight. There was a GI riding a horse. You should have seen that beautiful nag. It was gray and it had legs on it like a real racing thorobred. He held his head up like a king and strutted like a show horse. Really a fine sight! [*Probably an Arabian.*] By the way, the GI could really ride that horse. (Gad! These jokes are really getting me down. They are good. Too bad you can't be here to enjoy them!)

By the way, I haven't received any mail for a hell of a time. The trouble is something we can't figure out. It really is tough. I am so damned anxious to hear from you, to listen to your ideas and your new job. Darling, one of these days let me hear about those castles. I know I haven't told you not to, but just let a few sneak out so that I can figure a few things out for us, if I can possibly do it.

I think I'll close, Darling. I can't seem to think very capably. I promise you that I'll make up for this short letter. The head is really pounding. So long, Gal, give my love to your Ma. Take care of yourself. May God Bless you. Love, Mike. Don't forget, APO 760.

October 12, 1943 [*Tuesday*]

Hello Darling,

I wonder if I can make up for that miserable letter I wrote yesterday. Unfortunately, I didn't feel like a G. B. [*George Bernard*] Shaw. So naturally, that big head affected my hand. Then again that bull session distracted my attention and every time I got set to write something, they would tell a nice (?) joke and Hell I couldn't concentrate for love or money.

Sorry, Darling, I had to do a few things before I got around to finishing this letter. I even breezed thru' a book I had started. It was *Call Me Savage*. Queer, because the damn thing was about nothing else but sex and the thrill of intercourse and stuff. Personally, I liked it but why a guy wants to write about it. People know what it's all about so who the Hell wants to read about it. I didn't really finish the book. I laid it aside because I couldn't stand any more. Besides, in an environment like this, it doesn't do a guy any good to read such muddy stuff. Yeow! To top it off, one of my bunk mates has a bunch of pin-ups that would make a guy's hair stand on end. Guess this is just one of those horny periods I have. Fortunately, I am well protected by sand and sun.

Sorry, Darling, I didn't mean to write like that but I don't want you to feel that I don't have those periods. Thank God, I'm still human. We have never discussed that point but there are times when it seems hard to overcome. Your mention of it is subtle and sensible. You say that you miss me and easily overcome it with prayer. That is the easiest way out of this stupid yearning which has no outlet for satisfaction. The victory of will power and moral strength will taste sweeter when my time is served over here and we are together again.

Hell, Bette, I'm awfully sorry but I sound a bit mushy. It passes over easily.

One of the things that has gotten me to "griping" a bit is the fact that I haven't received any mail for a week. That deficiency is one of the biggest causes of low morale. Not too hard to overcome but it's there.

This morning I was thinking about what I should write to you. I wanted to be light and foolish. And yet, I remember times when you and I used to sit for hours and feel that we carried the world on our shoulders. Do you remember those long, windy sessions? There's an awful lot of power in those words that passed between us. It brought me one of the finest things in my life. The person who I want to share my life with. There I go again.

The whole damn trouble is that I am living a life of ease. When I am busy, I think a lot; when I am not, I relax and just rest. Stupid, isn't it but then again it can't be helped.

Dying from curiosity to hear about your new job. It's tough to be brought to the brink and then left with a "continued next week."

Well, Darling, this letter isn't striking the right tone. I'll close and see if I can do better later on.

Don't forget my correct APO is 760. So long for now, Darling. Give my regards to your Mother. Take care of yourself. May God Bless You. Love, Mike.

October 12, 1943 [*Tuesday*]

Dearest Darling,

When I received your letter [*September 24, 1943*] I was so nervous I could hardly wait to open it. When I did, the joy was so great that I thought I'd collapse from excitement. Thank you, Darling, we'll make a marvelous couple. I love you, and you are right when you say that you don't doubt it.

Let me answer a few questions before I go on. I received your letters of the 24th [*September*] (the acceptance of my proposal) and the letter from Knoxville, Iowa. Look Darling, do whatever you think is best with the Seagram's. I know how you feel because it is so significant to us. I think it is wise to keep that and my Xmas gift together. Things happen so rapidly one can never guess his next move.

I only passed thru' Des Moines. Did hear that it was a great soldier's town because of the WACS. But as a city itself, I hear it is quite a place. I do hope that you do get sent to New York State. At least, in upper NY. I have never been thru' it but I have always imagined those small cities as being great places.

"Darling, I miss you so much. You do everything with me. Hope you don't mind cause I just can't help it." How could I mind? The feeling is mutual. Whatever is in your mind, it is correlative with my ideas. Miss you, Darling. I am living for the day when we can be together. I was only kidding about my drunkenness and stuff. I can really be a sane person when it is necessary. I want to live such a perfect life with you that I feel lost as to how to show you what I mean. How unfortunate that we lost so much time.

You don't realize how good you make me feel when you say so much for me. You give me credit for so much. As if I have shown you a new life. That courage and strength, Darling, is to be the root of our love. We need no more but to be sure of ourselves. We have that. We can't miss.

Darling, there is one thing I must mention. You see, since our religions differ it will be impossible to be married in a Catholic church. We cannot have the flourish of a church wedding. We can be married in the rectory or the back of the church but not before the altar of God. Do you feel as though you would like to share my religion? I hope I am not being too difficult by my words. They are not demands. I never demand changes in a person's life, but they are merely obstacles that we can hurdle one way or the other. If you feel that you would like to be a convert to our religion, it is not difficult. If you do, we can be married with the fullest grace of God, and all the fullness of a Catholic marriage. I am asking you to accept this only as a thought. I shall give you all the guidance that I can. You have the heart for it and the strength to do it. Whatever benefits you gain from conversion, you will have to see for yourself. I can't tell you because it might sound like I was telling you what to do. Just consider the idea and see for yourself. If you wish to do it, you can get all the information from a Catholic priest. I am sure there will be one in any city you visit. Don't be afraid, Darling, you can see for yourself.

Gosh, I didn't mean to go thru' a long elegy. You have heard me say so much. I have always discussed religion from the human standpoint. I have never mentioned the technicalities. Do I sound like a husband already? I shan't be hurt either way, Darling, don't feel as if you must do it to please me. I love you for what you are; what you mean to me, and what you have done for me. My idea is to tell you all this so that you can choose for yourself. Believe me, it won't affect my love for you, either way you decide.

Gosh, Darling, every time I think of your "Yes" and the fine manner in which you said it, I get the nicest feeling in my heart and soul.

Whatever happened to us before only tends to make the future brighter for us. Whatever we missed before, we can make up for in the rest of our life time, and believe me, Darling, our life will be one of the nicest that two people could ever enjoy. I shan't spout about those castles in the air but merely of the fine companionship that can result from two people like ourselves.

I'll try to write to you again tomorrow. It is late now. I have been writing for 2½ hours and I am tired. Our task is easy, Darling, and the time will pass. Four months have gone by and they have passed quickly. The rest of the time that we are wasting apart will go just as quickly.

I am taking care of myself. Aside from an occasional "binge" I am in the best of health, and happiness is boundless by the thought of you.

Good Night, Darling. May God Bless You. Take care of yourself. I love you — Bette. Love, Mike.

P.S.: Note my correct APO is 760 — Just in case I haven't mentioned it before. M.

October 14, 1943 [*Thursday*]

Dearest Darling,

How you all? Every time I read your letters I can always pick up that phrase. It is a quaint sounding affair!

You know I always refer to some of my letters as being mushy and yet I have never told you how pretty your eyes are and the rest of the stuff that poets speak about. I will admit that I always enjoyed to run my hand thru' your lovely blonde hair. But what I am trying to lead up to was a description of this African moonlight. The other night when I answered your much-awaited letter, it was, as I said, quite late before I retired. I mailed your letter; in order to do that I had to walk to another barrack. I believe for the first time since I have been here, I noticed the moonlight. It was high and bright in the heavens. It lit everything so majestically, quite unlike the mental images of the eerie, dark Continent. It would indeed be welcomed by two lovers and believe me anyone who couldn't do justice to such moonlight is — well — just isn't. There you see the extent of my poetry. Oh! I forgot the most important. What I meant to say was that I just pictured the two of us under such a moon and I know that we could do justice to it.

Honestly, Hon, I haven't had so much rest since I was a civilian. Gad, what a horribly long time ago. But seriously, it feels good. The only thing that is wrong is that the more I rest the more I want. Unfortunately, since I had the chance to rest the weather changed and it got awfully warm. Here it is October and it feels like mid-July in Nebraska. Blood, sweat and tears. — The first is out but the second and third are true. The tears are shed because we are so far apart.

You mentioned a [*certain*] gal . . . . I thought that maybe that was some gal that I met in Okla. City. I didn't dance with her but what happened was one of the screwiest yet. (Or wouldn't that be me!) Someone called my room and started a conversation. After a while, some dame and a shave tail (Lieut.) walked in and had a drink with me. They invited me upstairs, and there were a couple more shavers and this dame. She was in bed, respectively dressed and she started to pop off. I never heard a more complicated, spoiled, temperamental brat in my life. She said that she was going to Childress, Texas, to see her husband. [*My brother, Tony, was commanding officer at Childress.*] We bantered back and forth while the Lieuts. just stood and drooled. Finally, I drank all the liquor (a good bottle of Old Taylor Bourbon) and made a graceful, if not too steady, exit. I never forgot that incident because it exemplified my stupid existence at that time. I don't remember her name but one never knows. Thank God that you came into my life. I didn't mind it too much (Life prior to our friendship) only it caused vanity and bickering. Too many people playing games. Thanks, Darling, I like games but [*you*] and I can fight it out for a life time. Does all that sound clear or am I just moanin' again.

Well, Darling, I must close. Again it is late and I must join the ranks of early risers. Gad! That is cruel. It shouldn't happen to a dog.

Good-night, Bette, take care of yourself. I'll need you as much in a short while as I need you now. I love you. May God Bless You — you big ugly 'ornery blonde Darling. (Eek! Is that me spilling over.) Love, Mike.

According to the 37th Troop Carrier Squadron's War Diary Summary for October 1943, the first three planes of the 37th left El Kabrit, Egypt, for El Aouina, Tunisia, on October 16, 1943 for the squadron's change of station. Using a shuttling service, the next ten days were required to make the 45 round trips necessary to move the entire squadron, less the squadron trucks and drivers. Each trip represented 3,600 miles. Two officers in charge of the truck convoy, carrying 32 enlisted men and equipment, left El Kabrit on October 26 and arrived by the end of November. The entire movement was made without incident, except for one forced landing. No one was injured, but some supplies were thrown from the plane when one of the engines failed.

During the month of October, more than 205 separate missions were flown. The flying officers each continued to average more than 125 flying hours monthly. The planes were being used to carry high priority cargo and passengers within 20 miles of the battle lines. The squadron's strength, as of October 31, was 52 officers and 218 enlisted men.

October 17, 1943 [*Sunday*]

Hello, Bette, Darling,

Say! I just received your card from Des Moines and I daresay, you weren't lacking for stamps. I am glad to see that you are traveling around this little ole' country of ours. Between the two of us, we will be a well-traveled family, although I wish we were doing it together. Probably when we meet again, we won't care very much to leave one spot we land in.

Darling, you know when I first wrote to you, I raved about all the little things I was doing. I said that I was going to sign up for Cadet training. Well, I haven't changed my mind but I have been wondering if it would pay to stick my neck out. I don't mean that I am chicken-livered but that training covers 16 months. We hope this damn mess will peter out long before that. And after we get married I will be content to just pass my time, until I am mustered out of the army. If you think that you would like me to go ahead with it, I will but if not I'll be content to stay GI and wait until they hand me that slip of paper that says: "Honorably Discharged." I'd like to go thru' the training but it may mean forestalling our union for a longer time. I mean that you might be an army wife after all the others are living a normal everyday life. Of course, all of this is premature but I'd like to hear your side of this. You keep telling me to be careful and it wouldn't be fair to let you sit on the ground and worry about me playing with the clouds. Darling, although our life is long, I'd hate to waste any of it as long as we can be together. Please don't try to be noble and give me the green light only because you feel I'd be happy. Tell me honestly what you feel. Our happiness no longer concerns just one of us but both of us. And let us not tear asunder what God is trying to put together. My hours in the air are mounting steadily and probably when I get home, I won't care to look at another plane except for a joy ride. I want so much to come home to you, I'll take my chances on being hurt by a car or falling off a stool at some bar. Believe me, Darling, my strongest argument against all that is not fear but the medium of time. And we have so much of that to make up.

I feel as if I could go on talking to you all night long. The only thing I have to answer you on is your post card. The mail situation is still bad but I know it is unavoidable [*probably because of our change of station*]. I only wish that I could write to you as often as you have promised and have written to me. Since my time is limited, I try to write as much as I can in that short space of time. Again I am hindered by the fact that I must do my writing at any hour and I can't linger with you too long because it is imperative that I get some rest. Sleep is a pretty important pastime over here and we usually try to make the best of it.

Darling, we are forever apologizing to each other because we try to spare each other. But you are ever in my thoughts and I miss you. Since our actions cannot betray our emotions, it is necessary to let our words do it for us. I know that you understand what I am thinking and saying, so I guess it is best that I cut this short. To realists like ourselves, words, no matter how deep, they are vague; no matter how satisfying, they leave a yearning greater than the human soul should be made to endure and yet they are the food for our patience and endurance. I love you, Bette.

Good-night, Darling, the hour is late; my body is tired but my heart and soul are hungry. Ole' man Morpheus will have to take a hand up and lead me to his dream land. So-Long. Give my regards to your Mother. Take care of yourself and keep me informed as to your progress in your new job. May God Bless You. Love, Mike.

October 19, 1943 [*Tuesday*]
[*Benghazi, Libya*]

Hello Darling,

It seems to me that I always complain, Bette, Ole' Gal, but again as usual it has been quite a while since I received any mail. The last semblance of a written word from the States was that post card from you.

Young Lady, you should be very proud. You know on those long trips we take, it is rather difficult to pass the time away. One of the best forms of time-idling is pictures. Every time I show your pictures, all I hear are Ohs and Ahs. I stick my chest out very proudly, a broad smile creases my pan and I announce: "We are going to get married as soon as I get home!" They look at me quizzically and wonder how the Hell I deserve the break. Can't explain it myself, just accept it as one of the most fortunate breaks of my life.

I have just finished a flowing description of the city of Benghazi to my folks. If I could go thru' the ordeal again. The old town is so shell-torn that it is hardly possible to tell anything, since there is nothing there. Nevertheless, seeing the city, amplifies the amount of strife that this part of the world has undergone. Those people who never realized what the boys went thru' should be forced to tour a place like Benghazi. When it is seen from a distance, it looks like a magnificent white cloak. But when seen from close range, the buildings or at least most of them are shells of their former selves. One part of the city is still inhabited by some Italians and natives. That part looks like those mysterious alleys that are shown in movies. It gives a guy the creeps just to walk up these streets. It certainly would not be wise to venture up there at night. Life is too valuable and short. This may be a wealth of education but the most important lesson that I have learned is that America is a great place. Not even the dead were left alone. The cemetery on the outskirts of town was a beautiful place, but it, too, was well-shelled. The thing that gets me the most of all is that I haven't any film with which to make a permanent record of all this. My last shots were taken in India, and I haven't developed those yet!

As always, the end of the month brings about the disappearance of that brilliant and beautiful moon I described to you. And again this part of the world is thrust into the darkness from which it gets its name. The only thing that betrays the existence of such a place is the fact that the stars still shine but they come no where near the light of the moon.

You know, Darling, I may sound awfully dramatic at times but it is the only way that I can express most of the things I want to say. In my effort to be picturesque, I may appear to be overemphasizing a lot of my ideas but it is the only way I can express things. As I said to my family — "Most of the things that once affected my moods, thrust me deep into moods, have disappeared by the fact that I am waiting to face a happy future." It sounds booklike but I can't say it any other way. You can see that it also affects the rest of my writing. Hell, I'm in a fump!

I hope you don't mind the way I write, Bette, but I know you want to hear from me. Again I am hampered by the lack of mail. I know that you write to me but dammit they never get around to sending it to us. One of these days I'm going to complain to the Postmaster. Gad! Darling, I feel good. Too bad you aren't around to feel the levity of my mood. I have been singing all day and this evening I feel as if I could devour a quart of bourbon, hold you in my arms, dance until the hours cease and forget that there is such a thing as night and day. It really is a bubbling mood and it is too bad it must be wasted in this sand and sweat. Hell! I almost forgot an important thing! A dream!

Last night, I was sleeping under the wing of my ship. (By the way, that is a very usual occurrence but I never mentioned it before.) My sleeping bag was cozy and warm although the air was cold and wet. I dreamt that you and I were married. It was impossible to take a honeymoon because I only had a 20-day furlough. (Don't mind the atmosphere I must present!) But we were lying (or is it laying?) in bed and my head was resting in the crook of your arm. I was talking but you never answered. It alarmed me. So I got up and got 2 cigarettes for us and then I came back and nestled in the same position. Finally, I said, "Bette, what the Hell is wrong?" By that time I was getting stewed up. Finally, you answered, "Mike. I just can't believe that you are home!" That's all there was to it. I was awakened by some voices and the dawn had broken thru'. But it was so good to hear you speak that I imagine that I was smiling in my sleep. That, my Darling, is what a soldier dreams of! Believe me, my spirits were very high throughout the whole day and you can see that that happiness still lingers now.

Darling, I must say, "Good Night." Thank you so much for you. You're great. Give my regards to your Mother. I hope you are faring well in your new job. Take care of yourself. May God Bless You. Love, Mike.

P.S.: I had a shot of genuine Seagram's VO last night — just a prelude to the day when we can douse that quart of Seagram's together. "What a glorious day for you and me, Dear —" So long, Bette. M.

October 24, 1943 [*Sunday*]
[*El Aouina, Tunisia*]

Good Morning, Darling,

So many things have happened since I last wrote to you and yet, this is the first time I am able to answer.

Before I go any further, you have to pardon this befuddled, sand-filled, sun-drenched mind of mine, but it seems funny that you are back in KC and you dismiss it all so easily and with no explanation. Not that I feel that I rate any but it would be a good course to steer me straight. But before I go any further, may I say that I miss you very much. If you feel that you would like to explain to me, please go ahead, I'll understand if I didn't and couldn't, I'd make a helluva husband. Hell! I'm all screwed up. I meant to say that I had received your letter of Oct. 3rd. It may be that you have already told me in a previous letter but this damned mail situation has everything upset. I receive one letter, and 2 days later I get an explanation. Oh well, I'd better go on to something that seems to be on your mind.

I realize that your situation with your Mother is difficult. As I said before, some people are better off merely by existing. Each day is like the next. Since our forthcoming marriage is so important to us and our love, as you say, is no joking matter, it is best that you leave well enough alone. The day that I come home to you will be surprise enough for your Mother. I couldn't be happy knowing that you are being jostled about so sensitive a point. That sensitivity has been an important part of both of us. So, Darling, that is your answer. Let it stand. Your happiness need not be shared, for it would be mishandled by people and hurt you. You are big to hold that to yourself and harbor it as a beautiful dream until I can make it a reality. Our next meeting will be glorious to behold and something we will cherish for our lifetime. I love you.

[*Half of the next page was censored.*] . . . I visited Tunis and I must say that I am less than intrigued with these cities. The less I see of them, the better off I am. I am quite content to stay in the small, snug surroundings of the radio compartment of my ship. I am quite satisfied with the rugged outdoor life I am forced to live and if anyone suggests a camping trip, I shall be compelled to bash his head in.

I am eager to ask what your future plans are but as I said before, I'll be better off if I wait until I hear from you again. Your letter was the first to reach me in 2 weeks. Haven't heard from my family and I am not really worried. Our new surroundings are a bit nicer because the country reminds me of Pennsylvania. It is a bit cooler than my former station and the days are shorter. In due time, I'll be able to give you a full description of our last camp. I am saving that for a later letter. Here I go again, but the letter received from Knoxville was dated the 27th of Sept. This one the 3rd of Oct. I know that you must have written one in the meantime.

Gosh, Darling, that letter was as refreshing as the morning dew. . . . I know that I need not worry about you. The feeling is identical. For if I had only a fascination and not love for you, I wouldn't care very much if I was faithful or not. Since my feeling for you is so strong, I have no urges and I don't care to have any.

Your explanation of religious backgrounds is very correct. Mine is strong. You are right when you say that you do what is expected of you. Religion or the strength of it, is based on the distinction of knowing right from wrong. The technicalities are merely further armor to make it easier for me to combat our human failings.

Every time I reread my letters, I sound more and more as if I were giving a theological sermon. But again these discussions only give us both a clearer picture of some subjects. We shan't ever argue about them. Discussions are more apt to produce the necessary effects.

Again (Repetitious me!) Every time I go off on a tangent, I want to tell you about my surroundings and about what your great, big hero (?) is doing, but, again, I am hindered because I can't supply the missing words. (Censor's idea.) It would all make such boring literature anyhow.

Say, Gal, I am curious to know what that censor said to you. What was his name? [*This was a reference to Nick Pappaeliou's comments in my letter of September 18, 1943.*]

The kid who is on my ship now is a hell of a nice guy. He knows all about you and he follows our progress as closely as if he were a part of it. [*Here I was either referring to Clete Carmean or Julie Ziankiewicz, my crew chiefs.*] "Dirty Gertie" [*from Bizerte*] our ship is our constant companion. She has a naked gal painted on her nose, and believe me she's an exciting woman. "JIPPA" has gone and left us. [*The plane may have been transferred to another outfit.*] "Gertie" is the envy of the gang and we are trying our best to keep her a virgin as long as we can. She still has a lot to learn and she isn't ready for this cruel world yet. I hope you don't get jealous of her. Besides, she's a red head and she has a hell of a temper. She has a terrific cough when she gets started in the mornings. (Too much liquor and smoke.) [*I was referring, of course, to the natural engine reaction of start-up — sputtering, followed by a blast of blue smoke as the engine catches.*] She's a good ship and we are proud of her. She can't woo me, though, I am already in love. A guy can't expect to run around with a red head and expect not to get burned. That's enough for "Dirty Gertie." You'll hear more about her.

Well, Darling, I must close. Again I am busy as Hell and I try to write as often as I can. I guess that succession of letters last week or was it 2 weeks ago, really surprised you. I just had to talk to you. These ants over here are not very interesting (18 letters, Gad! What a word!).

Good-Night, Bette, take care of yourself. Give my regards to your Mother. Don't worry about her. She has lived 40 years plus and she is satisfied. Don't try to change her, she would be hurt by it. Please write and write until there is no more paper in KC. May God Bless You. Love, Mike.

October 26, 1943 [*Tuesday*]
Somewhere in Tunisia

Hello Darling,

Another day and yet no mail. You'll have to excuse my shaky hand but I can hardly close it. It is just slightly blistered from digging a slit trench and putting up a tent. We finished most of the tent last night and just in time because it rained like Hell. We put the finishing touches on by digging a drainage ditch and slit trench, raked up the front yard and generally straightened out. All in all, the place can at least be called home, if there is such a thing.

There is one thing that seems strange about this place and that is the fact that the night seems to fall so early in the day. I know that the statement sounds damned silly but it's the truth. By 6 PM, it is practically time to retire. I don't know if it was the rain or the coolness of the air but for the first time in over a month, I had a good night's sleep last night.

You know, Bette, I didn't realize how aimlessly I wrote until I started this letter. I'll be damned if I can see one inkling of sense in all the words I have written. It would be impossible to put into words exactly how I feel. Oh, what the Hell! A guy has to say something. But at any rate, you can sell all the words I put into a letter when I do receive one from you.

It seemed rather funny but it isn't far from wrong. Almost continuously, there are planes that [*are*] coming or passing overhead. When we get home, it will be necessary to live near an airport so that I can sleep. Darling, if we were to spend our life in a trailer, I'd be right at home. [*Our camp was located right at the end of the runway of the field at El Aouina, Tunisia. Hence, the constant hum of incoming and outgoing aircraft.*] Between tents and sleeping on and under the plane, a civilized, soft bed would be bearable. I guess you had better put rocks in the bed. I'd really rather be at home.

You see what I mean, just words. Sometimes I wonder what the Hell a guy really thinks about. You can file this letter with the "incidental." Written because I want to talk to you and yet I have nothing to say. It is one of those moments a guy feels he is close to the one he loves, words are unnecessary, even an obstacle. Content just to sit with her, and feel that she is there. Appreciate and love her all the more, just because she is there. [*See the Valentine card from Bette on February 14, 1985 (p. 281), written four months before she died!*]

But, Darling, all these things — I mean I just don't feel like this letter is interesting. I'll close and do better when my hand is more flexible and my mind and body are rested.

So long, Bette, take care of yourself. May God Bless You. Even in a tent, your picture is beautiful. Brings the sunlight, where it can't possibly reach. Love, Mike.

October 26, 1943 [*Tuesday*]

Good Evening, Darling,

I received a one-page letter from you dated Sept. 28, and yet in answer to it, I feel I owe you an extremely long and assuring [*letter*], and above all, I shan't say, "I told you so."

You don't ask me to scold you because you scolded yourself, if it is necessary. Why? Darling, why? You did what you wanted to do and it proved well worth the experience. [*Bette had taken a job in Des Moines, Iowa, but it did not pan out, so she returned to Kansas City.*] Whatever the reasons, I don't care; nevertheless you [*have*] your reasons and you are satisfied by them. I often told you not to leave KC, not because you weren't prepared for it but because you would be lacking the companionship that you needed. I never hindered your freedom or thought or wish.

You would never [*have*] made a fool of yourself because you are too stable for that. New ventures are guesses, we don't always guess right. Whatever means of recovery that you feel are necessary, take them and really relax and make the best of them.

I'll admit that your letter was very vague. However, I know that you are wanting a few words of assurance. You have it wholeheartedly and extremely sincerely. You seem to feel so hurt by this last [*job*] experience. Don't Darling, it isn't worth it. Each mistake is a means of adding to our self-satisfaction (Good or Bad!) and to our self-consciousness, conversely to making us shy but fortifying ourselves to whatever else may even come to us. Darling, you speak as if I succeeded in everything I do. I didn't. I lost a Hell of a lot of time, and although it hurt me, I recovered — only to make a stronger thrust the next time. If everything we did was successful, we would become so sure of ourselves that defeat is not a temporary setback but a calamity and catastrophe. As long as we keep ourselves on the slight side of the blue ledger, we are doing OK.

Of all your words, I smiled and was best suited by those small and concluding words — "There isn't much to say except I love you and miss you." As if that isn't much to say — Only the means to keep a guy so happy that he can hardly sit quietly.

Those castles in the air — they aren't lost nor shipwrecked. You want to build more and bigger ones. OK! Go ahead — your castles in the air for me are to stay as beautiful as you are, as healthy as you are, and as you are — because I am coming back to you and not to a castle in the air. You are my castle, Darling. As they say in poetry and music, "You are the seven wonders of the world and some!"

You needn't worry about that fanning. As I said before, if you get the least bit ornery, I shan't hesitate to put some red welts on that — of yours. I guess the only time that you really will have that coming to you will be when you burn my steak (Are there such things?) or anything like that.

No, Darling, don't ask me to get angry with you or anything like that. Remember all I want is you. Look at me. I joined the Army and what have I gotten for it, except a lot of lost time and perhaps a few other things which we won't discuss. So you see, Bette, all our ventures aren't made of cake and sweet. The bitter sometimes makes life a Hell of a lot sweeter.

Must close. Have to get up early. Wrote you a letter earlier to-day. Didn't make much sense. I'll be waiting for more. If the mail gets going, we can discuss things as they happen, not a year later.

Good night, Darling, take care of yourself. May God Bless You. Love, Mike. P.S. At least you saw Des Moines and Knoxville. That's sumpin!

According to the 37th Squadron's War Diary, on October 29, 1943, one of our planes was involved in an accident while making a landing; two planes were damaged considerably. Our C-47 was turned over to the service squadron to be salvaged. The aircraft was "Dirty Gertie," but I had been sick with the flu when the incident occurred.

On October 31, a British bomber — a Wellington with unreleased bombs — which had gotten lost returning from a bombing mission over Italy, came in for a landing at our field, about midnight. The plane landed on the runway, but continued and crashed through the tent area. Several tents, personal equipment, and one jeep were damaged. One officer had a leg broken when the plane rolled over him.

October 31, 1943 [*Sunday*]

Hello Bette,

I don't want to hear another word about that last venture. You are driving yourself to a million and one apologies and they aren't necessary. Since you have already closed the subject, it should stay that way.

I kinda felt that you wouldn't be satisfied until you took that plane ride. It's funny but that whole area is one big front and the only thing to expect when you fly thru' it is bad weather. That vibration is due to the large engines those ships have. [*The rest of the thought was cut out by the censor.*]

Darling, you will have to pardon me if my letter doesn't sound too normal. I haven't been feeling so good the last few days. I have had a terrific case of upset stomach and all the effects. Fortunately, I am coming out of it and I'll be ready for duty in a day or so.

I received a letter from my brother, Tom. He wrote a swell letter and he gave me some thoughts to work upon. He said that if you feel the same way about me that I feel about you, he would be glad to add you to his list of correspondents. He won't be able to write you often because this coming year will be an extremely full year for him. But at any rate, you shall have gained a friend. He speaks of marriage as a lifelong job. That it is not a private affair but also a social affair. Darling, since we are content just to live normally, I can't see anything but plain ole' smooth sailing. If Lucy hasn't been writing, don't mind. She sometimes forgets to write to me. Enough of that for a while!

I finally got into Italy proper. We stopped at [*Bari*]. It's a city on the outside of the heel. I don't claim to be a linguist but my knowledge of the Italian language has been a great advantage to me. Everywhere I went, I was surrounded by an audience. They seemed to appreciate the fact that an American could speak their language. In order to eat chow, we had to eat at the Officer's mess (but we ate in the kitchen). At any rate, I had quite a talk with the cooks. The officers ate bully beef but the crew chief and I had steak. I expect to get into [*Naples*] one of these days.

I am sorry, Darling, but this "Sugar" report has to be short. I can't concentrate and every time I get my teeth into a meaty piece of news, I have to run. I have worn such a track from my tent to the latrines that they can use it for a drainage ditch. I hope that you have received most of my mail. For a while at the beginning of the month, I was able to write quite often and I did. Since I did such a miserable job of it, I'll try to do better tomorrow.

So long, Honey, take it easy. Miss you. May God Bless You. — Love, Mike.

[*This illness was the only time that I went on "sick call" during my three years of service. It was recorded in the 37th Squadron's Sick Report.*]

October 31, 1943 [*Sunday*]

Good Evening, Bette,

I'll take that bet. That makes $5. You owe me, Darling. You're marvelous. I received your letter of the 5th [*October*], the one in which you have enclosed the World Series dope.

I am glad that you are sending me the dope. You see, we knew the results but we never got the goods on how it was done.

Your letter, Darling, was better than all the medicines in the world. It sounded different and so much like yourself. This new job you speak of, may never make you a millionairess but you'll be happy. You see, Bette, since I never gleaned any fortunes, I was always skeptical of any big money. You see in civilian life, my salary averaged between $35 and $40 per [*week*]. I always had a Hell of a good time and very little worry. So you see, Darling, that is part of the fortune you can expect. I was never overly prosperous. If you remember, one night, you and I spent a few hours discussing the lean years that our families had seen. I am not building you up for a letdown, as a matter of fact, I am telling you that our life may mean some struggle but odds say that we can always laugh and grin about it. You are game, so am I, future watch out.

Darling, I am proud of you. You speak of domestication, if I didn't think you had it in you, I wouldn't even [*have*] tried to see you as a lifetime job. I caught that subtle hint — "I don't mind doing it, but I don't like to work and do housework, too. It makes the day too long." I guess your letter gave me such a lift that I floated into one of those castles in the air. To me, the things that are happening now are incidental. This life that you and I are preparing ourselves for is the thing that counts.

Gad, Bette, everything that you said in this letter was so close to me that I felt like taking you in my arms, passing my hand thru' your lovely hair and kissing you so hard that your lips would cry for mercy. "Darling, let's go to lots of baseball games!" Just try to keep us away from them. I am afraid that I am not too noisy a fan because I scan plays with too critical an eye. To me, things have to be letter perfect to be great or even good. Eye of an expert, you know (Ahem!). Woman, Woman, how can a man help but be in love with you.

When I wrote to you this AM, it was rather torturous to write. But I am feeling a bit better, not yet quite like myself, but well enough to spill these words onto you. You know, Darling, I can see green grass, rolling hills, roses, gardenias, a little home, a few young Bettes and Mikes.

About those clippings, the only thing we could read was written by Englishmen. What they <u>don't know</u> about baseball could cover the world a million times. Just to read an American's words is good enough. And please, Darling, send me some pictures of that ugly pan of yours.

Hey, Gal! You didn't perchance drink that bottle of Seagram's after that last setback? Kind of figured you'd go on a binge just to forget. I'd never forgive you for it, if you did.

Well, Darling, I'm going to close. I'd like to write more but a lantern doesn't throw much light. Don't mind being in bad shape but don't feel like being a physical wreck! As you said about the film, just send them, let's join the ranks of veterans and do things before we write about them. It takes so long for letters to interchange.

Good night, Bette. Thank God for you. You are like the voice out of the wilderness. Give my love to Mother. I am taking care of myself, only occasionally, something like this is apt to happen. May God Bless You. Love, Mike.

The intelligence officer formalized the War Diary for the 37th Troop Carrier Squadron. In the summary, he notes that November 15, 1943, marked the completion of twelve months overseas. During this one-year period, the squadron flew for a total of 19,431 hours.

From March 14 through November 15, 1943, (accurate records for the first four months of overseas service are not available), the following statistics were recorded:

1. Passenger miles flown: 13,207,466
2. Pounds of cargo hauled: 9,003,446
3. Ton miles flown: 3,632,321 [*A ton mile is figured by multiplying the number of tons by the number of miles.*]
4. Passengers carried: 25,844
5. Separate missions completed: 1,241

The War Diary also notes that on November 1, six courier runs were carried out, by order of M.A.T.S. (Military Air Transport Service).

November 2, 1943 [*Tuesday*]

Hello Bette,

Had a regular jam session last night. Good ole' geetar and hillbilly yodeling. Yeah man! Really had a time.

I spent . . . 1½ hour[s] writing to Tom, my brother. In his letter, he asked me to write about you, so I did it good and wrote at least 4 pages about you. Lady, you should really be flattered. Since Tom will be writing to you, I thought it best that he know us and the happiness we are seeking. He really is a Hell of a swell guy and he cares about everything.

I received 2 letters from you yesterday, and they had the clippings of the 2nd and 3rd games in them. Are you sure the Cards are going to win? (Ha! Ha!) [*The Yankees won the 1943 World Series, four games to one.*] I daresay that they cost you a load of postage.

I can't understand what the Hell the censor cut out of that letter because I very rarely step out of bounds of info'. However, I guess these guys get a bullet stuck somewhere and they start cutting everything out of these letters.

I wouldn't worry about that job situation you talk about. You seem to do OK. It may not be the best but as I said before, as long as you are happy you can't go wrong.

If I did not send your mail air mail it will be because it will be difficult to get these envelopes. However, since you say it only took 2 days longer than usual, it isn't such a bad deal.

You were speaking about a vase you bought and asked me if I did like it or at least hoped I like it. Darling, I have seen your choice of clothes and knick-knacks, and I never yet have seen one thing that I thought was unmatched. You are one gal that can wear clothes and really make a guy's eyes pop out. It's no wonder you awed me when I first saw you. I haven't come out of it yet.

I haven't seen a show since I left my last base in the Nile Delta. And I don't miss them because the warmest place at night here is in bed and believe me, Darling, my ole sack is comfortable.

That Seagram's. We'll drink it. (Can't waste it, rationing!) The bottle will not receive the fate that all ordinary bottles receive. It will be red-ribboned and revered like a Buddha.

OK, about that ring deal. I'll see if I can match the ring on your finger. A wedding ring usually isn't so fancy, tho' is it? Mom wears an ordinary gold band. I kind of like the new custom that the man wears a ring too. Kind of makes things even, don't you think?

I had intentions of having Tom marry us, anyhow. You see in my letter to him, I told him about it. Obviously, you don't expect me to be home by next Summer. You see, Tom won't be ordained until May [*1944*]. He can't perform the ceremony until he is ordained into the priesthood. That will happen in May. But at any rate, I am glad that you resigned yourself to such a long wait. A guy can never tell how much time he's liable to spend over here. But it will be the nicest thing in the world if Tom does perform the ceremony. He'll do it too, no matter where he is. He will be there.

Gonna' close now, Honey. There is too much noise around here a guy can hardly concentrate. Native gals! Whew!

So long, Bette. May God Bless You. Take care of yourself. Love, Mike.

The War Diary for November 2 showed that the 37th Squadron carried out three courier runs, and that one new airplane had been assigned to the squadron. On November 3, there were five courier runs, and another six the next day. On the night of November 4, a British stage show was presented at the base theater in place of the regular movie.

November 5, 1943 [*Friday*]

Good Evening, Darling,

Night shades falling, kind of quiet and it puts a guy in the perfect mood for dreaming. When God made me a realist, He must have felt that it wouldn't be a bad idea if He added a bit of the dreamer to my soul. Unfortunately, at the time, He didn't tell me that a war would be interposed so that my dreams would take time to materialize.

Do you know, Bette, we didn't or haven't shared one holiday together. I guess I'll call this epistle, Holiday Issue, because Thanksgiving isn't so far off and it will take just short of that for this letter to reach you. My mood is not a melancholy one but one which can depict and foresee the niceties and warmth of holidays together. All of them. Surely God will be kind enough to give them to us next year. These that are coming up, we can put on the red side of the ledger and mark them up to unwanted experience. Forgive me if I must delve into my past to dig up my ideas but at least you will be able to see what I missed and wanted and therefore can learn thru' words and not our life together.

Stretch and I never took the time to walk down 5th Ave. or one of the busier streets and look and buy for the holidays, we were too busy taking care of our selfish selves to bring joy to those people that were close to us. Not for me, I like to gaze and buy. Then to present the gifts at the cheerful Christmas table and hear the "Oohs" and "Aahs." Even when Tony or Lou get a tie they hate the sight of. When I did it I did it alone because she wasn't interested.

Let me tell you of one Christmas so that you can see what I have to make up. It was the year after I graduated from H.S. [*1939*]. I didn't even know Stretch, so that she isn't part of this. But that year, the Ingrisanos were really on their royal, and Mom didn't know where our next turkey was coming from. "Doc" was still a struggling med student and the rest of us were just struggling. "Doc" told me that he had $1, and he wanted me to help do the Christmas shopping for both of us. We went out and bought a dozen peppermint canes and paper and cards. We locked ourselves in our room and proceeded to wrap our Christmas gifts. In the process, we had more fun than we had had for our lifetimes. Came the big dinner and we presented our gifts. In the "Chief's," my Dad, we added a few 5 cent stogies, Italian style. To Mom's we added a few more sweets. The rest of the gang, Tony, Ted, Tom and Lucy, just received a single stick of candy. Since no one knew what to expect, the surprise was great. The presentation brought out so much humor that it hid the grief of that miserable year. In all of that, we still retained our fine sense of humor. Everything was a success and we had a great time.

You see, Darling, this is just one of the things I want you to help me make up. There will be a few changes in the next Ingrisano holiday because it will be Tony, Sheila and "Rebel" (maybe more); Lou ("Doc") and Sally [*Koch*] (and maybe more); Ted and Louise and their babies, Stella Ann, and Thomas Michael; Tom as Father Tom; Lucy and ?; you and I (?) (no comment) and the Chief and Mom. Quite a clan, isn't it? You won't mind too much, will you, Darling? They really are my hidden love. So again, you see, all that is what a guy looks forward to, and I don't intend to do it alone. That's why I always include you in my plans. You are the hinge that is going to swing open the door of my future. Our future. I always see you as the gal that is swinging along side of me, arm in arm. The gal with the lovely hair that I love to run my fingers thru'. The lovely woman with the pug nose and sleek body who knows how to wear clothes and isn't ashamed to admit that she loves me and who I love so dearly. I am not being mushy, Darling, just grateful to you for bringing me such happiness and unfortunately, it has to be so short-lived. But that was just a prelude of things to come.

You see, Darling, after all these words, why all the things I am doing cannot be interesting because they bring me close to a world of destruction, ruin, grief, and poverty. I want our world of beauty, grace, gentleness, and love.

I am going to close. It is dark and am getting tired. Sleep and another day has passed and I am getting closer to you and home.

Good night, Bette, May God Bless You. Take care of yourself. Give my love to Mother. Love, Mike.

The War Diary's report for November 5-8, 1943, showed more courier and special missions carried out. On November 5, one plane was slightly damaged by fire and one radio operator hospitalized as a result of an explosion caused by using gasoline to wash down oil spots inside the plane. Chaplain Richert, the Group Chaplain, arrived from Sicily on November 6. The next day, he conducted Protestant services in the mess hall, and, the War Diary noted, was very "well received."

November 9, 1943 [*Tuesday*]
[*Sardinia & Corsica*]

Hello Darling,

I received your very marvelous letter of Oct. 22. But before I go much further I must apologize because my letters will be a bit short for a while. It is for no reason except that I must snatch moments to write to you and paper is short. But above all, I must add my assertions that ours will be a life. (Mail call — No Mail — damn!) I wouldn't doubt that it was one of our ships that was in that picture. We got around there so often that we could have landed on the Pyramids without blinking an eye. I didn't get all the baseball clippings, *i.e.*, I only got as far as the third game. I can't imagine what is screwing up the mail works. We can keep in pretty good touch of the football season thru *Stars and Stripes*. The latest was that N. D. [*Notre Dame*] beat Army and gal that is pretty late.

Well, Darling, your soldier boy is at it again. You can add two more to my list. Sardinia and Corsica. Can't blame you for being jealous of me, I get around so much but home is the only place in the world. You lucky people. I daresay that all my travels are a wealth of education because I see so many different things. There are so many strange people, customs, and places, and since I can speak a little French and a Hell of a lot of dialectic Italian, it is more interesting to me.

Corsica, my Darling, is a picture-book island. Snow-capped mountains, green hills and weather like our states at this time of the year. The [*Ajaccio — city name cut by censor*] is built in the lowlands, shrouded by green, heavily-foliaged mountains. In order to get to any point in the city, it is necessary to climb uphill. For the first time, I regretted the lack of a camera because that city had a wealth of good snapshots. I was able to procure some postcards but I can't send them home. It is truly a tourist's city. The place is splattered with memorials to Napoleon and his brothers and predecessors. We couldn't find his home but we saw enough to assure us that he really loved [*it*] there. We visited one of their night clubs, [*censored*] and Darling, I never saw so many shady characters in my life. I expected any one of them to suddenly start to dance the "Adagio." And, believe me, Bette, that one place had as much atmosphere as anyone could possibly want. We sat and drank 2 bottles of good champagne (at $12.00 per). With all that, I can readily see how the French were so inspired to paint. (The Corsican gals are quite an inspiration at that.)

Well, Bette, I wish I could write more but really you will have to abide by me and the circumstances. In face of all this temptation, I am still a good boy. (Or did we promise not to discuss that.)

You surpass anything I have seen and one need not wonder why I love you as much as

I do. With every passing day and temptation, I look forward more eagerly to the fine life we will share. Feels so good, it hurts to think about it. I was afraid that I might get home-sick. Can't do that because it is injurious to my morale. (Am I preaching?)

Well, Bette, must close. Give my love to Mother. Have you sent any mail to my <u>correct</u> APO 760 yet? Haven't heard from home in 2 weeks — Drives a guy nuts. Can take anything but that.

Good night, Darling. May God Bless You. Miss you. Ever, Mike.

Four courier runs were made on November 10, according to the War Diary. A truck convoy with 28 enlisted men and one officer arrived from El Kabrit, Egypt, also on that date. Four enlisted men and one officer remained at Gabes, Tunisia, with a gas truck that had broken down. Except for the gas truck, the entire 15-day trip had been made without incident.

November 11, 1943 [*Thursday*] (Wish it was 1918)

Dearest Darling Bette,

I received a slew of mail to-day. Four letters and of course one of them from you and Thank You, Darling, for the 2 marvelous pictures. Gad, Woman, you are truly a beautiful gal. Often wonder how I rate such a break. I just gotta love you and I am glad for the re-taliation.

I don't know if I can ride, Darling, because I have never done it. If I were ever to get on a horse, I'd probably be telling the wrong end to go. But I'll try anything once. Never yet have I refused a dare.

Darling, you bring the future right into my tent every time you speak of a home and how hard you are going to try to make it everything I want. I ask very little, Darling. When I get home, we will be separated only because of the Army; but once I get mustered out, I want you to be with me all the time. Darling, I am not the type of person who likes to wander by himself. When I am alone, my mind is my companion. Since we will take the vows to love and honor, I hope to include, mentally, to remain forever together until that reaper calls harvest. Bette, do you realize that it will be so perfect? We are the same temperament. The only time I ever forgot an obligation was when I decided to get drunk but I never had anyone to hold me to my duties. Now, there is no reason to drink alone. You will always be there. No, Bette, this story book life we are planning shan't be spoiled by anything. Both of us realize what we want and we know how to hold it. We are not the type to spoil something we so carefully cherish now. Our mutual make-up is so sensitive that foolish-ness on any one of our parts would cause a complete crack-up of our normal selves. Do you see what I am trying to say, Darling? I don't want to continue writing in that view be-cause it adds morbidity to a joyful scene of happiness. We know how to laugh and we will never forget it.

I mentioned [*cut by censor — possibly Algiers*] on my way over but I never had an opportunity to see the town. Finally, it came. [*Algiers cut by censor*] is a typical French town. People are white and believe me that is rather strange in No. Africa. The only difference is that they don't speak English. As I walked down the [*street name cut by censor*], I felt as if it was no different from 5th Avenue. I wouldn't trade it for the dirtiest, muddiest backwoods road in the States. When tongues differ, there is no bridge that can make the breach. That's why I am so partial to the Italians because I can speak to them and understand them. My French is limited and I stammer every time I say anything.

By the time you receive this letter I guess you will have put on 10 lbs. From a tremendous Thanksgiving meal. Enjoy it, you lucky people. We hope to get turkey but as luck will have it, I'll probably be busy that day and miss mess at my base. Nevertheless, one day over here is like the rest. One never worries about the day of the week or the month.

Well, Darling, must close, snatching again. Has my sister written to you? If she hasn't I shall proceed to ball the Hell out of her. After all, you are going to be her sister-in-law.

Good night, Bette, take life easy. I feel great and happy but not enough until we meet again. Give my love to Mother. May God Bless You. Love, Mike.

On November 11, the squadron carried out six courier and special runs. The War Diary reported that Captain Milstead, the Group Intelligence Officer, arrived with Staff Sergeant Wells, who had been a prisoner of war in Italy since December 9, 1942. Staff Sergeant Wells was taken to the 12th Air Force Intelligence Office for interrogation.

Four courier and special runs were carried out on November 12. All glider personnel — 13 enlisted men and one officer — were transferred out of the 37th Squadron, while the remainder of the truck convoy, which had been stuck in Gabes, arrived in camp. Thirty "Escape Money" pouches, each containing 600 Algiers Francs, were also forwarded to Group Intelligence Officer on that date, according to the War Diary.

November 13, 1943 [*Saturday*]

My Sweet,

I have washed my face (surprise!), combed my hair, loaded and lit my pipe and now I am going to tell you how marvelous you are. I received 4 letters from you in one day and Honey, that is the epitome of satisfaction.

First of all, though, you are putting me on a pedestal. You are making me supernatural and superhuman. I'm not. I want you to think of me as the guy who loves you and hopes to spend his life making you believe it. The way you throw adjectives at me, makes the scale tip off balance, no 50-50. Don't think I'm not flattered and that I don't like it. I do and why shouldn't I. I never disagreed with my conceited self. But, Darling, we will be trying to overdo each other by our use of adjectives. But I understand that we must write like that because it brings us so closer together. Words are our only medium. I want so much to say "I love you." But you must hear it from my pen.

Your letters speak of the type of person I have always wanted. Laughs, tears, struggle and stupidities — all those we must share or it won't be complete. We can't conceal things from each other. Some foolishness may occur but in time we will discuss them. Time has always won over me and my conscience was always cleared by it. A lot of the things that I write about may not make sense now. But I will never leave you in the dark so that your mind will do flips. In our young love, we have already made one mistake. We should have been married in Ft. Wayne, but really the mistake was mine. I had to clear one situation, honestly, before I accepted the future that our destinies had drawn for us.

Since we have already closed the issue about our gallivanting, there is no reason for me to add more. You did it and rid yourself of the evil of pursuit.

You probably have already taken the pictures you speak about. Your Mother is right, your hair is to be worn long. Darling, those 3 extra inches mean more hair for me to stroke. (Sounds like I was currying a horse, but I know you understand the idea I am trying to convey!) 6 lbs., that's not bad. Are they in the right places. Nevertheless, it shows that you are gaining weight and that that nervous condition is leaving you. Good Gal!

Your one letter speaks about a quiet Saturday and Sunday. How I envy you! And how bitterly I feel because I can't share them with you. You see, Darling, again, why there is so much time to make up. To us, over here, there are no such things as days. Every one is like the next. It's not bad because we don't say, "the weeks are passing but the months are!" Since the month covers more, it makes the time pass — easy deduction, isn't it?

"The Lord's Prayer"; "Ave Maria"; *Nutcracker Suite*; *Symphony Pathetique*; the lighter vein — "B.B." [*Begin the Bequine*]; "You'd Be So Nice to Come Home to"; "White Christmas"; "Velvet Moon"; "Black Magic"; "You'll Never Know"; and thousands of others. Bette, you don't realize what I'd give to sit my seat down in a comfortable chair and entertain us with that kind of music. The Lord only knows how much I miss those things and the atmosphere that has always surrounded them.

Darling, again as before, you do as you like. If you want to tell your Mother about us, go ahead. I'm sure she will be prouder of us than to use it as a jest. Your thoughts on that are more effective than mine because you know your Mother better than I do.

"The only thing that is in this house is rum and coke." — Don't do that to me. Gad! My throat gets parched when you talk like that. This damn wine over here will make a guy's teeth fall out and his ears wiggle. But I'll show you. I'll put you on a diet of coke while I absorb enough rum and bourbon to make up for this surmounting thirst. When I reach your level you can start to join me. Say, Bette, let's decide on one brand of cigarettes so that we needn't worry about having different kinds around the house. Philip Morris has been my brand for 6 years. And I like Camels, if you prefer to stick with Camels. At any rate, it will be a good reminder of my stay in this part of the world.

Thanks, Bette, for the Christmas present. I can't say the same that I am sending you anything. I haven't received it yet but I guess I'll get it sometime next summer. Nevertheless, the thought is there. I was wondering if you'd like it but do you think it would be a good idea if I had a bracelet made for you of the coins that I have collected. Can't do it here but when I get back. Got enough so that I could probably make a necklace too. Think it's a good idea?

I received the 4th game. Thank you, Darling, for remembering my liking for statistics. You really are pouring them in. Save that $5 so that you can buy me some drinks in the Plaza Royale.

Say, Bette, think about that Literary Guild. See if you can get a complete or nearly complete set of [*Ernest*] Hemingway's books: *Sun Also Rises*, *Death in the Afternoon*, *For Whom the Bell Tolls*, *Farewell to Arms*, *To Have and to Hold*, and others. I have read most of them but they make a Hell of a collection. You'll enjoy *Song of Bernadette*. I think I have already written about that. Literature and Music are good hobbies.

Memories — What a grand feeling when one can turn back the days and laugh or cry over something that has happened. Yes. I clearly remember the night in KC on the corner of 14th and Main. I'm afraid we were both stiff. And after we finally got a trolley, we went to Memorial Park and talked a long while. I couldn't take you home that night because I would have been late for bed check. You tried hard to convince me that it was OK for you to go home alone. I haven't forgotten. And many's the time I got flustered because you were not home when I called you up. It was a tough disappointment when you weren't in and I had nothing to do. Never again, Darling, you'll be home because it will be our home.

So long, Honey, must close. Light is bad and gotta save these eyes so that I can look at you.

Give my love to Mother. May God Bless You. Take care of yourself. I love you deeply. So long for now. Love, Mike.

November 13, 1943 [*Saturday*]

Hello Darling,

Here I am back again but I just can't help myself. Seven letters and one Christmas greeting in one day. That's almost as much as a guy can stand. Someone must have heard our plea for some decent mail service.

Your spelling, yes, Darling, I have noticed a few mistakes and they are simple ones. You are too anxious to convey your ideas, consequently, you get careless about your spelling. However, I wouldn't worry about it. Any gal that can write to me as often as you do, my Sweet, needn't worry about a little reproach because of bad spelling. I know what you are saying and that's all that matters. Righto!

I haven't heard any ruling which says it is necessary for you to get an OK to send pictures that size. Take it, try to mail it, if no one says anything. OK — and I needn't worry about the situation because I know that you will take care of it.

Yes, Darling, the final reports on the Series are in and you are out $5.

Darling, don't worry about our reading material. It isn't the latest but it is something to read. I can't say that I can wrap my hands around any current *Reader's Digest*s but I'll get one sooner or later! It's fun to read about places where the war was and I have just visited. Kind of 2nd hand but it is interesting. I never did find that month's *American* magazine that would conclude that story which I was reading. Probably catch up to it sometime next year.

Thanks for the Christmas Greetings. A little premature but at any rate it brings the odor of holly and Christmas to my extraordinarily large snout! Don't worry about your shrunken pay checks. At least you eat. Why worry!

I haven't heard from the family concerning [*my brother*] Lou. But I did hear that he has been relieved and sent to a rest camp. He has been overseas for at least 18 months now. Gad! I hope that same fate doesn't fall on my shoulders. That's a Hell of a long time to go. Only 15 months to go.

Darling, you mustn't worry when you don't hear from me and above all don't let your imagination run away with your head! (It's too lovely!) We both are so sure that I'll be all right so why should we worry about it.

I am so glad that you like your work. You see, Bette, after all that fretting and fussing, everything turned out OK. I don't know what PBX is but I'm glad you like it. Is it something to eat? Or is it a new brand of liquor on the market. (Excuse, please, just jesting. Feel frisky and can't help but inject some levity into these terrifyingly morbid (?) epistles.)

My descriptions of these mysterious places seem to enchant you. You seem to revel in these slinking, dark, uncomfortably dirty scenes. Darling, is there a Hyde personality in you which I know nothing about? (Don't take a lot of my words seriously this evening, it seems I'm in the mood for leg pulling! When I start that I'm liable to write anything that is nonsensical!)

No question about the job situation, the defense rests. (See what I mean. I'm answering your letters, word for word; anything can happen!)

Darling, my lovely Bette, no matter how much rest I get, I shall never be able to make up for my loss for a Hell of a long time. I can't sleep later than 6 AM. But when we snuggle together on those cold winter nights, I don't think it will be hard to shed my army habits.

I am still on the ball, only once in the while, I roll . . . but it isn't serious. Only one serious thing in my life and that's you. It isn't just being in love, it's being in love with the right person!

As you are waiting, I am waiting to come back so that we can live the normal life of 2 people in love. My idea of perfection and the goal to steer was shown to me by a couple which I knew very well. Mr. Allen was 80 yrs. old, and Mrs. Allen was 75. Their married life was one big love affair. I watched it as long as I knew them. I shall never forget the examples that they set. Mr. Allen died not so long ago, and Mrs. Allen said she would join him very shortly. Darling, it was the loveliest, most perfect love affair I have ever seen.

The reason that so many people fail to see the future is that they have no incentive to do so. It can develop into something worthwhile and good when a reason is found. Our reason is forever present — us! We will be living in the present and thinking of the future because everyday we will be striving to make the next better than the previous. It is simple, Darling, we will be building a utopia which will be climaxed only by the grim reaper.

Hey! What's this idea of a cook. Never made any bones about being a millionaire. Besides, those domestic squabbles will be something to laugh about. After eating this army chow for so long, I'll be able to stand anything. There now, does that make it easier for you?

Darling, I would like to go on but I suddenly feel so tired that I will surely make a blotch of this letter. My eyes feel strained and so tired.

Please excuse me, I'm so sorry. Good night, Bette, miss you and love you so much. May God Bless You. Love, Mike.

P.S.: I'll answer the rest of your letter as soon as I can. REALLY TIRED!

Four courier runs were carried out on November 13, and the 316th Troop Carrier Group's Commanding Officer, Major Leonard C. Fletcher, and aides "made a careful inspection of the entire camp and personnel" according to the War Diary.

The next day saw six courier runs and an announcement that a V-mail "Christmas Greeting," which had been drawn by Corporal Carl A. Sands, was being copied on the mimeograph machine to insure sufficient copies for everyone. A USO stage show was presented at the base theater that night.

On November 15, three courier and special runs were carried out, the War Diary reported. Captain Cooney blue-lined the essential sections "North Africa Theater of Operations United States Army (NATOUSA) Circular No. 86" concerning regulations and restrictions of the mail for all military personnel.

November 16, 1943 [*Tuesday*]

Hello Darling,

Let's see, what am I going to start this letter with and what am I going to say? First of all, I want you to apologize to Mother because I couldn't send her a special Christmas greeting instead of putting both of them in the same letter; but, you see, Darling, just like everything else, they, too, are rationed and I had to spread them as far as I possibly could.

Now I think I can complete the answer to your letter. I really couldn't write another word last night. After I finished I was quickly absorbed by the arms of Morpheus and I slumbered deeply until I was awakened the next morning. In your last letter you mentioned that you had no brothers, sisters, nieces or nephews to share with me. That's wrong! The family is yours as well as mine. True, it will be by adoption but nevertheless, it will still be shared. You can easily see that you are taking the bigger share. They really aren't a bad lot and the kids are lovely. I got a report from Louise, my sister-in-law, about Thomas Michael, my nephew, she says that he doesn't seem to be getting bigger but he has the nicest blonde hair and he is so damn cute. When I saw him last June, Gad!, he was quite a kid. I can imagine what he must be now!

That problem of yours. Surely your Mother must suspect that something is on since we are constantly corresponding with each other. And surely your faithful letter . . . must strike some note of knowledge. To top it all, I don't think that your Mother will be very displeased by our love affair. I can't say that I have been treated coldly by her and I daresay, it was always quite the contrary. Your Mother treated me like a son. (Excuse the parallel but Stretch's Mom and Dad hated my "guts"!) On the face of things like that, I often wonder what kind of character I must be. I wonder if my moods differ so obtusely that I can also be loved by one and almost hated by another. It makes life interesting and the world all the more queerer. Ah Woe!

I hope you like your Christmas cards. They aren't fancy and there is nothing else we can get. However, they convey an international feeling. This is a nice time back in the States. In this heathen land they don't know life from death; and yet, it seems strange, since all the things we celebrate at this time of the year were formulated on this side of the world. Sometimes, I wonder why God didn't wait a few years and then He could have been born in the States and really He would have been appreciated. But I can't very well rewrite history so I shan't try my surmising on anyone.

I have written to my Ma, and for the second time today, I don't seem to recognize myself. My words seem to belong to an intelligent person and that's not me. Trying to inflate my ego but I'm the only guy that's here to appreciate it and I bore myself too often. Sounds stupidly circular, parallel, rectangular, and (eek!) flat. But there I go again, babbling and saying nothing. At least a brook has water and can satisfy his thirst. I spout words and can't even eat them.

Darling, you will have to excuse my stringing along. But I have exhausted all the info I can spread about the things done and seen and besides, it's so routine. Just itching for a heavy night's loving and a chance to drop off into the world I once knew. Never had a worry, didn't give a damn, and we had so much fun. Even in that struggle of married life, I think we'll make a game of it. It's so much like us to do things thataway and why not, we only have 50 years to live.

Well, Bette, Ole Gal, I am going to close. So many things heap up on me at one time, I have to take out some time to get everything coordinated.

Sorry I couldn't make this a more interesting letter. Want to say so many things but I am afraid that I am weakened to sentimentality and it ain't good. Not today, anyhow. I'll try to make up for misgivings in my next letter.

Good night, Darling, give my love to Mother. Take care of yourself. May God Bless You. Love you and miss you terribly. Patience is a marvelous thing. If I were president, I'd take the word "war" out of the dictionary. Love, Mike.

On November 16, six courier and special runs were carried out, according to the War Diary, and several new pilots were assigned to the 37th Squadron.

The next day, the War Diary showed six courier missions. Also on that date, Captain Cooney and Staff Sergeant Wells returned to camp.

Eight courier and special runs were carried out on November 18. Captain Cooney was appointed Provost Marshal of the 37th Squadron, in addition to his job as Intelligence Officer.

November 19, 1943 [*Friday*]

Hello Darling.

All thumbs. Gad! Woman, I love you. I am afraid that I must disappoint you because I must make this epistle short. I may sound like I am racing thru' it but can't help it.

Just finished *Kings Row*. Read it. It will lag in parts but it is one of the keenest studies of character that I have ever run across. I don't believe that you will be shocked by parts of it because the trend is human and humans aren't always normal. I am not ashamed to admit that I was moved to tears by some parts of it. It's a funny thing but little do we realize what friendship is until someone puts it on paper and we read about it. And, Darling, (Forgive me if I plea ignorance) but I didn't fully realize that a woman could love a man so deeply. (That misfortune of not knowing is attributable to the fact that I never had the time to find out. We'll admit our love is new, we have yet to fully realize what we mean to each other.) I can't make my point too clear because words can't cover the thinness and sensitivity of the subject. Since we never had the time to feel the depth of our emotions, we must feel it and believe it now in separation, and feel it and understand any emotion in life when we are together.

Wow! Listen to Socrates or Aristotle, take your pick. That subject, my Dear, involves hours of brain-wracking and it is best done, I believe, when our heads are together. It is such a meaty subject that I want you to remind me to discuss it thoroughly. Save my letters and when we get a chance to read them, we can broaden on every phase. They are only an outline of my activities. When my words are again brought to my mind, I'll be able to tell you what really happened at the time.

For now, my Love, I must ask your pardon. I warned you that this would be a short letter. Not thru' wish but thru' necessity.

Miss you, love you, and pray for you. Still in there pitching and I am healthy and happy. Give my love to Mother. Tell her that her little (?) boy is taking good care of himself. May God Bless You. Take care of yourself. Love, Mike.

The War Diary recorded six courier and special runs on November 19. The 316th Group Headquarters, under Special Order No. 111, dated November 16, 1943, appointed the following enlisted men to the next grade: Technical Sergeant Donald N. Grantz to First Sergeant; Staff Sergeant Thaddeus J. Urbaniak to Technical Sergeant; and Sergeants Daniel R. Emery and Ernest W. Womack to Staff Sergeants.

November 20, 1943 [*Saturday*]

Good Morning, Darling,

I won't apologize for my vague letter last night because I think I covered that quite ably.

It is a rather fine morn'. The sun is shining and there is a tang of autumn in the air. In the midst of all that splendor, I stood stark naked and took an ice shower. Gad! Woman, you'd never realize what a horror it is. And still I don't know whether I am numb, stunned, or should I be glad I am still alive. Picture it. Open air shower, the sun (not too warm) and stark naked. Now that I think of it, I don't see why I did it. What human impulse led me to such foolishness. Ah Me! Ah Woe! Ah Life!

I guess I was slightly affected. I feel gay and stupid; and yet my letter will probably be one of morbid and serious words.

I am afraid that I stumbled on quite a subject in my letter last night, but it will really be a good topic of discussion. But when you and I do discuss it, we will be on the inside looking out.

There is another literary recommendation I'd like to make, not because it is a fine piece of work, far from it, but because it gives us an idea that there are certain types of people in the world and that they can be forcefully driven by their emotions. The book is *Postman Always Rings Twice* — simply, a bit on the lewd side and maybe not too fantastic, and definitely a picture of the ironic side that such a life might have. I am not going to tell you anything about it. It would spoil the entire plot. Just read it and comment.

Do you remember the day we went thru' that art gallery [*the Nelson-Atkins Museum of Art*] in KC. I just wondered about that. Technically, we know nothing about art, but we can feel it and that's why it was painted. But if we ever (and you do recall my leaning toward the impressionists — [*Gauguin*], Van Gogh, [*Toulouse-Lautrec*], and such of that period) want to get an idea how those people lived, read *Lust for Life* by Irving Stone. When I read it, I realized that there is a fine line between sanity and insanity. I can see that most artists or at least the geniuses of their work (music, art, or literature) are perfect examples of that.

I am just picking up bits of ideas but one leads to another. "I have a rendezvous with death" was written in the continent I am now in. I have seen places that can be compared to Segar's idea of his rendezvous. "At some disputed barricade" — was the battle front — "— and apple blossoms fill the air." He was thinking of his home and not of this desolate desert because there are no apple blossoms here. Don't I sound awfully toned?

But really, Darling, part of the things I want together, touch on the things I have said. Legitimate plays, concerts, art galleries, I have always had an idea that I wanted to broaden myself on those subjects because they can induce such interesting conversations. If one pleads ignorance, it takes the color out of the subject.

Honestly, Bette, I don't want to sound classy but these things come in handy. I can just as well sit in on any ball game and know what is going on. Not to know everything but to know a little and in turn learn a lot.

You see, Darling, you never know what my letters are going to lead to. I could just have written . . . "whose little, itty bitty wovely is 'ou?" and stuff. (That sentence makes me laugh. It happens too!)

Well, Bette, My Sweet, I must close. This letter was sneaked in on some of my spare time. That spare time is all absorbed, so I must sneak out.

I sent your Mother a card which I got in Italy. I hope she gets it. Give her my love.

So long for now, My Darling. Take care of yourself. May God Bless You. — Love, Mike.

The War Diary for November 20 through 23 notes a total of 11 courier or special runs carried out, in addition to censorship and other routine section duties.

November 23, 1943 [*Tuesday*]

Hello My Dearest,

Darling, you are a beautiful woman. I received your pictures and I couldn't help but gasp at your sight. I have them propped up before me as I scribble this note. Your Mother is a fine looking woman. Darling, you are marvelous. I often wonder how I was so lucky to have met you.

I can imagine that you must be well aware of the fact that I have changed my ideas. In my other letters where I state that I don't ever want to leave you again, I'm not kidding. We can always manage something and there is no reason why we should ever be separated. Isn't this enough? Since you feel the way you do, and that's the way I want you to feel, you will be with me "whether it's the Everglades of Florida or the Mahore [*Mojave*] (or sumpin') desert of California." My life is devoted to you and I shan't have you away from me. Darling, you don't know how much I love you. This is one of those times when I let down my veil of patience and get as mushy as porridge. I have missed you, Bette, I have missed you terribly. Night after night, I dream of the marvelous life we will share someday. I think of little things that make the joy of living, forgetting all strife and trifle of life. Dreaming of the talks, the fights (if there are any), the moments, the surroundings, laughs (no tears), everything, and they don't make me feel melancholy, those thoughts make me feel so good because I know that they are still ahead of us and we have yet to share them. Many's the time I have regretted the fact that we didn't marry before I left. Yes, Bette, I'm letting the veil down because it never hurts to discuss one's feeling once in a while. I have felt like this often but I don't like to say it often because it won't do us any good. We are so far apart that it would only hurt the more.

Don't ever ask a question like that again! Not for a long time. Bette, we shouldn't worry about my getting back, just let it go and I'll be back before we know what has happened. It's November 23rd and only last year it was Nov. 23rd. Do you see what I am driving at? You'll be forewarned by a wire so you will have plenty of time to get ready. I even know how I am going to word it. So you see that's another thing that I think about. I have every angle covered and someday I'll be able to put them together and complete this unnecessary jig-saw puzzle of time. (I just noticed my first line in this paragraph. I didn't mean to make it sound so harsh! Just using it as an expression not a reprimand.) I'll drop my veil for a while. Remember, Darling, pray and pray hard. The patience will come to you easy enough. Remember that old word we talk about "STRENGTH" — It's so easy to find. I promise, Bette, above all, I'll make up for lost time. We must store up our happiness so that when God sees fit to join us, we will be happy — we'll be like 2 kids at the circus of life. Save that, and if I ever fail, show it to me — I hope and know that you will never have reason to use it.

Ha! So my favorite gal is being courted. Can't say that I blame the young sprig! Wish to Hell, I was younger, so that I could be in his boots. Why don't you see him and tell him that he is a bit too late. Break the bubble so that he can blow another one.

I have noticed the cross. I couldn't miss it and thanks. Darling, Gad, you look so beautiful. I never saw that suit before. Don't you think you ought to [*crossed out*]. That's all wet. As if I can advise you about clothes. Just wanted to mention wearing dark clothes more often because it makes your blonde hair stand out more.

While you are having an album made for your Mother, you might make one for us, although, I have two; one I got in Jerusalem, and one in India. I like pictures and like to keep an album. I took loads of 'em in Chicago but someone else has them.

I guess I have already worn out my welcome. But seriously, Bette, I must write to my sister. She has a problem and she wants to discuss it with me and I must answer her. She has a lot of faith in my words and I can't let her down.

Remember, Darling, we'll get married as soon as I get back and we can arrange it. You'll be as near to me as the circumstances will allow. I love you so much.

Good night for now. Give my love to Mother. I miss you terribly. May God Bless You. Love, Mike.

On November 23 and 24, the 37th Squadron continued with its courier runs and special missions, while the War Diary noted, "Censorship and other routine duties carried out."

November 25, 1943 [*Thursday*]

Good Evening, Bette,

I imagine I ought to be able to get off a long letter. I just finished our big Thanksgiving meal and I feel quite content with the world. Believe me, it was a big meal. Thanks to you people back home, we had all the turkey we needed, all accessories added.

I thought I had described all the parts of the day to you. Sunsets in Tunisia are rather scarce. Since the season has changed, the weather is cold and the sun is a rare sight. But nightfall is pretty. Clouds, not light, but heavy and black give the blend of blue. Shades and shades of blue from the deepest in fathoms of the water to the lightest boy-baby's clothes. Blended not in uniformity but scattered and shattered like the prism in a broken glass. Sunset is the cruelest time of the day to fly. Especially when you are flying into the sun. The dust gathers on our windshield and it necessitates a good amount of judgment to bring 'er home.

Hell! I forgot the most important thing. I received 4 letters from you. I received all the pictures you sent. I haven't received but one roll of film, but I'm very much in love with the prettiest girl I know. You are the most marvelous person in the world. You are right, there is no reason why we shouldn't be the happiest couple in the world. Darling, I am eagerly looking forward to the time that we can make these words reality.

Since you are showing so much interest in my religious discussions, I know that you are expecting as much clarification as I can give. First of all, Darling, if you went thru' with your instructions, how long or short it may be, it would at least be that much done. You will be an accepted convert and our wedding would be before the altar. Whatever more there is, we can discuss together. It will be interesting to probe because we can both be learning at the same time. Don't forget, Honey, there's a Hell of a lot to learn. You know religion for a married couple is quite different from a single life. But, at any rate, go thru' with your instructions. I don't think it will take longer than 2 months. When you receive your First Holy Communion, you will feel something you have never realized in your life. I can't describe it because it is something that each of us must feel individually, a levity of soul and heart that puts aviation to shame. I am hoping, Darling, that we can be married by Tom.

Our wedding. My Love, I am not an exhibitionist. Parallel to your ideas about sacredness of marriage, I believe our wedding should be a quiet affair. All we need is the best man, a gal, and the priest. I hate formality and I hope we don't have the Holiday Crowd at Ebbetts Field at our wedding. All we want is the grace of God and not the awe of a crowd. Yes, Darling, it won't be a big idea. As a matter of fact, I'd like to just fade after the usual congratulations are over. Only one thing, my family is so big, they constitute a crowd. Gosh, Bette, thinking like that makes time seem such an insurmountable mountain. But, the time has passed quickly so far, it won't be so long. Darling, it's so nice to look toward the future. It will be perfect. I am sure of it.

I can understand your idea about lost time. You are right. We are passing the "awkward" stage far apart and yet it is being done and all that's necessary is that we just get married. Whatever loose ends are left dangling by these letters, we can smoothen out on those long winter evenings.

You needn't be too proud of my money saving. As a matter of fact I intend to do better than that. Yes, we have a piano. But to copy a word, we will have each other. We can manage the rest of it.

Hotel President Drum Room. Gad! How well I remember. "There will be other times like that!" We needn't worry. Gad! Honey, there are so many things for us to do.

We really do get as much out of life as we put into it. My family has always told me how considerate I was. I should get an awful lot out of life. But, Gosh, Bette, what should a guy do but be square, and on the level? I never lived under any other code. Wish I could do more.

I did ride a camel and I have a picture to prove it but I can't get the damned thing developed. It is the most awkward feeling in the world. They roll like a ship on a rough sea, and the sensation is most like something else I can't mention. But when they get up or lay down, they never seem to rise high or get down. So many joints in their legs that it feels like a sliding ladder. I guess it takes about 6 movements, either way.

"I'm going to enjoy fixing things you like." That really [*sounds*] good, and Darling, I'll enjoy doing things that you will enjoy. I am not going into that fully. That's another castle in the air. Save it until I can put a sky hook on all those castles and lay them in your lap.

I showed your pictures to all the gang. You are my favorite pin-up. I notice that you are getting a bit rotund. 10 lbs. That's great. Darling, if I have done anything for you, I can at least say I helped you put on some weight. You ought to try to get well beyond 130. It will help you. Imagine Bette as the big, buxom blonde! I like popcorn too.

I saw a very interesting art exhibit the other day in Italy. It was great. The artist was there. He had the usual run of fruits and self-portraits. He was quite a technician. I like the way he applied his paints. His harbor scenes, the fury of storm at sea, country scenes, alley scenes, and the roadside home were great. Unfortunately, I can't buy any because I can't carry them all over the world. It would be nice to have a few in our home or apartment, whichever we can afford at the time.

Well, Darling, I must close. Lucy promised to write to you. My family is happy by my announcement of our proposed marriage. It's going to be a Hell of a family when we get together. She sends her love and apologies.

I received a letter from Joe Huss, the kid I met at the station in KC that day. He's in the Pacific Theater and I was surprised to receive a letter from him so quickly. I must answer him tonight.

Good night, Darling, give my love to Mother. Don't let things get you down; we will get together and the time will be forgotten.

The Guys were kidding about the pictures, wondering when you were going to send some "leg art."

So long for now. Bette, I love you. May God Bless You. Take care of yourself. Love, Mike.

On Thanksgiving day, as I recall, I flew early carrying a load of turkeys as our cargo. We went somewhere in Italy, perhaps Naples, near the Salerno front. We got back by evening in time for our own festive dinner. The War Diary for that day, November 25, shows three courier missions.

Eight courier and special missions were carried out the next day. The War Diary for November 26 also shows that orders had been received from the Commanding Officer of the 316th Troop Carrier Group for a change of station to Borizzo, Sicily. Five planes with complete aircrews, which had been on detached service (DS) with us from the 45th Troop Carrier Squadron, were dropped from our rolls that day to return to the 45th.

November 27, 1943 [*Saturday*]

Good Morning, Darling,

Now that I have completed most of my daily chores, I guess we can sit down and talk. You don't realize how I slave all day long so that I can have something to put on my back. I just finished shaving and showering and I washed a Hell of a load of laundry. Gad! What a life!

There isn't much I can write about. I received 3 packages yesterday. One from Mrs. Smith, an old friend of mine, one from my Cousin Sue, and from my brother Ted and his wife Louise. Except for those things, there has been nothing exceptional to write about. The weather. Ah! The weather — Damn it, it has been miserable. I don't know how my wash is going to dry because it is raining. Wash it one day, and it dries a week later. These domestic troubles can certainly get a guy down. Listen, Bette, My Sweet, I don't want you to get any ideas. The only reason I do these things is because I have no other choice. I don't cherish the idea of breaking my back over a hot stove all day long.

We had quite a discussion last night and it centered around the civilian lives we all left. We didn't talk about ideas or jobs but merely clothes. Our biggest puzzle was what we would look like when we get to put on "civvies." I am so damned used to khaki and OD [*olive drab*] dress that I can't imagine myself in a business suit, white shirt, navy blue, knitted tie, navy blue sox, a fancy pair of Paris suspenders and a nice pair of brown dress shoes. It all seems so remote. You know, Bette, you have never seen me dressed as a civilian. First of all, I hate hats. I never wore one and I never intend to. (Barring this army life which I had no choice!) I prefer sports clothes or very informal dress to a consistent clean-cut dress. My tastes are rather expensive and I have been told that my choice of clothes is very good. My shoes are costly. (My feet are so big, I couldn't get a cheap shoe.) My suits lean toward conservatism (looks like it is spelled wrong but I corrected it with the use of a dictionary.) I very rarely wear solid colors but plaids and herringbone. My shirts were almost strictly "Arrow" (Sussex). My preference in shirts was white or striped. (My sport shirts were all solid colors and blue was my favorite.) (For fishing and the beach, I had a yellow (bright) (turned white after a strict washing) terry cloth, long-sleeved, droop-shaped old shirt. Ties, knitted preferred in colors of wintergreen, navy blue, maroon, and then combinations to my taste. I usually like to blend my ties and sox. Sox, anklet affairs because I hate garters. The colors on these varied parallel to the colors of my ties. Shoes were usually brown, and I never had much choice of style. I said that before. I bought a new overcoat just before I came in and I hope Mom is taking good care of it because I like it a Hell of a lot. It is a black box coat with two diagonal pockets. It is well lined and comfortable as the devil in Hell. My trench coat is a honey. I used it as a top coat because it could suffice as that and I didn't like my top coat anyhow. It was a pepper and salt affair on a green background. I was drunk one night and got it soiled with oil in a car. It was never [*completely*] cleaned so I practically discarded it. For puttering around, I preferred an old pair of pants or shorts, my terry cloth shirt and basketball shoes. I guess that just about covers my wardrobe. I don't want to be fancy but I really never had more than one suit at my disposal at one time. Just prior to my enlistment, I was starting to broaden all of my personals but I figured that it was so very silly to go to any extremes. Had my eye on a Hell of a fancy suit. I was all set to cut capers and then bang! I was a soldier, dressed in the worst fitting outfit you ever saw. I am not in such bad shape now. Most of my clothes fit me better. I have exchanged most of my khakis and ODs and really don't cut such a horrible figure. Seriously though, Darling, I never had much of anything, so you see, you aren't getting yourself the pick of the crop. However, my ideas and ambitions are keen and sharp. I can try hard enough to get enough done. At least, with whatever else I have left over. I buy a bond every 3 months and my brother, Doc, owes me $300 and odds. I imagine I have saved close to $700. But I have urged my Mom to use whatever she may need. I believe that some of my money will be used when Tom is ordained. That is the least I can do for him and family. I guess that you will receive an invitation to the ordination. I doubt if I'll be home by then but it might be a good idea if you can get away and get to meet my family at that time. It will be nice to have one of us there.

Well, My Sweet, Lovely, Bette, I am going to close for now. I hope you don't mind my buzzing your ear this way, Bette, but it just gives you an idea of this character that will be the man of your life someday. The only thing I have on the black side of the ledger is me as you know me. People have said that I am kind, considerate, even-tempered, and easy to get along with — one more thing is that I love you very much and it is one of the greatest incentives to make the perfect formula for a happy life.

So long. Give Mother my love. May God Bless You. Take care of yourself, Darling. Love, Mike.

November 27, 1943 [*Saturday*]

Good Afternoon, Darling,

I just received a letter from you and I am surer that your mood wasn't one to cope with. But then again, it is the easiest thing in the world to feel nasty. I just wonder about crying. Any time you want to boo-hoo on my shoulder, I'll be there. Anything at all, Darling, I'd rather you got that way with me. Just spill your troubles, big or small. That, my dear, is part of the union. You weep, I soothe. I cuss, you ease the strain.

You're right, Bette, this [*name omitted*] must be looking for a sucker and I know just how you feel. I had the same kind of friend (?). We used to go fishing together. I always carried $25 or $30. He used to come along. At the end of the week-end, I'd find that I had quite a hole in my sock, and he had a good time. To top it all, he tried to steal my women. Fortunately, he didn't get them but I always considered that if he pulled that sort of stuff, he'd do anything. We quit after a while. I decided I could find better friends than that. As a matter of fact, I damn near knocked Hell out of him. It's a good thing we didn't go fishing any more. The only thing on your score, Darling, is just don't be too quick on opening your hand bag. If she is so well loaded, she can unload some of her dough. (Think of the future —). Seriously though, don't let her get away with it. You'll get stuck in the long run and you'll probably lose a friend.

As far as that Cadet situation goes, I wonder? We can discuss it when we get together. There are an awful lot of sides to the situation and we can gaze at it from all sides.

Inspiration. Hell we don't need any moonlight. I think I covered that quite fully.

That fanning that you talk about. I told you once that if you needed it, Darling, I shan't hesitate to apply the pressure. If you recall, I have an awfully large hand and if I recall, you are awfully small. (in those parts.) Some combination. It won't hurt me as much as it will you.

Talking about sleep. I am still a bit hazy. I just knocked off a few hours of "sack" detail. I feel a Hell of a lot better but, again, the more you get, the more you want.

Luckily, the *Stars and Stripes* keeps us well informed about the football scores. The Big Red of Pennsy [*University of Pennsylvania*] has been my favorite outfit. I saw the Navy-Penn game in '37 or '38. It was swell game. Penn won 16-0. They had a great backfield. It was quite a spectacle. Navy put on a swell show between halves. I want to take you to one of the service games because you'll be thrilled to watch 2,000 cadets or midshipmen come strolling into a big stadium. It gives you a thrill you'll never forget. I'll go into that more deeply when I write again. I am going to close now but I'll be back sooner than you expect. I try to write as often as I can when the opportunity affords it. Gotta keep up your morale and combat those ugly moods.

So long, Honey. May God Bless You. Tomorrow's chapter will be entitled, "Sports as seen by M. Ingrisano." After I finish, you'll probably want to see every type of ball game they can have — that's not a bad idea either! — Love, Mike.

According to the War Diary, no missions were carried out on November 27. The next day, an advance echelon consisting of four planes left for the 37th Squadron's new station in Borizzo, Sicily.

November 29, 1943 [*Monday*]

Hello Darling,

I must make this a short letter but at any rate I must write because I missed my sugar report yesterday. No wonder there's a sugar shortage, all the guys and gals use it up in their letters. I'll have to postpone that sports saga for a while because I need plenty of time when I write about something like that. I have seen so many events that I must concentrate. I'll put it all in words so that someday you can see for yourself.

I picked up an old sports page. The baseball season had just "wound up" and football had already started. After reading some of the scores, I realized the kind of season that I missed. I didn't think there could be so many upsets and that teams like Bohunk Teachers could knock off the big colleges. That's like when little Washington & Jefferson went out to the Rose Bowl and knocked off one of those big Far Western Conference Champs. But then again, I didn't think I'd ever see No. Africa & the rest. I guess things like that do happen.

This little poem I am sending is self-explanatory. It was sent over from the States and I am sending it back. We never think of ourselves being like that but it is not hard to see how parallel our actions are. I don't mean us, you and I, I just mean generally. People do things. Read about them. Laugh at them and then discover that it was written about them gener-ally.

Our conversation the other night drifted toward Christmas and past Christmases. It didn't make us homesick but I'll bet 10-1 that everyone of us was dreaming of what the next one will be like. We aren't [*so*] busy at the business of war and stuff not to be able to dream. And dream we do.

Darling, I must close. I don't want to rush off like this but I must. I always try to make up for these short notes. I think I have done a fairly good job of it. Haven't I?

So long, Bette, give my love to Mother. Pappy [*Addison Agle*] sends his best. Miss you and love you. May God Bless You. Love, Mike.

The Wolf!
If he parks his little flivver,
Down besides the moonlit river,
And you can feel him all a-quiver,
Baby — He's a Wolf!

If he says you're gorgeous lookin'
That your dark eyes set him cookin'
But your eyes ain't where he's lookin'
Baby — He's a Wolf!

When he says you are an eyeful'
But his hands begin to trifle'
And his heart bumps like a rifle'
Baby — He's a Wolf!

If by chance when you are kissin',
You feel his heart a-missin',
And you talk but he don't listen,
Baby — He's a Wolf!

If his arms are strong like sinew,
And he stirs the gypsy in you,
So that you want him close agin you,
Maybe —You're the Wolf!

P.S.: You can see it's not all work but some play. But there aren't any women around here, so we can't very well refer to them. All the guys are in the army back home, except 4-F [*the designation for those rejected by the draft board*], so we'll call this a pre-war or post-war bit of Kipling.

The War Diary entry for November 29 reads: "Shuttle service between El Aouina and Borizzo continued in operation. Eleven trips being made this date."

The next day, the War Diary reported that the air shuttle service was operating smoothly, and that one warrant officer, along with 22 enlisted men and a truck convoy, were awaiting ship transport to Borizzo from Bizerte, Tunisia.

Chapter 2

Somewhere in Sicily (December 2, 1943 to February 13, 1944)

*F*ROM DECEMBER 1943 to February 1944, while troop carriers continued to fly supplies and personnel in support of the Allied armies in Italy, other forces and matériel were being stockpiled in England in preparation for an invasion of mainland Europe. Allied bombers destroyed the historic Benedictine abbey at Monte Cassino in Italy, which was being used by the Germans as an observation post and after the bombing as a fortress.

Also during this time, Soviet troops reached the border of prewar Poland, the Royal Air Force bombed Berlin, and U.S. forces in the Pacific continued their "Island Hopping" campaign, taking Tarawa and Makin in the Gilbert Islands late in November 1943. Allied forces landed on Cape Gloucester, New Britain, December 26, 1943.

The following is the 37th Troop Carrier Squadron's War Diary entry for December 1:

> **46 Glider personnel, 23 Officers and 23 EM** [*enlisted men*] **assigned this squadron. Move from El Aouina was officially completed this date. 49 round trips of 300 miles and 7 one way trips of 150 air miles were required to move the entire**

**squadron plus equipment, except for the truck convoy which is await-
ing ship transportation.**

December 2, 1943 [*Thursday*]
<u>Somewhere in Sicily</u>

Hello Darling,

So sorry for being Peck's bad boy. Couldn't write any sooner and God only knows how I hate to let too many days pass by so that you might worry.

You will have to excuse me if I don't go thru' any excessive descriptions about this place; as a matter of fact, I'll eliminate all except that the weather is [*horrible*]. I get tired of hemming and hawing and being so general about it when my word bombardment is limited and suppressed. I get rattled and I usually "blotch" up the whole situation. We will have plenty of time to talk and believe me, it will take a Hell of a long time for me to get these travels out of my system. Hope I am not getting anyone mad at me! (The Censor can put away his scissors!)

Got myself another crew cut and I am not far from bald. It feels good though. Feels cleaner and lighter.

One of my tent mates [*Max Gilliam*] and I had a long discussion the other night. He had been married for 13 years and he is a swell guy to talk to. It's good to be able to speak to one like him and to realize the bliss and happiness that is in store for us. I realized it always but it just adds another stone to the foundation. I love you, Darling. It's great to hear about the things that people can share and know and feel the improvements that can be added. Gosh, Bette, since I feel like a veteran over here, the "sweating out" period has begun. From the day a guy leaves the States, he starts a down hill march to the day he will again see the beautifully inviting shores of his homeland. The symbols of home become magnified and the people he leaves at home become the incentive for his struggle and sacrifice. Like the baby who promises never to leave home again, we promise to make this world a better place to live in so that our sons never have to leave. Pity the first 4-F who tells me that I was lucky to see the world; his scalp will be hanging from my GI belt.

Darling, I wish I could go on and on. But every time I get my teeth into a subject, someone comes along and starts to bother me and tries to coax a conversation out of me. I can't be rude but —

It has been nearly a week since I heard from anyone. I shan't curse the mail situation because you must be fed up with my consistent blubbering. It's not your fault, Darling, because I know you write so often. It is just the mail gets tossed around so.

Well, Bette, my Love, I am going to close. However, I'll try (haven't you heard that often enough!) to do better.

Give my love to Mother. May God Bless You — I love you and miss you so. Love, Mike.

The 37th's War Diary for December 2 recorded round trips to El Aouina and Castelvetrano, in southwestern Sicily. One new plane was assigned to the squadron that day.

No missions were carried out on December 3, according to the War Diary, though orders were received that day to start the new glider towing program. And the first movie, it was noted, was shown at the new base.

December 4, 1943 [*Saturday*]

Good Morning, My Sweet,

I missed writing to you yesterday because the day passed so quickly and my unmeaning activities were so many. It rained so damn hard that I thought our baggage would float out of our tent. (I know the two thoughts are far apart but I didn't want to dedicate a whole paragraph to the weather.)

I received 4 letters yesterday and to make the day incomplete, not one of them was from you. I shall expect better results today. I sent you $25, so that you could get a Christmas present, from me to you. It may reach you after Christmas but it was meant for that purpose. I hope I can do better next year and that I'll be able to give it to you personally. For the time being, I am with you spiritually and my love for you grows with every day we are apart. Darling, if I could only tell you, if I were only fluent enough to tell you how much you mean to me.

Lucy told me that she had sent you a card. She has explained her difficulty to me because she has been so busy with her Nurse's Aide work. However, she wrote two beautiful letters which made my little ole' heart feel good. She said that although she doesn't know you, she will love you and respect you because you have done so much to make me happy. Once you meet, I'm afraid that I'll be thrust into the background and left to twiddle my thumbs. Mom and I had a heart-to-heart talk last nite and you were so thoroughly and beautifully lavished with adjectives no one could help but to love you the way I do. Tony wrote and said that he had heard of you before because he had seen your signature on the check that you cashed for me in KC. Then he goes on to say that I must have it bad (and he isn't wrong), and then finishes his quote with, "Ah, Youth!" The old Fogey! (Pardon me while I brush my flowing ? locks out of my eyes — you ought to see my nearly bald head, it's cute!) I hope that I don't bore you with my tales. You see, Darling, I'm so proud of you that I want my family to know you even though they haven't had the opportunity to meet you. And since my family and I share everything, why should they be denied the privilege of knowing such a fine person as you? I love you.

There's a boy who lives in the next tent from mine and he is one of the most interesting fellows I have ever met. We seek each other's company so that we can have our usually long conversations. Principally, they cover the arts, music, art and literature. I have gained some great info' from him and in turn he from me. (Sounds like poetry, doesn't it?) I shocked him when I admitted that I had never been to the Metropolitan Opera House or to Carnegie Hall. The only explanation for that was that that my companion had no love for that sort of entertainment. However, I am sure that you and I will cover all the points I missed. When I told him all that, he assured me that I really had something to go home to. He made me read some realistic poetry he had written. Frankly, and I told him so, it didn't make sense. You know my definite opinion of surrealistic art. But all in all, our views are somewhat parallel and our taste of music is almost evenly matched. He had helped me to pass away many interesting evenings and I am grateful to him. When we get drunk together, we try to harmonize; someday we will sound good! — (maybe!).

Gosh, Bette, here I am blowing my top and I have completely forgotten you. I never ask about your health because I know that you are feeling OK. Especially since you are gaining weight. I hope that your nervous condition is well under control. Darling, you are happy! I know I am. Time the unconquerable will pass! I live for the moment when we will be together again. The thought of you is forever with me and I don't care who knows it. Be content to just exist for a while, Bette, I'll help you to live a life time. When one of those weak moments comes along, just pick up a memory and things will slide along. God and His Blessed Mother are fine for solace. They can set a guy straight so easily that you hardly know how it's done. That's the end of my philosophy for the day.

I must close now, Darling, because I want to write to Lucy and a friend of mine, Bill Knapp, who is in India. I'll be able to dash off a few lines this afternoon. I don't know what I'll say but I know that it feels good to talk to you.

So long, My Sweet, give my love to Mother. May God Bless You. Take care of yourself. Love, Mike.

The War Diary entry for December 4 is:

First day of training program completed. Instrument and Formation flying, morning and afternoon session. Night flying called off due to adverse weather.

December 5, 1943 [*Sunday*]

Hello Darling,

Another day and no mail from you. The postmaster and I are going to tangle if he doesn't get on the ball and gets my sugar reports to me. But whenever I complain, I usually get mail the next day; I am hoping that the rule stays with me.

I received a letter from Tom and he told me that he had written to you. Lucy said that she had sent you a card but promised to do better. Tom told me that he didn't quite know what to say but I am sure his letter was interesting. They are always. If you want any information about [*religious*] instructions, he's the boy. As a matter of fact, he asked if you would like him to instruct you. I guess he can do that thru' the mail.

I have been doing a lot of thinking lately. The one thing that struck me was the fact that I have added some pen pals to your list in the form of my family. Darling, I don't want you to feel that I am forcing anything on you. You have told me more than once that whatever I do is all right with you. Therefore, I have taken the liberty to introduce you to my family thru' the mail. Everyone of them knows about you and when they write back and tell me that you must be marvelous to affect me the way you do, I feel so proud of you. Really though, I don't want you to feel that I am forcing anything on you. These friendships that I am helping to create are for the good of all concerned. It is unfortunate that we must do things like this but we have no choice.

I have written quite a few letters recently and a good part of them have been to my family. It is a means of clarification, and I hunger to talk to them concerning my future, which is you. There are no elaborate pictures, merely sound, easy ideas that have been formulated in my fish-like Brain. Tony, Tom, Ted, Lou (Doc), Lucy, Mom & Pop all know you. From Tom in his letter to-day, "I know she (you) is a great girl because you say so." You see, they are in for a greater surprise when they meet you and again I shall be forced to take the background.

Bette, My Sweet, I am sorry that I didn't write to you yesterday afternoon but again circumstances postponed that pleasure for me.

Darling, I miss you so. Lucy writes about Harry [*Koch*] and in turn I write to Lucy about you. I don't even know Harry; I never met him. He is my sister-in-law's [*Sally*] brother. By some quirk of fate he came to visit Sally at my home and met Lucy. He didn't know her very long then he left for England. He is a ground officer in the A. C., a Captain. But it seems that he can't get her off his mind and he is sure that it is love. Lucy is tickled pink and she lets me know it. Harry is taking his instructions and he keeps up a constant correspondence with Tom. There I go again. But, honestly, Bette, it is such a nice circle that I can't get out of it.

I got to thinking about the last time I saw you before I left for this side of the world. It was 5 AM on a Sunday morn. You were sitting on your suitcase and you were oh so-o tired. I was standing by and I had my hand on your head. Every so often, I would lean over and kiss your cheek or neck. We didn't say much. I don't think we realized that we were parting. Surely if things were the way they are now, our parting would have been tearful and tragic. I guess it was best for both of us that we accepted it as just a short "so long." In our gaiety, it was hard to say "Good Bye." When I left you, I went back to hotel and wrote my sister a long letter and I told her that I was finished with Stretch, and that I was determined to marry you. The weeks that followed were a nightmare. Drunk and yearning. Then I left. How often I dream of the day when you will come running down a ramp again, throw your suitcase like a bowling ball, and hit a strike when you rush into my arms and say, ever so beautifully, "Hello, Darling!" They can force us to live like dogs, send us to countries where only shells live, drive us to almost hopeless despair but just one memory can restore everything that we so often feel is lost. I love you, My Dear, and no one can change that!

But there I go again. Every time I sit down to write a light, stupid letter and the only funny thing is just that thought, and I never do.

I am not in a mood, Bette, I am merely trying to tell you that I love you. In my seriousness, I feel no remorse, but happiness because I can say it. My nicest moments are shared with you. When I feel ugly, I don't write. I usually cuss someone and start a discussion about this stupid mess they call war.

My loveliest critic, I must tear myself from you and try to shave some of the whiskers from my face. It has been nice to talk to you, but I must perform some earthly duties and consequently I will require some of my time. I say, *Adieu.*

So long, Honey. Give my love to Mother. Not all of it save some for yourself. Take care of yourself. And May God Bless You. Love, Mike.

P.S.: I hope to start reading *Keys to the Kingdom* by A. J. Cronin. I'll let you know how it is — I love you. Mike.

On December 5, the War Diary showed the following:

> **Training program: Instrument and Formation flying in the morning, Glider towing in the afternoon. Capt. Richert, Group Chaplain, held Protestant Services in the mess hall this evening.**

December 6, 1943 [*Monday*]
[*Almost half of this letter was censored!*]

Good Morning, You Lovely Wench,

It's a miserable morning. It will probably rain like Hell but I feel good and to me the sun is shining and it is a pretty little tune in my heart.

I went next door to borrow *Keys of the Kingdom* ("of" not "to") and since no one was home my task was made hard. I couldn't find it so I ended up reading 3 comic books. *Don Winslow, Superman,* and the *Hawk.* You know that literature that paints the nasty nazis so cruelly. Gosh! They were good. But later in the day, I was able to get the book. I started it and so far as I have read, it has proved to be a very well written piece of literature. [*The rest of the thought and that following on the next page were censored.*]

This fellow I wrote about in one of my recent letters brought in a book with a collection of nudes by Roye. Some of the women were beautiful and some were hags. Nevertheless, looking at it from the angle that the photographer meant, he rarely made mistakes as far as lighting and shadow. Women romping on a beach, laying in hay stacks (or is it lying?), staring into the blue, coming out of houses, might say that the pictures were taken at a nudist colony for women. My favorites were a brunette on a torso shot, and blonde who was reposing in a beach chair. Not only were their bodies attractive but their faces were beautiful. I won't say anything about some of the cracks that were passed. I'll let you imagine what a soldier or a bunch of them would say under the circumstances.

Well, My Pretty Maiden, I am cutting this letter short. I am eagerly awaiting our mail call, and hoping that there is a letter or more from you, and dreading the thought that I may again be disappointed. However, the better thought overcomes the possible feeling of remorse.

My Darling, again I bid you *A Riverdeci*! Give my love to Mother. Take care of yourself. May God Bless You. Love, Mike.

P.S.: Love you and Miss you. Not as an afterthought but as a reminder. M.

According to the War Diary, the training program's morning session on December 6 was called off due to weather, but instrument and formation flying resumed that afternoon. In the evening, Captain Cooney delivered a lecture to all officers on security and censorship regulations.

The War Diary's December 7 entry read:

> **Training program: Morning, afternoon and evening sessions of Instrument and Formation flying. The American Red Cross girls served coffee and doughnuts to all personnel, before the show this evening. The movie shown was *All This and Heaven Too*, with Chas. Boyer and Betty [*sic*] Davis. Eighteen bags of Christmas packages were distributed, a little early but nonetheless welcome.**

December 8, 1943 [*Wednesday*]

Good Morning, Bette,

Today is a Holy Day of Obligation, The Immaculate Conception. Prior to going to Mass, I decided to talk to you for a while.

As I said in my letter the other day, as soon as I start crying about the lack of mail, I get a few letters. I received 3 letters from you, Nov. 8th, 12th, and 13th. You're marvelous, My Sweet, but your praise of me is beyond expectations. If you keep telling me how good I am, I am liable to believe it. We all strive for perfection but we never reach it. It's hardly possible. But I am happy to think that our love is evenly shared. No strings, no doubts, just us.

Lucy had told me that she had sent you a card but I am afraid that she is apt to be a bit partial in her words of me. I can imagine that she planted the halo around my near-bald head and planted a picture of all roses and sweet. There is nothing I can say to that for after all she is my sister and it is to be expected of her. However, I am glad that she wrote to you, even though it was [*a*] card.

I was surprised to hear that you had to wait so long to receive a letter from me. However, there are apt to be certain lapses of time, they are circumstantial and there is nothing I can do about it. I try to make those periodic halts but it can never make up for those empty days when mail doesn't come. I know. A week and no mail, and then suddenly 3 letters or more. The joyous feeling is great, but then comes the moments and days of expectancy and anxiety which tear the very soul out of a simple man.

I am so glad that you are enjoying [*Franz Werfel's novel*] the *Song of Bernadette*. Purely thru' conversation, I learned that *Journey Among Warriors* is another enjoyable book. I shall hope to get to read it. That "Embraceable You" that you speak of is one of my favorite tunes. Many's the time that I went swinging down the street humming, singing (?), or whistling it. You must learn it. Reading thru' your letters, I can only say, "Woman, you flatter me beyond words." And yet, what more can one want than to be told that he is loved by so fine a woman as you are. I am most grateful to you, Bette, my life will be spent proving that you are not mistaken in your judgment.

We discussed our first meeting once. We were sitting on the porch, the question of the moment was first impressions. You said that you thought I was so polite and said that my background must have been good because of my tactful manner of introduction. You don't or maybe you do recall my anxiety to share the night with you. To get you out of there and to talk. We did sip a few bourbons but you kept insisting that you had to join your friends. It was the first and only time I was angry with you. Not because of you but because of your insistent loyalty to a bunch of children. If again, you recall, the entire evening was a nightmare. [*Name omitted*] and that slut; the insistent, stupid kid of a cavalryman and you and I had a premonition that we hadn't seen the last of each other. That we made the pair of gloves, one without the other, made one so worthless. As I speak of it, it all becomes so vivid in my mind. I don't think I kissed you that night, except when we were dancing and all I did was crease your forehead. Damn! That sailor, he insisted on dancing with you and when you were out of my arms, the moments were indescribably endless torture. I was jealous and it was so strange to feel that emotion toward a person (you!) who I knew so vaguely and whose mystery I was so anxious to probe. Our next meeting was supposed to be a party at your home. You remember that I "bitched" at one of my instructors and was restricted for a week-end — fortunately, the restriction was lifted and I saw you. Then Oh, Darling it happened so quickly, so unashamedly and it was then I knew I could never lose you. You were in my blood. I was ready to forget all my past, ready to assume the responsibility of this somewhat moody, almost hard to understand woman who so easily yielded to our mutual flood of the moment. Bette, you were mine, and I wasn't ever going to let you forget it. I began to feel the weight of the obligation in the East. You recall the struggle, I broke all my beliefs and tried to tell myself that you were just a game. I was wrong and I was glad of it. I know you felt the same way. Don't be surprised, at first you so carelessly answered my phone calls, then slowly you felt that you must temper this wild, warm, hot-tempered, happy-go-lucky fool — the subsequent result, someday, and with the grace of our Creator, someday soon, I will be married to that lovable, lovely, beautiful, moody, almost hard-to-understand woman who is the symbol of what I almost failed to accept and cherish. I love you so deeply, My Darling, my words and soul yield so easily to you and I want you to accept them and me, as humble as we both are. You see, MY Love, I don't forget, my game was not one of light words and lighter moments but of a man making love and fully realizing the meaning of the word.

I didn't mean to write so much, but your one word of thankfulness brought on a surge of words I couldn't control and which I wanted you to know. Words which I so feebly tried to tell you, so flimsily and awkwardly said like the Saturday night in Ft. Wayne when I said that I loved you. I shall never forgive myself for the impish manner which I courted you. Quite contrary to the ordinary, we will be married and then you will be courted as a woman whose lover is begging for her hand.

Darling, MY Own, I must close. Perhaps I will have time to answer your letters later today. This was for you.

Give my love to Mother. May God Bless You. Take care of yourself. Love, Mike.

December 8, 1943 [*Wednesday*]

Good Evening, My Darling,

Cry, weep, sweat, cuss, and the mail pours in. Darling, I love you. I received your letters of the 9th and 11th of Nov. I received your pictures and you look wonderful. It feel[*s*] rather strange to receive shots of KC and realize that I often walked thru' those alleys (rolled!), sat on top of the steps of the Liberty Memorial and dreamed of days to come. Many's the time that I wish I had called you and asked you to join my reverie so that I could unleash my soul upon your defenseless being. But they are memories. Tonight, I feel I must divert myself to present fact, answering your letters. By the way, I also received one letter from my former secretary, my sister and 2 from a friend of mine.

The History of a Stove. In this blustering, blowing, chilling weather, we innovated the idea of a stove for our tent. We cut the top off a bomb case, stole 2 long pipes, "borrowed" a used reel (wire reel), welded everything together and behold! A Stove. For fuel we use a combination of gas, oil, benzene, water, salt (sounds like a salad, doesn't it?). But the thing is we can't get the right concoction. Every time we light it, it blows up and we all run like Hell for the nearest exit. Really, Darling, it's the funniest thing you could ever see. Four guys jamming out of a tent door. "The Hell with everything, let's get out!" But as I write, our stove is puffing away quite cozily and magnificently warm. Perhaps by the time I finish this letter, I'll be "blown" out into the midnight blue.

Bernadette's secret [*in the **Song of Bernadette***] was the miracle of the Visitation. Surely, who would believe that a French peasant would be graced by God to have His Mother visit this frail human being. After the Visitation, the stigmata that she bore and the life that she lived were proof enough that people could see her secret. It was not to be shouted to the house tops but to be realized simply — The Work of Christ is the work of a humble Man — significantly of what He expects of all of us. The feast of Lourdes is celebrated every February 11 thru'out the world. (Do you like the thin end of my pen?)

Woman, I say again your flattery is beyond all words. You leave me speechless and henceforth deprive me of the quality that you find so intriguing. But a comparison to [*writer and explorer*] Richard Halliburton is like comparing or giving me the riches of Croesus. I hang my head in modesty. But, indeed, R. H. is truly the King of Description. Washington Irving was the master of our childhood hero of words.

Darling, I wish I could share you and your Mother's feelings. To me, a long time is a short time when it is over. That sounds vague but I mean that when we look back, the time that has passed is merely an interlude for the future we so often crave. You won't need to tell Mother of our intentions, Babe, surely, that anxious look for mail and the fact that it does come must certainly betray all that we are keeping from her. Mother is not blind, and she can see thru' that veil of patience. I am grateful to hear that she thinks well of me and that she does care for men.

When I showed Max [*Gilliam*], my tent mate your pictures, he said that the weather looks cold and that you should wear a scarf to protect your lovely neck. I am ever so proud to show the fellows your picture. Since I don't see "Pappy" [*Agle*] too often, it is hard to keep him informed of our progress. By the way, Darling, what is your full name? That sounds foolish but I never did know. You should devote one letter for information concerning yourself. There are a lot of things, material things, I know nothing about you.

That conversation on vibrations. Are you sure that Marg. wasn't talking about mental telepathy. Conveying of thought by thought. Personally, I like your idea. The voice is all that is necessary to convey thought. It is a nicer way. After all, wouldn't it be Hell if I just look at you and you are to assume that I am telling you I love you. We know that expression can convey a thought. The eyes have it. Ask Marg. how long these vibrations are? Maybe we can correspond without the use of letters. It would be faster and we needn't have to wait for weeks to talk to each other. I'd speak to you all the time.

Darling, don't talk about Seagram's. I haven't had a drink since I left Ireland. I had gin in Ismailia once but truly that was "rot-gut." However, it is not the Seagram's, it is what it stands for. It means so much to us.

I do hope that my letter this afternoon was right. I tried hard to convey the thought, I didn't want to spoil it.

Last night we had a show, picture — *All This and Heaven Too* — but what I am driving at was the moon. It was sitting up there in the cold, blue sky, in the middle of a perfect circle. It looked like, and pardon my expression, the perfect head-on view of a woman's breast. It was rather a large replica, I admit, but that was the impression. You can see what one thinks about. Anything can "pop up" in this warped brain of mine.

Good Night, Bette, My Sweet. Do give my love to Mother. The Blessed Mother look over you and ask her Son to Bless You — Good Night, Honey, do miss you and love, Mike.

P.S.: Waiting for that stove to pop. Sounds awfully furious. Keep your fingers crossed. Just fumed and smoked like the Twentieth Century Limited pulling out of Grand Central. Hell it does keep us laughing though. We are one big family and we love to laugh. Wish you were here. Mike.

❧❀❧

The War Diary for December 8 described the continuation of our training program — formation and instrument flying in the morning, glider towing in the afternoon. Catholic services were also held at the Group mess hall. Also on that date, a small fire destroyed one of the sleeping tents, though no one was hurt. It was noted that ten men would be permitted to visit Trapani, a city on the northwestern coast of Sicily, each afternoon from 1300 to 1730 hours.

The entries for December 9 and 10 follow:

December 9: Training program: Glider towing in the morning, afternoon session called off due to weather. By order of the Wing Hq., four planes went on a mission to Palermo, Foggia, Pomigliano (Naples) and return. Capt. Ellis made a physical inspection of all personnel this morning and in addition gave a lecture on sex morality. Twenty more bags of Christmas mail were distributed this date. An EM's [*Enlisted Men's*] club is being formed. . . .

December 10: Training program: Instrument and Formation flying in the morning, afternoon and evening sessions called off. Five Officers and five EM left for a rest camp near Naples, Italy, on the Isle of Capri. Cpl. Phipps had an accident while driving a two and one-half ton truck. . . . A passenger, was slightly hurt. Heavy rains for the past four nights flooded several tents. AMGOT [*American Military Government of Tunisia*] turned over to the squadron Special Services Officer some furniture for the Enlisted Men's Club Room.

December 11, 1943 [*Saturday*]

Good Afternoon, My Love,

I have just scribbled a few lines to Mom and "Doc" and so I must give You a moment of my time. In reality, that is a fallacy. I wish I could give you all of my time. I love you, My Darling.

I finished Cronin's *Keys of the Kingdom* and Bette it is a "must." Read it. I believe the reason that I enjoyed it was because I read it so thoroughly. Usually, I am like a race horse straining at the leash, I read so fast. But I read this book as carefully as I could, not cover to cover but word for word. It is the story of a <u>man</u>, a priest. Any normal person could not help but to understand his broad-minded view of religion, men and life. He was a character that would be easy to admire. However, I'll wait until you have read it and you can judge for yourself. I am going to try to read more of Cronin's work. Lucy sent me a copy of *Love at First Flight*. It is a comedy and it is the life of a Naval Air Cadet. I had read a condensation of it in *Coronet* but I was hoping to get a copy of the original. I got it! Could it be mental telepathy? Or am I serious? I haven't started it yet. I preferred to read a copy of *Sporting News* first, just to see what the Hell is going on in sports.

Latest report on our stove is that we got the damn thing perking as it should. It isn't perking right yet but we don't have to keep one eye on it while we are trying to pursue our other activities. But another problem has arisen, the rain. Gad! It's awful. Since my feet are so big, it is a problem for me to keep from getting stuck in the mud. They have had to use a derrick twice to get me out. I carry a shovel with me all the time, for an emergency, just in case the derrick is busy pulling someone else out. After all, I'm not the only one with big feet. Growing another mustachio, and it's a humdinger.

Seriously, though, Bette, the outfit has begun to organize an enlisted men's club. We are all for it. It will give us somewhere to relax after a hard (?) day's work. The officers have their club, we might as well have a place [*censored*] too. Besides, we have to have a meeting place for holidays and stuff. It's a very good idea. If we had some Wac(k)s around, they could act as bar maids and maybe put up curtains and stuff. See, give a guy heaven and he wants heaven, earth, and some Hell, too.

Well, My Sweet, I have exhausted all my stupid words. — Oops — The Greek sent home a picture like the one I sent you. His girl friend took it to the office. Amid all the Oohs and Aahs, they started to compare us. It seems that I look like Tyrone Power with a dirty face. Now, you see, I told you you were marrying a good bargain.

Well Darling, I must close. Give my love to Mother. Take care of yourself. May God Bless You. Miss you — Love, Mike.

December 11, 1943 [*Saturday*]

Good Evening, Darling,

My Sweet, I received 3 letters from you this evening, Nov. 4, 5th, and Nov. 23rd. You can see how screwily the letters come to us. Now, I know that yellow blouse or suit you were talking about. There are so many things that you say and I get puzzled about then I receive the letters you refer to and the ideas you write about.

One thing, My Darling, you start off so beautifully on the subject of love. My heart jumps a beat, my brain starts to throb and bang, you stop and I have to wait for the next chapter. I don't mind terribly, I am not angry but it seems so funny to be left hanging by your heart strings. I will admit that I write too much. Really, Darling, I'm not bawling you out, only I get so much enjoyment to hear you speak the way you do that I hunger for more.

Darling, you needn't worry about the amount of rest I get. If I was so tired, I could hardly stand up, I assure I wouldn't let you down. I claim no grand years of experience or experimentation; however, the power of love and its wealth of emotion can drive a man to superhuman strength. It is not so much what happens but the unexplainable feeling. Darling, we shall never be at a loss for the proper words. We speak of how moods are parallel. Words are not necessary to explain. Look back at our love. You can see that words were never necessary. We need not resort to that oft-spoken mental telepathy, dual hypnotism or the language of love, all that is necessary is two people who know what they mean to each other. Do I make myself clear? Or should I display my talents and draw pictures?

My hands have recovered from all that hard (?) work I had to do. It would be a Hell of a thing if we asked the infantry to do our work. Those poor — have enough to do, Thank God, I'm in the Air Corps. I wouldn't have any part of that outfit unless I led an entire army and I didn't have to wallow in the mud, sweat, and forget how men really live. No matter how torturous our lives may seem to be, the infantry is really Hell. But "The next door neighbor's garden is always greener."

My Favorite Blonde, you know damn well that I don't intend to sleep on rocks. You don't guess wrong when you say you know me. I like my comfort. I like everything that a normal guy wants. When this "shebang" is over, there are going to be a lot of lazy men. The guys won't want to get out of bed and I think I'll be one of them. When you sound "wifish," I love it all the more. Your words are the words of a woman who is ready to make a home for me. Surely, I'd be a fool to refuse it. Your words are the words of an angel of my dreams. Darling, surely you know and I am sure I have spoken about it, that nothing could suit me more than to live quietly, peacefully, and above all comfortably.

Yes, Bette, that same dog was in KC with us but we never paid much attention to him. As a matter of fact, I don't even know his name. Nope, Johnson wasn't with me the day I came to KC from Tulsa. I struck up an acquaintance with "Ax" [*Chalmers Johnson, my crew chief*] only just before we came over.

I picked up a rather nice souvenir the other day. It is an "Aviator's Prayer" but it is written in Italian and I can't read what it says. Nevertheless, it is a nice remembrance. It is a medal about 1½" by 1". It is silver coated or sumpin'. It has the picture of a saint shrouded by clouds with little angels' faces sticking out of the clouds and flying around there are 3 different types of Italian planes. On the back is a pair of wings, the Italian type with a crown in the center, and below the wings is the prayer. It really is nice and I had to talk an Italian Radio Operator out of it. It didn't cost me but $2.00 but I was willing to pay more if I had to. I couldn't resist it and so I didn't.

Well, Darling, I must close. I do hope that my mail gets to you sooner. I can do no more but to write it. I leave it up to the mail service to get it to you.

So long, My Darling. Give my love to Mother. May God Bless You. I do love you and miss you so much. The time will pass. Before we know it, we'll be laughing about all of this. Love, Mike.

On December 11, the War Diary reported:

> **Training program: Called off due to bad weather. Sgt. Moore suffered minor cuts and bruises of the left hand, when the jeep he was driving landed in a ditch. A list of prices for laundry service was posted and all personnel were advised to be guided thereby. Weekly rations were distributed at the PX and a long line waited patiently for their smokes and sweets. Map folders were rearranged by S-2 [*Intelligence*] and given to Squadron Operations, along with some suggestions to eliminate the usual confusion immediately before missions. A very [*satisfactory*] arrangement was reached.**
>
> **December 12: Training program: None. Eleven planes took off on a mission for Command Headquarters, carrying passengers and cargo to Italy and return. The open air theatre showed *Suspicion* with Joan Fontaine and Gary Cooper. A dance was held for sixty Enlisted Men at Trapani and was a decided success.**

December 13, 1943 [*Monday*]

My Darling,

Blue Monday? The 13th? Who knows? It isn't a mood I'm in, just a feeling of utter depression! Then, we'll call it a mood. Bette, My Sweet, I love you so much.

It's funny how easy one can be cast into funny shadows. The time when it is difficult to sleep unless after hours of torturous tossing. The tremendous yearning for your warm, comforting, soft arms; having your shoulder to rest my head upon, not a portrayal of morbidity, but just a tributary — Loneliness.

Tonight I feel like Poe, Shelley, and Shakespeare rolled into one. I could roll on with, "Ah Yes, Woe is me." Fortunately for you, I'm not one of those. You shall be spared the boredom of listless and useless yearning.

By the time I have completed the composition of this letter, I am sure that my mood will be reversed. I talk to you and my gloom fades like the smoke of a spent cigarette. You must pardon my endless chatter, My Darling, let me wallow in the muck of my thoughts — I'll talk out of it, but until that is done, you must bear with me.

My Loved One, how often the picture of you runs and stops in my mind. You linger and the beauty of you lingers like the smell of burning incense. Your eyes betray your emotions and I look at you helplessly and curse because I am so far from you and I can't help. But you are there and I know, I am with you.

Perhaps, if I curse the failings of centered mankind, I can relieve the pressure. Surely one cannot deny the democratic beliefs that we labor under. For the sake of our children, I hope that the young men and women realize the stupidity of this mess. Those damned bastards that believe in world power; those miserable dogs that can't stand to see people that are alive, healthy, and happy. Then again, how stupid my thoughts. Surely, I know that by these thoughts, I am aggravating my inner self. *Touche* — Then I bring the point to us, you and I, the loved and the lover. My Darling, as you pleaded with me, so will I plead with you. *Le Bon Dieu* can smile upon us. He will, I know because there are so many like us and He can't let us stray. You see, Bette, I talk with these words as I would talk to you. If we were together, my head would be buried in your breast. I would, no doubt, be shaking from the intensity of the emotion. So deeply do I feel my love for you, My Darling.

But I mustn't go on sounding like the cynic, hating everything and cursing it accordingly. My words are the words of love but they may sound distressing and perhaps a bit terrifying. If I were with you, I know that I would scare you or else you would have to suffer the consequences of untamed emotions. So, just read this letter and laugh and say, "Gad! He's at it again."

Darling, to get back to reality and out of the arms of this ruthless god of dreariness, you must realize that we will be separated for a long time. We have never talked about the time we would be separated. But let's say it will be a long time, leave it at that and be sensible. After all, Bette, my none-too-loquacious Blonde, I haven't seen you since July and it seems like a million years of yesterdays that I saw you in Ft. Wayne.

You know, Bette, if I had realized before what we meant to each other, I could have fixed things so that I could have stayed in the States for another year. I volunteered for all this. I was asked if I wanted to help start a new squadron in Missouri [*Knobnoster, Sedalia*] 60 miles out of KC. I was asked to stay with the 72nd [*Troop Carrier Squadron*]. I refused both and here I am. In both cases, I'd have more rank. Now, I'm just rank or is it rancid? Comparing it all to a prison stretch, at least, I have started my stretch and I hope I'll finish sooner than if I had waited.

Now, I'll devote the rest of this letter to making all my previous words void. Crazy, isn't it? Just one circle, no conclusions. Honestly, Honey, I am happy but I just get one of those fits of words, they mean something but they shouldn't be taken too seriously. All told, it means I miss you and love you.

You see, I told you once, I'm crazy. If I had some bourbon in me, I'd start to recite. I'd ruffle my hair, wave my arms, curse, yell, and then turn around and say, "Do you like gardenias?" I think you know those moods. You have seen me in them quite often. Sometimes they wouldn't be on the same subject. One night, long ago, I was taking a girl to see *Gone With the Wind* — But before we went, she insisted upon having a soda (no bourbon). I started to talk and I spent 3 hours telling her of the needs of strong-minded youth and the effect it would have on America's future. I wasn't radical, merely enthusiastic & sincere. She said the movie wasn't as "hot" after my 3 hour spiel. (Gotta flute, gonna learn how to play it, maybe!) See! All changed!

Goodnight, My Sweet. I love you so very much and I do feel so different. Give my love to Mother. May God Bless You. Take care of yourself. Love, Mike.

According to the War Diary, there were no training flights on December 13, but six planes took off on a mission for Command Headquarters, carrying passengers and cargo on a round trip to Italy. Six enlisted men received orders from the Ninth Air Force, the War Diary also noted on that day, and left the 37th Squadron to return to the States.

December 14, 1943 [*Tuesday*]

My Darling,

A new day, a new mood, a slight hangover from thought not liquor. Morpheus wrested me from the arms of Poe, etc., dropped me and nestled me to his bosom and off I went to dream land. But his sedative took time to work on my nervous system. I tossed and pitched in a sea of poetry. I defied Poe; I ignored Segar; I overdid Shakespeare, threw into my poetry a touch of Dali's surrealism and the finished product was a concoction called, "The Censor's Nightmare":

> Nip, Nip so I cleave
> How in Hell can I leave
> All these hearts upon their sleeve
> I hope it doesn't rain today!

II
Oh! these fellows how they bicker
makes me want to sneer and snicker
Long I linger, long I dally
I wonder what ever became of Sally?

You see, it went on endlessly. Nothing worthwhile for publication. No, My Darling, I wasn't under the influence of cocaine or any drug. It may be called silly but my mind contained all these thoughts. I am not working for a Section 8 (insanity). Perhaps as I write this epistle, I'll remember more of my verses. It's length certainly outran "Hiawatha" or "Evangeline."

Words, words by the score
Into millions do they soar
All I cut were 50 or more
Hm! Navy beat Army 13-0.

Silly, isn't it? Seriously though, I had to have something as a substitution for my thoughts. I tried to play the flute but later I decided that Sousa could use me as a drum beater.

Here they come line on line
"Oh, My darling, how I pine
I, forever, will be thine"
Oh, Clementine, My Clementine!

Now, let me get down to letter writing. Surely you must be annoyed with me. I thought about the time that you were going to visit me in Alliance [*Nebraska*]. I had reserved a room for you at the Drake Hotel, one of two that were any good. I was going to stroll down Main Street with you and I knew I'd have to fight off a squadron of paratroopers.

I finished reading *Love at First Flight*. It is a very breezy account of the training of a Naval Air Cadet. The author tries to touch off a spark to course a person to the lightness of *Private Hargrove*. I don't think he succeeded too well. At least, I didn't think so. I enjoyed the book but it wasn't what I would call a howling success.

I see that the basketball season has started. *Stars and Stripes* does a good job to keep us well acquainted with the news. In the Hockey League, Les Canadiens are running away with the standings. Navy beat Army 13-0, and I see that Washington U. is going to the Rose Bowl. I never had any favorite basketball teams because our local N.Y. colleges always turned out the best in the States: LIU [*Long Island University*], NYU [*New York University*], Fordham, City College, all these schools had good outfits. In basketball, as in hockey, it is merely the style of play and the individualism that impresses the fans. But in football, the various sections of the country varied as to style of play. East, hit hard and run over your opponents; Middle West, single and winged formations mixed with some football "savvy" and trickery. The South, and particular, the Southwest, wide open and plenty of loose, wide ball handling. Specialty, passing: Davey O'Brien, Sammy Baugh, Emory Nix to mention a few. The Far West, it was the "T" — now the whole country is trying it. My leaning is towards the Southwest. My ambition is to watch Rice, Texas A&M, Texas and few of the others play ball.

There again, you see, I had no reason to write about all this. It may be interesting or puzzling or just a lot of rot to you, My Bette, but to me it is years of study and interest. However, don't be too hard on me, I am apt to say anything. At least, it is better than that miserable poetry. I should dream and talk of love but there will be other letters and more of 'em. I could paint pictures so beautiful that the odor of gardenias would be evident. But, let me write one of these stupidly light letters I so often talk about. You know that I love you. So I hope that you will bear with me. "For better or for <u>Worse</u>."

Darling, I must close. I assure you this theme will not last too long. I am sure I will get back to normal. Oh, My Darling, I love you so much. If only I had had the chance to prove it the way I wanted to. I will though. Until then, you must hear the pounding of my heart and the sound of my humble words.

So long, Bette. Give my love to Mother. May God Bless You. Take care of yourself. — Your "Screw-ball" lover. Love, Mike.

Following is the War Diary entry for December 14:

> **Training program: Called off on account of bad weather. The EM Club was officially opened this evening and from all indications was a tremendous success. *Hold That Ghost* was at the open air theatre. This picture and many of the others have been seen three or four times before.**

December 15, 1943 [*Wednesday*]

My Darling,

This is your wittle, bwave, herwoe again. But I think I have settled somewhat to normalcy. Opened our club last night [*censored out a whole sentence*]. I feel much better. Besides I received 3 letters from you today and I really feel as if I hit the jackpot.

It seems that the first situation before the house is our children. Notre Dame is a good school and it is a Catholic school, but I'd like the young kids to go to a co-ed. Give him a chance to raise merry hell and enjoy life before some more bastards try to ruin it for him. All this is very premature, but Darling, I know that our feelings are the same and our children will get the best we can offer them. Besides, if he takes after his old man, he'll want to go to a co-ed school. Probably decide on Vassar, the wolf.

This [*name omitted*] that you speak of sounds like the ideal G.I. gal. Some guys go wacky for a screw ball like that. But it isn't worth the paper for discussion. Before I go any further, My Darling, I love you. I live for the moment when we will meet again. I dreamt that I was coming home. I wired from Florida and told you to go to my home so that we could be married immediately. When I reached Penn Station, you and Lucy were there to meet me. I kissed Lucy first and then I turned to you. All I said was, "My Darling. Oh!, My Darling!" Then I held you in my arms and the dream ended. You were so real, it seemed as if I could reach out and touch you & I didn't start to recite poetry.

I am so glad that Tom wrote to you. He is the picture of understanding and kindness. I feel someday he will be a saint. He is modern and understands the depths and workings of the modern human soul. He is ideal for the priesthood. Lucy writes and tells me that they are looking forward to his ordination. God Bless Him, he is so deserving of everything.

Yes, My Sweet, I figured out who the censor was. I figured by simple deduction that he is the only one who knew me well enough to make any remarks. The rest of 'em just stick to their cutting and scrapping.

The first year is the hardest, Bette, after that you'll get used to it. Time is a funny thing. At first, it is a big mountain. It takes so long to climb and once we get over it, we look back triumphantly and find that it takes but a few minutes of laughs to sum up the years of tears. And laugh, we shall; and live we will. I have so much to do for you, that I'll spend all my life making your life happy.

Your philosophies on life are great. Your sureness about the future warms my heart. You are not demanding and you make a simple plea for the one thing that can't miss — happiness. Some people demand all of everything and all we ask is to be able to live the way we did before I left. We just want to walk the same, laugh the same, and cry if we must. We look for no greatness. Everything is the picture of moderation, even if it must be lived in a stable. Yes, My Darling, life holds so much and we want so little.

No, My Sweet, we don't hear too much music and I do miss it. I'll have to spend a lot of time listening to catch up on it.

You should read Lucy's nice accounts about you. She and the rest of the family are happy for us. Her prayers are for my quick return and for our happiness together. It can't miss. All the guns of love are aimed at us.

Gosh, Bette, you must excuse me. I am afraid that my hangover hasn't left me. I still feel slightly dazed, my eyes are rough, and my stomach wild.

So long for now, My Darling. Give my love to Mother. May God Bless You. Take care of yourself. I love you and miss you more each day. Love, Mike.

The War Diary entries for December 15-17 noted routine training, promotions, and the delivery of Christmas mail:

> **December 15: Training Program: Instrument and Formation flying in the morning and Glider towing in the afternoon. Nineteen men were permitted to make a one day tour to Agrigento, Sicily. The men were transported by plane and had lunch at 52nd Wing Headquarters.** [*Squadron Commanding Officer*] **Major Fletcher posted on the**

bulletin board a copy of a letter received from Major Wm. H. Matthews, former C.O., now stationed in the U.S.A., congratulating the squadron on their first anniversary overseas and expressing hope that he would be ordered back with the squadron again.

December 16: Training Program: Instrument and Formation flying in the morning and Air work at night. One plane took off for Cairo on official business. The truck with one officer and 22 E. M. arrived late last night from El Aouina, Tunisia. The entire trip was made without special incident. The squadron Adjutant, Robert H. Edmunds, was promoted to Captain, effective date 3 December 1943. Just before receiving word of his promotion, Lt. Edmunds, was out playing football and fractured a bone in his left leg. He was flown to Tunis but due to the weather the pilot was unable to land. The same thing happened when they tried to land at Palermo, compelling them to return to Borizzo.

December 17: Training Program: Instrument and Formation flying, morning session only. Forty-six bags of Christmas packages arrived and part of them distributed this evening. Captain Cooney gave a lecture to all Commissioned personnel on Escape.

December 18, 1943 [*Saturday*]

My Darling,

This is Saturday but it should be a nice quiet Sunday afternoon. It is raining and if the surroundings were pleasant, it would be a pleasant rain. A day after the night before. A big time Saturday night, a good night's sleep, Sunday Mass, a nice breakfast, a little horse play, a nice dinner, the Sunday papers have been read, there is some soft music on the air, it's cozy and warm, the chair is comfortable, we are alone, you are sitting across my lap and the world just moves on. Dear God! Make that a prayer, when will it happen?

The rain beats its monotonous tone, beating of a distant tom-tom, breathing words of love and happiness. A world of peace and tranquillity amid all this death, slaughter, famine and poverty. Why?

A man can dream and must dream to overcome a picture of wet and cold, false happiness. Thank God I'm not in the infantry. I could go on deriding the picture in its true entirety and yet I don't want to because it would sound like I was crying. I don't want to, I just want to curse again. Surely, somewhere, someone must be ignorant of all this. Is there a Shangri-La or do we wait for our death to find an eternal peace?

Ah, Yes, but Peace on Earth and Good Will to All Men!

Well, Bette, My Darling, I will be straightened out as soon as I get some mail. I'll close this and start on a good theme, this afternoon.

God Bless You — I love You. Love, Mike.

December 18, 1943 [*Saturday*]

My Darling, Bette,

I promise you that my mood won't be the same. I received your roll of film, finally. I hope I can get some good shots with them. Damn it's too bad I couldn't get a load of film. I get so damned trigger happy, I like to shoot everything. But again, no mail. Sigh!

You know, Darling, I kind of like that rainy Sunday scene. We discussed the way we like to walk in the rain. I know I do, but if it's Sunday, and I'm not at a ball game, I might rather sit and enjoy the sound rather than the feel. Hell! I don't know, if I keep up like this I'm liable to start reciting poetry again, and if I do, I know that you'll divorce me even before we are married.

It really isn't anything and I don't want you to be disturbed by this useless banter. My sister knows me. She even wrote in one of her letters that it would be great to watch me pacing the floor and letting off a lot of steam. Might wring my hands, flay my arms, stroke my hair, smoke chains of cigarettes and say so much that means nothing. You know that even when I am sitting and my ideas are excited, I swing in all directions. I have never been a neurotic, just habit. There are a lot of things about me, Darling, but they are really harmless.

I love you, My Darling. And it is needless to say that the days pass and my love for you mounts like a thermometer on a hot day. But then again, I leave all that unsaid. My usually boisterous manner has been subdued like the waters of a fiery sea, calmed by the sun and a soft wind. A calm outer and a tumultuous inner.

I was thinking about something funny but there are some scenes that I can't possibly tell in a letter. Scenes that are directly caused by inconvenience. Someday, I'll sit down and go thru' the whole thing. I don't think that they will be as disgusting as they will be funny. However, for now, you will be spared these somewhat horrifying tales.

Well, Bette, My Sweet, I must rush now but don't fret, I'll probably go thru' endless lines of chatter that will make torturous reading. Can't give out right now. I will.

Give my love to Mother. Take care of yourself. May God Bless You. Love, Mike.

On December 18, according to the War Diary, bad weather forced the cancellation of the training program. That day's entry concluded, "Very heavy rains all day make even walking a hazard."

December 19, 1943 [*Sunday*]

My Darling,

I love you. You must forgive me for the monstrosities that I call letters. A vague, blank, unthinking period that is brought about by some foolish emptiness. One cannot help but to go thru' such a period. It is the first one for me in over a year. I was even accused of being quiet and justly so because not even words can I force to overcome this feeling.

I got a haircut today, and the local barber was the type that sang folk songs, romantic numbers and such, all in Italian. It reminded me of Eric Rhodes, the actor who played in a few of the Astaire-Rogers pictures. You know, the sleek Latin with the accordion and "E Donna Mobile" on his lips. In turn that reminded me of an incident that happened a few years ago.

We were giving a party for one of the boys that worked with us [*at Sears Roebuck*]. He was being drafted and he was the first one to leave our department. We had bought him a beautiful wrist watch and the party was to be held at the "Beachcomber" an exclusive nite club in New York. We sort of knew that the prices would be steep, so we decided to have a few drinks. There were about 10 fellows and we were going to meet the rest of the gang at the party. Naturally, everyone bought a round and the mood became a very merry one. We reached the "Beachcomber" — all sails to the wind. I just about staggered to my table. After we had eaten, I got a hold of this buxom Russian gal and really gave her a good swing. Finally, they burst into a Conga and believe me, I never wrapped my hands about a better pair of -er, -er hips. That finished all too soon. The stage show came on and Eric Rhodes was the MC. Quite inappropriately and ungentlemanly, instead of clapping, I booed. Finally, the watch was given to Rhodes and he made the presentation, but I was called upon to give the speech. I guess I must have overdone myself or something, at any rate, they had to give me the bum's rush and I always promised that I'd knock Rhodes' ears off. I never got back there because the place closed a week later. I must have been drunk because I paid 95 cents a shot for Scotch all nite. I didn't really get violent, just good-naturedly wild and they took me wrong. See, My Darling, I was quite a Gay Blade in my younger days.

There now, do I sound a bit different?

Six more days to Christmas. Last year, I was in Chicago. I did a little thinking about this past year and I often wonder why my life was as it was. I had so many opportunities to steer a different course. And yet, I realize that we were destined to meet and I am so glad for it. If things had gone as they appeared to, I would never have met you, and so we did and My Darling, it shall never change. Surely when the phrase was said it was meant for something, "You were meant for me." So many tricks of fate, and life could have made that 2 different people, but no, we were put together. I never did intend to go to that dance [*at the USO*]. If you'll remember I was going to see Glen Gray and I saw Bette Hill and no one else. It seems and seemed so strange that I started to put you in every phase of my life. You know, Darling, we could have gotten married that first night and we wouldn't have been wrong. I think often of this obliging nature of mine and I see how often it has caused me to choose the wrong path. Me and my nobleness. Now, I don't care for that, I want to be selfish and in my selfishness, I want you and only you. You know, Bette, I may be a very jealous husband, and I believe I have a right to be because I have waited so long for you. I love you and miss you so very much, My Darling.

Another thing, Bette, that made my quiet mood so pronounced was that I was hungry for conversation. Not in a letter but face to face. I wanted so much to talk about the things

I like. I couldn't be satisfied for reasons I can't explain just yet. I'm not a snob but there are times when shop and the talk about women just don't strike the right chord. I don't mean the women we love, just women. It brings out the same topics and nothing can be reached. Can't even get excited by the thought of it. A sort of mutual sterility and angelic stroke. I love to talk but my conversations must be varied or I find that I become rutted and the sides are so hard to climb out of.

Well, Bette, My Sweet, I must say "Good Night." Give my love to Mother. Pray for me. May God Bless You. Love, Mike.

The training program continued on December 19, according to the War Diary, with group formation flying in the morning and squadron formation flying in the evening.

On December 20, the War Diary notes, the training program included squadron formation flying in the morning, but the night flying was called off due to weather. Captain Cooney gave a lecture on security to all enlisted men before the movie in the evening. Also on that date, eight men left for the rest camp at the Isle of Capri in Italy: Second Lieutenants Addison D. Agle ("Pappy"), Marvin L. Finch, Robert T. Quinn, and Robert F. Scott; Technical Sergeant Claude L. Fuller; and Staff Sergeants John N. Henshaw, George M. Shera, and Sam Friedman.

December 21, 1943 [*Tuesday*]

My Darling,

Nothing to answer to. I haven't received a letter this week. Nevertheless, it doesn't hinder me from sending in my sugar report. Did you ever read, *For Whom the Bell Tolls*? If you did you recall a good part of the book depicts life in a sleeping bag. I could never understand how Maria and Jordan got along in that damned thing because my sleeping bag was so small that I just about got my long body into it. I was issued another one and now I can see that Hemingway knew what he was talking about. Not because I have experimented but by some simple logic, I can see that it is possible. As for me, I'll take my love in a good, ole'-fashioned bed.

Remember the night that I wrote you the first letter — It was a Monday night and I had seen you Saturday and Sunday. I was Charge of Quarters and I had just phoned you and quite impulsively I said that I was going to write you a letter. I didn't know whether it should be short or long or what it would be about. I still don't remember what I wrote but it was probably some corny philosophies. That was the night that you asked me if I'd like to talk to Mom on Mother's day. That Saturday night, I bought you your first orchid and we spent the better part of that night over a big discussion on religion.

It seems so long ago but it really isn't so long. How well I remember waiting for that street car at any hour of the night and the way I had to rush on Sundays so that I'd get back to quarters early. You know, Darling, there are a lot of amusing incidents I think about. I can't write because they are for us. I don't cherish the fact that a censor's eyes have to scan these words. Someday we can sit down and look over those happy months and it will be easy to admit that we are two funny people who don't give a damn about a lot of things.

You must excuse me, My Love. I have to cut this short. I had intended to write a long letter but it was cut short.

Give my love to Mother. I love you and miss you. May God Bless You. Love, Mike.

War Diary entry, December 21:

Training Program: Squadron formation flying and Instrument and Formation flying in the morning, night session called off due to weather. . . .

December 22, 1943 [*Wednesday*]

My Darling,

I had wanted to write a long letter yesterday because both the mood and the weather were fitting. Unfortunately, I had some visitors and when they left, it was too late to really think. I am hoping that you are saving most of my letters because there are a lot of things that I'll be able to elaborate on that I can't possibly talk about now.

Thank God, the sun is bright and it feels like a July day. It is amazing how quickly weather can change from a rainy miserable day to a bright sunny one. But all that is passé and hardly worth the lines.

It's funny, but at one time I used to think so very deeply about the future. I don't mean the near future but so far ahead that it is that well-known "castle in the air." I could do so because there were facts that made it possible. My ambitions and circumstances built that future for me. The war destroyed all that and it is necessary to start all over again. But this time I no longer think about that house in the country and all that sort of thing.

My thoughts are to the day when I'll see you again and the joy of sharing a bit of blissful happiness with you. I refuse to look beyond that because there are no facts nor trends of thought that I can work upon. Perhaps and justly so, I have become a skeptic to that chain of thought. I am not the same dreamer. I am more of a realist. I know that when I come back, we'll be married. I know that whatever honeymoon that we will have will be in a congestion. You will share me with my family. We don't know what kind of or how long a furlough I'll get. Then when that is over, we will be together as often as my duties will allow. You see, My Darling, we should realize that the war will not be over with my return; therefore, we must be prepared to set our course of life accordingly. When this mess is over, then we will put on our dream caps, mix it with reality and try to find the formula for our future.

Darling, I am not trying to frighten you. I only want you to see that we must go thru' this period of life. We'll go thru' it together and when Unk Sam gives me my discharge then we can start our civilian life. For the while, I'll still be a soldier and you'll be a soldier's wife. Once I am out, then we can see what I have to offer the world and in turn what is to be offered to me. Whatever happens, we can see it together and Gad! They had better look out.

My Darling, I don't think I have changed. My outlook on these matters is much saner and more intelligent. I haven't forgotten how to dream, and I haven't forgotten that our love will keep us as lovers always. To me, it is the only way I can live. For outsiders and such, we are husband and wife, but I shall never forget that you are the person I love. It doesn't seem so strange to say that because there are so many men that accept their wives as the keeper of the house. How Foolish!

Have I made myself clear, Bette? I love you so much that I don't want anything I do to make it seem different. Whatever little mistakes I make will be because I cannot and never will attain perfection. But Damn if I won't try to come close to it.

Say, Bette, I don't know if I ever mentioned it but I'd like to have a large picture of you. One of those things that just steps out and says, "Love me, for you are mine!"

Well, My Sweet, must say so-long. Hope to Hell I get some mail. But I'll keep waiting until Hell forgets that I'm a Saint. Give my love to Mother. May God Bless You. Please enjoy the holidays. As they say in Brooklyn, "Wait 'til next year!" and we'll really raise Hell. — Love, Mike. [*For some reason, there is a postmark on the left side of the last page which says: "Kansas City, MO, Stn 6, Feb. 1, 1944.*]

On December 22, in addition to reporting formation and instrument flights as part of the training program, the War Diary read:

> **General Clark, 52nd Wing Commanding Officer, along with his Staff Officers, made a general inspection of all personnel and departments and at the same time presented several awards to three men of the 316 T.C.** [*Troop Carrier*] **Group.**

December 23, 1943 [*Thursday*]

My Darling,

I received your package. I do hope I can put it to use. In this Hell-hole, washing is incidental. And if I ever do use the soap, I know damn well, I'll be a hit with the boys. Of all the packages I've received, the film that you sent me was all the film I got. Kinda' got under my skin. I was hoping to reap and "shoot" plenty.

Usually in our "bull" sessions, the talk gets around to the post-war planning that we read so much about. We have read a lot about this "mustering out" pay and bonuses. It all sounds like a lot of bull to us. They are bickering so much about it that it sounds like a pre-election promise. Since we feel that the war will last beyond another administration, we'll be forgotten by the next bunch of politico hoodlums. To remember the results of the last war, the father (?) of our country must feel that the intelligence of this war's soldiers must be on a par with the warped brain of a 3rd grade moron. "Let's give them $300. And a bonus besides!" "Let's set up a system whereby they can get a year's training, free!" "Let's make it so that they will be able to come home to a new America!" Surely they are jesting or at least they are doing a lousy job of keeping our morale high. I am speaking from a purely political standpoint. Not as a "gripe" but thru' the eyes of a person who feels some interest for all this "hullabaloo." They know damn well that when this mess is over, the future will probably take care of itself.

Sorry, My Sweet, a discussion such as that is like a discussion of music. One brings comfort and ease, the other discomfort of mind and status. We are having Midnight Mass tomorrow night and I recalled the many times that I was present at these marvelous ceremonies. The sound of young voices singing ["*Adeste Fidelis*"], "Holy Night." The sound of a sweet, almost shrill trumpet playing the "Credo." I got back so far as to remember myself dressed in a cassock of red, a white lace surplice and a "Lord Fauntelroy" (I think it is spelled that way!) collar and a red, silk scarf-bow. My cheeks would burn from the light and the excitement. My hair would be brushed, my shoes shined, my face as bright as the candle light and my voice cracking from the transition to the young manhood stage. (Oh! I forgot the white gloves!) It was a marvelous picture and the grandest sensation I've ever felt. Who was it said, "Youth is such a wonderful time, too bad it has to be wasted on the young." Surely, we could never appreciate then, and when we become older, it is too late to recapture our younger days.

"White Christmas" — the odor of holly and incense, the taste of that so-carefully prepared dinner, the feeling of satisfaction, the joy of living. "Peace on earth, Good Will to all men." "Gloria in Excelsis Deo." If only we are taught never to forget it again. I am not homesick by these thoughts, I just feel so triumphantly good because I have these memories. Oft-repeated, "They can't take that away from me." The privilege of being above the animal, the ability to think has provided the food of existence that fades only with the end of our lives. It takes circumstances such as we are now feeling to make us realize that we spend a good part of our lives just wasting time.

And so I close, My Darling, all I have are memories and a deep, almost indescribable, knowledge that I'll be coming back to a new life and to you. I love you so very much.

So long for now, Bette. Give my love to Mother. Have you received the money yet? Don't get too drunk, you'll miss the enjoyment of the holiday.

Take care of yourself. May God Bless You. Praying for us. Love, Mike.

Following are the War Diary entries for December 23-26:

December 23: Training Program: Squadron Formation flying,

afternoon and evening sessions. A publicity report on Major Childer's promotion was forwarded to Group S-2.

December 24: Training Program: Squadron Formation and Instrument flying in the morning, Group Formation flying at night. A Christmas tree was lit up in the Squadron Day Room. Midnight mass was held at the Orphanage in Trapani.

December 25: Training Program: Group Formation flying, morning session. Two large boxes of assorted crackers, candy, chewing gum, etc., were contributed by all personnel for distribution amongst children in the vicinity of the camp. Christmas dinner consisted of the following:

Turkey, dressing, giblet gravy, sweet potatoes, peas, cauliflower, ice cream, apple pie, nuts, candy, oranges, cranberry sauce and coffee. There were seconds for all who could walk back for it. Protestant services were held in the mess hall after dinner.

December 26: Training Program: Squadron Formation and Instrument flying in the afternoon. Squadron Formation flying at night. Lt. Rayburn received minor injuries when the jeep he was driving crashed into a tree, on the lane from Squadron Hq. to the main road. The jeep's windshield and top were torn off and the steering column was loosened.

December 27, 1943 [*Monday*]

My Darling,

My holidays were fine. The mail that reached us made the holiday perfect. You were celebrating Thanksgiving (in the mail), and I was bloated with Christmas turkey. When I hear of your Christmas, my new year will have already started. It's great to have two holidays in one. Of all the 13 letters I received, 4 of them were from you. So I must answer them. But before I do, I want to apologize for not having written for the last 3 days. My celebration started early and ended late, with one day necessary for recovery. I'm in good shape now. Just so that the tax payers won't feel they are being cheated. I'll give you the articles of our Christmas meal — Turkey, mashed sweet potatoes, boiled cauliflower, carrots and peas, beets, apple pie and all the ice cream we could eat. Everything was perfect and it made it so easy to take. Our bar was well stocked with bourbon, and I proceeded to get well plastered. It was a very full and very wet holiday.

The way you talk about the Cards beating the Yanks next year makes me think that you have no faith in "Dem Bums." You know that Brooklyn is going to win the pennant next year. You sound like a Rebel.

Darling, you speak about a ring. I didn't quite get it. Have you already got a ring and don't expect a wedding band from me? I don't mean anything by it but I always thought the man gives the girl the ring. Of course, that's just one of those things. You can straighten that out when you answer this. Make it just a bit clearer. I get dense every so often and I never know what's going on. —

My Darling, don't worry about a thing. We said that we'd like Tom to marry us. But, if by the Grace of God, I do get home before May, then we won't wait. This is long enough. I couldn't dare think to be back in the States and not have you as my wife. Lucy told me that she had written. I am glad that they are on the ball. She's so crazy about her captain that her letters are naturally full of him. I always talk about you, so I guess it's mutual.

I wouldn't worry about flirts, My Love, the day that you cease to be attractive to men, will be the day that your creator takes you away. You know men are wolves.

I like your expression, Darling. "I was feeling low, so Mother suggested I buy some clothes. It did help." That's keen. Women are so lucky. Men get drunk, have a hangover, and look like the last victim. Women buy clothes, and look twice as beautiful. The effects are the same but the women do look better.

So glad you were able to get more film. I really have a wealth of shots I'd like to get. I do hope that you get a chance to see the "Russian Ballet." Although I have never seen it, I'd like to, just once, because ballet is not my forte. My sister sees it every year. But you can be sure that we'll see the stage shows. That is one thing that I really enjoy. Even "Ten Days on a Barroom Floor."

I have heard about *A Tree Grows in Brooklyn*. I didn't hear much just the title. But if it's about Brooklyn, it must be good. I never heard of *Victoria Grandolet*. Sounds like a stuffy affair, but then again you can't judge a book by its name.

Tell Mother not to worry about me. If I couldn't stand the "gaff" then I wouldn't worry about it.

Darling, you must forgive me. A letter like this is used to answer your letters. When I don't hear from you, I go into my philosophies. So I try to give you 2 to 1. All I know is that I haven't received all your letters. One is dated Nov. 22, the other 27, one 30 and one Dec. 5. Heaven only knows what happened to those in between.

Darling, I must close. I'll try not to let so many days pass before writing. Sometimes it isn't my fault that I miss a few days.

Love you and miss you very much. Give my love to Mother. Take care of yourself. May God Bless You. Love, Mike.

The December 27 War Diary entry noted only the usual training flights — squadron formation and instrument flying in the morning, and group formation flying at night.

December 28, 1943 [*Tuesday*]

My Darling,

I hardly know what to start writing about, but in time I'll probably fill pages of senseless words. I never had the chance to tell you a lot of things, Bette. Oft times while we sat on the porch at your home, my words were about someone else. You must realize that I told that other person how much I loved her. But here I am repeating myself to you. Deep down in my heart, I feel the difference, if I can only find the words to tell you, I'll be happy. Instinct is a big part of the human mind, regardless of how often it has been tested and has been tried for disapproval. It is a full feeling. As we know it, almost indescribable. When I was away from Stretch, she was a forgotten person, not entirely because time had seen to it that I had acquired a habit. My love for you, My Darling, is not a part time job. When we were together, there were a lot of indications of my affection. My words, my actions showed you that you were not an obscure creature. But when I left you, I couldn't or at least you couldn't see my thoughts. You set the example for my actions. When we were together, we were building all that we have now but it wasn't until we separated did the realization of the dream become fact. Oh, Hell! I sound like a Columbus Square radical. What I am trying to say is that I love you so very much.

When my sister writes, it is easy to see what her thoughts are about. She dedicates pages upon pages to words of her captain. What a lucky man he is to be loved by her! At first she professed a bit of skepticism because of her last affair. It didn't work. But this guy showered her with every thing in the books. Naturally, she is flattered by his actions but she is also made so happy that it is a feeling she has never had before. She thinks it is all so very crazy because she has known Harry such a short time and then again she can't describe her happiness. But I told her that you and I have known each other such a short time and there is no doubt in our minds. Her conclusion was that it is such a great thing to find so much happiness in such [*a short*] time. What more can one say?

I have been told that the Rebel is such a beautiful child. What do they expect, after all, look at her uncle. Just kidding. If she [*saw*] my haircut and my ivy (climbs all over) mustache, the poor kid would be scared to grayness.

I heard a swell program last night from BBC (British Broadcasting). Just heard such songs as "Begin the Beguine," "You'll Never Know," "Woodchopper's Ball," "In the Mood" and a Hell of a lot of good swing selections. It really makes life interesting.

I haven't had a chance to do much reading lately. I can't seem to get my claws on anything. It is hard to ask a bunch of guys if they have anything to read. So I just act the part of a crow and do a good job of scavenging. So that just about limits me to comics and *Stars and Stripes*.

Well, Bette, My Darling, you must forgive me but I must close. Give my love to Mother. Take care of yourself, Darling. May God Bless You. Love, Mike.

The December 28 War Diary entry read:

Glider Formation flying in the morning and Glider tow at night. At the open air theater the picture *Cairo* was shown, starring Robert Young, Jeanette McDonald, and Ethel Waters.

December 29, 1943 [*Wednesday*]

My Darling,

I received your letter of the 2nd but I forgot to mention some thing and here it is. In one of your letters you mentioned [*that you had*] seen a short on Portugal. You said it looked pretty, but you added, "I wonder how it smells." I thought that was rather amusing but I can see that I have influenced you on that score. No kidding, though that is a question!

Your letter said that my words seem to bring me into the room. If I were only a "genie." Then I could do that, I wish that I left you for only 2 or 3 days, then I could come back and tell you all I have seen — we wouldn't have to worry about censors. Sorry again about those little gremlins of our mail. Just can't lose 'em. Besides in your figurations, you were all wrong. But I won't hint and let someone get inquisitive. Let it go. I'll tell you about it when I see you.

I was surprised to hear about your Dad. After all, our country is built upon traditions. My Dad, The Chief, is a rugged guy but I have yet to see the day when he didn't feel the real meaning of a holiday. My Darling, I can really see what you have missed on that score. If it were not such a great thing, why would we, who are so far from home, attach so much significance to those days. Regardless, of all, My Darling, we will never miss the fullness of these days as long as we live. I cannot help but to drop a tear, smile a smile, or laugh boisterously, because that day was our day. It is like the memories you and I hold of our short and marvelous love. To those we will add more and then our waning years will be spent in the memory of our youth. Surely an anniversary is worth remembering. So far, we have none. I don't recall the date I met you. (I know it was a Saturday night.) I don't remember the last time I saw you except that it was a Sunday morning sometime in the early part of July, maybe 15th or so. But I can tell you most of the things that happened and how I felt. Some day, we will add dates and really how important is a date except to know that something happened and the feeling still lingers in your heart & soul.

I was glad to hear about that "sans curlers, sans cream" habit of your[s]. At any rate, I should have remembered that. Darling, forgive me if I seem rude and it really isn't rudeness because it is something I will always remember. But you know, you and I lived as lovers or as husband and wife for 3 days. It was great. I was happy and I hope that you were too. That, My Darling, was only a preview of the life we will live for 365 days of the year. No one can take that away from us and no one will take the future from us. I do love you so, Bette.

Look, Honey, I must close. I'd like to keep on but I can't. Thank Mother for her greetings and tell her my Xmas was Merry but not white. Take care of yourself. May God Bless You. Love, Mike.

In addition to noting the day's flights, the December 29 War Diary entry described "another successful dance" that was held at Trapani, Sicily.

December 30, 1943 [*Thursday*]

Good Morning, Darling,

I had a marvelous sleep and a long one and I am ready to take the day by the horns and toss it for miles. Showered, washed and sang a song. My mustache is starting to curl at the ends and it really is a beaut.

Ah! The great Postal Service. I received your Thanksgiving Day letter. I presume the day was well-worth spending, especially in the middle of the week. In the army, we say, "In the middle of what week on what day." Days, dates, and months are forgotten and years take so long to pass.

You slipped up on one cue, My Dear, when you said that I'd be driven to "tears" by your writing about your sewing. You should have said that I'd be driven to "tatters." It took me all night to dream that one up. Speaking of dreams, I've had some "lulus" lately. My God, Woman, you're nasty — making me wait so long. I woke up before we had a chance to spend our "first night" together. I don't mean that in any way except that it seemed as if we spent our first night in a bed roll, somewhere in Grand Central Station and to top it all someone tried to steal my pillow and in the argument that followed, I was really banged up. But, you see, a guy is apt to have some crazy moments (couldn't spell weird or wierd, so used crazy. Too lazy to look it up.) But, My Darling, one fact is certain and that is that you are very beautiful. Can't help but love you so much.

Bette, in two days, another year shall have passed. Another year of war and misery for a lot of people. The year '43 will always be a pleasant memory in my book because of you. Even amid all the tears, God provided for some laughs because He realized that the human mind could stand only so much. The coming of this year brings me closer to my 23rd year, and you to your 22nd. If I am not mistaken. Our birthdays are 9 days apart. Yours is on the 19th of March, Right? And mine is on the 28th. So in one week, we will have two things to celebrate. There is only one thing wrong with such a memory, each birthday means a passing year. Our years will be so full of happiness that I know that it will be hard to watch each year pass. Tempus Fugit! Sometimes, we wonder why!

I stopped for a moment to have a spot of breakfast. We had a few cans of fruit cocktail hanging around and so we opened one and had a spot. Of course, we had the usual hard-boiled eggs in the tent but I couldn't dare to eat one so early in the AM. Before I got over here, I couldn't look an egg (hard-boiled), an onion, or a pepper in the eye. Now I cut up an egg, slice an onion and pepper on it, douse it with salt and pepper, two slices of bread, and I munch. It is amazing what hunger will do to a man. I could never take that for a steady diet — But soldiers can't be choosers.

Well, Bette, My Love, must close. Give my love to Mother. Thank her for remembering me in her prayers. Take care of yourself. May God Bless You. Love you and Miss you. — Love, Mike.

December 30, 1943 [*Thursday*]

Good Evening, Darling,

Early morning, early evening and my pen begs me to talk to you. It doesn't have to twist my arm because I will and here I am. I just wrote to Mother and I do hope that she will be glad to receive my note. (Do you like me in blue or black?) (I kinda think the blue is more becoming, don't you?) In my letter to your Mother, I sort of gently hinted that I was coming home to take you away from her. I do hope that neither of you mind too much. Oh, Yes, tell her that she should not mind my stationery because I just used anything that got into my big mitts.

It really is cozy at home tonight. The old stove is perking to beat Hell and I really can't complain. Feel just perfect only lack one thing and that is to have you in my arms. What I'd give to be sitting in front of an open fireplace, a nice cozy chair, no lights just the flicker of burning logs and you in my arms. (One arm, the other holding a bourbon and coke.) Oh Joy! Why life can't be one pleasant interlude after another. But then again, one must suffer his purgatory on earth so that he can find his dreams on earth.

I don't know if this letter will make sense or if it will be a series of stupid remarks. I know I have said this so often before, but I can't help it. Can you imagine what a task it would be if we were unable to repeat words which we have already used? *Je t'aime*; I love you; *je te amore*; *l'amore per te e grande*. No matter what language, it says the same.

Oh, My Darling, My Loved One, how I wish I could go through books and books full of pages painting dreams, each one different from the other. How often I curse myself for wasting all our time. To think that for a short time I had you. I could have whispered sweet nothings into your ears. Sweet words that would have been so "gooey" that you would have needed gasoline to clean the sugar out. My Love, all for you, and all that missed because I was such a fool. But I'm coming back to you.

I have changed, Honey. I have changed a lot — only because I realize how and know now what I didn't know then. More than once I have pleaded with you, and again and again until the day Our Creator calls me — Don't ever leave me! As I will be to you, so shall you be to me, a shadow, a shadow that cannot be lost in darkness.

Do I sound like the maniac? Well, I'm not. I am merely telling you the words of the love I feel for you —

So you see, My Blonde Wench. It is not as stupid as I thought it would be. My love is not explained by geography (as deep as the ocean), not by astronomy (as bright as the stars), but by words that are known to you and me and lovers the world over.

So Long, My Pretty, I shan't waste any more of your time. I do hope that you receive these letters. I have been writing faithfully as circumstances will allow. Sane again — What a horrible feeling.

Take care of yourself, My Lanky Cleopatra — May God Bless You — and my name is not Anthony — leave that to history. Love, Mike.

Following are the War Diary entries for December 30 and 31:

December 30: Training program: Glider Formation flying, afternoon session only. Censorship and routine duties performed as usual.
December 31: Training program: Glider tow morning session only. Payday as usual, on the last day of the month in combination with New Years Eve, sort of helped to get the boys into the holiday spirit.

January 1, 1944 [*Saturday*]

My Darling,

Happy New Year. Perhaps the first part of this year may not be too great but with the help of God, maybe the latter part will be filled with the happiness we want so badly. Perhaps, we ought to entitle this new chapter, "Our Love — 1944." It is a new year and the leap year, so My Sweet, here's your chance to "pop" the question to me. Of course, I may hem and haw but I guess, I'll say, "Yes."

I wrote a nice long letter to my Mother last night and tried to sum up a few things of the past. It was the first really long letter I have written to her in such a while. I had meant to write to you but I had so many interruptions that I couldn't possibly concentrate. (I am writing so small because my hand is so cold, I can't possibly write any larger!) I stayed sober last night. I know that sounds unlike me but as I explained to Mom, there were only a few people I wanted to be with none of them are here now. So, to fully feel the moment, I didn't want my brain numbed by alcohol. It would have spoiled everything.

I slept late this morning. Went to Mass, received Communion, and I am ready to consume a large dinner that they are preparing for us. Dinner is late today, so I know I'll be ready to "dig" in. All in all, Darling, I feel much better than if I had gotten "loaded" and forgotten. I feel happier and in good shape this new mysterious year.

Darling, I love you. This is another one which we have missed. This is another one we must chalk up for future reference. Postponed, "On account of the teams not showing up!" Another day to grit your teeth and wait. I thank God over and over again for giving me the patience to endure this. I never prayed so much in my life. I won't forget. Whatever I didn't do before, I'll make up to Him now and in the future. It isn't really tough, Bette. My mind had told me that enough and my body has followed suit. What more can one do?

I can't say that this weather is perfect for the occasion. Sunny Italy and such. Bah! Wading around in inches of mud, trying to keep dry, and it's tough as Hell to keep warm. But so what? They say, these things make a better man. I'd rather take mine in easy doses, in a better place.

It's awfully hard to write because it is so hard to conceal my true emotions. Again I feel like telling you how much I care. Not in three words but in three thousand words and yet I don't want you to think that I am unhappy. I am. But a guy likes to keep telling the gal he loves, the same thing over and over again. Now, I know why the ole Hemingway devotes three and four pages to a "Good Night" scene. Words are hard to find when they mingle with our deepest emotions, so instead of action, we find ourselves repeating the same thing, yet, not knowing that it is being done. My Darling, I do love you and miss you so very much.

I hope you have had a nice holiday. Give my love to Mother. Take care of yourself. May God Bless You. Love, Mike.

All flying was cancelled on January 1, 1944, but the War Diary still had something to report:

> **. . . Heavy wind storm last night and today damaged all our Gliders, eight in all. New Year's dinner, except for the ice cream that didn't arrive in time, was a duplicate of the Xmas dinner, plenty of everything for everyone.**

The next day, as the War Diary shows, things returned to normal:

> **January 2: Training program: Formation and Instrument flying, afternoon session only. Lt. Arnie A. Maki was relieved of his present assignment and appointed squadron Adjutant. Lt. Robert Roman, in addition to his present duties as assistant Intelligence Officer was appointed as squadron Special Service Officer in place of Lt. Maki. Both appointments effective 28 Dec. 1943.**
>
> **January 3: Training program: Formation and Instrument flying in the AM, Group Formation flying at night. 2nd Lt. Marshall C. Wells was recommended by the Group Commanding Officer for both the Air Medal and Silver Star.**

January 4, 1944 [*Tuesday*]

My Darling,

I received your letter of December 7th and I am glad that you are satisfied by the receipt of my two letters (11 pages in all). I didn't write for the last few days because there were a few tasks that presented themselves and I couldn't possibly shirk them.

Since you so forcefully state and rebuff my remarks, I can't do anything else but accept your flattery and like it, too. Darling, you can whip all the adjectives you like at me. The most I could do is spank you for it and you are too far away for me to do that. "Cause when I talk, I don't talk to myself." Yes, Dear! No, Dear! That's right, Dear! — Ha! Sounds like I was getting a verbal lashing. If we were together, I could silence you with a kiss, now, I can't do anything but accept. You brute! Taking unfair advantage of me.

I have had a chance to read some lately. I finished a book called, *Leonardo Da Vinci* —

I don't recommend it. It left such a small impression that I can't recall the author's name. But I did read a swell one. *The Ever-Widening Stain* by W. Holinbrooke Johnson. It is a different type of mystery which is so cleverly written that it is most interesting. I have two more which I intend to dig into next. The first I will read is *Hungry Hill* by Daphne du Maurier, and the next is *Man the Unknown* by Alex Carrel. I can't venture an opinion yet because I haven't started but as soon as I finish this letter, I'll go again into the dreamland of fiction. Your paragraph about *Pathetique* aroused my slight outburst. It is unfortunate that you didn't accept the great opportunity to hear it. Don't fret, that kind of music never dies and we will have a lifetime to unfold. Marvelous thought, isn't it, Bette?

You are right about that library of recordings. Tibbitts has a fine voice but I would rather hear him sing something from *Barber of Seville* — "The Road to Mandalay" is OK but Hell, I've seen enough roads. Don't get me wrong, Darling, I like it — Just pulling your leg. (Pretty one, too!)

Darling, My Love, I like your passion for jewelry and perfume but that kind of jewelry runs to astronomical figures, doesn't it? I shan't woo you with diamonds of Tiara but Woolworth's has quite a collection, hasn't it? (Do not hold what I say against me, unless I talk about your figure!) (Can't seem to get serious — I'll try!)

Bette, I am sorry that I impose upon you so often. When I asked for a large picture, I didn't expect you to rush off and have it made. I realize that it is expensive. Take your time, as long as I receive it some time. I am happy with the snaps. I wasn't really complaining, just being natural.

Darling, love is a thing we are lucky to have. Surely, one who has never felt the supreme emotion, cannot be blessed by any other emotion, except those that depict the more horrible things in life. The more that you think about it, My Darling, the more you will realize that we are not experimenting. To a degree, we are accepting certain things, such as, the mutual acceptance of worldly likes and dislikes. Aside from that we know the equality of life we are so eager to accept. . . . Temperamentally, we could never find a better match. We realized that the first laugh we shared. Never a dull moment, never a ragged, forced moment; an ease, forever noticeable, which came to us like a breath of fresh air. Physically, one blonde, and black hair is the only contrast. One does not need to hear it said; it can be felt, "What a lovely couple." You see, Bette, it doesn't take much to start me. Whenever I talk about us, I seem to drift into a world that is so beautiful and so easy to understand that it obliterates the finest rain drop that falls. My words come so easily that my pen cannot move fast enough. My Darling, I love you so —

(Continued next letter.)

You see, can't get too deep. I feel it though and those words I have written are from my heart. Webster's new meaning — "Love" — "That which is felt by Mike for Bette." (N) (V) (Adv.) (Adj.), etc.

"Pappy" is swell. Returns your greetings —

Must close. So sorry to leave. Give my love to Mother. May God Bless You. Love, Mike.

January 4, 1944 [*Tuesday*]

My Dearest,

You must excuse me for taking so much of your time, but when I started writing this afternoon, I felt so good that I wanted to keep going. I said I was going to read. The first thing that I engaged was a comic magazine. Then I started *Hungry Hill*, read a few pages and then fell asleep. I awoke because it was "chow" time. We had a very enjoyable meal. (By the way, Darling, did I ever tell you I like chocolate pudding.) Watched a "Black Jack" game for about 15 minutes and decided I'd like to talk to you. If I were courting you at home, and it wasn't a date night, I'd probably call you or drop a line. Did I ever tell you I was a very persistent lover. Never give a woman a chance to forget me. After all, in like manner, it shows that I haven't forgotten the woman. Fair exchange, if she like[*s*] me enough. Catching snatches of a bull session, kind of makes concentration hard.

Well, My Sweet, I guess I can get back to this letter. The conversation was very interesting. No, it wasn't about women. It was a subject that concerns us more than women, at the present time.

Speaking about the KC Philharmonic, I read an article that stated that KC is coming into its own as a center of music. Its Philharmonic is rated with NY Phil., and a few of the better ones. It wasn't so surprising to read because it seems only natural that the American people, generally speaking, should turn to the finer arts. America is a symbol of a near perfect world, therefore it should lead the world's arts. However, it still is not extraordinary for these Italian kids to ask me if there are still plenty of gangsters in America. Funny though, kids will be kids regardless of nationality, color, race, or creed.

"Our love will always live with us and our children." That's one of the nicest things I have heard you say, Darling. I had never considered us as being people of a family. That is to say, to have children. You know I have always admired kids. I don't mean in score but as individuals. I imagine we ought to make pretty good parents. You know, Bette, a baby or two might be good for you. I mean physically, and I don't mean during the bearing period. But the effects of bearing might help you to blossom out some weight. Can't see you with ten kids hanging onto your apron. "Mommy, why is Daddy always drunk?" You know, Darling, if we had met sooner, we might have started a family. I want to admit something — Do you remember the night in Ft. Wayne when you found it so hard to sleep? I was curious and I asked you some questions. One of them was about pregnancy! I want to tell you what I felt. In that split second of thought that supersedes such a question, I hoped that you were because I wanted to marry you on the spot. Not to save our honor but because it would have fulfilled a desire that I felt from the day I met you. I know that sounds fantastic. But really, Bette, I did so much thinking about us that I covered all the angles. Maybe because I was afraid I might lose you, I don't know. All I know is that I wanted and still want you so very badly. Do I explain myself? I am afraid that I am explaining this very badly. I am trying to make you sense what I feel and I don't want you to misunderstand because it is ticklish and could be easily misunderstood. But if you look at it in the light I want you to — it'll sound as good as I wanted it to. There now, that's a lot of words to use to tell you that I love you —

Good night, My Darling, If I could only send my heart to you. It could tell you what my tongue finds so hard to say clearly.

Take care of yourself. May God Bless You. Love, The Big Brute.

Following are the War Diary entries for January 4-6:

> **January 4: Training program: Formation and Instrument flying in the AM only. Monthly Unit History and War Diary forwarded to Group Intelligence Office. A third rate picture was shown in the open air theater. Whenever transportation is available, squadron personnel will be permitted to travel to Trapani by truck to see the movies.**
>
> **January 5: Training program: All scheduled flying called off due to bad weather. Special Service arranged for the Officer's first dance at Trapani. From all indications it won't be the last. Major Milstead, Group Intelligence Officer paid a visit to Squadron S-2.**
>
> **January 6: Training program: All training schedules called off due to inclement weather. One plane took off for Castelvetrano and return on official business.**

January 7, 1944 [*Friday*]

My Darling,

There is nothing to answer to and I must make this as short as I can. Things have been quiet, same old routine and I must spare you a paragraph about the weather. Just a few words, it's not so good!

I finished *Hungry Hill* and I must say that I enjoyed it. It covers 5 generations and there is quite a bit of significance to it, if you want to look at it. It is slow reading but for once in my life, I didn't admit defeat and surrender the book. I finished it and enjoyed it. I am skipping *Man the Unknown* for [Alexandre] Dumas' *Twenty Years After*. Carrel's book is to be read in moments of deep concentration. Since I cannot profess to that right now, I am leaning toward fiction to ease the waste of wasteful days.

I am going to beg your forgiveness for this weak imitation of a letter but I am sure you understand. All I know is that I love you and miss you very much, and I don't drive myself at this moment to tell it to you in better words.

So, My Darling, with your forgiveness, I bid you *Adieu*. What more can I say? Take care of yourself. Give my love to Mother. May God Bless You. — Love, Mike.

The War Diary recorded the usual business of the 37th Squadron in its entries for January 7-9:

> **January 7: Training program: Formation and Instrument flying in the AM, afternoon session called off due to weather. One plane trip to Palermo and return on official business. Captain Cooney, Squadron Intelligence Officer, gave an interesting and instructive talk on SECURITY and ESCAPE to all Enlisted personnel.**
> **January 8: Training program: Formation and Instrument flying in the A.M., night flying called off due to weather. . . .**
> **January 9: Training program: Glider Formation flying in the AM. Group Formation flying at night. Lt. Robert Roman, Special Service Officer, is interviewing Enlisted personnel for the purpose of enrolling for Army Institute Courses and also with a view to enroll in some College Correspondence courses sponsored by the Army. The movie *Hers to Hold* played at the open air theater.**

January 10, 1944 [*Monday*]

My Darling,

I shan't go thru' any long discourse of apologies but really it wasn't my fault that I didn't write sooner. I'll try to make up for it in the best manner I possibly can. This picture which I am sending is one of the most recent we have taken. I hope it doesn't scare you to death.

The mail situation has been miserable but by some quirk or mistake of some postal clerk somewhere, I was lucky to receive a letter from you last night. It was dated Dec. 12 and you are still talking about your Christmas, while we are 9 days past our New Year. News really doesn't travel very fast these days, does it, Bette?

Gosh, Honey, I love you so very much. It's true that I haven't put it into words of late but I feel it so deeply that you occupy every empty moment. My prayers are for us. Every word, every feeling are for us. God must be tired of listening to me. Well, as one of the boys said, "The first 6 or 9 months are the hardest."

I am sorry to say that it is a rumor when one speaks of 300 combat hours. Perhaps, if it was in heavy [*censored*] bombardment or medium [*censored — possibly bombers*] — it might be true. At any rate, I would have been home months ago. But, Darling, again, and I will keep saying it, we must forget the medium of time. All we can do is look forward to the day I come home. Once I reach the U.S. — 1 year or 2 years will be forgotten and we will start to count the days when the war will finish and we can begin to live a normal life.

We had a show the other night. I saw part of it. It was *Hers to Hold* — Deanna Durbin and Joseph Cotton. She sang "Begin the Beguine" and it really did bring back some great memories. That song will be my lifetime best. I spoke about reading Dumas' *Twenty Years After* — The reason for my anxiety to read it, is that many years ago I read his *Three*

Musketeers. I looked everywhere for the sequel — *Twenty Years After* and never found it until now. I am reading it slowly and I am trying to recapture the theme lost by 5 or 6 years of neglect. Man or boy, I did always like Dumas.

Darling, I was in a wretched state last week. I decided to dry out my barracks bags because they were soaked from the Sicilian "Sunshine." I had your letters in one of them. They were dripping and since they were no longer legible, I had to throw every one away. I have only 2 of 'em. They are your most recent. Gad! You should have heard me curse. I was so damned mad, I couldn't find enough cuss words to describe my feeling. Nothing like a shrug of the shoulder and a sigh of resignation.

You are right when you say that there isn't much to say. One cannot help but feel the void in his life when the most important person in his life is missing. Life apart like this, My Darling, is routine. We care nothing for the principles we are fighting for but for the people. We are doing a duty which is universal and tends to invite moments of extraordinary let down. When two people are together, even if they are silent, they can feel the security of each other's presence. It is the joy of nearness that creates a cloud of happiness that no one can feel but the two people. Darling, it is a thing we cannot avoid. We must try to overlook it and smile because we know that our love is something created and is untouchable by anyone but us; but this mess of a war is man-created and it is muddled and badly handled universally.

You say that I spoiled you. "Darling, no one can smile like you, no one can drink like you, and no one can dance like you." (You fail to mention "no one can love like you" — I happily accept that because I know you aren't experimenting.) The smile, my physical make-up, that was created by God. My drinking ability, years of practice — You forget that I do get drunk occasionally, and I did cause you a Hell of a lot of trouble. Dancing, thank my sister. I was so damn girl-shy, I was afraid to ask anyone to dance — If you had added "Love" — my answer — My Darling, I don't need the teachings of a mortal. Within one's heart is a space reserved for that one blessing. Truly, you filled it. I needed no prompting nor coaching. All I needed was you. (Consider the other. Left for the miserable mortal, egged on by the weakness of man and the strength of vice. That spot is created by a feeling which must be strengthened by alcohol or any drug — then man succumbs to the kiss of Satan and is left to sorrow forever after —)

Must close — I'll try not to let so many days pass before my next letter. Forgive me. Give my love to Mother. May God Bless You. Miss you & Love you. — Love, Mike.

On January 10, according to the War Diary, the training program included formation and instrument flights, as well as a night navigation flight — "cross country to Sicily, Cap Bon, Pantelleria and back to Borizzo." The showing of the movie *Keeper of the Flame* at the theater "was not a success due to trouble with the projector."

The January 11 War Diary entry described the usual training flights, and noted another dance for the enlisted men at Trapani.

January 12, 1944 [*Wednesday*]

My Darling,

I received your letter of the 13th. Little by little, with never increasing pace, your epistles find the way to this side of the world to the guy that waits so anxiously for them.

Sallying back and forth, I must say that your ideas are clear about the subject of art. One point I must add in the judging of a picture, etc. It is true that the artist tries to convey his ideas merely through his mood. But to judge, one must be open-minded and exceptionally broad-minded. Surely to view a variety of themes, one must leave his mood in the background and as he drifts from theme to theme, experience the change of the artist's mood. If, at that moment, he cannot do that, then he must try to resort to the meager technical background that he has at his disposal and judge by technique, lines, grace, and color.

In music, for the average listener like myself, it is not always necessary to know the composer's temperament. As a listener, my ear tells me my leaning. I credit myself with a sense of balance that I hope helps me to enjoy the beauty of a piece. However, that is neither here nor there. I like it for what it stirs in me, regardless of what the author meant to tell me. An independent soul, eh wot?

I have been feeling rather comfortable of late. Not physically, that is almost impossible in this climate, but mentally, and morally. I just have an easy, happy-go-lucky, "Oh, Hell, Why worry" sort of mind ease. I pray more than I ever did in my whole lifetime. Not a night passes that I don't say a word for us. It's funny, Darling, but I have just accepted the feeling normally and without fear. I am content, lean back, light my pipe and reflect on life and us. To make the picture complete, all I need is a smoking jacket, a pair of slippers, a cozy chair, and you. It isn't that I don't miss you, but since I can't have you, I am content to live with the thought of you. Oftimes, I think of the wild blood of our veins. I have to laugh, not sneeringly nor maliciously, but happily, when I think of some of our untamed emotions. Strange, how evenly they are dispersed between us. We are really a very evenly matched couple. It makes it all so easy to love you. Without doubt, without strain, just like a shortstop on a fast play that moves like greased lightning. So easy, and yet so beautiful to behold.

"Sad Sack" is one of our foremost comics. He is known to every man overseas. Fresh out of *Stars and Stripes* and always in a predicament. Kinda thought this one was cute.

I have devoted this afternoon to letter writing and I must answer a lot of people. I am sorry, Bette, but I must cut this short for fear that writer's cramp will set in and many friends will walk out if I don't answer, I promise you that I'll never send another letter like the one I sent a few days ago. I couldn't help it, really. One of those bad days we feel every so often. Tell Mother that I am glad that she liked the card. I should have written sooner. (Don't you like the way I change the subject so often.)

So long for now. Take care of yourself. Praying for us. Love you — May God Bless You — As Ever, Mike.

January 12, 1944 [*Wednesday*]

Bette,

I have wasted as much time as I can possibly waste and yet I have too much of it on my hands. I don't know what I am going to say because I have no plan for this letter. It may be a lot of foolish, useless words but nevertheless, I felt that I'd like to talk to you. I could spend the rest of the afternoon with a book but I am afraid that I have read too much and I am causing a strain on my eyes. Every time I start something like that I go into it deeply and feel it.

In his letter, Tom speaks of you quite admirably. Naturally, I didn't expect him to speak any differently because you are a person to admire. In one line, he remarked that you weren't quite sure whether you wanted to become a Catholic or not. That is OK with me because as Tom says we don't want to force a thing like that on someone unless they are sure and ready for it. My understanding is that you do but you want me to be near so that I can be some guidance to you. Remember, Darling, I want to be fully understanding. Do not think I am reproaching you! I am afraid that I jammed something down your throat and I am sorry if I was too presumptuous. Do whatever you feel is right and above all do not lose contact with Tom, merely because of a slight disagreement and it really isn't much. It is just one of those things that we can thrash out once we get married. Believe me, Darling, I don't mind. We pride ourselves by our levelheadedness. So, therefore, I wouldn't think of being a "stuffer" on that score. But enough is said. I have talked about it entirely too much and I shan't approach the subject again, unless you will it so.

I love you. Or haven't I told you so? It is a fine thought and definitely worth the time that lovers think about it. It is a great thing that it offers so much food for thought. Many is the time that I lay in my old bedroll and think about us. Mentally, I plan a life so perfect, that, at times, I am afraid to think of it. Now with this contented feeling I have, it makes the thought all the nicer. I love you —

Darling, I almost started to write about an awfully morbid thought. Even in the worst spot, I have yet to feel fear. I am not brave but I just don't bother myself with those thoughts which I feel are foolish. Maybe I'm from Brooklyn but my idea is Missourian. I have to be shown before I worry about it. Just as stubborn as a mule when it comes to that.

Well, My Sweet, for the 2nd time today, I say *Adieu.* Things aren't so tough — especially when one's mind is so pregnant with happiness. May God Bless You — Love, Mike.

The training flights consisted of glider towing on the morning of January 12; the formation flying at night was called off due to weather. On January 13, according to the War Diary, there were instrument flights in the morning and navigation flying that night.

January 14, 1944 [*Friday*]

My Darling,

I received two letters from you and another roll of film. I don't know what I am going to do with you. You'll spoil me. The letters were dated Dec. 10 and Dec. 17.

In the earlier letter, you growl so that I can hear you over here. Don't feel too badly about it, Honey, those bad days are very apt to shine thru'. Man is so funny, it just can't help itself when it gets like that.

I wrote to you the other day about our religious discussion. As I told you in that letter, I am leaving everything up to your discretion and I shan't forward another word until you have decided everything for yourself.

I haven't heard from my family since Christmas, and suddenly I receive 4 letters. I don't mind but I wish they would send them thru' by degrees. I do hope that you like our (Chicha [*nickname for my sister, Lucy*] and my) gift. She says that the stuff has a gay smell and that she liked to think of you as always being gay. If she knew you, she would easily realize that her choice was ideal. I never think of you in any other way. Your face is always smiling at me. I have never seen you frown and I hope I never am the cause for you to frown. At any rate, it sounds like you gals are getting along and that is great to hear.

I have heard that "Fats" Waller had died. The British Broadcasting Company dedicated a program in his honor. I must admit that I didn't like his style very much. You see, Darling, my taste is in the blend of many musical instruments. I never could go for Goodman's Quartet; Shaw's Gramercy Five or any shallow gang that makes music on a washboard. My pleasure is in the blend of many saxs, a few trumpets, trombones, etc.

Yes, My Darling, it is 7 months since I saw you. And yet, everything is so vivid in my mind that I ask God to keep it that way. It has made everything so easy. My memories have never been dulled. If they were, I should proceed to go slowly and definitely mad. You wouldn't want to marry a madman, would you, Bette? These last seven months have passed so quickly that it doesn't seem hard to take the next, who knows, how many months.

My Darling, I am sorry but I must cut this short. Don't worry about those short letters you send. They are letters and they are from you. "I love you." What more need you say?

Give my love to Mother. May God Bless You. Take care of yourself. Praying for us. Love you and miss you — Love, Mike.

The January 14 War Diary entry noted the usual training flights, plus "radar instruction in the afternoon and evening."

Glider towing continued on January 15, as well as a training flight to Malta. There were also radar approaches and simulated paratroop drops. A new movie — *Coney Island* with Betty Grable — was also shown that day.

January 16, 1944 [*Sunday*]

My Darling,

You must forgive me if I make this a short letter. I had intended to answer your last two letters but my time became limited and so I must compensate. However, I won't answer those until I have more time, and I am writing this to tell you that I love you.

I feel that I am not entirely neglectful. I was able to get you a dog statuette and if I can find some good wrapping paper, I'll be able to sent it to you. I can't tell you where I got it [*Malta*] but at any rate, it is from this side of the ocean. (I know you'll die of curiosity but I can't help it.) It was mounted on a black base but clumsy me, I kind of got my left hands working and tore it asunder. It is a cross between a setter and a sheep dog. The lines are perfect and I am sure you will like it. You can remount it. I can't because I haven't the implements to do it with. I do hope that my search was not in vain and that it reaches you in one piece.

There is one thing that I failed to mention to you and that I found to be very quaint. Most of the travel in this country is done by mule, horse, etc. They have a type of donkey over here that is very cute. He usually has a gray coat. A very soft, almost velvet gloss. It reminds me of the gray gown that a gal wore to our prom. She was my heartbeat at the time and I thought she looked lovely. Regal gray and a hooded cape of the same color and material to go with it. Don't you like the way I skip subjects? If that gal knew that I was comparing her to a jackass, she'd be very hurt. Sometimes I wonder if the comparison does fit her or should the jackass be hurt? Back again. His stomach is white and head is usually a smattering of gray, white and black. His tummy is as round as a barrel and fits the appearance perfectly. To top it all, he stands about the height of a well-built St. Bernard dog. I have often remarked that I'd like to put a leash on one of 'em and walk down 5th Avenue. It would create a fad. Honestly, Honey, you should see them. They are really cute. The loads which they drag are usually 3 to 4 times their size, if not more.

I had to tell you about it because every time I see one, they fascinate me more and more.

Darling, I can breathe more easily now. I shaved off my mustache. It isn't that I wanted to but damn! — it was such a bother to keep trim. Since I must shave with cold water and little time, it is a pain to bicker and quibble about a hair, here and there.

Well, Bette, Old Gal, I must close. I promise you a better letter soon. I just had to write and I had to squeeze it in as fast as I could. Hope I can send the dog soon.

Give my love to Mother. May God Bless you. Take care of yourself. Love you and miss you. Love, Mike.

The War Diary entry for January 16 reported: "Training Program: Glider formation flying in the afternoon, Night Formation flying at night. The EM [*enlisted men*] attended another dance at Trapani."

January 17, 1944 [*Monday*]

My Darling,

I can now answer your letters. They are dated 18 and 19 [*December*].

Forgive the small writing; my hands are cold and I can't write any larger. But large or small, I love you.

People, regardless of location, race, creed, or color are no different. Thru'out my entire life I have believed that. The good and bad of one people are evenly scaled with another. It is true that I have moved about a lot since my first thought on the subject. However, it has made no difference.

No, Darling, I have not seen a camp show since I saw Jack Benny [*in Tunisia*]. But it doesn't bother us too much. As long as we can see a picture once in a while to remind us that people are still as they are in the States, it is enough to keep us happy. My best enjoyment is to see pictures of football games and one short had a few shots of the World Series. Really good!

Ssh! Don't look now but I hear rain drops.

I want to thank you for the compliments that you extend toward my Mother. You couldn't have said a truer word. She has been the backbone of all of us and I know that she has done a great job. Not by looking at myself but by watching the progress of my brothers and sister. You'll love her as much as we do.

My lovely Darling, in your letter you say, "I've tried to keep this letter light but I've never felt my love so strongly as I do now." Surely, it is not so seriously heavy. It is serious but it provides a lightness of heart and soul that we cannot describe. It is the memory of it that forces a light of a smile on our faces, even in the depths of the most morbid of moods. Yes! We can put it on paper but how? We do it because we must. It doesn't bring us closer because words can never satisfy a hungry soul but only for the moment. Then, in all this absence, we build up an emotion so great that it will burst only when we are together again. I could never tell you how much I love you. You have never known how much I love you. You can see that you are in for a great surprise. I promise you, My Darling, I shall never, never be able to do enough for you. In God's name, I shall never forget the torture of these empty moments, and I pray to Him to give me the power to fulfill everything so completely as I hope to. I love you.

Gosh, Bette, honest, you must forgive me. Even the warmth of these words can't take the stiffness and coldness out of my hands. This is the first night letter that I have written for a long time and things have really changed. I mailed your package yesterday. I hope it gets to you safely.

Good night, My Love. Take care of yourself. May God Bless you. Love, Mike.

The January 17 War Diary entry recorded glider formation flights that afternoon and "Night Formation flying (V of Vs) at night." For the V of Vs, we would form into a Vee, with a lead plane then the two wing planes. The next Vee would be off and behind the wing of the plane on the right, and at a slightly higher altitude to escape prop wash (turbulence).

The other Vee would be off and behind the wing of the plane on the left (and slightly higher). The reason for the Vee of Vees was to have the flights in a relatively concentrated area so that when troopers were dropped they would be reasonably close together on the ground to form a fighting force.

January 19, 1944 [*Wednesday*]

My Darling,

Joy of Joys! I received 5 letters from you, dated Dec. 21, 29, 31, and 2 for the 1st [*of January*]. The worst part of it all is that I can't answer them the way I would like to. It is amazing what little time a guy can have to himself at times. Darling, your letters are marvelous. They express the most pleasant moods; they sound so nicely different; they are my extremest pleasure.

We have a recording of the Boston "Pops" Symphony Orch. — "Jalousie." It is one of my favorites. And a recording of Sammy Kaye, recording with Tommy Ryan singing, "Begin the Beguine." I needn't tell you about that.

Bette, your letters were perfect. I have no visions of expansive living but your words make my future like a garden. Too beautiful to behold. Day after day, you become my perfect companion. I can see nothing but our life together and it is perfect. My Darling, you can't make me love you because I have so much love for you now that I wouldn't know where to put it. Believe me, Bette, I am thrilled beyond words. You needn't worry about my anger. I never throw anything but words and God has gifted me with the use of them. They are biting, stinging, and the depth or height of sarcasm. You needn't worry. I don't get that way often and never if I am not coaxed.

I can't very well imagine what happened to those letters between Nov. 20th and Dec. 4th. Someone is mishandling the detail and I don't know where it is. They will get to you in due time. I am so glad that you received the money. Use it the way you wish. I only wish that you enjoy it as I meant it.

Do you know? I think that you were trying to get me to fall in love with you. You knew when I left you. I knew it but I wasn't sure. If you remember, way back in April [*1943*], I told you that we had to be careful. We were playing a very tough game. As a matter of fact, if you recall, I didn't see you for one week end, and when I did, we were such nice people. You devil, I believe you tricked me into all this and I love you all the more for it.

I think that you are pulling my leg. Bad enough that the mud is bad but then you have to send me poetry about it. Kind of adding salt to the salad. Then asking me if snow shoes would help! Huh! Just laughing while I suffer, eh, Nero — Fiddle while Mike sinks!

So you cut your hair! Why don't you wear it in braids, schoolgirl style. With that funny little nose of yours, you will really be in style. Then to rub further, you start to describe a little white world. Snow, Snow, the one thing we miss here that makes January look like July. (Seriously, Darling, you did justice to the picture. I like to hear those things and [*I'm*] just playfully retaliating.)

Darling, it would be nice to have an identification bracelet but I have two wrist watches.

My own and GI (Government Issue). I have three rings (my high school ring, a souvenir ring which I just got and a ring with the head of Mussolini on it which I never wear) and to add, a bracelet which I picked up in India, which I never wear. Hell! I'd look like an overdressed Caesar. Besides, with all that on my arms, how the Hell would I lift my arms.

I never read any of Woolcott's works but from what I have seen of him, I imagine he is extremely dry. Boringly so! *Johnny Get Your Gun* is fine book but don't send it to me. Since it is a depiction of the horrors of war, I don't think it would be appropriate over here, although it might make excellent reading. I have started *The Sound Wagon* by T. S. Stribling and I find it very amusing. Halliburton has a fine style but his appeal to me is passive.

Darling, I must close but don't fret, I haven't started to answer your letters. That process will involve countless pages —

Good night, My Love. May God Bless You. Miss You terribly. Love, Mike.

Following are the War Diary entries for January 18-19:

January 18: Training Program: Glider Formation flying in the AM only. Another movie at the open air theater, *Pardon My Sarong*.
January 19: Training program: Instrument Flying in the AM. Group Flight Plan flying at night.

January 20, 1944 [*Thursday*]

Hello Bette,

Look, Mom, that man's here again. Here I am. I told you that I would need endless pages to answer all those letters of yours. These are a few of the ends to end all ends.

One thing I must scold you about, Darling, and that is your spelling. It doesn't happen often only occasionally. "Loosing" is spelled with one "o" not 2. Unnecessary is spelled in just that manner. But it isn't so much your spelling but the fact that you are rushing thru' an idea and you get careless. There! That ought to hold you.

I came across a rather nice sentence. This girl had just interviewed a small-town, Roman Catholic priest. He had left a very fine impression on her and it made her quite meditative. In this, the author portrays her thoughts, at least explains them. "The girl sensed her own future lying pregnant in the womb of time. What it was; what manner of birth it might be, lay inscrutable in the pines, the pond and the invisible air."

Often I have been brought to a reverie by my surroundings. I don't "sense" the future, I visualize the possibilities of that surrounding to the future. The other eve', I was watching a very golden sunset and I wondered how often we would watch such a sunset together. At the moment, there was no necessity to feel the beauty of it but just an urge to hear and feel your presence so that you could share that sunset with me. It is like the manner you express yourself "— if I could feel the strength of your body and arms about me, just once more, I'd never ask another thing."

Ah! Reality! The more time we have on our hands, the more conscious we are of it. And so it is. Wasted, useless use of time. But I am content. I have seen this period pass quickly. It is a lift because I realize in 6 more months, I shall have seen a year pass and each tick brings me closer to the end of my sentence and into your arms.

My letters are also a guide. It is as if I am writing a novel. An autobiography being handed over to you. Each letter is a chapter. Surely, it can't be far wrong because my letters are my very mood. My novel will be completed when I send the last chapter with an "I am coming home" ending. From there on, let the future, the untouchable, carry on.

From what you say in your letters, I am sure that we will have a good start on the library for our home or whatever it may be. I shan't apologize for recommending these books because no one was ever harmed by sensible literature. They cover a variety of suggestions and I do hope you find them as entertaining and as helpful as I have.

There must be something wrong. In one of my letters covering that period you speak of, Nov. 20-Dec. 4th, I wrote some poetry titled, "A Censor's Nightmare." Surely the old goat, whoever it might be, is not lacking a sense of humor. If so, he isn't qualified for the job. I read an article or at least an order, issued by the War Dept., urging people to report anything written in letters or otherwise that are censored. The reason for it, is that it shows that our letters are being read. They aren't supposed to be. They are to be "censored," which means that anything of military importance is to be omitted. Why the Hell should some stranger read things that are purely for you and me? As for me, I don't give a damn anyhow. If I feel like saying something that is for us, I don't give a damn who hears it. Besides, I love you, and that's my business, not his.

Well, Darling, I must close. Didn't mean to gripe. Just angry because you don't get all my mail. The Hell with it, one of these years, we won't have to worry about an intermediary. So long for now. Take care of yourself. May God Bless You. Love, Mike. (Hope you can read some of that scratching!)

On January 20, the War Diary recorded training flights for that night only. The entry also noted that the movie, *Let's Face It* with Bob Hope, played that evening.

January 21, 1944 [*Friday*]

My Darling,
    Another day, another letter, another mood, same you, same me, no sentence, need a verb.
    As I look over these articles you sent, I see that most of the teams that did play in the bowls, didn't have very impressive records. I do know that So. Cal. [*Southern California*] knocked Hell out of Washington U. in the Rose Bowl. There really wasn't much

mid-western in the articles. I like the powerhouse idea of the M.W. My taste varies a bit. What the hell, I'm only one guy out of 130 million. Basketball has about hit its peak by now, and Hockey is almost finished. Baseball will be in the air soon and I do hope I get a chance to see a few games before next season ('44) is finished.

I heard a record made by Enrico Caruso, an aria from *Pagliacci*. It was excellent. I can't very well paint the scene and therefore it will be impossible for you to recapture the mood. However, it was truly enjoyable. I hate to suggest so many things but most of them are purely suggestions. This is a must. Darling, I want you to get Ernie Pyle's book, *This Is [Your] War*. Don't send it to me. Keep it for our library. I believe it costs about $2.50. Pyle describes the desert war, Tunisian, and Sicilian campaigns. His style is great. While I was in KC, I read his columns with the deepest enthusiasm. He is human and real. His depiction of scenes and men are as vivid a picture as one could possibly want. It will be nice to have so that in later years, we can remember what our boys did and where!

I feel most content today. I don't know why. It is one of those days when a guy can say, "It's great to be alive." The atmosphere hasn't changed any. (Except that the mud has subsided to a great degree!) It is just a feeling so superb that the least bother will spoil it. I wonder how much I have changed. My love for you grows more intense as the days go by. I wonder often if I am slowly but surely feeling the transition to the Puritan state. Not really "holier than thou," just sensibly sensible. I have quit drinking because I dread the morning after. Wine can really knock Hell out of a cheerful mood. I still cuss like a trooper, but it's like a vent for excess energy. I seem to sense that I am building up to a mental eruption that will make Etna look like a water spout. No, I'm not going crazy!

I answered a letter to my secretary. (You know, I did have one, once!) She sort of reminded me of my civilian days. She said, "You know, Mike, I miss the feeling I used to get when you would call 'Mom.'" I did that quite often and I never cared for privacy. At times, I'd have her pick out a horse for me so that I could lay my two bucks on a hunch. You see, Honey, I had my vices but they never did me too much harm.

Last night I wrote you a long letter. Not actually, but in my dreams. Now, I can't remember a word of it. I do recall that it was a very nice letter but the thing was that you were peeking over my shoulder when I wrote it. Of course, that wasn't fair play because I had to be very flattering.

I promised you that I would spank you one of these days. Wish you were here, I feel in just that mood. You see, I am still unpredictable as I was always.

At one time, when I was at a loss for words, I would build pretty castles. I can't do that any more. I believe that I have lost some of that dreamer in me. I like to look at things realistically now. I never thought I would stray and here I am thousands of miles from the people I love and miss so deeply.

Darling, I must close. It will be near Valentine's Day when you receive this letter. Since I have no cards (Had one I sent to Mom.) and I can't send any big heart-shaped box of chocolate, you must add that to your list of "he must, next time we are together." Give my love to Mother. Take care of yourself. May God Bless You. Love, Mike.

January 21, 1944 [*Friday*]

My Darling,

I received your letter of January 4. Strange to have received so many in one month. (That is to say, I usually receive them from month to month and very seldom do I receive any in the same month that I am writing!)

Yes, it is leap year and I am not too undecided about my answer. I guess I might as well say "Yes!" You vixen, you have captured my heart and I couldn't dare but say anything else.

I think that I mentioned the film in a few of my previous letters. Nevertheless, to repeat, I have received 2 rolls so far. I believe that is all that you sent prior to the beginning of this year. It is so damned hard to keep track on so many things that it is easy to lose them in transit.

You asked me a question in your letter that I felt I must answer. Funny, but no matter what it may be I never waste time to answer something I know that you want to hear. This is one of those intimate situations that I spoke of. However, whoever may read it, it is purely an opinion. I feel that you were prompted to ask this question because of the literature that Tom sent you. The Roman Catholic church is against birth control. Perhaps the profession of my belief will sound hypocritical of me. But barring the issue of religion which we should not rightfully do, I believe in the exercising of birth control. I am trying to answer your question as it refers to us. The sex temperament that we both possess would give us a family unequaled in world history. We find pleasure in each other and in each other's touch. At times we are fanatical. It can't be helped, that's us. We both know that we'd like to have a family. How big lays in the Grace of God because He alone can judge that. I know that our rate is moderate (2 or 3). The broad minded reference is, what do we do in the meantime? You know me well enough to know that I speak openly and with utter disregard for other people's convention. We want to enjoy the fruits of life and that we will. It isn't that we are careful but that we are human. Human beyond the rights of many men. Darling, honestly, I wish I could speak as openly and frankly as I'd like. Bringing forth revelations we both know, but which would help us to further my point. I am more than understanding when it comes to something close to me. Bluntly, we like to sleep together. A joy which is commonly basic to happiness. Resorting to control would be our method of, shall we say, living. I'm sure that we are sensible to know when we want to start our family and when to continue it. Personally, I hope you don't mind if we don't take too much time to start it. But that is a question to decide mutually.

Darling, I hope I have spoken sensibly. It is ticklish and extremely difficult to write under these circumstances. If you analyze our short past, you will realize that the question is easily answered.

In the past, I have been reluctant to offer an opinion on any thing. But your questions make an answer imperative. Do not lose sight of me and they will be answered more clearly. By that I mean, see the intricate workings of my stupid mind and you will discover the key to a lot of your questions. If I have not fully answered your question, tell me what I have omitted and I'll fill it in.

There, I covered three pages for that. It requires lots more but I need a prod and further questions to forward more.

Your religious duties are a subject which I have talked about often. I won't say more until you read all my letters on the subject. I am sure that they will clear all the questions in your mind.

Remember what I told you, it still goes and always will. I love you. My understanding is part of that love. It is not just one word, love, no one could ever asseverate just one word with a multitude of emotions.

Darling, I must close. This is the second letter for today. Still many more to follow. Gotta save some for the next letter. Good night — May God Bless You. Love you and miss you. Love, Mike.

Flights continued as usual on January 21 and 22, and included instrument, formation, and squadron flight plan. On January 22, there was also one plane trip to Castelvetrano, Sicily, "on official business," and Red Skelton in *Whistling in the Dark* played that evening.

January 23, 1944 [*Sunday*]

Dearest Bette,

It is a quiet Sunday afternoon and I can't find one coherent thought. They are just as aimless as a brook that starts somewhere and ends somewhere. No one cares either way.

I didn't write last night because I wanted to wait until after mail call. I didn't receive any letters, so I got into a homey conversation. It got cold and it was too late to write. I tried to get some reading material and ended up with a *Superman* magazine. Really brain food.

Somehow or other, I feel I should be getting some "sack" time. But since, I didn't get up until late this A.M., it is only right that I try to stay awake. The weather mingled with my feelings are making me drowsy. Warm sun, contented cow, quiet country scene. Nothing to do, should take a walk but here I am, no set plan, nothing of interest to say and I want to speak to you.

In church this morning, I prayed for everyone and I asked God to give me peace of mind. I didn't expect Him to make it that peaceful. Right now, I don't give a damn what happens or when it happens. I am leisurely puffing on my pipe, every so often my attention is arrested by the drone of a plane overhead and onward I write to someone I love dearly and who is only 5,000 miles away. If they would let me borrow a plane, I bet I'd shorten that distance, dead or alive.

The table I am writing on is set directly off the center of the tent. On it is a box of tangerines (we just bought them.), a couple of boxes of crackers, and pen, paper, ink and me. I am facing the opening. On my right are two empty cots. One is mine and the other is

Clete's [*Cletus Carmean, my crew chief*]. His cot is littered with a dirty towel, dirty fatigues, a heavy fur-lined flying jacket and a summer leather flying jacket, and a mess kit. Between our beds is a small end (?) table and a shelved case, littered with a lamp, my mess kit, our toilet articles, writing paper, a few books, my basketball shoes, Listerine and old letters. On my bed is *Superman* and my heavy flying jacket. On my left are two more empty cots, separated by a shelved case. Rollo's [*Rollo Blue, crew chief*] bed is littered with heavy gloves, *Reader's Digest*, a gun, and blankets. His bed roll is airing in the sun. The partition shelf has a pipe, toilet articles, paper, tobacco, soap, chewing gum, tooth paste, and old letters. Max's [*Max Gilliam, Rollo's radio operator*] cot is made. He has just a mess kit on it. That just covers part of our home. I don't want to go any further. As soon as I finish this letter, one of the cots will be occupied, mine. I have a *Newsweek* which I haven't read. I never thought I'd be so interested in politics, but anything can happen here. I [*have*] never read as much in my life.

Well, Darling, you must forgive me for taking so much of your time. Just wanted to tell you that I love you and miss you. From my letter, you can see how empty my thoughts are.

So long for now. Give my love to Mother. May God Bless You — Love, Mike.

The Squadron activities on January 23 included glider formation flights and a dance in Trapani for the enlisted men. The next day, there was instrument flying in the morning only, and the movie, *More the Merrier*, with Jean Arthur and Joel McCrea, that night. The January 25 War Diary entry reported training with instrument flying in the morning, and night flying was postponed due to weather.

January 26, 1944 [*Wednesday*]

Hello Bette,

There is nothing much to talk about. The mail has slowed up again so I just have to create my own ideas.

I wonder if I can describe the women over here so that you will have a fair idea of the competition that the American girls have. In the first place, our girls have a distinct advantage because their education is unlimited. Before Mussolini, it was necessary to be of rich parentage before it was possible to attend school. He had started to install free education but the war soon ended that. So, although they are not ignorant, they aren't bright.

I can't very well describe their clothing because I am not too well versed on that subject. Consequently, you must forgive my naïve description. Hats are almost nil. For the younger girls, a kerchief seems to be the mode; hats are reserved for little children and elderly city-bred women. (Remember I am describing the city gals, not the peasants. They have no style — an old dress, a shawl, maybe shoes, maybe not!) Since Italy has been at war so long, black is a common color. But as for dress, they seem to quite up-to-date and color scheme is fair. Stockings are a luxury. Most times, if they are worn, they have been often repaired for "runs." For some reason or other, whenever I see a girl with a good pair of stockings on, I get the impression that she is being "kept" by some American Officer or enlisted man. Shoes, there is only one style and that's all I have seen. They are those damned "wedgies." The most clumsy, the most ugly horrible sight of those shoes. As for under clothing, I can't describe that because I haven't investigated too deeply. It seems that most of the women have ugly sores on their legs. I guess it must be from lack of vitamins. It must be strange that I should notice all this; but, after all, you can't blame a guy for looking and when he stops looking, it is time to call the diggers, right? Ever since I have been over here, I have become a very noticing person. Very little detail passes my eyes. I guess I'm just curious.

There you are, My Darling, that's the best I can do and now I must rush off. I try to write as often as I can but there are times that I must miss.

I must close for now. Hope I get some mail tonight. If I do, I'll probably write again. For now, no more to say except that I love you and miss you.

Give my love to Mother. Take care of yourself. May God Bless You. All My Love, Mike.

On January 26, the training program consisted of instrument flying in the morning only — night flights were postponed due to weather. The next day's War Diary entry noted:

Training program: Double Tow Glider and Formation flying in the AM. One plane trip to El Aouina, Tunisia, on official business. Night flying called off due to weather.

There were instrument flights the morning of January 28, with squadron formation flying that afternoon. The movie *Mr. Big* was shown that night.

January 28, 1944 [*Friday*]

My Darling,

I received your letter of the 4th and I was glad to hear that you had gotten so much of my mail.

I got a letter from someone that sort of got me "hot under the collar." She speaks of the Café Rouge, La Martinique and a few other points that she visited with some Merchant Seaman. The fact is that she seemed to flaunt all these things in my face. I don't mind if people have fun. Why shouldn't they? But it was the manner in which she said it. It seemed that this seaman had quite an impressive record in the invasion of Sicily and he received the DSC (Distinguished Service Cross). She had her picture taken with him, and all that sort of stuff. The guy's a hero and she made me know it. My answer wasn't very abusive, but my thoughts were indignant as Hell. It makes me mad to hear people say, "What did you do overseas?" and the answer is of no consequence. Hell, every time I think of a boy sweating 18 months here and even if he sits on his ass, he goes home with only a campaign ribbon and he's considered a dud. Just being here is enough. Then I think of a guy that has 1,000 hrs. in the air and he doesn't even rate an Airman's medal. We don't give a damn about the ribbons, home is our best reward; but why the Hell people must always be impressed is beyond me! Well, I guess one person's opinion doesn't mean much. It is the people that mean something that count. I am not "griping." I am just showing you how people react.

Darling, that was a nice letter you wrote. It's a swell idea to send me those sports columns. I enjoy reading them. I can't answer all your questions. A lot of times I go off on a tangent and it covers all your questions. If I don't answer, I'll unconsciously say everything that you want to know. The reason for that is that I hate to make my letters look like news items. Short paragraphs to say a few insignificant words. I drum my brain to rhetoric heights and then I am ready for my revelations. Darling, I don't want you to be angry but I put in an application for Cadet. My reasons are plain and logical but I don't want to discuss them because the censor will probably delete most of it. Since their system of handling these things overseas is so flimsy, the application will probably be of no avail. However, I want you to trust my judgment and we'll let fate take its course.

I don't know what's wrong but I feel in a sluggish mood to-day. I hadn't intended to write because I feel that way. I feel lazy, Honey. It is one of those things you will have to contend with. One of those "breakfast in bed" moods where I'd need a house full of maids, valets and footmen to serve my needs. But my letters couldn't possibly be too uninteresting, so I write. I want to make it a point that you hear from me because it might set your pretty blonde head a frettin' if you didn't.

Clete and I are naming our ship "Bar-Maid Nell" in memory of that famous woman of disreputable character. The alcohol and smoke caught up to "Dirty Gertie" so — But there will be more about Nell as soon as I get on the right track.

I am going to close. My ideas are too sketchy and incoherent to make this worthwhile. So, My Darling, *Adieu*. Love you and miss you. May God Bless You. Love, Mike.

On January 29, the training program consisted only of glider towing — the squadron formation flights were called off that night. The War Diary also noted that applications were being accepted for qualified enlisted personnel to apply for Aviation Cadet Training.

The War Diary entry for January 30 read:

Training program: Glider Tow and Formation flying in the AM. Group formation flying at night. Some personnel were transported to Group Headquarters to see a British Stage Show plus a movie. All departments have been instructed to get all their boxes and crates painted and lettered properly for a contemplated move. The use of a gymnasium to play basketball has been arranged by Special Services. First practice session held this date.

January 31,1944 [*Monday*]

My Darling,

I love you. I am so sorry that I missed so many days but so many things distracted me that I couldn't help myself. Yesterday, I got into a hot 2-hour workout that took up most of my free time that I couldn't write. It is not very often that I can get any exercise and I hate to miss the opportunity. Besides you wouldn't want to see me get lazy and fat. I was never the type of guy that regretted a good bit of exercise.

I received 3 letters from you. Dates 23, 25, 27 of Dec. and one from your Mom — 27th. Thank her for me and tell her that I'll try to answer as soon as I can.

You can see the crazy order in which our mail gets here. I have already written that I had gotten your letters of Jan. Now, I start to get the Dec. mail. Screwy, isn't it? In your letters you say that mail is plentiful. In your Jan. letters, there are complaints, so you see, we can't seem to get together.

Bettyjeane Louise, very pretty, indeed, as a matter of fact, quite delicate in such a small frame like yours. We are going to put "Betty" on the cowling of the right engine or on the loop antenna housing on "Barmaid Nell." We decided on the picture and I think it's a good idea. It is the picture of one of the "Gay Nineties" gals. Big plumed hat, big hips and big breasts, holding a parasol in the right hand and a dainty silk handkerchief in the left hand. She is quite the dainty dame and I do hope she comes out as we picture her. The paintings will be done soon and I'll let you know how it looks. I'll try to take a picture of it when it is done. Someday remind me to sing that song to you. Ole "Bar-Maid Nell" was quite a gal. There will be more about her. Just like an old time serial.

I am glad that you liked Lucy's gift. That night gown that you talk about excites me but I like the effect of the blue. The reason I say that is that when my Mother was sick, I bought her a blue bed jacket. It was just the color I wanted and somehow I felt it would suit her. Mind you, I know nothing about female clothes & such. When I visited Mom in the hospital, she had on the jacket and she was asleep when I walked in. I thought that I was looking at an angel. Her hair is gray and her cheeks were almost blood red. Gad! I couldn't help but be breathless.

Now, Bettyjeane, don't threaten me. My hair is growing and it is starting to shape up. If you ever cut your hair, I swear I'll divorce you. Seriously though, Darling, I look better with short hair and you look so beautiful when your hair is just streaming down your neck. We'll compromise that ought to satisfy both of us.

Your revelations, My Darling, are so very reassuring. But surely you would never expect me to be content just to have you follow me around. I am not that conceited. Maybe it's because I'm so democratic but I like the 50-50 method of doing things. We'll laugh, dance, drink, and make love and it will be our world, equally ours, no questions asked and no quarter given. It will be our duty to ourselves to strive for the perfection we are so eagerly planning.

Darling, it isn't extraordinary that you should be attractive to men. You are so beautiful that it is a natural thing for men to want to "wolf" you. I'll never let them bother you. I'll just sneer and scare them away. If I feel ornery, there'll be plenty of busted heads. Why worry?

I didn't think that you wouldn't enjoy my poetry. Although it was really Shakespearean, it did sound like it had possibilities but if you really don't like it, I'll stick to prose.

Darling, I must close. I'd like to go thru' more detail on a lot of the ideas I have but I can't just now. I'll try not to let too much time lapse between letters. I am forgiven, aren't I?

Give my love to Mother. Thank her again for her letter. Take care of yourself. Praying for us constantly. May God Bless you. Love, Mike.

Over the next few days, the 37th Squadron's activities included the completion of glider training, and the first mention of the eventual move to England:

> **January 31: Glider Tow in the AM. Group Formation flying at night.** *Tornado* **with Chester Morris and Nancy Kelly played at the open air theater. Pay day as usual caused a buzz of activity in the card room and the PX. In addition to past lectures on SECURITY, Captain Cooney (Squadron Intelligence Officer) instructed heads of all departments to call a meeting of** <u>all</u> **personnel in their respective departments and to impress on each and everyone the vital importance of SECURITY and to be especially careful not to mention or even discuss contemplated moves now or at any future time. Special emphasis being placed on correspondence.**
>
> **February 1: The Glider Training schedule being completed, all Gliders were transferred to the 313th T.C. Group. One plane took off for Castelvetrano and return. Lt. Robert Roman, asst. Intelligence Officer, attended a conference of officers at Group S-2.**
>
> **February 2: One plane took off for Algiers, RON** [*remained overnight*]. **One plane transferred to the 313th T.C. Group. At the open air theater,** *Five Came Back***, starring Lucille Ball. Major Fletcher, Squadron C.O. called a meeting of all department heads to discuss a pending move** [*to Cottesmore Royal Air Force Base, England*]**.**

February 3, 1944 [*Thursday*]
<u>Sicily</u>

My Darling,

I received your letter of January 14 and your opening sentence was a wow! I have been thinking of the same thing. It's funny how a restless feeling can come over a person and he realizes how much more he loves another person. Instead of dreaming of a meeting in Grand Central, I didn't dream; as a matter of fact, I couldn't get to sleep. Every time I think that someday we will get together again, I get a quickening of the pulse that makes my heart jump out of the skin.

You talk about those hard-boiled eggs. I may eat them but I haven't said that I have entirely learned to like 'em. I'll take mine sunny side up any time and after all, Darling, you don't want a guy to starve. At any rate, as long as you, at least, promise to scramble them, there isn't much more I can say.

I am not angry about the fact that you opened your Mother's letter. I knew it would happen because it was the natural reflex for you. However, Bettyjeane, you mustn't fret. Your Mother had to know sooner or later. It is OK for people to wait and then take up where they left off. But the day of slow motion is over. Surely we would wait but we'd be living together anyhow so why should we be doing an injustice to everyone including ourselves.

You must forgive my blunt manner of expression but I rarely pull my punches. It may seem crude but it really doesn't sound as figurative as I write it. We will be wasting all this time but we are apart and then when we meet again, there will have to be a period of reconstruction. No! This is it! You are mine. You won't be any different from when I left you and I shan't be changed. Why should we waste an eternity of days just to find ourselves? It will mean more months of separation. Aren't these enough? I am not saying all of this as a scold. It is just an opinion I know that you share with me. Whatever it may be, it can't change our ideas. You needn't worry about Mother. She may worry but it is all so useless.

Darling, I know the situation and I regret that you must labor under such a handicap. But we are grown people. We know where our future is and how we want to share it. Surely all these months of planning should not be for naught, so that we will have to do all of it over again. I love you and I want you to be my wife. To share all that I have. To be able to guide and be guided and to live as happily as God is giving us the grace to live. We are so revolutionary that it doesn't matter anyhow. We'll do as we please and wait for repercussions and that, too, will fall on our deaf ears because we will be living the life that is being created in these pages in all these months. If you haven't said your piece clearly, have I helped to clarify it in any way? Darling, when I am speaking of something I know to be the truth, neither hell nor the lack of ink or paper can stop me. I'd write on toilet tissue if it were necessary.

These things don't bore me, Darling. They are the type of things we must try to straighten between ourselves. You speak of your stone wall. You know why you love me. Mine was never made of stone, but by a suppression that caused inferiority. I am saving that for a talk with you. It is not a piece of conversation for a censor to be tossed about like scramble of eggs. That is only one thing. Morally, I don't know how to stop thinking about you. In the eyes of God, I am sure He accepts you as my earthly Guardian Angel. But again, I shan't cover more on that. I am ready to hit the sack. Tired!

Well, Sweetheart, Good night. Give my love to Mother. Take care of yourself. May God Bless You. I love you and miss you. Love, Mike.

The War Diary for February 3 noted that "all personnel were busy packing, crating, stenciling, etc." in preparation of the squadron's move to England.

On February 4, according to the War Diary,

> **"Dinghy" drill was held at 1030 hours for the Air Echelon in readiness for the move by air.** [*"Dinghy" drill was a training exercise to prepare for an emergency landing in water. It was the job of the radio operator and crew chief to inflate the dinghy that was carried on board and anchor it to the plane.*] **A severe wind storm at the open air theater caused no apparent damage. A movie was shown at the open air theater. All personnel were ordered to have everything in readiness, personal baggage, etc. Another dance for the EM was held this evening at Trapani, Sicily.**

February 5, 1944 [*Saturday*]
<u>Sicily</u>

Dearest Bette,

Again, I give you a word of forewarning because I don't know what this letter will look like when it is finished. As usual, the mail has been pitiful. I haven't had a letter from home for such a Hell of a long while. It isn't because they don't write but because it just isn't getting here.

I happened to be in town [*Trapani*] and I saw a set of Tech. Sergeant's stripes. They are really "big time." They were made out of heavy gold braid. Clete, my crew chief is a tech, so I thought it would be a good idea to surprise him. They cost me $1.00 (100 lira). I had them sewed on over his regular stripes on his OD blouse. They looked like a neon sign. You should have seen the look on his face when he saw them. I don't think he will ever forgive me.

I haven't done any reading lately and so I can't discuss that at all. Believe me, I do miss it. I finished *Twenty Years After* and since I enjoy all of Dumas' works, this was no exception. There was an article in *Reader's Digest* which proved to be very interesting. It was an article written by a Catholic woman concerning Birth Control. Her ideas were very good. I believe it was in the Oct. or Nov. issue, 1943. She said that if people did want to practice control, it should be done in a sensible manner. Since a woman is fertile at certain times during a period, it would be best to abstain from intercourse during that period. On a whole, the article was very good. It has a decent twang to it. It does not advocate abstinence except for birth control but as I said she believes in restraint during the period of fertility. Read it, I am sure it will help to form an opinion.

Gosh, Hon, honestly, it is tough as Hell to write. I hate to leave a page unused but I can't seem to get the words to fill it. Rather than have you suffer from boredom, I'll close and then write to you later, perhaps, when I can really get my teeth into it.

So, so long for now, My Darling, I love you and miss you ever so much. Take care of yourself. May God Bless You. Yours, Mike.

February 5,1944 [*Saturday*]
Sicily

My Darling,

Good Evening, My Sweet, wrote to you earlier in the day, received a letter from you this evening and so here I am again. I heard from a few friends of mine, too, I have answered their letters already. It really makes my day complete when I receive a "sugar report."

Nope! I haven't heard that new song. It takes a while to catch up to us. I haven't heard the radio as regularly as I used to. Just sort of catch snatches once in a while. Always good to hear! "Embraceable You" — one of my many favorites. I liked T. Dorsey's or was it J. Dorsey's arrangement of it.

You speak of Bear Mountain. That is really a nice place. We never go there in the winter time because we aren't active participants in winter sports. But in the summer time, The Mount, is really a lover's paradise. You see, it is right on the Hudson River. Every Sunday there is a daylight line that runs a boat up to Bear Mt., Indian Point, etc. And in the evening, they have a moonlight sail. It really is so very cozy and nice. I guess it is a 2-hour ride and there is an orchestra abroad ship. My H.S. used to have a sail every year and we raised Hell. I haven't been on one in over 5 years. Too busy trying to be a business man, and liked my sleep on my day off. Not to forget the ball games.

I'm afraid I can't say much about my ability as a skier or skater. I have skated a few times and I really wrecked myself. Never skied in my life. Tried to roller skate a few times but again I was a flop! Really, Darling, I prefer the team sports or at least body contact. I like to watch ice shows and Hockey games, though. Sonja [*Henie*] puts on a show every year at Madison Square Garden, and it really is a sight of beauty. I miss my hockey games as I have missed all the sports. The baseball season isn't too far off. Kind of lose touch of things but I really don't worry. The day will come when we will be seeing all this together. Gosh, Bette, it makes my heart light to think that amid all this turmoil, a person can see the brightness of the future. And not alone, either, every time I think of you on my right arm, it makes these empty days pass with the speed of light — But —

Well, Good night, My Love, don't fret about your big hero. He has the situation well in hand but he wishes to God that He would help me pass the buck to someone else.

So long, Bette. Give my love to Mother. Love you and miss you. Take care. May God Bless You — Ugly, Mike.

The War Diary entries for February 5 and 6 described weather problems:

All scheduled flying called off due to strong winds and rain. Ration day as usual was a very busy day for PX personnel.

February 6: All cabin tanks on Squadron planes were tested. One plane to Castelvetrano and return. Group Formation Flying at night. Rain, rain and more rain all day and night, and mud! By order of the XII Air Force, letter dated 28 January 1944, the following named officers were promoted to rank shown:

TO Captain:	1st Lt. Noel S. Bennett	ASN 0790497
	1st Lt. Frank B. Waters	ASN 0790108
TO 1st Lt.:	2nd Lt. Nicholas Pappaeliou	ASN 0805328
	2nd Lt. William L. Ballard	ASN 0797441
	2nd Lt. Harold K. Bailey	ASN 0798488
	2nd Lt. Marvin L. Finch	ASN 0669464
	2nd Lt. Manuel M. Freedman	ASN 0744889
	2nd Lt. Richard J. Gosnell	ASN 01703990
	2nd Lt. Ralph P. Janes	ASN 01703884
	2nd Lt. George R. Robertson	ASN 0805328
	2nd Lt. Robert F. Scott	ASN 0666835
	2nd Lt. Billy M. Smith	ASN 01703998

Sicily, February 7, 1944 [*Monday*]

My Darling,

You see, I told you, screwy as Hell. I received your letter of January 11. And to relieve your anxious heart, My Love, I also received your 3 rolls of film. Thank you, My Sweet.

Wait a minute. What makes you think that the Cards are going to win the next pennant. Don't forget, my Little Chickadee, Brooklyn is still in the league. I hope that I'll be home so that we can see a nickel series, Yanks and Brooklyn. Or don't you know what a nickel series is? You see there are three teams in NY — Yanks, Giants, & Brooklyn. If the Giants or Brooklyn win in the N.L. [*National League*] and the Yanks in the A.L. [*American League*], it cost only a nickel to get to anyone of the stadiums by subway. So there, you can learn something every day.

You needn't worry about that bourbon. Our supply didn't last very long. Things get tough. I had to start drinking cognac and lime juice. Not bad, but I don't recommend it for weak stomachs. Mine must be made of iron and I bet that it is rusted from that rot gut.

Woman, My Woman, that ring you speak of must be a honey. As one of the fellows said, "If I had that ring on my finger, I'll have a gun under my arm!" We'll try to match the shape, but I don't know about the value. Couldn't you pick something in Woolworth's? I don't mind wearing platinum but it will have to look masculine. After all, My dear, people might think I'm queer. Whoops! Or am I?

If you didn't have to get back to KC we probably would have gotten married. Don't forget, too, Bette, our financial status was in dire need of uplifting. I came over here $50 in the red. I took care of that easy enough. You know, Darling, since I have been over here, I have formulated a lot of ideas about advice I can give to the generation that we will make. Such things as extreme hesitation with extraordinary prior thought. It isn't so involved but it requires endless stressing to drive the point. If our children are like us, they will be extremely impulsive. We will have to tame that a bit but not suppress it entirely. I'd hate like hell for our son to miss so much just because he had to tear everything apart just to find the ultimate result. The poor guy will be abnormal. I know now that the stupidity of "why do today, what we can do tomorrow," trend has caused me many anxious moments and many a disappointment, dull, and hurt moment. But I shan't preach. We must learn to practice all this for the sake of those who are still unknown, not yet started and are wanting to be brought into our world by us. The children we hope to create out of love and with the full grace of God.

Well, Bette, My Sweet, must close. Give my love to Mother. Take care of yourself. May God Bless You. Still waiting for that weight report. Love you and miss you. Mike.

P.S.: You didn't spell "mutual" correctly. You spelled it with one "u" (mutal). Careless you. Love, M.

There were no scheduled flights on February 7, according to the War Diary, which also noted that the first volume of the "316th Troop Carrier Group News" appeared on that day. The Enlisted Men's club was closed "due to the necessity of getting things packed and ready to move."

The February 8 entry read:

Planes were tested for "Slow Time" flying in the morning. Movie at the open air theater: *The Man From Down Under*, starring Charles Laughton.

To familiarize the new pilots with the performance of a C-47, it was necessary to go through all sorts of trials to determine various characteristics. "Slow time" flying would be to throttle back (slow) the aircraft to determine when it would reach stalling speed — that is, when the power would cut out.

Another practice stunt was for us to fly at a high altitude (say, 5,000 feet) and "shoot landings." Since the airfields were busy, one could not shoot landings on the field itself. Hence we would go to the higher altitude and simulate all the conditions for landing, such as throttling back (slow time) with gear lowered to get the feel for actually landing. Once the plane was "landed," the pilot would then power up as if he were taking off again, call for the gear to be raised, and off we would go. We would also kill (shut down) one engine to simulate a hit, which would cripple that engine. The pilot and co-pilot would then make adjustments to keep the plane flying on one engine.

February 9, 1944 [*Wednesday*]
<u>Sicily</u>

My Darling,

I received your letters of the 7th and 10th last night. So you see, I have to answer your mail in a rather backward fashion.

I heard from Lucy and she tells me that she and Harry are engaged. It is one of the nicest bits of news I have heard. It seems that my brother, Lou, is due to arrive one of these months. That, too, is most encouraging. All that makes life worthwhile. And, Darling, I am waiting with utmost anxiety for your picture. I presume that it has already been sent. Gosh, Bette, you are so thoughtful that I can't help but learn to love you more each day.

Thank you so much for your extreme faith in my ability. It is true that I was part of the business world before this. But believe me, whatever I lacked, I have found. It will be a bit harder to persuade me that things just can't be done. I am not overly boisterous, but I do realize what I want and how I can obtain it. Surely, I never hope to be taken as anyone's fool.

Darling, it is OK if you can't send anything. There really is so little I need. The picture is one thing I want. The film is for our personal records. I don't like to weigh you down with things that are unnecessary and so much bother. If I really need anything very badly, I'll ask but until then, don't bother. — Your description of that home was very fine. It's funny that as I read it, I noticed that you had misspelled "dining" (one "n" not 2). I must be a prude for that sort of stuff but I can't help it. You must forgive me if I am such a nuisance. As far as that bottle of bourbon goes, it gets wet enough around here on wine. Drinking bourbon in this atmosphere would be like painting a picture in the bath room. I'll develop my thirst until I can really satisfy it in the right place.

We had an egg fry in the tent last night and all the fellows were here. For thirst quenching we had six bottles of wine, — some sweet, some dry. The party really warmed up and by the time we were ready for bed, there wasn't a sober person to be had. It was cozy and really enjoyable.

Heard from a buddy of mine who is stationed in China. He promised to get drunk with me, the next time we met in the States. Told him about you and he sends his love. Our favorite censor [*Nick Pappaeliou*] made 1st [*Lieutenant*]. And he returns the love you sent him. Sounds like a vicious circle, doesn't it?

Lucy said that they had sent you an invitation to Tom's ordination. You must go, Darling. It won't cost much because I know that you can stay at my home and that all our humble hospitality will be at your disposal. It will be a great event and I know that you will share my family's happiness. Tom is the best. Couldn't find a better guy and I know you will be at ease with the gang.

Well, Honey, I must close for now. Sorry if I sound parched but after last night (?) and I woke up early and played ball for 2 hours. Kinda gets a guy down. Give my love to Mother. Take care of yourself. May God Bless You. Love you — Always, Mike.

The February 9 War Diary entry recorded one round trip to Castelvetrano. It also noted,

Roll call continues to be a headache for the EM. Morale in general appears to be good however.

On February 10, one plane was sent to El Aouina, Tunisia, on official business. The War Diary concluded: "Rain continues to be the main topic of conversation these days."

February 11, 1944 [*Friday*]
<u>Sicily</u>

My Darling,

I have written to Lucy, Harry and Sally (my sister-in-law, Harry's sister, and Lou's wife). I received your letters of Jan. 11, and Jan. 25. There are so many things happening at home that it seems to require all my attention, all at the same time.

An interesting point in your first letter which I think needs some clarification. I am not angry. Hell, if my words can do someone some good, they are welcome to them. The things that puzzle me are what views and what opinions? You must make these clearer. Though I don't write for the purpose of publication, I'd like to know what sort of stuff Mrs. Huff is using. One thing, My Darling, whatever I say it is nothing more than what I feel and think. I have never been afraid to approach anyone for any reason. If I gripe about something, it is because it affects me and the men I must work with. If I praise something, it is likewise for myself and those about me. I am a GI, one with many millions. If it were not for censorship, I should not hesitate to speak my mind more fully and with a clear conscience. But Hell, you know that better than I do. So there is no sense for me to go beating off into an elegy of my own. One thing they can't censor nor deflate is my love for you and I most certainly will be your Valentine. My heart is yours, My Love, don't beat it, just caress it; it will last longer that way. Again, I wait for your picture with anxiety unequaled.

Vain Creature, even if we were stranded on a desert island, you'd have to have lipstick. You forget to mention a couple of cases of good bourbon. At least you rate me above a phonograph.

You can tell those gals in your office that if you ever change your mind about me, they needn't worry. If you ever changed your mind, women won't want to know me. There is a lot behind that statement, accept it as you wish. My ideas are too devilish, brutal and barbaric to put on clean paper.

There are 4 people with the same thoughts, Lucy, Harry, Bette, and myself. We are all hoping that we can meet at the same place for the same purpose — marriage. Chicha [*Lucy*] is so gloriously happy. Four happy people, in four different corners of the world, surely it can't be too long before we converge. What an explosion of happiness. It should be heard all over the world.

So I see I have made a lot of people literature happy. Tell that bunch of female wolves to read *Lust for Life* by Irving Stone. They can see how a man reacts to things. It's fairly short and I am sure that they can discuss it to its fullest. Tell them that you all should read the same books at the same time and then you can compare your opinions.

Well, Honey, I must close for now. I have a dental appointment I don't want to miss (?) Take care of yourself, Darling. May God Bless You. I love you and miss you. Love, Mike.

There was no scheduled flying on February 11 because all planes were preparing for takeoff on short notice. The movie *Lucky Jordan* was shown, and all personnel were restricted to camp due to being "on alert." Newspaper releases for all officers were forwarded to Group "S-2" — Intelligence.

February 12, 1944 [*Saturday*]
<u>Sicily</u>

My Darling,

This is one of those nites when I don't know what I can write about. I have no plan of letter, whatsoever. My thoughts are sparse and unevenly dispersed — one of those nights when I yearn for your comfort and cry for your presence.

The weather is miserable, the stove is ornery, my feet are cold. I am not sad nor am I happy. I could yell or I could be so quiet that the echoes would drive me mad. I can't read because the love stories in *Colliers* serve to deepen my feelings. If I had a bottle of bourbon, I'd drink it to the last drop. It would have no effect but to serve as a nightcap for a good, solid night's sleep.

The night is black. The mud is knee deep. It seems as if the entire camp is asleep. Every thought of you becomes so pronounced that I hear "You," "You," "You" pounding thru' my brain. This sounds ever so dramatic. If it were, I wouldn't write because I don't feel dramatic. I am so much in love with you. This is one of those nights that if we were together, I'd love you to death. A night when friends wouldn't dare to visit for fear of being tossed out. A night when soft music and soft (?) drinks and soft talk, and soft embraces are the epitome of life. A night when war and trouble are but fading clashes in the gloom. A night that God made for lovers alone. A night when we discover what has been forgotten and lost, and is regained with all the intensity of new love. My God, Woman, I'm in love with you and there is nothing in this whole wide world that can change it.

But I mustn't go on like this. Realize my mood. I am not lonely. Not really. I can't afford to be and I mustn't be. I feel all the things that I should feel when I am with you. It is so easy to forget when we are given the things we want. If I can go thru' this, it will be a long, hard road to forget. This is the moment of masculine putty. Yours for the asking,

My Darling, you [*don't*] know how much I miss you. Yes! I know it is wrong for me to speak so. But Hell! A guy can't be firm and cold all the time. There must be some vent for emotions, even if, it is only words in a letter. A mental intercourse that can't be excused and above all must be substituted.

Every so often, I burst into song, some unintelligible ditty that is nothing more than a scream imposed upon a tune with stupid words.

My Darling, if I could only say what I wanted to. If I could only put into words what I feel. If I could make you laugh with me, I could make you cry with me. If you could hear me bitch or praise, you'd know how I feel. It is like a sudden push of blood to the brain. A period of semi-coma that cannot bring anything but the giddiness, stupidity, futility non-sensical, morbid, pitiful depth out of a wasting soul. A feeling of helplessness that seems carried by inactivity of the cells that God has poured into our bodies. A feeling that deems a wasting soul to create a wasteful body, if it could be so.

But I won't go on. I'll stop. Send this and when the sun shines again and I've had a good night's sleep, I'll be OK. Even if I got drunk, it wouldn't help. I felt like pouring words onto your already over burdened shoulders, and so I did. The best that you can do is tear it up but you mustn't because some day you'll want to show this to me. When you do, I won't laugh. I may be pensive because I'll recall the night of Feb. 12th somewhere in Sicily when I felt this way. It will only mean another kiss for you and perhaps a broken rib because I'll have you then.

But Good Night, My Darling, don't be restless because of this letter. Just get an extra 40 winks and say, "He's at it again. Why do I love him? Or is that why?"

May God Bless You. Love, Mike.

Preparations were made on February 12 for two planes — the advance detail for the air echelon — to leave the next day for England. All departmental equipment going by air was loaded on the planes.

February 13, 1944 [*Sunday*]
<u>Sicily</u>

My Darling,

Strange as it may seem, this letter is an answer to your letter of February 3, 1944. Some-one must have slipped up somewhere because it got here so quickly. However, I must make my answer short. I can't help it.

Darling, you mustn't worry your pretty blonde head about that jewelry and stuff that you speak of. I attach very little sentiment to things that are of the material world. There are very few such things that I cherish. So you see, I don't mind at all. I give my entire faith to a person who means so much to me. There is no reason why I shouldn't. I trust that their love is strong enough to return that faith and trust. The things that are important are the teachings that are passed from person to person. So you see, Bette, I don't mind a bit about those pieces of jewelry. Whereas that ring that I'll put on your finger someday, it will be significant of the love that will be passed between us. But it won't be the ring but the depth of the feeling. See? You needn't worry about my jealous streak. Surely, I didn't have to know where you got it. And the very fact that you tell about it is enough to warrant the understanding that goes with the admission.

I don't know the censor who you are referring to because there are a few of the officers that do this work. However, it doesn't make any difference if I know him or not. If the man cuts stuff that is incidental, that's his business. We have a word in the army that covers that perfectly but I won't bother to mention it here. So the Hell with it, let the guy have his fun, he'll probably cut paper dolls when the war is over.

You aren't just kidding when you speak of the days passing. I was thinking about it the other day. Each day we are closer. Each day adds more to any already full love. It isn't so bad. We can knock this stretch of time over in the same manner that we have beaten time before. It isn't so tough.

Your letter got here so fast, it felt as if we were closer. But I shan't put too much faith in that speed, it probably was a mistake.

Gosh, Honey, I must close this. I'd like to go on but I'll continue as soon as I can. There are so many things I feel are unsaid.

Well, Gal, must close again. I haven't received your picture yet. It will get here in due time.

Take care of yourself. May God Bless You. Praying for us. Love you and miss you. Love, Mike.

The War Diary entries for February 13-16 described the preparations for the 37th Squadron's move to England:

> **February 13: Two planes departed Borizzo 0900 hours. No. 34 was cleared to El Aouina, Tunisia, and No. 30 was cleared to Gibraltar. Personal baggage belonging to the remainder of the Air Echelon personal was loaded on the planes.**
>
> **February 14: All planes loaded and in readiness for the move to the UK [*United Kingdom*]. All work being finished on the line, the supplies and equipment of Engineering, Communications, and Tech Supply were moved to the Squadron camp area for crating. The supplies could also be more conveniently guarded.**
>
> **February 15: Ten planes departed Borizzo for the UK, with all the remaining personnel of the Air Echelon. One plane and complete crew being held for Lt. Col. Washburn, Jr., Group Executive Officer. Captain Ralph E. Shadwell, Jr., ranking Officer automatically became Commanding Officer of the Ground Echelon.**
>
> **February 16: All crating and packing being completed.**

Right: Mike — and daisies, *ca.* April 1943.

Below: Bettyjeane Louise Hill, April 1943.

Bette Hill and Corporal Mike Ingrisano in Kansas City, Missouri, *ca.* April 1943.

Bette in May 1943.

Mike, March 1943.

Bettyjeane, *ca.* April 1943. This picture was cut down to fit into Mike's celluloid cigarette case.

Bette and her big hat, *ca.* April 1943.

Chapter 3

Somewhere in England
(February 24 to May 11, 1944)

$\mathcal{O}$N EARLY 1944, Troop Carrier Groups left Sicily for England to continue training with U.S., British, and Polish airborne and glider-borne troops for the pending assault on Fortress Europe. The target date was set as May. German resistance in northern Italy remained fierce.

Elsewhere in the war, Soviet troops crossed the Dneister River on March 19 and retook Odessa on April 10 and Sevastopol on May 9. U.S. bombers began daylight attacks March 6, using the classified Norden bombsight, first developed in 1927. U.S. and British forces relentlessly hammered at the Japanese in both the Pacific and China-Burma-India (CBI) Theaters.

Following are the War Diary entries covering the move of the air echelon of the 37th Troop Carrier Squadron in February 1944:

February 15: Ten planes of the 37th Troop Carrier Squadron departed Borizzo, Sicily, at 0645 GMT [*Greenwich Mean Time*] for Oran. Moderately rough weather was

encountered for most of the flight, along with scattered showers and a low ceiling. The Squadron reached Oran at 1245 GMT and remained there over nite. Most of the Squadron personnel attended the base theater which was showing *Is Everybody Happy* with "Ted" Lewis. At Oran plane No. 328 rejoined the Squadron. It had departed from Borizzo two days earlier.

February 16: The Squadron, now consisting of eleven planes, departed Oran at 0800 GMT bound for Gibraltar, arriving there at 1100 GMT. Most of the flight was made at an altitude of 5000 feet and approximately five miles from the coast, good weather was encountered for the entire trip to Gibraltar. Immediately after landing all Officers and Enlisted men were assembled and given instructions as to their dress and conduct while on the base. After the assembly all personnel were given their lunch by the RAF Unit stationed there. Most of the men spent the afternoon resting or helping the Crew Chiefs to rearrange the loads for the over water flight to St. Mawgan. After supper, all pilots, co-pilot[*s*], navigators and radio operators were briefed by an RAF Officer for the flight to the UK. At Gibraltar, plane No. 503 rejoined the Squadron. It had left Borizzo two days before the other planes to act as the advance detail. At 2150 GMT, the Squadron, now consisting of twelve planes, departed Gibraltar.

February 17: Continuation of flight from Gibraltar to St. Mawgan. Because of winds stronger than had been anticipated a number of the planes were blown off course and as a result they were one to two hours over their original ETA [*estimated time of arrival*]. Immediately after landing at St. Mawgan, all personnel were served with hot coffee and doughnuts by the American Red Cross. Everyone was given a physical inspection by the Medical Officer on duty. After the physical inspection each man was assigned billets for the nite.

February 18: All planes departed from St. Mawgan at 1115 GMT for Cottesmore Air Base, arriving there at 1400 GMT. Personnel were assigned billets. Personal baggage was unloaded and hauled to the billets area.

February 19: Freight and office equipment was unloaded and the offices set up. This Squadron was assigned [*hangar*] "B." Other men who were not helping with the unloading cleaned out the billets where the Enlisted Men were to live.

February 20: Routine Squadron duties were performed. The engineering department checked all planes and carried on the inspections that were due after the move.

February 21: In addition to routine Squadron duties some orientation flights were made to familiarize the crews with the surrounding area. In the evening the USO show, *On With the Show* was given in the Enlisted Men's mess hall.

February 22: Routine Squadron duties were carried on. More orientation flights were made, enabling other crew members to become familiar with the immediate area. The Squadron received fifteen new English bicycles to help relieve the transportation problem.

February 23: More orientation flights were made this morning. In the afternoon, a lecture was given to the Squadron, both Officer and Enlisted personnel, on German Uniforms and Equipment. All types of uniforms were shown along with the various insignia of rank used by the German Army. From 1600 hours to 1700 hours, the Enlisted Men received instruction and training in close order drill. PX supplies were rationed out to the enlisted personnel.

Somewhere in England
February 24, 1944 [*Thursday*]

My Darling,

I love you. I am so very sorry, Bette, for not writing sooner but you can see that it wasn't entirely my fault. Darling, I am so very sorry again to have to remind you that these things happen and you mustn't be worried by them.

Things are a bit different. I don't think I need to say that it is much more comfortable. One need not worry about stepping out of a tent into a mud hole up to his chin. There are many more conveniences than we are accustomed to. At least we can get all the cokes, donuts and coffee that we want at the Red Cross. Unfortunately, due to circumstances beyond our control, it is impossible to be too elaborate in my descriptions. The weather is typically English. What more can we say!

Darling, I am making this note short because I want you to get it as soon as possible.

Above all, Darling, I miss you more than ever. The last time that I waited a long time for mail from you, it was before we realized the change in our life. Day by day, you mean so much more to me. Regardless of what I may do or [*where*] I may go, you are the first and foremost in my mind and heart. God only knows how much I miss you.

If at any time, there is another lapse in my writing, you mustn't worry about it.

So, so long for now, Bette. Give my love to Mother.

Take care of yourself. I am feeling fine. May God Bless You. Love you and miss you ever so much. Love, Mike.

War Diary entry, February 24:

Routine Squadron duties were carried on. Orientation flights were made in the morning. In the afternoon at 1400 hours, the Squadron was given a lecture by the Base Security Officer on Security and

Censorship. Until this lecture was given, no member of the Squadron could write or send out any mail.

Somewhere in England
February 25, 1944 [*Friday*]

My Darling,

Again I must [*beg forgiveness*] because my letter must be short. I know that you don't like the idea but I can't help it.

I don't remember what I said in my letter yesterday because I wrote it so fast. I do know that I told you that I loved you. That stands, I can never forget that. I did mention that we had a lot of conveniences. It isn't every post that everything is so handy. You can find it all, the entertainment, right here. There is a dance every Saturday night and the women aren't too ugly, at least, they speak English. The food is definitely an improvement. Chicken every Sunday and we needn't worry too much about a constant diet of C-rations and Vienna Sausage. We can get beer at the NAAFI [*Navy, Army, Air Forces Institute — the British equivalent of the American Red Cross*]. It isn't American beer but English beer isn't so bad. Oh Yes! One of the most important things that I forgot was that we needn't go miles to take a bath. As a matter of fact, it's like home. Why worry?

I met a friend of Harry's and believe me, he gave me quite a build-up. Really I am most anxious to see him.

Do you remember the morning I came into KC on a X-country [*cross-country flight*]? I had flown all night. I pleaded with the pilot to stay long enough so that [*I*] could see you and we could have breakfast together. He said no! So I had to be content with a phone call. Well, I met him and bawled the Hell out of him. As a matter of fact, that was the first thing he thought of when I saw him. Both he and the co-pilot got a big kick out of telling the story. Told them our intentions and they didn't feel too happy about the whole deal.

Well Honey, I must close. But as soon as I can get settled, I'll write often and make up for this laxity which wasn't my fault.

My Darling, I love you and miss you ever so much. Take care of yourself. May God Bless you. Love, Mike.

The War Diary entries for February 25 to 29 described the transition to life on the new base:

February 25: Eleven planes of this Squadron were sent to Stanstead to pick up freight and personnel to be taken to [*Mullaghmore*], North Ireland. All planes departed this station at approximately 1300 hours. Eight of the planes were loaded and remained over nite at Stanstead while the other three brought the crews back to this station. The first

passes were issued to Enlisted Men since arriving at this station, six of the men went to Leicester on 12-hour passes. Mail was censored and sent out.

February 26: Mail censored and other routine duties performed. No flying due to unfavorable weather conditions. A dance was held at the American Red Cross Club for all enlisted personnel on this base.

February 27: Mail censored and other routine duties carried on. No flying due to bad weather. At 1700 hours, all Officers of the Squadron attended a reception for Brigadier General Clark, 52nd Wing Commander.

February 28: Ten of the Squadron planes departed on a freight and passenger mission to Mullaghmore, North Ireland. One plane was forced to return because of engine trouble. This date three new planes were assigned this Squadron.

February 29: Mail censored and other routine duties performed. All personnel paid, the Enlisted Men in the morning, and the Officers in the afternoon.

෫෯෯෫

This write-up on the transfer of the ground echelon is found at the beginning of the March 1944 Squadron War Diary:

The Ground Echelon, consisting of 28 Officers and 168 EM were still at the staging area at Mandola, Sicily, awaiting ship transport to the UK, with captain Ralph E. Shadwell, Jr., in command. At the staging area, the men were able to catch up on their letter writing along with that eternal laundry problem. A few late movie releases were also in the offering. For a time an epidemic of colds and fever threatened to interfere with the troop movement. Nevertheless, on Sunday, 5 March 1944, the men were transported by truck to the dock area where they boarded the *Monarch of Bermuda*. In a large convoy of other troop ships, airplane carriers, battleships, and cruisers, the journey to the UK began. It wasn't long before the good sailors were separated from the bad. The seasick received sympathy instead of relief. The balance of the trip may be said to have been smooth and uneventful, and on the evening of Wednesday, 15 March 1944, the transport arrived off the coast of Scotland, the troops being quite relieved and happy at the thought of arrival. Because of unavailable transportation, there was a delay of three days. Finally, on Saturday, 18 March 1944, the men were taken ashore, where they boarded trains and arrived at Oakham at 0200 hours on Sunday, 19 March 1944.

The War Diary in early March 1944 showed that with the resumption of mail and regular flights, things were returning to normal:

> **March 1: The Air Echelon personnel received their first mail since arriving in England, part of it was direct from the States and the remainder from Sicily. At approximately 1400 hours, the planes and crews returned from their mission in North Ireland. A dance was held at Victoria Hall, Oakham, for the EM only.**
>
> **March 2: One plane carrying freight and personnel left on a mission to North Ireland. Squadron formation flying in the afternoon. Two bags of mail direct from the States were received and distributed.**
>
> **March 3: The Orderly Room and the Squadron Commander's office were moved upstairs leaving Intelligence, Supply, Engineering and Operations in the room downstairs.**
>
> **March 4: At 1000, a Group Formation was held for a review by the Commanding Officer, Lt. Col. [*Burton*] Fleet. Plane left for North Ireland on 2 March returned. Group Formation flying in the afternoon.**
>
> **March 5: Five planes took off for Gosfeit [*Gosfield airfield*] to move fighter unit to Beauliew [*Beaulieu airfield*]. Three new crews and one navigator were assigned this squadron.**

March 6, 1944 [*Monday*]
Somewhere in England

My Darling, Lovable Bettyjeane Louise,

Before I even start to apologize, my correct APO is 638. Now, I can start. I really have no excuse except to blame circumstances that were entirely beyond my control. I am sure that you understand and above all, I can't help it. Darling, I love you so very much.

I have received loads of mail and I do know that I should start to answer but first I must make up to you and Mom, the letters that you missed. I received 10 letters and a Valentine from you but I won't even start to answer them. As a matter of fact, most of your letters are in answer to mine and therefore I am required to start new subjects. That will come later on because I want to devote this letter strictly to incidental and other things. The circumstances upon which I have received your letters are rather funny. However, I can't tell you about them, so you must be left to linger on the scaffold of curiosity.

One thing happened that left me quite happy. Do you remember, in one of my letters, that I mentioned losing that cellophane cigarette case? If you recall I had 2 of your pictures in it. The loss was one which hurt. The other day, one of the fellows asked me if a case was mine. As soon as I saw your pictures, I knew it was mine. I had lost that some months back. So when the guy found it, he must have put it in his barracks bag. He must have found it then remembered to return it. I was most grateful to him.

I haven't had much time to read. I can't possibly do much of that now but I would like to have a copy of Betty Smith's *A Tree Grows in Brooklyn*. That's a request. By the way, Darling, Williamsburg is quite a prominent part of my fair boro. I haven't received your picture yet but I am patient and hopefully expectant.

When I read your episode of the night gown, I didn't fail to see the humor of it but for a some none too apparent reason, I started to blush like Hell. I never blush so I couldn't quite understand the reason for it. But I guess those things will happen.

I do suppose that you must be wondering when I am going to tell you how much I miss and love you. I do ever so much. There are so many things I want to say. It is as if I want to tell you so much that I feel like getting drunk and start to forget because I can't. Oh! My Darling, you mean so much to me. It is so like us to want to fill pages of love and yet we know how each other feels. If I could just hold you for 15 minutes, I'd be happy. You know that I love you but I feel so weak because I can't prove it to you. Again, one of these periods when the fullness in my heart must burst because I can't find an outlet for my emotions.

Darling, I must close. It is imperative that I write to Harry. One never knows but that I might see him. I will write tomorrow. That's a date. Forgive me for not being too personal. You know me. I am not always like that.

Give my love to Mother. May God Bless You. Take care of yourself. I love you so dearly. Miss you beyond words. Love, Mike. [*The second page of the original is stamped in a circular form with "Kansas City, MO. Mar. 17, 1944, Sta. 6" initialed by CWB.*]

❦❧❦❧

On March 6, five planes were taken up for instrument flying. According to the War Diary, all pilots, co-pilots, and radio operators attended a lecture at the base cinema. Four planes were sent to Fulbeck air base in England to pick up gliders, but there were no glider pilots, so they returned without them.

❦❧❦❧

March 7, 1944 [*Tuesday*]

My Darling,

I love you. I feel like the rose that has passed its bud and is grown, alive, healthy, and kissed by the bright rays of a sun, unknown to him.

You should have seen your future husband pressing a pair of OD pants. I am not truly an amateur but I am not the epitome of perfection. But, the job is done, not too good but not so horrible that I can't wear the pants.

My Love, you must forgive me. It is nearing your birthday. I haven't sent you a card. I am unable to buy a gift and all in all, I am so far from being a good lover that I am utterly ashamed of myself. In our whole courtship, I have yet to give you anything but my love. That may be sufficient to you but to me it is vague and I feel so miserably helpless. I have tried to satisfy your curiosities by small things of hardly any value. And even at that I failed. I sent you one statuette. I tried to get one recently but the price was preposterous. £2-10 Shillings ($9) for a dog. As it is, I came over £12 in debt. Or at least, the total of my present month's pay. You see, I raised my allotment to $75 per mo. So that we can have a fairly good start. My salary is approx. $50 per mo. There isn't much I can do with that, but it is worth it as long as you and I can get our feet planted. No excuses. They are plain, cold facts.

Gosh, Honey, I've missed you. What with no mail and then not being able to write to you, it created a void which did me no good. When I go off the beaten track, I don't spare the rails. But time marches on and we are, each day, getting closer to each other. Even in my lonely mind I can see primrose paths, quiet days, mounting happiness, and the strength of your companionship. One need not ask [*for*] more. Oh! My Darling, I shall never forget, no matter what the circumstances may bring.

I am so glad that Tom has written to you. Lucy has received her ring from Harry. You have nothing from me but my heart and soul. Someday — I promise I'll make everything up to you.

As good as I may feel, I didn't have any breakfast and I must get some chow. I'll close now. I have kept my date, but, believe me, I am not entirely satisfied.

So long, Honey. Give my love to Mother. May God Bless You. Take care of yourself. Love you — Love, Mike.

P.S.: Don't forget, Honey, My correct APO is <u>638</u>.

On March 7, the War Diary notes, nine planes took part in a squadron formation flight. Also that day, pilots, co-pilots, and radio operators attended a lecture by the Intelligence officer on security and censorship.

March 8, 1944 [*Wednesday*]
England

My Darling,

Your mail is really pouring thru'. I guess it has to because there was such a lull for such a long time. I received 3 letters from you last night. It is really great hearing from you. Letters are our only contact with you people. Of course, we think almost incessantly of the people we love but those letters are the closest we can get to you. Of late, I have been dissipating [*crossed out*] (Can't spell it; at least it doesn't look right.) "cutting up." I guess that happens when everything seems so new. The feeling will pass. I'll have to cut it out or I'd be a wreck. But really, Honey, the beer over here tastes very good. I'd trade it all for a moment with you. I love you ever so much, My Darling.

In this letter you speak of dogs. I don't recall if I ever mentioned that Mom has a cocker spaniel at home. She's a thorobred and has a title as long as nobility. But Mom calls her "Queenie." Little Stella Ann, my niece, started to call her "Keenie" and the name stuck.

The dog is a good creature. She understands Italian and English and she is a good comrade for Stella Ann, Thomas Michael (my Nephew) and the rest of the family. However, a spaniel such as that is a good house dog. I can't say that I like beagles. The slut or female is just that — ill-tempered and badly mannered, as a rabbit hound they are OK but — My favorite dogs are the Irish and English Setters, Labrador Retreiver [*crossed out*] (Damn! I can't spell worth hell this AM) retriever, the German Police dog [*Shepherd*], Dalmatian, and of course, the ever-gentle St. Bernard. My setter was called "Major" (or "Big Red"). He was a Hell of a fine field dog. I have no intermediate taste because my preference drops to the smaller dogs, like spaniels, terriers (not the Boston Bull) and so on. As a parallel, I have no love for the chow, spitz, dacshund (can't spell anything), and the Mexican hairless. So you see, My Dear, my liking falls to the field or man's dog array of animals. That's that for a while.

Gosh, Honey, I miss you. The English girl is a good sort but there is something lacking that sets a distinction to the clean-cut American girl. Your manner, your poise, your entire anatomy is so much to my [*liking*]. It surpasses anything that I have ever seen. Really, Darling, I can't help myself, you are my love, my real love.

All this may sound unhinged, but that's why I am so anxious to see Harry. We have so much in common. We have two women waiting for us who love us, and who we love so dearly. It will give me a chance to talk about something besides a skeleton.

Well, Bette, don't worry about that pregnant urge. It was merely an urge, like my sudden desire for chocolate. Surely, I can't be pregnant.

So long for now, Bette. Give my love to Mother. Take care of yourself. May God Bless You. Love, Mike.

The flying schedule for March 8 was cancelled because of bad weather. That afternoon there was a lecture for all flying personnel on radio briefing and navigation aids. The enlisted men practiced close order drill.

The March 9 War Diary entry read:

> **Flying personnel were lectured on chemical warfare and Engineering. One plane was sent to Edinburgh, Scotland and another to Barkston Heath to ferry gliders to the 315th T.C. Group. Squadron orders read: "Effective immediately, one complete crew will be available for emergency duty from 0800 to 1900 hours daily."**

March 10, 1944 [*Friday*]
England

My Darling,

I can't kick because the mail has been coming thru' quite regularly. But the one day that is missed, calls for definite gripe. Seriously though, Honey, I am "sweating out" the arrival of your picture. Can't wait to see that lovely face.

One of the more pleasant things around here is the fact that we hear a lot of good dance music. And there are plenty of dances about, so we can stay in practice. The majority of the English girls are good dancers. The whole trouble, in most part, it is difficult to understand their talking. I learned a new step the other night. It is a local step but good to know. I don't know what they call it. You take 3 full steps to the left. Stomp your feet 3 times; a full 3 steps to the right, 2 steps back, dip and twirl your partner around once and finish off in a waltz. That is repeated thruout the entire number. The one thing that makes it so entertaining is that the entire crowd does the same thing. It is really picturesque. Looks like [*how*] a mass waltz would look. (Diana [*sic*] Shore, "Sunday, Monday, Always.")

Darling, you must forgive me if I sound as if I am enjoying life. My brain was slightly warped from some things. This is such a pleasant change. My heart is in Kansas City. My body is in England. Gosh, Honey, the only thing that is wrong is that when I hear all that good music and watch all those supposedly happy faces, I get so that I miss you so terribly much. I know that may not sound so manly but it is the truth. When I watch these things happen, I want to sit down and have a good cry. I know when all this internal reaction is happening because the muscles in my jaws tighten so much they hurt. You can't blame me, My Dear, you are all I am asking for in this little ole' world, just as I found you and realized that you were it, I was on my way to a world I had never dreamed I'd see. It's true that it is a world of experience, but typically, of a peace-loving nation, I am content to find my experience in my own back yard, in the manner that I see fit.

Lucy writes to me and she tells me of all the planning that is going on at home. She tells me of all things that are being passed from person to person at home. When I hear that I think of you. You must plan alone. The only one you can tell it to is me. At least, I am the only one who appreciates how you feel and vice versa to you. One thing that we did decide upon was the fact that we wouldn't plan anything. So it shall be. But we will be married as quietly as we met. We will share our happiness together. You are all I am living for. I was never an extremist as far as plans go. My idea is that people know what they are expected to do. Do it and let the rest of the world hurry by. We have never painted pictures for our future, except to say that we will be content with each other and that things will be done once we are together again. We can't look beyond the immediate future. What more can we do? Sensibly speaking, we know that the future is not the brightest thing in the world because my name will be a number for a few more years. When we get to the end of that term, then, Woman, we can cease to be Sgt. & Mrs. But <u>Mr.</u> & <u>Mrs.</u> It's a great thing to look forward to. Oh! My Darling, I dream of it. I pray for it. I ask God to give us peace and the strength to go thru' these chaotic years and let us live the way He has always meant us to, in accord with each other, no animosity, no hatred and a distinct tolerance toward all races, creeds, and colors.

You must forgive my pen, Darling. There are so many ways to tell you that I love you. This is one of them. I must close for now. But there is more where this came from.

Give my love to Mother. Take care of yourself. May God Bless You, My Love. Oh! God! How much I love the Woman! Love, Mike.

March 10, 1944 [*Friday*]
England

My Darling, Bettyjeane,

This will surprise you immensely but I just felt like talking to you. Besides, I didn't write yesterday so I had better make up for it. You mentioned the good mail service in the letter that I received tonight. I am inclined to agree with you. For some reason, the service has been exceptionally good. Your letters are rather up to date, February 28.

We were discussing the various types of wives that some men get stuck with. Since it was purely a man's conversation, we didn't bother to degrade husbands. The most thoroughly discussed woman was the type that married and ran. We don't mean the kind that deserted but just the type that didn't give a damn. True! She sleeps with the man she marries but she'll sleep with anyone for that [*matter*]. Another was the one that told "John" what to do and when to do it. You aren't that type, are you, Honey? I mean can I wear the pants in the family. I am not skeptical because I believe that we are both level headed enough to decide things clearly, understandingly, and for the interest of both. Believe one thing, Darling, I shall never want to do anything, unless you are included.

You were speaking about this "Stinger." I had only one in my life but I was too drunk to taste it. I had run down the list of cocktails and the last one was just that. So you can see that I was nearly cold-cocked by that time. It didn't make any difference what I drank. It will be a long time before I get a chance to taste a legitimate American drink. Alcoholic drinks are almost a thing of the past. Beer is about the only thing of quantity that you can drink over here. And it is only like a watery beer. Warm and not too tasty, they have an excessively violent effect upon one's organs. They don't make you sick, purely well bloated. Don't be shocked, Darling, but most of my drinking has been wine, cognac, grappa, gin, and for the Christmas holidays, an excessive amount of American bourbon and Canadian Club. That, unfortunately, didn't last long. The other stuff that I mentioned is the kind of stuff that makes a young man age quickly, causes bunions, falling hair, and arches, tumors, softening of the brain, teeth, and finger nails, weak ankles, soft muscles, diluted pupils, and any sort of sickness that is a 4-F's dream. However, I am still alive and 1-A. Still fit to fly and still able to cause as much Hell as ever. Not to mention the fact that it hasn't made me the least bit sterile nor killed my feverish emotions.

Well, Honey, you might call this a drinker's parody but, at any rate, I talked. Must write to Mom. Love you so very much. May God Bless You. Love, Mike.

P.S.: Millionaire is spelled that way. (not "air"). OK. I must write to you and thank you for your fine thought in one of your letters. "You are my gift from God." It is indeed complimentary — Thank you so much. That will come later. M.

On March 10, the morning flight schedule was cancelled, so all combat crews were given a lecture on weather, according to the War Diary. There was one flight to Prestwick, Scotland, and three planes were being used to ferry gliders from Fulbeck to Spanhoe airfields. That night's orientation flights were also called off due to weather.

The March 11 War Diary entry read:

> **There was a Group Formation in the morning at which time the Officers and EM were reviewed by Brig. General Clark, C.O. 52nd TCW [*Troop Carrier Wing*]. The Group Executive Officer, Lt. Col. [*Walter*] Washburn, Jr., inspected the billets and offices. There was a Group Formation flight in the afternoon and one squadron plane made a night orientation flight.**

March 12, 1944 [*Sunday*]

My Darling,

It is Sunday, and it would be a wonderful day for making babies because the weather encourages indoor love.

Can't complain about the mails. I receive a letter from you almost every day. I have gotten your letters of Feb. 21 and 28. If it keeps pouring in this way, I'll be very happy. I am so happy that your nerves have settled down, at least I have accomplished a few things. I know that we are not wasting time, My Dear. It is just that it happened to me before, only then, the love that was, started to slip instead of gain. Each day to me is the same as it is to you, my love grows more intense. I am made unhappy only when I think that we must do all these things separately. I feel so strongly about our union. It is truly my idea of the perfect companionship. I have waited for this all my life. Each time I left you, I looked forward to seeing you again. Before you, my dates used to be distasteful at times. I dreaded the thought of what was to happen and above all the climax. Really, all in all, it was the emptiest feeling in the world. If you can imagine me as being a person who lacked enthusiasm for happiness, then you readily see what changes were prompted upon me. All this may sound strange to you but it is all very true.

In the summer, to counteract and avoid a lot of embarrassment on my part, I used to spend my weekends on LI [*Long Island*], swimming and fishing. Never with the person I was supposed to be with but with my friends. When I went to a ball game on Saturdays, I'd take little Mickey, my kid cousin, because I could have a vent for my joys. On Feb. 22, 1942, five of us went out for a drive on LI. It was beautiful, a typical pre-spring day. We had dinner in a big roadhouse on Sunrise Blvd. Since the music was so beautiful and we were having a great time, we stayed very late. Next day, I was accused, very distastefully, of endangering the young lady's character. That was trust from people who were supposed to know me well.

One time, prior to my enlistment, we went out to have a big fling. Most of us were leaving for the service. The young lady I was with got drunk and gave me the cruelest treatment I had ever had. Perhaps, I told you about that. What I am trying to say, My Darling

Bette, is that, more and more each day I review my past and I see why I love you so much and why I appreciate you all the more.

You must forgive me if I speak the way I do but I want you to know me as I know myself. Since all these things have happened to me, I want you to know them. I ask for no pity. Hell! It's all in a course of life. I want you to know that I thank God for you.

Must close, My Love. Take care of yourself. May God Bless you. I love you so very much. Love, Mike.

The March 12 War Diary entry continued to tell of bad weather. All morning flights were cancelled, and "All personnel had the afternoon free."

On March 13,

The engineering department began the installation of pararacks on all squadron planes. Afternoon schedule called off. In the evening seven of our planes participated in a Group Formation flight.

March 14, 1944 [*Tuesday*]

My Darling,

You are going to listen to one of the proudest GIs in the whole USAAF. Darling, I received your picture. There are no words that can explain my elation. I strutted like a peacock. Showed your picture to everyone. It sits proudly on top of my locker and I have requested that everyone must remove his hat, if he wishes to gaze upon your very lovely countenance. Maybe I'm wrong or maybe I'm showing my conceit but it does look as if your expression was meant especially for me. Bette, my morale quota jumped 99%. One percent off because I can't be near you. No kidding, Honey, I can't tell you how much your picture meant to me. Every chance I get, I just sit and look. To boot, you couldn't have added any better words. I have put your small note in the frame with your picture. The day I come home, I am going to make those words stand.

Darling, you mustn't fret. We have been apart a long time. Thank God, the time has passed quickly. I must ask you to stay patient. If only in this God-created world I could tell you something definite, I would. You must be prepared for a long wait. As much as I hate it, I must keep telling you that. There is no sense to kid each other. We are too old for fairy tales. This mess has made us older. We are told to face the inevitable and that we must. We must let our love be our standard. I know that it is strong enough to help us beat off time passing. You are living on a promise. I am living on a hope. Between us, we are being asked to do something which our democratic minds are used to repelling. We don't think of the next person because he (or she) think the same as we do, only in accord with his (or her) ideas. Darling, I do love you. I do miss you. I do want you. There is nothing more in this whole wide world I care for. I have told you this often but I repeat it because the circumstances of the times push the point. I know that my words sound feeble, but in repetition, unlike the oft-used coffee bean, I hope that they, my words, gain strength. We are battling from two sides of this world. We are both the typical American. We can't lose. As I said before, they can try to beat us down physically and mentally but they can't make us forget what we have to go home to. You are my shining light. Each day that passes you shine brighter. Someday, with the help of God, you will again be my pillar of life and light of my soul. To the ears of the critic, my drama may sound like the "Ham" in Hamlet but to me, they are my only depth of description. Bear with me. I am yours.

Darling, I must close. I forgot to mention that I received your letters of January 16 and February 17th (the one with the regular stamp). I'll answer those as soon as I can. You know my conception of soon. I rarely waste time. Love you so much. May God Bless You. Gratefully in Love, Mike.

March 14, 1944 [*Tuesday*]
England

My Darling,

Received 3 more letters from you and a birthday card. Letters are dated February 24, 25 and March 3rd. Thank you so much, My Love. Gosh! Honey, I do love you. I know I said that earlier in the day. If the guy reads this doesn't like it, well. — Besides, I never grow tired of saying it.

Quite to the contrast to the fact that you have cut down on your cigarette consumption, I smoke nearly a pack to a pack and ½ per day. I don't know why. I wish I could get some exercise. I might have a chance to cut down.

I meant to tell you, Darling, I enjoy those columns but I just about get time to read them. I have cut down quite a bit on my reading since I have been here. I don't know why but it just happened.

I understood your viewpoint about sterility to the utmost. Men are different. If they are constructed the way I am, there is no such a thing as periodic moments. Sometimes I wish I wasn't that way but I can't very well combat something that has been built into my organism.

That remark I made about skating was just as I meant it. I am a flop. You mustn't fret about those sports events, My Darling, I shall never let you out of my sight and I do want company wherever I go.

One thing I'd like to straighten out. I realize that it will be a financial burden to go East to Tom's ordination but under the circumstances you must. I have instructed Lucy to send you the money if it is necessary. And even if you are short when you get to my home, you will never have to worry. Gosh, Honey, I do want you to go. Not only because of the fact that the occasion is an important one in our lives but because the change will help you. You see, you will be my representative. Since I cannot appear, someone has to be there from our, yours and mine, side of the family. Bette, do think it over and discuss it with me and

Chicha. She has control of my finances as meager as they are. She will see that everything is under control for my sake. Please give me an affirmative answer. It isn't too often that I ask you to favor me.

Well, Honey, I must close. My hand feels like it has been thru' a potato masher. I have written so much I can hardly straighten my fingers.

Give my love to Mother. Take care of yourself. May God Bless You. Love you and miss you ever so much. Love, Mike.

The War Diary entries for March 14 and 15 read:

March 14: Squadron Formation flying in the afternoon and evening. A lecture on chemical warfare was given in the afternoon.
March 15: All squadron Enlisted personnel moved from building No. 42 to building No. 40 to provide room for the Ground Echelon when they arrive. One battalion of paratroops arrived on the base to take part in a practice paratroop mission drop on Friday night. In the afternoon Instrument and Navigation flying.

March 16, 1944 [*Thursday*]

My Darling,

I received your letters of 13th and 14th of February. I imagine by this time, you must know my current address.

Your letter of the 13th told me of your fall and injury. It's tough, Honey. I hate like Hell to see people fall. It renders them so helpless and at times those damn falls can really be very injurious. I do too wish that I was there to treat your knee. I had forgotten of the last event when I treated Mother. It is strange that time can put dents into one's memory.

You talked of that stew. Ugh! I am afraid that the army has done much to put a deflation on my palate. Food tastes commonplace. It is no longer a treat to sit down to a good meal. I was never too heavy an eater but I do enjoy a good meal. Remember the night we had dinner at the Hotel Keenan in Ft. Wayne? The only thing we could get was shrimp cocktail. That was one of my last contacts with good American food. Ah Woe!

It seems as if your mail service isn't so bad. According to your letter of the 14th, you received my letter of Jan. 31 in good time. Darling, again, I must remind you of your spelling. Think I'll have to conduct a special course for you. Don't be too angry with me, I get conscious of those things occasionally.

You do ask a few questions, don't you? [*One entire paragraph was razor censored.*]

I think that Bettyjeane is a very nice name. You see, you can't spite me by calling me

Michael because it is the name that most all of my friends called me. It's a nice name but rather a sticky one. Mike's OK.

You know, Honey, I think I'm putting on weight. I can't seem to get any exercise and it beats the Hell out of me. Seems the English people don't care for basketball. It is hard for us to locate a court. That weight is only a temporary condition. I don't suspect that I'll have it as easy as I have. Things are changed though. I felt that we had pioneered a lot of things before. Now, everything is laid before us.

Well, Honey, I must be rushing off. I'm afraid that I have some sleep to catch up on. Can't seem to get enough of that and I haven't been goofing off. Just one of those periods when I can't seem to be satisfied.

So long, Darling. Give my love to Mother. Take care of yourself. May God Bless You. —Love you and miss you more each day. Love, Michael.

On March 16, the War Diary recorded a chemical warfare lecture in the morning, squadron formation flying in the afternoon, and group formation flying in the evening. Engineering personnel continued the installation of pararacks.

There were no flights on March 17, because all planes were being readied for a practice mission, though it was called off due to bad weather.

The March 18 War Diary entry noted:

> **Ten planes took part in a paratroop drop mission at 1400 hours. In the morning the glider pilots arrived from Sicily. Preparations were being made for the remainder of the ground echelon scheduled to arrive at 0200 hours tomorrow.**

March 19, 1944 [*Sunday*]

My Darling,

I had intended to write one of my unusually long letters but right in the middle of all my corresponding, I was rudely interrupted. However, your mail is still catching up to me, the latest that I received were dated February 6th and 11th.

You needn't worry about the fact that I might lose my taste for that golden liquid. The more I refrain or at least the more I don't get a chance for it, the more I thirst. That bottle of Seagram's will be like a drop in a bucket. You needn't worry about "just looking at it." So you went out and bought a few new, floppy, big hats. I guess you must have been in a mood of some sort. You did say once before that you went shopping when something went wrong or if you didn't feel just right. Good sport, if you can afford it.

You know, Darling, it's funny but I never thought of the fact that you worry about me. I accept things as they come. I worry about things that don't affect me physically. As far as something that might come from this nasty ole' war, it never bothers me. I still contend that that is the only way to feel. I don't like to lose sleep because something might happen. Let it, then it will be too late to worry. But that is too morbid a thing to discuss. I like to look into that future. Kinda' like the odor of orange blossoms, lilies of the valley, etc. The idea of a cozy living room, all the perfection of our home and above all the kindness that will be given, the kindness of life.

You talk about the substitution of religion for love. Aside from those that are gifted by the love of the life of the religious, we can accept that as being, just partially true. Those that turn to religion must be also gifted. There are so many times that disappointment in love can cause an opposite effect. You know, the drunkard, the heathen driven by lost love, the sex-crazed. When a person turns to religion, he must give up a lot of the pleasures of life as we know them. He prays for strength of mind. I can't seem to put my mind on the subject, so I'll drop it. But if you ever decide to leave me, I think I'll turn to drink. Gosh, Honey, I do love you.

Darling, I can't seem to make my words strong enough in this letter. All I know is that I miss you terribly. Chicha writes so often of her plans. It hurts to think that we must wait so long. We are getting restless. It is a very normal reaction. Let time pass, OK! But keep us going so that it will pass. It is fine to think but one can't be left to do too much of it. Your picture is a great comfort to me. It looks down on me. A lot of times, I control my tongue so that I don't cuss in front of you. The other day I let out a stream of words that would make Satan look up to Heaven and pray for me. I swear, I saw you frown, Darling. You look angelic. If I didn't know you so well, I'd swear that you were an angel. My Darling, I miss you and love you so very much.

I am going to close only because my tone doesn't ring right in my ears. So I shan't bore you any longer.

Give Mother my love. Take care of yourself. May God Bless You — Love, Michael.

The ground echelon personnel arrived on schedule on March 19. They were given a hot meal and assigned billets, according to the War Diary. That afternoon, three bags of accumulated mail were distributed.

The next day, Captain Joseph Sotak gave a lecture on "Driving Regulations," while the ground personnel were given the day off to rest from their trip.

The March 21 War Diary entry noted the beginning of mission planning from the squadron's new base:

> **Defense lecture for all combat crews. Captain Cooney, Intelligence Officer, gave a lecture on Censorship and Security to the ground echelon personnel. Combat crews were assigned for a paratroop drop mission. Planes were loaded at 1100 hours and all details of the proposed mission were covered very carefully. Pilots, navigators, radio operators, company commanders and jumpmasters participated. Mission called off due to inclement weather.**

March 22, 1944 [*Wednesday*]

My Darling,

Haven't received word from you for a few days but I am really not kicking. [*I crossed out the following: "I just got back from"*] All I know is that I love you more each day. It is a very tough deal but every time I see some of these English gals, I get more and more homesick for you. It leaves such an empty feeling within me that I just can't help myself. No one can come close to you, My Dear.

I saw *Pride of the Yankees* last nite. I had seen it over 2 years ago but it was the idea of having something to do. The picture impressed me more now than it did then. I guess it must be due to the passing years. The passing years that tend to mature the mind to the realization that life holds so much. You know the story of the picture. Above all, I couldn't help but to be grateful for what their love meant to each other. It is necessary to experience all that before the feeling can have any depth. Darling, I feel so deeply for you. Somehow or other my mind is blunt. It cannot help me to express what I want to. It cannot tell you how much I love you and miss you. It cannot tell you how I feel when I see so many things happen and I can't tell you of it. My mind revolves around us. I get fed up with the pettiness and stupidity of some of my associates. But all in all, there is nothing that I can do to alter my ideas or theirs. One must drift with the tide of the present because he knows that one day he will be on an open sea and he will be able to navigate toward his own goal. All this may sound circular and unattached. I can't help that because there is so much I have to leave unsaid. I realized last night that I shall never be truly happy until I am with you again. You are my whole life. These are not just words, they are my heart.

I cannot help but to make this a short letter. I am going to close for now but I assure you that I won't stay away from this pen and paper for long.

So long, My Darling, take care of yourself. Thank God the time is moving. It is spring our hearts feel it, but the feeling is numbed by the distance.

May God Bless You — Love, Mike.

The March 22 to 25 War Diary entries detailed practice missions, lectures, and entertainment:

> **March 22: At 1900 hours, 12 C-47s took off carrying pararacks and fully-equipped paratroopers on a practice drop. One plane returned to the field due to one engine cutting out. Paratroops on this plane were transported by truck to the drop zone. The other 11 planes carried out their mission successfully and returned to base at 2300 hours.**
>
> **March 23: After having lived in tents the men appreciate sleeping in barracks and feel that this base compares favorably with any back**

in the States. **Glider Tow in the morning and afternoon. Two planes dropped paratroopers and one plane cross country and return. All combat crews attended a lecture.**

March 24: Capt. Sotak lectured on "Driving in the British Isles." Two planes dropped paratroopers in the afternoon and one practiced night landings and flight check. A directive was posted advising all personnel that passes would be issued for one 48-hour pass per month and more frequent passes for lesser intervals.

March 25: A dance was held for EM at the A.R.C. [*American Red Cross*] **Club with the A.T.S.** [*Army Transportation Service — the British military service for women*] **girls in attendance. Two planes dropped paratroopers in the morning. All other scheduled flying called off due to weather.**

March 26, 1944 [*Sunday*]
APO 133

My Darling,

I haven't received any mail from you the last few days and I haven't been able to write. I hope you noted my correct APO <u>above</u>, APO 133.

In your letter of the 12th I noted your paragraph about English women. You mentioned that the women back home were angry about these Anglo-American marriages. I can't blame them but what can they do about it. You see these women have so much in common with our girls back home. Really the only difference is that we are Americans and they are English. The most important thing, though, is where our boys hearts are. I have seen many beautiful English girls. I have spoken and danced with many. But I'm afraid they can't even carry a candle to you, My Darling. I am not impressed. We share too much to even make me forget it. You know, Bette, I was never a lady's man. I never cared for conquests nor was I always "tagging" after a skirt. I know where my happiness is. Even in this temporary world, I hate temporary happiness. You and I have set our standard. A standard which was mutually agreed upon. One which would set us both for life, a happy, full and satisfying one. What more could one ask for? It is like my brother Lou said, "You know Mike, I am resting now. This inactivity is of no value to me. Even a few dates don't help because my heart is with Sally." And it has been two years for him. My words are inadequate to tell you how much you mean to me.

Darling, I am cutting this short. I must write to Harry and thank him for some envelopes and other things that he has sent me. I promise you I shan't let so much time pass between letters. Again it was circumstances. You must be quite used to that word by now.

Well, Honey, happy dreams. I love you so much. In another week it will be a year since our meeting. If we could only turn the clock back.

Take care of yourself. May God Bless You. Love, Mike.

On March 26, two planes dropped paratroopers, while another flew to Hendon air base in England and back. Another paratroop drop was called off at the last minute due to weather. The War Diary also noted that the men of the rear echelon who had been assigned to the baggage detail arrived and the bags were distributed.

Nine of the 37th's planes were used to drop paratroopers the afternoon of March 27. Intelligence Officer Captain Cooney and Sergeant John Henshaw from S-2 accompanied the mission as observers. These missions, which were carried out with the 506th and 507th PIRs (Parachute Infantry Regiments) of the 101st Airborne, were named "Curveball I, II, and III," according to the 45th Squadron War Diary.

March 28, 1944 [*Tuesday*]
APO 133

My Darling,

I knew that it couldn't last too long that's one reason I refused to be too excited by the whole thing. So again I complain for the lack of mail. It is almost a week since I heard from you. I must be content with a memory of my last letter from you.

I had started to write to you yesterday but there was so much confusion that I couldn't get started. To top it all, I concentrated on a book, found it so enjoyable and entertaining that I finished it completely. It is *Turnabout* by Thorne Smith. He is the author of the *Topper* series. This book was made into a film but I don't think the film quite covered the perfection of humor. If you recall, thru' some medium of earnest wishing, man and wife change sexes. The picture climaxes with the husband's pregnancy. Hell! The book practically starts there. All in all, it was one of the funniest books I have ever read. You must read it.

In my letter yesterday, I had started on a tangent about the weather and then I branched off to a discourse on my early life. I didn't get near to finishing the letter. But the weather was beautiful yesterday. It would have been perfect to walk arm in arm along some country lane and welcome the first signs of spring. Today, a knife as sharp as life's best wits couldn't cut the fog.

23 years ago today, Bette, your lover became a reality. Some times I wonder if it should have happened. Seriously though, Darling, I am happy to be alive. I don't have too much to kick about life. Describing the smaller things of life, I can't complain. So far I have done everything any normal fellow would do. I have felt every emotion that life has to offer except the one that climaxes life. Except for a few things that have happened to me singularly you are the brightest star in my entire existence. You have given me more than I have ever hoped for. Family love means a lot to a person but there is a certain amount of irresponsibility that is attached to it. Small things like war make a person reckless. But once he has added something more to his life, it is necessary to think

of a different road. I am prepared, as you are, to start a new generation and to start ourselves on an independent life, dependent only on ourselves. I like the idea tremendously. Don't you, Bette? We have never been pessimistic but if anything happens to disturb our plans, don't feel badly about it, Darling. I want you to realize that we have something, if anything alters our plans. At least, we have had it. But I know you don't like to discuss it and I don't like to talk about it. It seems so foolish to nip a bud before it blossoms. I love you.

Well, Bette, My Little (?) Chickadee, I'll say *adieu* for now. I do hope I get some mail tonight.

Give my love to Mother. Take care of yourself. Young Lady, you are beautiful. If you keep looking at me like that, I'll have to marry you. You are making a lot of guys jealous of me.

May God Bless You. Love, Mike.

On March 28, six planes were used for glider towing and one plane dropped paratroopers. According to the War Diary, Captain Cooney gave a short talk on "Current Events" at the cinema before the evening performance, and Captain Sotak lectured on "Chemical Warfare."

March 29, 1944 [*Wednesday*]
England — APO 133

My Darling,

I guess I can call this a red letter or at least a many letter day. I received 5 letters from you today. Dates — March 4, 7, 8, 10 and 20. I especially like the idea of the 20 — only 9 days for your letter and it was to [*APO*] 638. Aside from that I received a long-awaited letters from Tom and Tony. Tony sent a bunch of pictures of "Reb," Sheila and himself. Reb is 3 months old. She's an adorable baby. Sheila looks much prettier than she ever was and Tony looks just like old Tony. Tom's letter was most welcome as most letters are but in his letter, he writes rather glowingly of you. It is so very good to hear. I have told him that he will meet you at his ordination but definitely.

Darling, I do things so stupidly at times. I should be more considerate. Your birthday passed and I didn't think a thing about a gift. What I mean is that I didn't send you anything directly but I could have had Chicha pick out a gift for you. I feel so miserably stupid about my failings. You know that I love you so very much and I hate to feel as if I am not doing enough for you. And I'm not. But really almost always my hands are tied and I can't move at all. If I could do some good cussing, I would certainly put my head under all my vows.

Darling, you are a heartless creature. You go thru' a short discourse about that poor kid who hadn't heard from her husband for such a long time. You admit that made you feel badly, too, and then you turn around and say that you hadn't heard from me for 6 days. Sounded like "I work hard all day over a hot stove and you, big lug, you go out and get drunk." Seriously though, I'm sorry you haven't received that dog yet. Damn this mail service, sometimes they are so miserably slow about mail.

You know I never did tell you much about this country. One of the most important things is the pubs. They open at 11 AM-3 PM and 6-10 in the eve. It is almost impossible to buy whiskey (which they call spirits). My favorite beers are Guinness Stout, and Worthington Ale. The beer costs 1 shilling (20 cents) per glass. Most of it is very watery. There is no such thing as a bar. They usually serve you thru' a cubby hole. You carry your glass to the smoke (smoking) room and drink at your leisure. By now, you can be assured that the pub is one thing which I have made an extensive study of.

Next, they drive on the wrong side of the road. Their cars are small and not too unlike a small Crosley or Austin. One of the things that has impressed me most of all is the fact that most of their homes are wonderful structures. Most of them look like "our little home in the country." Above all, cleanliness is definitely prominent, Thank God. The English like their beer and dancing. The beer for the elders and the dancing for the younger people. (Bette, did you once mention the song, "How Sweet You Are"?) I just heard it, it's beautiful.

I know you want to know about the women. To be honest about it, I can't do too good a job about description. Very much like all men of any nation, the women are no different; that is, for a variety of facial and physical characteristics. The women here are well dressed. Silk stockings are rare but the English women do not like to expose their legs (I guess that must be due to the changing atmosphere). Stockings, I do believe are mostly cotton or at lest a good imitation of silk or nylon. The clothes, outer, are like our American styles, except that they aren't as stylish. Black is used here as in America, not as mourning. There are a lot of low shoes and a lot of Dutch wooden shoes. Why? I don't know. Gosh, Honey, I can't say much more because I haven't made too close a study. Would you want me to get deeper into the subject or would you be jealous?

The phone booths are funny affairs. They are usually outdoors and look like a policeman's booth. When you make a call, you call your number and when you are answered you deposit the money. There are 3 slots for money. 1 pence (2 cents), 6 pence (12 cents), and one shilling (20 cents). There is an abundance of 2 pence and 6 pence stores (5 and Dime stores) owned by Woolworth's, of course. Walking down main street of one of the larger cities is just like going down to the Plaza [*in Kansas City*]. You can do a lot of window shopping. All stores are closed on Thursdays. In the larger cities, the ballrooms are much like the Trianon and Aragon in Chicago but they aren't quite as beautiful. Well, Darling, do you think that will hold you for a while? After all, you have to give me some chance to see more.

Sorry about the wrong spelling of your name, Bettyjeane. In your letter of the 7th, you mentioned the fact that you were going to see *Student Prince*. There was a little place on Long Island (or was it NY?) that we used to frequent. Almost every time, they would put on a show featuring excerpts from the operetta. It was truly beautiful. The voices were excellent and the music perfect. I know that you will enjoy it extremely. (Do you notice all the scratching I've done on this page? I can't help it. These guys don't know how to keep quiet.)

I do wish that I could be part of the GIs in that picture *Familiar Haunts*. If I were, we would be together again. Darling, in 2 more days it will be a year. Of it all, we have been apart 8 months. 8 months of the loneliest, unhappiest days of my life. I don't mean that in the depressive sense. Merely that I have felt lost without you. I missed you from the day that you left Ft. Wayne. When you left that Sunday morn, I didn't feel like sleeping, even though I was tired. I had the emptiest feeling in the world. I knew that day that I had lost something that I had to come back to reclaim. I wish you had never left. Why didn't we get married? You could have come with me to NY and then when I left for overseas you could have done what you wished — NY or KC. Maybe you would have had something real to remember me by. Something that could have made up for my absence. Something to love and look after until I got this mess cleared up. Now you must live on a mental memory. Darling, we could have had 2 or 3 weeks of the completest happiness in the world. Darling, I love you more each day. As I told Lucy, I am madly, deeply, blindly in love and I am happy for it. I'll be back, Darling. They say that if you are determined to do something, you can. I am determined to come back to you, more determined to do that than anything I have ever wanted to do.

Darling, I love you. My words are for you and they symbolize what you mean to me. Never have I felt so excited about anything. I want you and I <u>am</u> going to take you and make you my very own.

Good night, Darling, you must <u>forgive</u> this <u>very</u> <u>short</u> letter. Give my love to Mother. Take care of yourself, My Darling. May God Bless You. Love, Mike.

All scheduled flying on March 29 was called off due to weather. The War Diary also noted: "A lecture on 'Familiarization with Base Defense Plans' was attended by all personnel."

March 30, 1944 [*Thursday*]
APO 133

Good Evening, My Darling,

I guess I haven't talked myself out yet. Of course, there is no definite course for me to steer this evening but I'm sure you don't mind if I let out a spiel or two.

It is rather quiet around here tonight. The usual "town goers" are gone or getting ready to go. A couple of the boys are playing Solitaire. There is the usual bull session going on. You see a bunch of us live in one large room. There isn't as much room for privacy. These boys are the most carefree that I have ever known. You couldn't possibly feel low because they won't give you a chance to be. We have a set of trap drums, a violin, an accordion, a flute, and a mandolin. It seems that there's music around here all the time. I do mean noise. (You must forgive me, Bette, I took time out to see a movie. *Passport to Suez* or something like it. I never saw so many characters in all my life.) Unfortunately, a break like that usually throws me off my subject. Now, I'll probably think of something new.

You can see so many characters in the army. We have one kid. He is only 19 yrs. old. He is as tall as I am, weighs 150 lbs., has a size 14 foot (That's big!). He's a virgin and you should hear the ribbing he takes. When he talks about the fine art of intercourse, he will go thru' a long discourse, use the words of Webster's special and say nothing that is of any importance at all. It really is something to laugh at. Last night, one of the guys showed me one of those lewd stories that concerns the young widow and the farmer's son of 15. I couldn't possibly help but to have the usual reaction of a normal (?), growing (?), young (?) boy. The kid didn't even know what the Hell was going on. Maybe it's better to be that way.

Remember the noise I was talking about. It's started. I can't help but to be distracted. You can blame these guys if my letter falls apart and sounds like a mumble jumble of words. Thank God. He's stopped. One of the guys came in drunk and he started to chew my ear off. He was just about able to stand. Gad! It must be good to get in that condition. I never get like that (?). Oh, Well, a guy can't stay sober and enjoy life.

Darling, Id' like to go on and speak endlessly to you. But ole' John [*Underwood*], and Wild Bill [*Toohey*] are starting to "goo-goo" and fall all over each other. One guy is in good shape, the other, eek!

Honey, I must close. Damn those guys. A guy can't concentrate. Good night, Darling. I love you so very much. I miss you so very much. Give my love to Mother. Take care of yourself. May God Bless You. Love, Mike.

On March 30, there were more practice flights, and, according to the War Diary, another lecture on "Chemical Warfare."

The next day, all personnel attended a group formation and passed in review for the Group Commanding Officer on the parade grounds. One additional plane was assigned to the squadron; two were taken up to check equipment, and twelve were used for training personnel. That evening, the British Special Service arranged for a piano recital at the American Red Cross Club, which was "well received."

The following was placed at the end of the March War Diary, with no author noted:

> **Remarks: Entering the ETO** [*European Theater of Operations*]**, as a tactical organization, high in morale and proud of its record of accomplishment during the 17 months of previous Foreign Service in the Middle east and later North African Theater of Operations, the enlisted men of this squadron are confused and dismayed at prevailing conditions at this station. The enlisted men of this troop carrier Squadron are mostly Technically Trained and have built up**

their enviable records in Foreign Service in pursuit of this training. Now, however, these men are daily being assigned to duties that are basically those of a service squadron and the work of basics that this squadron lacks. At the same time, the men are called upon to perform all the technical and administrative work required in the operation of the Troop carrier organization. In a theater where it is apparent that every stress is being made for improvement of courtesy and discipline, it is felt that this condition is not best for good morale, pride in their work or the incentive to repeat a fine record.

April 1, 1944 [*Saturday*]
<u>Someone's a Fool Day</u>

Dearest Darling Bette,

Since there is a big black-jack (cards) game going on, I guess I'll be able to dash off a note. I erred. I got no further than one line when a friend of mine walked in. I met this guy many months ago when I was still in Alliance [*Nebraska*]. I tried to locate him for many months. Next thing I know he walked in on me. I have had long talks with him. It is nice to know a guy, haven't seen him for a long time and then get to discuss things that have passed. But, nevertheless, that doesn't come close to the subject I wanted to write about. I know that I shan't be able to concentrate so I won't even attempt to be the author of one of my long letters. After all, Darling, this is our first anniversary. I wonder often what power was at hand to bring us together. I never intended to go to that dance and I never did see Glen Gray. It was a pleasant turn of affairs. Such a meager turn of affairs that it changed our whole life. Gonna' make this one page long but I'll make up for it. Somewhat like that cocktail hour (and how I would like a juicy martini), this is just a bunch of mingled ideas. I tried to send you a few of "Sad Sack's" antics but it seems that too is a restriction. So you see you must be denied a laugh or two.

Honestly, this is a miserable old letter. I'll just end it and start over soon. I think I can do a Hell of a better job than this.

Take it easy, Honey. Miss you. May God Bless you. Love, Mike.

A dance was held at the American Red Cross Club on April 1, according to the War Diary, with a 15-piece Army band performing. The SIDECAR mission — a training mission to drop British paratroops — which had been scheduled for early Sunday morning, was postponed due to bad weather.

April 2, 1944 [*Sunday*]
Palm Sunday

My Darling,

I received your letters of the 16 and 18 of March. It has been a long time since this date. Just a year, but it seemed like such a long year. Today is another nice day for making babies. Unfortunately, you are in one part of the world, and I'm in another part. You were talking about that "Liberty Street." There is such an avenue in Brooklyn. I think I forget whether it is Liberty St. or Ave. It isn't very far from my home. Gosh, Honey, I've been interrupted at least [*ten*] different times. It's no wonder I can't get a decent letter written. I didn't mention that I had received your snapshot, too. Darling, I can't help but to repeat that you are a very beautiful girl. There is nothing like pictures. One of these days, I might get a chance to get a few made, one never knows. You did always have a flair for large hats. Some people don't like that but I think they are perfect. Especially something that is that color. In one of close-ups, there is a very definite curve exposed. Darling, you must forgive me but I couldn't help but to have a funny feeling. One might call it a touch of excitement. I guess that is a woman's duty. At any rate, you can see that I study your pictures closely. A long frame like yours needs a lot of weight to show. The more I look at your picture, the more I love and miss you. You did spell one word wrong unintelligent has two "l's." Glad to hear that you got a raise. Someone has to make the money in this family. Don't worry about the Cards. They aren't even going to get the pennant next year. Especially if I get home to root for the Dodgers. Darling, you needn't ever worry about getting one letter a week. I feel miserable if I don't write at least once a day. When I miss that day, I feel as if I haven't talked to you. I never want to do that. I want to be with you always.

One year ago today, the sky was clear, there was still a war going on and one lanky corporal was on his way to meet one lanky blonde. They were all set to go on a course of the nicest two months any people ever had. And when that was over, they were going to spend each day falling harder and harder in love with each other. Really, Darling, the climax for me came on my first visit home. Then I knew that I was missing something. On my second visit home, I was sure. I never did see you before I left. If we only knew. But that isn't what I started to say. We met and the next day, we walked and talked. I don't think we had a drink. Bette, I can't tell you how grateful I am for all that happened during those few months. If I never enjoy any more of that life, I want you to know that I loved you every minute of it. I never doubted, never shall doubt that we were meant for each other. When I come home, we will be inseparable as two peas in a pod. We have a long wait, Darling, but we have been separated for 9 months and only a short while ago, so it seemed, it was 3 months. The time has flown. I pray to God that He will continue to make time pass.

Well, Darling, I must say so long. Give my love to Mother. Take care of yourself. I am being as careful as the times will allow me to be. I love you and miss you so very much. May God Bless You. Love, Michael.

The SIDECAR mission was rescheduled and cancelled again two more times, on April

2 and 3. Lieutenant Robert Roman gave a lecture on April 2 to new personnel on censorship and security.

The War Diary also noted on April 3 that Captain Cooney, the Squadron Intelligence Officer, left to attend Intelligence School at Ascot, England, southwest of London.

April 4, 1944 [*Tuesday*]
APO 133

My Darling,

Received your letter of the 14th. You can see that the mail situation hasn't straightened itself, yet. I got a letter from Lucy today. She told me that the date is set for Tom's ordination, June 6th. He'll say his first mass on the 11th of June. She also stated that they had written to the Red Cross in an attempt to get me home for the great day. As much as I'd like to be home, I wish they hadn't done it. However, you can see how big the day is for us. The reason I say that I wish they hadn't done it is that it is purely a matter of principle. Do my stretch like everyone else and get it over with. God! It will be a great day. I told all the guys about it and they are all pulling for that one chance. I'd be happy just to see Tom's first Mass, see all of you and head back to the theater that my outfit is in. Honey, I couldn't possibly tell you what I feel. My heart is so full of joy for Tom that I can't put it into words. When something like that happens, I am not as eloquent as I am usually. You see, My Darling, we have waited 10 years for this. It is much easier to tell you of my love for you because it is new. It won't be stretched over such a span of years. Once we are married, it will be a lifetime of keeping it a new love. Do you see what I am trying to say?

I meant to mention that our favorite censor promised to wring my neck if I didn't send you his love. He asks about you always. Pappy has been sick and I can't get to see him. It has been 3 weeks since I saw him last. He hasn't seen your picture yet. As soon as he is well, I am sure we will sit in for a long jaw session.

I am hoping to see Harry soon or have I said that already? He is in the Air Corps. He's a ground officer.

I would like to have gone to the Art gallery with you. There will be a million and one things to discuss. It will be nice to learn things together. It's true that our art education isn't too extensive but it isn't hard to learn. You'll recall how deeply impressed we were with the Easter special at the Gallery last year. The lighting effect was perfect. The way that cross looked, one could not help but be left breathless by the exhibition. If I'm not mistaken, we made a few quick quips about the armored suits that were in that large room.

Darling, I must close for now. Gosh, my letters have been pitiful for the last few days but you must realize that it isn't my fault.

Give my love to Mother. Missed a letter and forgot the most important words. I do love you so very much. Take care of yourself, Darling, miss you. May God Bless You. Love, Mike.

The SIDECAR mission, consisting of 13 squadron planes participating in a Wing paratroop drop mission, was successfully carried out on April 4, according to the War Diary. Major General Royce, Commanding General of the IX Troop Carrier Command (TCC), visited the base on a general inspection tour. A dance for enlisted men was held that evening.

The April 5 War Diary entry read:

> **Lecture on Chemical Warfare. Two planes cross country; one secret, the other to Stanstead** [*air base in England*].

April 6, 1944 [*Thursday*]

My Darling,

Stopped right there. It is one of those funny letters which I have no ideas whatsoever. I wrote to Harry this afternoon. My cousin [*Ben Alfieri*] and a fairly good friend of mine [*Dr. Nick Ippolito*] are over here. With all the people I know over here, it's no wonder I don't find one of them. You can guess why I am writing like this, haven't received a letter from you for quite some time. I haven't done any reading for quite a while and I can't very well discuss that. I have read a few Perry Mason, Ellery Queen, and Charlie Chan mysteries, but they are hardly the things that call for discussion. All I know is that I love you very much.

When Harry wrote, he asked me if I could suggest anything for my sister's birthday in June. Hell, Honey, you know I couldn't possibly suggest anything. I'm so ignorant about those things. That's one of the first lessons that you'll have to start teaching me. You know consideration of people and how to treat them. You needn't worry about yourself. I know how to manage or did I do a bad job of keeping you happy? I don't mean physically — I am talking about my etiquette and stuff. I never did court you with flowers and candy, and stuff. The only thing I ever got you was an orchid. Little did you know that it knocked me down to the last sou I had. I was really left quite broke. What a love I am! But you can't say that I starved you or let you get thirsty. I think between the two of us, we nearly drank Kansas City dry. Gosh, Honey, there are so many things I can think of. So many moments of pure joy that made my parting days from the states a joy I'll never forget. The words that sounded like drops from heaven were the words that hit me like a thunderbolt. "Mike, I think I'm in love with you." You know, Bette, I think I believe in that woman's intuition that they talk about. Remember when I met you. I mean the time right after that, when I insisted that it was just a game. I said that it would be you that would be hurt. You said you didn't care, that you would take a chance. Even then, I'll wager, that you knew that our friendship wouldn't [*fade away*] . . . when I left KC Gosh, Honey, you were right. When I got back to Nebraska, I couldn't stop thinking about you. Even when I thought I was going to get a furlough. I tried to figure out a way that I could stop off in KC for a few days. That X-C [*cross-country*] trip I took to NY settled everything for me. If it had happened a little sooner, I would have never volunteered to come over. I'd have been better off in my old outfit. But since this is a love letter and one for reminiscences, I shan't cry over spilled milk. You know, Darling, I am rather crude. Most of my words are rough and none too cautious. You must forgive my outward temperament. It is the only way I can express myself. It is the only way I ever did express myself. There is no sense for me to be like sugar and cream because you know I cuss like a trooper. There's no sense for me to pretend because you would find out sooner or later. I am not talking in the present. You have already heard my acid tongue. But, Darling, remember even in my rough house manner, my love for you will be as tender as your love causes me to be that tender. I am tempted to start building that castle in the clouds but it would be going against our promises. Just wait until I get home. Please remember, My Darling, that that time may be a long way off. —

Must close. Take care of yourself, Darling. Give my love to Mother. May God Bless You. Love you and miss you — Love, Mike.

Glider towing flights were called off on April 6. Personnel from the 316th Troop Carrier Group passed in review, and several awards were presented by Major General Royce, according to the War Diary.

On April 7, four planes were transferred to the 31st Transport Squadron. The morning flight schedule was cancelled, though one plane dropped paratroops in the afternoon, and another was returned to the 315th Troop Carrier Group.

April 8, 1944 [*Saturday*]

My Darling,

I received your letter of the 28th and I think the stationery is beautiful. (Or is that the word with the ary?)

Again and again, I must repeat that you must be patient. It is unfortunate that the mail passes so slowly. Then again you must realize that there are times that there are good reasons for me to be lax.

You asked a few questions about the Red Cross which I'll try to answer. I cannot complain for there have been many instances where the R.C. came in very handy. In a lot of the places, they offered us a place to flop. In every instance that that was true, the prices were liberal and only used as a security. The money was returned upon departure. It is necessary to pay for your food but it is so cheap that one could hardly bicker about the price. In most places, the R.C. set-up was ideal. Here on our post, it is perfect. It is a place where one can sip his coffee or coke and gnaw on a doughnut and have a good bull session. (The coffee, coke and doughnuts are not free, but there again, it is not a matter of bickering.) There is a dance every Saturday night, discussion once a week and various forms of entertainment that one can pursue. Of course you realize that this is not true in all the cases but it is more true than untrue. There hasn't been one R.C. that

I have been into and you know by my travels that I have been in many, that has been all out to grab a GI's money. In the larger cities, the R.C. is a hangout like the canteens at home. Any touring GI can spend a whole leave in one of these places and still have a Hell of a good time. (In any case, I enjoy a nip once in a while and the R.C. is one place that you can't get it!)

The other question that you ask is one which is touchy. A lot of people would not agree with me. However since you ask, I am at your service to answer and debate. (Since this sounds so much like a quiz program do you mind if I interpose a few words and tell you that I love you so very much! — I do.) We must remember that every doctor is sworn to the oath of some Greek — can't recall his name. — Aristotle of Hypo — something. That oath is based on the fulfillment of a doctor's duty — to serve to preserve life to the fullest degree within his means. Secondly, from the Christian outlook, man cannot make himself like unto God to take life. In the case of life and death, we can do no more than to stand by and accept the processes of nature. To a Christian — the Way of God. He judges our life and our nature of death. Remember you asked me the question — ordinarily my answer is not prejudiced by religion or otherwise — however, in this case, I agree [*thoroughly*] with the church. It is the same as in the case of abortion. The church by the law of God forbids abortions but only in the case when it means the life of the mother in the natal stage. Then it is a case of saving a life which is actual and a life which is in the stages of being. So you see, My Darling, as heartless as it may seem, [*name omitted*] must die normally through the normal expiration of her life breath. Unfortunately, she must suffer — who are we to judge the nature of her death? In my religion, we pray that God will bless us with an easy death, so that we may not spend our last moments in a Hell on earth. — Have I answered your question?

Ole Nell [*nickname for my aircraft*] is doing OK. As a matter of fact, I couldn't ask for any better. She's a good gal and she seems to be very much in love with me because she hasn't caused me any trouble at all. Really a good kid.

Darling, don't be angry but I butchered my head again. In the first place, it was too much trouble to keep neat. Secondly, I lost my good comb so I'd rather not worry with having it to comb at all. Besides you know that I'd be too much competition if I flashed those waves of mine around. Conceited, aren't I? I have not decided to raise another mustache, yet! I might get around to that too.

Darling, I must close. Do not fret if you do not hear from me. It is natural. There are times when I "cawn't" help myself. Well, Darling, so long for now. The guys send their love. And I, my love rides to you on the wings of the air mail stamp but it is like the dove, tender and soft.

Give my love to Mother. Take care of yourself. May God Bless You. I am being as careful as I can. — Love, Mike.

On April 8, Lt. Colonel Burton Fleet, the Group Commanding Officer, made a general inspection. There were group formation flights that afternoon, and a dance at the Red Cross Club for enlisted men that night.

April 9, 1944 [*Sunday*]

My Darling,

No mail but that won't prevent me from writing. After all, you did mention that mail has been so spasmodic that I like to try to ease your worrying brain. First step is to tell you that I love you very much.

Happy Easter, My Darling. It is Easter Sunday. I heard Mass and received Communion. You know who my prayers were for. It's funny but I seldom pray for myself. Figure that I'm here so I can see myself do whatever is right and wrong. Above all, I am alive and healthy. I pray for your safekeeping and that your health will remain good.

You mentioned in your last letter that the weather was starting to change for the better. Your words said something about hoping we could walk, talk, laugh, and just be Bette and Mike. Yes, My Darling, I yearn and hunger for those days. How nice it would be to hold your arm, saunter along slowly and watch your beautiful face and hair glitter in the sunlight. Darling, if you only knew how much I miss you as each day passes. I am falling more in love with you each day. I learn to love you each morning. I pray for you each night. I am controlled by you each day.

I cannot talk too long this evening. I am going to have a hard day tomorrow and I want to be prepared for it. I'd like to go on for a long time but I have been reading quite a bit from *Bedtime Esquire*. It is a series of articles and stories from *Esquire*. They are a bit naughty but nice. But even such kind of writing can make a person's eyes tired.

So, My Darling, Good night! Take care of yourself. Give my love to Mother.

May God Bless You. Love, Mike.

Sunrise Easter Services were held at the Base Chapel on April 9. There was one flight in the afternoon, but did not drop paratroops because it was unable to locate the drop zone (DZ) due to bad weather. Captain Cooney, the War Diary noted, returned from Intelligence School at Ascot that day.

On April 10, three gliders were exchanged for CG 4A's (the designation for the American-built glider) at Greenham Common air base in southern England. Two planes dropped paratroops that morning, and another was sent to Spanhoe with personnel.

In the afternoon of April 11, two planes were used to drop paratroops, six participated in radio navigation flights, and nine were used to fly squadron formation that night. Two planes were placed on detached service, one to Folkingham airfield and the other to Grove airfield.

April 12, 1944 [*Wednesday*]

My Darling,

I am not going to complain about mail because I am not in a position where I can receive any for a few weeks. However, I know that it will keep "stacking up" so I don't mind it so terribly much. If I don't answer some of your questions, you can see why. If you ask me if I love you, you know that you can receive the answer to that always. You needn't ask, I'll tell you.

Finally, I saw Harry. He's tall, almost as tall as I am. Black hair, straight, rather Roman featured, that is they are long. Well polished, clean cut and neat. I can see very easily why sister loves him so much. He's a fine chap. Damn nice to talk to, swell to listen to — all in all the short visit I had with him, made me very happy. I wasn't able to discuss very much with him because he is a busy person. However, that one visit is leading to more, in a very short time, and we intend to make the very best of that period of time. I didn't realize that he was such an important guy. In an army sense, I was much stunted by the rank that I saw. The entire atmosphere left me awe-stricken and embarrassed and it made me feel how important Harry is. But our next visit will be on mutual ground in an atmosphere that God created and where He is the owner of all He surveys — fresh air and wide open spaces. There isn't much to say except that I was very glad to see him. It was something that I have written to you about often. A feeling that I was a bit closer to home.

My Darling, the weather has been beautiful. It's funny that the things that are beautiful are the very things that make us feel so low. It is these things that tell us that we should be so close to the one we love so dearly. I can think of nothing but of being with you. The time is passing, My Dear. Again as I have repeated for the last 9 months, I get the funniest feeling when I think that perhaps some day soon you will be in my arms. Love has a great effect on a person. It can be the one thing that makes his soul take as much as it does. It is easy to see when I notice so many guys that haven't that someone to go home to. To think that man is trying to ruin the very things that God gives us life to accomplish.

It would be so easy to forget the things that I have known and what I want so much. But the relief would be only for a day or night. You are mine forever, Darling. I don't like to think of real happiness unless you help me to share it. I like the sun and spring but when we are apart as we are now, these are there merely because nature saw fit to let them have what we have. It is tough to be dropped from one environment into another especially since it is against our wishes. I don't want to sound too solemn, Bette. I want to tell you how much I miss you. I guess I must have done that for almost every day I have been away. Let me speak as I wish and I will be happier. That is one freedom that no one can take from us.

Well Ole' Gal, I must close. I am busy but not enough to stop me from writing entirely. My letters will be short for a while but please don't mind that too much.

Give my love to Mother. Take care of yourself, Darling. May God Bless You. I love you very much. Love, Mike.

Glider towing and formation flights were made on April 12. The next day, in place of the regular flying schedule, there was a Wing mission to Greenham Common to pick up gliders. The War Diary continued:

> **. . . a 24-hour alert went into effect and no one was permitted to leave the camp. The expected Air Evacuation move was called off. Captain Cooney attended a class in Aircraft recognition.**

April 14, 1944 [*Friday*]
APO 133
[*Written from radio school at Greenham Common, England*]

My Darling,

Since I still cannot answer your letters, I must make my letters on the tune of self-made. It is rather hard to create, especially since I am taking life so easy and nothing is really happening to me. No, I'm not on furlough, I am merely taking a refresher course. A guy can forget a lot of technicalities when he hasn't looked at a book for over a year.

Speaking of furloughs — that is one of those strange words that has never happened to me in my army career. I am glad of that because when I do get home, I'll have more time at home (I hope). According to the Air Force plan which we have heard about, a GI (Air Force) returning from combat is not given a furlough but is given 20 days to get to a re-distribution center. In my case, Atlantic City, New Jersey — it takes approximately 6 hours to get there by train from my home. You know, Bette, I want to get married as soon as I get home. If I'm not mistaken, you feel the same way. You can bet your sweet life that I don't want to waste any time at all. Once I get reclassified and sent to my new base, from what we have discussed already, you will come to that base so that we can be together.

But there I go talking about the future. Every so often, I can't help but to forget our past that we won't discuss those things. All I want is to get home to you. I wish this damn mess was over so that we could get home. But I guess, there must be a couple of million guys that feel the same way.

Darling, really I can't think in this atmosphere. Besides, I miss your letters. I can get ideas from them always. So for the next little while, you'll have to be content with these farcical sketches.

So long, Bette. Give my love to Mother. May God Bless You. Love you and miss you so much. Lil Mike is being a good boy — Love, Mike.

The regular flying schedule on April 14 was called off by Group Headquarters, but there were formation and radar and instrument flights that afternoon. There was a live show at the Red Cross Club that evening.

On April 15, two additional planes were assigned to the squadron. Five planes were flown for instrument checks that morning, and eight were used for formation flying in the afternoon. There was also one Horsa glider assigned to the squadron, according to the War Diary.

All scheduled flying on April 16 was cancelled due to weather. And, starting that day, all passes were limited to 12 hours.

April 17, 1944 [*Monday*]

My Darling,

I spent a very fine week-end with Harry [*in London*]. I know that we have added a very fine person to our social clique. I won't go thru' any details of our visit together but I will say that we talked about everyone and everything that we know of. I do know that there were 2 women, one in Brooklyn and one in KC whose ears must have burned horribly because they were very much talked about. This meeting was the nicest thing that has happened to me since I have been overseas. Everything was perfect. I was able to talk about the people that mean something to me. The people that I love above anything in my life. You may know how I feel, My Darling, but I felt so all alone until I saw Harry. So many things passed before my eyes that the very ground was no longer England but it was my home.

Bette, you must bear with me again. Forget that there are words that are oft-repeated but that they are words I want to say to you for the rest of my life. And I would be saying them to you if we were together. I love you, My Darling. I love you more each day. I'd shout it to the very tree tops if these English people knew what I meant. It is merely a matter of watching the time pass so that God will be good to us and join us as soon as He sees fit to make man see the end of this cruelty and stupidity. I am afraid that I sound a bit dejected, but it is because of the marvelous cloud I was floating on yesterday. It seems cruel to see the bubble burst and find that I am thrust back into this materialistically upset world. It felt so good to hear my words as I pictured our future. Those days of unbelievable happiness, those moments of quiet and peace and solitude, I could feel my arms about you as I told you of my love that is endless. Yes, My Darling, all this and more passed thru' my brain as I talked to Harry. It was as if I could tell him all this and he understood because he felt the same way. Darling, really the time is passing; all those thoughts will be soon actuality rather than purely dreams of a brain warped by loneliness and solitude. We cannot measure that time in days or months. But with every letter it is a week — the weeks will make the months, as they have passed for us already and then one day — you will be really mine and I, yours, not in words but in actions. But I guess I shouldn't go on like this. We know how we feel, we talked about it, but —

I went to a movie this evening. The picture may have been old. I don't know. It was *His Butler's Sister*. Deanna Durbin, Franchot Tone, etc. I like Deanna and I enjoy her voice. In one scene especially she sings a Russian Folk Song, and then "Two Guitars." It was beautiful but — This ETO (European Theater of Operations) seems to be made up of a bunch of over-sexed morons. When a woman appears on the scene, particularly, in a scene where she is depicted as a woman in love and she looks as only a woman in love could look, these dirty bastards feel it is time for them to howl like the banshees of old. Where I was before, it was understandable because we never saw women who could excite us. But here where there are any number of beautiful gals and they seem willing to please these young beasts, there is no reason for them to conduct themselves like morons. We were much better disciplined and well-mannered. They gripe about Spam, Frank Sinatra, and general comforts. Since I have been in England, I have never eaten Spam. As a matter of fact, I never ate better even when I was a GI back in the States. Most of 'em have never heard of C-rations and K-rations. They talk about Sinatra as if he was the worst bum in the world. I don't know Sinatra personally but I know his life and struggles. I also know as well as anyone else that he is happily married, has a nice wife, two children and a nice home. If the women want to fall all over him, I don't blame him for capitalizing on his good fortune — it is damn good business sense. He was once a pauper. He can make a good fortune. God Bless Him. These rookies are the type that cry because they know their women like a guy like Sinatra. And yet they are the same guys that will "goof off" every night, play with every woman, have children by them, and leave their wives stranded in the States.

I am not trying to sound like a guy that's showering himself with self-pity. It makes me laugh, that's all. Probably you read about all this and worry about me because of it. "I've had it, Darling." This is a breeze. Half of these guys don't know what it is to watch their shoes float out of a tent or step outside of their tents and flounder in knee-deep mud. Hell! Most of 'em don't know how to pitch a tent. They don't know what it is to slip into your sack at night and battle the sand fleas until you are so tired that you don't give a damn. That isn't even hardship compared to the kids in New Guinea, Cassino [*Italy*], and Anzio [*Italy*] where life is really rugged.

All those words came from one single thought that I had at that movies. You must forgive me if I bore you. But if you should ever hear some Son's Mother say that Johnny is suffering so in England, tell her that you were just wondering about those poor bastards in Italy.

Guess I've chewed enough of your ear off and I haven't seen anything compared to those guys. Darling, I must close. I got a code in the node and I must get some sleep to combat it.

Give my love to Mother. Take care of yourself. May God Bless You — Love you and miss you ever so much. Love, Mike.

The War Diary entries for April 17-19 read:

> **April 17: Two ships were used for night formation flying and one plane test-hopped.**
> **April 18: In the afternoon and evening twelve planes were used for Instrument Flying; group formation flying at night. A meeting of all squadron Public Relations Clerks was held at Group S-2.**

April 19: Effective at once, Lt. Robert Roman was relieved of his duty as Special Service Officer. One plane was test-hopped and one instrument checked. Two planes to North Witham for Radar check.

April 20, 1944 [*Thursday*]

My Darling,

Thank God the days have passed. In a few more days I'll be able to get my mail. I guess they figure that these few days of training have made a better radio operator out of me. If they wanted to see a guy really go to town on this radio stuff, they should have sent me to Kansas City. It really is tough not to get mail for a solid two weeks and know that it is around somewhere.

I am not as loquacious (or is it spelled differently?) as I used to be. This country doesn't appeal to me for description as my former haunts did. There was such an abundance of things that I could see to talk about. I'm afraid that I am accepting England as a vacation, for the time being. Those that are stricken with grief and are truly war-ridden offer so much to a person who is used to observation. It is true that this country is beautiful, but that seems to be as far as it goes. Everything strikes me as being too sissified. Contentment as such is apt to fray a person's nerves, and keep him perpetually rutted. There, I seemed to get so many things done without the help of civilization. I don't read ½ as much as I did. I don't see anything. I guess I got so used to living like a gypsy and vagabond that inactivity gives me a loggy brain and fat ass. There is nothing to gripe about. The food is too good over here. No mud to contend with. No reason to go and get "stinking" drunk. As a matter of fact, most of the time I am too lazy to get off my sack. Darling, to top it all and very sincerely do I say this, the women have no appeal for me, whatsoever. They seem to be a bunch of nonsensical ignoramuses that know of nothing but gaiety and free love. From hearsay, it seems that the fellows don't even have to work for a good piece, it comes naturally. Ugh! You must pardon my very bold and brazen manner, but from one so ignorant, I cannot think of any abler way to express myself.

But to Hell with all that! The other night, I decided to compare some of your pictures that I carry with me always. Darling, you are changing, more mature. I can notice an increase in weight or is it because of the darker clothes? You get prettier each time. When I showed your large picture to Harry, he smiled and said, "Mike, you can't miss." As if I didn't know. I guess that after 10 months, you may be anxious to know how much I might have changed.

Your received the pictures I sent many months ago, taken in 2 different places, after a good lapse of time. You'll notice that I look quite tanned and in pretty good physical shape, although I didn't have one of the comforts of home. Now, my tan has vanished, my cheeks are fuller and although it would never show in a picture, I am a Hell of a lot flabbier. All because of the lack of exercise, and the lack of the facilities to get exercise. I managed always to sneak in a basketball game or kick a football around, now it's "me and my sack." When I don't work, it's because I can't work, or it is impossible to do anything. One of my best friends, a boy I knew in the states and who I was very fortunate to find over here (He knows you well because I talked about you so often), remarked the other day that I had a lot of gray hair and he wanted to know why. God alone knows, I don't. I don't think I mentioned it before but I got another one of those very short crew cuts. I don't know why I did. It is just a bit more comfortable. Besides I lost my good comb and this saves me the trouble of combing my hair.

Whatever changes there may seem to be, they do not alter my deeper feelings. Nothing could change them. My love is still the same. It may be and is a bit more pronounced. In a very short while, I shall have finished my 20th month in the service. I am getting the urge more and more to settle down to a peaceful home life with you. Even with all the squabbles and hen-pecking, it will seem like the voice of an angel to my ears. Promise you won't scold me more than once a day and please never before bedtime. There is too much beauty to that period of the 24-hour day.

Darling, I must close. I am going to try to do some light reading before I retire. Give my love to Mother. Take care of yourself. May God Bless You — My love for you is like [*Vesuvius*] in eruption — I do love you ever so much — Take care — Love, Mike.

On April 20, the squadron was preparing for a Wing "paratroop & parapack drop [*training*] mission" called OPERATION MUSH. The "Liberty Run" trucks, which took men on leave to Leicester, were cancelled because of the limitation to 12-hour passes.

OPERATION MUSH was carried out on April 21. Thirteen planes from the 37th Squadron participated in the mission, which was, according to the War Diary, "completely successful."

Flights on April 22 and 23 included instrument, radio navigation, radar training, and instrument checks.

April 24, 1944 [*Monday*]

My Marvelous Darling,

Surely you could never realize my profound joy when I found two week's mail. Twelve (12) letters from you + your book. Then at tonight's mail, I received 4 letters from you, the latest dated April 18th.

I hardly know where to start. I had a marvelous time with Harry in London. We had a chance to get to hear the London Symphony Orchestra, conducted by Malcolm Sargent. I shall send you the program in a later letter. In the meantime, I'll try to answer your questions. I love you.

I do know [*name omitted*] but I have not seen him over here. He went to KC with me. Never knew him so well, good kid but a wee bit conceited. We were with the same group in Alliance. I do know that he is not stationed near me.

Darling, I'd like to send you a subscription of *Yank & Stars and Stripes* but I must find out from the censor if it is possible. I do know that Harry sends Lucy all of that and I am sure that it will be OK for me to do it. I shall check and get things rolling for you. It is our one source of information. I know that it will bring you closer to our theater and I know that you will feel as if you are a part of it, thru' me.

Darling, don't worry about "Sports' Comments" because I have been receiving a splendid supply of *Sporting News*. That paper covers everything. Besides, again, since we get a daily copy of *S&S* there is all the information we need. Also, you must not worry about film. I have an abundant supply to last me for a while. Harry and I took one roll in London. It will take 6 weeks for them to be censored. When I get them you will be sure to receive my pictures. Can't promise any Gables but it will be a few pictures.

I don't blame you for "griping" about the lack of mail, during the period that you spoke of, but someday I'll be able to tell you why. You must trust me. You realize that I don't let too many days pass without writing, but when I don't you know that I just can't help myself. Enough of that, OK?

I am glad that you received that statuette, finally. Thank Mother for her letter. I have so many letters to answer that I'll try to answer her as quickly as I can.

Darling, don't worry about those awful moods that you talk about. It is not unusual to walk around in a fog. Being in love is a funny thing. Day by day, the anxious moments of our love become more and more pronounced. It is not unusual to feel as if the world is just an ugly, ole' sphere in which we are forced to live. Our thoughts are for each other and there is nothing else worthwhile thinking about.

In most of your letters, you worried about hurting my eyes from reading your letters. Surely, Darling, you must be dreaming thru' a bubble. I could sit here all night and read your "uninteresting words."

Hey, Bette, where the devil did you get that name for the dog, "Pido." I can't seem to associate it with anything that I know except that it is one of your quips.

Before I try to answer any more of your letters, I am going to describe Westminster Cathedral where I heard Mass Sunday morning. Harry suggested that I go there. When I walked in the side door, I thought that either he gave me a wrong steer or I was in the wrong place. Then I walked toward the center of the vestibule and then I was truly amazed. It was gigantic and beautiful. There are 4 altars on each side and then a great big altar in the middle. I went to confession and then received Holy Communion at one of the smaller side altars. Then I heard Mass at 10:30 at the main altar. I was never so impressed in all my life. There was an all-male chorus. I think the Mass was said by a Bishop. I can't tell how elaborately beautiful it all was because my vocabulary is not sufficient. I wanted to take some pictures but I was embarrassed because there were so many at Mass.

Darling, you must forgive me if I close. You see last night Harry missed his train and he couldn't get one until 5:00 AM this morn. I stayed up until then and we had a good bull session. Since I had to get up so early, I didn't get any sleep. Feel rugged.

I'll do better when I am rested by tomorrow. Good night, My love. Take care of yourself. I love you so very much. May God Bless You. Love, Mike.

War Diary entries for April 24 and 25:

> **April 24: Glider tow, morning, afternoon, and evening. Liberty Run to Leicester in effect once more. The following named officers were promoted to 1st. Lt.: Addison D. Agle and Eugene Wilger, effective 15 April 1944.**
>
> **April 25: Glider tow and radio navigation flying in the morning. Nine ships used to pick up gliders at Greenham Common and two ships cross country and return.**

April 26, 1944 [*Wednesday*]

My Darling,

I received your letter of the 20th of April. Unfortunately, you speak so often of the lack of mail that I hardly know what to say. Try as I do, I can't seem to write often enough and this lack of mail is not really my fault. I have devised a new system whereby I write to you at least once per day. I write to my other correspondents during the morning and write to you each evening. If, as in this case, there is any change, I alter my plans accordingly. Honest, Honey, you'll have to excuse my very vague explanations but there isn't a damn thing I can do about it.

You don't realize the favor you did me when you sent me the book [*A Tree Grows in Brooklyn, by Betty Smith*]. I am reading it in spots because I can't read it as much as I want to. It is one book which I am reluctant to set aside. In one of the chapters that I read, Smith describes Bushwick Avenue. That is where I live. She captures the picture so beautifully. All the moments of reading seem to have one basic background thought which they leave me. "It will be great to show Bette all these things some day." Darling, I realize day by day the more I love you, how much I am leaving for you to desire. Lord knows that I have been a very poor judge of your desires. I do not feel wholly guilty because I am going to make this all up. I want you to tell me all your heart desires once we are together. Please, Darling, to really appreciate what you want me to be. I want you to live by that patient feeling of our future to come. Even my letters sometimes leave me defeated to purpose. They lack the words that you want to hear and I try ever so hard to please. I am not lax because I want to be but because I am forced to by my actions.

One of your letters asks a question which I feel that I must answer. It is a question which I want you to ask because it is a natural question. All we have ever said is yes. We will be married. Above all that is the smallest question. We will be. Then you ask, "Then what?" You said once that when we get married that you never wanted to be apart from me again. I have assured you of that as far as I can foresee. You know that as long as I am in the army and in the <u>States</u>, we will take up quarters somewhere near my base and live as Mrs. & Sgt. Ingrisano. The army does provide for dependents and especially for wives. We will be given what is known as quarters & rations. I don't hope to be only a buck sergeant as long as I am in the forces. Cadet is out. Looks like they don't need any more pilots and they don't particularly care to give a guy who has been overseas a break. However, we will be drawing a fairly good upkeep. I have some money saved and there will be more by the time we are married. It may be a bit of a struggle for a while but others have done it. I know that we can. Once I am discharged, I have a job and we will get ready to set up our home. Remember, My Darling, I have never promised you a home of gold and wine but I shall never let you down. I will have some land on Long Island on which I hope to build a home someday. All in all, our future is as rosy as two middle class people can hope to have. These are my ideas. There is more to it but since you ask for only a skeleton, I give you that. Much more can be added but I want to plan it with you. I'm not very good at it. I hope to provide the service and let you provide the ideas and results. One idea which I don't want to discuss is about my army career. But I do hope to try for my commission when I get back. That we will leave for later days.

I cannot blame you for thinking about these things. Everything is so uncertain. I cannot plant definite ideas in your mind but I can reassure you of what we want. You must suffer and hate the life of an army wife as much as I do not relish the idea of an army career. We will make that as easy on ourselves as we can by feeling as we do, that as long as we are together, the rest of the world will have to manage by itself. We'll take care of our end. Since we are both merely existing now, we will continue to just exist until I am free to do as I wish. But that temporary existence will be easy to take because we'll be taking it together. It isn't going to be too pleasant a life, but we can make it or break it. Since we know each other so well, since we feel as we do, how can we do anything but make it ideal? It isn't easy to live on words just now, Darling. I know it isn't easy. My heart becomes bitter at times. You are alone; so am I. I feel as you do. I hate this stupidity. What can we do but accept the life that has been thrust upon us by the gods that rule our bodies? My soul is free. If I could, I would leave it with you. I love you, Darling. It is all that we have now. Those words and our memories, we can and must live on those. If we can't, we might as well yell, "Uncle" and succumb to the weakness of our souls, the weakness which brings us shame. I'll never yell "Uncle," Darling. You are too much a part of me. Hell, high water, pain, torture, or —. I'll never let you go. If I feel that way then I can live on those words and I am doing just that. There you are, Darling. That's Mike speaking. Do I sound like that firm character which you fell in love with?

I must close. If ever you feel you want to ask me any questions any more and you feel that my words will be any help — ask, I'll answer. I don't have to make words. I feel what I say to you. They are not the flesh but the heart and soul.

Take care of yourself. May God Bless You. I love you and miss you. Always, Mike.

April 26, 1944 [*Wednesday*]

My Darling,

I have already written you [*on this day*] but I want to overwhelm you with as many letters as I can as long as I have the chance.

There are any number of things I'd like to talk about. You mention things to me that I accept but then you never broaden the idea. You know that the ulterior idea in our minds is our marriage. But it isn't as easy as all that. You have agreed to be married in the Catholic Church. Not as a convert but with your religion as it is. We'll be married not before the altar but in the rectory of the church. You agree with all of that thoroughly, am I right? You know that I'll never argue or dispute any point that you mention. I don't want you to accept everything without a say so. That's why I want to understand you and have you understand me. It must be complete, consoling, affectionate, and satisfying. I never want to hurt you unconsciously, accidentally, or purposely. You are my whole life. You are the one person who I want to make totally happy. Once we are together, we will run the show. It will be our life, once we are married. And it shall be so until we are married. Since you have been so honest to admit so many things, so I shall be outspoken as I have always been. I never want you to be hurt by any careless words. Remember, Darling, trust my humble judgment and any time there is anything that you want to say that you are afraid might hurt me, say it. I'll judge the extent of the hurt if there is any.

You are probably wondering what I am talking about. I'll tell you. Harry and I talked a lot about you and Lucy. I have explained any number of things to him and he agrees with my ideas. (First of all, remember, it is I who love you. It will be you and I who will be married. We will be left to independence, dependent upon each other.) When I had seen Harry and left, I received a letter from my sister, Lucy, that I found was very much of a disillusionment to me. It hurt. It was one of those things that pass in a family that must be thrashed out only by those individuals. I wrote an answer and told [*her*] what I felt and how I wanted it accepted. Regardless of whatever feeling, I've said my piece and shall act accordingly to my ideas, our ideas.

What made me think of all this was the fact that you mentioned in your letter that Lucy has asked about a white wedding. You and I decided to have a small wedding without any fanfare. You are sure you will be satisfied with that. If you do want a noticed affair, it shall be so. Since we are not demonstrative people, it would be best for you and I to be married quietly and as originally planned. Our wedding will be merely a day to remember. Our life will be one to truly cherish.

Now, Darling, I have said so many things I don't want to frighten you. Answer me as you want. Openly and without fear of reprimand. You know how much I want to make you happy and I know that I must and do understand you. Do not fear that family shadow that looms behind me. I love my family but they will not be my guiding stars forever. I am grateful to them for all that I have learned and will continue to learn but if I did not interpose my own ideas of life, then truly I'd be tied to Mom's apron strings and you would never be happy with me. No, My Darling, all that will happen will be for us. Everything, laughs, tears, worries, and pain will be ours to share and not ours to share with my family. Please do not be afraid to speak to me. I won't & do not stand for carelessness on anyone's part toward you. My love, My Darling, is something that may take even a long time to understand. But it is my love for you.

If I sound wild-eyed, stop me. But Tony once told me that to understand everything about yourself and the woman you love, you must talk everything over. Regardless how small or big it may be or how it may hurt or may not.

Sometimes I think that I pushed my family before you too often. I'm sorry if I've been too enthusiastic, but I wanted a thorough understanding. First of all, I want that with you. Gosh, Bette, I never want to look like a fool in your eyes. You must realize this but this time overseas has matured me more. It has opened my eyes to a lot. It has made me understand a depth of life that I was reluctant to believe. Above all, it has brought all the people I love closer to me. Most of all, you because I found that I need you and love you so much more than I have ever needed anyone's love. I can never forget how much you mean to me, how much I owe you, and how much all our memories have really been an opening to the real life before us.

I must close, Darling. Please answer whatever you feel. You said you loved me; I have said I love you. It's about time that we really knew it. I knew it a long time ago. It has been growing so much. One of these days, it's going to knock us down. A lovely thought, really. Good night, Darling, Michael.

April 26, 1944 [*Wednesday*]

Good Evening, My Darling,

Here I am again ready to send you a few lines [*third letter of the day*]. First off, I want to satisfy one of your questions. I have inquired everywhere about the possibilities of getting you a few *S&S* and *Yank*. I find that I can't get a subscription and it is still impossible to send any sort of manuscripts to you. I know that Harry does send any number to Lucy but I guess a Sergeant doesn't rate nearly as much as a Captain. So you see, My Love, I have tried my best but it all seems to no avail. However, I shall keep trying. I read a few pages from your book and believe me, Honey, every word so far is typically Brooklyn. It didn't change for a long time after the period of 1911 that Smith writes about. Although her language is also typical, there isn't a word I can say to disprove it. But I won't add any more. I can't read as much as I did but when I finish, I will give you a complete summary to compare the differences, if there are any. I doubt it. The streets that she mentions are not fictitious. I know everyone of them. As a matter of fact, my Aunt [*and Uncle Dominick Alfieri*] lives on Devoe St. and another one [*and Uncle Frank Alfieri*] lives on Graham Ave.

Tom mentioned that he had received your picture. He approves thoroughly. As if anything such as any approval is necessary for me. My mind is made up for our future. There is nothing in this world that can change it. You needn't worry about that "wrinkled old hag" that you are talking about. Darling, I'll love you always.

No, My Sweet, I don't feel any older. I don't [*think*] any more about anything but the day that I'll come home. What more is there to think about? Don't worry about the fact that I may leave you alone. Impossible! Darling, I've said it once, if I have said it a million times, I never want to leave you again. Remember the army has a temporary hold on me. But your hold is permanent. Whatever the occasion, you'll be at my side.

Darling, thank you again. You know what I have written in some of my previous letters. Nothing is scarce here. We have enough chocolate to satisfy us. I don't ask for any because I'll only get sick from too much of it.

No, I haven't got a twin but since my puss is so commonplace, it is only natural that you may have seen someone who looks like me. I wish to Hell I was the guy. He can take my place any time. But Hell, I'd hate to have his conscience. I guess we'll survive the time element, Bette. It is passing, you know. It may not be too long before you'll see me in "civvies." Besides, you'll have a life time to correct my very lax dressing habits. Besides, if I did have a twin brother, just think how jealous I'd be if he was taking my place. I'd be left holding that well-known bag. Besides, it's impossible there couldn't be two equally handsome (?) men in this little world. Furthermore, Mother wouldn't hold such a secret from me.

I can see your point about the ordination. Since there is nothing I can say further, I shall remain silent and wait for the time to pass to watch the developments. Please, Darling, don't feel as if I don't understand. I do. It is so difficult for you. I understand perfectly. To be really honest, I'd be so proud and honored to be the first to introduce you to my family. However, if the arrangements are satisfactory on all sides, I'd like to have you attend what will be, I know, one of the most beautiful rites in the church. Besides, you'll have the opportunity to see New York. Or would you rather see it with me? Enough. I'll go into it in detail when I hear about the ceremonies.

Perhaps you are right when you say that it was best that we didn't get married. We won't discuss the points about getting married. We know the joy that would be ours if we had. But we didn't. You know our parting wasn't too hard on us, was it? We left as if it had to happen, and, Thank God, we accepted it just as that. All in all, I find that we are very sensible people. We will have all of this behind us and that everything will be waiting for us to take and make perfect.

"Pappy" [*Agle*] is feeling better but he is going back to have his tonsils removed. Congratulations are in order. He has made his first [*lieutenancy*]. It couldn't have happened to a better guy. He's a damn good pilot and he loves it. There couldn't be a better combination. I gave Nick your love. He thanks you and returns. "Pappy" is glad to know that you still remember him. He too sends his love. All in all that makes 3 of us.

Darling, I must close. I have answered 4 more of your letters. Don't fret, one of these days, I'll devote one letter, just for you and I. You know that my love rides on the wings of every stamp and letter I send you.

Take care of that cold and yourself. I feel great, never better. Give my love to Mother. May God Bless You. — Love, Michael.

On April 26, in addition to test and instrument flights, there was a radio code class for radio operators, navigators, and pilots. The day ended with group formation flying that night.

Radar training began the day on April 27, according to the War Diary, followed by glider formation flying in the afternoon. One plane dropped paratroopers, and five picked up gliders at Greenham Common. Lieutenant Robert Roman read the Articles of War to all personnel.

April 28, 1944 [*Friday*]

My Darling,

I don't know what day it is or date but I do know that I haven't written for days. For-give me. I played softball last night, slid into home plate, ripped my coveralls and my knee. Later, I had to slide into 3rd base, came in on the seat of my pants and my right fore-arm, one bruised elbow. Feel stiff, black and blue, well bandaged but happy. By the way, we won 9-0. These extra-curricula activities were the things that I was griping about. Since the weather has been nearly perfect, I decided to take advantage of them. Really, Darling, you must forgive me but you don't want me to get too fat, do you? Nothing new about that *S&S* and *Yank* business but I do know that you can buy *Yank* back in the States. It is pub-lished in New York. If you order it, you can have all of your favorite pin-ups, "Sad Sack." (Alias Dear Mike.)

I'll try to answer more of your letters. In one you talk of Spring. We are having it here, in a mild sort of way. I do notice that the trees are budding. I love that kind of weather, too. New York doesn't get too damn warm but it is nice enough to keep pleasantly happy. That land that I spoke of is set in a rather nice part of LI, at least I thought so. When a breeze whips up, it is as nice as anything you would imagine.

I finished the book. It was excellent. I have already loaned it out. There is a long wait-ing list for it. When it is returned to me, via a squadron of readers, I shall read it again. Again, as I said before, Miss Smith has captured the idea of Brooklyn. A strong sense of civic pride which makes us feel as if we are set apart from the entire world. Darling, hon-estly I am going to show you, someday, what I mean. But I shan't try to cram anything down your throat. It took me 23 years to learn. And a war to make me believe.

Yes, you asked about "Maisey Doats"! — Gad! What dope fiend ever thought that one up. This "Besame Mucho" is marvelous. I have heard so many of these wonderful songs and yet, I don't know hardly one name. Methinks, I am going to devote a lot of time to lis-tening to music, as soon as I get a chance to really relax.

Darling, you were speaking of the ball season and hoping that we'd get a chance to see some games this season. It sounds like an impossibility but the season is long isn't it? It would do my heart good to sit up in the stands and yell my heart out for "Dem Bums." Oh Well! This war can't last forever.

In another of your letters, you are telling me of having dinner at the airport. Then you recall the day I came thru' from Tulsa. Then you utter a prayer, it looks like a dreamy thought because at that moment, you must have dropped your pen, and there is a differ-ence in the color of the ink. I shall never forget that kiss as long as I live. Darling, I think of all the circumstances and conversations that passed between us and I realize more and more that it all would lead up to a final and definite conclusion. Oh God! If He had only told me then. I love you.

In your next letter, you ask a series of questions which are interesting and provide a lot to say. It is a questions of moods, and lax functioning of the brain. You feel that it all comes from physical tiredness. I don't believe so. After all, our minds can be trigger sharp when our bodies are exhausted. Our minds are forever working. At times they are overworked. It tends to bring on a fit of tears, remorse, loneliness, and any number of good and bad reactions. Most of the times, as in your case, a terrific longing for each other, a loneliness that appears unbearable. As an interception, we can feel an unseen hand which casts a spell over us and leaves us listless and our minds a total blank. If we were not given a rest from this soul-torture, our inevitable end would be a breakdown. Since it is not fitting to destroy ourselves physically, and since we have no control over our mental self — this blank must interpose. It is not so noticeable that someone drops a screen before our brain but it can be felt when we realize no matter how hard we try to think, we gain no conclusions. That is why, at times, you receive these uninteresting, uninformative letters, not from physical weariness. Hell, I sleep for hours and days but from that blank mind that cannot even force a decent word. I think you understand that because you can read it in my words. Even if I never mention it, you can read it. I'd bet that if you look over my letters periodically, almost like clock work, you can see the extent of that blank — Besides, I'm almost always a total blank.

Darling, I am going to close. I am sending you that program [*of the London Symphony Orchestra*] I promised I would send. One of these days, I might be somewhere where I can take a picture and you will have one pronto. I'll have to wear a hat so that you don't notice my curly (?) locks or I'd better wait until it grows. But please, Darling, don't cut your hair. I promise never to cut my hair short again.

So long, Honey, take care of yourself. Give my love to Mother. May God Bless You. Ever yours. Love, Mike.

April 28, 1944 [*Friday*]

My Darling,

Here I am again. Just a bunch of rambling thoughts. Perhaps, foolish, perhaps stupid but they are simply thoughts. I don't know how long this missile is going to be. I may say, "I love you" and end it. But surely you won't like that a bit. I was looking thru' *Coronet* magazine. There were a few pictures in it which prompted my ideas for writing and secondly brought about a thought which I had long since forgotten.

As you know, photography in *C* is excellent. In the last few (2) issues that I have seen, they have had some perfect pictures of good-looking, handsome children. And as I said before, it prompted an idea in my meager brain. It seems funny to plan a family even before we are married. But looking at these children and hearing about my nieces and nephew and seeing their pictures, makes me feel more and more tender toward little children. There was a time when I was quick tempered and intolerant. But that was long before I had any ideas that some day I'd be a father. Since you and I have decided to be one, I have looked forward to the day that children would be of great importance to us. Born in a free world out of the love of two people. You have never heard a whisper of patriotism from me. Not because it means nothing to me but because I believe that I am typically American. We accept our love for our country deeply, unconsciously and with no eye toward reward and no outbreaks of over emotion. To us a mere thrill or slight tear is enough to keep our faith in our flag and country. I thank God that He made me a part of a great country. But my overall thought is not for myself nor my gratitude. What I am thinking is that two peasants were able to bring six healthy children into a country that offers them every opportunity in the world. And how we, their offspring, will in turn do the same for our children. Only with more of an advantage because we are taught and have seen the greatness of our country. In these days of turmoil and war, I have no fear for the ultimate end of our U.S. Even if I am not able to share the happiness of victory, it will be gratifying to know that I have lived my full life under circumstances unequaled thru'-out this immense globe. Our children will be very lucky. At least, they cannot help but to be healthy children and if they lean slightly toward their mother, they will never have to fear the taunts of society. Darling, I love you.

Darling, My Bette, I don't think that you need to worry about our plans. Even when you ask me to quote, I cannot do it too proficiently. For people like ourselves, we never need extensive plans. If you just look back over the days that we spent together, you will realize that we didn't ask, "What shall we do?" We did it and forgot that there was a question that might have been asked. Woman, I love everything about you. There has never been a doubt or question in my mind. There has never been a hesitation nor anything that might have been an impulse. Everything that had happened has been done as if it was supposed to, with no reason to question, as naturally as if we had known each other from the day we were born.

I am not speaking words because they look good but because I have thought of every thing that has gone by. Things which are the backbone of our love. Things which are cementing a foundation of love that is as great as we could ever imagine. Things which I do not speak of in my letters because they are for you and I and not for the intermediate eyes of a censor.

Darling, I am closing. But you have shared the thoughts which I formed because I looked at the picture of a little child. A thought which should be shared only by you. And is shared purely by you.

Good Night, My Darling. May God Bless You. Love, Mike.

The War Diary entries for April 28-30 read:

> **April 28: Formation flying and glider tow in the morning. In the afternoon there was an instrument flight check, glider tow and paratroops drop.**
>
> **April 29: There was a personal inspection of personnel by the Group C.O., Lt. Colonel Fleet. There was a meeting of all Staff Officers with the Squadron Commander. A lecture on Escape was given to all Air Crew personnel by an American Officer who had just returned**

from enemy territory. Special Services arranged for a guided tour of Stratford-on-Avon.

April 30: Practice landings in the morning, afternoon schedule canceled on account of pay day. One plane cross country to York and another to Wrexham and return.

May 1, 1944 [*Monday*]

My Darling,

Here I am back again. I see by my records that I have finished nearly all your letters. It takes a lot of high, hard letter writing but I'm succeeding. I feel pretty good today. My ole' tent mate, Max [*Gilliam*] and lil' Moe [*Dan Emery*] and myself managed to bribe a bottle of "Highland Queen" scotch out of some guy and I do mean a good time was had by all. No scars, no fights, just a good time not even a big head. After I finish your letter, I am going to hit the sack for a few hours. Had to get up early to do some work. Bette, I meant to tell you that "Ole Nell" [*nose art for my aircraft*] can't be painted. It seems that they removed most of our women. But I'll always think of her as just that even though she won't sign her name to the form. I guess that's about all of the local dirt for the time being. No mail today but tomorrow is another day. Nothing bothering me for the time being. As a matter of fact, My Love, I am a man who is happily in love and not a worry in the world.

I am glad that the mail is getting to you. However, I can't explain why it comes to you in such a static form. It may be that when they herd all the mail in the P.O., they become well mixed up and in the general melee, the later letters get to you first. I wouldn't worry though, as long as you get them.

I was glad to hear that you are reading so much. It will never hurt and it really is one way to get a liberal education. At least, it is a pleasant way to do so. Even though I can't do as much heavy reading as I used to, I can, at least, read my *Sporting News* from top to bottom. Keep my nose in the sports news. I sent your suggestion on to Harry. I haven't heard from him yet, but I am sure he will appreciate it. Since my sister does not smoke, the compact will be ideal.

You ask me to cure your cussin' habit. I'm afraid that's one place I can't help you. If I don't clean up my own tongue a bit, I'd never be able to help you. Besides that, I am afraid you would be a bit annoyed with my language. Since your picture is on my locker and you are forever watching me, I try to cuss as little as possible. After all, I should try to set a good example.

Oh Yes, Bette, I am sorry I cut my hair. I want to get a picture made but I hate like Hell to sit before a camera with this mop. I don't want you to think that you'll be marrying a convict. It won't be long before it will be grown back in. Sorry, Darling, I'll try to do my best to get my curls (?) back again!

Let's see, now, I think I discussed that Cadet idea before. Everything has been "scrubbed." "Washed out." I had heard that about most of the boys are being sent to infantry units but I didn't believe it. I thought that it was one of those latrine rumors that we hear so often. But since then you have mentioned it and I have heard it from other sources. What the Hell, might as well wait until this show is over.

You mentioned a few lines about psychology. Don't worry about it. I'd hate like Hell for someone to look into me. I am liable to find out things that I'd rather not know about. Besides, I spend enough time with myself to know me well enough. To top it all, who gives a damn. I got to live with myself a long time after so there really is nothing I can do about me. Do you get my idea of repetition? Everything that would ordinarily happen with some-one else will happen within me. (Barring the sexual entries.) Crazy, isn't it?

Really, Darling, I am awfully sorry if this letter sounds sketchy but I'm afraid that that scotch and heavy meal I had are catching up to me. I'll close now and start again when I am refreshed. I may be busy for the rest of the day but I may also be able to squeeze in a few more pages later on.

So long, Honey. Take it easy. May God Bless You. I love you. Mike.

On May 1, nine planes were used to fly a squadron formation in the afternoon, and five were sent to Greenham Common to pick up gliders.

Eight planes were used for radio navigation flying on the morning of May 2. At night, 12 planes flew in squadron formation. Special Services arranged for a trip to the New Market race track. The weekly staff officers' meeting was held in the squadron comman-der's office, and an NCO (Non-Commissioned Officer) meeting was also held that day, according to the War Diary.

May 3, 1944 [*Wednesday*]

My Darling,

It is a quiet morning. Everyone seems to be asleep. Resting after a series of strenuous activity. So sorry, Darling, I never did get a chance to write again the other day. After I woke after a bit of a catnap, I felt just like that something the cat refused to drag in. I do mean I felt rough. But I feel more like a human being now. I had a funny thought at breakfast this AM. You seem always to worry about appeasing me that your cooking will be satisfactory to me. After eating this GI food for so long, I don't think that I'll be so very difficult to satisfy. I really feel good, Darling. For some reason or other (ink spot!) I feel extremely happy. Maybe it isn't happiness, but it is a keen feeling of satisfaction. Now, I'll see if I can finish answering the rest of your letters. By the way, the mails have slowed again to a snail's pace, [*will*] probably get hit with a pot full in a few days.

You mentioned that Lockheed Transport that broke a record on a transcontinental flight. I haven't heard about it but I have seen pictures of Douglas' Constellation. It's a big 4-engine job with a twin tail. She really looks like a sweet ship. They say she can go too. I think Douglas has the right formula for transports. They know how to make them.

I know that it didn't miss your eye. But did you notice that Brooklyn got beaten by the

Giants by a score of 26-8! If you don't think I didn't take a ribbing, you're crazy! Gad! I thought that the guys would never stop. But the way I feel about it, if they've got one bad game in their system, it's best that they get rid of it. Just wait until they tangle with the Cards! Ah Ha.

It is about time that you decided to smoke a good cigarette. After all, that means that we can have just one brand of cigarettes in our home. Those little things seem to be so important. It feels so good to be able to talk about small things that appear to be so unimportant. Simple little things like a mutual feeling toward candle light and bourbon; Philip Morris; ham and eggs and things like it.

You mentioned in your last letter a few things about the beach and ocean. You have heard me mention over and over again the amount of fishing I used to do. You have heard me speak also of Long Island. I did a lot of surf casting on the Island. It isn't a big place but it is beautiful. The Island is approximately 12 miles wide and 120 miles long. There is a place about 95 miles out on the North Shore called Mattituck. There is a huge bay which is part of Peconic Bay. It is ideal for swimming. The water is crystal clear and the sand is as clean and white as it can be. When you swim under water, it seems as if you see for miles. Around the outer side of the bay is a breakwater. It is a long brick [*stone?*] wall that extends for about a ½ mile out into LI Sound. The beach that surrounds the area is long, clean, and occupied. It is an ideal place for beach parties, etc. On a clear day, you can look across the sound and see Connecticut. The beach is about 200 yards wide and it blends in an abrupt manner into a larger cliff which is about 100 to 200 ft. high. In this one spot, the beach extends for miles. It is a lovely spot, a place that needs no one to beautify it. It would welcome a few but despise many. Along this North Shore that I speak of, there are any number of such places. Centerport is the home of the annual sail boat regatta. It is the ideal vacation spot. Then there is Stony Brook and Rocky Point. — Rocky Point is one of the liveliest summer resorts on LI.

Somewhere about 75 miles out in the middle of the Island is a fresh water lake. It is called Lake Ronkonkoma. It too is a resort spot. It is a lake that is a few miles around. I have spent many a careless and carefree day out there. We would leave on a Friday night. Just a couple of guys. No women. We would do some bowling first and do a little bit of drinking. Then about midnight we would head out. It was a beautiful drive. Eddie [*Brown*] had a model A Ford convertible, 1930. It was an ole wreck but it satisfied our means. A couple of gallons of gas were all that we could afford. After we reached my ole' hut [*Wyandanch*], we would either sleep or drink some more. The next morning we would be off to Ronkonkoma. The days were perfectly spent. A little swimming, a little playing, occasionally some of the lighter sex, not too often, tough really. We would get back to the city on Saturday or Sun. Depended upon what was on the schedule. All in all, Bette, it was an experience that made the depth of my youth. I liked to swim, above all, I like a deep tan and a healthy, clean feeling. Oh well. It isn't the end of my life. There will be many days like that. It's true that it won't be done with the zest of youth, but you and I, even as mature people, will never be old.

Well, Honey, I must close. I have a special reason to write to Chicha.

I love you, Darling. Do take care of yourself. May God Bless You. Love, Mike.

The May 3 War Diary entry read:

> **Formation flying in the morning; one cross country and return; one plane used to drop paratroopers; Dingy drill and Link Trainer** [*flight simulator*] **instruction in the afternoon. Up to two 24-hour passes permitted each month beginning today. Weekly dance with the 316th TCG** [*Troop Carrier Group*] **orchestra furnishing the music. A trip to Stratford-on-Avon made this date. Three airplanes were transferred to the 31st Transport Group.**

On May 4, the weekly officers' meeting was held, at which time Captain Cooney, the Intelligence Officer, talked about censorship and security, according to the War Diary.

May 5, 1944 [*Friday*]

Hello Honey,

Here's that man again. You must be rather tired of receiving those pint-sized letters of mine. If I recall correctly, you were tender toward a quart. I wouldn't mind sloshing thru' a quart of good bourbon!

I received a nice letter from Lucy. She tells me all the preparations that are being made for Tom. You can understand that this is going to be a long discussion among my family members until much time has passed. I guess you know already that the dates have been changed. I suppose that you and Chicha have already finished or discussed plans for your visit, if you have decided to do so.

Whoa! Is my face red! You know you discussed that transport that had done such a fast trip across the states. Well, I turn around and tell you of another that was just as good. Now, I discover that we were talking about the same ship. What rattled me was that I thought the ship was a Douglas craft. My mistake. Sorry, Darling!

It is a quiet afternoon but by far one not suited to inspired writing. Again that mood of blankness. It seems as if I couldn't think of anything even if I tried. I can't seem to get any foundation for a letter. Just try to put a few scraps together and I'm afraid that you'll have to be content with what may appear as a letter. I see by the paper that the Brownies and Cards are leading the leagues. The Blues are 4th. But the league has started only recently so by the time that the season starts rolling, Brooklyn should be right on top. Hell, the Cards haven't got a chance. If they weren't so physically incapacitated they wouldn't be able to field a team. One of the guys got a musical clock. It plays 2 tunes — "Wooden Soldier" and "School Days." They call it "The Nickelodeon." There is one unoccupied bed in our bay that we use for card playing and general lounging and bull sessions. That we call the USO. That's just an example of the ingenuity of the American Soldier. A fighting man (?) who can acclimate himself to all and every environment.

I slapped a pin-up gal on the wall near my bunk. Some dame by the name of Leslie Brooks. One of these gals with bedroom eyes, expect that one of these nights, she'll creep into my sack. The horrible creature.

Say, Honey, I meant to ask you about this Sinatra rage that we hear so much about. Or have I mentioned it before? We hear the American Forces Program every so often and there is a program on it called, *The Barracks Bag*. Somewhat similar to a request club. It seems that they play a lot of "Frankie's" records. In one of them, "Shoo, Shoo Baby" the record was made with a lot of women sighing, moaning, and just yelling, "Frankie!" It gets so bad in one place that Sinatra actually laughs in their faces. He must think that they are a bunch of jerks. I can't blame the guy, but it is a Hell of way to earn a living.

Random thoughts but no where to ramble. Haven't had any mail from you for a few days but what the Hell tomorrow is another day. Now I can understand why the Cocktail Hour should remain as a permanent American institution. There is a part of the day when there is nothing to do but engage in some silly, useless talk. After all, the British have their Tea hour; the Mexicans have siesta. You can see by this note that I haven't a care in the world. Darling, I do love you. That is the one thing in my thoughts that is permanent and prevalent. It is there like I am here. Never forget nor do I care to forget it. When they send a guy to a place over here, they should allow him to take a treasure with him. You are mine.

And so with that pleasant thought, I conclude my lecture for the day. Doesn't it sound so shell-like.

Give my love to Mother, Darling. Take care of yourself. May God Bless You. Love, Mike.

On May 5, the War Diary reported, an officer's mobile post exchange was in camp to supply the officers with shoes, clothing, etc.

May 6, 1944 [*Saturday*]

Good Evening, Darling,

Saturday night. I could be at a dance but I feel so restless that I'd much rather not. I'd probably make an ass out of myself. Besides I feel like a good drunk and since I can't get a spot to drink, I can't very well get started. So here I am. Believe me, Darling, not as a last resort but as the best turning point. I went to see the *Constant Nymph* earlier this evening but I had to walk out because the sound was so miserable that it was impossible to enjoy the show. Guess it's just a useless, stupid feeling I am not getting around the way I used to and I am not seeing as much as I did. The final feeling is one of nervousness and restlessness. The feeling will pass today or tomorrow or the next day but it will pass. I shan't worry about it too much.

I received your letters of the 24th and 25th. The funniest thing I read was that all of you are betting on the future show [*the invasion of Europe*]. Funny because it sounds so much like a big ball game, I'll bet that Lloyd's and Jack Doyle's and all the big betting houses are reaping a fortune from this affair. It seems so silly because there will be so many mothers' sons involved. It makes us feel rather angry to think that we are being used as pawns for a bet. Then to think that it will all be broadcast. Just as if Army and Navy were playing their annual game at Philadelphia. Yes! Folks. It's a great day. They are lining up to kick-off. There goes so and so. He just got tackled and hurt on the runback. Exciting and ever so gruesome, isn't it Honey?

What the Hell! Might as well let it go! Darling, so sorry that you complained about the lack of mail again. But I do think that my recent letter explained the entire situation. I see by the papers that New York had an extraordinarily warm day. 80 degrees and in May, too. It sounds like the middle of summer. It must be a marvelous time of the year. I saw so many years of Spring and Autumn and I love both times of the year.

Darling, you speak of [*the writer of travel literature Richard*] Halliburton. I know that you are as much a lover of travel as I am. I hope and pray that God will provide us with the means so that I can make your dreams an actuality. I know that I have said it before but I'd like to show you many of the places that I have seen. Above all, I'd like to see a lot of America. It isn't the idea of just seeing these places but it is a matter of seeing them all together. Darling, I love you so much. Believe me, now, more than ever I dream of the days that we will be together. Gosh, Honey, I miss you so much. (I left for a minute or two to devour a sandwich of Spam and a few anchovies, tuna fish and a nice slice of pineapple.) Now we are looking for a snort so that we can blow our tops. Really, Darling, it isn't just me.

But, Thank God, Bette, the days are passing. We can wait and wait. Each day becomes longer than the next but they are passing. There is no reason to complain. There is no sense to look to anyone else, consider ourselves and let's just cry about the whole thing. Darling, I am looking eagerly toward the day. Everyone can talk about D-Day but all we talk about is De' Day. I love you, I miss you. I shall never stop loving you, You are mine and I don't give a damn for anything else.

Darling, I am reading an awful lot. I've started, *My Son, My Son* by Howard Spring. It's a great book. It appears to be rather dry and yet I don't seem to be able to leave the book alone. It isn't dry. The author writes in the first person and he writes in such a matter of fact way that you can't help but to enjoy it. I'll tell you more about it when I get further on. Have you read Ernie Pyle's *This Is Your War*, yet? Think you'll enjoy it. At least you will be able to re-live some of my days.

Must close. I'll pick up my book again. Might as well relax. Give my love to Mother. Take care of yourself, Darling. I love you so much. May God Bless You. Love, Mike.

The May 6 and 7 War Diary entries read:

May 6: Instrument flying in the morning; group flying in the

**aftenoon. The Squadron Commander made a personal inspection of
all personnel, in the barracks.**

   **May 7: Squadron formation flying in the morning; in the after-
noon, Link Trainer and Group Glider Formation flying. One cross
country flight and return.**

May 8, 1944 [*Monday*]

Good Morning, Darling,

   Definitely is spelled with an "I" not an "a." Such as a definite liking with a mutual interest can be easily said, I love you. I received your letters of the 26th and 28th [*April*]. I
do mean that is quick service. Darling, your letters made my happiness unbounded.
(Someone is getting a hot foot!) (It didn't work!) I am really glad that you and Mother are
going to New York. By the time that you receive this letter, you shall have seen what I have
talked about for the last year. It seems so funny that I'll have to speak in the past tense because you won't get this until you get back.

   Well I can't start to talk in the passive because I don't know what you have seen.
I'll let you explain everything to me. Tell me about everything, be sure not to miss a
trick. The places you see. The people you meet. The way you feel about everything.
And above all, don't be afraid to give me your frank opinion about all. Gosh, just
knowing that you are going makes me feel as excited as you are. I have pictured you
always among the familiar scenes of KC. I can't imagine that you will be in NY.
I had planned to be the first to show you our fair city. But I am so very glad that you
are going. It will be such a great change for both of you. I am sure that you will like it.
I hope that you will be satisfied living in the atmosphere I have known for so many years.
You'll be able to walk thru' the streets which sheltered my birth, youth and pre-mature
adult stage. You'll marvel at our sights and get lost on our subways. You will probably do
a lot of shopping and undoubtedly get a stiff neck looking at our stratospherically tall
buildings. Believe me, Darling, I don't want to brag but you'll feel as if KC is a dwarf
among the ruins when you have seen the monstrosity of our city. I do know that your
week will be well planned. I am sure that Chicha will take good care of you. Dad will
use his best wine, if he has any. Mom will feed you 'til you burst. She will feel that
you need those 10 or 20 pounds which we talk about so much. My Aunts [*Tess and
Maggie*] will be bubbling over. Tess will talk about everything. Maggie will be typically
shy and my cousins will scrutinize from stem to stern from port to starboard. You
needn't worry, just be your plain self and they will love you as much as I do. I am sure
that you will have a dinner date with the Smiths [*longtime friends of the family*]. You
will be duly impressed because their apartment is a nice place. I am sure that you'll
enjoy that. You will meet all those plus Ted, Louise, the babies, Sally (my sister-in-law,
Doc's wife, Harry's sister.) and the Koch family (Harry's family and Lucy's future
in-laws.) and of course all your future in-laws. I do hope that you like all of them. Then
you will see people who will appear insignificant to you. People who typify the section

of Brooklyn from which I come. People who are not intelligent, speak with little English but who love my family and have watched it progress as closely as they have watched their own families. People who have always been important to us in a minor sort of way. They are not perfect but they are proud, proud of us all. Casual but you know that they are there. Darling, I am as thrilled as you are and I am looking forward to your visit as much as you are. I can't wait for the day. I will feel every moment of it. And to top it all, you are flying across. I do hope that your reservations are made. But I do know that you have taken all those precautions. If you should have some need for some extra money, don't be afraid to ask Chicha for it. I, too, have made reservations for that. I don't want you to sink too deeply into a mire. I want you to accept any help, with no feeling of shame or humiliation. After all, Darling, what is mine is yours. I do have a few bucks saved so don't be afraid to approach Chicha. She has all my instructions.

Gad! If the feeling is as nice to you as it is to me, you will be overjoyed.

Darling, I am going to close. I'll be on pins and needles until I hear about everything. I hope that you and Mother have a time which you will never forget.

Take care of yourself. Give my love to Mother. May God Bless You. I love you so much. Love, Mike.

War Diary entry, May 8:

> **Radio Navigation and Radar training in the morning. Link Trainer and glider formation in the afternoon. One plane test-hopped and another used for high altitude flying.**

May 9, 1944 [*Tuesday*]

Good Morning, Darling,

Well, here I am again. I have spent some rather enjoyable hours. It may be because I am in one of those moods that calls for expansion. I don't know. But I have noticed always that I never like to waste time or precious moments. Many years ago when I read John Kiernan's life (Kiernan of the *New York Times*, and "Information Please," one of our modern geniuses), I learned a very valuable lesson from him. He spoke of time and the value of it and how stupidly we waste and abuse it. In a mild sort of way, I have tried to accept that as a lesson. I notice that most of the fellows around here like the ole' sack. They get up early for roll call, eat breakfast, clean the barracks and if they aren't busy, hit the sack. To me, that is like rotting in cotton. I like to read and when I'm not reading, I am writing. I read late into the night and I started early this morning. This book, *My Son, My Son* by Howard Spring, is a good novel. It is funny but I have found it is almost impossible to describe such a book unless the one to whom you speak has also read it. It is the kind of book where you feel as if it is so hard to read and yet harder still to lay aside. I have read no more than 300 pages of it and still I am thrilled and excited to find out what is to happen. I shan't try to describe any part of it but I do know that the main character, it is written in the first person, is a very queer and somewhat nasty character — as mean and inconsiderate and thoughtless as may be. I cannot help but feel that the end of his novel will leave him as a person to be pitied. But that is neither here nor there.

I had meant to write to you again last night. Your last two letters left a few words that amused me. Not amused as we think of it but with a feeling that I must answer to it and comment. It is a parry and thrust of conversation that is not silly prattle but an enjoyable *tête-a-tête* of light conversation. But there I go again, sound as if I was taking my reading too seriously and that I was trying to duplicate a novelist. I get a kick out of it every time that you mention that you are eating a lot and that you are hungry always. I like to kid you about being pregnant. Funny that as long as we knew each other before I left, I never think of the times we supped together. I don't think that we ever really sat down to a good meal. We spent most of our time just picking up something small, then came the drinks. Most of all, I recall that we loved, laughed and were infinitely in good spirits. You know, Darling, we did have fun. We did get serious once. That time in Fort Wayne. It was the one time we laid our hand out to find out what the score was. I guess, now, I know that we found that the cards were loaded. Darling, I love you. Do you remember the night in KC when those high school kids had just returned from their prom or some sort of dance? Do you know, Honey, I felt old that night. It was one of the few times that I realized that a few years have passed by. I think we were sober that night, weren't we? I do know that we had a Hell of a time with those kids. Remember the night I damn near had a fight with that Looie. It's a good thing he left. I think there may have been some trouble. Every time I see a P-38 pilot, I think of the "John" that you tried to give the hot seat one night in the Tropics, Hotel Phillips. (That's the name of the place, isn't it?) Just one line from you and I think of a hundred and one things to say. You mention on the next line about not wanting to cut me up with those bones of yours. You forget that I am rather soft in part. If you recall, I had an operation many years ago on my abdomen. It pouts out like the sack of a Kangaroo. Maybe I ought to wear a girdle. When I get to feeling very low and I think of all the comfortable moments we spent, I can remember those periods of extreme emotional upheaval that seemed to earmark our parallel sex complex and I miss you more than ever. Maybe we are crazy but no one can say that we denied each other anything. We played hard and we loved harder than that. I had never experienced anything so real and definite before. I know that the realization of that fact is mutual to both of us. Every moment was a moment of beauty. Things that we will cherish all our days. Just being with you is something I shall never forget. Darling, we should have made it stand but whatever failings we had before, we will remedy. I love you. I love you more each day. I miss you deeply. If they were but words, I should feel cheap but they are my deepest feeling for you which makes the beauty of it all ever so rich. As rich as the color of your hair, as soft as the touch of you, as real as you and I can be. I love you.

Must close, My Love. Give my love to Mother. Take care of yourself La Locks [*of hair*].

Meant to tell you Nell has changed sex — she is now Lil' Jackie. I'll tell you the facts in another letter.

May God Bless You. Love, Mike.

According to the War Diary entry of May 9,

> **... Instrument and radar flying in the morning; group glider formation flying in the afternoon and squadron formation flying at night.**

On May 10, all passes, leaves, and furloughs were cancelled by the Group Headquarters. One plane dropped pararacks that day, while two were sent to North Witham airfield for radio checks.

May 11, 1944 [*Thursday*]

My Darling,

I don't know what kind of a letter this will be. There is a lot of noise going on, hence, a possibility of the lack of concentration. I have finished Howard Spring's book. Believe me, Darling, I think that it should be a must. It is somewhat on the style of Daphne du Maurier's *Hungry Hill*, but instead of covering a vast amount of generations, it covers just one. (I should say 2 but we never consider father and son as 2 generations!) If you have some time, you should try to read it. I have started *Burma Surgeon* by Gordon Seagraves. It is not the fastest tempo but I feel that I must try to mix some non-fiction in my reading. The title is enough to hint the story or at least the facts.

I must tell you about "Little Jack" [*my plane, which carried the serial number 43-15510*]. "Nell" stayed by us but since we couldn't officially christen her we decided to give her an offspring in herself. You see, our flight surgeon [*Dr. Jack Ellis*], is a Hell of a fine skate. By some mutual agreement and by some mutual affection, we decided that the name be of some consequence to him. One of these days if we can procure a bottle of Scotch (?) then christening will be final. However, we don't intend to smash anything save the empty bottle on the snout. So you see, Honey, we get around. "Little Jack" looks like his mother.

That seems to be all as far as the local news go. I love you. This weather is perfect, Darling. There is no further desire in my heart but to have you in my arms. It is so perfect that one could desire nothing more than to walk forever. No special goal, just meander lazily, as carefree as the atmosphere would permit and with you by my side, I shouldn't care to give a damn for anything. We did it so often when we were together. Do you remember the first time that we went to the memorial [*near the Union Station in Kansas City*] to take some pictures? We wanted to be alone. Just as we settled down to a cozy locked in each others embrace scene, a bunch of kids came up and decided to take pictures right where we were! Darling, I hate myself for living under such a foolish pretense as I did when we were together. Everything was so perfect. It would have been even more perfect if I would have known myself. That's why your visit to Ft. Wayne was so perfect. It had been so long since we knew each other, and I knew what I had felt for a long time. That visit really made our love as we know it now. It was what we wanted always and what we shall have always — I love you so very much.

Darling, I must close. Gotta' work once in a while. Give my love to Mother. Take care of yourself. May God Bless You. Forever Yours, Mike

[*A note by Navigator/Censor Nick Pappaeliou at the bottom of this letter reads: "P.S. Mike's been a good boy."*]

The War Diary entry for May 11 describes OPERATION EAGLE, which was the rehearsal for the invasion of Normandy:

Eighteen planes were used in a Command Mission, dropping paratroopers in a practice flight; take-off time 2315 hours. OPERATION EAGLE.

Chapter 4

EAGLE to TRANSFIGURE, Normandy to Greenham Common (*May 13 to August 31, 1944*)

SUMMER 1944 MARKED the turning point in the European Theater of Operations. Troop Carrier and Airborne forces completed training in a dress rehearsal May 12 for the vertical assault on Normandy. On D-Day, in Normandy, June 6, 1944, in OPERATION OVERLORD (airborne phases were labeled NEPTUNE), airborne and glider-borne troops landed behind the German lines after midnight. Seaborne troops began the horizontal assault of Normandy at Omaha, Utah, Gold, Juno, and Sword beaches under the command of General Dwight D. Eisenhower.

Allied troops continued to press the retreating German forces. OPERATION TRANSFIGURE, scheduled for August 17, was planned to drop troops and gliders west of the Seine River to block the German escape route, but it was cancelled when Allied troops moved beyond the Seine.

Concurrently, in OPERATION DRAGOON, Allied forces successfully attacked the French Mediterranean coast with airborne and seaborne troops.

In mid-August, on the Italian front, Allied forces kept moving northward. In Eastern Europe, Russian troops reached the border of East Prussia. In the Pacific, the Biak operation in New Guinea was successfully completed August 20.

The 37th Troop Carrier Squadron's May 12 War Diary entry describes an accident that occurred during the rehearsal for the invastion of Normandy, OPERATION EAGLE:

> **The paratroops drop mission [*OPERATION EAGLE*] was completed at 0435 hours and was successful except for an accident not involving any of our planes. The Group Commander [*Colonel Burton Fleet*] and Group Chaplain [*Captain Floyd N. Richert*] were among 14 men killed [*including two paratrooper/observers*] when a 36th T.C.S. plane collided with one from the 44th T.C.S., after the paratroops were dropped.**

May 13, 1944 [*Saturday*]

My Darling,

The weather continues to be as beautiful as it has been for the last week or so. Can't complain at all, I feel healthy and I am getting more exercise than I have had for a long time.

I received your letters of the 30th and 1st. Although it isn't the best service, the mails are much better than they were. I must thank you for your glittering remarks about me. At least you concede that your lover is a man of some caliber. You speak of Halliburton and where you put him next. I can see that you are getting a wealth of travel education from him. Perhaps my description of the African moonlight was sufficient. You must remember what and who I had in mind that made my words easy. As long as there is a driving power, the mind is easy to control. Darling, if I sound sketchy, forgive me. I just crawled out of the sack.

I do hope that you tell me a complete description of the visit to my home state. If it can be more romantic, throw a kiss into the Atlantic, eventually it will land on the shores of England. I have never seen the Pacific Ocean but I have seen enough of the Atlantic and other bodies of water. If you ask me, I think they all look alike. Same color, same purpose, same danger just like a glass of water after a big night, they can have the same comforting effect. I must thank your Mother for her grand thought. Since I have been such a miserable son-in-law, I am doubly grateful. I guess I am justified to think that I am accepted.

Sorry, Darling, but since I had such little time in London, I didn't get a chance to see anything too historic, above all, a castle. Someday, I'll tell you a lot of tales but since I am limited to certain subjects, I'll leave all of that to personal talks with you.

Thank God, My Love, the time is passing quickly. When I reread my letters, I shall see how often I have said that to you. Yet it is a thought that occurs at least once a day. I love you, Darling. I am grateful for that because if I had no one, each day would be an eternity. Your visit to New York has done a lot for me. I can vision all your actions. In that way,

I place myself with you. How much I miss your tenderness! How easy it is to take this waste of time to know that one day I shall have passed all this and you and I will be living our life together. I hope that your thoughts of me have made life easy for you. When I feel mellow, I don't have to sit in an easy chair, light a pipe, and hold you in my arms. I merely think of it and the feeling fires within my very lonely and hungry soul. Yes, Darling, love is a funny thing but without it there would be a lot more funnier people.

Take it easy, Honey. Give my love to Mother. You'll probably have a lot of reading to do when you get back to Kansas City. May God Bless You. Love, Mike.

On May 13, a funeral was held for the 14 men who died in the plane collision the day before. They were buried at the Cambridge cemetery. The War Diary notes that "transportation was made available for all who desired to attend."

May 14, 1944, Mother's Day [*Sunday*]

Hello Love,

Since you aren't a Mother yet, there is nothing I can say for you on this day. However, my deepest regrets to Mother because I cannot do the same this year as I did last. This day also reminds me of the great favor you all did for me last year. Unfortunately, there is no one of such kindness with me now. Darling, I do love you so deeply. Although I haven't heard from you for the last few days, I shan't gripe. I have received mail from other sources, home and Harry and a few other of my friends who are overseas. So you can see that I am not lacking for correspondents.

"Pappy" and I swallowed a quart of Irish whiskey which we were lucky to procure. Believe me, I felt like Paddy's Pig this AM. Things kinda felt ruff this morning. As a matter of fact, I had to sleep all afternoon to recover. I still don't feel in the best of shape but a Hell of a lot better than I did. Guess I am getting old. If nothing else, when I ever get home, I'll be a connoisseur of liquors. (Had to look that one up. Use the word so often that it is best that I know how to spell it.)

Me and my big mouth. At one of our post dances, I was doing a tour with one of these English gals. They played a rumba, so I suggested that we try. I explained the step and told her how to use the lower part of her anatomy. I called it "fanny." She looked at me and said, "Do you know that you used a word that is considered almost unspeakable in the English language?" Later I recalled that the word has something to do with feminine anatomy and shouldn't be used as regular conversation. Was my face red! After all, how the Hell am I supposed to know everything about these people? To cover up, I had the gal believing that I was an old ballroom dancer, etc. etc. Gad, Honey, never thought I was such a bull artist. These dances do help to lighten some of the boredom.

I don't know why, Bette, but I have been feeling light of mind these days. I have been thinking a lot about us. It is the nicest feeling in the world. Being in love with you, is one of the best things that I could ever hope for. I never thought that it would be so easy to live on memories. But I find myself smiling about us. I can hear a song, put the appropriate memory to it [*and*] I can feel it all over again. It is comforting to know that someday I shan't have to put my thoughts on paper. All I'll have to is draw you to me and whisper some sweet nothings into your ear. Joy of joys!

Well, Darling, I must conclude. Think I'll read awhile before I hit the sack. One night I drink myself into a stupor, the next I read myself into one. I think that that is the better.

Good Night, My Love. Take care of yourself. One more week, you'll be in N.Y. May God Bless You. Love, Mike.

The War Diary entries for May 14-16 read:

> **May 14: Major Fletcher, Squadron Commander, requested all personnel to be sure to write home on Mothers' Day. All scheduled flying was called off and instead there was a meeting of all officers of the 316th T. C. Group; called by 52nd Wing Headquarters, at which Lt. Col. Berger was named as the new Group Commander to replace Lt. Col. Fleet. Captain Cooney, Intelligence Officer left for the British Prisoner of War School at Highgate for a six-day session.**
>
> **May 15: ETO [*European Theater of Operations*] orders restricted all personnel from 0001, 15 May 1944 through 0600 hours, 17 May 1944.**
>
> **May 16: Received orders, IX TCC [*Troop Carrier Command*] that all personnel, equipment and supplies were to be packed up and ready for a simulated move by 0600 hours, 17 May 1944.**

May 17, 1944 [*Wednesday*]

My Darling,

I know that I haven't written for the last few days but you mustn't worry. No cause to, every time I settle down for a session of reading, I get called to some sort of duty. The days passed so quickly that I didn't realize that time passed. I managed to finish *Burma Surgeon* and I immediately started *Also the Hills* by Frances Parkinson Keyes. Darling, that is another "must."

To top it all today, I received 4 letters from you. The latest is dated May 9th. Your May 2nd [*letter*] which was an answer to my previous letters was a long, enjoyable, interesting and very informative one. Your words give me an insurance which you may feel I don't need. Darling, you must let me confess things which I do not have a thoro' understanding for. These confessions from time to time may amaze you but you must not forget that I must live to learn. At times, our forthcoming marriage has been of much concern to me. Not from the frigid standpoint but from a view which is normal to any young couple. You see, Darling, I want to do everything right. I don't want to make any mistakes whatsoever. I want so not to be a disappointment to you. My recent literary trend has done much to assure me that my thoughts are not uncommon to others. Things that I feel, things that I have thought of always. I hate to think that they are cheap and base. Above all, I love you and I want you to love me in the same manner. With as much fever and feeling as I have. Since our thoughts are mutual, I feel that you too are the same way. I sound jumbled, I know but I am trying hard to make myself understood. I have found that I loved you not for a day but want to for always. That as we both noted, each day adds more to us. I think I am growing up, finally. We shall have our struggles but [*they*] will not hurt us. I think that we are too big (literally not figuratively) to be beaten easily. I had felt that I would not be able to please you. Your reassuring words make me see how stupidly wrong I was. I want you to understand that whatever you say to me, you must believe it in reverse. What I mean is the credit that you heap upon my shoulders. Remember, Darling, since you, — my well-balanced ledger of favorable feeling has been due to you. For once in my life I seem stumped for the proper words to say. I want to thank you so often for you that I hardly know how. Believe me, Darling, it sounds so stupidly unlike me but I guess I just haven't got it tonight. I haven't started to answer your letters yet, so you can see that I have much more to say. I'll leave it at I love you for now but that isn't all.

So long for now, Darling. Gosh, I feel slow tonight. I want to go on and on and I can't even get started. —

Take care of yourself. May God Bless you. Love, Mike.

P.S.: Try to read that book, *Also the Hills*. Read it carefully — it is well worth the time. I love you — M.

On May 17, trucks carrying equipment and personnel departed and returned on the simulated move that had been ordered the day before. All other personnel were inspected to ensure readiness. The War Diary also noted: "Combat crews' pictures were received from Group S-2." The restriction that had been enacted on May 15 was called off.

May 18, 1944 [*Thursday*]

Good Evening, Darling,

Guess I must be in love, for the second time in almost a week, I have addressed your letters as KC, New York. Gonna go crazy soon if I keep that up. We had a funny incident the other day. We found a mouse in the barracks. Hell it was a riot to watch the fellows try to capture it! A guy's got to pass the time somehow.

Today is Ascension Thursday, a Holy Day of Obligation. Since it was also Tom's ordination day, I not only went to Mass but I received Holy Communion for his sake. It is all a means of prayer, My Darling, so you can feel that you too were not forgotten.

You must forgive me if yesterday's letter seemed to be full of a lot of distractions because it was. Aside from a lot of jumbled thoughts, there was a lot of noise and I could hardly concentrate. But I do want to thank you again for your very reassuring words. It leaves me little to desire except you — I have been quite content of late to bask in the sunlight of my many happy moments.

I received a very nice letter from Chicha. She is quite excited about your visit. I imagine that all of you will get along so famously. I see by one of your letters that you intend to stay at the Astor if it is possible. I can readily see that you and Mother are really making a grand fling at it and I can't blame you. I have often lolled about the bar at the Astor but I never stayed there because there was no reason for it. When you mentioned that Harry James was at the Roof, I was jealous and homesick as Hell! In the flash of that momentary thought I could feel you in my arms as we danced to his marvelous music. I do think that we did quite a bit of dancing and the more I danced with you the prouder I was of you. Pardon my boldness, Darling, but we do make a handsome couple. Not only such a meager descriptive adjective as handsome, but strikingly so, your blonde, beautiful hair and my dull black mop. I like to think of you in the atmosphere of the surroundings which I loved for so many years. It couldn't have been more perfect. I am thrilled and happy that your decision was as it is. It was left to your judgment and it was my very wish. I do love you so very much, My Love. You have made me and kept me so splendidly happy. God! You are too good to me.

Darling, I must close. Forgive me again if I seem to be rushing. I can't help myself. Take care of yourself. My Love to Mother. May God Bless You. Love, Mike.

On May 18, the War Diary recorded only that nine planes had been used for formation flying that day.

May 19, 1944 [*Friday*]

My Darling,

I have finished *Also the Hills*. It was longer than I expected but it was well worth it. I discovered in part that it got "mushy." But the underlying thought and characters are perfect. I have found that I enjoy to read, not for the plot but for the knowledge I might gain of the character and personality of people. Then, too, as I mentioned before, the openness of thought that is revealed. Some of the words which I have said to you are words which were written before but they express the meaning which I try to portray. Surely it would be marked conceit if I thought that my thoughts were extraordinary and virgin.

I was glad to read in one of your letters that you were so completely changed insofar that you are more relaxed and much happier. I know that I studied you very closely. But it is hard to determine a person's failings in so short a time. It takes a lifetime. People are always lacking something which they need so badly. We found what that was. Perhaps, we discovered it the hard way. Nevertheless, we found it. It is pleasant to think that we have what we want, we shan't need to start over again. It will not be hard to make each other totally happy. I believe it will come easy to us. After all these months of separate planning, Hell! It will slide into mutual assent so easily. I want you to come to me whenever there is anything that may seem to bother you. After all, Darling, understanding is one of the greater parts of love.

You mentioned a few words of wonderment as to whether we would get a chance to see some ball games in NY. Darling, baseball is the symbol of democracy. It is one trait and pastime that is purely American. It will live as long as America does. Maybe we won't see a game this season or next but the years won't tarnish the novelty of the game. Since sports are another of our mutual liking, we won't be lacking for it. Bet, ten dollars to one that I'll convert you to a Bum's fan.

You spoke of "our" bottle of Seagram's. I have never forgotten it. I just recounted the story to one of my buddies. Perhaps it is just as well that we never did get to that party. At any rate, when you and I decide to drink that bottle, we can drink a whole quart of toasts to the guys that would have drunk it. It seems only natural that that bottle should be so significant to us. We did always enjoy a good spot of stuff every so often. I am glad that you are keeping it well dusted. Hope you have a nice red ribbon around it. It's a shame that it will go so quickly. — It is as if I were coming home to Bette and our baby, — or our dog — This is new. I will be coming home to Bette and a bottle of Seagram's, standing side by side.

Well, Honey. Cheerio Ole' Gal. Take care of yourself. May God Bless You. Love You — Love, Mike.

Ten planes were used for glider formation flying on May 19, and there was an S-2 (Intelligence) officers' meeting at the 52nd Troop Carrier Wing Headquarters, according to the War Diary. That evening, a USO show was presented in the enlisted men's mess hall.

May 20, 1944 [*Saturday*]

My Darling,

I feel exceptionally good this evening. I have exhausted all my reading material. My eyes are well rested and hence, My Love, I devote my words sans music to you. Last night we went on another "tear." I felt perfect this AM so no disastrous results. We managed to squeeze 2 bottles of Scotch and 1 bottle of Old Bushmill's Irish Whiskey. That was just about the capacity for 4 of us. Since we don't bother to leave camp and we don't bother to bother anyone, it is an easy choice to merely walk 10 steps and fall into bed. (I shall be most thankful for the day when I shall be able to sit comfortably with a well-mixed drink in my hand and drink slowly and enjoyably. Not for the sake of getting drunk but merely to enjoy it. By some trick of fate, I ended up with a bouquet of red and yellow tulips. We didn't steal them nor did we get into any trouble.) I cut the stems shorter, put some water in my canteen cup and put them before your picture. In my most rhetorical manner, I spoke reverently of their significance — the yellow tulips for the color of your hair — the red tulips for your lover's heart which bleeds so to have you in his arms. So you see, My Love, even when my brain is paralyzed and I am supposed to forget for the moment, I can't forget — No, I can't forget the love that has nourished me thru' out all these months. You are smiling more today, too. You did like flowers, didn't you?

I am sending you this clipping from *S&S*. I do hope they let it get thru' to you. You can see what they think of Frankie. Every time I look at it, I laugh harder. The GI's have the perfect expressions and the WACS — In our barracks we have a different expression for these actions of these women. Unfortunately, it is rather base and I shan't mention it in my letters. However, it is expressive and in one of our solitary moments, remind me to tell you of it. At any rate, if anyone sold buckets, he could make a fortune in one of these audiences. [*This may have been a Hubert cartoon. The males are absolutely stone-faced while watching Frank Sinatra perform; while the females in the audience are going wild with enthusiasm.*]

Darling, right at this moment, you are winging your way across the states. Flying is a dangerous habit, isn't it? Seriously though, I can visualize it. All day I have followed your steps. I think there is a 6-hour difference. At this moment, it is 9 o'clock in the evening here. In the States, it should be 3 in the afternoon. You aren't so far out of NY by now — in a short while you will be at my house. Honestly, Honey, it doesn't hurt — as a matter of fact, it feels good to me — But you can't blame me if I feel slightly jealous. I pray that your visit will be perfect. Chicha has told me that she is taking an extra few days off to entertain you. I must thank her for her kindness. I shall trace your days until you return to KC. Then I want a full report of everything. I love you.

Darling, I must close. I owe Harry a letter. Take care of yourself. May God Bless You. — Love, Mike.

May 20, 1944 [*Saturday*]

My Darling,

I know it felt good to wake up in a strange bed in a strange city and know that the world feels so good, especially since there is someone who loves you so much. Everything so far is ideal, isn't it? Travel the easiest and quickest way. Meet a bunch of nice people, find that you are fascinated by the grandeur of the biggest city in the world and still someone loves you very much. Excited and exciting, isn't it? The first time in New York and know that you won't be lacking for company and something to do. Up early, breakfast leisurely, ride a subway to Brooklyn, a lot of gushing and extravagant talking, so much to say, so much to do. Church, strange edifice of so many hidden mysteries and hopes, surprised, stunned and amazed by a rite that is as old as our days. All that, every thought and every move, above all of it, the shadow of someone who loves you. Oh, Darling, I know it so well. I wanted so much to share it with you. I wanted so to be the one to say: "Mom, Pop, Chicha, this is Bette, my future wife." — Alas and alack, Woe is me, *Tempus fugit*, etc., so all this happens and I can't be a part of it. No, I'm not hurt nor jealous, just eager. I wish above all things that soon I'll be able to retrace all your steps. I hope that I can make you come to NY for the second time in one year. Darling, I love you. But I shan't dwell on it. I know that between you and Chicha I will receive a detailed description of your entire week. Not a care in the world, no worry about the material loss, the cost — Mike wants it this way and so it shall be. You will see all the relics of your lover — things that I haven't seen for such a long time. I hope you can feel what I have left behind. Darling, I want you to learn as much about me, merely by being able to see the things and places I have known all my life. But I think I have said all this before. You take it from there and give it to me clear and packed.

I have written to Harry and Chicha and I feel as if I have written a novel but I had to write to you. Not for anything but just because I felt like talking to you.

Most of my tulips are gone except two which I have stuck in the folds of your picture. I have pressed 2 into a folder of my own, so that I can preserve then for a future tale. Getting sentimental in my old age aren't I? But I haven't seen flowers for such a long time that I didn't realize how much I missed them. I still haven't answered all of your latest letters, so you can see, Bette, how much more I still have to say.

At this time last year, we were getting ready to wind up a very lovely friendship. As I look back, I can remember that you wrote to me every day then as you do now. Funny you may have known then but I didn't realize what was to become of that friendship. If I had you would have been Mrs. Ingrisano by now. But I guess it wasn't the true spirit to talk about what should have been. Sundays were always our best days, weren't they? They were a climax of a very anti-climactic Saturday evening. It is amazing how quickly we recovered from those rough Saturdays. Now, I'm sorry that I studied so much and that I didn't see more of you. Hell! Look what all my studying got me and think of all the time we would have had together if I had studied less. Perhaps, it was all for the better. We know what we missed, and it makes us all the more grateful for what we are to look forward to. Darling, I love you, or did I say that before. I guess it's normal.

Flashing thought — You must have been awfully disgusted with my eagerness the first day you came to see me. Or were you flattered? I know it isn't the thing to talk about but look beneath the surface and realize the beauty and meaning of that long-awaited meeting. I owe you a million and one apologies for some of my actions. Someday, Darling, remind me to go thru' all the days from the time I left you until the time I saw you again in Ft. Wayne. First of all, remember that there wasn't any inkling of what is now. I won't tell you in a letter. There was nothing wrong with my actions, but my brain was in a whirlpool of emotions.

Gonna close. Gotta wash some clothes. Take care of yourself, Honey. Give my love to Mother. May God Bless you. Love, Mike.

⁊⚘⚘⚘

The War Diary entries for May 20-22 provided more details on the mid-air collision of May 12:

May 20: Lt. Roman gave a lecture to the new personnel on Escape, Censorship; and Security. Ten planes were used for glider tow formation flying in the afternoon.

May 21: Squadron personnel attended Memorial Services for those men who were killed recently. Captain Cooney returned from school at Highgate.

Oprep 'B' No. 1 for 24 hours ending Sunset <u>12 May 1944</u>.

Narrative of Operation:

"Eagle Training Exercise called for seventy-two (72) aircraft of the 316th Troop Carrier Group to transport a token paratroop force from Cottesmore [*our home base*] via March, DunChurch, Cefn Llechid [*in Wales*], boat #1, boat #2 [*checkpoints just off the coast*], and on to the DZ [*drop zone*] near Devizes [*in southern England*]. Three paratroopers were on each plane, two of them jumping over the DZ. The operation proceeded smoothly. The paratroops being dropped on the DZ at the appointed time with the exception of one man who refused to jump. On the way home after the jump, two of the Group planes collided in mid air resulting in the loss of all personnel on both planes." [*Troopers were from the 504th and 505th Infantry, 82nd Airborne Division.*]

Following is the official description of OPERATION EAGLE, called "Mission Report, 316th Troop Carrier Group (Consolidated) EAGLE Mission, May 12, 1944," filed under Record Group 18, Entry 7, Box 124 at the National Archives:

EAGLE called for 72 aircraft of the 316th TC to transport a small paratroop force from Cottesmore, via March [*the 52nd TC Wing assembly point*], over DunChurch, westward for 159 miles to Cefn Llechid, Wales; then south for 50 miles to a marker boat in the Bristol Channel; and east for 55 miles to Devizes, which was the IP [*initial point*] prior to the final move into the DZ.

The idea behind OPERATION EAGLE was to use training missions to keep the Germans guessing. By taking off as if we were headed for the Continent, German radars would be able to pick up the flights and think that the invasion was coming. There were several checkpoints, all in England or just off the coast, so that the lead navigators could tell that the planes were on course to the drop zone, which was near the city of Devizes.

On May 23, the War Diary noted:

Air crews are being trained in glider pick-up. There was radar training in the morning and formation flying in the afternoon.

May 24, 1944 [*Wednesday*]

My Darling,

I haven't written for the last two days. I got into another one of those lazy spells. Plenty of sleep, a little work, very little play and no mail. All in all it's a very bad situation. I hope for the best so I shan't gripe. I haven't told you about our embryonic kennel. It now consists of 2 cocker spaniels and one Scottie. The Scottie is female and she is called "Bonnie" — a good natured gal but at times she can be very ornery. One spaniel is a black male called "Snowball" (Register as Prince Blackstone). He is full of pep and vinegar, a lot of Hell, playful and healthy. The other male (spaniel) is a light coffee colored brown with white markings on the breast and right hind leg. His name is "Fudge." He has distemper and we had to send him to a hospital. The poor guy had any number of fits and froths. We are hoping that he can be cured. In the meantime, the other pups (all are from 6 to 8 weeks old) are well pampered. Everyone of them has a pedigree a yard long. At least. This is one diversion that keeps the fellows in good spirits. Once the gang of pups are thoroly housebroken, it will be easier to care for them. I guess that just about covers the gang.

Can't understand this lack of mail. I do hope that the next mail call will yield fruit. I guess you must be feeling the end of your visit by now. I know it's only Wednesday but time seems to go so quickly in cases like that. I wish to God I could look forward to the end of my stay here. But Hell compared to some of these guys, I'm in good shape.

I am not going to hang my head in shame but "Dem Bums" aren't in such good shape, are they? The ball club isn't as good as it used to be. As a matter of fact, the line up looks like a bunch of foreigners to me. Ole Dixie Walker is really slapping the apple around. I hope he has a good season. The Cards are right in there but I don't want you to start, "I told you so!"

I am glad that you are assenting about the idea of children. At the time that I mentioned it to you in KC, I had no idea that some day I might be the cause of your future maternal pains. My ideas were the same as yours. I never did think too deeply about children. But as you say, it is a normal reaction. The reason I believe for our mutual feeling before was that we were too interested in ourselves. When a person thinks alone, that's just what he does. After all, why think about our offspring when you can't even decide a thing for yourself. But when you find your mate (crude sound, isn't it?), it is natural to think of the future — what is better than to include children that are born out of love into the future with us. Hell, we'll probably end up with a set of sextuplets!

You mentioned *Mrs. Parkinson* in one of your letters. I read a condensation of that in *Omnibook* many months ago. I don't think I ever mentioned it. I found that it was a most enjoyable piece of literature. (Dungeon is spelled with an "eon.") I do hope you get Pyle's book. Don't send it to me. I'd rather read it later on when the memory of these days is faded rather than when they are still fresh in my mind. I do hope that you are saving my letters. There are so many things to discuss that I could never cover. I try to save as many of yours as I can.

Darling, I must close. There are a few things to do. Haven't forgotten that I love you very much.

Give my love to Mother. Take care of yourself. May God Bless You. Love, Mike.

The War Diary recorded on May 24 that glider pick-ups had been made from the air for the first time; the flights were successful. That morning, there was also radar training, followed by formation flying in the afternoon and at night.

May 25, 1944 [*Thursday*]

Hello Darling,

Note the fancy writing paper. It isn't local stuff. I got it from home. Finally got a package of stuff I had asked for. Glad to get it, too. (*Barracks Bag* is playing Harry James' "Velvet Moon." Remember the number, Darling?) Since I wrote to you last night, we had an addition to our wolf pack. One of the kids [*Tony Cimmino*] got back from London and bought a mongrel back with him. Cost him £2 ($8.00). We named him "Gremlin II." Cutest thing you ever saw. He stands knee high to a grasshopper. He must be about a foot long. He is black with white toes and a white diamond on his breast with a pinhead white point on his tail. He's so young, he still can't see perfectly. Cutest thing you ever saw. He's got all these thorobreds beat. We made up a phony pedigree for him. We had it typed up, put a phony signature on it, had "Grem" put his foot print on it — put an English stamp on it and officially made him a class "A" mongrel.

I got your letter of the 10th of May. You aren't kidding about the idea of saltpeter. It's true that most of them are kids and naturally and typically American hot bloods but it doesn't excuse their conduct. However, your other idea is the blow that hits the nail squarely. Idleness is the perfect cause for bad conduct. But that is not for us to say. The Gods and rulers are the ones to determine the management of these kids.

That character of rank that you talk about must be a page out of Runyon. You aren't kidding about that cigarette smoking. At times, I have smoked as much as 2 packs a day. In most part I try to stop it by lighting my pipe. It helps. However, about things being rough, it looks rougher from that side of the world [*than*] it does from here. I was surprised to hear that he was an Air Corps man and that he believed in such a rigid attitude toward his men. Especially since he was supposed to have done all the things he says that he did. He surely must realize that there are 4 other guys besides himself. When his number is up, it wouldn't make any difference if he was a general or a buck private, but he'd go the same way. I've seen a few examples like that. If he feels that way about it, he not only is in the wrong army but he is wearing his rank in the wrong place. Surprised it doesn't pinch him every time he sits down.

I am glad that you liked the program I sent you. I rather thought that it was as complete as one would expect. After all, a composer doesn't write music unless there is a definite story behind it. We would hardly be expected to know the story unless it is told to us. Then it is easier to blend story to music and the appreciation is fuller.

Promise not to cut my hair again. It has started to blossom again but I'd never guarantee any raven locks. I don't get those floating waves of the dream man. The silver threads are there but they denote age, not always dignity. You don't want me to be old and useless, do you? I don't think you'd be happy with me! Maybe we can live on love (?).

That quote you sent me would be the kind of a thing to show to that "big time" son-of-the-devil. I doubt that he'd appreciate it. Surely I do. When the time comes, Darling, I want to go first. But that is to be left to the future. You will always be a thing of beauty in my eyes. You will never cease to be so as long as we live. This love that I feel for you is one that is mounting and it reassures me with a feeling of permanency that cannot be overcome.

It's Thursday. Three more days and you will be on your way to KC. Gosh, Honey, I've been praying that everything is perfect for you. I know that I am being repetitious by saying that but it is just the way I feel. I want you to leave NY with the most pleasant memories, aside from ours, of a lifetime. Going back to it and me will be easier.

Darling, must close. Take care of yourself. Give my love to Mother. May God Bless You. Love, Mike.

A glider practice mission scheduled for May 25 was postponed for 72 hours due to weather, according to the War Diary. The next day, there were glider pick-ups in the morning, as well as two cross-country flights. That afternoon, there were instrument and radio navigation flights. A meeting of all combat crews was also held that day. The War Diary entry for May 27 noted squadron formation flying in the morning and parapack drops that afternoon.

May 28, 1944 [*Sunday*]

My Darling,

It has been days since I wrote to you. I'm sorry. I reserve writing to you until I have written everyone else. But as has happened for the last few days, I have been called to do something whenever I was ready to write. I love you. I received your letter of the 21st. It is one that I shall try my best to preserve. It was written from NY. Darling, you talk about your hop like a veteran of thousands of hours. From the sound of it, you were fairly well "bumped" across the entire country. At any rate, I am glad that you were fortunate to get to LaGuardia.

Of course, your letter was inadequate but I understand perfectly. You have loads of time to give me every description you can think of. I can see that you met most of my family and I am glad that you did. I have never met Mr. & Mrs. Koch. I can't imagine who this Frank is unless he is my cousin-in-law and I don't know who Fr. Lacy is. At any rate, you must [*have*] felt rather pious to have such nice company.

So you like Mom and above all her cooking. I knew you would, Darling, she's a grand person. You mustn't worry lest I don't get along with yours. If I recall correctly, you don't do so badly. I am glad that Mother and yourself got off to such a smashing good time. I know that everything will be OK. You can't miss. Especially if you top it off with a ball game under the lights at Ebbets Field. Brooklyn won that game, 3-2, didn't they?

I can't elaborate much on what you said. The most I can do is surmise. But I am still looking forward to the rest of your letters concerning your visit.

Darling, I was going to continue this letter tomorrow but I'll finish this and then write again. You see, I've got a wee bit of a hangover and to boot, it is so hot this evening that I've got a Hell of a case of Spring fever. I know that I can't make this letter very interesting. I just don't feel anything but ruff tonight. I do know and I can say that I love you very much.

Right at this moment you are on your way home. It must be a hell of a feeling. I hope that you have enjoyed yourself so much that it is a torturous feeling. Not because I want you to suffer but because I want everything to [*be*] so perfect that it will make everything so much easier for you.

Darling, honestly, I must close. So sorry for this horrible letter. I promise to do much better. A good night's sleep and I'll be in good shape. I'll explain everything in my next letter.

Take care of yourself, Darling. Give my love to Mother. May God Bless You. Love, Mike.

May 28, 1944 [*Sunday*]

My Darling,

I know that I have just written to you but since I don't want to retire yet, I am writing again. The weather has been beautiful today. Someone said that it was 100 degrees in the sun. There is a nice balmy breeze blowing thru' the window and I can think of no better pastime than to write to you, My Darling. Not only have I got a dull feeling in my head but just as I was sitting down to write, one of the guys called me to show me what "Grem" was doing. As I leaned out the window, I leaned too quickly and not low enough. Gad! What a horrible shot in the head. That dull feeling I was talking about is a direct result of over-indulgence. I'm glad that [*it's*] over.

I received a letter from Sheila, Tony's wife. She sent me a bunch of pictures of the Rebel. My little Honey is really growing up to be an adorable child. Kinda' makes me feel old to think that she is growing. She is 11 months old now. Darling, just think, if we had played the game the smart way, our baby would be at least a year old. You'd have a companion. From a look at the size of us, our children ought to be a pretty big bunch of kids. Oh well, we have years to start.

So you saw the Bums play. How did they look in their new satin suits. Really must look classy under the lights. I always did get a big kick out of night games. Very seldom missed any of them at Ebbets Field. I used to travel over to the Polo Grounds in New York to watch the Giants whenever they played a night game with the Bums. One thing about it, was that when I would come from work at night, it was a treat to divert from my normal course of life. If I had thought of it, I was going to suggest that if you did go, you should have taken little Mickey [*my cousin, Mike Petruzillo, now DDS*] with you. He's a good kid to watch a ball game, smart as a whip. I used to get a big kick out of it to take him down and listen to his enthusiastic chants ("Kill the Ump." "Yer Bum." etc.). Don't mind if I talk this way, Honey. Just the thought that you are doing the things I would like to do with you, gives me a nice feeling. It almost makes me homesick.

I am glad that your (can't spell tonight!) hotel suite was satisfactory. You sound as if you had a Hell of a job getting your plane. They really have some fancy names for their kites, don't they? I always thought they used the word "Flagship" in all of their names. An airliner is a really a classy looking ship, isn't it? The way they handle them, well polished and waxed, they can get at least 170 to 190 M.P.H. That's a good cruising speed for any plane. It beats riding a train any day.

Well, Honey, there's my little line of chatter. I think I can creep into the ole' sack and sleep it off. Take care. May God Bless You. Your tattered, well-beaten Lover, Mike.

The May 28 War Diary entry noted only "glider tow flying in the morning and afternoon."

May 29, 1944 [*Monday*]

My Darling,

Good Morning. I don't feel as badly as I did. I slept a long night thru' and now I feel like the first bloom of spring. The weather is still beautiful. I've got a lot to do but I had to write this AM just in case I am not able to write later. I must make this short but Darling there is a special request I must ask from you. Here I go again and I am sorry but I promise to make it up to you.

Little Rebel, Our Niece, will be a year old on the 22nd of June. Again I am at a loss for doing the right thing. Would you be so kind as to get her something? I don't know what to suggest, maybe a piece of jewelry, a necklace or bracelet or something. Have it inscribed from Aunt Bette and Uncle Mike. I don't know what to suggest except what I have already said. I leave it up to you. Address it to:

Mrs. Anthony Ingrisano
Section B — 1225 Unit
C.A.A.F.
Childress, Texas.

Please do that for me, Darling. I owe you so much I hardly know where to start being grateful.

As I've said already, the weather is perfect. Gosh, Bette, it is one of the loveliest days I have ever seen. Do you remember the day we went to that Memorial Park in KC? The day when we just strolled easily along the streets. When we got to the Park, we were bothered by kids and dogs. We took some pictures, too. You remember the one where you decorated my hair with daisies and clovers. The reason that I think about it is that today is just that sort of day.

I have to laugh about that sentence of mine about strolling easily. I don't recall one time that we did anything else unless it suddenly started to rain. You know, Darling, we never seemed to have a care in the world. Who would have thought that a year later I'd be on this side of the world? That's what I liked about us. Carefree, easy-going, unworried, everything accepted as normal, as if we were 2 other people. If you think about it, there was so much security and good in the whole feeling. One cannot say that we didn't know how to get serious. Darling, I love you. I love you for everything that you are and what you have done for me and what you mean to me. I can never forget you as long as I live.

Darling, honestly I must run off. My free time is up for the morning. I still have a few things to do.

Give my love to Mother. Take care of yourself. May God Bless You. Ever requesting something, Your Lover, Mike.

P.S.: Thanks again for the favor. I know you will handle it as ably as you have everything else. M.

❧❀❧

On May 29, ten planes took part in a Wing glider mission, according to the War Diary.

❧❀❧

May 30, 1944 [*Tuesday*]

Good Evening, My Darling,

I feel at a loss for words this evening. I don't even know what tree to bark up. I don't know whether to dream, to be philosophical or just to write. Since I have done nothing interesting for such a long time, I can't give you any ideas of what I may have done. Fortunately, I have been busy enough to keep my mind occupied. The weather still is ideal. As a matter of fact, at this very moment there is a refreshing breeze blowing thru' my window. But even at that, that doesn't create enough words for an interesting letter.

Decoration Day today, the official beginning of summer. All the resorts, pools, lakes and all the recreational spots are opening. This is one of the nicer times of the year. Nope! I can't even get started on that. Looks like you'll have to be content with a variety of nonsense. Even at times, nonsense is hard to think of.

Darling, sometimes I think the fates played a dirty trick on us. It took us so many years to meet. We are wasting some of the better years of our life. Lord only knows how many more we may waste. Don't think that I'm griping, I am running aimlessly over a number of thoughts of a guy who is thinking of nothing else but of the girl he loves. Sometimes, we are apt to feel that people have placed too much drama on this play of life; yet, look at these words which I have imparted to you. So often have we seen scenes of the soldier thinking of and writing to the one he wants to go home to. If I could be photographed at this moment, I might just as well be that soldier. I'm not unhappy, far from it, my thoughts of you have done much to keep me in good spirits. It is just that I am putting these thoughts on paper especially for you. I know that you go thru' the same thing. Very often I think of you and your actions. Surely you must feel the same as I do when you are writing to me because you have said so, so often. Curled up in that comfortable settee or sitting at your table in the kitchen I can see the pen stuck between your teeth as you so deeply try to tell your lover how much he means to you. Sometimes I think it is better if we just say it in three simple words, "I love you," and leave it at that. No, that isn't right, there are too many ways to say it. It would be so nice if I could help you to say it personally. We must promise now and never forget it — we must make our future perfect — so perfect that these days will be forgotten as they started. I do love you so very much.

Hope there's some mail tomorrow. Sweet dreams, My Love. Take care of yourself. Give my love to Mother. May God Bless You. Love, Mike.

The War Diary entries for the last two days of May read:

> **May 30: There was glider pick-ups in the morning; also two planes were used to fly cross country. Two planes were transferred out of the squadron. Nine planes were used for squadron formation flying in the afternoon.**
>
> **May 31: Eighteen squadron planes took part in a group formation flight at night.**

June 1, 1944 [*Thursday*]

My Darling,

I received your letters of the 17 and 19 of May. Darling, you must never worry that you might say too much about New York. After living there all my life, it is easy to understand that I hunger for any sort of news. Especially since you are foreign to New York, it is a novelty to hear your opinion of the bold and lordly structure on a rock.

This [*name omitted*] that you speak of is one girl who has seen enough hard luck for a while. That is the whole trouble, trouble seems always to concentrate on one group. They are feeling the war and naturally the next guy doesn't give a good damn. If it is any good, offer my felicitations. I can understand fully how they must feel. But surely, Darling, don't you think it would have been much better if the girl's baby had lived? I don't intend to preach about it because it is of no connection to you and I. But the baby would have been theirs. As it is, she would have been with his shadow but time helps to make people forget. The baby would only remain as a symbol of the past, not the sign of a person, but the sign of a world that is living so stupidly and will forget as easily. In all events, if she remarries it will be an ex-serviceman. I daresay we have a fairly good understanding of these things. If she had the baby, her next husband would surely understand the circumstances. Remember I'm not preaching. Today is one of those perfect days to talk so many things out. At any rate, there's a memory she will never forget. Gosh, Bette, here's where I change. I love you.

As I said before, this is one of those days. It is raining. I haven't a care in the world. I can think of nothing better than just to talk to you.

Darling, those pictures that I spoke of seem to be a thing of the past. It burns me up to think that just for the sake of having a few pictures of no consequence developed, I have to wait for the duration plus. I have heard nothing about them. Lord only knows when they will be done. I'll send them immediately, when and if I ever get them.

I understand perfectly that you would be unable to write as long as you were away. Since you are my most frequent correspondent, I miss your letters but it makes it easier for me to understand how you feel when I can't write over a short period of time. Don't worry about it, Darling, patience is one thing that I have developed. It is one good trait that I am thankful for.

"Nell" is a thing of the past. "Little Jack" is entirely overhauled. So much so that he is a new person. I want you to remember this day because it is the first day that he officially joined our family. He is a pretty good "Joe" at that, though I know nothing about him yet. It won't take long for me to know his faults, etc. Darling, another month has passed. Chalked that one up. It passed rather quickly. You must have wondered a long time about my Sgt. Rating. Obviously, if you didn't you must be as tired as I am about writing the same one over and over again. Next month, July 1st, it will be exactly one year since you sewed my three stripes on. What I mean is that I made it one year ago next month. Keep your fingers crossed. I hope to add one more next month. At least, I hope so. After all you may cease being proud of me if I don't add something new once in a while. The extra dough is more than anything. After all, the more money that we have, the better start we will have for future insurance. To be honest, Darling, I'm not too worried about it. As we have discussed so often, we can't miss. I love you, I love you more than these words can ever express. You know, Honey, I feel like a veteran. This is my 21st month in the service. It isn't a long time but I may have had a fairly good start in civilian life by this time.

How do you like that line of chatter? I don't think I can do much more. We just finished swabbing down the barracks. The place really smells clean. Even cleaned the windows. Washed and clean, feel like a baby out of bath.

So long, Darling. See you tomorrow. Some day we won't have to say that. Take care of yourself. Give my love to Mother. May God Bless You. Love, Mike.

On June 1, the War Diary recorded:

Three planes were used for cross country and three were radio checked in the morning. All afternoon and evening schedules called

off on account of weather. Test No. A., B., & C. on aircraft identification was given to all combat officers by S-2 personnel. Thirteen glider mechanics (EM) were transferred out of the squadron to the 53rd T.C. Wing.

June 2, 1944 [*Friday*]

My Darling, Bette,

I received a letter from Tom today. He sounds excitedly thrilled. I don't blame him. It was dated the 22nd of May — two days after his first Mass. He said that you are charming and Ted admires my taste. As yet, Tom hadn't spoken to you, so I expect another letter shortly. Am so glad that everything turned out so wonderfully. Spottily but steadily I am starting to piece together that little drama that took place at my home a short while back. Oh! Darling, I prayed so hard that everything would be perfect. I feel like resting my head on your lap and hear you tell me the whole story. I love you, Darling.

I know that [*there*] are going to be a lot of things which you will fail to mention. You can't help it. I'll ask some questions. If you have answered them already, answer them again. I never tire of hearing of my home. How do you like our sturdy old brownstone? I imagine you had the usual share of sessions in our living room. It is one of the coziest places in the house. Many a night we sat around talking about stupid little things or solving problems that appeared so big for us. Long winter evenings and short summer nights, never did the charm of that marvelous place leave me. I spent many quiet and pensive moments there. I won't ask about the gang because I know that you'll cover it. I don't imagine that our neighborhood was very impressive. But there is more to it than you can see. I could turn over stones and tell you a story. How did you like our small, inadequate but fruitful back yard? Even in a crowded place like that one could find a lot of solace and relaxation in that little ole' spot. Oh, Bette, there are any number of things I could think of. The more I do, the more homesick I'm afraid I'll get. When I get home, Darling, we must go thru' all of it together. I guess the family pulled out the album and showed you Mike at 3, etc. I wonder if Mom showed you that picture of me in the Teddy Bear suit. I was only 3 and it is one of my favorite poses. And of course, you must have seen the one of me at 10 yrs, wearing a pair of goggles [*flying goggles used by older brother, Tony, when he was in the old Army air service at Mitchell Field*]. Thought I looked "snazzy." You could [*not*] miss seeing my high school picture and my portrait. Pretty sharp character, wasn't I? I can tell you where they are. My H.S. picture is on the china closet in the kitchen or dining room. (We never are formal!) My portrait is on the piano. There was plenty of me around, I am sure. I don't think you were at a loss for memories. Thinking like that, puts me right in my front room.

Darling, I must close. The mood is perfect but torturing. There is a lot of time yet to discuss everything. Take care of yourself. May God Bless You. I love you. Love, Mike.

War Diary, June 2 entry:

> **Instrument flying in the morning, one plane test-hopped and two planes cross country and return. Nine planes were used for formation flying in the afternoon.**

June 3, 1944 [*Saturday*]

My Darling,

I received your second letter from New York. "The Crossroads of the World," how I wish I was standing right in the middle of that cross road. The traffic might be heavy but I'll be damned if I'd care. It must have been strange to be in a black-out. I've been in so many, feel like an owl. It will take some time to get my eyes adjusted to the light.

So you saw [*Charley*] Spivak. I don't know if his band has changed any. It has been so long since I saw him that I wouldn't know. But as long as he puts that trumpet to his lips, I don't think there would be any change. The last time I saw him, he played [*Jules*] Massanet's "Elegy." That trumpet sounded like St. Peter's Golden Tone. It was the first time I ever saw an audience really appreciate it too.

Let's see, 73rd and Riverside — I can recall the joint you are talking about but I don't know who runs it. Mayor La G[*uardia*] lives up there someplace but I don't think it is his place. On the East Side, near 5th Ave. and 74th is another beautiful place that is owned by the Vanderbilts. Talk about a joint, that really has class. I don't think I'll ever be able to buy one like it for you. I am glad that you were impressed by the grandeur of that part of our city. It is the nicest part of town.

I didn't think that PFCs [*Private First Class*] were allowed on the Roof Garden [*Hotel Astor*]. It surprised me that you didn't say "General" or such. But the Garden is a nice place, isn't it? Harry James — need one say any more. I am glad that you were entertained. I'll trade all my fortunes (?), my stripes, my position to have been that PFC for just one minute. Some guys have all the luck.

You didn't think that you'd get lost. As long as you manage to keep your eyes on the signs, it's the easiest town to get around. It never cost me any concern at all. But I guess, I'll have to excuse the Ole' Hick. Darling, you're marvelous.

Cherrystone clams are not a delicacy unless you eat them in the proper atmosphere. Even if they are seasoned properly, they cannot come close to an oyster or shrimp cocktail. However, when the fishing is dull and the sea floor is sandy and you dig a few out of the sand with your toes. Insert a knife cleanly but firmly spread his jaws, free the meat from the shell and start. Gad! They aren't bad at all. We'll try it someday.

Darling, I must rush off. I'll try to get off a longer note later. I'm not very busy but there are a few things I must attend to — Take care of yourself. May God Bless You. Love you and Miss You. — Mike.

War Diary, June 3 entry:

All personnel were restricted to camp as of 0900 hours. Ten radio operators were checked in Rebecca [*guidance equipment which allowed planes to find paratroops on the ground who had landed earlier*] **training in the AM. Another trip to Stratford-on-Avon. Six new glider pilots were checked out in Horsa gliders in the afternoon.**

June 4, 1944 [*Sunday*]

My Darling,

The shades of evening are slowly being lowered. Sound like an author, don't I? Really, Darling, today has passed so quickly and quietly that there is no room for thought. I have lived today thru' all our memories that I find that it is hard to put them on paper. I love you. To add to the solitude of thought the day has been filled with soft music coming from our radio at the end of the room. It has been wonderful today, Sammy Kaye, Andre Kostelanetz (I think it is spelled that way) and any number of other types of dreamy music. You know, Bette, I have heard James' "Velvet Moon" any number of times. The thoughts and memories behind that song are enough to drive any man mad.

Oftimes, and pardon my veering from the subject, I notice my limited vocabulary, my use of simple English, my broaching on simplicity. Many years ago, when I was a student in my last year of high school, my teacher in English praised my usage of ordinary language. She contended that the meaning and not the magnificence of the word was the ultimate goal. Ever since then I have never tried to overstep my knowledge nor flaunt my intelligence.

My Darling, and again I am back. These last few days have been yours. Hardly a moment passes that I dare to look from your eyes. Please believe my words as the words of a mature man and not of a love-struck boy. You mean more to me than I have ever realized. How often women have been a passing mode, an exit for my passion and the meaningless depth of my emotion — These thoughts no longer exist in my happy brain. I want to love you as fully, as passionately, as honestly, and as sincerely as I have always dreamed I would love the woman who is to share my future. Remember always, My Dearest, that I have never put myself up as the model of perfection but if ever I ever wanted to prove myself to anyone, it is now and to you. Someday, which day we are so patiently awaiting, I'll be able to do more than to put it into words. I shan't try to spear this mood with the physical, at this moment, that, too, is too materialistic. I want you to think of my love as a love for you, not for your beauty but for your heart and soul.

Darling, I hate to drop this as I have. Like everything else, my letter must come to a close. Don't even let these words pass from you, though. They have imbedded themselves so into my heart that only a world's end would put them to a halt.

I love you.

May God Bless You. Mike.

On June 4, one plane in the 37th Squadron was used for radar flying, while two flew cross country. The War Diary entry for that day showed that 22 glider pilots had been transferred out of the squadron.

Also on that day, General Dwight D. Eisenhower, Supreme Commander of the Allied Expeditionary Force, postponed D-Day — the invasion of Normandy — 24 hours, to June 5-6, because of unfavorable weather forecasts.

The War Diary entries for June 5 and 6 read:

> **June 5: Eighteen planes took off at 2315 hours, loaded with para-troops and parapacks, which were to be dropped over France at 0157 hours, 6 June 1944. Captain Shadwell, executive officer, read messages from Gen. Eisenhower and Brig. Gen. Clark to all remaining personnel.**
>
> **June 6: All eighteen planes returned from their drop mission over France [*Ste. Mere Eglise*]. Several planes were damaged by machine gun fire and flak, there were no personal injuries. All paratroops and parapacks were released over DZ and the entire mission was carried out successfully.**

June 7, 1944 [*Wednesday*]

Good Evening, Darling,

Here's that big goon of yours again, Darling. I love you. I'm sorry if you worried because I didn't write. Darling, you must understand that I'll try to write as often as possible. I've been too busy getting sleep and eating in my spare time. It seems so long since I last heard from you. I got a letter from Harry. He's been promoted to major. In his letter, he sent me a letter that my sis had sent to both of us. It was a complete description of Tom's mass and the reception. It was wonderful to read. I got Harry's letter on the 6th, yesterday. I shall preserve that day and letter for a long time in my memories. Before I forget. Did you receive "Pappy's" letter? I'm anxious to know what he had to say.

Darling, I love you. I don't know if you recall what I said when I left you last July. If you can, I can't repeat it. I want you to remember it always. You have heard me say it often and over again but allow me to repeat — there is more power in prayer than I ever realized. You have said it to me, too. Darling, I've thought of you an awful lot. In one of my spare moments, one of my most definite thoughts was a conclusion which was made as firm and as secure as I'd ever want. Darling, you are mine. You are going to be my wife. I thank God over and over again that He has made me so happy and secure. You may be wondering what I must be thinking of — Feel it, I know that you do. It is the same as I have repeated over and over.

Darling, you must forgive me if I make this short. The same as I said to Mom, I had to write to both of you. You must be content with short letters for a while. Right now, I am going to head for the sack. You keep scolding me about sleep. So I shall try to get as much as I can.

Good-night, Bette. Take care of yourself. Give my love to Mother. I love you. May God Bless You. Love, Mike.

War Diary entry, June 7:

> **Thirteen planes were used to drop parapacks, containing ammunitions and rations for the troops [*that*] landed yesterday AM. Three planes had to return to base due to bad weather, the other ten planes carried out their mission successfully. Five planes were damaged by machine gun fire and flak. The navigator of one plane received a bullet wound in his left leg. There were no other casualties.**

June 8, 1944 [*Thursday*]

My Darling,

I received your first letter from home. I can see quite definitely that your visit was not as successful as I had prayed it would be. True, you were impressed by our city but that I expected. It is novel and gigantic. I am glad that you enjoyed that part of your vacation. As far as anything else goes, I must try to be as understanding as I have tried to be always. I'm afraid I'm a bit let down, not because of you, Darling, but because of what you wrote. Remember always, I love you. I love you dearly not as these words go but as my heart feels. It, our marriage, is my ultimate dream — Even in my moodiest and darkest moments, I find it is my only source of sunshine and light. But I shan't try to flower your concern by words.

Let us think of ourselves first. We have agreed always to talk things over. I'll try to give you my ideas but I want you to tell me all the circumstances that prompted your letter. I am sorry that your experience was so bad that you were willing to divorce me, even before we were married.

I cannot imagine what must have been wrong because you don't mention it. But I shall tell you what I think. You can supplant the circumstances and we can see how serious all of this is.

Someday, shortly I hope, you are going to be my wife. We will be two people living independently of everyone else. Marriage will enfold a new world to us which will be foreign but it will belong to us, our own creation to do with as we please. Remember me as a person mature enough to know where his future happiness points. In the play of life, it takes certain events to prove to a man what act belongs to him. I've found it, you are my leading lady. Many years I played the appeaser, the second rater whose only glory was a bow at the end of the play. I respect my family for everything they are, for everything they have done, but the part they play in my mature life, ceases to be a major part but purely a minor part. They are in the background as far as I go as an individual. My wife comes first. — Tell me what was wrong. I must know. As a middle man or should I say at the bottom of this totem pole, I am supposed to know what to do.

I was sorry to hear this. In these days when I have my mind left open to pleasant dreams, it is unfortunate that we have a problem. But it is best because it can be straightened out now. My plans are being altered slowly. I shan't tell you of them, Darling, but you can be sure that they will be beneficial to both of us.

I am closing now. But whatever there is, tell me everything. I must know.

Take care of yourself. Give my love to Mother. I love you so deeply — In moments like these I miss you more than ordinarily. May God Bless You. I'll make you happy, believe me. Love, Mike.

June 8, 1944 [*Thursday*]

My Darling,

It is quiet. There isn't much to do but to think. Perhaps, it is best if I think out loud. This is the second time that I am writing to you today. I have reread your letter often. I'm afraid that I'm a bit stunned. Since I cannot understand what has happened, I hardly know how to alter everything or anything.

I'm afraid I handled the whole situation raggedly. It is all my fault, I guess. I don't know how to say how sorry I am. I thought that by my insistence, I was doing the right thing. I guess I'm all wet. I think a lot of my good work was spoiled by people who didn't realize my efforts, [*did*] not understand my meaning. I do love you so much, My Darling. I promised that I'd never hurt you and here it is so that I must try my best to alter something I know nothing about. You must have been hurt or you never would have written the way you did. What can I say? I feel so much at a loss. I am so far away I couldn't possibly do a thing.

This is the first time that anything has ever interposed, ever troubled our quiet, happy love affair. I am hoping that you will face it as I am trying to. Believe me, Darling, I am your first concern. Have these last events caused you to lose any respect for me? I must know. I crammed something down your throat and I can see that I was wrong. Trust me, My Dear. What you have done for me cannot be discarded like that old shoe. I have tried my best to be tactful. I have pampered and coaxed. In the middle of my fondest dreams, a bubble burst so loudly, so fully that I am left gazing stupidly at something I have worked so hard to create. Not only for me but for us.

I spoke of an alteration of plans. I might as well tell you. We are going to be married but it will be so quiet that our only company will be you and I. You are afraid that my debt to my family is so great that I dare not move unless I consult them. Darling, you are wrong. You are going to be my wife to be shared by no one. I will be your husband to be shared by no one but you. We needed no one to prompt us before. We shall need no one now. If I could only make myself as forceful as I feel. I am limited by censorship — I cannot tell you what is in the pit of a cavity I always considered my heart. Believe me, Bette, I'm not kidding. Perhaps what I said before about my family can cause you to doubt me. Don't! I was never so serious in my life as I have been to you in these last few letters. Let me see you smile. Forgive me. My prayers have been my sole source of comfort. They have proved to be successful so far. What more can I say or do.

Good night, My Love.

May God Bless You. Your Own, Mike.

June 9, 1944 [*Friday*]

My Darling,

I received your letter of the 15th of May. Just a straggler that finally reached me. I am inclined to forget the unpleasantness of the last few days. Not because I want to but because it seems to be the best for me to do. Believe me, Darling, again I repeat. I am sorry.

In your letter of the 15th, you complain of the heat. Does it really bother you so much? I don't like intense heat but I can stand a good sun to bronze my body.

You ask me if I'd like to live in California. Personally, Darling, I've been thinking of setting home somewhere in any small city. I don't mean some little out of the way place but someplace where we can have a good social life. My ideas and convictions are slowly being confirmed. I think that we will both be happy somewhere alone. Honestly, Bette, not because of what you told me but because I have thought of it a long time. We agreed never to discuss the future. In lieu of what I said, you must feel that I change my mind quickly. I am trying my best to make you happy. My ideas have been scattered for a long time. My yen for New York is slowly waning. To be honest about it, I never was crazy for lights and noise. Darling, everything will be OK I promise you.

The weather leaves me a day of peace and quiet. Now, I am getting plenty of rest. Sleep like a log, eat fairly well and don't give much of a damn about anything.

Bette, I am worried about what you must think. Never in my life have I ever been so concerned about what someone thinks or how much someone cares. Everything was going along so beautifully for us. We didn't care for anyone else or anything. Now, because of some of my stupid blundering, I have almost destroyed a thing that is so sacred to us both. I am eagerly awaiting assurance from you that you don't feel badly and that you care only for what I have done for you.

My letters will seem very sketchy for a while until I hear definitely from you. Feel like I'm sitting on a world of needles.

Until tomorrow. Take care of yourself, Darling. I love you.

May God Bless You. Love, Mike.

P.S.: Excuse the laddie — for things have been a bit screwy around here lately. Give him a few days to recover & he will be the same Mike who left Fort Wayne, when you were there. Nick. [*Pappaeliou, navigator and censor! His references were obviously to the D-Day mission to France.*]

There was no War Diary entry for June 8. On June 9, two planes were test-hopped and two flew cross-country and returned.

The June 10 entry read:

> **Pass restriction partially lifted, part of the combat crew members were permitted to go on the Liberty run to Leicester. Three planes were transferred out of the squadron.**

June 11, 1944 [*Sunday*]

My Darling,

"The Day We Parted" — Tommy Ryan and Sammy Kaye. We were lucky again to catch Kaye's *Sunday Serenade*. It's 5:20 PM but time means nothing to us. If I were to accept my present mood firmly and strongly, nothing would mean much to me. "My Sweet Embraceable You."

Darling, I received your letter of the 22nd of May. Slowly but surely, I can piece certain things above all, I notice a decided absence of mention of my Mother and Dad and Lucy. Since as yet, I know nothing, I shan't even bother to pry. It worries me to Hell but since there is so little concern I don't mind. Darling, I love you. You must understand that above all. You said that you trusted me to do the right thing. As I have said in so many ways, this is the one time in my life that I want my judgment to be true and sure. I knew that you'd like Tom and Mickey and Lee, Mr. & Mrs. Smith, Dan and Gert. I have had some raw deals pulled on me in my life. I have taken everyone willingly and smilingly, regardless of whether it was justified or not. One of these days, the ever-loving, humble Mike will start a young revolution by himself. So many of the things that I have said are not self-explanatory but you must be patient, My Dear. Just relax, let me do the thinking. You forget about everything.

The time is passing. I am still over here. My biggest regret is that my ideas did not materialize because my ideas were known to no one. Again I ask you, My Darling Bette, to trust my judgment. I have too much behind me and ahead of me to fail anyone this time.

I was so sure that you would be impressed by so many things. If I was there, I could have helped you so much more. I can't imagine why but I can see that you weren't helped much.

I must write to Tom and thank him for his decency. I am glad that you think that we are so much alike. He and I get along famously. We never mince words when we are together. I am sure that we understand each other perfectly. He has never tried to impress me with much. He has accepted me as a human of a single brain and body.

For the first time in a while, I had a pass. My only mistake is that I didn't get totally blind drunk. I'll do a better job next time. It's so easy and forgetting is simple and enjoyable that way.

Darling, My Own, I love you and miss you so terribly much. In these troubled days for you, I want so much to be at your side, so that I can comfort you as much as possible.

Take care of yourself. May God Bless You. Love, Mike.

There was no scheduled flying on June 11. An amateur show was presented at the Navy, Army, Air Forces Institute (NAAFI) by members of the 316th Troop Carrier Group and the 316th orchestra, according to the War Diary.

June 12, 1944 [*Monday*]

My Darling,

I had not intended to write to you today but I can't help myself now. I love you, Bette. I received your last letter from New York and the letter of June 2nd sent from KC. I guess my prayers were answered. You see, Darling, for the last week and for this one coming, we are having a special Novena to the Sacred Heart. All of those words may appear as a mystery to you. But it is one period of time when we devote our hours to prayer of deep devotion for which we ask for peace of mind and whatever else we may want. As always, I never pray for myself. I am here. I know what may or may not happen to me. But since I am so far away from all of you, I don't know how well all of you are faring. Above all, my primary interest of late has been that everything would straighten out at home. Your letter assured me that you aren't angry with me. Your attitude also assures me, and I admire you deeply for it, that you are willing to analyze and discuss whatever faults you or anyone else may have.

Now, I guess I can tell a few things I have never discussed before because it concerned solely myself. You see, Bette, in most part, I am the scapegoat of most *affairs de famille*. If anything goes wrong, even if I am so innocent that I am ignorant of it, I am the first one that catches Hell. It is not a new role for me. I am so used to it that I don't notice it but when it comes so close that it reflects on the person who I am going to marry, then my fangs show. You ask me if it is your fault. No, I don't think so. It has happened so often that I couldn't possibly feel it is so. When I hear from home they will ask me why you were so inconsiderate not to call. (It is part of the typical Ingrisano conceit to feel that we must be catered to — not cater.) I have heard the song before, (Why doesn't she call? If she thinks I will, she's crazy, etc. etc.). I've heard it so often, it's sickening at times. Always, it is the other person's fault. Above all, My Dear,

I appreciate your attitude. Although your letter of June 1st was blunt and definite, I accept it as an afterthought. Your letter of the 27th of May was perfectly clear and understanding.

As I have said before, I haven't heard from home for such a long time that I feel like the lost sheep. Harry sent me a 5-page letter from Lucy for our double info'. It was a complete description of the Mass. And yet, since everyone or at least the affair concerned me more, I haven't heard directly from home yet. Lucy is right, Harry gets the mail more quickly. As for other affairs, they have been heaped so heavily on my shoulders that I feel like Atlas. So you can see, Bette, you know my gang for only a week. I've known them for 23 years and I know them less than you do. The funniest part of it all, I am the youngest. The rest of my brothers have done what they wanted and when anything comes up — Mike has the broad shoulders. I am not apologizing for anyone but that's my family. God Bless 'Em. Trust me, My Darling, time is passing, anything can happen, but please trust my judgment.

I am glad to hear you say that it was I who you are in love with and that the adjustments can be made from there. That's the first time anyone ever said that to me, regardless of circumstances. I, and I again say it, appreciate your marvelously understanding statement. I am not going to get mushy and tell you that I love you so much more for it. In all your words, I detect a sense of practicability and so I shall keep it on that plane. The most interesting and most decent point is that you don't try to push the blame over on anyone. You are skeptical because you are afraid that you might be wrong. Thank you, Bette, it makes everything so easy to see. You are right, never pull any punches. It is best that we iron everything out now. As for the toast they gave for everyone and neglected to give for me, it's OK. What the Hell, I know it hurts but my beer is watery enough for tears. It is easier for me to take because I wasn't there. But I know how you feel. You were hurt because that big goon hero of yours was forgotten. Those things do happen, Darling. Can you see my attitude, Bette? I know the story. I could have written it before it happened. I could repeat myself over and over again. I've seen the play so often, I can play every part. I want to hear from you about those letters because I want you to let me know if I have covered it from stem to stern. Then we can let the incident fly and get back to normal people. I could tell you things from the age 1 to 23 and yet it would do no good. There will be changes and the first will be made not in a letter but by myself when I get home and I can assure that I'll be looked upon with awe and admiration.

Of all these words, behind all these thoughts, I have written and thought in a light mood because you did enjoy your trip. Reviewing the ultimate outcome, that was ½ of the idea. Since nothing more seemed to be accomplished, and no gratitude was shown for your trip across the States, you can at least say that you have seen NY and it is a good joint, at that. I must warn you beforehand, Darling, it isn't your last trip.

Well, I must close, Bette. Give my love to Mother. Thank her for me for being such a good skate about everything. Take care of yourself. May God Bless You. Love, Mike.

There were no War Diary entries for June 12 or 13. On June 14 and 15 the report was:

> **June 14: One plane cross country and return. All personnel were permitted to leave camp from 1700 to 0600 hours, 15 June 1944. Trucks left on the Liberty Run for Leicester at 1800 hours and returned at 2300 hours.**
>
> **June 15: Two planes cross country and return. Trucks left for Leicester at 1800 and returned at 2300 hours.**

June 16, 1944 [*Friday*]

My Darling,

I must make this a brief note, Bette, because there are a few things I have to do. I tried to write last night but the guys lured me out to town and I got slightly planked. However, I am in good shape now. I'll write a nice long letter later this evening. I received your letters of the 5th and 6th of June. I got a few letters from Chicha and she sent me a few pictures. She said that someone else had the pictures you were in; but she would send that as soon as she gets hold of it. By the way, Darling, she doesn't mention a thing about anything. The one thing that you must not believe is that whatever happened must not and will not make any difference to us. Dear Bette, again I ask you to trust me. Those things can be altered eventually and in due time they mean nothing whatsoever. I love you, Darling.

Gad! Honey, where do you get those rumors? 14 months and they send you home. Someone must be having a pipe dream. It would be nice to look forward to; I'd just have about 3½ months to go. I wouldn't rely on those things though. Our latrines always uncover those well-known rumors. The Army is one of the greatest places for that. Look at my brother, Lou, 26 months in the Pacific and still no relief in sight.

You must be on pins and needles waiting for news about me. From what all of you have said, our mail was held up. I'm glad that it is now starting to seep thru'. I was in the first wave of planes that went over France on the big day. I can see the headlines in the KC *Star* — "MNI, fiancee of Miss Bette Hill of KC etc., etc." — Don't bother, Honey, I was not alone. They'll probably make me a general or at least a staff sergeant. I hope that that helps to relieve you a bit. Your big, handsome (?) hero is in good shape and still kicking. The only thing this guy wants is a chance to marry his big blonde and be happy forever more.

Well, Honey, I must close for now. I promise to make up for the few days that I missed. After all, a guy has to celebrate once in a while.

Give my love to Mother. Take care of yourself. May God Bless You. I love you. Love, Mike.

June 16, 1944 [*Friday*]

Good Evening, My Love,

I promised that I'd write and so here I am. Just shaved and showered and I feel like a million. Your complaint about the lack of mail must be cleared by now. I don't think I need to explain. I wish I could tell you about my baptism [*of fire*] in great detail but I'm afraid I'd get called down for it. I flew over France with one of the first bunch of paratroopers. Nice work if you care for it.

You mentioned in your letter of the 4th that you felt as if there would be a difference somewhere that we would have to solve. The one solution that makes everything easy is that we are big enough to handle it. It isn't really a solution but a realization that we can take it. Accordingly, we will act as we see fit but only before it is discussed thoroughly and satisfactorily. There is no difference, Darling, believe me. As far as any dictatorial attitude you speak of, you may well forget it because I am not and never intend to be. I don't believe that anything can be accomplished in that manner. The family hasn't mentioned anything because they know how strongly I feel toward you. I believe they wouldn't dare to say anything. Remember those horns I mentioned before. My family knows them very well.

You must forgive me and accept my most humble apologies. New York is not the biggest city in the world. You know how it is, when a guy comes from such a big place, he can't help but exaggerate a few minor details. Bette have you heard this new song, "Lily of the Lamp Light;" or "Lily of Marlene" [*Lily Marlene*] or something like that. I never could catch the name of that song. I heard it long before it became popular in America. Only we heard it in a foreign language in some very different environment — Cute tune, isn't it?

Darling, do I detect a tone of stubbornness? After all, you did say that New York is a nice city and it would be different if I was there. If I were to come home in the near future, you wouldn't want to lose all that time apart. Honestly, Honey, I promise you again and I'm not kidding, it will be different. It is a pity that my entire idea went astray. Perhaps, I'm too much of a dreamer. But everything would have looked so changed. As Harry said, you would have been seeing everything thru' my eyes. If your visit would have been my descriptions, my arrangements for you and we would be together. Central Park would not have been just a park but a place for us to steal a moment of solitude in an atmosphere suited for two lovers. Harry James would not have been just another band, the Roof just another gathering spot. They would have been a place for us to dance to the music of a band that gave us part of our memories. "Velvet Moon" and a multitude of other pleasant moments that can be thought of. "Toffenetti's" would not have been just a place for dinner but a refuge for so many things we would have wanted to discuss. Don't you see, My Darling Bette, there are any number of things I could show you to explain my point.

And as far as my family goes, they would have met you thru' me not as a person who is strange to them. I can do no more than to apologize for their actions, of which I know nothing. 142 [*Somers Street*] would not have been just another place in Brooklyn. It would have been the home where I would have shown you the last 21 years of my life just as you showed me your life in KC. Perhaps, again, I was the dreamer. I thought that you'd feel my presence because my home is so full of everything that molded me. You see, My Darling, I wanted someone to do all that for me. I can see that they failed. Perhaps thru' ignorance, indifference, or whatever have you. Do you think that it will be much of a struggle to convince you what I want to do to help us? Do you think I could do a good job of making a trip like that worthwhile? I am hoping that it will not be too long before I can prove my points. I love you so dearly.

I can't say much for the comparison of the women of KC and NY. You see in KC, I was limited to one lovely blonde. There, I admire beauty but I must be awestricken before I explore beyond just looking. In New York my interests were so diversified that I never cared to study the female beauty of my fair city. Only those that interested me were those that I saw as beautiful or otherwise. But you are right on one point. Lee is a lovely girl. It has been a long time since I saw her. Since a girl grows so quickly at her age, I am sure that she must be so much more lovelier than when I knew her.

Thank you, Patient, I am glad that the Ole' Doctor wasn't wrong on all points. I should have felt thoroughly disappointed if everything went wrong.

Darling, I must close. Promised Chicha a letter about Harry. He and I are growing closer and closer together. He has proven to be a fine guy. Our friendship has become cemented because of our mutual interests, and our mutual exchange of advice. More about that later.

Good night, Darling. I do hope I have done some good. I love you. Take care of yourself. May God Bless You. Love, Mike.

June 19, 1944 [*Monday*]

My Darling,

I received your letters of the 7 and 9 of June. I appreciate the fact that you didn't write too expansively of D-Day. It is one subject which can dry up so quickly and which loses its interest much more quickly. So we shall let it go at that and accept the days to come as normally and as formally as the interest strikes us. All we do know and as you do say, each day that passes brings us closer to each other.

I am glad that you appreciate my elegy on tulips. Perhaps, I could have done a better job but at times my words become limited. They did last a long time; the memory of them will last a longer time.

What I meant when I said that flying was a dangerous habit, was that it is always the first trip that is the hardest. It seems that that is the one trip on which we worry that everything might happen. It is just the psychological effect perhaps. You speak of 2500 air miles; I'm not laughing but I won't attempt to dwarf your record by stating any statistics. However, I agree thoroughly with you, there is no other way to travel. It is the easiest, quickest, safest and cheapest way to move from place to place.

Gad! Woman don't tell me that you don't know who "Dixie" Walker is! Yes, he is from Georgia and a Hell of a fine ball player. His kid brother, Harry, starred in the outfield for the Cards last season. Harry has been drafted into the service but "Dixie" still lumbers on. At present, he is slapping the ball at a .405 average, which is good in any league, even against Cardinal pitching. Give the Bums time, the season has a long way to go.

I'd like to read *Razor's Edge* but I'm afraid you'll have to wait. I can't read as much as I would like to. Hold it for me; I'll be back to you. On one of those quiet evenings at home, I'll be able to read it. After all, Darling, there is still a lot of life to live.

"Pappy" and I went down to see Harry and "Pappy's" uncle, a fellow by the name of Hamel. I felt rather shy because I was the lowest ranking man in the whole bunch. However, that made no difference to anyone, and I accepted the challenge to speak as openly and as directly as I wished to. Harry and I spent most of our time in personal chatter. The whole day, Sunday, was ideal. It was a very odd day in England; the sun was shining. Their billets are ideal. They are in a beautiful private home. Very much like any estate in our country. We sat in soft chairs, set in a lovely garden and drank scotch and water, smoked cigarettes and chatted idly. You can't imagine how great it was. It was the easiest way in the world to get homesick.

It seems that any time Harry and I get together, we start to dream. Our conversations are of no one but Lucy and yourself. He told me that Lucy had consented to get married if Harry ever had a chance to get a leave. I don't mean a permanent leave to the states but just so many days and then report again to duty. I thought it was a sensible idea. But of course, all of it was supposition. Hell! The only way we can live these days is on supposition. Darling, would you be content to have me for a few days and then see me march off again? The way I see it and it is just as Harry and Lucy see it, we would have at least lived in that short period of time. But all of that is a pipe dream but it would be good to know how you feel about it. Makes a guy feel good to know that he can dream and have the girl he loves dream with him. Enough!

Darling, the pups are growing up. They are a frisky bunch. We are giving Gremlin the Purple Heart. He is in the hospital. Poor kid has worms. He should be in good shape in a few days. I'd like to take one of them home with me but I don't think it is possible.

Honey, must close. Take care of yourself. Give my love to Mother. May God Bless You. Love, Mike.

The War Diary recorded no information for June 16-18. The entry for June 19 read:

> **Colonel Berger, Group Commanding Officer, presented the Air Medal to the following named glider pilots for their participation in the Sicilian invasion, in the initial stages: Second Lieutenant Louis A. Browning, F/O** [*Flight Officer*] **Samuel Fine and F/O Kenneth A. White.**

There was no June 20 entry.

June 21, 1944 [*Wednesday*]

My Darling,

This may be the first day of summer but you would never know it here. All we had was a short burst of beautiful weather and now it has again simmered down to typical "Blighty."

I received your letters of the 12 and 13th of June. I am glad to hear, Bette, that my mail has started to pour thru' to you. You must forgive me if I do not write too regularly. It is just one of those things that doesn't take any explaining whatsoever. I never realized that anyone would read a book because it was poor literature but it shows a decided interest of determining what is good and what is bad. It is the only way to become fairly critical of everything.

I'm afraid that we couldn't possibly bring the hounds back with us. You see, they are purely a pastime and we use them for a diverse sort of companionship and pleasure. The trouble that would be confronted to make them citizens isn't worthwhile.

Darling, I was surprised to hear that your Mom's going or at least is thinking of going to Calif. Perhaps, the change will be beneficial. But I am glad of your decision. It will be hard for you but I think you can manage aptly. There are so many possible reasons I could give you for staying in KC that I shudder to think of it. However, it is for the better that you stay in KC.

The reason that I have never mentioned that your letters were inadequate is that that is you. You don't believe in being explosive. However, whenever the subject necessitates that, you do well to answer all I ask. What more would I want? I am fortunate that you write to me often. I am grateful that I can depend on Bette to keep me well-informed, happy, questioning and having her loving me. And since you did ask the question, I do love you. You can ask it as often as you want but I don't think I give you any reason to ask, do I?

I'm sorry about my consumption of cigarettes. I notice it, too. If I am in a place where it is warm, I notice that my throat gets extremely dry. Under the same conditions, I cough a lot and my mouth tastes like the morning after. For the time being, there is nothing I can do to stop the habit. It is a case of restlessness and funny reaction of nerves that cause an almost chain like sort of fiend. To boot, I couldn't step out 3 rounds without puffing like a locomotive.

Darling, there could never be another you. It is so odd that at times, I can realize my love for you more than at other times. It is just during those periods of mental relaxation when everything about me becomes lax. Darling, I love you as fiercely, as honestly, as dutifully as I have always. Every time I think of it, I can see that the time is passing. Each day seems like a year but each day teaches me more, makes me a veteran and brings me closer to you. Aside from everything, discarding all passage of time, it seems like yesterday since I last saw you. Every so often, you must send me pictures so that I can see if there are any changes in you. It has been a long time since you sent me a weight score. It is summertime and I know that you do lose weight now but just keep plugging, Honey. Remember what I always said about the figure I like. (or need I get nasty!) Gosh, Bette, you'd never know me. Hell! Sometimes I think I'll get so fat, I won't be able to bend over. I don't know if I've put on any weight but I do know that whatever muscle I did have has softened up considerably. Oh well, I don't think I'll ever get bald.

Must close, Darling. I'll try to do better with my letter writing. Forgive me. Give my love to Mother. Take care of yourself. I love you so very much. May God Bless You. Love, Mike.

Though there was no entry on June 21, the War Diary's June 22 report noted that nine planes made a trip delivering mail and ammunition, "landing on French soil for the first time." I recall from this trip the nurses going after poppies in minefields, and seeing body bags on the plateau near Omaha Beach, waiting for decent burial.

June 23, 1944 [*Friday*]

My Darling,

I'm sorry if I missed writing to you yesterday but it was completely beyond my control. I received your letter of the 14th. It seems that the service over here is a Hell of a lot better that it ever was. Our barracks is like a morgue tonight; the quiet and solitude is almost maddening.

Yes, Darling, the weather is perfect for strolling. I like the months of August and September best in the states. At that time of the year, the heat of the summer has subsided a bit so it is naturally cooler. It is pleasant to think that someday I'll be able to stroll with you every day at any time and to any place. Darling, I love you so much, miss you as much.

Thanks a million, Bette, I knew I could depend on you to take care of the Rebel's birthday for me. I left everything in your hands because I knew that you could handle it so aptly. I couldn't ask a better person to handle such affairs for me. It leaves me so little to desire.

There are so many things I'd like to say but unfortunately I can't. It will be a break to be able to write without censorship again. The one thing that hurts above all is that when I write of something personal concerning you and I, one of those characters walks up and asks me what the trouble is. What puzzles me is that they are supposed to censor the mail, not read it thoroughly.

Things are quiet again. There are any number of rumors that can stir a guy's blood. I wish to hell that I'd learn someday to rely only on things that actually happen instead of listening to rumor. Oh well, life is pleasant with a little slander thrown in.

Darling, I must rush off. Any number of events these days cut my letters to short notes. I'm so dreadfully sorry for it but I can't help it. The only thing I can do is to promise.

Take it easy, Honey. May God Bless You. I love you. Love, Mike.

On June 23, the nine planes returned from Normandy. The War Diary noted that there were glider tow flights that day.

The entry for June 24 read:

25 members of the combat crews, ten officers and fifteen EM were ordered to return to the states on an extended leave for rest and recuperation. Captain Cooney, intelligence officer, gave a lecture on Security, stressing conduct and things to be remembered especially on extended leave.

My buddies, Dan Emery, Don Harris, Sonny Rice, Ernie Womack, and Urice Underwood were among those headed home — hence the "quiet" and lonely feeling that I wrote about in my letters! These men had been overseas for 19 months and had from 800 overseas flying hours up to 1,600 hours, with five campaigns behind them.

June 25, 1944 [*Sunday*]

My Darling,

I must beg your forgiveness for not writing but it seems as if I have been to both ends of the world. The last letter that I wrote to you must have taken an eternity to write.

I received your letter of the 16th of June. Service is good; that letter took 8 days to reach me. I owe you a decent letter. It seems as if I am as inert as a bear in hibernation. The funniest part of it all is that the days are passing in a whirl and they leave me in a daze. Above all, Bette, dazes, whirls, seeming inertia, etc., I love you so very much.

What I meant in my last letter about censorship was that I disapprove with the fact that my letters are read so thoroughly. If I were disclosing anything of a military nature, the censorship would be understandable. But when I am asked about my personal troubles, especially since I don't discuss them, then I cannot help but voice my disapproval. That is one of the biggest reasons why such letters seem taut and strange. I try to say what I can without disclosing the real nature of our discussion. Oh well, it can't last forever.

In one of your letters, you mention that you aren't capable of drinking as much as you used to. I don't think that that is too bad. I've drunk everything from rot gut to poison. Hereafter, I am a teetotaler. The strongest drink I'll have will be coffee. Just like everything else, I'll save it until I get home; then you and I can pitch a good drunk. Although we did drink a lot, I don't remember once when we got unruly. We came damn near close to it though.

Darling, I wish I could give you something definite about the time I have spent over here, etc. You and I are fortunate. It has only been a year for us. There are some who have double that. The only thing I can keep saying is that we must try to be as patient as we can. Lord only knows, there are times when it drives me crazy, but what can be done; nothing except to relax and try to be decent about it. It is unfortunate that we are unable to express our opinions as we see fit but again that is impossible. Brave spirit but what more can I say. Some day we'll be able to laugh at all these years that are passing. We must continue to find comfort in the thought of each other until the day comes that we will not think of what is to happen but we will be experiencing the love that we speak of so often.

Thank you for the compliment about this writing business. I aim to please. I like to write as often as I can and when I do I like to make it worthwhile to the person to whom I write. Surely you know that there isn't anyone who I write to more often than you. There are times when I could go on and on. You remember how often I used to rip off 6 pages without flashing an eyeball. I am glad that you are satisfied with my meager attempts. I'm glad that you got the gift for Rebel. It is always best to insure packages like that. I know that Tony, Sheila, and the Rebel will be pleased.

Thanks again for still loving me regardless of my rank. I'm afraid that you'll have to be content with buck sergeant for a while. From the looks of things, I'll stay the way I am. There isn't a thing I can do about it try as I may. Just like everything else, it doesn't pay to complain. Just get to a point where I accept anything, any time, in any manner. Then again anything can happen.

That's all the dope for now. Well, Darling, I must close. May God Bless You. Take care of yourself. Love, Mike.

There were no entries for the rest of the month of June. I do recall, though, that on June 30, 1944, an A-20 fighter/bomber crashed on our field.

England, June 26, 1944 [*Monday*]

My Darling,

I can't say what kind of letter this may be but here goes. Saw Pappy this AM. He told me that you had answered his letter. Told me that you still loved both of us but he's a bit jealous because you lean a bit toward me. Of course, my answer was as typical as I could make it and that was that since it was I who is going to marry you, it is only natural that you should love me more.

It seems like a funny thing, Bette, but this is one of those periods when I feel as if I have exhausted all my subjects of conversation. I haven't read anything lately; I haven't heard any music worth talking about. Everything seems so drab except my work and I can't talk about that.

I went to a place the other day where the pubs stayed open from 10 AM to 10 PM [*Blackpool?*]. The bar was actually loaded with Gin, Scotch, and Irish Whiskey. So I went right ahead and got well plastered. Suffered no hangover, thank God. It is a strange thing, Honey, but I think I have forgotten how to drink like a gentleman. You recall the concoctions that I spoke of once before, cognac and fruit juice, wine and brandy chaser, etc. The kind of stuff that would royally set a guy on his royal. Over here in Blighty, it is a normal thing to feel rough after a heavy night's drinking. The usual mixtures are thus — Scotch and beer chaser (before I go any further most of this stuff is drunk straight). In most part, I like to chase my hard liquor with a stout which is a bit stronger and heavier than the regular beer. After the Scotch has been exhausted, it is normal to start on the gin supply and work down thru' brandy, cognac, etc. You can see that the effects wouldn't be too satisfactory. The one time I drank in a decent manner was when Harry and I were in London. We had Scotch and soda and spiked by a few ice cubes. Ice is one thing that the English do not believe in using too readily. If nothing else, I am sure that I'll be an authority on liquors. Don't fret that Lovely, Blonde head of yours. I have cut down considerably and I intend to cut down much more. The one observation which is noticeable is that we don't drink for the pleasure of it but purely to dispatch ourselves into another world and give us a chance to forget this existence. I found it always so pleasant to drink with you because on the rare occasion when we overtaxed our capacity, we would be involved in some sort of mischief. Always full of Hell and never a laugh missing. I do miss all that so much, My Darling. I love you.

I must have done something drastic. The other day I bought a pair of low cut dress shoes. It felt so strange. My ole' dogs used to give me a Hell of a time in "civvy" street. I had to quit playing ball one season because they wouldn't stand the strain. For two years, I wore nothing but G.I. shoes. My feet feel as if they can take anything now. So I decided to shop and there you are, the magnificent owner of a pair of shoes. Exciting, isn't it?

I must write to Rebel. This is her first year on this world. She picked the worst time in the history of mankind to choose her life. I pray to God that she will see no more but what she will read in her history books. I hope our children will be under the same circumstances.

Gosh, Bette, looks like I've run thru' all I can think of. Things in these parts are normal again. No matter how hard I rack my brain, I can't think of much more. I don't want to write a love letter because I'm afraid I'll break down. Foolish feeling, I know but what more can I say.

Well, Darling, see you on the morrow. Give my love to Mother. Take care of yourself. I love you. May God Bless You. Love, Mike.

June 28, 1944 [*Wednesday*]

My Darling,

I don't know if that is the correct date; I've lost all track of time. However since no date is different from the other now, it doesn't make much difference, does it? I received your letters of the 19 and 20 of June. Again I must compliment the fine mail service. Honestly, I don't believe it. You must ask Mother to forgive me. I didn't know that her birthday was in June. Sometimes wonder what the Hell I do know. I am glad that you did get 5 of my letters at once. The trouble with that is that you'll probably have to wait any length of time to receive more. As long as they are getting thru' and you so know that everything is perfect with me, that is the main concern.

We have discussed music often. In most part, it has never concerned our future pleasure but just short technical exchange of knowledge. You can recall how often we did that and how infrequently we never thought to do anything about it. However, as you say, music will be a must in our future budget (spelled with a "d"). If our future is even slightly financially rosy, you can bet that our entertainment will be well varied. There are any number of things that can be done. It is a shame that so many young people prefer the indoor spots rather than a variety of other sorts of fun. Your cocktail hour intrigues me. Unless we could be clairvoyant and see that great future, it would nicer to talk about. I'm afraid at times the Army tends to stunt a man's dreams. At this moment, there are so many tributaries to the river of life that it is hard to choose the lake and smooth sailing of a canoe. Nevertheless, dropping the materialistic and seeing life with you, it is not hard to imagine any sort of difficult pattern. Do I sound like Webster wound up to burst?

I must thank you again, My Mutual Dreamer, for the abundance of compliments that you heaped on my ugly dome. I cannot realize how wonderful I am but the extent of my tenderness, kindness, and gentleness do not go beyond you. It is because of you that these noteworthy characteristics of my rather Jekyll-Hyde personality are so prominent. My love for you, Bette, could not be otherwise. I share you with no one. You are my light house in this storm. Everything I do and have ever done since I met you has been patterned because of you. It isn't so hard to understand, is it, Darling? I'm no different from anyone else, lovers have done the same as I have done. It is the essence of the love, the true core of one's feelings. Surely you would never be content with me if I dominated your life in a hard sort of way. Now, Bette, you wouldn't want to be beaten before every meal and twice before every meal on Sunday. But you would want to be loved as strongly, as surely and as gently as I can do all these things, before and after every meal and especially all day on Sunday. So you see, life isn't so hard to handle, is it?

You talked about the Roof Garden [*at the Astor Hotel*]. I can see and I always noticed it before; we both like as much atmosphere as can be had. You have never seen the Trianon and the Aragon Ballrooms in Chicago — the Marine Grill of the Hotel McAlpine — the fury of the Atlantic on a typical early Spring or late Autumn day. — You have never heard the sound of a crowd as only a noisy crowd in Brooklyn (Ebbetts Field) could ever make such a sound. — You have never ridden along beautiful highways and watched nature change clothes. — Yes, you have and so have I but we have never done all these things together. The atmosphere must be perfect but the companion must be suited. Even "Sloppy Sam's" on Sand Street near the Navy Yard could be a castle in heaven if the right two people are together. Yes, My Delightful Dish, we go on dreaming; it shall never hurt us.

The reason I mentioned the fact that PFCs and Generals mixed is [*interesting*] because for the most part on this side of the world, it is taboo. Oftimes, it is a written law to segregate the enlisted men from the officer. I shan't bother to go any further on that score because I know the censor will not like what I have to say. Someday or at least on one of those cold winter nights when I'm priming Michael III for West Point, you can listen in on a man's conversation and find out why I'd insist that the child be an officer rather than carry the rating his old man carried in World War II. Off the point of that, your words of reassurance are like a [*breath*] of Spring which I cannot feel in this damn weather. Our love for each other is strong. It has nothing to combat but the element of time. And that we must endure because we are part of a world. We know that a lot of time will pass between us. We must be content to let it go and not worry about the proverbial spilled milk. We know what we mean to each other. How much we have to live for. What more on God's Green Earth can we ask for? My Prime Petal, I ask you to stay as firm as the rock of ages that have been washed by the sea for centuries. I am coming back to you. I am going to bring all that I took from you. I am coming to reclaim all that I left behind. I am coming back to prove that "I love you" is not just three words.

Darling, I haven't finished answering [*your*] letter but I must close. I leave you with my heart, soul and thoughts. Handle them gently because they are of you.

Give my love to Mother. Take care of yourself. May God Bless You. Love, Mike.

June 29, 1944 [*Thursday*]

My Darling,

It is a quiet morning and so I have a little time to dash off a fast note. One of the fellows managed to sneak off with a small basket of strawberries. It was shared by as many as we could include. Took our strawberries to breakfast, had corn flakes, aha! A fine mixture of flakes, strawberries and cream (?) + sugar and a meal unlike the feast of Kings and Presidents. Really, Darling, that's the first time I've had anything like that for centuries. After such a fine repast, I showered — feel like a million bucks.

I finally got those prints back from the base censor. I don't know how to distribute them because I only have one of each. I think I'll send you the one of Harry and I and then I'll have a few more prints made and send them off to my folks when they are returned to me. I do hope you like our photograph. I thought it was exceptionally good. It has been passed by the base censor, so I am sure, it will pass easily to you. It is the first snap I have sent you for a dog's age. Note the crease in my pants. Must have been a mistake. Didn't think I could be so neat, especially since I must rely on my own cleaning and pressing. Guess I'm not too much of a rookie at that.

Let's see, where was I? Oh Yes. I went to see *4 Jills and a Jeep* last night. Gad! How the Hell do they expect people to absorb and believe that sort of rot. I guess they get away with it, so I guess it's OK. At any rate, the music was good. "You'll Never Know." Shades of Ft. Wayne. Darling, do you remember how often we heard that tune. It was so damn popular at the time. How do you like this "Serenade for Strings." Or is it, "Holiday for Strings"? Whichever it may be it [*sounds*] good. Harry James is playing. "Carnival of Venice." Really good! Looks like I'm "blotching" most of my spelling this morning. Can't imagine why? The numbers that you mentioned are all strange to me. I haven't heard one of them. It takes a little time for those things to travel across the ocean but eventually they get here.

In your letter of the 20th, your words of reassurance did my heart a world of good. I am glad that whatever actions may have occurred, you did not lose any respect for me. I am gratified to know that rather than lessen it, it has grown more firmly. The consoling thought is that you did enjoy your stay in New York. I am dreadfully sorry that everyone made you feel so strange. I had such high hopes that I was twice as disappointed. Nevertheless, I shall endeavor and I am sure I can succeed to rectify the entire situation. Darling, as I have said before, our own love is strong enough to combat such frivolities of life. It is a pity that Tom declined your invitation. That is another one of those things that can arise at any time. But since we understand everything so perfectly, I am sure we have discussed it enough. So we shall let it rest 'til one of those long winter eves.

Must close for now, Darling. I'll try to write later if I can. Give my love to Mother. Take care of yourself. May God Bless You! Love, Mike.

June 29, 1944 [*Thursday*]

Good Evening, Darling.

I love you. Good start, isn't it? Feel good, not a care in the world, except that I miss you and love you very much. As if that isn't anything to cry about. Funny thing, every time I feel like writing a long letter to you, I light up my pipe. My thoughts usually run so fast that I hate to interrupt them by stopping to light cigarettes.

We went to the show this evening. The name of the show was *Ladies Courageous*. How the Hell do they expect people to eat up that sort of bohunk? The only interesting thing about it all was that they had some good action shots of all types of planes. The women got too mushy. The one amazing thing that I noticed above all was the vast amount of knowledge of aircraft that I have acquired since I've been overseas. You recall how enthusiastic I sounded when we'd watch some crate go lumbering by. It is so much different now. I just don't see the outside but I can see the heart of the plane and the guys that fly these planes. Experience is a great teacher. You'll probably have to listen to more spiels than a bunch of recruits in basic. Guess a guy has to do something.

We had a funny incident happen a few nights ago. Most of the guys have a cigarette before they pile into their sacks and peel off to dream land. One kid takes longer than the rest of us to wash, etc., before he gets into bed. Well, we ask him to recite the "Raven" before he gets to bed. He has a deep bass voice and most of his enunciation is exaggerated, such as, "Once upon a midnight dreary (pause) (dreary is said with a roll of the tongue, etc.). He does that quite often. One night "Sluggsy" [*Jesse McGahan*] across the room, interrupted him and said that he (Sluggsy) would like to give his version of "Dangerous Dan McGrew." Well, it was a riot. The version he gave was not exactly the essence of sainthood but it was perfectly clever. To make it ideal, you must know the type of dry voice S. has. Here's an example. He used to be a Staff but was busted for some reason. He remained a private for a Hell of a long time; then one day they made him a PFC. When he came into the room that day, we all roared with words of congratulations. We asked him to say a few words. With a sober look on his face and in the driest voice that his vocal chords could emit, he let forth with the following classic remark: "Their generosity overwhelms me!" Really this gang is a riot at times.

Darling, I must be stymied. But I am going to close. I have a full day ahead of me and I'd like to read a bit before I retire. You will excuse me, I'm sure.

Good Night, Sweet Angel of My Dreams. Take care of yourself. May God Bless you. Your Lover, Mike.

P.S.: Looks like my words at the beginning of this letter are not true. But I didn't realize I was so tired. At any rate, my pipeful is almost finished. I love you. Good end, isn't it? Mike.

The War Diary entry for July 1 showed only formation flying in the morning and the weekly trip to Stratford-on-Avon. The next day, the first squadron picnic was held at the park near Leicester. The War Diary noted, "Transportation was furnished to pick up the girls and to take them home."

There was no entry for July 3.

July 3, 1944 [*Monday*]

Hello Darling,

Gosh, it has been so long since I heard from you. I shouldn't complain because it has been 3 days since I wrote to you. I am awfully sorry but the days have passed so quickly.

This picture I am sending you is one which was taken just a few weeks ago. I'll send more as soon as I can get a few reprints. There aren't many of myself. As a matter of fact, just one but I shall send it as soon as I can. You see that my hair has started to grow back in. You can also see that I haven't lost any weight. Look rather plumpish, don't I? As usual you can't see my eyes. That seems to be normal with me. You can see the 9th Air Force patch that Harry is wearing. It isn't very plain but you can see it. It is a classy patch. I haven't sewn any of mine on but as soon as I can I will. I never seem to get anything done, do I?

Hell, the rain has been miserable. The sun must have forgotten us. The squadron had a picnic yesterday. Everything was going along smoothly until the rains came. By that time, we had enough beer in us not to care for rain or snow. It was held in some sort of park. There were any number of young deer running about. The scenery was ideal. Every one had a good time. Must admit I felt pretty happy.

Honey, I'm sorry for not writing. I still don't feel too energetic. I guess it must be another one of those periods when I don't give a damn about much. I get so damn lazy. I assure you that the mood won't last too long. How do you like our fancy stationery? I think it's pretty classy. The Old Goose looks good, doesn't it?

Well, Honey, I am going to close. I'd like to go on but I do have something to do. Pardon my inadequate note. But you said as long as I just said, "I love you," it would be OK. I do love you and miss you so much.

Give my love to Mother. Take care of yourself. May God Bless You. Love, Mike.

July 4, 1944 [*Tuesday*]

My Darling,

Before I go any further, I suppose you have noticed the address of my letter. Darling, maybe I will be one of those 4-star generals. A year ago, I made Buck and a year later I am a staff sergeant and I'm as proud as Hell. It also reminds me that it will be a year since I saw you last. One whole year and we could pass it off as a day. I spent the better part of this afternoon sewing my stripes on my OD blouse. That, too, refreshed my memory that you had sewed on my buck stripes. I must admit that I didn't do as good a job but it must suffice for the time being. Gad! It feels good to see the three go. Sorry if I sound so childish but you must realize that it is an event in this rather drab life of ours. To me it is a triumph and I have no one to share it with until you hear or at least receive this letter. I should be out getting gloriously drunk but I don't feel as if that can be any solace to me.

To make my day more complete, I received a letter from you. As I said before, events pass and yet they are brought back to mind by the passage of these letters. If they are a bit distasteful, it is necessary to feel the counter effect. I am sure that everything is settled. Tom told me in his letter to you that he had written to you and explained a variety of things. I do hope that he is understood. I can see now that there was a necessity for strangeness because of the strangeness of character and familiarity. Everything seems so ticklish, so very ticklish that I do wish I could drop it. I am left holding a controversial bag. So many events may change our plans that it seems silly to plan anything. If I could put my heart on this paper, you could see that there are so many beautiful thoughts there that they could last us a life time, and we would have nothing to do but laugh at what appears to be so serious now. I love you.

It appears that everyone misunderstood you as a person. I never thought of that. I had become so accustomed to you as the person I know and understand that I never considered the fact that other people would see you thru' different eyes. I had no idea that I missed the most important thing. But again I repeat myself, we are big enough to cope with even the greatest indifference. I am so very sorry that the cards turned so much against a smooth sail.

I am glad that you have decided to continue or at lest renew your interest in the piano. I was hoping that you would accept something to divert your attention from the time passing. I envy you because I had so often burned the desire within my soul to do something constructive with music. I guess I'll have to devote my time to singing. (My letter is toned so seriously that it seems wasteful. Unfortunately, things do sometimes disrupt a dream, don't they?)

Darling, I hate to correct again but it is spelled "literally." I shall have to spank you.

I am going to close for now but I shall write early tomorrow. I want to spread the news of my good fortune to the family. Again, I apologize for seeming so childish.

Give my love to Mother. Take care of yourself. I shan't worry about a thing. I love you so much. May God Bless You. Love, Mike.

On July 4, the War Diary reported:

Nine planes were used to fly group formation in the morning and in the afternoon there was one cross country and four navigational flights.

July 5, 1944 [*Wednesday*]

Good Evening, Darling,

I received the letters of June 21 and 26. You are most flattering in your praise. Darling, I am not that great to be a General. As a matter of fact, I feel so small in this great show, it isn't even funny. I doubt very much if your presence in Washington would be influence of any sort. Wish it were, I wouldn't mind sweating out 14 months and then the Hell with the rest of it.

Darling, I know that the subject should have been dropped long ago. Your words are perfect. You confess that you love me so much. It is so good to hear that. It never hurts to hear it said often and over again. But I'm afraid that you misunderstood Tom's letter. That's why I hate to see ticklish subjects like that discussed in letters. Word of mouth is the only way to talk these things over. When he said that the family would accept you as you are, he didn't mean anything except that they must learn to know you. That seems to be the most important failing of all. How can people disagree if they don't even talk to each other? You see, you people don't even know each other. That's what appears so difficult to me. When he says that you must accept my family as they are, it is the same thing. You don't even know them. It is like starting from scratch. I am not going to try to explain anything thru' a letter; it doesn't do much good. Unlike God's words to St. Thomas, you must see to believe. The same for my family, it must learn to know and love you as I do. This will show you. Tom asked me about your clothes, wondering if I'd ever be able to afford to keep you as well dressed as you are now — I told him that you made most of your clothes. You see, Darling, you must impress people of being rather extraordinarily extravagant. Hell! You know as well as I do how we go in for the higher classed things. We are ordinary people. Our family lives were parallel by the fact that we both felt the pangs of that wolf long ago. You see, Darling, all these things are misunderstood. I shan't try to rectify it. One cannot do things like that in letters. Believe in me and trust me. I promise that I'll show you differently.

You even said yourself in your letter that when there are two people in love, they accept each other. Consequently their families fall in line. Well that comes in time. But when we are separated like this, no one can line up if we can't even see each other. It sounds vague but the idea is there. I am glad that you agree with me when I said that we are big enough to handle the situation.

Whoa! You are asking me to stay away from you on a furlough. (Gad! What a word.)

But it isn't as easy to do as to say. From the circumstances, I know it can't be done. I cannot tell you much more but you will see where it is impossible.

Really, Darling, I cannot do justice to this letter. There are so many things rushing me that I can't write favorably.

I know that you will wait for me, Darling. You'll wait for me 'til Hell freezes over. I know that. Believe me, I am so grateful for it.

I am going to close. It sounds abrupt but I must stop.

I love you, Darling. I shall love you always. It is something I can't put into words. It is something that is not man made. I sound stupid and crazy if I mention it. I told it to Harry and he was kind enough not to laugh at me. I must go now. My head has been in a whirl because of all the events of the last few months, I want to forget it all. Forget the torment that these troublesome days caused me. What I want to say I want to say before all of you. Not individually because it is what I know would clear everything so easily. It all happened before I got your first letter that sounded as if everything went wrong. That's why I cannot take it all so seriously because I know that you and I must be married regardless of friction, fits, disruptions or bowel movements. Oh, My Darling, My Darling, if I could put it into words. If I could only impress you with the depth of it. I know that you would not tell me to spend my time alone with my family. I want you to share that time, if only to hear what I have to say. My story of God's kindness to make me realize <u>our</u> future. Damn this censorship. It is nothing wrong, Darling. Don't concern yourself. It is just that it was so important to you and I. Nothing on God's green earth could ever make me change my mind about us. I tried to tell my family but I'm afraid again I couldn't put it into words. I shall never forget it. Since I cannot paint any picture, I can tell you that your name, you and everything about you was my guiding star, my guardian angel. Save this letter, Darling, save it. Never lose it. I need it to put into words, to substitute what I felt. Believe me, My Love, if you could have my mind for an hour, you would never doubt me. You would say "yes" to whatever I propose. You would never let the events that caused you so much concern bother you at all. If you were me for that hour, you would laugh because the happiness in your heart and soul would not permit you to cry. That's all, simple, isn't it? I know you will be left in the dark by this letter but believe all I have said. Never forget it. When and if and I am not commanding it, I don't command anyone, I ask because of what I have said above and will have to say when and if I get home, you will see NY again and you will be with me, happily married and everyone's blessings will be with us. I promise.

Good night, My lovely Blonde. May God Bless you. Love, Mike.

The "mystery" which I could not relate because of censorship centers around an incident which happened to me on D-Day. As we approached the coast of France at about 12:30 AM on June 6, 1944, I looked forward from my seat through the front windows of our aircraft. I could see lights and what appeared to be anti-aircraft fire coming up from the ground. I then looked to my left out of the small window at what is normally the navigator's position. I saw what looked like a white image sitting near the tip of the wing. I got up, moved across the aisle, and looked closely, fearing that fear had caused me to have illusions. As I looked closely, I determined that the ghost was Bette, sitting there, and clad in a white gown. She smiled at me and said: "Don't worry, Mike, you'll be OK." The image then disappeared. I do not now recall, 50 years later, what my reaction was then. I remained frightened whenever we faced critical situations in combat or in just plain flight but I was never harmed. None of my crew was wounded. We took some pretty good hits then, as well as in Holland and Germany, and we flew in weather conditions that not even the birds would fly in. But despite the fear, I seemed to always have the feeling that Bette's reassuring words would see me through those days, and that I would go home to her eventually.

Forty years later, she died of cancer. Two weeks after her death, my brother, Ted, who had died in 1982 of a heart attack, came to me in a dream and said: "Mike, don't worry about Bette. She is with the family." This is not a fairy tale. It is as vivid today as it was when both of these visitations happened.

On July 5, the War Diary recorded a trip to Stratford-on-Avon and to the New Market race track (dog racing, I believe). There was also radio navigational flying that morning, as well as a cross-country flight and glider pickups that afternoon. The squadron finished the day with local flying and a group formation flight at night.

The July 6 entry read:

Horsa [*glider*] towing and local flying, morning and afternoon, also a group formation flight at night.

There was no entry for July 7, 1944.

July 8, 1944 [*Saturday*]

My Darling,

I received your letter of the 27th of June. I can see by your letter that the thought of your previous letter is still there. I shan't dispute anything that you have said. In my letter to you the day before yesterday, I explained the whole situation. That letter and a few more things to boot may help you to decide differently. If that does not help, I shan't bother to press the idea any further. We shall do as you have planned. It is most unfortunate that the tide has run low. I was hoping for a satisfying conclusion for all concerned of such a delicate situation. I was hoping that everyone would bend slightly because of the mutual love for me. However, I shan't, and again I repeat myself as usual, I shan't dispute anything in any way. But remember, Darling, I won't give up hope until you have received that last letter. Read it carefully. Again trust in me, it is no trick to lure you eastward. I feel that it is important enough to warrant extra consideration from you. Amen, so it shall be. The subject is dropped until further notice. I feel too good and I love you too much to concentrate on that pin that almost burst our dream bubble.

The ole boy still has plenty of punch in him. I just finished a good 2-hour workout. I'm trying to cut down some of this excess beef that I have developed in the last three months. Played some baseball; I can still smack the apple a fair distance.

I didn't know that you were so interested in politics. Learn more each day from you about you. I never interested myself too much until recently. You know by now that I have done a lot of reading. A lot of that has been magazines. I usually read *Time* and *Newsweek* from cover to cover any time I get a hold of a copy. What amazes me about myself is that I have learned to concentrate on all that stuff. Normally, I never bothered about how the government was run. I left it in the hands of the men who were picked for the job. As far as the forthcoming election goes, I can say nothing about it. My only voice would be to vote, which I am not doing. I do believe that it will be a closely contested affair but I think that FDR [*President Franklin D. Roosevelt*] has the upper hand. There are too many people who believe that it is foolish to change presidents at such a critical time. Dewey is a good man. In four years, he will be our next President.

I am glad that I made you something to be proud of. In an outfit like mine, there isn't much more a guy can do. Who knows one of these days they may decorate us. I'll look like a walking Christmas tree. So far, I wear the usual Good Conduct ribbon, the European-Africa theater ribbon with 2 bronze stars; under my wings I am supposed to wear a blue patch which designates combat of some sort and now I see by the papers that we are allowed to wear a bar on our left sleeve for overseas duty. One bar designates 6 mos. service overseas. After next month, I'll be working on my third. The Staff stripes I sewed on look like neon signs. Gad! What the well dressed soldier will wear. By the time I muster out of this man's army, I'll look like a second MacArthur. Oh! I forgot instead of the usual Air Corps patch, we are allowed to wear the 9th Air Force patch. It really is a snazzy looking job. Enough!

Well, Honey, that's about the extent of the talking I can do to-nite. I have forgotten the most important thing, not really forgotten it, just saving it for last. I do love you and miss you so very much.

Good night, Bette. Give my love to Mother. Take care of yourself, May God Bless You. Love, Mike.

War Diary entry, July 8:

> **There was practice in new type dispersal** [*a method of forming planes and then dispersing them for landing in low visibility*]**, under instrument flying conditions. Two planes cross country and four navigational flights.**

It was on this day that we witnessed a tragic incident involving Polish paratroops and the 315th Troop Carrier Group. We had been sent to Scotland on a supply mission. As we approached our home base, and called the tower for landing instructions, we were told that two planes had gone down in the near vicinity. We were tasked to find the wreck. We did very shortly. Two planes from the 315th (a sister outfit) had collided and gone down. The accident occurred almost in our back yard.

We landed, dumped our cargo, commandeered a jeep, and drove to the crash site to find that two of the 315th planes, carrying 13 Polish paratroopers in each, had locked wings in a tight vee. When they tried to separate, both must have had engine failure and went down from an altitude of approximately 1,300 feet. The only survivor was the radio operator from one of the planes. He had been wearing his parachute and was heading toward the rear of the plane when the action took place. He was fortunate, he jumped and landed safely in shallow water. (We never wore our parachutes. They were too cumbersome, and besides at the altitudes that we flew, we would not have had a chance to survive if the ship was critically hit.)

While surveying the brutal scene, the Polish general arrived with his staff. All of them cried at the sight of brave men who did not get a chance to face the real enemy. All told, 26 troopers and 9 crew members died. There is a memorial in Tinwell, England, near Stamford, for the dead men.

There was no July 9 War Diary entry.

July 9, 1944 [*Sunday*]

My Darling,

I received your letter of the 28th of June. I am glad that you appreciate my abundance of mail. At times when I am forced to miss a day of writing, I feel guilty because of it. I try my damnedest to write as often as I possibly can. There are a few times when I feel "blah" about writing. Oftimes that accounts for a variety of hellish letters you receive from me. I am happy to be able to write to you as often as I do. It is pleasant to me to be able to discuss so many things with you.

I don't know when I'll see Harry again but it would be easy to write to Chicha and ask her. I guess you will write the usual letter of thanks, regardless of circumstances, and you ask her for Mrs. Koch's address. But at any rate, I'll ask Harry in one of my letters.

Hey! Doll, what is this 118 business? Thought I told you to get up in that high weight category. I told you to reach that 125 mark, at least. Anyhow, Darling, I'd love you if you were a wisp. It is only for your own health that I worry about. I guess I must weigh about 200 now. It is a good weight for my height but Hell I gotta convert some of that fat to muscle. I'll probably try some of those sitting up exercises. Bette, I don't think you ought to send any more film for a while. I haven't as many interesting subjects here as I had before. I still have gangs of film. But I want to shoot something worthwhile. Hate like Hell to waste the stuff on countryside. The world over, countryside is beautiful and not different.

I am happy that you so positively gave me such a positive answer to my question of marriage. It was merely asked to see what you thought of such a subject. You are so much like me when it comes to making the most out of life. It changes the whole complex of life that seems so upset and rushed. Even in our hurry, we would be able to share those few fine moments together to the greatest extent. It is such a fine feeling to know that we are giving our happiness to each other. There is no reluctance whatsoever in what we want and what we want to do for each other. I love you just as strongly as you love me, My Darling. Our future is what I have lived for all my life. It is a sense of mental security. It is the ultimate ending of all the tumultuous living that causes us so much to want. It is the beginning of a life we are so eager to share. To share unselfishly, under the concept of every code of the real world. I am yours completely. However mushy that may sound to the realist, it is as honest, as sincere as I can say it. As far as your vanity to the extent that you even know what you are going to wear, I should be nasty and say that I wouldn't care if you didn't wear a thing. But I shan't, leave it to a female to think so far ahead.

I cannot tell you why I want you to stay in KC. However, I can say that it is best if Mother be on her own for a while. My reasons are not personal. They are more of a materialistic nature leaning toward distance rather than anything else. You will see that more clearly when a few more things materialize, things which I cannot say.

Well, Darling, I must close. Need some sleep. Am anticipating a busy day. I love you.

Give my love to Mother. Take care of yourself. May God Bless You. Love, Mike.

July 10, 1944 [*Monday*]

My Darling,

I love you. Gad! Three days and no mail from you. Yet I feel so good. Not because of the lack of mail but because the world feels so light and giddy and I'm not drunk. I'm in love, more than you'll ever know.

I wrote to my brother, Tony, not so long ago. It was during one of those rather distracting, distressing moments of mine. I received his answer today. Words of comfort in a taut sort of way; he "bawled me out" but it was comforting because it was a direct, honest view. As sure as I was of so many plans, he made me so much surer. I am tempted to send the letter on to you but the words are not fit for your ears. He speaks to me as soldier to soldier, leaning enough toward our brotherhood to make his words worth listening to. Please don't be angry with me if I quote a few lines but you must remember that we never cease to learn. And learn I do. One of his lagging remarks, after he had said so much to remove the tautness and strain of family lines, was this: "Ignore everything and write to Bette and plan for the future." We are so happy when we do that. How right he is. We live in a world set aside just for us. We put our hearts and souls into it. Nothing means anything but us. And so it should be and shall be forever on. Whatever I have said before will not stand because there may be any number of alternatives to our immediate plans. We will do what is best and what Tony has helped me to see is best. The things you suggested that would be our best plans. Yes, My Darling, you and I first. The world and rest will have to wait for us.

"If it is Bette that you want then by God get her, but don't burden her with your family troubles. You'll have enough of your own when you get married." And so I see another mistake of mine. And again I say: "and so it shall be." I want you and by God I'll get you — no strings attached. How can I ever mend the wrong that I have done. I must ask your understanding — and forgiveness. With that help — we can forget it, — forget it thoroughly, I shall never burden you again.

You see from these quotes that Tony knows what he is talking about. Consider it as I have, not as a brother, but as an older person talking to me. He covers every point — listen to this; "If she wants to be a Catholic, all right. If she does not want to, that is all right, too. This is America. Freedom of religion and all that sort of stuff we are fighting for. Let Bette be what she wants to be. Only one thing. Give the kids a religion. One religion. Whatever it may be. I don't believe God is so fussy over what religion, do you?" You can see in those words how tolerant, how understanding, how definitely right he is. My mistake is that I was misguided to some degree. A splitting, tormenting splitting of views but if I continue to be that way I'd be wrong. I was wrong, Darling. I want you fully; I do not want to be wrong. I love you and I am to consider you first, as you have always considered me primarily.

There you are Bette. I have quoted. All in all, Tony's assertions are mine. It is the way it must be. I can see it all so very clearly now. In view of what happened to me, I can see that we are not on the wrong track. Let us talk of the future, not the near future but those days when we will be together, ready to start the life that we will plan in these letters. I love you.

The baby received the gift. They were thrilled. Tony says that he and Sheila think it is lovely, such good taste and exquisite. Thank you so much, Darling. It was from both of us. You're grand. He asked me if you'd like to write to him or if I'd like he'd write to you. I think it is best that he writes. You have done your best on every score; the process must be reversed.

Well, Honey, I am going to close. I love you and miss you. there is so much more to say but it must wait. Give my love to Mother. Take care of yourself. May God Bless You. Love, Mike.

The War Diary entries for July 10-13 read:

> **July 10: One plane was used to tow gliders, five for radio navigation and one for cross country. The Red Cross club held a dance with WAAF girls in attendance and the 316th T.C. orchestra.**
>
> **July 11: Two planes were used to tow gliders and two cross country. Nine planes for group formation flying at night. Two crews were given "gee" training** [*this was the signal acceptance system on board the lead plane that allowed pilots to "home in" on the drop zone*]**.**
>
> **July 12: Three planes cross country, one navigational flight, five planes in the afternoon and night. Two crews were given "gee" training.**

July 13: One plane was used for checking weather. Captain Cooney gave a lecture to all personnel on Censorship and Security. Captain Ellis gave a lecture on sex; Chaplain Jones also spoke at the same meeting.

July 14, 1944 [*Friday*]

My Darling,

You must forgive me for not writing these last few days. I was catching up on some well earned rest and I took a holiday last night. Went into town and I saw, *Higher and Higher* with Frank Sinatra. Regardless of what they may say, I liked the show. The music was perfect. Everything was good about it because it left me in a giddy feeling, the fast moving of the film, the few dance steps and the singing of Sinatra was superb. And, of course, the songs were ideal. Enjoyable, Indeed!

My Darling, in your letter of the 29th, you speak of an inadequacy of words. Don't ever let that bother you, Bette. You ask me not to let you get in the first word. My Dearest, do you think that either of us will be able to say anything? Don't you think that the least important thing will be words? After the usual, "Oh, How I have missed you and I love you so!" — there will be a silence that neither of us will care to break. After that, the words will flow so easily that I pity the person(s) who tries to break into that conversation. My Darling, you can talk until your hair turns gray. I won't stop you, I promise.

Bette, your thought of possibility and my suppositions certainly do help to keep a guy's morale sky high. The whole trouble is that after a few years, we start to look for fact. What the Hell, it keeps a guy happy for the time. I have so many memories to live on and the fact that I can look for so many more, keep me very happy. That should be said in the plural but I know that you understand. (A couple of characters begged me to sit in for a game of pinochle. I played until someone else showed up. Played for about a ½ hour.)

We were talking about the things that make America so wonderful to all of us. Since we all have someone we love at home, we don't speak of them. They (you) are usually our silent thought, a background of everything we say. The conversation ran something like this. "What I wouldn't do to 6 hamburgers and a couple of milk shakes." "How about some good scrambled eggs, toast and a good cup of coffee." (Delayed again for 4 hours only; this time for business. I tried to continue there but it was too bumpy!) Let's see where was I? Yep, then it ran so, "Gad! For one good shrimp cocktail, well iced with plenty of fresh lettuce — "Not to forget, lettuce and tomato on toast." And so on.

I'd like to go on, Honey, but I must stop right now. I have a full evening ahead of me. I shan't be able to continue until tomorrow evening.

Give my love to Mother. May God Bless You — Love, Mike.

War Diary entry, July 14:

Three planes were used for Wing missions and one for a group mission. There were two navigational flights. Nine planes were used to drop [*Polish*] paratrooops in a group formation flight at night; six were used to drop gliders, carrying airborne infantry. The entire mission was a success.

July 15, 1944 [*Saturday*]

My Darling,

I received your letter of the 24th of June. Since they all arrive in a sort of helter-skelter way, I try to answer them in the manner they come, not in that manner do I answer them. You mentioned that you were sick. Gosh, Honey, do take care of yourself. . . . Baby, things aren't too rough. If it is that time, it is understandable, but for any other reason, heads up, Bette, the time will pass. Ole Doc Mike will be around to handle the situation as well as possible. I love you.

Since I did not want to appear too eager, I waited until I came to the second paragraph to tell you of my decoration. I have been awarded the Air Medal. It is not an unusual decoration; nevertheless, it is something to be proud of. I wasn't present at the presentation. I was busy but I'll get it soon. The fellows told me that my name was called but I was absent. No fault of mine. A gang of us got it but it is nothing to be ashamed of. I'll describe it best I can. — It is suspended from a ribbon of blue and gold, — blue background with 2 vertical gold stripes. The medal is bronze, with an eagle clutching two thunderbolts, one in each claw. The background is a bunch of pointed peaks, 16 in all; I counted them. The medal is attached to the ribbon with a fleur-de-lis. It is rather heavy and has a flat, circular back. (My description is not from my own medal but from one of the other fellows.) The box is about 3 [*inches*] wide and 8 [*inches*] long. Included with the award are 2 ribbons to be worn on the chest instead of the actual medal, — an extra piece of cloth for replacing a worn ribbon and a small lapel button which is worn for civilian life. The ribbon is the same color as that of the medal ribbon. Believe me, Honey, as low as it may be rated, it is something to be proud of. (The back can be used for an inscription.) I am already trying to figure out how to have it made into a bracelet or necklace for you. It is heavy and that end remains to be seen. Like it? Aren't you proud of me?

Now for your letter. You misunderstood me, Bette. It isn't that there isn't a love of some sort in my family. It is just that we know each other so well. The very fact that I speak as I do, can show you that we know each other's flaws. Knowing what is wrong with a person, and understanding it, is one of the easiest [*ways*] to realize a love that is not stagnant. Surely you must realize this. If I did not <u>love</u> you, would I trouble my head to understand you as I try to. Easy and yet so right, isn't it? The reason I ask you not to be angry with me is that I felt as if I had pushed you so much your way. So glad that you feel the way you do.

Darling, I must apologize for causing you so much concern. I promise not to drink much any more. I've seen the light of temperance. I'll save all those headaches for that bottle of

Seagram's plus. I do miss you so very much. Rather than think about it too much, I take off the cork and go on a good tear. Forgive me. I'll do better. I promise. I promise with all my heart.

You are so very much right. This small emotional upheaval has brought us that much closer. I see things so much clearer now. It is a feeling of maturity I have never had before. It is things like that that make us grow up quickly and realize that life is more than a bourbon and coke. I am extremely grateful for it and so much the wiser.

Again I must thank you for a job well done. I received a letter from [*Tony's wife, Rebel's mom*] Sheila. She sent me pictures of the little Darling and the card that you enclosed in her gift. Perfect, Bette. Listen to this. [*Sheila describes all the gifts that were sent, then writes,*] "But the daintiest and sweetest gift of all was that little gold cross that Bette sent. It was the first to arrive too and Michael it is simply precious." You see, Darling, they are so appreciative of it. You're marvelous. (Only you should have said Uncle Mike and <u>Aunt</u> Bette!) Remember one of these days you will be my wife.

Must close now. I'll write tomorrow. Take care of yourself. I love you and miss you so. May God Bless you. Love, Mike.

On July 15 and 16, the War Diary reported:

> **July 15: The squadron Commander presented the Air Medal to all crew members who crossed the channel on either the first or second night of the invasion of France. . . .**
>
> **July 16: There was a 13 plane mission, carrying infantry soldiers to and evacuating wounded from Normandy. Four planes had to return with their load due to bad weather. The remaining nine planes carried out their missions successfully. S/Sgt.** [*Staff Sergeant*] **John M. Olden, NCO in charge of the Parachute Dept., made a free jump for the first time from 2,000 feet.**

July 17, 1944 [*Monday*]

My Darling,

Say, Bette, if you ever notice 2 letters with the same date and you receive them ages apart, forgive me. A lot of times, I forget the date and just put down the first one that I think. Then I'll get ambitious and ask someone. Then, I find out that I'm all wet. Crazy, isn't it? Just show you the way I feel sometimes. I love you. Not a care in the world. Not a worry on my mind. The only thing that makes me unhappy is that we are not together. The consoling thought is that you are well but there and I am in good shape and here. Hell! What's wrong with me? These thoughts sound so childish. So may it be. Amen!

You decided to be a pianist. Very good. I can't think of any better way to keep well occupied. Savage turmoil in your mind can be appeased more easily with the striking of a sweet (?) note. As far as getting out of the corn fields, sometimes I wonder if that is good idea. Meant that for a crack; I won't bother to say any more.

Yes, Bette, it is a year. Nothing has dimmed in that year. Everything that you and I shared has been relived over and over again in my brain. What little we ask out of life, I could never want any more than a repetition of those days. They were happiness in all its splendor. You can see how easy it is to satisfy people. I don't want much more out of life but to be able to spend it with you. Everything went so easily. No cares, no worries, no tears. Do you know, Bette, I sometimes think that you and I are the most irresponsible people in the world. Looking beyond ourselves, as we are, I don't believe that personality of ours will be injurious to us. Sometimes, I wonder about our financial happiness — it doesn't frighten — most times it amuses me but I do think that we will fare well. I know that I'll have you by my side. It makes everything look easier. I think you are more capable on that score than I am. Gosh, Honey, whenever I think that some day this war will be over and I will be coming back to you, I get such an impatient feeling that it ought to hurry and help me to stop wasting time.

I must close for now. Again I am lacking enough sleep. But before I try to make it up, I want to answer as much of my mail as I can. Lord knows I am gangs behind it.

Give my love to Mother. Take care of yourself. May God Bless You. Love, Mike. I love you.

[*After this letter was written, Doctor Ellis gave me a physical and decided that I needed a change from so much flying. He found that my ears were troubling me, and that my hearing was slightly impaired. I was sent — along with Ed Tuman and Bill Toohey — to Torquay, England, for one week of rest and recuperation.*]

෧෪෬෧

The 37th Squadron kept busy in the weeks following D-Day, as the War Diary entries for July 17-25 record:

> **July 17: The four planes that failed to carry out their mission yesterday did so today. Two planes were used to drop paratroops and five for local flying. Three planes were instrument checked.**
>
> **July 18: Captain Cooney gave a lecture on Censorship and Security to the nine officers and five EM who were assigned this squadron. Nine planes were used to drop paratroops and six for glider formation flying in the morning. One plane was used for double glider tow in the afternoon and evening. Nine planes were used for glider formation flying at night.**
>
> **July 19: 19 planes were used to fly squadron formation in the morning and one cross country. One plane was used for "gee" training and three each for transition and instrument flying. A squadron party and dance was held at DeMontfort Hall in Leicester, with the 316th T.C.**

Group orchestra supplying the music. Food, drinks, etc. Combined with dancing helped to make the party a big success.

July 20: Six planes and gliders were used to fly group formation, eight were used for transition flying and two for cross country in the morning. There was a double and single glider tow. Five planes left for an air evacuation mission in the early evening. The following officers were promoted to 1st Lieutenant: William C. Hopkinson [*"Hoppy"*]; and James L. Campbell [*"Soupy"*].

July 21: Ten more planes took off to complete air evacuation mission to Normandy. Lt. Roman gave a lecture on Censorship and Security to two new officers. . . .

July 22: Two planes on cross country and return. Two planes are on DS [*Detached Service*] and the fifteen planes on the evacuation mission have not returned as yet.

July 23: Thirteen planes returned from the evacuation mission, two RON [*remained overnight*].

July 24: The two remaining planes returned today. Five planes were used to drop paratroops at night and one plane for a cross country hop.

July 25: Six planes were used for a supply mission to Normandy. Eight were used for glider formation in the afternoon and three cross country; one returning and two RON.

July 26, 1944 [*Wednesday*]

Hello Sweet One,

Now, don't get angry with me. I haven't written for one solid week. And I know when I tell you what I have done, you won't mind. My Love, My Very Lovely Blonde, I've been on a week's vacation. At least I accepted it as thus. I discarded all sort of connection with anything. I didn't pick up a pen once. In all the beauty that surrounded me, I hungered so for your company. But since you weren't there and couldn't be, I let most of my thoughts stray to idleness and nothingness. It was the first leave I have had in such a long time. I made the best of it. For seven whole days, I was treated like a human being again. Slept as late as I wanted to, in a good soft, clean bed. (So soft I had a job getting used to it.) I had a swell hotel room; plenty of fresh air, light and comfort. Not one MP stopped me to ask for a pass or anything connected with the military. Served hand and foot in the dining hall. The food was excellent. Everything was so beautiful and peaceful. A typical vacation, resort town, although the weather wasn't always ideal, it didn't bother me in the least. To top it all, there were 8 letters from you awaiting me when I got back. I'll answer those in the course of time.

The place [*Torquay*] I was at was ideal as I visualized it as a spot for a honeymoon for us. One day as I was walking, I stumbled on a spot that made my heart cry for my younger days. It was so much like the places I frequented for my fishing joys, for my days of peace and quiet. Water, surrounded by steep cliffs and at the base, a beautiful beach. Gosh, Honey, it was the first time in the last 3 years that I had seen such a familiar scene. Unfortunately, I can't go thru' any detail but I did take some snaps. I can't send them but I'll save them for my album. You'll hear and see all about these things someday. There, now, I hope you haven't worried. I do hope that will set your mind at ease. It would have been the model of perfection if you had been there to share all these things with me.

Thank you for your congratulations. I can't make you stop being proud of me. Every so often, gotta' do something to remind you of your hero. I hardly know where to start to answer your letters, so I'll "bat" around until I am set to do your letters proud. I am so grateful to you for your letters, Darling. Nothing in this whole wide world could make me stop loving you. I thank God for our meeting and for your comforting thoughts. I pray that He will see fit to bring us together as quickly as possible. Things are shaping up. Maybe someday this mess will end. I do love you so much, Bette. These few days have shown me how much I can miss you; how much I need you near me. Yes, My Darling, the time is passing. Each letter, each day, each week shortens our anxiety for the moment when we will be together again. We will be together not as before we parted, but as husband and wife, ready to give this little ole' world a boot in the ass and a merry whirl.

I am going to close, but not for long, I hope. I expect to be busy but I'll do my best. One must pay for "goofing off." Give my love to Mother. Take care of yourself. May God Bless You. Yours, Mike.

July 26, 1944 [*Wednesday*]

Good Evening, My Darling,

I didn't think I'd write again this evening but I did so much want to talk to you. There is nothing special on my mind except that I love you so very much. There is a dance on the post and the music is good but I don't feel like dancing with anything I know I can't enjoy. I want so much to hold you in my arms and let the evening while away. Just to swing around in our foolish manner, reminisce when the music is sweet, and laugh when we can't maneuver (I think that's right!) one of those steps reserved for the younger set. It seems strange to say that but there are people younger than ourselves, aren't there? Gad! I can't write too much tonight; the time is passing and it is later than I expected. Black-out time will approach and I'll be left in the middle of a wonderful dream. Carry on, Ole' Boy!

Darling, you know those songs that you mention that are on the Hit Parade, I have never heard one of them. Perhaps it was because we were lacking a radio until now. Our other radio is out of commission. Thank God, we have this one back. It sounds so good to hear that damn thing thunder. We will do well on that score; I like to listen too. But comedians must be good before I really like to listen [*to them*]. Dance music is my forte. Had an excellent chance to meet a girl who liked to talk about something interesting. We discussed music but I found that she was vague and shallow. She was an intense reader, so we changed to that. The one point that caused a holler was the difference of titles on a book that you just sent me. The English have distorted *A Tree Grows in Brooklyn* to *A Tree in the Yard*. Fortunately, that is all they changed. Why? I don't know. Perhaps they don't know or don't like Brooklyn. Believe me, it hurt me to the core. All in all, it was a very crazy thing to-do. Let's see, where was I? Oh, Yes, I love you. Gosh, Bette, I don't think I'll ever be able to tell you how much you mean to me. No matter how I try or tried, my words wouldn't be sufficient to express my depth of feeling. As many times as I have said the same thing, the theme doesn't vary. It's you, My Darling, no one else. All my thoughts are centered about you. You mean everything to me. But I am not going to go on like that. Every time I start off like that, the time over here seems that much longer. Well, Darling, I'm not doing too badly on that score. The time is passing, isn't it?

Happy 4th of July, Aha! It isn't that easy or at least it wasn't. It didn't even feel like the 4th. Hell, Honey, I've a multitude of holidays to make up. In the first place, it didn't even feel like the 4th I remember at home. No holiday has felt the same. The customs are so much unlike. Besides, that Day of Independence was declared because we declared our Independence from England. Look where I am!

Gotta tear off now. The time has passed and I still have so much to say. But tomorrow is another day. Good night, Bette. May God Bless You. Love, Mike.

On the morning of July 26, the two planes on cross-country returned, six planes were used for instrument training, and five planes took transition flights, according to the War Diary. That night, ten planes were used to fly in group glider formation.

July 27, 1944 [*Thursday*]

My Darling,

Here I am again! Listening to "Dance of the Hours" — beautiful. I rested well, got up, got another short (not too short) haircut, shaved and showered — I feel like a million. And so I must try to answer some of your many letters.

I am most happy by the fact that most of my letters these days are arriving in one piece. I was getting rather provoked by the fact that so much of my stuff was torn. At any rate, there is no reason to cut any more because of the difference in the activities of my life. It seemed that I saw so much more before that I tried my best to convey it to you without covering anything that might disclose the wrong words. Whatever you wish to do to that creature is perfectly OK with me. However, with time and a change of clothing you can leave all of that to me.

In one paragraph of your letter, you spoke of the rotating system of the Air Corps. I won't go into that because it seems like such a long discussion that has so many different aspects and views. I'd be able to go on indefinitely and all that would be left would be more heartache that it doesn't pay. However, you go on to refer to something I said. It has such a beautiful thought to it. It is great to have our laughs as a memory. Since there were no tears in our companionship, we are lucky. Not even when we parted did we so much as think of it is as a parting but just as a short reminder of distance. The world could be so decent if everyone could laugh as hard and as honestly as we did. Love you so for those memories because you made everything so easy to take. So —

Yes, Bette, if you can get some more film, I would appreciate it. I am running low now. And above all, do send me more pictures of yourself. You speak of taking a picture at the Art Gallery before you leave KC. Do you intend to go somewhere and tell me about it? Or do you mean that once we are married, you feel you won't see KC for a while? One never knows, does one? Especially since you mention a picture in that lovely dress; I think that it would be perfect. Funny, but when I saw you that night, I felt a spirit of possessiveness. For some reason or other, in my subconscious mind, I felt that no one was going to mar that beauty in any way. Pardon my enthusiasm but you must have been labeled "Mrs." that night. Now, I can't bear to think how I would have felt if I was backward and if you were someone else's love. Marvelous how the trick of fate plays into the right hands at the right times.

Thank you for the compliments, Miss Hill. I didn't think I was so handsome. Yes, I do believe I can carry that extra weight. It gives me the lift comparable to the vitality of a pregnant woman. Of course, I could never get that way but being pompous adds some color to a drab personality, doesn't it? Whatever other pictures I have taken, you must wait to see those. I can't send them thru' the mails. They disclose a few things. However, in due time, you will see me in every shape, form and mood. Sorry, no nudes.

I didn't think that it was so difficult to get cigarettes. We are rationed to 7 packs a week — that isn't enough for a guy that smokes as much as I do, But since it is the best we can do, it must be done. I manage well. Are you still smoking P.M. [*Philip Morris*], or did you tire of my brand? I can't seem to change. I've smoked them so long that anything else tastes "blah." My only alternative, unless I am offered a cigarette, is Camels. Strange that even smoking makes good conversation for us. I don't think that you'd look too bad smoking a pipe. You need a big one, though. Since we are both so tall, a small pipe looks sheepish silhouetted (I think that's right.) against our long frames. Besides a cigarette smoker makes a lousy pipe smoker.

Well, Darling, must toddle off. I'll be back as soon as I can. Take care of yourself. Give my love to Mother. May God Bless You. — Love, Mike.

July 27, 1944 [*Thursday*]

My Darling,

I should date this letter back because I am trying so hard to do justice to those days that I didn't write. The censor will probably be driven to insanity especially since this is the 4th I've written in the last two days. There is no one I'd rather write to and since there is no one she would rather write to it makes everything a balance. I just pounded the sack for about an hour, so I feel quite refreshed. Since I have nothing to do at the moment in the line of duty, here ah am.

You see, Bette, you are getting old. Just because you clean out some of the ole' locker, you get stiff for a week. What you need is some good, vigorous exercise, such as sitting in the Plaza Royale and downing about 20 bourbon and cokes (with a dash of lemon, please!). If I've done nothing else, you can say that I developed the muscles in your right arm from lifting a glass from the bar to your lips. (Decrepit is right.) You just give me a lifetime, though, and I'll show you how to give that frame a workout. Now not the way you think. In the first place, you like to swim. We will teach you how to do the fundamental movements, that is, if you haven't forgotten. Secondly, we'll (note the we — me and myself.) (All courses free of charge.) show you how to handle a 9 ft. casting rod in a pounding surf — you aren't afraid of worms, are you? Simultaneously, we will learn how to golf. One thing you must show me is how to ride horseback. I've always craved for it but Hell never got around to it. Should have been a Westerner — But gad! Why carry on so? There are so many years ahead of us. It will take us a few years to adjust ourselves to that lost time — after that, time marches on.

Oh, Yes! The Pups — Don't know why but things aren't going so well for the little characters. "Snowball" and "Fudge," the Spaniels, are still hospitalized. Not for too long. They're OK but we want them in good condition. Little "Gremlin" came back but he caught pneumonia. The vet is feeding him sulfa — he's coming along fine. Poor little bastard has a towel wrapped around his chest and neck. He will be in good condition in a short while. "Bonnie," the Scotch terrier, is the best of the lot. She is sporting a cute plaid necklace and romping and raving all over the place. Since "Grem" is the only male around the place, we are trying to cook up a love affair for him with "Bonnie." But I guess as time goes on and they grow older, they will take care of it themselves.

Changing the subject myself. — I have a cigarette burn, one on each hand, on the middle finger in each case. They are really ugly, nasty bruises. Damn cigarette sticks to my lips and the next thing I know, flesh is burning. Horrible, isn't it? How the Hell do you manage to get them on your leg? Anything can happen, can't it? Listening to a good program of Spanish music — tangos, boleros and rumbas — Aha!

Glad to hear that V.A. brother-in-law has been found. As a German POW, he will be treated well, — especially since he is an airman. They have a lot of respect for our Air Force. — Kaltenborn shouldn't report such rumors. He should have more sense that that. At any rate, it is good to hear. Rumors are hot and heavy, aren't they? Someday they will come thru'. Everything must come to a head.

I knew that you would like "Holiday for Strings." Have you heard it sung by a duet? It really is sharp. Finally heard one of the numbers that you mentioned; it is "L'Amour." It's OK — Yes, Darling, we have lightning bugs in NY but only in the suburbs not in the city proper. Didn't think you could do things like that to them. I just like to see them dart from place to place. Wonder if they know where they are going. Talk about random thoughts, aren't these? And it isn't too hot to think and I still can't find any remarks to go with your mind.

Must peel off, Darling. Cheerio and all that sort of rot. — May God Bless You. I love you. Yours, Mike.

The War Diary entry for July 27 notes:

Seven planes used for radio and instrument flying and one for cross country in the morning. The night glider schedule was called off.

July 28, 1944 [*Friday*]

My Darling,

I am a bit "peaked" this evening but I must write. Since I hate to miss, I try my best unless it is utterly impossible. That, too, happens. I love you.

In your letter of the 11th, you talked about that stationery. Yes, it does look good to see those [*parachutes*] but it certainly doesn't stir any adventure in my soul. I'd like to hit the silk, too, but only for the sensible, that is, if I had to. It would be a thrill to fool around like that but that thrill is the kind that is short-lived. Personally, I'll take my thrills in easier doses. However, the first jump must be the easiest, so I am told. Can't let my letter get too technical; you'll hear more when I get home.

Again in the same letter, that same discussion comes up but I'm refraining because the situation is as dead as last year's Christmas tree. Hell! The only thing that concerns me is that I love you, that I am waiting for the time to pass and that when it does we shall realize the first of our many beautiful dreams — doesn't that seem enough to care about?

Funniest thing again in that same letter you say that it will not be impossible for me to learn to play. And since it (piano) is a part of our furniture, I should try. I will. But that isn't the part that worried me or appeared funny. Last nite when I hit the sack, I was thinking of what we would do until we set up housekeeping. Lord only knows what circumstances will determine that. You see, I've already started to be the man of the family. Worried before we start. But as I said before, who knows? I'm sure we don't know what factors will determine so much for that near future.

You know, Bette, the more I look at that list of songs, the more I realize that I have heard some of 'em. However, since I don't listen to titles and since they don't mention them too often over here, I don't pay much attention to them. But they must be good, if they are the choice of so many people, the great, wonderful American masses.

I spoke to a buddy of mine about Estes Park. Asked him if he ever heard of it and had he ever been there. Guess we have to go there. He told, too, that it was very beautiful. If it is anything like my conception of the beautiful western part of our country, it must be great. Especially since we will be together; it would be my idea of perfection. You know, Darling, we won't be the richest (financially) people in the world but we will try our damnedest to do some things that we wish now. When I get out of this man's army, I intend to rest before I assume my place in the business world. It may not be long enough but enough to make it a honeymoon for us. A sort of readjustment for me and a rest for you. After all, the army is leaving a trace on me that I am going to try my best to shake off. A place like Estes Park sounds ideal for that sort of thing. Not a place where there are millions of people because I am seeing plenty of them. But a place where you and I can be to ourselves. Give us a chance to play, talk, laugh, and love and to rid ourselves of the memories of the years that will pass with me in OD and you the waiting, patient woman of my life. And so it must be. We must allow ourselves that bit of freedom. I am sure that by then we shall have earned it, not that we haven't earned it already. It sounds so good to write like this that I hate to stop. It puts me in a world I seem to have forgotten. A world I yearn to join so quickly. A world we are fighting for and which means and has meant so much to all of us prior to this war. Fortunately, we can join the many millions who are able to stand these days of separation. Fortunately, we will be part of the millions who will be able to rejoice when that day of meeting comes. My Darling, I love you so very much. These days over here have taught me to respect and cherish the love I have. I have learned the sensibility of warmth and decency. Gad! Woman, you are marvelous.

Honey, I must close. I feel an extreme desire to relax. Give my love to Mother. May God Bless you. Love, Mike.

On July 28, 12 planes were used for supply and evacuation flights to France. According to the War Diary, three planes were test-hopped and six were used to drop paratroops.

There was no War Diary entry on July 29.

July 29, 1944 [*Saturday*]

My Darling,

No letters from you for the last few days but it gives me a chance to answer those letters that you wrote in my absence. It is rather quiet this afternoon but it is purely because it is after lunch and all the fellows are resting before going to work. I can't make this letter too long because I haven't got too much time to myself. The news is spouting over the air and here I am — very much in love with you.

I stopped in the middle of the letter of the 13th and from there I carry on. When I relaxed last night, I couldn't find any good literature, so I picked up a comic book and really did some intense and deep reading. I can easily understand your thirst for knowledge at times. The mood hits me often but it is easier said than done. Finding the proper reading in these parts isn't easy. I don't mind too much — can't pack everything into a short space of time.

In that same letter, you mentioned that it was 366 days since I saw you last. My fondest memory of that day was the sight of both of us waiting for your train. Darling, you know how reluctant I was to see you go. We should have been married then, but typically of my stupidity, I didn't think it was wise to risk the separation. How foolish! Perhaps, it isn't so bad, after all. All this time has passed and we still have many days to look forward to.

If you notice in my letters that I don't answer your questions immediately it is because I go about it methodically as I can. It gives me a chance to concentrate on what to say. I know that you are as practical as I am. Therefore, I knew that your answer would be the affirmative. You would come to NY, I know. It would be criminal to waste even a minute of any time that I might get. Gosh, Bette, I may say it many times but time is time. Whatever we have lost now, we have to try to make up as often and as many times as we can. God knows how much we miss each other — why prolong any sort of misery. We were meant to be the strength of each other. That strength becomes so magnified when our presence becomes actual. Bette, My Darling, I love you as deeply as any man's heart could love a woman. Everything about you sends a thrill up my spine. In my most sentimental mood, enveloped in a mood of soft music, fascinated by a web of pleasant dreams, you stand above it like our famous Lady of Liberty. The beauty of our friendship has elevated me far and beyond any height I have tried to attain and as my foothold I have your spirit — you.

You must forgive me but I have to manage my time and I must carry on to the materialistic. May I leave that dream for a while?

Take care of yourself, Darling. May God Bless You. Love, Mike.

July 30, 1944 [*Sunday*]

My Darling,

Harrumph! No mail from you for 3 days but so I shall carry on. Not bitching, Darling, I'm way beyond that stage. Guess I've been over here long enough to know how the mail system works. Had a letter from Tony, yesterday. He made Captain. Guess your S/Sgt. ranks lowest in his family. You'll have to take a back seat with me, Darling. Hope blood is thicker than water. I love you, Darling.

I am trying or at least going to try to make this letter as light as possible. Don't think I can succeed too easily. This day is perfect for reminiscing. There is a definite overcast, the kind of Sunday which is ideal for making babies. The music adds a definite touch of peace and solitude. We are listening to the German Overseas Station. They are playing some soft and light symphonic music. It really is great to be able to be at such ease with the world. If I could spend the rest of my life with you in such a mood, I wouldn't give a damn if the rest of the world wasted itself. Gad! The peace and quiet around here is inspiring. But before I try anything, I should try to answer the rest of your letters.

Many times I have felt that the day is too short. I haven't experienced that for a long time though. The emptiness of the past months and the fact that I pray for the time to pass have helped me to lose the faculty of short-lived days. Believe me, inwardly, I haven't died. It is that strange, strong urge that beckons every soul far from these places. Darling, my realistic and practical nature makes the present easy but my soul rebels often to that realism. In those moments, my entire self strays to you. I am tempted to see the "bah" of life and care only for those thoughts that bring me closer to you — But there I go again — I'll carry on.

You speak in one letter with pride of my achievements. Talking about "guts," etc. Darling, my hair isn't getting gray because I'm a brave warrior. Believe me, fear is a great thing. I speak not of cowardice — that's weakness. I mean fear. That emotion that causes cold sweats, itchy skin, unintended prayer and a dry throat that aches because it is strained beyond endurance by that emotion. Hell! Honey, I'm lucky, that's all.

So you want to bet on the coming elections. I don't know what to bet. Personally, I think FDR is in but I don't know what to wager. Those election bets are sometimes hard to pay off. The hell with a bet. The only thing is that I'd like to be home in time to collect everything personally. The best bet is you against me. Pardon my conceit but neither of us can lose. Although, I think I'd get the better of the deal. I love you.

Hey! Bette, get off that stuff about your writing being dull because nothing exciting ever happens, "after what you've seen and been through." Ugh! You make me sound like a knight on a white charger. You know yourself there is nothing more exciting than buying a new hat, walking thru' a city crowded with laughing people, listening to good clean American humor, the tone of an American Orchestra, reading about the forthcoming elections, noting that the Kansas City Blues and Brooklyn Dodgers are in last place and that the Cards and Browns are in first place. What could be more exciting than that? Do you think all the things that I described in my letters of the places I've been were exciting? The only thing exciting about an odor (stink to a Brooklynite) is the smell of perfume worn by a beautiful blonde, the odor of freshness of a gardenia worn as a corsage or in that person's hair. The thrill that one feels when he walks down a quiet street after a heavy rain storm and he can smell the freshness of the green about him. The thrill of holding his favorite's hand, that look in their eyes, the happiness, and glitter of companionship — those things, My Darling, and only those things are exciting. The Hell with those other "stinks."

In your latest letter of the 17th, you spoke of doing something to Mother's hair. Do you remember the night it turned green? Gad! I think we laughed so hard it was pitiful. I do hope we didn't hurt her feelings. At any rate, it would have been a good fad! Fried Chicken, Ah! Do I like it? Just serve it sometime and you can have my answer. I promise that I'll break every rule in Emily Post's book; go at it hands and feet.

Wait a minute now; Brooklyn is still playing this season. Of course, they aren't doing as well as can be expected but they can't be good every season. At any rate, "Dixie" Walker is still slapping the ole' apple. Sure the Cards are on top. The rest of the league is resting. They feel that St. Louis ought to have a city series once in a century. Lord only knows, I share your prayers. I'd like to see any kind of a ball game. It doesn't have necessarily to be a series game. Who knows, anything can happen.

Well, Bette, I must close. Give my love to Mother. I love you and miss you very much. Take care of yourself. May God Bless you. Your Lover, Mike.

On July 30, 12 planes flew in group glider formation, and eight were flown cross country and back. The War Diary entry for the next day, July 31, read:

> **A four plane mission to Prestwick; seven planes supply and evacuation mission to Normandy. Two planes had to land at a different field, RON, the other five returned OK.**

August 1, 1944 [*Tuesday*]

My Darling,

I received two letters from you yesterday, dated July 18 and 22nd. Bette, your pictures are great. You look wonderful in white (or is it some other color?) Looks white. It's a shame but in order to make your pictures fit in my wallet, I have to cut them down a bit. But, believe me, that doesn't cut down the effectiveness at all. Boy! Am I lucky! Didn't realize that I'd have such a lovely creature for a wife. At one time, Bette, I'd be backward about taking so much loveliness out of the world. Now, I've attained a selfish streak. Let the rest of the world take care of itself. Wonderful! That background looks familiar. Honey, isn't that the school near your home? It brings back memories only because we were together — aside from that everything seems crude and so much unlike us. But we are honest people, it has happened and so the events are a background of so much to happen. I do love you so very much. You are quite photogenic, aren't you?

I'm sorry that I didn't write to you yesterday but I was up from early dawn to late night. When I finally hit the sack, I didn't spare the horses. I didn't get up until 10 AM this morning; took a shower, shaved and waited for dinner. I was a pretty tired Boy, I assure you.

Got paid yesterday. Received £22. About $88. I paid off my debts for my rest [*leave*] and I had 2 shillings, 2 pence left. (about 25¢). Kinda left broke, wasn't I? But it was worth every cent of it. I don't worry about it. I'll give you an idea why it doesn't bother me. My monthly pay amounts to $172 per. I send $75 home as an allotment. It isn't used but put aside for me — if my family needs it, they are free to do so. I buy a War Bond per month, which is another $18.75. All in all, that is approximately $100 that I don't see. All that dough is a start for us. Every so often I give you my financial report. I feel that you should know what is going on on that score. I don't think we will do so badly. After all, two heads are better than one. We can manage well. When I get out of uniform, we will set our plans for that. Gosh, Honey, it sounds so good to be able to talk that way to someone. It sounds cruel to speak of cold figures in place of a warm love but that is one of those necessities that do have to be discussed, isn't it? I don't know what my overall savings are but why worry. At least, it isn't one of those starts from scratch. Do you think we'll be able to handle the situation aptly?

My Darling, I stand corrected on my interpretation of some of my letters. I am glad that they are what you like to hear. There are times that I go off the deep end; everything sounds so harshly brutal. Lord knows I get "cranky" every so often and my letters are not the epitome of loveliness. I am glad that I have done so well.

Bette, I think your Mother is right. Tennis is too strenuous a game for you. It is so hard for you to gain weight in abundance. Tennis is a fast game; it is meant for losing weight not for hardening. Swimming is better because it helps to develop the body on a whole. It is not a continuous grind. When one gets tired, it is easy to rest — whereas in tennis, the action is instantaneous and then there is that quick letdown. Tennis concentrates on the legs — for a woman it is strictly legs and hips, the most vital part of a woman's organs for birth, more or less. Swimming is good for the development of legs, arms, chest and stomach muscles. It is said that it is the one form of exercise that puts every muscle into movement. That's what you want. We do hope to start a family, don't we? With the Grace of God, we hope He will bless us and not let any misfortune befall us. You mustn't get me started on that score. You know I could talk for hours.

Well, Darling, I must close. I still haven't answered your letters. I must leave for a while. I'll try to make up as many letters as I can.

Give my love to Mother. Take care of yourself. May God Bless You. Love, Mike.

According to the 37th Squadron War Diary entry for August 1, eight planes were used to tow gliders and five to drop paratroops.

The 316th Troop Carrier Group (TCG) War Diary entry for the same day read:

> **Two aircraft flew to France, A 22 C, carrying freight: left Cottesmore flew to Valley and Prestwick and then to A 22 C.** [*"A 22 C" was the designation given to the airfield at Colleville, France, which had facilities for accepting courier planes. After the Allies had gotten a good foothold on the Continent, airfields were immediately constructed and captured fields were opened. The designation system was thus: "A" meant a U.S. field and "B" meant British, followed by a numerical designation, followed by a letter that indicated the type of facility: C = courier; N = night landing; D = air depot facilities.*]
>
> **This has been a month of movement, flustration** [*sic*] **and change. First, there was the forming of a new Airborne Army** [*the 1st Allied Airborne Army*]**. This being much the kind of thing that existed in North Africa, for there we had Americans and English and Poles in a lesser degree. To most of us here this new Army is the only reasonable thing that could have happened, though many of us resent the wearing of the black and gold tab** [*shoulder patch of the 1st Allied Airborne Army*] **which is now the new order.**

August 2, 1944 [*Wednesday*]

My Darling,

Here's your Ole Man again! Say, I resent that. True, I have a few more gray hairs but I'm still full of life. Gad! Woman, I've got gangs of life in me. I'll prove that when I get home. Alas and alack!

Say, Bette, I don't know what I'm going to do to you. You'll have to keep that weight of yours up. I can't think of any way to help except me. That one way isn't effective unless we are together. You can read between the lines as I shan't bother to explain.

That political discussion is acute, isn't it? I daresay it is hardly the way for a VP to act. So damn many things happen and after all I guess we can consider Wallace as human. Personally, all the fuss and ado can hardly be of any effect upon the election. As I said before, Dewey will be the man for '48 but it will take a terrific upheaval to [*vote*] FDR out of office. However, if he stays in much longer, the coming generation — the Rooseveltian generation won't know of any other man except FDR. If he could age as much as a High Lama, and be as wise and as learned as one, there won't ever be a change. Although I disagree with a lot of his actions before Pearl harbor, I am inclined to stay with him until the gang we are up against now is beaten. Don't let my words sway your vote. Believe me, only because of the present circumstances do I say what I have said.

I have never heard of Lt. Jack Collins. Besides it would hardly be my place to correct him. I am sure that he must be gentleman enough (By Act of Congress) to show some consideration for his family. That is purely up to him not for some stranger to remind him of it. I used to know a Lt. J.J. Collins but he has long since gone back. If it's the same fellow, which I doubt, he must have seen his family.

So you like to eat crackers in bed. Well, I won't kick. Personally, though I like to have my snack before bed time. It's OK to eat crackers or a Dagwood sandwich if you are doing some reading but who the Hell is going to read in bed? That privilege is reserved for our old age. As long as we are on the subject of food, I do like corn on the cob. One of my fondest memories dates back to a year when I was just a little squirt — can you imagine that? My Dad took us out to our shack on Long Island. We went out to the Elk's Club and Pop got a mess full of fried chicken and corn on the cob (oozing with melted butter!). It was late, so we sat in the old Model "A" Ford, listened to the Tunney-Heeney fight and ate. Gad! It was good. Funny I can taste it this very moment. Do I like Corn and Fried Chicken?

I had a chance to see the *New York Times* book review section. I see that this *Anna and the King of Siam* doesn't rate very high. [*Bob*] Hope's book is well rated. That would be natural; he is so damn clever, it's a wonder it would be any different. That man is one of the Marvels of our Age. Thank God for men like that.

You talk of a headache in this latest [*letter*] but since I didn't get your earlier letter yet, I don't know what it is the result of. Whenever I hear of headaches, I think of 1st, a hang over; and 2nd, woman trouble. Whatever it may be, take care of it, Honey. I'm pretty fortunate on that score. My headaches are self-made. (Hang over). Haven't had one for quite a while so I can't kick. Did quite a bit of drinking on that rest (?) leave but not once did I awaken with a head. Guess I must be quite immune to that alcohol treatment.

Well, Bette, I must close. There is too much noise in this house of mine; can't think.

Give my love to Mother. Take care of yourself. May God Bless You. Love, Mike.

On August 2, three planes participated in a formation flight, according to the War Diary. The weekly 316th Group dance was held at the NAAFI hall.

August 3, 1944 [*Thursday*]

Good Morning, Darling,

Ah! Yes, so I must write this AM. I am going out with "Pappy" tonite to celebrate our anniversary [*one year since leaving Baer Field, Indiana, for overseas duty*]; so I don't think I'll have much time to write this evening nor do I think I'll be in such good shape. Alas! I must be allowed that much after all this time.

I can't understand the lack of mail from home. Honestly, it is irritating. But that's one of those things. I've stopped complaining about that lacking because it seems so much in vain.

Gosh, Honey, it is rather difficult to write this AM. Life has been rather uneventful. It is amazing how quiet everything can get. Just listened to the news. Now, I can go on. I never comment on that because it isn't in the books. The only thing that interests me is the end of this mess.

Rather "soupy" [*bad flying weather*] today so we can take life easy. We've spent a lot of these past days playing pinochle. We have had some rather hot games. Though they are inexpensive, they are a Hell of a lot of fun. Darling, you needn't worry about that lack of money I mentioned in one of my previous letters. I've got about 5½£ now (about $22). That's enough to last me until next pay. Don't like to have you thinking about my meek financial affairs.

Got to thinking last night about Christmas. I was kind of wishing I'll be home by then. It has been a long time since I've spent a good one at home. The first away from home, I got stinking drunk on egg nog. (It was good! Gad! I couldn't leave the ole punch bowl.) To boot we hustled a few extra bottles in — Don't know if it was gangs of fun but I numbed to everything. I do know I got home about 5 AM. Last year, the atmosphere was changed, but the spirit was the same. If you recall my letters then, it was rain and snow that made it a wet but not white Christmas. Fortunately, we had a gang of good American bourbon. I may have drunk a lot of whiskey straight but I do miss my bourbon and coke. (Just a dash of lemon, please!) But I guess of all the times of the year, Christmas is the one time that brings everything so close — "Gloria in Excelsis Dei." "Peace on Earth, good will to all men." All these things in one little thought. Really is great what any mind can think of. I love you more and I miss you as much. I become more and more thrilled by the fact that time is passing quickly. It seems as if it can't be too miserably long before I'll be home. I mean the months are passing. The rest that are left whatever they are, surely will pass just as quickly.

[*The previous Christmas, we were in Sicily. On the eve, I am ashamed to admit that I did get drunk. We then went into town to hear midnight Mass at the Children's orphanage. When I heard the familiar hymns, sung by the children, I burst into an uncontrollable flood of tears — a crying jag that lasted until I got back to my tent.*]

Well, Bette, I am going to "carry on." This letter is very much comparable to your random thoughts letters. Just tattling on. So long for now. "This is a Hell of a way to spend an Evening." — Here by myself. Take care of yourself. May God Bless You. Love, Mike.

The August 3 War Diary entry simply read: "Seven day rest leaves were discontinued."

August 4, 1944 [*Friday*]

Hello Bette,

Played a couple of strenuous games of volley ball. After I finished, I took a shower; that moment decided a change in my routine. I noted that not only was I gaining weight but I was getting loose. That's one thing that I can't stand. And I know that if you saw me in the flesh that you'd divorce me before you married me. So we have devised a schedule of training — every night from 7-9 PM. I worked out this afternoon so we aren't starting until tomorrow eve. This training schedule consists of 2 rounds of 2 minutes each of rope skipping, calisthenics, shadow boxing, punching heavy and light bags and some body contact boxing. We are concentrating on the stomach. Really, Honey, looks like I was developing a business man's paunch. Hell, I haven't weighed myself in years and I bet I am close to 220 lbs. That's out. I am going to try to cleave approximately 30 lbs. off. My normal weight should be 190. Hell, you lose weight and you shouldn't. I'd be ashamed to come home in this condition. — But if they ever wanted to send me, I wouldn't bitch. I don't imagine that you'd be too angry with me.

Well, we went out last night, "Pappy," Nick (our favorite censor) and a few more fellows. Unfortunately, I had a headache before I started. By the time the evening was over, it was magnified. Funny incident occurred. When we got back to base, we stood around talking like a bunch of "queers" — high-pitched voices and dirty old talk. As we were talking, this RAF Corporal passed and listened in. He joined in and asked a few typical questions. He actually thought we were serious. Finally, we broke up and I started toward my barracks. This character followed. As high as I was, I wasn't that drunk. So I turned around and in my normal base voice, I said; "If you think I'm queer, you're crazy. If you take another step in the direction I'm going, I'll set you down on your royal." After he heard my natural voice, he "peeled off" and headed in another direction. Didn't think that he took us all that seriously. Besides he shouldn't have just put his nose in the conversation. Aside from that, the evening was swell. We did an awful lot of reminiscing. We decided that, at least, we have so much time behind us. I love you, Darling.

Gosh, Honey, if it weren't for you and a few other of my friends that write, it would be a fairly dreary existence. Your letters are like clock work. There are very few days when I don't receive at least one. I haven't heard from home for about a month. Can't understand it but Hell as I said before, my griping days are over. Now to go ahead. I received your letters of the 19th, 23rd, and 26th. I got your pictures, too.

Darling, you look lovelier as the days go by. If I can get you up to about 130 lbs., I'll be a good press agent for your Hollywood career. I can't believe that I could be so fortunate. Darling, I love you more and more. Showed your pictures to all the fellows, a lot of guys are jealous of me. Can't blame them. What are those three birds on your left side? Wearing chickens; didn't think you were yearning for a colonel. I've meant to ask you for a long time, but I never have. You don't wear anything that has any connection to me, do you, Bette? It's true I've never sent you anything and I am sorry. It's impossible to get anything over here any way. Not that it makes any difference. I've got a few things that I could send but I'd rather wait until I get home. I tried to get a small pin that is a duplicate of our 9th Air Force patch but I couldn't get the damn thing. Well, I guess that is another example of our lack of demonstrative nature. Just carry me in your heart, the way I carry you. We have that much wealth. I guess it can carry us for a long while until I get back. Hell! I haven't even put a ring on your finger yet. We shall see.

You asked me a question about your job. (My face is burning. I guess I got a bit of a burn today. Don't mind my off-hand remarks!) That all depends, above all, this is a supposition, if and when I get home, it is just a furlough, a leave, it would be best that you just got a leave to coincide with mine. Because once my leave is over, I'd have to return to the wars and you would be left idle. Of course, I'd make arrangements for allotments, etc. for you. But you could go on working and save the money I send for that rainy day. But, and again a supposition, if I were transferred to the States indefinitely, then we could keep our earlier promise that you'd go wherever I go. I don't ever want you away from me again. (I'll try not to get sentimental but I do feel it.) Wherever I go, we can decide, then, our plans. I am sure that you won't be an army wife too long — this can't last indefinitely. Besides with S/Sgt. pay, we can't do too badly. To be honest about it, Bette, I'd like to get enough overseas time to guarantee that I'd never get sent over again. I assure you that as long as I must be here, I want as much as I can get so that I don't ever have to go back anywhere out of the USA. It is the best way. True, we are apart now, but we can stand it a little longer and then assure ourselves an uninterrupted future. Besides, I've got enough time now that whatever more I've got to do, it will, more or less, be on the down grade. Take "Doc" for instance, he's been overseas in the Pacific 28 months — but the consoling part is that his time has passed. He can't be over much longer. I hope to Hell that I'm not here that long but so far my time has passed easily, hasn't it? (Confusing is spelled with 1 s.) Is that ample answer to your question?

Your last three letters are great. Not that your others are not deeply appreciated. It is simply that these latest letters have been such a comfort to me. I think it's the pictures that help so very much. Not only that but they have a touch of home that is indescribable. You've said things and asked questions that make everything appeal to me so beautifully. Perhaps, it is that you tell me that I am so close to you, that you make me feel the same way about you, Darling. Our enthusiasm hasn't waned the least bit. We are so eagerly looking forward to the future. Day by day, our love grows stronger. It is helped by our anticipation of so many things that are due to happen in the near future. The anticipation of things that will make our dreams come true; things that help to keep our morale high and our spirits undaunted.

When I left you, I told you that I'd be back. When? But I'd be back in one piece and unchanged. Your prayers will be answered as will be mine, Bette. He isn't so childish that He won't look after me. My return to you is His gain. I think of it that way always and it makes everything so easy.

I should go on and answer the rest of your letters but your words have a way of inspiring me to a warmth I so seldom feel. I guess it must be love. It may sound foolish but how many people really know what love is? Even my dreams these days are nothing but of you. Every action, every word. It is a feeling that I cannot fully describe. At chow, I wonder what your cooking will be like. How it will feel to sit across from you and enjoy every meal together. I am not asking what kind of cook you are, that is secondary. It is just a feeling of wanting to know how all these things will be with you. Whenever we have a warm, beautiful day, I sense your closeness. What it will be like to walk and laugh again? On miserable days, I wonder what we will talk about; what we will plan; how we will do everything. You see, darling, I am not that homesick that it affects my days. It is merely that I can think the way I do, that I can include you in every action on my part. It is those very thoughts that keep my heart laughing and that smile on my face. I told you what I thought about at that rest camp. How much I would have enjoyed it if you were there. To show how I betray myself, the hostess there asked me where I got such eyes and why did they sparkle so — I wasn't drunk — I was merely drunk with happiness that the thought of you could bring. I miss you so.

Darling, I am going to close. I must answer some of my other mail. I do hope I haven't talked too much.

So long for now. Take care of yourself. May God Bless You. Love, Mike.

P.S.: A letter this long is a censor's nightmare. But sorry, Ole Boy, when a guy feels the way I do, he has to tell someone — Right, Bette? M.

The Group War Diary entry for August 4 read:

> **Another beautiful day, very unusual to have so many in a row. Ideal afternoon for the P.T.** [*physical training*] **program, everyone was out trying to absorb as much sun as possible. Had a good volley ball game and soft ball game between EMs and Officers. As usual the Enlisted men won. Mission of the 1st was completed today. Group had glider formation in the afternoon, flew from Cottesmore, Ramsby, Wisbeck with LZ** [*landing zone*] **at Cottesmore. Forty aircraft participated. Whenever the weather is permissible a daily training program is carried out dropping Paratroops on DZ at Ashwell.**

The Squadron War Diary for the same day read:

> **12 planes participated in a glider formation flight and one plane made a cross country flight.**

The next day, August 5, 1944, the Squadron War Diary recorded a simulated drop mission involving 18 planes, plus the regular weekly flight to Stratford-on-Avon.

August 6, 1944 [*Sunday*]

My Darling.

No mail from you for 2 days. What are you doing, laying down on the job? This is just that period of time between mails. I know that I don't have to wait too long. It is as regular as meal times. One consolation of my lack of mail from home, I got a letter from Harry yesterday. He gives me all the dope. It seems that a buddy of mine from Boston [*Dan Emery, who had been sent home in June for an extended leave*] called my home and gave them some dope. [*Harry*] also said that my brother, Lou, had received his orders to return home. Lou is probably enroute home now. At least I get that dope from some source. Now, by the time, I get it from home, it will be old news. What the hell, I still hear it.

Just finished supper and I am resting before I start my evening's training. Don't know if I can cut down my weight but I get plenty of aches and stiffness out of it. See what I go thru', Darling, to keep in shape.

Funny I feel as if there is so little to say this evening. One of those nights when we would do little talking. Listening to Tommy Dorsey, Frank Sinatra, and some beautiful music — "For You." Everything is so peaceful and quiet. Weather is ideal for lounging but I don't intend to do that. My activities have been limited of late to everything in general and nothing in particular. I love you.

I had a funny dream the other night. Everything happened on the 26th (of what and when, I don't know). Listen to this queer assortment of ideas. I landed at LaGuardia Field. I don't remember who my pilots were; all I do know is that they went home and forgot to tell me when to get ready to come back here. Well, all I had to do was to head for Brooklyn, 20 minutes by cab. But before I left, I told the pilots my phone number so that they could call me when they were ready to leave. When I got home, everyone was sitting on the stoop in front of my house, included in the bunch was my bro., Lou. Well we battered around a bit, as dreams will have it; they leave us such little time to do anything. Funniest thing Lou was in civilian clothes and he was ready to renovate the house to renew his practice. After a while, I went indoors to call you. I said I was going to call Kansas City. When I walked in, I noticed all the furniture piled up, and on it was a sign, "blackout sale." I asked Lucy about it; she just winked and walked out. I called your number and waited. Just then a bunch of typical English people walked in and started to look over the furniture. I started to talk but decided to keep quiet. Then some character walked in and said, "You have to take that test today; it's the 26th!" I turned around and started to shout, "Dammit that's the 3rd thing I have to do on the 26th!" (I don't know what test nor do I know what else I had to do!) My mind was so preoccupied while I was waiting for you that I didn't know what decision to make — since I didn't know when I was to return; I didn't know whether to tell you to come East or not — when you answered, I said, "I love you." that's all — someone did something that caught my eye — I dropped the phone, ran over to him and started to argue like Hell! — Then, I woke up. — you figure it out; I can't.

Darling, I am going to close. Most of the guys are ready so I don't want to keep them waiting. Give my love to Mother. Take care of yourself. May God Bless You. Love, Mike.

The War Diary entries for August 6 and 7 described the move of the squadron's air echelon to Greenham Common airfield:

> **August 6: All personnel restricted to camp as of 1400 hours. Two local and three cross country flights.**
> **August 7: The air echelon, consisting of 83 officers, 50 EM and 20 planes were ordered on DS to Station 486 (Greenham Common), per letter 52 TCW** [*Troop Carrier Wing*]**, subject Orders dated 7 August 1944. . . .**
> **REPORT FROM GREENHAM COMMON: Air Echelon arrived 1445 hours. Upon arrival men were transported to Site No. 7, assigned to them for a billeting area.**

August 8, 1944 [*Tuesday*]

My Darling,

Received your letter of the 21st. It really is great to get those letters, Darling. If I complained about letters from you, I must be crazy. If I just say that I haven't heard for a few days, believe me, Bette, that isn't a complaint, it is purely a statement. Lord knows, you do so well. Better than I could ever hope. The same for myself; I try my damnedest to write every day. As in some cases, it is impossible. You must understand that. There are times when I do work, you know. Finally received some mail from my home. Two letters that were dated July 23rd and 28th. Good service but what the Hell happened between those days. Called Harry last night. I have some very good hopes of seeing him often. Just one of those lucky breaks for me.

Darling, I feel like a million bucks. The weather has been perfect. My arms are tanned and I've tried to get myself some body tan in my spare time. It will take some time for me to do a good job of that. Funny thing but as long as the sun shines, I can lose weight and I feel great. It must be my sunny (?) disposition. It is just as my sister said about my gaining weight that I can lose it just as easily. That's no lie as long as I get a chance to see sun and I am able to perspire and release that excess energy, I do well.

You asked me if I had remembered your phone number. Hell! I can't forget it. I got it so that I'll have it for any emergency that may arise. I don't intend to be standing short. I don't think that Tony will ever get up in your area because most of his flying is done in the Western part of the States. Don't worry, as soon as we start out housekeeping, we'll see plenty of Tony and Sheila.

Darling, I love you. I am not going to write too much this evening. I am going to save most of my answer for tomorrow. I see myself clear to be able to write early so I want to make sure I'll have gangs to say. One thing I cannot exclude is that I've never felt so buoyed in all my life. Truly, I can't understand that buoyant feeling but I'll keep it as [*long as*] it wants to stay. Believe me, I have you to thank for it. It is no wonder that I am planning my whole future with you. There is so much of it.

Good night, Honey. Give my love to Mother. Take care of yourself. May God Bless You. Love, Mike.

The August 8 War Diary entry included a report from Greenham Common air base:

> **The air echelon was to work in conjunction with the 89th TCS [*Troop Carrier Squadron*] ground echelon. In the afternoon two planes were dispatched to Cottesmore to bring back six officers and 16 EM; mainly engineering personnel to help on the line. Eight planes were sent to North Witham to pick up freight. Two 2½ ton trucks were dispatched to Cottesmore for use of air echelon on this base, arriving 0100 hours, 9 August 1944.**

During this time, we were preparing for OPERATION TRANSFIGURE (which would eventually be aborted). In the Intelligence briefing, after we were given the mission details, which I do not recall, we were told to expect *85 percent casualties*! The number was reasonable. Our crew chiefs and other engineering personnel were installing gas tanks, which were not self-sealing, immediately behind the bulkhead, and right behind my position. These tanks, I believe, were to hold from 50-100 gallons of high-octane aircraft gasoline. They were made from pressed cardboard, painted black, and linked in circuit with aluminum piping with valves so that the fuel could be forced into the wing tanks, as required. We were going to do a double glider tow. To provide ourselves with minimum protection, we wrapped flak jackets around the tanks, hoping that a direct hit by shells or small arms would be stopped by the metal jackets. Ironically, at mail call that afternoon, I received a financial statement from Sears, Roebuck, my civilian employer, informing me that I now held approximately 19 shares of Class B stock in my profit-sharing account. My own thought was: "Who the Hell cares!"

August 9, 1944 [*Wednesday*]

Good Morning, Bette,

Here I am again. A bright sunny August day, plenty of fresh air, light classical music, all the comforts of home (?) and you to talk to.

I am gratified to know that you agree with everything that I said in reference to Tony's letter. Our line of thought has run parallel always; the only advantage he has over me is maturity. I believe I have his letter salted away somewhere in my files. I'm getting so absent minded these days, it's no wonder I can remember anything. At times, it is a distressing feeling. At other times, it is advantageous. They say that two [*heads*] are better than one. Your letters prove that in the most definite way. I am so content to know that I can rely on your levelheadedness. It is that moral strength that I have felt so seldom in my young life. A feeling of independence that makes the world so easy to see. It is so damn easy and intelligent to say that other people must step in line with you. That harmony of personality adds to the greatness of our love and fits so perfectly with our capabilities of unity.

I was most concerned by your statement of your health. . . . Take care of yourself, Darling. Health is the one thing we cannot have unless we work for it.

I can still feel that elated feeling about me. It really is great, honestly. I love you so much. I miss you as much, but I feel as if there is a closeness that I cannot describe. The funniest part of all that I feel is that I am so much at a loss for words that I can't possibly just put my ideas on paper. Bette, being in love with you is one of the greatest things in the world. And so.

I must close. Perhaps, I'll have time to write again later on. One never knows. Give my love to Mother. Tell her I'll be as good as I can. Good enough to make a worthwhile husband for you. Please do take care of yourself. May God Bless You. Love, Mike.

The War Diary entries for August 9 and 10 read:

> **August 9: Two planes were dispatched to France and eight planes participated in a glider formation flight. Five planes picked up gliders at Membury** [*an air base in southern England, which also had a large hospital nearby*]**. The two planes dispatched yesterday to France returned at 1430 hours. Eight planes took part in a group glider flight, loaded with airborne troops and equipment.**
>
> **August 10: REPORT FROM GREENHAM COMMON: General** [*Dwight D.*] **Eisenhower inspected the officers and EM of the air echelon; because many of the men were not wearing their campaign ribbons, the general ordered that in the future they would be worn while in Class A uniform. Two planes were dispatched to Cottesmore to pick up glider tow ropes and laundry. Captain Cooney, Intelligence Officer, received orders transferring him from the 37 TCS to 9th Air Force Headquarters. Lt. Robert Roman, assistant Intelligence Officer, arrived from Cottesmore to replace the Captain as squadron Intelligence officer.**

August 11, 1944 [*Friday*]

My Darling,

I didn't get a chance to write for the last few days. Aside from my lacking, I've been fortunate to receive 2 letters from you, dated 24th and 3rd of August. That is really good service, don't you think? In your letter of the 24th was included your last picture. Darling, you know your slimness makes you appear short in the picture. If I didn't know you, I'd think that I was marrying a short gal. I love you so very much.

I don't know if this is permissible but since no one has said anything I thought I'd mention it. We attended a formal review and Gen. "Ike" Eisenhower decorated a few of the boys that are closely attached to us. He is a rather nice chap. He went thru' the ranks and talked to a lot of the boys. I wasn't in the ranks because we were detained by some unforeseen circumstances. But when he called us all around the stand, I was standing close by. He spoke informally and splendidly. No sense to tell you what he said because I am sure that you'll be able to read his speech in the papers. There was a lot of fanfare and rank attached to the whole shebang. I saw Ike's Scottie — he has 4 stars on his collar just like his boss. All in all, it was very impressive. [*In reality, we were late because our truck broke down on our way to Hungerford Common. We stood immediately behind the general and his staff, including Kay Summersby. When Ike spoke to the command over the speaker, he called us the Air Transport Command and not the Troop Carrier Command. We did not take this goof too kindly. The Air Transport Squadron were not really a combat unit. They did not drop paratroops as we did, nor did they tow gliders.*]

You must have misunderstood my letter about what I mentioned about America and such. It is quite natural that I made a mistake because I seldom reread my letters. Only when I am dealing with a "touchy" subject do I do so. But ordinarily it is easy for me to exclude "not" when there should be one and to put one in when there shouldn't. Bette, I don't think I'll ever be able to catch up on the luxuries that the States have, that we haven't had in all these countries. Forgive my mistake.

You mentioned the fact that it was very hot in KC. You said that you don't practice the piano "cause I stick to the bench." Silly thought but what a Hell of a situation if a guy's seat was left after he got up. What made me think that, — I was thinking of one of these formal parades when the soldiers are made to pass in review. When they pass the reviewing stand, every eye turns to the right; naturally, you don't see where you are going; what a mess if there was a hole, a deep one, in front of you — what a guy can think of sometimes.

I was glad to hear that Sheila had written. I knew that she would come thru'. Tony, Sheila, and "Reb" have been very nice to me ever since I joined the service. They have been very attentive. I can always expect a letter to any I write and more. It is one of my nicer correspondences. I really enjoy writing to the gang. Little Reb is my favorite gal. You see, I'm her God father, by proxy. Or have I told you that before? You see I must be especially attentive to her.

In your letter of the 3rd, you said that you hadn't heard for a week. I have told you why already. Another example of your skill with clothes. That house coat must look good. Rose colored; it must be a soft color, isn't it? That icy shade may look good but I know that I can depend on your judgment. I think I told you why I like blue so much; it appears so cool. It gives a woman an appearance of freshness that nothing can change. Believe me, Darling, your "homey" remarks do something to me. It gives me such a close feeling — as if you could read my very thought. So you are low on night gowns; do you really think

I thought what you think I did? (Funny way to put a question, but that's the idea!) It isn't so much the maliciousness of the thought but the fact that it is said in such a normal manner. The same easy manner that everything else happens and will happen. Those little things that sound so natural, that make time seem like an unimportant thing. I promise I won't let you go to bed with wet hair. I'll sit up and help you dry it. You know how much I like to stroke your long, lovely hair. That is one thing that fascinates me so. I assume from what you say that you've seen a Dr. I do hope that you've been able to rectify whatever has bothered you. I get that same sort of nervousness that you speak of. That's why my nails are bitten so often. During those periods of time, I smoke a lot. It is one of those damnably hard periods to get over. Thank God, it is easy to get into a torrent of thought. I love you so much, My Darling. You needn't worry if I think you need a good fanning. I won't be afraid to give it to you. Gosh, Bette, if I just had you in my arms there would be no need for any fanning or anything like that. I think that the warmth of our love will be enough to take care of any condition. I don't worry about a thing as long as I know that time will pass. I'll take care of your health as carefully as I would a little child. I'm even willing to bet that I'll be able to get some weight on that lanky frame of yours.

Darling, I must go. Give my love to Mother. Take care of yourself. Don't worry about me; I'll be OK. Taking good care of myself. May God Bless You. Love, Mike.

On August 11, according to the War Diary, two planes were dispatched to North Witham, with extra crews to pick up two additional planes. Engineering personnel continued work on their 100-hour inspections. There was a glider mission involving nine planes. The day's entry concluded: "All personnel worked late installing pararacks for the Wing Mission No. 101. (Greenham Common.)"

On August 12:

> **Twelve planes departed for the far shore carrying supplies in executing Mission No. 101. Supplies not needed but each plane returned with patients. 1st Lt. Robert Roman was made squadron Intelligence Officer and 2nd Lt. Gordon McShane was made his assistant.**

August 13, 1944 [*Sunday*]

Good Evening, Darling,

I wrote to a buddy of mine yesterday. I was going to start one to you when I was interrupted to go to work. The buddy I speak of used to be my tent mate back in parts where we used tents. His name is Max [*Gilliam*]; I mentioned him before, you must recall. He sent me a letter from the States. Kinda made me feel sort of homesick talking about the Statue of Liberty and cold bottles of Budweiser. Really hurts to hear it. But I'm glad he got a break and is enjoying himself. Some guys do get breaks but he had it coming to him.

Let me explain, My Love, before I go any further that my letters are scratchy and not so frequent as before; it is not too much my fault. Aside from enjoying the weather as often as I can, I am busy. Darling, I'm changing colors, getting a bit of a tan. Keep it up long enough, I'll have myself a good, black tan. I don't mind. It makes me feel a Hell of a lot better. Been playing a little ball, too.

I got your letter of the 4th. That really is good mail service. Glad that you are getting my mail now. True, I goofed off for a while but you know now why I did so. I was serious when I said that I wanted to take a vacation when I get out of [*overseas duty*]. I think we ought to be able to do well. There isn't any reason why we can't enjoy life freely. After that, we'll still enjoy life but there will be the question of work. Eek! Gad what a horrible thought. Talking about that *Tree Grows in Brooklyn* and the English version, I never thought of it as you mentioned it but their name does a take a lot of appeal out of it. Lord knows! As much as they jest about Brooklyn, a lot of people still like to hear about it.

Gad! I don't blame you for not wanting a picture at that price. Sounds like robbery. Hell! Bette, they should be flattered enough to pay you for taking the picture. I can see that you are really cutting down on your cigarette smoking. I wish I could do the same. I've never tasted these Phantoms you speak of. Someone just gave me a pack of Sheffield cigarettes. I think I tasted them once before. They are dry; but Hell, cigarettes are cigarettes. If I stay in the army much longer, I'll be able to smoke anything.

That's a good idea. I'll trade those lessons with you. I think it is less painful to learn how to fish. From what I hear that horse back stuff is rugged. Plenty of aches and pains after a few hours of that. Darling, I meant to ask you this but do you know how to drive a car? I expect that we'll want a car for ourselves. I think you'll do most of the driving. Even though I know how, I don't trust myself too much. Strange as it may seem, I seem to be allergic to cars. Feel a Hell of a lot safer in a plane. I don't know why but I don't do well at that sort of thing. I do OK but not as well as would be expected. We'll let you handle that side of the family. Besides, someone has to drive this drunk home.

I've written 2½ pages and I haven't told you I love you. And I do so very much. God knows how much I'd like to have you with me right now. I get such of a Hell of a fine feeling just thinking of that great day. Guess what makes me feel so good is that, again I repeat, the time is passing. Now all I'm doing is adding more and extra time to what I have already.

Must say Good Night. Give my love to Mother. Take care of yourself. Do hope you are over your headaches. I love you and miss you. May God Bless You. Love, Mike.

On August 13, according to the War Diary,

Lt. Roman and Lt. Weiss gave all personnel necessary instructions pertaining to voting. (Greenham Common and Cottesmore.)

The August 14 entry was a report from Greenham Common:

Lt. Roman attended a meeting of the S-2 [*Intelligence*] **officers at Group S-2. Gliders were towed to** [*Welford Park*] **during the afternoon. Eight planes were dispatched to France; two carried whole blood and six resupply. Effective at once personnel were restricted to the base.**

August 15, 1944 [*Tuesday*]

Hello Darling,

Just a busy little beaver. I wish I could explain. You'll have to be satisfied with my meager letters these days. I love you, Darling. I have been feeling good these days. Nothing much to think about except us. That is the only and nicest thought in the world. There's a bunch of characters around that are chattering like a bunch of hens at a sewing circle. I haven't had a chance to do much sunning these days but I still feel good. Some times I think that hard work can't hurt a guy too much.

You know, Bette, this time of the year is the one time a guy can dream and dream in an atmosphere of balmy weather. Of late, my sleep has been disturbed by dreams. Not really disturbed but pleasantly. Had a nice one last night. Dreamt we were at a beach somewhere; as usual, I was resting in the sun and you were sleeping somewhere about. I was trying to think of something to do to trick you for a joke. There were a few other couples with us. As I recall this is the way it went. You had fallen asleep in a shady spot. It was getting late and time to go home. I told a buddy of mine to awaken you. But I told him to say some sweet words and pretend it was me. So he put his arms around you and said, "Wake up, Darling, it's time to go." Without opening your eyes, you muttered in a ½-sleepy manner, "Yes, Mike." Put your arms around him and kissed him. But the guy had a mustache, Hitler-style; you felt it and jumped up; your face was flushed. For the moment you were angry and then when you saw that I was laughing, ran over, put your arms around me and said, "Oh! Mike" and I kissed you. It may all be a dream but how often I reflect on those days when I'll be able to get you up mornings with a kiss. You must excuse me, Bette, if I appear to be talking in a fantastically childish manner but I think about things like that so often that it can't be funny. This morning while I was washing, my mind strayed — I was thinking about us and I walked off still in a daze and left my towel behind.

It's a wonderful life. Everything I think of is pleasant. So far away from the mess that surrounds us on all sides. The meaning of us is so much clearer to me than it has ever been. Oftimes, I think of the night when I'm liable to come home drunk (got into a discussion of the war and what I had done, etc. — you know. Had a drink with a few of the boys!) — the blunt idea is that as a typical wife you will start raising Cain and deride me for my actions — suddenly the wife pulls out the pre-marriage romantic letters with the inevitable, "And you told me all this!" It is amusing to me because I know it won't happen. To me, it is just an idea of what a day can be and what it may be like. Funny little incidents that make waiting so hard. I guess you feel the same way too. Bette, I love you so very much that I hope and pray that I'll be capable of making your life as happy as I want it to be. Lord knows, we've got one of the finest foundations for it. I pray to God that He will let us see the end of this quickly so that we can make all those dreams come true. A world that can be subjected to this much surely can be a Hell of a lot a better one and come thru' a lot.

I am going to close for now. Expect to be busy for a while. Give my love to Mother. Take care of yourself. May God Bless You. Love, Mike.

P.S.: Sent for my ballot yesterday. Even if he doesn't win, [*Thomas E.*] Dewey will get mine. — M.

War Diary entry, August 15:

REPORT FROM GREENHAM COMMON: Captain Maloney, 88th TCS Intelligence Officer is to assist Lt. Roman in preparation for a mission over France. All 29 planes are in readiness as are all combat crews and glider pilots.

August 16, 1944 [*Wednesday*]

Good Evening, Darling,

Beautiful evening, nice breeze and quiet and I'm in love — my heart desires nothing more than to be able to tell it all to you instead of having to write it.

Just got a late letter from home. It seems only a certainty that Lou is on his way home. I envy him but I shan't even let it bother me. Wish you were hearing the same about me but who knows it may not be too long off.

I am trying to think of so many things to say but I don't think my mind is functioning too brilliantly or quickly. It's a queer feeling. Something I haven't the power to express. I don't feel much but realistic and slightly tired. Maybe it's because I haven't heard from you for 3 days, — maybe its tiredness. All I do know is that in all my realism I want so much to have you in my arms. Bette, my words are insufficient, as I feel my actions would be too. Perhaps after a while they would prove differently. You must be able to read thru' and beyond my words. It is at times like these that our memories haunt me with their beauty and comfort. Luckily, we can laugh deeply, think softly, whisper sweetly and in our dreams and letters love intensely. [*It is*] One of these nights when I feel I could do Shakespeare justice and out Barrymore Barrymore.

Look Darling, I hate to shove off this quickly. But it is best that I do. My mind needs relaxation. I hope I don't sound too temperamental.

Good Night, Sweet Dreamer. Take care of yourself. May God Bless You. I love you and miss you so very much. Love, Mike.

The Squadron War Diary's August 16 report from Greenham Common recorded one cross-country flight and return. It also noted that group pictures were taken of all combat crew members.

The 316th TCG War Diary entry for the same day read:

> **Preparation underway for "Transfigure" mission. Rumored as a bigger event than the airborne landing on "D" Day. Very little confusion in preparation this time. Mission postponed another 24 hours. The 44th, 45th, and 37th Squadrons had their briefings.**

On August 17, the 37th Squadron War Diary noted:

> **"Transfigure" mission was called off completely. Four planes on DS were returned to Grove; one additional plane went along to return crews. There was a glider pick up under actual field conditions.**

The 316th Group War Diary entry that same day read:

> **Everyone anxiously awaiting news of the mission and finally word came to postpone it another 24 hours. Later on in the day it was scrubbed altogether.**

August 18, 1944 [*Friday*]

My Darling,

I received your letters of the 6th, 7th, and 9th of August. I can't kick about a shortage. You can understand my beefs but they aren't too strict, are they? I don't sound off because I know that the minute I open my mouth, it is stuffed with mail. Just called Harry. I'll be seeing him soon. Good to talk to someone I know. Tells me that Lou isn't on his way home but was sent to another island and is being reassigned to another unit. Poor guy; he'll never get home. Makes me so damn mad to hear those USO commandos "bitch" about how tough it is in the States. Well!

Your letter of the 6th was opened because they said that it was in bad condition when it was received. Don't think they read it though.

In your letter of the 7th, you went on graciously and beautifully of the grandeur of the States. Unfortunately, you stopped too quickly. You should have kept it up. Really sounded good to ears attached to eyes that have seen beauty but not the beauty I love and enjoy. Surely these countries have a lot, but Hell, Woman, they aren't America. Darling,

I'd like to do everything and go every place that we would like to go. God willing, we'll see to it that we'll never be inactive. Even in those quiet moments, we won't be at a loss. I don't promise a thing, but these dreams that we are dreaming now will formulate to one of the nicest things in the world.

Darling, forgive me again. I am going to close. You may be surprised at the brevity of my letters but it isn't my fault. I can't explain the situation, please understand.

Harry sends his love. May God Bless You. I love you. Mike.

The August 18 report from Greenham Common, from the Squadron War Diary, read:

> **ETO restriction was lifted at 1200 hours. Eight planes were used in a Wing mission to France. Six planes left for Cottesmore to bring back quartermaster personnel and supplies; three returning to make a second trip. One plane cross country and return.**

The next day, except for two planes that went cross country and returned, all flying was cancelled due to weather.

August 20, 1944 [*Sunday*]

Hello Bette,

Gad! It is about time that I wrote you a decent letter. This is the first chance that I've had to concentrate on a letter to you. For this last week, it seemed as if I haven't had time to do anything, let alone eat and sleep. I had a good night's sleep last night so I feel as if I can get along here and tell you how much I love you.

I saw a movie last night. I don't recall the name of it because it was some sort of screwy affair. The thing that attracted me most of all was that the heroines were good sized and lovely women. I don't know what their names were but one was blonde and the other brunette. It is hard to judge size on the screen but they certainly did look to be 5´9˝ or over. Truly lovely girls! Maybe it's my mood but they made my heart feel heavy because they reminded me so much of you.

When I wrote to you the other night, I said that I was going to retire early. I was going to but one of the fellows came in with a guitar and we sat around and sang all sorts of melancholy tunes. Something that might sound mournful but really has more depth for thought than anyone can imagine. Unfortunately, as tired as I was, sleep didn't come too early to me — just as I started to relax, duty called and we were hustled out in the middle of the night. Ah me! Ah Woe!

I thought of you an awful lot these past few days. However, I couldn't put those thoughts on paper because I was afraid to spoil them. The reason I was afraid I would was that I was tired enough to jumble everything. It would have been pitiful to disturb all of that. For some reason, it has seemed so easy to relive whatever memories that will be ordinary for the future. That sounds rather mixed up but it isn't. It isn't hard to imagine our future life. It isn't hard to see the happiness and pleasantness of that future that doesn't seem so far off.

That mournful wail of a lonely heart. I know it isn't right to veil my thoughts behind a laughing mood but it is best that I can do. It is as hard for me to write of how miserable I feel sometimes as it is for you to read these letters. God, Bette! I miss you terribly. It isn't too much the physical absence but just you. Just to have you near me, would be the epitome of my happiness. I guess it is a lacking of normal living that does that. I feel as if I've lived a hermit's life so long that I'll be afraid of people when I come in contact with them again. I haven't even bothered to drink & forget. Just a good little boy.

Well, Darling, I am going to close. I wish I could tell you what is occupying my time but I'd only cause more gray hairs for the censor. Take care of yourself. May God Bless You. Love, Mike.

Two planes were dispatched from Greenham Common to France on August 20 on a blood bank run, according to the War Diary. Four planes left that evening on a resupply mission and returned that night.

August 21, 1944 [*Monday*]

My Darling,

My Lovely Woman! Woman that I love. Please forgive me for my stupid moments of these last few days. In the face of disappointments, I'm afraid I let my mask fall and my writing surely must have shown it. I love you.

I received your letter of the 14th of August. You can see that there is no need to kick over that sort of service. Don't apologize for the lipstick on the paper, — wish I could wipe some of it off my mouth. Well, I'm proud of you. I do hope that the change to a non-smoker isn't too difficult. If I give it up, I'd bite my nails down to a knuckle. I am glad that your appetite has developed so for the best. They say that that is one of the best ways to put on some heft and beef. My solution is one of the best but I wouldn't want you to try it without me.

It would be good to get seats for the World Series but (pessimistic me!) I don't think it will be me who helps you yell for the <u>Browns</u>. But I am sure that if I can't help you enjoy it, I'm sure that Mother would enjoy it. It is the custom when one buys seats for a WS to buy them for all the games. I don't believe that they will sell less. It is almost compulsory to buy for all especially if you want to get a good seat. Don't think I'll be able to see a good ball game for a while. Sounds gloomy, doesn't it? But I wouldn't worry; anything can happen.

Well I must say $1,100 is nothing to sneeze at. We can always see Benny and hock that stuff. Darling, are you sure you wouldn't wear a plain ole' gold band from me to show that I've given you that little at least? You recall my report on my status financially. I received a statement from Sears. It seems that I have about $150 in shares with the company. I won approx. 3 shares. I also figured it out that I was making $33+ per week with them and my prospects looked good when I left. Considering the present salaries that looks paltry but to consider the post-war salaries, wouldn't be doing too badly. Everything seems so upset as far as servicemen go that I don't know what the Hell we'll decide on for the future. At any rate, I do know that we won't have too bad a start when this is over. Not to forget an additional $300 for mustering out pay. Sounds mercenary, doesn't it? I hate to speak of everything in terms of dollars & cents but it does make some sense.

Bette! The Hell with all that! Who wants to look at the heavy side of everything. From what we have seen of each other, we do know that that part of the future will be the easiest thing in the world for us. For once, I sound optimistic but perhaps I've a right to. I miss you so much. Everything about me appears unimportant. I got a letter today [*in which*] I was asked if I had changed. My tone sounded so unusual. Surely what is to be expected of us over here. We put our chins forward but there are times when it gets socked and socked hard. All I know is that I miss your arms about me. I miss the way your hair tickles my nose. I miss the way you say I love you. I miss the tenderness of the moments we shared. I miss all of that and a multitude of other things that made Mike love life. Surely I am allowed my moments when I am apt to forget that life is made of strawberries and cream. Surely I am allowed those moments of cursing, yelling, screaming and ill-temper. But beneath all that, there is still me. The one who told you that he'd be back. The one who wants to move heaven and earth simply to be allowed to live that simple life he loves. Darling, is it so hard for me to put this in words that are understood?

Time, that oft-spoken word. That word that means that a little part of our life is slipping away. Time which we pray to have pass and cuss if it does. There are going to be many trying months between now and our union. So far that much has passed. So much more may have to pass but above all our cursing, all our torment, all those emotions that are tossed about by a trick of a mind, we can see us just as we left it in a memory of beauty and love. My whole life is for you, My Darling. I shall never disappoint you. Never fear for me — my assurances are not just vague words, easy to say because we are apart. They are as easy to say as every bit of truth I have ever let slip from my lips. You are the only person in my life. I found that out over a year ago while I was sitting in a plane somewhere in the desert. I was more than sure of it one night not too long ago when I was in one of the hottest places [*D-Day, June 6, 1944*] in heaven or earth (It wasn't Hell!). That is, the place wasn't; the ordeal was. I've seen it and heard you in every place in this lil' ole' world I've been in. I never thought it could be so — like St. Thomas, seeing was believing. I've seen it. In my most skeptical moods, in my worst wretched moods, I've seen [*your*] head and shoulders above everything I have ever known or loved. Are my words understood, Bette? After all my miserable letters, I had to tell you that I loved you and missed you in more words than just those six. And so I leave you, My Darling. Good Night.

Take care of yourself. May God Bless You. Love, Mike.

The August 21 War Diary entry reported:

> **One plane took off** [*from Greenham Common*] **for weather observation; one for the courier run to Cottesmore and eight for a resupply mission to France; picking up their load at Membury; they were unable to continue due to weather and returned to camp.**

August 22, 1944 [*Tuesday*]

Good Morning, Me Love,

Just a beautifully miserable day. The best thing for me to do is to dash off a note to you. As long as I am sure not to be disturbed, I can be sure to get more than one page out. After I reread my letter last night, and slept over it, I realized that I said many things that may appear roundish. That is, far off the point. The reason for that is that it is impossible to be blunt in a letter. First of all, there are too many circumstances which are directly in line with the subject and yet it is impossible to mention those facts. I make myself really understood when I can look a person eye to eye and say what I feel. You know that from experience, Bette. Sometimes I wish I could not be so damned downright factual. However, I've lived that way all my life so I don't expect to change. A few more years of this censored living, I'll forget the freedom of speech. You can imagine me in the middle of a revealing statement and suddenly hear me say, "Now this is strictly off the record, I can't tell you directly that I love you (censor's orders) but you'll be able to understand in time." What a Hell of a life.

Heard from a friend of mine, Dan Smith. Finally made the grade. He is over here in England, helping me to win the war. Wants to get together, doesn't realize it isn't as easily done as said. He'll learn.

Well, Darling, I'll close. This is just one of those dashing notes from your dashing caballero. (Or is it spelled differently?) Give my love to Mother. May God Bless You. I love you. Love, Mike.

There was no August 22 entry in the Squadron War Diary, but the Group War Diary entry for that day read:

> **Rumors from the grapevine say that we'll be returning to our old base once again which will be appreciated by all. The food has proven to be quite excellent here at Greenham Common; but the distance between buildings and transportation facilities are very bad. If and**

when we return to Cottesmore, we'll know how to appreciate a good base.

August 23, 1944 [*Wednesday*]

Good Evening, My Darling,

From the news I'm hearing, this is an eventful day in the history of the world. [*Paris was finally liberated August 25, 1944.*] But since one cannot tell what significance it may cast on our future, it is best to let it go at that.

I received your letters of the 31st of July and the 1st of August. There are two cartoons on the one page so I don't know which you are referring to. I take it that you mean "Terry" [*Terry and the Pirates*]. It has been unanimously decided in these circles that "Terry" is one of the cleverest of its sort. As a matter of fact, it is considered the best. It is the best portrayal of the sort of life we lived and live. No one could come closer. The informality and close relationship of crews is ideally shown. Even we, as the slow Joes of the Air Corps, have our Hot Shot Charlies. Maybe they haven't got Burma or Willow to show off to but there are women regardless of race, creed or color. It is normal for men to be hot rocks. Let them flash something and they feel as if they've made a conquest. We are lucky. Of all the comic strips, "Terry" is the one which is in the *Stars and Stripes*. It may be a bit late but it gets to us.

I am sorry that you haven't gotten any mail. But the events of the last few weeks are reason enough for my laxity. Sorry, Darling.

I can't imagine Bette in tears. Not because of anything except that people don't cry over me. I don't mean that for self-pity. Darling, I love you so much. Your tears are not in vain. I can imagine how you felt especially since everything about you were things that we shared. I can't feel things like that because I have nothing actual to remind me of our past. But, believe me, our memories have a lot to give me. Every so often I think of that bottle of rye and the events behind it. I wonder so often if we will drink it or stare at it. If I know our thirst, we will have an empty bottle for a shrine. That anxiety (and you spelled it right!) that you feel hurts but it feels so good to know that we can begin to get anxious. It's a great feeling, isn't it? One of the greatest in the world, one that makes life like this so easy to face. Darling, I miss you just as much as I have ever.

Your estimate of my time of departure is just a few days off but it is close enough. Every day adds more to my time here and brings my stay closer and closer to an end. Gad! Just the thought of it makes my spine tingle like the bells of Big Ben. But again, we mustn't think too much along these lines.

Your Mother needn't worry about your treatment of our children. I don't believe you could be any crueler toward them than I could be. Sometimes I appear to have little patience with them but children have a refreshing sweetness that is hard not to love.

Gosh, Hon, hate to run but I gotta. See you soon in my next letter. Take care of yourself. Tell Mother I am doing well. I am being a good boy. May God Bless You. Love, Mike.

The War Diary entries of August 23-27 told of the squadron's return to Cottesmore from Greenham Common:

August 23: 20 planes were dispatched on two resupply and evacuation missions in France; 16 planes returned this evening. (Greenham Common).

August 24: REPORT FROM GREENHAM COMMON: The remaining four planes returned this noon. Orders were received to return all personnel and equipment to Cottesmore. A convoy of five vehicles, with the remaining personnel and equipment also left for Cottesmore.

August 25: 18 planes were dispatched on a resupply and evacuation mission.

August 26: All 18 planes returned after RON at Greenham Common. Two planes dispatched to Greenham Common to bring back two gliders and two planes cross country and return.

August 27: 18 planes were dispatched on a resupply and evacuation mission.

August 28, 1944 [*Monday*]

My Own,

Yes, My Darling, I know I haven't written for days. No one knows it any better than I do. Hell! I haven't slept in my bed for almost a month. I have been so nastily busy that I don't even think about it. I've received your mail in so many different places that it isn't funny. Above everything, Bette, I do love you so much.

There are any number of your letters that I must answer but I want to let them stay to one side. I have your letters of the 11, 14, 15, 17, 18 of August. All of them have made excellent time but I haven't had the free time to answer them. I am not even going to try to answer them this evening. One night last week, I went over to our club. I tied on a drunk like no one has ever seen before. I paid for it, too. I had to work the next day and . . . I didn't recover my normal senses until 3 PM. I got stinkin' and I had it coming.

Since I haven't written any letters for the past few days to anyone, I've had a chance to think about the little I've said since I've been in England. I was rebuked so often for saying things I wasn't supposed to that I decided many months ago to level off and keep my tone light, easy and unimportant. But recently I've been back to the life I lived before, a nomadic life of letting days pass. I haven't cared if I needed a shave, nor could I. I've eaten irregularly, slept any time I got the chance, admired the stars from my sack and kept so busy my head is in a whirl. You ask about exercise, — I haven't had a chance. I feel trim and tired. At that time, I had plenty of time for 1, 2'ing [*group calisthenics*]. I only wish I could make my letters as interesting as they were.

Bette, the other night, I was talking to this kid Lt. [*Milt Bostwick*]. I don't know what it was but from his manner, he prompted me to talk. I jabbered for hours. He and I were under the wing so it was plenty quiet except for occasional outbursts. I spoke of you and how much you meant to me. Darling, as I was talking everything that we knew (you and I) came back to me. I was living my moments with you over and over again and they were like a memory so fresh that it made my flesh tingle. Oh! Darling, how much I love you and miss you.

Must close, Bette, there we go again. Give my love to Mother. Take care of yourself. May God Bless You. I love you, Mike.

August 28/29, 1944 [*Monday/Tuesday*]

My Darling,

Here I go again! I had to dash off a few more lines before I hit the sack. Feel like a new man. I took a shower and I feel good. Felt crummy, dirty, tired, got a bit of a head cold. Things didn't happen as quickly as I thought.

In one of your letters, you clearly outlined step-by-step where I'll be able to contact you, just in case. You needn't worry. I'll cover every spot in KC if I returned.

August 29, 1944

I stopped abruptly last night. Turned in and slept like a log. Woke up this AM and I had a beautiful head cold. Got myself some drops; hope I can cut out the lousy feeling. Weighed myself and found that I am down to 200 even and I feel good. Guess I am big enough to carry that much. Hence, I carry on.

I've read of the terrific heat waves that have hit the states. Wish to Hell we could have an abundance of heat and more sun. It's hard as hell for a guy to relax so that he can garner some of that vitamin "D." Oh well, someday I'll have plenty of time for that.

You were speaking of low-flying aircraft. It is unfortunate that some guys can't control a plane. It really is a lot of fun to hedge-hop. Sometimes, it is the only way to enjoy life. I saw a plane hit a hay stack back in the States. Fortunately, the worst that happened was a gear-up landing. When Pappy and I went to his home town last year, he gave me plenty of thrills. We buzzed Belmont, NH [*New Hampshire*], like it has never been buzzed before. It is a bit nerve-racking but plenty of fun. The safety of it depends on the pilot's judgment. I'd rather get killed in action than [*in*] foolishness.

That was a clever cartoon you sent me. Sometimes those troopers aren't lucky enough to fall into a pair of panties. My Buddy came back out of the front not so long ago and he had some interesting stories to tell [*a friend from 505th Parachute Infantry Regiment, 82nd Airborne Division*].

I am glad that you are doing so well with your smoking and everything else. It will never hurt you to eat as much as you do. I've found that I can't get to food easily. Cigarettes will go a long way to eliminating my appetite. I haven't truly enjoyed a smoke but a few times in my life. However, I've never made any attempt to eliminate the habit. I've been smoking since I was 17. That's a fairly long time. I don't know how injurious it is to me but I am cutting down. It isn't that easy. I like the way you say that we'll get our weight to where <u>we</u> want it. Is my opinion that important?

Darling, the reason that I haven't mentioned film is that I don't need any just yet. I may want some in due time. I wish I had a speed camera so that I could get more interesting shots. I've added a lot to my collection. Adding more each day. But you can be sure that if I need any, I'll write and I'll make it one of those short requests especially for you.

I am glad that you like to listen to me talk, Bette. Really, I am not the most talkative person in the world. But I do like to open my "yap" when there is something to say. As long as I don't put my foot into it, I am glad. I've looked over the amount of letters that you sent me for the month of August. It has been the same for the last 13 months. I can't tell you how much I appreciate your consistent attentiveness. Except for the few that caused so much discussion, the rest of them have been perfect. Darling, you should never feel that your letters are inadequate, no matter how short they are. No one can realize what a light, breezy letter means to a guy over here. I'll admit that I don't do justice to all of 'em but I try. I like the way you discuss things and the very fact that you are willing to talk about things makes everything more perfect. I love you, Darling. I love everything about you. I am getting used to the idea of being away because I know that no matter how long it may be, I still have so much to look forward to. If we can feel that, Bette, it makes things easier to take. Miss you truly, but —

Must close. Give my love to Mother. Take care of yourself. May God Bless You. Love, Mike.

The War Diary entry for August 28 read:

16 planes returned, having RON at Greenham Common; three of the original 19 are still out.

On August 29, two planes dropped paratroops and three returned from France. There was no entry for August 30.

August 30, 1944 [*Wednesday*]

Good Evening, Darling,

I received your letter of the 20th. You can see that your mail has been coming thru' as steadily as anyone would want it.

You asked me about my plans for our future home. I have a multitude of ideas. It will take time before we can decide anything. My job is in New York. We will need some means of livelihood. However, My Love, I am not too eager to stay in New York. I had a good chance to get a personnel job in Sears and eventually that would have meant a transfer out [*to Syracuse*] of the City. You understand that it will take some time to acclimate myself to the changes that have occurred due to the war. Fortunately and I'm not bragging, I am quick to learn. At the time of my departure, I had an overall knowledge of the entire line I was in. For the way we like to live, New York has its advantages. The social life is complete but one's overhead is tremendous. I doubt if we will be able to afford a home of our own for a while but eventually we will manage that.

Darling, let me interpose for a moment; believe me, I like for you to ask me questions such as this one. It is like planning a new life. It gives me a chance to forget my immediate environment and a chance to drift off to a world that will be so complete with you. It's like planning a campaign. If we slide over the "ifs," we can accomplish much. The primary understanding is that everything is assumption, subject to immediate change by circumstances. But I go on — You see my plans are based on my past life. Since I, nor anyone else, cannot foresee the future, I must use my past as a crutch. I don't believe it will be well for us to live in Manhattan, New York City, proper. We can easily find a place in one of the suburbs, Queens or Brooklyn (no comments, please!) I cannot say anything for certain but if I must stay with Sears, I'll try damn hard to transfer. You see, Bette, you must trust me implicitly on that score. I do believe you'll be happy there because first of all, we'll be together; secondly, it isn't the most monstrous existence in NY. I believe you may fret about family troubles. Again I ask you to trust me. I've done a tremendous amount of thinking and I've formulated a vast number of ideas on that score. It is an easier problem than we think. Of course, we did start off on the wrong foot. But please, Darling, don't consider it. There is another thing. Joe Huss, a buddy of mine, and I have worked on a few ideas. It may be possible that we'll strike on something there. He lives in Utica, NY. That's upstate, a very lovely city and a nice part of NY state. But that is purely a mental picture he and I painted. One never knows what will come of it. I know that in all I've said, I haven't said anything too definite but what is definite, except love and hope, these days. Those are my ideas, what do you think?

Darling, I do love you so. I was lying on my sack this afternoon. This cold I've got has given me a choice headache and pain. But I was thinking how nice it will be to be with you again. It seems that that is all I can see, you and I together. Those thoughts give me my happiest moments because it is the only worthwhile thing to think of. Being together again will give me a chance to recapture myself. It seems as if I've lost so much since I've been over here. I know a Mike that is as strange to me as anyone I've ever known. Believe me, Darling, at times, it isn't the nicest feeling in the world. Fortunately, it is just a passing thing. If it hung to me, I'd give up. I am glad that my letters are good to you. I try so hard to show you day for day how I feel. My love for you mounts daily but my words can never be enough to tell you my true feeling. I am the most fortunate person in the world to have someone like you to tend to my morale. You've done a great job, Darling. I hope that with time, I'll be able to repay you for everything. I love you and miss you.

Heard from home and find that my brother, Lou, was sent back to New Guinea. Nice, isn't it? I feel sorry for Sally, his wife. They were married 3 days before he left. Fortunately, we had more time than that. I hope that I'm not away as long as he is. I don't think

I will be. The Air Force's policy is much different from the Infantry — besides he's a doctor and more important than I am.

Well, Darling, must close. Tell Mother to take good care of my lovely blonde. Give her my love. May God Bless you. Love, Mike.

August 31, 1944 [*Thursday*]

Good Evening, Darling,

Payday and a bunch of card games going on. I am not taking part in that nefarious pastime because I've gotten 2 letters from you and I'd rather talk to you than cuss and sweat over 5 cards. I guess you must be wondering how I came out of debt last month. Well, I collected 7£s for my rest leave and later in the month I hit a slick lick with the bones [*a dice game*] and cleaned up about 14£s. I hope you don't mind my gambling, Darling. I'm just broadening my education. As it was, I ended last month with my crew chief owing me 2£s. Gotta send little Stinky [*my nephew Mike Petruzillo*] $10 so he can buy a pair of basketball shoes. Since he is taking my place in the family sport's circle, no reason why he shouldn't be well dressed. It will be a sort of inspiration to him. I know how I felt when I got my first pair, went out and scored 12 points in the first game. It will do the kid a lot of good to get a good start. Got a picture from Louise, Ted's wife. Ted looks good but I hope I never look as good and healthy as he does. He's powerful as Hell but a wee bit too fat. Louise looks great . . . and has a heart of gold. There's my report locally.

So ole' [*A.V. "Sonny"*] Rice got married, can't believe it. Of all the guys that hit the states, 6 of them got married. Rice was the last one we expected to get hitched. I am glad that he wrote but he promised to call. He must have been busy. I hope his news didn't make you too optimistic as much as I hate to say it, Darling, plans are changed so easy. A lot of water has passed under the bridge since he left. Believe me, at the time, our morale went up 100%. It has deflated a bit. Sorry about his dog. Snowball never did recover from his distemper. He had to be destroyed. Gremlin reached the same fate. He never recovered from his double pneumonia. "Fudge" is going great. Full of p — and vinegar. I'll give Rice your congratulations, if he ever returns to us.

Darling, I love you. Everyone of your envelops has a wee smear of lipstick. Why don't you put a big blob of it on your letters so we can all enjoy it? But that isn't why I love you. But let me get on to answering your letters.

I'll do that little thing for you. Nick [*Pappaeliou*] is getting married over here on the 9th of Sept. As yet, I haven't received an invite. But I'm sure it will be forthcoming. I don't think he'll forget me that easily. . . . Pappy is still prodding along. Doing well.

Darling, I'm sorry they feed the public such news. These grandstand generals give me a pain in the rear. All of you know that you must wait for time to pass. I don't know why they pass on such heartbreaking rumors. If they don't come true, it makes you feel twice as miserable. The same for these commentators that are sitting in plush chairs in the States and fill the people with assumptions, their own opinions. Who the Hell gives a plug nickel for their opinions? Ours are just as good if not better. Lord knows, we'd all like to see home for Xmas but why think about it 'til it comes true. Don't worry, Bette, we'll make up for every holiday that we've missed. Maybe not this year but there are other years. (Darling, riged is spelled rigid.)

Thanks so much, My Love, for your words of encouragement. Your words make love so perfect. I didn't think I could have so much charm and have a person love me so. It makes everything so easy to face over here and it makes the future look so easy to cope with. You are right, we do have so much more than money can buy. We both have a part of each other nothing can change or remove. It fits in perfectly with every ideal I've ever ventured to think of. We've got an advantage not too many people have enjoyed. That freedom which we enjoyed has made things a bit easier. I believe that we respect each other more for our straightforwardness.

. . . Learn something new about you each day. It amazes me every time I think of it, how easily we can pass thoughts so easily. Almost without a flicker of an eye. It makes me think of a few other things that I shan't mention. (Third party.) But what I am thinking about is another example of our mutual and easy understanding of things that may not seem too important but add a sense of propriety that helps to add respect to two people in love.

Tell Mother that that March 26th is a better bet than my 26th of August. I do hope that it refers to me. That would suit me fine — 6 months isn't too horribly long to wait. It fits perfectly. Glad to hear about your smoking report. Sorry I can't share your love of peanuts. They give me heartburn. But I do like potato chips or pretzels and a good cold glass of beer. (Ah-Men!)

So your coloring is much better. I don't know what more you can do to improve yourself. I can't think of anything. Your skin was always clear. I particularly like that little mole on the right side of your face. Your hair, as I've said before is one of my fondest pets. <u>Don't</u> ever <u>cut</u> it! That dimple on your chin is superb. Gad! Woman how much more do you want? . . . Pardon me if I kid you once in a while, Darling. Just a bit playful. I promise not to be fresh. Love you.

Well, Bette, My Sweet, I'll shut my trap until tomorrow. Give my love to Mother. Take care of yourself. May God Bless You. Love, Mike.

The Squadron's War Diary entry for the last day of August 1944 was as follows:

> **Four planes to Greenham Common for supplies and one to Spanhoe to pick up a glider. Five planes for local hops. There was a meeting of all flying personnel re personal equipment. Pay Day as usual, the last day of the month. Movie shown at NAAFI.**

The plane "JIPPA" and Mike's original flight crew, North Africa, August 1943. Back row, l to r: Ralph Parker, Nick Pappeliou, Addison "Pappy" Agle. Front row, l to r: Chalmers Johnson, Michael Ingrisano.

Mike — in his winter flight dress outside his "home" tent — Tunisia, North Africa, *ca*. October 1943.

Below: Mike's quarters in Sicily, December 1943 and (right) message written on back to Bette.

darling, say you will marry me before you look at this! Me, my moustache, my haircut and my home. Unusual day — the sun was shining
Love, Mike —
Sicily — 1943

Read 'em 'n weep —

Hotel President

Kansas City, Missouri

Sale of the following items as long as they last.
Limited to one to a room.

Fleischman's Preferred	Qt.	$4.70
Fleischman's Preferred	Pt.	2.35
Seagram 7 Crown	5th	5.05
Schenley Reserve	5th	5.05
Schenley Royal	5th	4.25
Four Roses	5th	5.00
P. M. DeLuxe	5th	4.95
Park-Tilford	5th	4.85
Black Gold	5th	3.85
Paul Jones	5th	4.30
Kinsey	5th	4.10
Sheffield Dry Gin	5th	4.50
Hartley Brandy	5th	4.30

Above prices are subject to Missouri Sales Tax.

September 1944—2000

The price list from the Hotel President in Kansas City, Missouri, September 1944.

Bette in Miami
Beach, Florida,
December 1944.

Mike Ingrisano and Don Harris on leave in Bradford, England, February 1945.

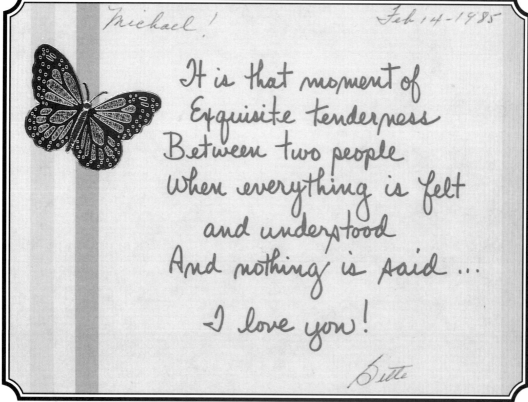

Michael!

Feb 14 - 1985

It is that moment of
Exquisite tenderness
Between two people
When everything is felt
and understood
And nothing is said ...
I love you!

Bette

"And Nothing Is Said."

Bette and Staff Sergeant Mike before their wedding in Brooklyn, New York, May 1945.

Chapter 5

MARKET GARDEN and More
(September 1 to November 28, 1944)

BY LATE 1944, Belgium and France had been liberated, and the Allies pressed into the Netherlands and Germany. In an effort to secure a bridgehead over the Rhine River, under the overall command of General Bernard Montgomery, OPERATION MARKET GARDEN was launched September 17-26. Troop Carrier planes dropped British, Polish, and U.S. paratroopers and towed gliders into the area around Nijmegen, Eindhoven, and Arnhem. Although the operation was unsuccessful, it gained valuable ground and improved Allied positions.

Around-the-clock Allied bombing (U.S., day; British, night) was destroying German industrial centers.

By late November, the Port of Antwerp had been opened to traffic. Fighting continued in northern Italy and along the Adriatic coast.

September 1, 1944 [*Friday*]

My Darling,

Back again and I don't think I have too much to say except I love you. But

I'll carry on. Played in one of those card games last night. Didn't lose, didn't win! Just passed off a lot of time. Then we got around to a big discussion, business, politics, the war. Ended up hitting the sack at 1 PM [*AM*], and I intended to go to bed early. Bing Crosby is over here; he's broadcasting from the new canteen in London. Do hope he comes up our way. He's still the world's best crooner. Just dashed off a note to my Dad. It's funny, I hardly ever write to him and I'm sure he must feel like the lost soul. Just batted the breeze with him, fishing, politics, and a few odd items. Just got an Air Mail letter from my sister today, dated August 2nd. I can't understand it. Almost a month and people wonder why I bitch sometimes. Your mail does splendidly except for occasional empty spurts but when they start rolling, you do very nicely, Darling. I'm glad you can say the same for me.

It's amazing how you disclose things. So your Mother and Dad went to school with Ike's brother [*Milton Eisenhower*]. It seems almost natural. Oftimes I do forget that you come from the Middle West. I guess that I've traveled so much that one place is like another to me. Distance seems to be the easiest thing to cover. A thousand miles are like going to the corner drug store for a cigar.

That dog story you told reminded me of the one I just read — a guy went over to see his friend and he saw his friend playing chess with his dog. The fellow was amazed. The players were battering back and forth, moves, rebuffs, etc. Finally, the guy said to his friend, "You have a very smart dog there, Joe." To which the friend replied, "I don't know. I beat him 4 out of 5 yesterday!"

Well, Darling, I have to make this short and sweet. I promise to do better. One of my off nights; too much lamplight discussion.

I love and miss you. Take care of yourself. May God Bless You. Love, Mike.

The 37th Squadron's September 1 War Diary entry read:

> **All personnel were restricted to camp. All S-2 Officers were briefed at Group S-2. Three planes were dispatched cross country and return. One new plane assigned to squadron, complete with crew. Eight glider pilots and mechanics were also assigned to the Squadron.**

Following is the 316th Group's War Diary entry for the same day:

> **Today a restriction was placed on the field and everyone knew by this time what to expect in the next few days. One plane on Wing mission #531 flew local paratroops training jump; 2 aircraft personnel and supplies to Membury on Wing Mission #533, while six aircraft transported personnel locally.**

On September 2, according to the Squadron War Diary, the combat crews were briefed by Group Intelligence. Three planes flew cross country and returned, and another plane was assigned to the squadron.

The Group War Diary entry for the same day, September 2, read:

> **After hurried preparations were made for operation "Linnet" to facilitate the handling of all Squadron personnel in the Group S-2 briefing room, actual briefing began and continued throughout the day. This operation called for several drops and glider landings in the Tournai, Belgium area. Six aircraft transported personnel to Ramsbury and one carried personnel to Greenham Common.**

September 3, 1944 [*Sunday*]
<u>Still Here</u>

My Darling,

This has been a rather queer day. I had hoped to do some good letter writing but fate and work intervened. Now I am here and it is perfect weather for making babies. Too bad it didn't set in sooner. I had started a nice letter to my sister but I had to cut it down to nothing because I was interrupted right in the middle of it and for hours, too. Oh Well, a guy can't have everything. I've got you and I love you, what more can I ask?

Really, Darling, everything was so perfect early this afternoon. Nothing has changed but a few hours have passed and moods can cool easily. I'll try to paint it. Everything was quiet. There were a few card games going on, a chess game, some letter writing and Sammy Kaye's *Sunday Serenade* was on. That's one of my favorite programs; naturally I felt ideal. My heart was set on some choice love making in my letter. But —

Anyhow my thoughts didn't perish. I thought about you all the time I was seeing the blue-gray comparable to beauty of anything living. I was thinking of the days to come. It seems that the news would naturally make a guy's eyes turn toward America. Big thoughts about little things that make life so easy to see as beautiful. It makes life something we can look forward to so eagerly. Or have I said that once? Guess it's because I do feel that way. Repetitious but in my constant repeating, the feeling becomes stronger. I looked thru' all the pictures that you've sent me since I've been overseas. Those pictures bring you closer and closer to me. I miss you, Darling.

Today is my second year in OD [*Olive Drab — in service*]. I don't expect to get out before I have a hash mark (3 years) but I do hope it isn't much over that time. A lot of things have happened in 2 years. I've seen an awful lot of this little ole' world. The biggest change in my life has been you. Aside from that, there isn't too much to note. Naturally I'm like a million guys like me. We want to go back to the life we have always known and loved. However, I want to go back to all that but with you at my side. It excites me beyond control to think of everything and with you to help. You'll never know how much you mean to me; how much you meant to me this last year and a half since I've known you. My prospects appear so much brighter. Not because they have changed any but because you've given me more incentive. I love you.

Darling, I must close. I had meant to make this better but —
Take care of yourself. May God Bless You. Love, Mike.

In addition to recording one cross-country flight, the 37th Squadron War Diary entry on September 3 noted that OPERATION LINNET had been cancelled.

September 4, 1944 [*Monday*]

My Darling,

I received your very nice letter of the 26th of August. Gad! Mail comes so quickly from you. It seems as if we hardly have time to ask a question but that it is answered. So much the better. I shan't complain as long as the condition continues to exist. Sounds like a walking advertisement, doesn't it? Feel perfectly at peace with the world. It seems as if I must do a million and one things and although I haven't a thing to do, I wouldn't do them if I had to. (Sounds screwy and complicated. Read it slowly; it is as easy to understand as it is to say!)

I read a small book that has been circulating thru' the barracks. It is called, *Sex Factors in Matrimony*. It is written by an English Female Doctor. She surprisingly speaks very intimately of what exists or should exist behind those doors. I agree with her in most part but she has missed a few of the angles, figuratively speaking of the sex act. It isn't nor is it meant to be a smutty outlook. It is the basically simple bared truth. Everyone of the fellows have read it and the opinions are the same. We have a hillbilly Kentuckian in here who was married a short while before he came overseas. He insists that the book is complicated. He's the only one that made that observation. Perhaps, he can't read. Think so? . . .

Enough! Now to answer your epistle. So you really like the cold weather. You should live in England. If you had been thru' the mud and slush of the other countries I've been in, you'd love Florida in the heat of summer. Darling, ever since I was down under [*in Sicily and Tunisia*], I never seem able to keep my feet warm. Believe me, it is a most distressing feeling. I used to be most proud of the fact that hot or cold, I never had cold feet. If I get them the least bit wet, Gad! Seems funny to mention it but I'm just warning you that I can make it miserable for you on cold days. Imagine icy feet on your back. No divorce, please! Seriously though, it may be a vitamin deficiency. Who the Hell knows? Maybe it's because my heart has been so cold over here. If that is the case, the condition will change the moment I see you again. Great day! (Darling, riding is spelled with one d.) Do I like to bowl? Haven't I ever mentioned it before. Little gal, you all is speaking to the greatest bowler this side of the Gowanus Canal (Bklyn). No, seriously, I do like to bowl. When my feet folded up the last year I played basketball, I had to turn to bowling to get my winter, indoor exercise. I'll show you how; I promise it will develop some points (no pun intended) and cause not too much fatigue. It's OK with me, if you care to compare me with a muffin. If you make it warm (even hot), I don't mind. So you don't want to resist me. Half of the battle is won. Since it is mutual, we've won the entire battle. Are you sure you won't resist me once (once in a million years, say!) in a while?

Fireplaces, My Darling, are an American Institution! Just like baseball, hot dogs, or hamburgers. Fireplaces, not only keep a person warm, but they are pretty good things to have for enchanting the moment of love.

Look, Honey, I do want to keep on. Lord knows, I want to go on forever — Nope, I won't end yet! The Hell with the Censor. Feed him beans! If he wants to listen in OK. No objections! (Fascinating is spelled with an s.) I'll make a Rhodes Scholar out of you yet! It is not only the flickering of the fire nor the heat but, to be philosophical for the moment, it is a picture of our lives. Together the slow process of warming (the knowledge of) life and gradually going into and knowing the fullness (the extreme heat) of life — (I'd never make an author! My ideas fully shown aren't consistent.) Then the burning out of life — The climax has passed. We are happy to watch the fire (of life) die out because we have had that much. (We cannot be too selfish to expect the perpetual flame! The hereafter will give us that!) Nonetheless, together we have lived the fullness of the fire — (To divert, let me be nasty — and so the lights are out and off to the warmth of bed.)

Really, My Love, I must rush off now. I wasn't jesting with you. My mood forbids me from going on endlessly in a tirade of the finer things. I love all of that, believe me. Pardon my occasional lightness.

Good night, Bette. Take care of yourself. I love you. May God Bless You. Love, Mike.

The September 4 War Diary entry noted a few promotions, as well as:

> **. . . Liberty Run and after duty passes in effect once again. There was a USO stage show at the NAAFI for all personnel.**

The Group War Diary, on the same day, explained that the LINNET mission had been cancelled "due to the fact that ground situation had advanced to and beyond the point where the airborne troops were needed. . . ."

There were no War Diary entries for September 5.

September 6, 1944 [*Wednesday*]

My Darling,

I received your letter of the 24th. My Lovely Creature, you needn't apologize. You've done such a fine job of writing to me that I could never kick. You mustn't overdo yourself. I don't mind if you miss a day or so. Your letters are so regular that I can expect at least one a day or if you miss, soon after one will follow. No, Ma'am, I can't kick.

Seems so funny to hear you speak of my tan and yet I haven't been in the sun since then.

But the ole' tan hangs on for quite a while. You aren't kidding about that gym and ball diamond. You know, Bette, a guy does have to move around to keep in fairly good shape. It's taken me years to get in practice. It's hard as Hell to forget 23 years of training. You wouldn't want me to be a flabby ole' puss in the corner. Can you imagine me as the type of guy who did no more than play a heated game of chess?

I am glad that you can handle a car. You needn't worry about those terrific drunks. I don't think we'll ever get in that sorry state. Besides there are cabs! I don't think I'd ever get disgustingly drunk in your presence. It doesn't become me, Bette. Maybe it's because we can handle our stuff; but I never recall one time when we appeared "lit." Besides it takes most of the fun out of everything. If I know us well enough, we wouldn't want a coma to ruin our evening. Remember the night I damn near passed out cold! I still don't know how it happened unless I just went into a weakened condition. I wasn't really embarrassed but I wasn't too proud of myself. Wasn't I in bad shape? I could have fallen asleep anywhere. If my legs could have taken it, I could have fallen asleep standing up.

It surprised me to hear you speak of my absence as ending in just a matter of weeks. I do hope you are thinking in terms of many weeks, which, in turn, will mean many months. Hate like Hell to speak like that but it isn't mutually healthy to cut down time. Sometimes it pays to extenuate the period so that if it should be shortened it will make everything appear nicer. If you noticed in most of my letters, I don't speak of my time over here but I speak of the day we will be together. You know like they speak of D-Day, V-Day, H-Hour — so it is best we speak of T-Day (Together). Let this time pass, it will because it already has. Oh! Well! I'll be a real veteran. Just think of our day and it will make time pass easier. We have done a good job of it. We will.

What have you done to your writing? It looks smaller. Maybe you've gotten a new pen (?). I don't know what has been wrong these last few days, Honey. We sit up for long bull sessions and I can talk for hours but when it comes to doing anything, I feel as inert as Hell. I can't seem to concentrate on much. Nothing too much wrong. Must be I'm so much in love with you.

So I am going to close. I promise I shan't write too many letters like this. Just getting loggy as Hell.

Good night, Bette. I love you and miss you so much. Take care of yourself. May God Bless You. Love, Mike.

The September 6 War Diary entry read:

> **No scheduled flying yesterday. Two plane mission to France carrying personnel, etc. One plane used to drop paratroops in a practice drop. Weekly EM dance at the NAAFI.**

The September 7 entry noted only that two planes had been transferred to Saltby. The Group War Diary, though, had more details in its September 7 entry:

Briefing and preparation for Mission "Comet" was made today but an indefinite delay went into effect. During this period regular administrative runs were made. 2 aircraft with personnel to Telkingham; 3 aircraft flew personnel to [*Saltby*] and 3 aircraft to Spanhoe. Restriction was again imposed on the personnel of this field.

September 8, 1944 [*Friday*]

Hello Bette,

Another one of those lulls when I can't seem to write a decent letter to anyone. It is a distressing feeling but one which I can't help. I wonder sometimes if you suspect what brings about such moods. Unfortunately, I can't explain myself but I know you understand.

I see by the papers that they have already decided a method of demobilization. I haven't got one qualification which will assure me of a quick discharge. Except for a decoration, service overseas and home — I'm pretty much at the base of things. And to add to a guy's morale, the Air Force is considered a pretty important branch of the service. Outfits like my own, I imagine are pretty important for post-war uses. Oh Well, as I've said before, it is best that we just sweat out everything. Let time and fortune take care of things. Perhaps, this separation will do us a lot of good. It will give us a damn good conception of what we mean to each other, as if we don't know already. But we certainly will appreciate each other more, as if we don't already. What the Hell am I saying? Sounds like I'm agreeing with everything I shouldn't! Oh well, Darling, if this doesn't teach us anything, it certainly should teach us patience. I don't feel like bitching. Honestly, Bette, sometimes it is just as well to shrug our shoulders and wait. I volunteered for this man's army, so I might as well do the best of it. Thank God I have you to wait with me. We can't complain too bitterly; at least, I'm still healthy and sane. I do love you so very much.

I received your letter of the 22nd. You speak of a dream or something. I'm afraid I'm at a loss. It must be in one of your other letters. I am gratified to know that you aren't the nagging type. I never did think so. I think we are very much alike. If we were to be of a nasty temper or nature or were the nagging type, those bad characteristics would take a lot of the gloss from our temperaments. I hate like Hell to think of wasting so much happiness by being that way. You are right, we can't help but be very happy. Especially if occasionally we look back and see all the time we have already wasted. Darling, it is our duty to each other to make the rest of our lives as enjoyable and as pleasant as God will allow us. Really, there isn't a worry in the world except to wait for the time to pass. Easy, isn't it?

I got a letter from a buddy of mine who recently arrived in this theater from the states. If I bitched the way he did, I'd have shot myself long ago. He spent 2 years in the States and in that time he was home for 3 months. Compared to my 5 days, he didn't do too badly.

Well, Bette, I must rush off. Really can't help myself. Take care of yourself. Give my love to Mother. May God Bless You. Love, Mike.

September 8, 1944 [*Friday*]

My Darling,

Here I am back again. I told you earlier that I just can't drive myself to write but I received 2 swell letters from you and I must answer. Good service, too, August 28 and 31st. Not much more than a week plus. I am glad that you understand that I am busy occasionally. At certain periods of time, it is necessary that I relax completely. During those periods, my letters are scarce. You see, Darling, I am not a man of iron nerves. Naturally, I try to relax, forget everything so that things will come easily to me. I know you understand.

In your letter of the 28th, you asked about the possibility of my getting a discharge at the end of the war over here. I think I explained that in my earlier letter. Looks like I'm stuck for the duration plus. However, I do hope and I am praying that I don't spend that duration here or in the Pacific. You state that your discussion was futile because none of you knew enough about it. You are not alone. I guess this is one time when we are moronically ignorant.

I know how you feel, Darling. It is difficult to put emotions on paper. I know what you are thinking and that assurance alone is enough to overcome whatever defeat I feel is coming or has come to me. We have put ourselves on paper now for over a year. At times we are apt to become impatient. But we must continue to strive on. You say that it is making you impatient that is "it" the thought of the wonderful days we have ahead of us. Think of those days but don't let them affect your daily life. Lord knows, I need not preach morale to you but let me tell you how I get over my blues. How I try to overlook the time.

My time is, at times, almost as wasted as yours is. I turn to whatever recreation the base has to offer. (Believe me, the worst moments, those that I am speaking of now, come when there is a lull in my work.) When I feel low, I try to mingle with the guys more than I do ordinarily; a card game, bull session, normal courses of barrack life. Occasionally, when I can get some literature, I read. The worst moments are when I need physical comfort. Hell, I don't know exactly what I do but I usually wait for the normal discharges of the male body. It always relieves a guy. (Pardon my very definite frankness but I am normal and I know that I can't shock you because you understand the normal male.) If I can't get over it that easily, I try a drink or two. If things get very, very bad, I think of us, shrug my shoulders because I know I can't do a thing about anything and I keep telling myself that the time has passed and this life can't keep going on. At times, I mutter silent prayers that help a lot. The very fact that I can express myself in letters has done me a world of good. If I can talk to you and I can always in my letters, ¾ of the battle is won. It isn't easy, I assure you but what comes easy to anyone? Especially when people are in love as we are; we must accept the bad with the good. We know it is made easy because our love is there to carry us on. Gosh, Bette, there are a million and one things and they all add up that I love you and miss you and I know that someday (when?), I am coming back to you and that

that union will be enough to make all these days seem like a far forgotten nightmare. I love you.

Oh! Yes! Those letters that I receive so late. That is hardly a thing to worry about, Darling. After all, there must be millions of letters that pass over this ocean. It is easy to understand that some of them must stray. I've heard of Roosevelt's outfit but Lord knows where they are. Except for a goose ride, I don't leave the post. It isn't worth it. But, if perchance I should get anywhere near a Bomb Group, I'll make inquiries for Lt. [*Julian*] Rice. It isn't too easy but I do try my best especially when it is a chance to meet someone who can talk of things that we both might know.

I am glad that Seagram's is bourbon. I haven't got too much of a taste for rye. Your suggestion is swell. However, that is one bottle which will not be shared by anyone but you and me. We've talked about that bottle so much that it is part of the family. It has a story behind it that no one but we will enjoy. It isn't fair that anyone else should try it. Am I right?

That's a good discussion for you. I am sure that those piano lessons are helping to keep [*your*] mind occupied. Besides you are improving your playing. I wish I had something like that to help me pass my time off. As for making me proud of you, I couldn't possibly strut any more like a peacock than I do already. Just having a person like you love me and loving a person like you is reason enough for my chest to pop.

Don't thank me for that vote. It will probably be the one that puts Dewey in. You can talk about nice weather. If I was any colder, I'd be [*polar explorer Richard E.*] Byrd's twin. (Darling, riding is spelled with one d.)

Must rush off. I'll be back as soon as I can. I love you and miss you. May God Bless You. Love, Mike.

The September 8 War Diary noted that the COMET mission had been postponed, and that the weekly lecture at the American Red Cross Club on the war situation had taken place. On September 9, three planes flew cross country and returned, and 18 planes flew a practice drop mission.

The Group War Diary entries for September 8 and 9 are:

> **September 8: Briefing continued today on mission "Comet," the assault area was the Nijmegen, Holland area. Very similar to the mission "Linnet." 3 aircraft to North Witham on administrative to carry personnel.**
>
> **September 9: Mission #549, 14 aircraft flew to Neitheroven transporting supplies: one aircraft to Northolt with personnel. Although the parapacks were still on the planes and since the majority of the planes had not flown since August to any extent, a Group formation was flown today.**

September 10, 1944 [*Sunday*]

Good Afternoon, Darling,

It is one of those rare, sunny, nice Sundays in England. So nice, in fact, that I feel as if I could sleep endlessly. But I've decided on a different plan. I've secreted myself in a remote place so that I'll neither be disturbed or bothered. "I want to be alone." There's a song which has driven this theater crazy. It is "I Walk Alone" sung by Lily Ann Reynolds. (I think that's her name.) She sings with Louie Prima. There is a program called *Duffel Bag* on the American Forces Network over here. It is somewhat of a request club. Not one day passes that they don't play that number. At times, it has been played over and over for 3 times, at least. It really is a swell arrangement.

You must pardon my sketchy ideas today, Darling. I proceeded to tie on a bun last night and I did a good job of it. In our day room, we have a swell bar. They had a good supply of scotch; so I decided to relieve my taut nerves and I doused a good number of glasses of that golden liquid and a bit of soda, please. As the evening wore on, we played some "oldies" on the phonograph we have. The tears fell like rain drops and then we raided the mess hall. We didn't eat well, but did you ever taste ketchup and peanut butter as a sandwich? Don't try it. Death cannot be far off. Fortunately, I woke this morning feeling as crisp as last night's collar on a humid summer evening. I am feeling much better now and mentally greatly relieved. The circumstances haven't changed any but my outlook is lighter.

However, great or small, happy or unhappy, I cannot help but feel thrilled by the thought of us. You know, Bette, we will have a wonderful life together. I know that both of us have differences which we cannot help but they are so easily overcome by our mutually understanding personalities. We are so damned nonchalant about many things that it would frighten people who don't know us. Who cares if it rains or shines? I've spoken to you often of those little things I think of. I shan't repeat myself but I never cease to thrill at the renewing thought of those little impersonal, or personal things. You are a wonderful person. You know, I can't help but to love you. A love to me that is so beautiful that it seems criminal to have time pass. I should have found you years ago. We would have had an even more wonderful start and a longer, more glorious road to an end. These love letters of mine are a great help to me. Just being able to talk to you is a privilege I share and don't wish to share with anyone. You have a good number of reasons to catch me in a breach of promise, haven't you?

Let me swing over to a lighter vein, if I may. I've seen two fairly good shows on the post last week — *Gaslight* and *Lady in the Dark*. Both of them were cleverly done. You may wonder why I don't discuss literature as often as I did but I haven't been able to get my hands on anything worth reading. My subscription to *Sporting News* comes thru' regularly. I spend much time over my much-loved statistics. It is a good way for me to keep contact with a sport that is so close to most American guys. Whatever happened to the St. Louis Browns. If my memory serves me correctly, the KC Blues aren't doing too well this year. Isn't it sort of damp in that cellar. They've been there so long. I see by the papers that the football season is ready to start. The kids go back to school tomorrow. Wonderful days, nicest of our years. Ernie Pyle wrote his last article in *Stars and Stripes* yesterday. He is returning to the States. He has been overseas 29 months and in combat a year. We'll miss his frank coverage of the news. Very humanly he says that he can't take it any more. He needs some rest. Blankly stated that if he hears one more shell or sees one more dead man, he'll go mad. He must be a great guy to know. He did a swell job as long as he was over here.

Well, Bette, I must leave. I want to write a few more letters if I can. Take it easy. Give my love to Mother. I love you and miss you so very much. May God Bless You. Love, Mike.

September 10, 1944 [*Sunday*]

Good Evening, My Love,

I just sat in on a rather drab account of a man's life. A picture by the name of *Roger Touhy, Gangster*. Just one of those things. At least it helped to kill a few hours. They had a short with it, Music by Johnny Long, the left-handed violinist. I remember the time I saw him in the New York Paramount when his "Shanty in an Ole' Shanty Town" was very popular. It seems like centuries ago. The one number that really struck my fancy was his arrangement of "Jealous" (Jealous of the stars that shine above, ta ta ta, etc.) He had four clarinets playing in megaphones. It was the sweetest thing I have ever heard. I made a mistake on that girl's name; it's Lily Ann Carroll. A kid just sat on the bed opposite mine and started to count the number of £s he had won in a poker game. He seems to be incensed with the idea that card playing or gambling in general, is the only way to enjoy life. He never knew what poker was until he joined us overseas many months ago. The poor bastard will go crazy trying to figure out the angles of the game. Little does he know that he can't top it. Got some good rumba music on. Period! I had some good music on. Can't get the station on clearly so I cut out all the static (hear enough of that!) and shut off the radio.

Received your most comforting letter of the 30th of August. Darling, it was ideal. You are a most marvelous person. It is surprising how uplifting a letter like that is occasionally. It reassures me of so many things and makes life seem so remarkably good. Of all the things, Bette, that you asked me for, you asked for something I have but one of. Only this afternoon I asked my sister to send me another pair of wings. We can't get any over here that are worthwhile. The only pair I have is the pair I bought in Ft. Wayne just before I left the States. I'm dreadfully sorry, Darling, but as soon as I get those, I'll send you that pair I have worn for so long. The way packages travel, I'll probably be able to deliver them personally. When I was back in the States, I never went in for those things and now when I want to send you something so badly, I can't. Don't I ever do anything right? Since you cannot wear gold, we'll arrange something when I get home. My idea is to get a ring that will be alike for both of us. Since I can never equal your diamond, the best I can do is try to get something that will be significant and a bit more lasting than a bottle of bourbon.

I daresay that you weren't kidding when you said that you had a lot to say. The reason I never try to infect you with things that bother me is because I cannot really put them on paper. Whatever may arise that hurts my pride, I'd rather discuss it vocally. Hence, I steer clear of letters on that score. I've had my lesson once about how dangerous a misplaced word can be. I prefer to let things stand. I know only too well that you can understand me but I hate to burden you with anything. If you recall, we decided to let certain things hang and stick to planning. Naturally, there are some things that we discuss but they fit into the natural pattern of our exchange of letters.

Thank you, Darling, for your encouragement and understanding. I am glad that you feel that I have changed. I am afraid that I cannot accept everything as cream and roses. You recall my letters of the various places I've been. I didn't adhere to the constant theme that everything was beautiful. I'd have to be blind not to see the horrors of man-made destruction. Some people are apt to think that this is child's play. How childishly foolish! But how true, when you say being in love changes a person's outlook on many things. Here's the way I feel. With our love, I associate everything that runs parallel to it. You and I know the tenderness, the beauty, the joy of our love. To that we fit the description of a lovely moonlit night, a sunset that makes a heart grow warmer as the body gets colder; a city; a building; a home in which we'd think perfect for our kind of living. All those things surely are the epitome of our happiness — here or at home — But the change that people are apt to notice is the ugly. The changes of temperament that are brought about by nervousness, fear, tiredness, and anything concerned with war and its ugliness. They are not changes that are voluntary but are due to the fact that we cannot allow ourselves to be blind. The eyes can see; the ears can hear; and the fingers can touch; what these senses see, touch, or hear, I cannot say, censorship forbids me but they are almost every day life. I cannot help if they show up occasionally in my writing. When I get back to my barracks, I try so hard to shut all that ugliness out — I speak to you of love; I plan with you, I laugh and cry with you — For the few moments my pen lives the life that I and millions like me have loved for our whole lives. Then why cannot I be allowed to let some of the ugliness, which to them is fantastic and unreal, leak out? I'm human. But I shouldn't have to tell all of this to you because you understand. Then again, I tell it to you because you are the one person I can really talk to. My Darling, my heart is easily bared to you. That is another reason I can say I love you. These words run easily and evenly in a plane that has been so noticeable in our close association. You are my love, now and forever. Your prayers are not in vain, Darling. I do love you; always will and I do want you to love me. More than you'll ever know. I am not capable of prying deeply into this soul of mine that has given me so much comfort and happiness since you came into my love. I'll be back for you, Darling. I pray to God that He'll see fit to bring us together soon. Whatever His course, we are ready to steer — for we know at the end of it is the light of our lives. How beautiful a thought.

Good night, My Darling. I love you. May God Bless you. Love, Mike.

The Squadron War Diary entry on September 10 recorded two cross-country flights and one test flight.

The Group War Diary entry on the same date read:

Due to the weather, Mission "Comet" was postponed for a period of 24 hours. Wing Mission #550 was flown with three aircraft participating, going to Northolt, Glasgow and Salisbury respectfully, carrying personnel.

On September 11, according to the 37th's War Diary, there was a 15-plane resupply mission and an eight-plane mission to France. Twelve of the 23 planes returned that day, while the other 11 remained overnight. The restriction on passes was again lifted.

The Group War Diary entry for the same day, September 11, read:

Today the mission "Comet" was scrubbed altogether, much to the disappointment of the Airborne troops that were here on the field. Restriction lifted again and six and twelve hour passes were issued once again.

The next day, the 11 remaining planes returned from France. There was another 12-plane resupply mission to France.

September 13, 1944 [*Wednesday*]

My Darling,

Sorry I was unable to write the other day. Guess I gotta earn my keep once in a while. I do wish I could write about it but I'm stuck. It really is a damn pain in the royal exit. I can't understand the way this mail runs. I guess I'll be saying that as long as I'm overseas. But it is funny — plenty of mail will come in and I don't get one. I know that you write almost every day and my friends must write once in a while but damn. I don't know. But no use to kick; it doesn't help, I learned my lessons. I don't want to but I don't seem to be able to concentrate. I guess there's a little too much noise going on.

So I see you've gone back to smoking. It isn't the worst thing in the world. I do hope you never smoke as much as I do. Sometimes I feel like a furnace on a winter day. There's a crude expression that goes with that but I'll spare you a blushed face. I'm glad you agree with my idea for weight. It is the most pleasant but really not the most painful.

It is a most comforting feeling to notice the way letters pass between us. We are so eager to please each other's moods. Of course, that's how it should be but a lot of people make mistakes so easily that way. What I am referring to is how we can cry on each other's shoulders and know that we can make everything seem so simple by a few nice words. I feel sorry for a person who has no one to turn to. It must be one of the loneliest feelings in the world. I have felt greatly relieved by your last letter. It seems strange as Hell the way things have changed in my life. At times when I have a chance to reflect on my short past, I can see changes that bring me nothing but joy and happiness. You, My Darling, have left me with nothing but the finest memories in the world. I didn't think that things would change and really quickly too. I love you all the more for it, Bette. Believe me, I can never stop telling you how grateful I am for you. You're a great person, Honey. Do I sound like all sugar and cream? No kidding, a guy just can't help himself. I can place you side by side with every woman I have ever known and you stand out head and shoulders above all of them. Every time we get into discussing <u>our</u> women, the first thing that comes out are pictures. There hasn't been one time that someone failed to notice how nicely you dress. You can't realize, Darling, how proud that makes me feel.

Well, Bette, I'm sorry I must toddle off. I'm not doing a very good job of this letter. So I'll sign off and try to do better next time.

Good night, Darling. See you tomorrow. Take care of yourself. May God Bless You. Love, Mike.

On September 13, 11 planes returned from the resupply mission in France; one remained because of engine trouble. One Squadron plane was used to drop paratroops in a practice drop, and another flew cross country and returned. Squadron War Diary entry for that day also notes, "The 316th TC Group personnel put on their own show at the NAAFI."

The Group War Diary elaborated on that show in its September 13 entry:

> **Routine day — PT in the afternoon with a baseball game between the Enlisted men and the Officers. A show was given in the evening at the NAAFI by the Enlisted men and the NAAFI girls here on the base. The show was entitled, "A Handy Guide to the ETO," — completely original and very good.**

On September 14, 11 planes loaded with ammunition took off for Belgium; 9 of them returned because they could not cross the English Channel due to weather. One remained overnight in England and one delivered supplies and returned. Eleven more planes took off, picking up their load of ammunition, but had to return to base because of weather. The Squadron War Diary concluded this date's entry with: "1st Lt. Nicholas Pappaeliou (Navigator) was married to an English girl this date."

One plane was transferred on September 15, but all other flights were cancelled due to weather. The War Diary noted that Sgt. Les Goldman, of the 340th Service Squadron, gave his weekly talk on the status of the war at the Red Cross Club.

The Group War Diary entry for September 15 read:

> **Routine day here at Headquarters. Paratroops begin to arrive here on the base. Had a very good volley[*ball*] game in the afternoon during PT period. Dance held at the NAAFI in the evening with music by the 313th Orchestra, and the band proved to be very unpopular with the WAAFs, ATS and Enlisted men here.**

There was no flying on September 16, according to the 37th's War Diary. The entry continued:

All personnel restricted to camp as of this morning. A new motion picture, *Follow the Boys* played at the NAAFI. Eight new glider pilots assigned.

The September 16 Group War Diary entry detailed a new mission:

Field was placed under restriction again today along with preparations being made for Mission "Market." Briefing held at Group S-2 and it was announced that the assault area was still to be the Nijmegen [*Holland*] area, with huge glider landings after the paratrooper drop.

September 17, 1944 [*Sunday*]

My Darling,

As tired as I am and as busy as I have been, I must write to you this evening. It has been a few days since I've written but I am sure a sort of reassurance will make you feel better. As unimportant as this note is, I'm sure you don't mind if I tell you that I love you. The mail has been rather punk of late but I am not kicking because there may be a very good reason for it.

Time passes on, Darling. It feels so good that it does pass. Right now all the past seems so far beyond. (I might as well be honest, I'll be damned if I can concentrate.) I want to keep on saying, "I love you." "I love you." and keep on repeating it over and over again without saying anything else. It seems as if more and more so this evening I want you to know that. Every time I feel this way, I can dream of the most wonderful days that will be ours someday. It is quiet as Hell in here this evening and I still can't concentrate.

Hell yes! I knew I had something to tell you. Our favorite censor got married last week to an English girl. Naturally I was invited to the wedding and I was most anxious to be there. Unfortunately, something would happen to unable me to go. I was told that it was an elaborate and wonderful affair. Much to my delight and amazement, I was told that my name was mentioned often. Since Nick's wedding was of much concern to me, it was doubly disappointing that I couldn't go. Pappy was there. That made 2 of our former crew that could be there. Oh, well, maybe Nick feels the same way I do. I don't care if anyone is at my wedding, except you.

Well, that's all the dirt. Darling, I'll write a better letter as soon as I have a good chance to relax. Right now, I'm just miserably tired.

Good night, Darling. I do love you and miss you. Take care of yourself. May God Bless You. Love, Mike.

Following are the Squadron (WD) and Group War Diary (GWD) entries for September 17-19, 1944:

WD, September 17: 23 planes participated in an operational mission [*MARKET*] to Holland, dropping paratroopers and pararacks. The mission was a complete success; all planes and crews returned safely after making their drop over the DZ. There were no casualties and only three of our planes received slight flak damage. Two of the these already in operation and the other being repaired.

GWD, September 17: First day of mission. Briefing held in the morning. All but one aircraft returned home. Mission very successful. One aircraft ditched in the North Sea but all of the crew were picked up immediately after ditching and returned the following day to their home base.

WD, September 18: 20 planes participated in an operational mission to Holland, towing 20 gliders loaded with 82nd A/B [*Airborne*] Infantry, ammo., and combat equipment. 18 planes reached the LZ and discharged the gliders directly over LZ. One glider released itself over the channel landing in the water. All personnel, including the glider pilot were picked up almost immediately by the British air-sea rescue service. The glider pilot received minor injuries only and the tow plane returned to this station. All our planes were hit by flak and 12 of these were damaged extensively. Three crew personnel received personal injuries from enemy fire, only one requiring hospitalization. Of the two planes still out, one is missing and the other is reported down in Southern England with engine trouble after completing mission. The crew of this plane were not injured but the plane is unserviceable due to enemy action. Of the 25 Officers and EM who left on furlough to the States on 23 June 1944, 21 returned to this station. Two planes were used to evacuate wounded from France and are still out.

GWD, September 18: Second day of Mission "Market." This day is the most dreaded by all flying personnel of this group as it seems in the past that the worst casualties have been inflicted on the second day of any mission. The pilots ran into a great deal of flak and machine gun fire more than to be found on previous missions in which this group participated. Some casualties mostly from small arms fire. All in all the mission was very successful.

WD, September 19: A four plane paratrooper operational mission to Holland was canceled. The two planes on an evacuation mission to France are still out. No news as yet on the plane and crew that did not return from the mission to Holland on the 18th.

GWD, September 19: Weather bad today, heavy fog. Mission postponed for period of time. Rained in the afternoon.

September 20, 1944 [*Wednesday*]

My Darling,

It has been a few days since I wrote to you. I don't know exactly how long because my mind has been slightly befuddled. That shortage of mail still exists because they are holding it up but I shan't bitch. I'll just wait. It'll come soon enough. I've been kept fairly busy so I didn't notice the lack of mail until I was able to have a breathing spell. I was speaking to Nick the other day and mentioned the fact that I still haven't met his wife. He promised me that as soon as we had the chance, we'd get together. Find out her name is Betty, too.

Well, [*A.V. "Sonny"*] Rice got back and he feels all the better for his stay in that foreign country, USA. It feels good to hear the guys talk about the States. Never did think I missed it that much, until I heard all the familiar names, etc. He speaks nicely of his wife. Most of the fellows came back; a few stayed home. But don't let this move cause you any anxiety. It seems as if they've cut out that system. We hear all sorts of rumors but I'm afraid I can't get up enough pep to believe any of them. Just like most things in our lives, it is best to have it before you can believe it. Wish I could tell you half of the things I am doing so that I can make something of my letters. I've been so "geared up" lately that I can't even think straight. I should have a million and one things to say but I'm so fidgety I can't sit long enough to write. I'm not bad enough to be able to say how much I miss you and love you. You must bear up with me for a while. My letters may continue to be short. I can't help it. I'll be OK as soon as I can relax a bit.

So Darling, please forgive me. I do love you so very much. I keep praying for the day we will be together.

Give my love to Mother. Take care of yourself. Don't worry about me — Physically, I'm OK. May God Bless You — Love, Mike.

The Squadron War Diary entry for September 20 was:

> **A scheduled resupply mission to Holland was postponed for 24 hours. The two plane evacuation mission to France on the 18th returned today. The crew of the plane that made a forced landing in South England, after returning from a glider mission to Holland on the 18th, returned to camp by truck transportation.**

The Group War Diary entry for the same day simply stated:

> **Weather still very bad. Mission again postponed. Movie held in the evening at the NAAFI, *Iron Major*, with Pat O'Brien.**

September 21, 1944 [*Thursday*]

Good Evening, Darling,
    21st of Sept., 1st day of Autumn, I'll bet a meager fortune that the weather must be per-
fect. (By the way, Bette, things don't look so good for the Browns, do they?) Feel a Hell
of a lot better today but still feel a bit tired. I love you. Rather a speckled form of letter is
being formulated here. I don't know what's liable to come out of this pen of mine tonight.
Still no mail but I was told that things would be straightened out by tomorrow. Thank God.
It seems like a long time since the last letter was received. Really miss your mail, Darling.
You can see what it means to me.
    You know, Bette, I was thinking about things today. I was thinking about how we dis-
cuss money, etc. I don't recall how much I had when you came to Ft. Wayne but we did a
good job of it that time. Every so often I get to thinking about those wonderful days we
spent together. It makes my heart rush and my blood boil. I miss you so very much, My
Love.
    The kids that came back were talking about the amount of money they had spent
while they were home. It seems almost (incredible forgot how to spell it!) unbelievable that they could spend a $1,000 in such a short time. But they admit and it is not
hard to believe that money was no object because if they were tight it might be like a
restriction on their freedom. It was a nice feeling for them to be able to buy whatever
they wanted, do things whenever they felt like. That is the beauty of it all. You may
have a job tempering my nervousness but I'm sure I won't be too hard to handle. True
to form or should I say, naturally, all the fellows that got married while they were home,
lost weight and vice versa for the bachelors. Oh! well, maybe someday I'll be ready
to enjoy whatever those boys did. And with you, it will make every thing so beautifully
perfect.
    Darling, again you must forgive me. I'm going to hit the sack. I love you so very much.
Take care of yourself. May God Bless You. Love, Mike.

    On September 21, the War Diary reported:

> **Lt. Reed, the** [*glider*] **pilot rescued from the channel on the 18th
> along with his five passengers, returned to camp. 14 C-47 A/C** [*air-
> craft*] **are attached to this squadron for temporary service. The glider
> mission to Holland was postponed for 24 hours.**

    The Group War Diary also noted the postponement of the mission, and added that
the movie shown on September 21, *The Hairy Ape*, was "enjoyed very much by all the
men."

The next day, the glider mission was again postponed for 24 hours. The Squadron War Diary continued:

> **Glider pilots Lt. William W. King and F/O** [*Flight Officer*] **Philip M. Schott returned to base from their mission to Holland on the 18th September. Six airplanes were returned to the 315th T.C. Group.**

The Group War Diary's entry for that day, September 22, read:

> **Mission not flown again today and it looks doubtful as to whether it will clear up or not. Begin to clear some in the afternoon. Movie in the evening** *This Is The Army***.**

The glider mission to Holland was finally flown on September 23, as the Squadron's War Diary related:

> **24 planes were used in an operational mission to tow 24 gliders belonging to the 45th TC Squadron to the LZ in Holland. One plane after completing mission was forced to RON at Brussels due to engine trouble. All the remaining planes returned to camp. The 45th TC Squadron towed 21 of our gliders and 23 glider pilots to the LZ in Holland. Four of our glider pilots were also towed by the 45th Squadron in our own gliders. Three of our glider pilots flew with the gliders towed by the 36th TCS.**

September 24, 1944 [*Sunday*]

My Darling,

A beautifully miserable Sunday afternoon; nothing to do and for the first time in a week my mind feels perfectly relaxed. Relaxed enough to be able to write a decent letter. To top it all, I received 2 swell letters from you yesterday. I couldn't write last night because I was truly tired. While I was in church this morning, I was aware of the fact that this last week was one of the longest in my life. For the first time, I was able to look back over the week and it seemed like an eternity since I went to Mass last Sunday. Now I feel so relaxed everything seems like a bad dream. Above all, head and shoulders over everything, I know that my love for you is strengthened every day. Darling, I love you so very much.

In one of your letters, you asked me a question which is not too hard to answer. I do <u>not</u> intend to stay in the peacetime army any longer than I have to. It's true that the army is not a hard life but Darling, you and I have discussed so often the great feeling of independence. Regardless of how easy a thing may be, if a man cannot think or act freely of his own, then the ease is dismissed. Those kids that went home, say that the greatest thing of all was being able to move whenever they felt like. At heart, I'm a civilian — right now

— I'm in uniform; I must try to be a good soldier. But this next peace time will not be an easy one. ⅔rds of our men will be required to do duty overseas. Personally, I've seen as much of this world as I'd like to see. The next time I travel, I want to be with you. Don't you see, Bette, all these days I live in uniform are merely so that I can live with you out of uniform. Bad enough you'll have to be an army wife for a while; I wouldn't want you to live that way any more than you have to. I don't mind the leisurely, go to Hell, matter of fact manner of living but it isn't what I want nor wish to continue. Whatever struggles that may have to be faced by the present day soldier after the war, this is one guy that isn't afraid to tear into the world.

Gosh, Bette, we are planning most of our life on that future. I know it sounds mushy as hell but this is the way I think and what I believe, that home of our own, the chance to do what we wish, when we want to do it, the chance to raise our family off a post in the normal environment that all of us have had. All those little and many things that made our pre-war life so nice. When a guy has to reminisce, he doesn't dream of the army but of home and what he is looking forward to go back to. Army memories are day by day thoughts and actions which are always concluded with a definite, "I wouldn't do it again if I were paid double."

There you are, Darling, straight and clean. Just as I feel. I haven't made any reservations on what I said because there are none. My ideas are definite conclusions. It will have to take another war against us to change my ideas. Do I sound selfishly unpatriotic or is it a normal thought? I'm sure, Darling, that you agree with what I say. To me, my most important thought, is that this mess will finish so that I can come back safely to you. You are my whole dream; the army is my pastime and duty. I know I'm afraid of war but not afraid of a good fight if there must be one.

Gad, it's hard as Hell to concentrate. There is so much noise going on, I can't hear myself think. Talking about baseball pools, I've fooled around with them all season and still haven't hit one. Got a few tickets for the World Series pool; it pays off £100 ($400). Not a bad piece of change, is it? From the looks of things, seems like Detroit will back in as the American League winner. Right now, I'm thinking of the football season. Wouldn't mind sitting in on a few games this season.

Darling, I'm going to close. My hands are cold as Hell. I told you that the weather is great. Grr —

So long for now. Promise to do a lot better with my letters now that I'm settled a bit. Give my love to Mother. Take care of yourself. May God Bless You. I love you, Mike.

The War Diary entry for September 24 read:

> **One radio Navigational flight and one test hop. Seven ships were returned to the 315th TCG, and two additional planes went along, one to pick up equipment and the other to bring back the crews.**

September 25, 1944 [*Monday*]

Good Evening, Darling,

Since I have the chance to write, I am going to make the best of the opportunity. I've received gangs of mail from Tom. He's gone all out and he really is writing gangs of it. I always welcome it; mail is received with open arms always. Dropped my vote in the mail tonight. Dewey got it but he is the only Republican I voted for. The rest of the men on the ballot were guys that have done a good job for my State, consequently, my vote. To boot I received your letters of the 28th of Aug., September 1, 4th, and 10th. Really pouring, it doesn't make me mad. Now if I can answer.

Young Lady, you seem to be doing a lot of interior decorating. Well, at any rate, it is something to keep you occupied. It would look like Hell if I started papering these walls, pink, Ha! I'd get laughed right out of my sack. Glad to see that my letters haven't been cut lately. It is gratifying to know that you are receiving my letters in full. After all, there is nothing that I've written that could possibly be cut out. It's none of the censor's business if I want to tell you how much I love you.

About this teeth business. I've always liked a nice set of teeth. I went in for an appointment and I was told to come back Oct. 1st at 3 PM. — Great, isn't that? By that time my teeth will fall out. I know that I have 2 cavities that I'd like filled but who the Hell am I to say? As for what you say, it really doesn't pay to unnecessarily pull teeth but wisdom teeth can cause a lot of trouble. Especially since they are so big and can restrict space in a small jaw. If your teeth are close together, it is best to get rid of those teeth. I wish I had had it done. Do you remember the night I had so much pain at your home? Mother's Day or at least the night before, wasn't it? I chewed cloves all night. Gosh, Darling, it seems so far and long ago. I love you so much for everything.

You talk about being a glamour girl. Surely you must be kidding. You can make anyone of 'em look sick. Every time I look at your picture on my locker, I realize how lucky I am. Honestly, Bette, you are a very lovely person. I could never possibly find anyone that could come close to you. Everything about you makes my heart grow warmer. Just to have my arms around you would make me feel twice as young as I am. Honey, you're my dream, girl. (Pardon me while I light up a filthy, black cigar!)

You make some funny remarks at times, Bette. "It has rained for 2½ days. — It feels so wonderful." Sorry, I can't agree; I'm afraid I can't get enough sun. Hell, can't get any. Rain, eek! Wouldn't you look cute, all decked out in your Sunday-go-meeting clothes and all your "pink" wrapped in a handkerchief. It would look cuter if you tied a stick to the end of it and carried it on your shoulder. I don't blame you for yelling; I would not pay that much dough myself.

So you think I would like the idea of walking into that mess. Honey, if there was any chance of that, I could care less if a hurricane had passed thru' the living room. As long as you are there, it makes no difference.

Bette, I'm gonna peel off. Someday I'll have enough privacy so that I'll be able to write forever. That's one reason I liked tents.

Good Night, My Love. Take care of yourself. May God Bless you. I love you — Mike.

There was one test flight on September 25, according to the Squadron War Diary. The plane that had been forced to land in Brussels two days earlier returned on that date, and eleven glider pilots returned from the mission to Holland.

The Group War Diary entry for September 25 noted:

> **Field restricted again today; as long as the actual work continues there is never any bitching from the men. The Dance that was to be held at the Red Cross Club this evening was called off. Movie at NAAFI during the evening,** *Buffalo Bill.*

September 26, 1944 [*Tuesday*]

Good Evening, Darling,

Although I should crawl, if I can make it, into the sack, I must write to you before I retire. I just gotta tell you how much I love you. I don't promise to make this long but I know you understand. You know, Darling, a lot of thoughts pass thru' a guy's brain while he's in the blue. The best part of it all when I think, it is usually about us.

Bette, you'll have to teach me how to live again. My speech isn't what it used to be. After such a long time with a continued association with men, it seems as if every other word is a cuss. I don't promise anything but I'm sure it will take a little time to rectify my malfunctioning tongue. I'm sure you'll be able to stand me. Another thing, it seems like such a long time since I've mixed with any people on a social standing. You'll have to teach me to use the right fork, etc. Probably have to kick my shins or slap my hand every time something happens. The best advantage I have is that my teacher will be such a swell one.

Really, Darling, you will be patient with me. If you must scold me, remember that even in my ignorance, my love is strong. You know, Bette, thinking as I said I was has its advantages. It kind of brings out that extra soft spot that I am saving for you. It makes me miss you so much that it frightens me because it makes this separation seem so hard to endure. But don't worry, I'm here and I know there is nothing I can do about it. I was also thinking about the reading you've been doing. Darling, do you wear glasses? I've noticed that my eyes feel strained and I don't read ½ as much as I did. I wonder if it is tiredness. There are a million and one things which I thought of today — A million of them cannot be explained because of that 3rd person, the censor. But since I always believed in action rather than words, those thoughts can wait.

I am going to say, "Good night," My Darling. Give my love to Mother and Elpha [*Bette's maternal aunt*]. Take care of yourself. I love and miss you so. May God Bless You. Love, Mike.

The Squadron War Diary entry for September 26 read:

18 plane resupply mission to Holland; all planes returning OK. One plane test-hopped. 12 glider pilots returned from Holland.

This was not a "milk run." The Germans completely surrounded the area near Grave (or Keent). There were many planes trying to land with their mission matériel, but only 10 planes at a time were allowed to land while the remainder circled the area. A wonderful monument depicting the scene was dedicated in 1995.

The September 26, 1944 entry in the Group War Diary follows:

The mission "Market" was continued today resupply to the far shore. Pilots report small arms fire but very inaccurate. The movie *Standing Room Only* was shown at the NAAFI. One of the best films we've seen since being overseas.

September 27, 1944 [*Wednesday*]

Hello Darling,

I've so much mail to answer and yet none because I don't feel like writing to anyone but you. It isn't that I have too much to say but since I didn't write for such a long time, I don't like to feel as if I drifted away. When I am busy as I was, I forget everything and concentrate only on what I have to do. But inwardly I never forget that you are my love. My real, honest love to which I look to.

I have started to read *Dawn Over the Amazon*. I don't know who the author is but I do l know that it is a damn good book. It is dated the year 1950. The armistice of this war was supposed to have been signed in 1944 but it was hardly a settled thing. There is more unrest and we are again facing the same hated opponents, the Japs and Jerries. Only this time, we, USA, is faced with immediate danger. I haven't gotten too far but it is easy to see that it is a highly imaginative story. By the way, the love scenes are torrid.

You know, Bette, if the opportunity ever arose, what would you think of making a go of it in So. America? I forgot to mention it but the story does take place in So. America, as the title implies. Just a passing thought, I wonder.

From one of your letters, I can gather that our thoughts do run parallel. What I mean is that whenever one of us does anything, it is always with the idea that someday, we'll be doing it for each other. That thought is alone one of the most comforting in the world. There is little I can do over here but think. Actually I cannot formulate anything material because the army is not my life. But my brain drums incessantly of ideas and mannerisms. "If I can do this, I can get that for Bette." Etc. Things like that that will be the nucleus of our future. Believe me, Darling, it is great to be able to think about someone else. To know that someone is ready and willing to share whatever life we may have to face, be it good, bad or indifferent. Behind all those motives is the deep feeling of love, a love that is mutually satisfying and enjoyable. As I have said so often before and shall continue to repeat, knowing that you share my every dream has made my days so much easier to face. It is impossible to describe by words how much you have meant to me. Knowing that you are there has made everything I've done, no matter how small or big, seem important because it shrouds you, directly or indirectly. Whatever emotion, regardless of joy or disgust, has always had you looking at me in the background. You, your influence has done much to forestall my weaknesses and cement my strength. Yes, My Darling, it may not seem possible to you but if you could probe my stupid brain and sieve-like soul, you could easily see what I mean. I love you and miss you deeply.

So long for now, Darling. Give my love to Mother. Take care of yourself. May God Bless You. Love, Mike.

There was a 20-plane resupply mission to Belgium on September 27, and all planes returned. There was also one navigational flight, and another plane carried troops locally.

On the next day, September 28, the War Diary recorded:

> **13**[*-plane*] **resupply mission to Belgium; all planes returning OK. Eight additional glider pilots returned from Holland. Glider pilots returning from Holland were given a week's furlough. Six hour-after-work passes are in effect once again.**

September 29, 1944 [*Friday*]

Good Evening, Darling,

I know I didn't write last night but I still don't recall how long it has been since I wrote last. Believe me, Darling, it's not from negligence, but just a whirl caused by any number of continuing events. But to make everything complete, I must have received any number of letters from you and I hardly know how to start answering. Last night I had a million and one things to say and yet, I was so weary that I didn't feel like imposing any of my boredom on you. I figured I would get a good night's sleep and I'd be able to get off a few good letters but I was wrong. I was very rudely awakened at a very unsatisfactory hour. After a long day, I'm back but still tired. This has been the longest month I've spent overseas. Whoa! All that talking and nothing said — I love you.

I received your very bulky card of the 15th of August. Clever, indeed, My Dear. Only wish I could make all that come true. (Finished another [*writing*] Pad — Must make a million!) Thank you, Darling, for that great big lip print. I tried to adjust it just right but I'm afraid I'm a realist when it comes to something like that.

I was delighted with your frankness concerning the truth of love. I know that you'd tell me whenever you feel like that you love me. What angers me more than anything else is to see someone who can put things on paper but when they are face to face with a person, actually feelings are lost in silence. I can readily see that it is easier for you to say things than write. When it comes to wanting to hear the right thing at the right time, you have never left me in a quagmire. That is one of the qualities I like about you, Bette. You told me once that you loved me, and you showed it many times. The reason I say it that way is that as we look back on it, our relationship was so short, it seems even shorter. I'm not griping because I know what is in the future. You know me well enough to know that I shan't mince my words. Whatever mistakes I made then, shall never be repeated. I promise you.

I'm glad that you won't mind living in NY. But remember one thing, since the future is uncertain, we don't know where we will end up. Only God knows what the future has to offer. The only thing that is certain is that you have me and I'll have you. That isn't the worst start in the world, is it? Matter of fact, we have a damn good start. I love you.

Just thought I'd mention it, but I got a letter from Dan Smith — You must have met him and Gert and Mr. & Mrs. Smith [*Eleanor and Bill*]. He's in the ETO now and said that he expected to visit me in a few days. I'll have to teach the rookie how not to bitch. Every letter he has sent me has been torrid. But at any rate, it will be good to see him; it has been over 2 years and we did have a lot of good times in New York, even though I footed the bill a lot of the times.

Say, that was quite a dig about the Cards that you sent me. At this stage of the game, I guess they don't have to worry. Detroit looks "in."

Your letter of the 11th amazed me or have I said that before. Frankly, I like your open discussions. Sex is really a thing to be looked at openly. . . . But I'll drop the subject. That's another one of those things that I'll take in flesh and blood. I don't think and I believe that neither of us need worry.

Must close, Dear. I hope I can write tomorrow but it will be late. Give my love to Mother. Take care of yourself. May God Bless You. I love you and miss you. — Love, Mike.

On September 29, according to the War Diary:

> **16 plane mission to Belgium (resupply), due to weather 15 planes returned with their load from Kemble, only one plane completed mission. Seven more glider pilots returned from Holland. One plane was test-hopped; two planes resupply to Belgium.**

September 30, 1944 [*Saturday*]

Good Evening, Darling,

I don't know what this letter will sound like. All I want to do is talk to you. I dreamed of any number of themes; yet, I don't think I'll touch on anything important. I know you won't mind if I just jabber along. I should answer your many letters but I am sure you won't mind if I let them ride for tonight.

Last night, after I had written, I crawled into the sack at 8 PM. I read for 2 hours and then fell into a deep slumber until 7 AM. (big blob of ink: cute isn't it! Writing too fiercely!) I felt refreshed but not wholly rested. So I will follow the same course this evening until someone forgets to disturb me one of these days. My soul and body feel clean. I am not totally happy; I can't be as long as I am away from you; but I am doing as well as can be expected. My thoughts are running away from me this evening; my pen cannot move fast enough to keep apace.

I went to church this afternoon, preparing myself for Communion tomorrow. I felt haggard and dirty. So hours later, I stood before a thundering shower, cascading mountains or falls of cold water. There I was, stark naked, a man who had faced all the perils of the subway rush hour on 42nd and Broadway, the man who had elbowed his way to the best seats at Ebbetts Field, the man who fearlessly tackled crowds to order a scotch & soda at Schumachers, brave (?), so he thought, until he faced that cool, cold cruel water. Ah! What a debate — but the iron was struck; I had no choice, plunge and so I plunged. Gad! It was horrible — soap everywhere, water dripping from every crevice and precipice — Brr — It must be done — done it was. (Honestly, it felt good.) Then that poor, unfortunate soul, having spent every ounce of strength on that ordeal, stood before a mirror, saw his countenance freckled with blotches of a filthy 3-day growth of beard — Struggle, do you hear? Struggle and so with razor in one hand, lathered brush in the other, I gained new life and set about to rectify that awful sight. Totally weary, — it was done — and so, My Darling, I sit here and I want to tell you how much I love you.

What has all that to do with my telling you, "I love you" — surely, you would think ill of me, if I looked beggarly. (Do you think I read too much?) There I got that off my hairy chest. Seriously though, Bette, I'll warn you ahead of time — you had better have plenty of talcum powder around the house. As effeminate as this may sound, it's the truth. Perhaps, it is my childhood training but I do like to look and smell (pardon my crudeness as referred to nasal passages!) clean. Nothing is nicer than to get between 2 cool clean sheets and all about one's person, the odor of refreshing powder. Seriously, I mean that. It has been hard to keep up the practice in army life but as a civilian, I used to reek of that powder. Don't get me wrong, not disgustingly, merely in a nice manner. Does all that sound silly to you, Bette? But there I go off my subject. Whatever it was. I carry on like an insane person sometimes but really it's an outlet for some emotions I can't explain. Screaming and cursing don't do any good. I banter about like the broken record.

But all that is not what you want to hear. I so wanted to tell how much I have missed you. Even in all those stupid words up above, you may detect an inkling of what I feel. It is the wish to have you near me always. Since I can never get mushy, I like you to know those little thoughts that pass thru' my brain when it feels like it is in an unbearable vise. A headlock of strangling, confused thought. Darling, you are the one to whom I want to tell of my every waking minute. Perhaps, I don't do a complete job of it and perhaps I don't do it often but I know you understand these moods. The moods that make my arms burn to have you part of me. I'll never be able to forget the pleasantry of my thoughts the thoughts of you have provided for me — I love you.

So, Darling, I say "Good Night" — I am hoping for an easy day on the morrow — I'm afraid I'm a bit weary yet.

Give my love to Mother. Take care of yourself — May God Bless you. Love always and ever, Mike.

On the last day of September, the War Diary reported, 15 squadron planes left for a resupply mission to Belgium; all returned. There was one flight to Scotland to transport glider pilots who had been on furlough, and two planes were returned to Spanhoe airfield. One plane, with crew, was returned to the Pathfinder School of the 9th Troop Carrier Command.

Every squadron detached one crew to be part of the 9th TCC's Pathfinder Group. This group led us into combat by "setting up a path" and dropping paratroopers of Regimental Combat Teams (RCTs). The Pathfinders generally landed 30 minutes plus before the troop carrier planes carrying paratroopers flew into the drop zone. The RCT would set up lights and radio (Eureka) systems so that the troop carrier planes could "home" in on the signals and thereby drop their paratroopers on predetermined DZs. The Pathfinder School was where combat air crews and RCTs trained for this specific mission. The Pathfinder concept began with the drop in Sicily, July 9-11, 1943, and was used mainly in night drops like Sicily and D-Day over Normandy, France.

The Group War Diary, on September 30, 1944, read:

> **Aircraft which were unable to complete mission yesterday did so today. Pay call today. All personnel who were interested could apply for 24 and 48 hour passes. "So ends this month of September, 1944, a little tragedy, a lot of memories, a history that shall not soon be forgotten."**

October 1, 1944 [*Saturday*]

My Darling,

Here I am again. I did just as I promised last night. I hit the sack right after I wrote; I read about an hour and then snoozed. But my efforts were useless. About 1 PM [*AM*], a few drunks came in and woke me up. I had to smoke a cigarette with them. Well, then I passed out and at 5:30 AM, I was disturbed again by the fellows that had to go out. I tried to go back to sleep but I didn't fare too well; I got up at 8 AM and sat around until time to go to church at 9:45. Although I didn't get too much sleep, I felt a Hell of a lot [*more*] rested than I have for a long time. So I am dedicating most of my afternoon to letter writing. I answered 2 of my letters. One dame, I used to work with, the fiancee of one of my buddies, keeps insisting that I send her a picture. (Sammy Kaye's *Sunday Serenade*. What memories!) Naturally I can't send her a picture; I haven't even got one to send you. Where the Hell does she think she rates to you. — Got paid today and sent Mom $20. Her birthday is the 16th of October. After I pay off my debts, I ought to make this month closely. Darling, I bet you wonder where my dough goes. Well, last month, I pitched a few drunks at our club, it cost like Hell to get a shine on. A double Scotch or Gin costs $1.20. Gotta' learn how to drink less or get drunker more cheaply. You see, Bette, I haven't left the post since my rest leave, some time in May. I don't mind — I can't find enough to do to keep me occupied in town. The pub hours aren't long enough for me and the women aren't appealing. Easy, isn't it? Besides I'm too happy by the thought of you to think about anyone. (Have been wanting to ask you — You know this song, "I'll Be Around." What is it a 4-F number? I don't pay much attention to the words but who is saying it and what is meant by, — "I'll be around when he's gone"? Sounds like some GI is getting the wrong rub. Maybe I'm wrong! I love you.

Today is ideal for just this — Crawl out of the sack late, go to Mass, have a nice dinner, and head out to a good football game — after the game, have a nice supper somewhere — knock off a few quarts of bourbon and then dance 'til late in the morning. Darling, I dream of things like that. I feel as if it will be the nicest thing in the world to share these days, all days with you. Not too much of a dreamer, just so much in love and so very happy about the whole thing.

In one of your letters you said that you didn't think my heart had gone cold since I've been gone because I can write such warm letters to you. Yes, but that's because it is you that I write to. I've changed to the degree that very little means much to me. Don't feel as if I'm hard-hearted but it is a feeling of choosing what I want and striving to get it. I used to be considerate of everyone and everything regardless of what they meant to me.

Now I think nothing of telling some character to go to Hell. To you, My Darling, I cannot extend enough warmth in my heart to really prove what I am trying to say. Coolness to incidental persons does not necessarily mean I've become a bloodless Blue Beard. To you and to those that have made my life what it is, I am still the Mike you knew before. Perhaps, I am a bit more of a neurotic but I still care for the things that I have always, with some exceptions — Your memories of me cannot be changed because I haven't changed that much. I love you and miss you as much as I did the first minute after your train left Ft. Wayne —

Well, Darling, I'll close. Give my love to Mother. May God Bless You. Love, Mike.

P.S.: Someone just handed me *30 Seconds Over Tokyo*. Let you know what I think. I finished *Dawn Over the Amazons*. I'll give you a review of both as soon as I can stop for a moment from telling you how much I care for you. — M.

October 1, 1944 [*Saturday*]

Hi-Ya Babe,
 Here I am again and again and again, surely you'll tire of me — I dare you. I read

quite a bit of *30 Sec. Over Tokyo.* — really is excellent. I can feel every moment with the author. His ultimate end may have been just reward but personally I'd like to keep my body intact. Ah, Fate!

I received your letter of the 15th of September. Kinda figured the outcome would be in your favor. I like to shirk from work any time, I can do it. But about that matter of sleep. I don't think it will be difficult to break your habit of early arising. But now that you mention it, I recall that you do sleep restlessly. You know me, — it's like trying to wake the dead to get me to stir. Pardon my crudeness but I'm sure you'll enjoy your sleep once I get home. It's a good idea to awaken early but why strain at the halter. I like to just lazy around but with you at my side, the pleasure will be doubled. I'll bet it won't take too long to break your habit. Do you mind if I try real hard?

Really, Bette, it can't be difficult to put up with your "clutter" so cheerfully. I don't feel right unless I get mail from you. If I receive a stack of mail, I read yours last so that I can "soup up" every word.

You are being very considerate by your drive for a car stop. With your interest in politics and your concern for people like that, you'll land in Congress as one of our lady representatives. As far as that interest, I'm afraid I'll have to take a back seat. You'll wear the pants on that score. Of course, I'm not totally ignorant but when I start in on such a discussion, I end up cussing and yelling. Can't help myself; there are too many blind spots which burn my royal.

Yes, Darling, we have had a lot of fun. There are many instances we could speak of. Oftimes, I take an overall picture. I don't see each date but every wonderful thing that has happened for you and I. I can always place that into that warm spot in my heart and call it, "Memories of You." Pleasant, indeed, Darling, and so many more to add before we write "*finis*" to this life of ours.

Yep! I've read about the storm on the East Coast. (Just heard the football scores of yesterday's games — Gad! What high scores!) Hope it isn't as bad as the storm of '38. Really knocked the Hell out of my favorite fishing grounds. Trees, buildings, launches, speed boats, everything was ruined. I hear this storm has done a lot of damage, too. But I haven't heard exactly how much damage it has done.

So you'd like to have a bowling alley in the basement. Gad! Woman, you don't expect to live in a place like that, do you? It'll take a big place to have something like that. Of course, it could double for a ballroom. Or am I being too presumptuous. More about that though.

Gonna' close. Hope you don't mind my second letter in a day. Felt like dashing off a few words so you wouldn't think I'd forgotten. Cheerio for now. Love, Mike.

On October 1, a 14-plane resupply mission flew to Belgium and returned, according to the Squadron War Diary. There was also one local "hop." The entry concluded with: "12, 24, 48-hour passes now in effect."

The Group War Diary entry for the same day read:

Mission of fifty aircraft, carrying ammunition, to far shore. With the beginning of the month it brought on true aspects of fall weather, leaves turning and the flowers beginning to disappear.

October 2, 1944 [*Monday*]

Good Evening, Darling,

Here I am back again. Perhaps, I'm not in as good a spirits as I'd like to be. Think I'm a bit cranky tonight. But some silly bastard is playing with our cat and it is as annoying as Hell. Never told you about our cat. He's a stray that someone picked up and he has been with us a long while. His name is "Roundy" but I can't tell you why — Not that it's a military secret but his full name isn't for sweet ears like yours. There's another pet that is a base pet. He's a crow called "George." Really is a clever ole' black bird. He knows when it's chow time — he thinks nothing at all of jumping on a table and snapping at your food. One day while we were sweating out a line, one of the guys beckoned "George" on his shoulder — Since he isn't bashful, he climbed up on the kid's shoulder. I was studying the crow's feathers and mentioned that it looked as if he had been in a fight. At the same time, I was motioning with my finger, without even a casual glance, "George" snapped and clipped my finger. We really have an assortment of pets around here, haven't we? Sound like a bunch of crazy men.

One day a St. Bernard showed up from nowhere — No one to this day knows who the dog belonged to. Our little Scottie, Bonnie, took one look at that gentlest of gentle dogs, put her tail between her legs and ran off yipping like a coyote. That monster was truly a monster. In order to give him a drink, the fellows filled up a <u>bath tub</u> full of water. More fun that a barrel of monkeys. But all that isn't what I started to write. Those jerks are still acting like kids.

I finished *30 Secs. over Tokyo*. — It was great. I don't know if it was a good idea to read it or not. The author endured unlimited hardships. The man has to be admired. I can understand every one of his emotions and thoughts and yet I've never been thru' ⅓ of what that boy saw and done and had happen to him. I disagree with him on one point. I don't think the raid was successful or useful. But who am to say? That *Dawn Over the Amazon* was one Hell of a good book, too. The author's descriptions are excellent. His love scenes are torrid. Although the time is set as 1950 — the amour or technique is parallel to my conception of ideal. Ah me! To be able to love you again as we knew it before. I'll admit the book made me a bit "horny" but it's still practical. Someday, Darling, we won't have to live in our thoughts. It feels so nice to love you, Darling, even from so far a distance as this. There is always that consoling thought that our separation cannot last forever. Knowing that the years have passed us before, makes it easy to think that the years will pass and are passing now. The only regrettable thing is that we cannot watch this passing together. I love you —

Good Night, Bette. Give my love to Mother. Sorry to rush off so soon. Take care of yourself. May God Bless You. Love, Mike.

The following entries are from both the 37th Squadron War Diary (WD) and the 316th Group War Diary (GWD) for October 2-4, 1944:

WD, October 2: One 10 plane and one 6 plane mission to France; All planes returned OK. Capt. Joseph N. Rieger, Navigator, returned from a leave in the States.

GWD, October 2: Another large mission to the far shore of sixty aircraft, carrying ammunition. Administrative flight to Greenham Common.

WD, October 3: A 17 plane resupply mission to France; 12 planes returned, four RON at B-56 [*Brussels/Evere, Belgium*] **and one is still unaccounted for.**

GWD, October 3: With the weather turning cooler the job of building a fire will soon be a part of the day's routine for those who don't have central heating in their buildings. One plane sent to Greenham Common to tow a glider back to Cottesmore, and 66 aircraft carried ammunition to the other side.

WD, October 4: Five planes returned from Belgium; 11 planes resupply mission to Belgium; four planes returned due to weather and took off again (RON); the other 7 planes returned after completing mission. The 316th TC Group weekly dance was held for the EM at the NAAFI.

GWD, October 4: Sixty aircraft left today carrying ammunition. From the looks of things the group will have a busy month ahead of them. The regular Wednesday evening dance was held at the NAAFI for the enlisted men this evening.

October 5, 1944 [*Thursday*]

Hello Darling,

So very sorry that I haven't written for the last few days. If it had been possible, I certainly would not have "goofed off." I should answer more of your letters but as usual I can't concentrate on a thing. Not because I'm blank but because the gang won't let it stay quiet enough. I can't blame them. The World Series is on the air and they have the game on as loud as possible. It is a terrific temptation not to listen. But regardless of what obstacles I can't let another day pass without writing. At any rate, the Browns did win yesterday's game, didn't they?

I love you. I haven't been able to think of anything but that. I've been busy as Hell but I can always find time to think of you. Regardless of time, circumstances or what have you, the uppermost thought in my mind is you. The racket is almost unbearable now. — I hope I don't make too many mistakes — anything can happen. But what I am trying to say is this — just an idea of how many thoughts have passed thru' my numb brain. You know that I have seen many things and have been thru' many places. As I've said before, I try to discard all the disgust. But whatever has any semblance of beauty, I earmark for future days. Someday, who knows, we may have enough money to travel abroad — There are many things I've seen that I'd like you to see, too. Gosh, Bette, I hate to drop this subject like this but it is impossible to write. I'll close and I promise to write early tomorrow so that I won't have any interference.

Good night, Darling. I love you so very much and miss you. May God Bless You. Love, Mike.

The War Diary entry for October 5 read:

> **The four plane resupply mission that left on October 4th for Belgium returned this evening. A 13-plane resupply mission to Belgium was also completed. . . . A voting booth for voting by Federal Ballot was set up in Group Hqs with hour posted for voting. One plane test-hopped.**

The Group War Diary on the same day reported:

> **Once again ammunition was carried to the opposite shore with 48 planes participating. Liberty run in the evening to nearby towns.**

October 6, 1944 [*Friday*]

Hello Darling,

Thank God I've got a day off today and I must make up all the time I missed and the letters which were so pitifully written to you. I took care of the physical things this morning and now I must handle the morale end. Washed clothes and did other incidental things now I must write to you and make up for that "lousy" letter of yesterday. Really, Darling, so many things to say that I must have quiet to concentrate. I don't know what I'll say but you will bear with me, I hope.

I guess that you had guessed that we were in on that job in Holland. You can see from my writing that I am safe and well. However, I don't feel too keen about writing about it because I'd like to let it drift into the long lost past.

What I have been thinking about is us. I know that I've said this before. I've said so many things over and over again. But I know you don't mind hearing it any more [*than*] I mind repeating. We have already agreed that we will have a small wedding. I mean no fuss whatsoever. I've gotten to a point where I care about nothing else but to spend the rest of my days with you and you alone. I don't cherish the idea of having anyone gaping at us as if we were two puppets. Of course, since we are going to be married in the rectory of the church, there will be no one present except our best man and maid of honor. I am hoping and I know you feel the same way that you don't want a reception any more than I do. Honestly, Darling. I don't care for that sort of stuff. Especially since we've been apart for so long and it takes so long to arrange things.

Here are my ideas for "our" day. Let me know what you think because even if it doesn't happen soon, we will have time to discuss it. While you are on your way east, I'll arrange whatever has to be done. In the first place, a blood test is necessary according to the laws of New York. I can get my health certificate from my Flight Surgeon. You can get yours in KC because it takes at least 3 days in New York. Well that takes care of that. Since you are non-Catholic, I have to get a special dispensation from the Bishop. That takes a short time, especially since it will be understood that we want to get married as soon as possible. I am sure that Tom will perform the ceremony. We haven't decided on our best man and maid of honor. Is that for me to decide? I've got gangs of female cousins and my leanings toward any special one are varied. Little Lee would be swell or my cousin Sue or Lucy. Best man, I don't know-it may be one of my army buddies or Ted, my brother. (Handy to have a large family, isn't it?) Gosh, here I am babbling along and yet I don't know what you'll think of the whole idea. But, there is something that we must talk about. It makes everything so near, too.

Tony said speak of the wonderful future, isn't this it? And, honestly, Bette, I don't feel like wasting any time. I've promised myself that we would restrain ourselves until it was fitting. (Sounds hillbillyish but you don't mind my being slightly old fashioned!) As for the ring, well, I think it is best if you and I pick it out together. Gosh, Bette, I love you so much. Being able to plan like this is like talking to you of the nicest day of our many. It brings us so much closer together. Regardless of how much time may elapse between this writing and the actual day, it seems like nothing when you speak of it. My day seems to pass so easily. I've been wanting to say this for a long time but never did and since you never really mentioned definite plans, I never thought to speak of it.

We can stay in some NY hotel until my furlough is over. If I don't have to return overseas, you will come with me to my next base. That is one point which we are both definite about. I don't ever want to be too far from you once we are together again. I promise you I am using all my discretion in everything I've said. There shall be no middle way but one — just everything we will do will be for you and I as man and wife or as I've said before — as lovers. This subject is one of the nicest to speak of. I guess I've said that before. But it thrills the Hell out of me to think I can write evenly to you and know that you enjoy it as much as I enjoy writing it. (Funny, I've repeated myself again — feel as nervous as if this was the day before — but many times my enthusiasm runs away with my senses! Just like a babbling, drunken soak, drunk from the sweet liquor of love!) There you are for now. I'll wait anxiously for an answer. I do hope our thoughts run parallel. Everything will go so smoothly that we can have a great start.

To change, — not that I want to but — Well, I see the Series is tied at 1-all. Really exciting games, too. Really would be a series to follow. Oh! well, one cannot have everything. I have you. What more can I ask?

I expect to have tomorrow off, too. I can't leave the post because I am expecting Smith and I don't dare leave for fear of missing him. But I don't mind, really. It feels good to be able to relax. It gives me a chance to write, read, sleep and eat regularly. Must remember to tell you of a very pleasant experience I had in Brussels. But aside from that still feels good to be near my sack. Reading *Strange Fruit*. Rather raw and really not too interesting reading.

Well, Bette, signing off for now. Give my love to Mother. I love you and miss you so. Take care of yourself. May God Bless You. Love, Mike.

WD, October 6: A 16-plane resupply mission to Belgium; one plane returned from Kemble due to engine trouble; all other planes returned after completing mission. One plane cross country and return.

GWD, October 6: Two planes were placed at the disposal of the airborne today for practice loading by the airborne troops. Three planes dispatched to A-88 [*Maubeuge, France*] **carrying rockets.**

WD, October 7: 15 plane resupply mission to Belgium; Three RON and 12 returning after completing mission. One plane resupply mission to Belgium and return.

GWD, October 7: Sixty planes were sent out to the far shore carrying ammunition. As the evenings have turned noticeably cooler overcoats, scarves, and gloves are appearing as the men leave on pass in the evening.

October 8, 1944 [*Sunday*]

Hello Darling,

Gad! I've got a pot full of mail to answer and yet I don't feel like it. Just can't get up enough energy to write to so many people. Guess they will have to wait. I'm getting damn tired of waiting for that buddy of mine. He said 10 days or 2 weeks and it is past 2 weeks since he wrote and still no hide nor hair of him. I'm not too eager to get off base, so no sense to kick. Thanks a lot for all the cards — getting too lazy to write — Secondly, though nice having you love me and knowing that you are thinking of me so much. Darling, you're swell.

Your boss . . . must be a character. I can see that his mind must be full of little spots of dirt. It is strange what makes men like that. We expect it in the army because women are a rarity. But when a man is surrounded by women and can have one whenever he flicks a finger, he must be sexually distorted. Surely his thoughts can be segregated to time and place — But his compliment is true. All I have to do is look back over our relationship and I can see laughs and no tears. You never worried me once about things that concerned you. All our discussions were openly frank and pointed. Although they may not be directly related to disposition, those little things are part of the make-up. He needn't tell me, I know you are a wonderful person.

Went on a real binge last night, Bette. One of those forget everything affairs. We polished off 2 quarts of Johnny Walker Red Label Scotch. — Three of us handled it aptly. — Don't be angry with me but my meaning in forgetting everything means not what I love but what I'd like to put out of my mind. The trouble with those loads is that they cost so much. The two bottles cost us $36 — $18 apiece. Sounds crazy, doesn't it? But you can see how much we want to forget. I love you Bette. That's one thing that has occupied my mind so much in these last few months. In one letter you said that it was raining and when it rains you get so romantic. . . . When I look over things, I don't deserve you. You are too good. Coming to Fort Wayne the way you did; going to New York at my request; running yourself ragged for this big goon. I promise you, I'll make up for all of that. Perhaps, I haven't proved myself by doing all the little things that make things so nice but I am so much the realist. I like to prove my love to you personally — It isn't being dramatic or crowd loving, just that my strength is in my arms and I want you in them. I was thinking about it last night.

You wrote about your collection of dogs. I've only sent you one. It isn't that I've forgotten — Lord knows, I remember all those things but even as long as I've been in England, time has passed so quickly. Mentally, it seems as if I've never had a free moment. Always on the run and my brain in a definite whirlpool that often threw me spinning. Maybe I haven't fared so well but I've always seen the sunlight break thru' with my thoughts of you. I haven't courted you in an orthodox manner, showering you with gifts, etc. Humbly I beg your forgiveness. Asking you to bide with me in our love that has been and is so beautiful even if it came in a time that seems so inopportune; the days are so upset. I promise you as I've promised myself that I shall never have you regret this love, My Darling. But I shan't keep talking like this; kinda makes me feel low — I carry on.

I mentioned in one of my letters that I was going to tell you of my experience in Brussels, Belgium. When I visited there recently, we were forced to remain overnight because of mechanical reasons. I was hardly prepared — had a 3-day growth of beard, had on a dirty pair of overalls, no money and in general I felt crummy. I won't describe the city; I'll leave that for a later letter. We got a hotel room and then set out to look over this virgin territory — virgin to me. The beer is excellent and I got slightly charged up on some cognac.

In the meantime, I had wandered off and tried to locate the rest of the fellows. I walked into the Hotel Metropole looking for them. As I was gazing about, an elderly fellow walked up to me and asked me to join his party for a drink. He said that he and his friend, a lovely Norwegian girl, wanted me along. They took me to a private club. Obviously they were of a nice social standard because the club was a very lovely place. It was located in the Greek Market Square. The buildings that made up the square were the Town Hall or Municipal Building, King Albert's home, that is the equivalent of the Capitol in Washington — Where the King did all his administrative work and the rest of the square was made up of other official buildings. Quite an ideal location — the club was sited in a corner of the square. The club was two rooms which were drinking rooms and upstairs was a lounge and above that were apartments. It must have been an artist's hang out. (Can't seem to describe this the way I saw it.) Try my best. They had a nice bar and well stocked one at that. The walls were lined with old Dutch masterpieces — works done by Van Dooven, I think and other artists of that school — I believe the 15th century. Everyone of the paintings were originals. The people showed me the apartments. Just one big room. One might feel as I did that they (apartments) were not for actually use as a home but merely as a rendezvous. You know a place for lovers. There were antiques all over the place. From the window, you could get an excellent view of the Square. In one corner was a double bed that had a beautiful red velvet bed spread on it. And there was a light switch that was really a long cord that could be put into the bed — so that when you were ready to retire or just wanted darkness, it wasn't necessary to get out of bed. All the lighting was indirect. Then there was a small alcove, as Charles explained it, "Even among the antiques, we must have some modern furniture." This small room had a small refrigerator, stove, dishes, glasses, beer bottles and a sink. All in all, seeing a place like that was an experience in itself.

Now for the people, etc. As soon as I walked in, a redheaded girl, slightly tipsy from too much wine, ran up to me and gave me a big kiss, "An American" — That's all she could say, couldn't speak another word of English. After all the introductions were over, they asked me what I'd like to drink. — The bar had dozens of Three Star Hennessey's Cognac on it. My eyes damn near popped. We must have toasted America, Belgium, France, NY and every state in the Union and every other state. A few of them spoke excellent English. The national language of Belgium is French. I can speak a little French, enough to get along on. That Norwegian girl I spoke of spoke broken English. She would start to say something and when she couldn't think of a word, she would blurt out a string of French. It was cute as Hell to watch her. . . . The party broke up at 11. But not before I was given a couple of address and phone numbers and a standing invitation to join them for supper and a drink every time I happened to be in Brussels.

What amazed me was why out of so many they chose me. Fred told me that when I walked in, he and Dagny looked at each other and said, "That's our man." For an innocent and nice time, it is a memory I shall have for a long time. But I can talk about it better than write about it. Looks like you'll have to listen to me a long time.

Well, Darling, I'll close for now. Give my love to Mother. Take care of yourself. I love you and miss you. May God Bless You. Love, Mike.

On October 8, according to the War Diary,

Three planes RON at Belgium returned this date. One XC [*cross country*]. . . . **Two EMs were hurt in an explosion of a tank grenade while working in the salvage yard. 13 C-47As were exchanged for 13 C-47-Bs.**

The next day's War Diary entry read:

Flight Officer Chitwood, Glider Pilot, killed in action 18 September '44, dropped from rolls as of this date. One plane carried mail to Belgium and brought back some Polish paratroopers. Three-plane mission to Membury and return. 1 Plane transferred to 313th TCG.

The Group War Diary entry for that day, October 9, described an awards ceremony held for the 52nd TCW:

Dull overcast day with intermittent showers. Representatives from all squadrons and Group Headquarters went to Barkston-Heath, where General Williams presented decorations to thirty-five members of the various Groups and Squadrons of the 52nd Troop Carrier Wing. Among those decorated were Lt. Colonel Walter R. Washburn, Jr. who received the DFC [*Distinguished Flying Cross*]. **A practice paratroops drop was carried out by eight planes for those paratroops completing their qualifying jumps.**

October 10, 1944 [*Tuesday*]

Good Evening, Darling,

Feel like a million bucks this evening, a bit tired but what the Hell, that's to be expected. I went up to Pappy's [*Agle's*] room last night. He showed me your card and promised that he would write to you. He apologized because he was so lax. Well, we sat around, listened to the Series and generally batted the breeze until 1 PM [*AM*]. In the meantime, he had a half a bottle of John Haig Scotch and we drank right thru' it. I can always tell when Pap's feeling a bit low. That is usually the time we get together. I must ask Tom if it is permissible and I think it is but I've asked Pappy to be our best man — He said "Try and keep me away from NY on that day." Do you think you'd like that? I'm sorry, Darling, I don't think that we can be married in the Little Church. However, since we will be married in the rectory, it doesn't make much difference. You see, Bette, Our Lady of Lourdes, where Tom said his first Mass, has been our parish since I was born. Just as you say, I don't care who's there as long as we are together. It is easy to see that we are not hard people to satisfy.

I'm glad that you cleared that hangover easily. Believe me, it isn't the worst thing in the world to get a good binge on every so often. There is one thing. You are lucky you don't have to go into the blue with a hang over. It'll kill you. I know. One point that is lucky for you is that you can have variety with your drinking. We are lucky to get something to drink in one place. (A couple of the guys are bulling and naturally the topic is home. Just wondering how it would feel to sit up at 6,000 ft. and watch the lights of the cities pass under us. After all this time and experience, I wonder how it would be to see the States as we saw them so long ago.) Oh well, time marches on.

Sorry, Darling, I'm going to close. I am making this short because I am going to try to answer many letters that I should have answered long ago. The reason I beg off is that it is getting late and time is running short.

Good night, Darling. Take care of your self. May God Bless You. Love, Mike.

The flight schedule was busy the next three days, as the Squadron War Diary and Group War Diary report:

> **WD, October 10: Five planes were used to drop paratroopers locally. Nine planes picked up supplies at Kemble and returned to this base. Movie at NAAFI.**
>
> **GWD, October 10: Twenty-seven planes participated in mission to far shore. Six were called back as they were 15 miles from Brussels because of weather. Cloudy most of the day, cleared somewhat in the afternoon. Liberty run in the evening.**
>
> **WD, October 11: Nine planes resupply to Belgium and return. Five day furlough for all EM personnel now in effect.**
>
> **GWD, October 11: 26 aircraft flew resupply hauling ammunition to B-56. Rained in the afternoon. Three day passes and seven day furloughs were authorized for the first time since the Group has been in England. The Enlisted Men also had a pleasant surprise along with the good news of the passes. Ice cream and plenty of it, and even though it was a little cool for ice cream, it was more than enjoyed by everyone.**
>
> **WD, October 12: 13 plane resupply to mission to Belgium. One plane RON at B-58 [*Brussels/Melsbroek, Belgium*] for purpose of bringing back weather report tomorrow morning. Movie at the NAAFI. Four planes were used to drop paratroops.**
>
> **GWD, October 12: Normal day — usual administrative flights carried out. Movie in the evening. *This Is the Life*. If only life were like that.**

October 13, 1944 [*Friday*]
Friday the 13th!

Good Evening, Dream Girl,

My Darling, Bette, I love you. I had a swell dream last night. Discarding all future events, my dream started. I was home. I can't remember any of the facts but I do know, we were married and everything was perfect thereafter. I know damn well that the feeling lasted thruout the day because I could do nothing else but sing and feel like I was bouncing on a cloud.

I'm sorry, Bette, for not being able to write for the last few days. It seems like an eternity since I last wrote to you. I've been kept pretty busy and losing sleep again. But I see that I am going to be presented with my Air Medal tomorrow so that means I'll have the day off. From what I hear, we are going to get a cluster to it for our last job [*Holland*]. If I had my way, we'd get everything they've got plus a good rest at home. To add to my growing chest full of ribbons, I believe that we also have the Presidential Citation. At least, that's what my service record says. I think I've written about it before. It isn't an actual medal but just a blue ribbon enveloped in a gold border. It is worn on the right side. Contrary to all other decorations. But really, Darling, all I want is to have you in my arms. Please do me a favor, Bettyjeane, if you can still find them, send me some clippings and pictures of that latest airborne job in Holland. We've had pictures and columns written about our outfit and I'd like to see them. One of the guys got a column from home. It was in the *New York Times* and it was a cause of great humor around here. Publicity doesn't faze us. One fellow got an editorial from the Chicago *Herald Tribune*; it caused a big argument last night. Since it would never pass the censors, I won't tell you what it was about. Perhaps, it sounds like a smash at Anglo-American relations but since it is the truth, it cannot be denied.

I've started to read *The Apostle*. Life of St. Paul — by Sholem Asch. It is a long book and it will take ages for me to read it but since I've always been such an admirer of St. Paul, I want to read it carefully. I read a very short condensation of *Nana* by Emile Zola. However, it was an extreme condensation and it seems as if all the sluttishness was gathered from the book merely for the purpose of exciting the GI. Believe me, it wasn't hard to become excited by the book. Nana was quite a character. You remember our discussions of the impressionistic school of art. You can recall that I was interested in Van Gogh because of the unique life he lived. I believe he did a lot of his work in Arras, France. I've seen the town quite often. It looks like a bit of a mining town. I do know that the city was mentioned by Dumas (*The Three Musketeers*) as well as Orleans and many other French cities. It seems funny after all these years to see towns and cities that I have read of so often.

I see in one of your letters you mentioned the idea of a Red Cross Unit. Darling, one of us in uniform is enough. Funny, but I'm so afraid of missing you when and if I ever get home that the thought alone sends me thru' a spasm of fretting. That's the one nice part of so many things, the fact that you are home waiting for me. I keep hoping that you are enjoying as much of life as is possible. I realize that to each of us being apart leaves an open void that cannot possibly be filled unless we are together. Knowing that you are still enjoying some luxuries makes my dangers, whatever they may be, not too bad to take.

Darling, speaking of that complaining friend of mine, he still hasn't come to see me; — it is 3 weeks. I shall send him a perfect lashing tonight. You've never complained to me because your understanding of whatever I may be going thru' has been wonderful. Your one complaint was justified. Fortunately, we discussed it levelheadedly. It is one of our prime advantages. I can't see anything wrong with you, except that you are so lovely and so far away.

Say you are [*becoming*] a sportswoman. First you speak of swimming and then bowling. As I have said before neither of the activities will hurt you. I wish I could be with you, Unfortunately, indoor swimming has its disadvantages because of the lack of sun. You know me, I'm forever the sun worshipper. A brown body to me is a healthy body. The lack of sun is one of my greatest bitches against England. So many of them here speak of holidays. Yeah, good wet holiday. But I'm glad that you are getting that exercise. You'll have to improve your bowling score, not that I'm bragging but I used to roll a fairly good score.

I guess we are in the same boat, Bette. I thought I was in love once before but I was wrong. I didn't think a person could mean so much to me until I met you. I know exactly what you were speaking of in your letter of the 27th of Sept. My heart grows warm each time you tell me such things. You say that we have to prove so many things to each other. I disagree because to take up where we left off will be all our proof. Everything we ever did was done normally and without fear or shame. As you say, we have so much love and respect for each other that we cannot possibly miss. I need your help for the future we will have to face. That you will give all of your help to me leaves no doubts at all in my mind. You're wonderful, Dear, and I love you so very much. Oh God, how I miss you.

No thanks, Bette, I don't need snuggies. I use my heavy flying boots — still cold — can't help it.

Good night, Bette, I want to answer a few more letters. You can be sure of a letter tomorrow. Give my love to Mother. Take care of yourself. May God Bless You. I love and miss you — Love, Mike.

The Squadron and Group War Diaries for October 13-14 continued to record the work of the 316th TCG:

> **WD, October 13: 15 plane resupply mission to Belgium. One plane forced to return due to engine trouble; 14 completing the mission. One plane returned from continent with weather report, RON the night before. XC to Ireland, RON. F/O David C. Little, asgd and JD as of this date.**
>
> **GWD, October 13: Mission 462 flown to the far shore. Gliders were towed from Greenham Common to Cottesmore. On the flight one glider crashed and three personnel were killed: F/O Krohn; F/O Lucier and Sgt. Basham.**

WD, October 14: 15 plane resupply mission to Belgium. One plane returned from RON in Ireland. Glider department received four CG4A Gliders.

GWD, October 14: Dull overcast morning but turned out to be very beautiful in the afternoon. All aircraft returned from the far side safely.

October 15, 1944 [*Sunday*]

Hello Darling,

I take it all back. Seems as if the unpredictable Army has again made a liar out of me. Not only did they postpone the presentation but I had to work to boot. Since today was Sunday, I surmised that I'd have a day off — again I was mistaken. Luckily, climatic conditions made the day much shorter than I expected. Don't worry about my working too hard. I don't mind it too badly; it makes time pass quickly. However, a day each week gives me a chance to catch up on my domestic work. Working like this, cuts down my [*letter*] writing but I'm sure you don't mind too much as long as you understand that the circumstances are beyond my control. I miss you terribly these days, Darling. Just like that dream, all I can think about is you. But so I carry on.

Sheila hasn't written to you recently because she and "Reb" were in New York for a few weeks. I, too, was disappointed because of the lack of mail from that corner of the States until I heard of her visit. Tony hasn't written and I'm sure because he is busy, too. Ted and Louise sent me a few pictures of their children and my Mother and Dad. They all look great; the babies are growing up and in turn my parents are aging. It seems always impossible to think that the years are passing rapidly. Christmas is just around the corner, and although I am not too enthusiastic about spending another (my 3rd) away from home, there is <u>no</u> light in sight which tells me that I'll be home. As we've said so often before, we'll make up every holiday we've missed plus. My cousin Mike [*Fusco*] is getting married this month. It seems like only yesterday that I sat on the walk in front of my house and spoke to him of you. I don't know who his wife is but I'm sure they'll both be very happy. And so I go babbling on. People's lives change, and you and I wait for our transformation from the single to the plural. Patience is a great virtue, Thank God, we have been endowed with such a strong sense of it.

Without the strength of you behind me, Darling, these months would have been hard to take. Months no longer now, starting on that second year now. Say what anyone might like, there have been 2 occasions in my short acquaintance with you that I've spoken [*your*] name when I wanted you near me so badly. It may sound hardly masculine but when people are in love, genders are secondary — Once you came to me, that was in Ft. Wayne — my only disturbance then was mental. The other was in the midst of Hell breaking loose [*D-Day*]. I uttered your name; you could not reach me but your image did and I felt a peace that eliminated all my fears. Perhaps what I am saying may not make too much sense to you. One thing you can understand that it is a way of telling you how much I love you —

actually the events are dim to you. I will tell you of it one day. But believe me, Bette, in the hours of my worst ordeals, you came to me as if you were meant to be there all my life. You said that you didn't think that you were capable of ever loving a person as you love me — I thought the same — but I've learned so much, My Darling, being without you is like living with ½ a soul. I love you.

The fellows are teaching me how to play bridge. Don't know how much I'll learn because our time is so limited but at any rate, I'll know something of the game. It is one good house game to know, isn't it? Do you know how to play? One hears so much of those numerous tales of bridge clubs that I've always felt as if all women know how to play the game. Personally, I prefer strip poker.

I wrote to Mother the other night and told her of our wedding plans. The one thing that I stressed and which I know is a mutual thing between us, is simplicity. You know, Darling, I've seen quite a few things but I know that my nerves would snap if I had to face the ordeal of being pushed from hand to hand. No thanks to anyone; I've been away from you too long. This is one time I dictate, if it is agreeable to you and this is one time people eat out of my hand.

Well Cheerio for now, Bette. Give my love to Mother. Take care of yourself. May God Bless You. Love, Mike.

Squadron War Diary, October 15-16:

> **October 15: Of the 15 plane resupply mission to the Continent, 11 planes were forced back because of bad weather; three completing the mission; one plane still out. The . . . Glider Pilots, missing in action, 18 September 1944, are hereby dropped from the rolls as of this date. . . . Six EMs were awarded the Bronze Star Medal under GO** [*General Order*] **98, 9th, TCC** [*Troop Carrier Command*] **dated 15th Oct. . . .**
>
> **October 16: Flying was somewhat curtailed due to the weather. One plane returned after being forced to RON on the continent; One plane XC to Chalgrove for the purpose of transporting Capt. Floyd C. Miles, pilot; 1st Lt. Norman C. Herro, navigator, to Pathfinder on TD. T/Sgt.** [*Technical Sergeant*] **James M. Scoggins and Sgt. Ronald Roach were hurt in a trailer mishap out on the line. They are in the hospital for observation. Weekly dance was held at the American Red Cross.**

Group War Diary, October 16:

> **Very cold this morning and along with rising temperatures in the afternoon came the rain — a very heavy rain. Some of the Enlisted Men left for Scotland today on 72-hour passes. The regular Monday Red Cross Arrow Club Dance was held this evening. Among the guests**

were several civilian girls who kept the jitterbugs as well as the by-standers entertained.

October 17, 1944 [*Tuesday*]

Good Evening, Darling,

I took a little time this evening to see a show. Saw Bette Davis in *Mrs. Skeffington*. Damn good, I really enjoyed it. Besides the regular picture, they had a short newsreel, the invasion of Holland. I think that they'll show it to all of you eventually. I was quite proud to see it because it was the first time I've seen my outfit in the newsreels. It is too bad that all these pictures are shown and we're not able to see them and explain what is going on. Oh Well! Time & Fortune.

I still haven't taken life too easy but last night, I really let go. You must forgive me, Darling, but I had to let loose. We knocked off 2 quarts of Scotch and then some. But I promise, Bette, my liquid activities are going to cut down to nearly nil. Have a good time and forget but it isn't practical. One of the kids just got back from London on pass. He was a virgin before he left but as we call it, he got "studded." I guess the change will do him good. I'm afraid it was kind of prying on his brain.

I've received your letters of the 2nd & 5th of Oct. but I haven't had time to answer. I am writing a short note tonight so that you won't think I have forgotten you. If you only knew how much I miss you and love you. I am hoping to have a day off tomorrow. I am planning on it so that I can write a nice long note. I've got so much to do that I really need to take life easy. Received some long letters from home and I've got so much to answer to. There's a lot of bulling going on but I feel so damn tired that I don't feel like anything but to pound the sack.

So, Bette, My Darling, forgive me if I beg weariness. Believe me, I have so much to say. I'll let it hold 'til tomorrow. Give my love to Mother. Take care of yourself, Darling. Good night. I love you. May God Bless You. Love, Mike.

The October 17 War Diary entry noted the movie at the NAAFI, "including the official pictures of the airborne invasion of Holland." The entry also showed an 11-plane resupply mission to France. One plane, which flew to Prestwick and then France, did not return that day.

Group War Diary, October 17:

Weather was very bad most of the day. Some of the aircraft were unable to return because of weather conditions. . . .

October 18, 1944 [*Wednesday*]

Good Morning, Bette,

Sorry about that horrible missile last evening but I just didn't have the pep in me to write a decent letter. I was afraid I'd blotch the thing up. But since I had a fairly good night's sleep last night, I think I am in better shape to write.

In your letter of the 29th, you wrote very encouragingly of letting me have some peace when I get home. I don't believe my nervousness is constant or contagious. I still enjoy life as it is. But at times I am almost uncontrollably fidgety. I can't really understand it except that it may be a subconscious thing that is beyond me. There are times when I feel I must talk to someone, someone who knows and understands me. I think you know the feeling very well. You can remember my spontaneously talkative moods. I'd go for hours and when I was finished, perhaps, I'd said nothing but the mental relief was worth the effort. A few weeks ago, I couldn't get any Philip Morris so I had to get some Camels — just a point to illustrate, — I went thru' a carton and ½ like a stove. But I practically ruined myself — unnoticeably to myself of course but I was like a spirited horse. I find that I can still relax but the moments are rare. I know that just being with you would be enough to sober me beautifully. Since that is impossible, I have to make the best of those nervous periods. I don't want you to worry about it because it isn't a thing to fret over. My biggest deficit of late is sleeping. My dreams have been disturbed — funny little things, occasionally a nightmare but what the Hell. As tired as I am, I struggle thru' the night and feel refreshed the next morning. All in all, Darling, it isn't hard to see what is wrong — all I need is you. But our patience will be rewarded — time will pass and I should feel myself a perfectly weak personality if I couldn't take it. I love you. Don't worry. You won't spoil me — as it has been said so often before — you can miss things and yearn for them so deeply and yet when you have that one thing, it takes such a short time to make up for lost time. Tell Bonnie that she may think I look like [*Cary*] Grant — someone else said they thought I looked like Tyrone Power — if one should ask me, I think I look like the rag wheels of Hell.

I resent the manner in which you speak of Dem Beloved Bums. From rumor, I hear that the Browns intend to move to Brooklyn. They can, at least expect good support. We can stand an American League team there. The Cards are OK but wait 'til next year. I hope to be home by then and I'll be able to root for the gang — then watch them go. Darling, you needn't send me the clippings from the Series. I'll get all my info' from *Sporting News*. I renewed my subscription, so I can keep tabs on all of 'em. Looks like Notre Dame and the Green Bay Packers this year. The Brooklyn Tigers are not quite up there but it takes a few games for the kids to get started. I see that the National Hockey League starts Nov. 28 'til March 17 or so. Gad! I do hope we'll be able to see a few matches this year plus a few basketball games at the Garden. It will be swell to be in the stands with you. It will be as I had never been thru' all these bad dreams. I can readily believe what was said about misery, — it is easily forgotten.

You mentioned El Camino in one of your letters. Said it was closed for remodeling (with an e) (maybe 2 ls, I don't know — who cares!). I don't recall meeting Paul Larson there but wasn't that the place where those high school kids came in from their prom. They were all dressed in gowns and tuxs. — it was about midnight — We batted the breeze a while with them. I think both of us were feeling rather high — (how unusual). If I recall correctly, we pushed back the tables and showed the kids how to dance "Begin the Beguine" — One of the kids cut in on me and a young lady that was seated next to me told me that my girl friend was very lovely — (As if I don't know that!) Do you remember that night? Or is that another dream I wish had happened? Many were the days that we sipped cokes there. One thing those young gals that served as waitresses were awfully cute. Weren't they?

Darling, I'm glad that you agree with me about the Army. The lack of freedom is my best reason for getting out of it. There are so many things that can be exploited; so many ideas that were frustrated by the Army and war. Once this is over, I shall feel that I have done all that was expected of me as an American. Once the war is over, I shall feel as if I can take a passive interest in the events of our country. Keeping an eye open to make sure that the same mistakes are not made. Of course, I am one of many millions but I'm sure that a lot of guys feel as I do. I like the uniform and I'm extremely proud of what it stands for but some things I don't like to be thrown into nor the people I must encounter. The experience is worth a million but I am just as glad to make it a short million.

Well, Darling, I must close — must write to Chicha. Sending this free mail — gotta do it that way. Wait til payday and I'll be rich again.

Give my love to Mother. Take care of yourself. I love you and miss you. May God Bless You. Love, Mike.

October 18, 1944 [*Wednesday*]

Good Evening, Darling,

I've written so many letters today. I feel like a display in Macy's window. Two letters arrived tonight that I had to answer immediately. These people were so worried about me that I had to let them know that I came thru' this last one with flying colors. You must be wondering why I am writing to you twice in this one day but it is best that I take advantage of my free time and I just feel like talking to you. This is the 8th letter I've written today and besides that I washed a gang of clothes. You can see that I am not wasting any of my free time. One never knows where I'll be tomorrow and so —

Darling, I received your letter of the 8th of October. I am sorry to hear that you are bothered by such an affliction. Not because it is bad but because I am so far away that I can't do anything about it. One consoling thing is that it took so long for you to break out that way. It is almost 15 months since the last time I saw you. Gosh, Bette, it is rough, isn't it? I hardly know what to say. Before I knew I could do something about it. Now, all I can ask is that you be patient. But, at any rate, stay under the Doc's care until he has you fairly settled. Above all, it will give you a good chance to put on some of that weight. All I hope is that I'm not away so long that you'll look like a sieve from all the shots. You can tell the Dr. that I'll gladly take his problem child off his hands. Lord knows, I must have a touch of the same thing. I got the same nervousness but it is because of other things but I'll gladly blame it on excess energy, if they'd send me home.

It's rough, Darling, I know but as we've said so often before, if others can take it, so can we. It's mutual. I miss you as much. We have done very well, living in the future has done a great job for us. I am not promising anything but really, Darling, it can't be too very long. The first year is the hardest — that has passed and so we are a few months into our second year. I love you so very, very much. My days are made complete with the thought of you. As each day passes, I find myself talking more and more about you. If I look at your picture much more, I'll wear it out. As childish as it may seem, you must hear me tell you how much I love you. Every day before I leave, I say the usual, "Gad! I love you, Bette" Maybe I'm nuts, I don't know. Maybe I'm queer but things like that are important to me. You aren't being selfish when you say that those beautiful autumn days are meant for us. If you are selfish, then I'm disgustingly greedy. Everything I think of is perfect for us. Perhaps, Bette, you shouldn't tell me what you did because it makes me so damn mad to think what this damn war is doing to people like you and I. But that conforms with our policy. No holds barred, no punches pulled. Best to discuss things than let them hang non-supported. Just like you said once, "We know we are meant for each other because we are equal in so many respects. We'll never regret loving each other."

To go on — I see in *Stars and Stripes* that there will be 18 Garden games this year. I don't know if you have ever seen any of the basketball games but I do know that you'd enjoy them. I see from the schedule that there are going to be a lot of teams from various parts of the States that never played there before. Darling, you may think I'm a sports maniac but to me, that's as good a diversion as any. Unfortunately, I don't play ball well enough to make a profession of it but I do like it immensely. Hell, Bette, I'm so badly out of shape I couldn't run a ½ block without puffing like the KC Limited. Heard they are going to start a post basketball tournament (note the scribbling!) Hope they go thru' with it. It'll give me a chance to shape up and at least have something to do on these long evenings. I don't promise that you'll see every game but I promise to keep you well up on your sports. (How do you like the stupid spacing of my thoughts?)

Gotta peel off, Darling. Chin up, life isn't too hard to handle. Take care of yourself. Don't forget your shots. May God Bless You. I love you and miss you. Love, Mike.

War Diary, October 18:

> **Of the 15 planes originally dispatched on a resupply mission, three completed the mission. Dance in the NAAFI hall. 12 planes were forced back because of bad weather. Major Leonard C. Fletcher, Commanding Officer, promoted to Lt. Col. . . . One plane returned from [*Prestwick*] and the continent, sent out the day before.**

Group War Diary, October 18:

Only flights in the United Kingdom were flown today. Ships loaded at [*Prestwick*] for tomorrow's mission. Rained in the afternoon and evening. Social service held for the Enlisted Men at the NAAFI with 150 civilian girls as guests of Cottesmore. Most of the men were disappointed in the girls and decided they preferred the girls in the service to the civilians.

October 19, 1944 [*Thursday*]

Hi Honey,

Here Ah is back again. Something must be wrong somewhere, — two days off in a line. At any rate, the rest is doing me some good. The only bad point of it is that I get too much of a chance to think. The more I think, the more I miss you. You can see, I'm never consistent when I bitch; one minute I want rest and the next I yell like Hell. Of course, that's natural; the worse thing we can do is think. As long as I can leave my brain like an open tunnel, I don't do too badly. The only thing about that is that I can't get the thought of you out of my mind.

Looks like we don't have any luck with our pets. We think "Roundy" is dead. She disappeared a few days ago. Someone said she got hit by a jeep. Hell of a thing. So, kiddingly, someone suggested that all of us in the room fall out in ODs and have a formal service in her honor and that we fire a 32-gun salute in her honor. Oh Well, it gives us something to think about.

We wrote a dissenting letter to *Stars and Stripes* today. We were rather peeved at an article that appeared in it written by some character who just returned from a 60-day at home and was glad to get back to the ETO because of the attitude of the folks at home. The manner in which he wrote was similar to the baby who has had too much ice cream and has gotten sick and doesn't like it any more. Poor bastard, I'd like to hear the fox hole GI give that excuse for wanting to get back. I don't care what the next guy thinks, let him make his dough, have his fun, etc. I'm only interested in what the people I love think. It isn't a matter of being fed up or afraid to take chances with my neck, but give a guy something to shoot at. This policy holds so true with a gang like ours. Our records are untouchable. Bomber boys get their tours in and get ready to head home. Ours is not a matter of missions or anything else, yet. If half of these guys did ½ of what we did they'd bitch twice as much. But all that is hardly what I wanted to write. What's the use of thinking it. Let me be sheltered in your arms, and whatever filth has drifted into my nostrils will be forgotten. The request is simple, not that it is unattainable but seems so far off from here. But that again is contrary to the morale uplift. I love you.

I can sit here and think of a million sweet words I can whisper into your ears and yet to put them on paper, to be read by an eavesdropper is the utmost of sacrilege. Little familiar things that are familiar to you and I that would seem so "Oh Oh" to someone else. Miss you, My Darling, like I miss everything that should be a part of our lives now. Don't fret, I'm not losing my patience, just like to say those things to you. Can't get out of practice you know, Bette. I don't want you to think that I'm an amateur when I see you. Can't see myself being boyish if you were around. Gosh! It has been a long time, though, hasn't it, Honey? Hey! What the Hell's wrong with me today. Not that I'm saying the wrong things only — Must be the music we have on; it's a lot of sentimental stuff that makes a guy feel like swooning all over his sack. Silly, isn't it?

Hardly know how to go on, Bette. No sense to discuss the war news. I'd be called down for that but at any rate, it does look good, doesn't it? Don't get too much news about the political race. I'm afraid the English papers don't care too much about our gov[*ernment*]. Listen to what one said about football, "But football over here (America) has neither the speed and ball control one sees in Association football (English Soccer) nor the bustling vigour of Rugby (English Football) — Sides get into a series of huddles which seldom result in either gaining more than 5 to 10 yards of ground before the next round table conference is called to decide how they shall make their next play." Gad! Aren't we horrible?

Well, Bette, that's all for now. Give my love to Mother. Take care of yourself. I love you and miss you. May God Bless You. Love, Mike.

October 19, 1944 [*Thursday*]

Good evening, Darling,

Here's your lil censor's nightmare back again. You see how fortunate you are. Each time I have some time off, I try to talk to you as much as I can. Of course, it is a bother to no one but the middle man, the poor character. Just saw a fairly good "B" picture. Wallace Beery and Marjorie Main in *Rationing*. Don't mind the old guy's "muggin" — it's a welcome change.

I've progressed quite a bit on my reading of *The Apostle*. I am enjoying it immensely. As I've said before, I've always admired the works of St. Paul. Naturally, I welcomed the chance to read more about him. If I only had a better understanding of the Hebrew language and customs, I'd be better off. However, my familiarity with the rites of the modern church give me a spider web view of the old church. You know Paul brought the new religion, belief of Christ's arising from the dead and his Ascension into Heaven, to the Gentiles — whereas this belief was originally reserved to the Jews. Since Christ was a Jew, it was believed at the time that in order to receive His grace, it was necessary to comply with the customs of the Jews, that is, circumcision and abstinence from pork, etc. These customs were narrow minded because at that time, the Gentiles believed in the perfect body. It should never be touched or marred — consequently, they would not submit to circumcision. Again, at that time, since Jewish law set most of the religious laws, it was impossible for the Jewish to turn their face toward these "new" converts. St Paul's logic was that meaning of the Messiah, Christ, was to be known to all regardless of Jew or Gentile. So you see, we, as Catholics, owe so much to Paul who was a hater of Christ before his (Paul's) conversion — He even helped to persecute St. Stephen, the first Martyr. I hope this isn't boring you, Darling, you see Religion in fact or should I say as told with fact is like any other History. Even in the sacrifice of the Mass, toward the end of the Mass, the priest faces the congregation and says, "*Ite Missa Est.*" (Go, the Mass is ended.) Actually he speaks to the converts (Gentiles) and they are supposed to leave and then he, the priest, goes on with the Mass. However, thru' the years the customs have changed with the times. There is no discrimination whatsoever.

As a matter of fact, the Jews, the chosen people of Christ [*God*], still do not believe that He [*Christ*] came on earth and they are still waiting his arrival. That's why their year is something like 5900 B.C.; whereas, our year is 1944 A.D. (Year of Christ, 1944 years after His Birth). There are so many facts that are interesting, Darling, but it would take years and we do have so many years ahead of us. I don't want to talk you deaf and dumb so soon in our love life. If I did that you won't be able to hear my many million of endearing words that are still unsaid.

We got another bitch coming and I'm going to write the note to *S&S*. Seems some other kind of outfit is taking credit for a lot of our work. You see Darling, ATC [*Air Transport Command — not a combat unit*] are the white shirts of the air whereas TCC (Troop Carrier) are the dray horses. ATC has claimed to so much that we know damn well we did. The paper said that this ATC delivered some stuff to the paratroopers. Sure they did it but they get a big column spread but who the Hell brought the troopers there in the first place? We get 3 lines. Bunk! Sick of hearing it!

You spoke of the customs of the South American people, such as, beating your wife in public or anywhere, sadistic thought, isn't it? Maybe it isn't a bad idea — "Aha!" said the villain, "You'd better watch out." Seriously though, that brings to my mind some rather queer English expressions. I explained their rather curious meaning of "fanny." Of course, I didn't say it outright but I believe I delivered the general idea. Now, when an Englishman wants to tell you to look him up some time when you are in his vicinity, he'll say, "Knock me up when you are in town." You know damn well if a guy said that to a girl (especially if they weren't married) it would call for a slap in the face or is my mind in the gutter? Secondly, we saw something extraordinary or spectacular we would say, "Good Show" "Swell" "nice play" "good going" etc. whereas under the same circumstances, an Englishman would say, "Smashing" "Champion" or "Wizard." You figure this one out. — A fast number will be a "quick step." When cutting is allowed on a certain dance, they call it, "Excuse me dance." If something bothered us, we would say, "he peeves me." Or "angers me" "I got a bitch coming" or as the Army says it, "I'm p...off" The English would say "Browned off" or "Cheesed off" (Maybe because cheese is sour.) To us beer is beer, to them, it may be called "Mild" (That's the different colors, tastes, etc., as we would call brands like Budweiser, Schlitz, etc.). "Bitter," "Stout" (There are any number of stouts: Guinness'; Nutmeg; Milk stout, etc.) or "ale" (There are also a million of those.) Gad! Give me a bourbon and coke and — er just a dash of lemon!

That's all for tonight, Darling. I do hope this letter of fact and fancy is interesting. Again, I find myself with so much to say. Poor censor! It can wait. Really all I started to say was that I love you and miss you so much.

Good night, My Lovely Bette. May God Bless You. Love, Mike.

The War Diary on October 19 showed one test flight and a resupply mission to Belgium involving 12 planes.

October 20, 1944 [*Friday*]

Hi Darling,

Here I am back again. No, I am not taking life that easy, just got a break in the atmospheric conditions, so relax, my boy, relax.

It's a good deal, believe me. Bette, I am sending you this picture that I took a few months ago. Nope, I didn't mean to pose like a fairy; that's just how the pose came out. I tried to get my wings and stripes into it so you see how I had to achieve that effect. I'm sorry I never sent you a portrait. I just can't seem to sit for something like that. Maybe someday I'll muster enough strength to do it. I look kinda' chunky in this picture and there isn't much change from that picture and as I look today. I weighed myself today and I tip the scale at a mere 203 lbs. Figure a few pounds for clothes and that puts me about 198 or 200 even. That isn't too bad really. You can't see my eyes; that isn't unusual and the sun was not out. At any rate, this will refresh your memory of what I look like; cute, isn't it?

I've felt awfully elated since I heard some talking that may be good news. I think my letter of last night reflected that. I get a kick out of everything I think of. Those thoughts are usually thoughts of us. Just thinking how crazy both of us are and little things like that. Just a good honest feeling that gives me the impression that my morale is as high as it ever will be and Lady, that's high.

I see that your swimming lessons are progressing rapidly. As I've said before, I don't care for indoor swimming but it is a good way of getting exercise. Swimming is an easy sport to learn. Above all, get the fear of the water out of your head. If it goes under water, it is the easiest thing in the world to get above water again. I had to pull Chicha out once because she got panicky but never let your imagination run away with yourself. Breathing is easy as long as you concentrate. If you do the crawl, breathe under your right arm every other stroke. Breathe thru' the mouth and release air slowly thru' your nostrils. I was never a good distance swimmer because I've never been in shape long enough. I am short winded. Above all, form is important — [*yours*] is perfect. (A bit thin but not too scrawny.) Learn a bit, Darling, and I'll try to complete the job.

I don't know what to say about going to New York. You seem to be well set in KC. You have your friends and activities. Your whole social life is set. New York is big and cold. To avoid any repetition of what happened in June, I'd rather have you there only when I'm there. As long as there are cablegrams and phones, I won't have to worry too much about keeping you informed of my homecoming. Don't worry, Darling, the day that happens, I'll see to it that you'll have plenty of time to get ready. Gad! It's nice to think that someday that dream will come true. I love you.

No thanks, Bette, I don't need any gloves. I've two pairs of leather gloves plus a couple of pairs of heavy flying gloves. My feet are my worries not my hands. (chlorine was spelled right!)

I am glad that you appreciate my vote, but really I can't put my heart and soul into the election. True, we have a long distance view of the events of home but it isn't vivid enough to get your teeth into it. The lack of good American papers has a lot to do with that. There are so many daily happenings that I like to read them on the spot.

Well, Darling, I'll close. Give my love to Mother. Take care of yourself. May God Bless You. I love you and miss you. Love, Mike.

The Squadron War Diary entries for October 20-21 read:

> **October 20: No flying because of bad weather. The following lectures were given to all squadron personnel: Capt. Jack R. Ellis, Protecting against VD; 1st Lt. Robert Roman, security and censorship regulations; a talk was given by the Group Chaplain.**
>
> **October 21: One plane XC and return. Squadron formation was held for the purpose of presenting Air Medals and Purple Hearts. Under General Order No. 92, 9th Troop Carrier Command, dated 7th Oct., section three, the following named personnel were presented the Purple Heart: 1st Lt. Nicholas Pappaeliou, 0-805328; 2nd Lt. Dewey H. DeLaire, 0-832112; 2nd Lt. Marcel O. Gerdin, 0-705679. 14 Enlisted Men and 11 Officers were presented the Air Medal for the participation of the opening phases of the Normandy Battle. At the regular time of the other formation was held, these men were on Furlough to the United States. Movie at the NAAFI.**

The Group War Diary had only one entry for October 20-23:

> **Very bad weather during this period. No flights were made to the far shore and only a few local flights were flown.**

October 22, 1944 [*Sunday*]

Hello Darling,

I know that I wasn't seeing "red." Your new stationery is clever. Not that I'm tired of blue and white but the idea is a good one. As long as the ink doesn't run, you're OK. Finally got around to handing us our Air Medals yesterday. It has been such a long time since I tried to masquerade as a soldier that when my name was called, I thought my legs would cave in. When I walked up and saluted my CO [*Commanding Officer*], I thought I'd pass out from fright. The most interested spectator at the presentation was George, the crow. He really stole the show. I couldn't help but laugh. He'd look up and appear as nonchalant about everything and if he was in someone's way, he'd step away as gingerly as you please. Our Group CO gave us a short speech. He's a Hell of a fine guy, and old airline pilot and swell as they come. He commended us for our fine work. No windbag, whatsoever, he speaks softly and briefly but he can make you feel so much at ease. So to top the day off, we went to town and celebrated, not boisterously, not too soberly, but pleasantly.

Gosh, Bette, the days are really passing. Fortunately, I've been resting since last Thursday. I am taking advantage of the change but I'm ready to get going again. I can't understand it but my mail isn't as I'd like it to be. Fortunately, I can always expect at least one per day from you but it has been a long time since I heard from Tony that it isn't funny. I'm sure he must be busy as Hell.

Most of the guys that went home are receiving pictures from their wives that they took while they were at Atlantic City. It gives you the funniest feeling. I can't help but feel almost unbearably jealous but again my consolation comes from the thought that someday someone will be jealous of you and I. Just look at the white sand, gay people (so much in love) and you know that the sun is shining, makes a guy think that some time all this mess is worthwhile just as long as we can get back to all of that. When I look at those pictures, I can't help but go off into a dreamy mood and wonder what our, yours and mine, leave will be like. It is wonderful to think that we will be able to do nothing but lounge around for who knows how long. Gad! I won't believe anything until it happens. Can't help but feel that sometimes I'm laboring under a persecution complex; everyone picks on me. But that feeling only comes from being in the Army and being away from everyone. (I'm waiting for Sammy Kaye's program to come on. I like to write while his music is on. Heard the football scores. It certainly does sound like a wild and woolly season!) (I meant to mention it before, damn, I'm getting so forgetful but I have been toying with the idea of sending you my Air medal. But since it is so close to Christmas season, I'm afraid of getting it lost.) (I'd like to bring it home personally!)

You asked me in your latest letter if I had ever noticed how often our thoughts run parallel. Yes I have. I have noticed it very often. And it is very understandable indeed. Isn't it natural that since we are so much in love, our thoughts should be mutual? There I go repeating myself over and over. But each of us has a set idea of what we'd like for the future. Since we both know each other as we do, we plan for each other. Those thoughts are due to intertwine. (I don't think that word is right.) The other night, I had a rather queer thought. Especially in view of other close relations, I thought it was a funny feeling. It wasn't in the gutter, believe me, but I couldn't help but feel that I'd be like a blushing bridegroom on our first night. Ordinarily, I wouldn't think like that but it seems like such a long time that we've been apart. Don't fret, Darling, the thought isn't contagious. Typically of us, it doesn't take long to overcome certain barriers, above all, the barrier of time. We know so well that our separation had done nothing more than to bring us closer together. Closer than we ever thought we'd be to any person. We have both confessed that. It is a wonderful confession, too — that of loving a person and missing her.

Can't understand it. My thoughts aren't running as quickly as I want them to. Ah! Here's that Kaye boy — what a swell way to relax. Ordinarily, when I write to you, I go on and on. The only time I stop is when I exhaust an idea. You know well that it takes pages for that. I hate the idea of having to stop in the middle and think of my next word.

Well Darling, I am going to close. (Kaye is playing, "A Fellow on a Furlough" (?)) Take care of yourself, Darling. Give my love to Mother. I love you and miss you terribly. May God Bless You. Love, Mike.

On October 22, according to the War Diary, there was one test flight, and 16 planes were sent to "southern England" for loading.

October 23, 1944 [*Monday*]

Hiya Baby,

Really smell like a woman on the make. Feel so good, clean and fresh. Right after supper, I felt so sleepy, I was ready for the sack but I got going, took a nice cold shower and here ah is — Got my first Christmas package from my brother, Ted. Seems my family isn't getting my mail as I wished they would. Didn't hear for 3 weeks until they got my letter to my brother, Tom. I can't understand it. Gives me a pain in the royal to think that my mail may be going astray.

I had forgotten for the while that you must have met Dan Smith. At any rate, he still hasn't shown up. I'm wondering if they booted him over to France. That "down under" isn't any Army expression or maybe it is but the term is used when someone refers to Australia. You know, Australia is down under the world. Look at a globe.

You know, Bette, I had to laugh at one of your expressions. You were answering my letter about the use of talcums, etc., and you said something like "we'll smell nice together." But I guess, that's as good a way to say it as any.

They announced something about starting a football team in this post. I'd like to go out for it but I'm afraid of the shape I'm in. If I could go thru' 2 months of good strenuous training, I'd take a good shot at it. The body can take lots of punishment if it is ready to handle it. Fortunately, basketball doesn't call for as much body contact. Ordinarily, I'd be ready to call it quits for all athletic activities on my part but since I have no other form of exercise, I'd take anything to lazing about. Before, Darling, one good summer season of good swimming would carry me easily thru' the winter. Gosh damn this miserably miserable weather. The desert for all its inconveniences had this beat by a million miles. You must tire of hearing me repeat this subject, Bette, but playing ball does so much for eliminating a lot of restlessness. Nights are so long here that a guy goes crazy just bulling all the time. It gets me mad as Hell to read of other outfits in the ETO that have already started their seasons and here we are sitting on our dead ass. I know well that I am in worse physical condition than I've ever been. Since I've been in the service, you saw me in my best shape while I was in Kansas City. Oh Well —

Things look good in the news these days, don't they? The way things look, seems as if the Pacific war will end before this one. They are doing a great job over there. They seem to have the brunt of American power there; that's the best reason for such good progress. My hopes of this Christmas at home have long since vanished in the winds. Lord knows, my tour of duty has long superseded the usual requirements for a lot of outfits. But I'm not going to bitch. For some unknown reason, I feel as if it won't be too long before I'll be home to you. I figure that as long as I keep saying that the time is bound to pass. But really, Darling, I don't feel too bad off. We have gangs of time left yet. Both of us are still plenty young and what we have to look forward to is worth waiting for. Lord knows, I couldn't love you nor miss you any more than I do. But it is a nice feeling. The kind of a feeling that makes everything and anything easy to take. I love you.

Cheerio, Darling, I've got a lot of rummaging to do. Want to see if I can sort out any of my stuff. I do that every so often.

Give my love to Mother. Take care of yourself, Darling. May God Bless You. Love, Mike.

War Diary, October 23-24:

> **October 23: Due to bad weather all flights were canceled to the continent. Two planes were used to tow gliders in the afternoon. Seven Enlisted men were sent on DS** [*detached service*] **to Greenham Common. Weekly dance was held at the American Red Cross.**
>
> **October 24: 17 plane resupply mission to the continent, four of which returned. Two planes administrative mission to the continent and return. Two planes XC and return. . . .**

The Group War Diary's entry for October 24 read:

> **Ready for command inspection. Weather still very bad. First day of restriction is in effect to bring all AWOLs** [*Absent Without Leave*] **over the entire United Kingdom. The movie** *Canterville Ghost* **was shown for the Enlisted and Officer personnel at the Junior Officers Mess this evening. Almost all planes arrived back even though the field began to close in.**

October 25, 1944 [*Wednesday*]

Good evening, Darling,

Forgive me if I just dash off a short note. How do you like this fancy writing paper. Received it today from Louise's Mother. Got a few other packages and I received a pair of wings from home. I had requested them a while back, finally got to me. If you can be patient a little longer, Darling, I'll send my ole pair off to you. I always promise but it takes me such a long time to get things done, doesn't it? Must be my Southern blood! Got a short note from Dan Smith, — seems as if he was busy but he'll be aheadin this way in a little while. Can't seem to think tonight. That's why I'm just dashing off little unimportant things. I had a rather rough day the other day so I tied on a slight bun last night. [*Incident of the bad weather trip after carrying wounded to England and then trying to get home to base!*] You see, Bette, you are going to marry a drunkard. This country would drive any airman to drink. Wish to Hell I could see the sun long enough to blind me momentarily. For that very damn reason, I just don't feel right. I guess the lack of mail is another reason. Can't understand it. Gives me a royal pain. A few of the guys had to stay in a few of these French towns. Everyone of them said that the hotels in these towns are just made for nothing else but love and its counterparts. It is no wonder that the French people think of sleep as merely a pastime.

Well, Darling, good night. I'm sorry I can't do better job. Give my love to Mother. Take care of yourself. I love you & miss you. May God Bless You. Love, Mike.

On October 25, 12 planes returned after staying the night on the Continent. The War Diary reported on that day that the regular dance was held in the NAAFI hall.

The Group War Diary for the same day read:

> **Second and last day of the restriction. Overcast weather. 22 aircraft returned from resupply and evacuation mission. A practice paratroops drop made locally in the afternoon.**

October 26, 1944 [*Thursday*]

Good Evening, Darling,

Here I am back again but I want to apologize for that horrible missile I sent last night. I just wasn't up to it or anything last night. I'm sorry, Darling. Well the mail started to roll in again this evening. I received your letters of the 4th and 14th. You can see that it took a Hell of a long time for that first one to get here. Gosh, Honey, I love you so much. It isn't that I just love you; I'm crazy about you. Funny but in the letter of the 4th you speak of a Series that is about to start and here it is the 26th, the season of baseball is lost in the record books and the football season is ½ over. It doesn't make much difference who censors the mail as long as he is an officer, the privilege (?) is not confined to 2nd Looies and above. You were asking me if I wanted any fruit. It's OK, Darling, to be without it. I don't mind. I am building up a good stock of "what I am without." That great day of my homecoming and I'll check that mental list and see to it that I make it all up. I imagine that as long as I've gotten along without that forbidden fruit, I can manage without edible fruit. Thanks for the thought, Bette. But I don't want you to go thru' all of that trouble.

I just checked that "green" letter of the 14 and I see that you wrote it on the 14th and it didn't get postmarked until the 17th. Fine work, isn't it? Letting a letter stay in the box for 3 days. Oh Well, why worry. It's only going to a guy overseas. Lord knows I wait for every day to pass, hoping that there will be a letter from you.

In one of my letters, I explained my plans. I told you why I wanted to spend our honeymoon (?) in New York. I know you don't mind if we do it that way. I think that you will be quite benefited if you go to Florida. The change will be of a good sort because it will give you a fresh start on your patience. What I mean is that it will be something new and you won't mind the months passing. As I said before that if I am on my way back, I will certainly find a way to tell you of that fact. I have tried to damper my optimism as much as I can but I do wish that plans stay as they are. If so, I believe that I might be able to see you after or just before you get back to KC. The four month season at Sarasota will be ideal for you. And at the middle of March you will get a good chance to see some of the big league ball clubs. I believe the Boston Red Sox train there every year. You needn't worry, Darling, nothing can interfere with our plans. You see, Darling, I'd like it if you can do everything you want because it will help you to pass the time away. In the meantime, it will make me happier to know that things are going easier for you and at the same time you are enjoying yourself. Don't let my optimism enlighten you too much but I think that they may give us something to shoot at and I am shooting. Gosh, Honey, I love you and miss you so much.

Bette, I am going to peel off. But I want to dash off a few more short notes. Again I want to apologize for that miserable letter last night. Those moods don't come too often — you know that!

Good night, Darling. Give my love to Mother. Take care of yourself. May God Bless You. Love, Mike.

War Diary entry, October 26:

> **One plane returned from a two-night RON in Belgium with the weather report. Lt. Dean O. Davis left for the Zone of the Interior** [*the continental United States*]. **No flying because of weather. Show at the new station theater.**

Group War Diary, October 26:

> **Resupply and weather mission to the far shore with 2 planes participating. Movie in the evening, *Two Girls and A Sailor*. As the restriction was lifted today the pass quota for the evening was filled within a short time.**

October 27, 1944 [*Friday*]

Good Morning, Darling,

Just thought I'd dash off a short note before I went out this morning. There is a good possibility that I may not be able to write this evening. I wish Dan would show up one of these days. I'd like to take him on one of my sightseeing tours. Well to go on. I do hope that my letters were clear enough. It is hard as Hell to write about one thing and know that there are so many other things I'd like to say. Things that would make us both happier although they are only suppositions. You'll have to watch out, Bette, I've held so much back that when I do get home, I'll talk like a machine. The only time I'll break down is when I'm asleep. Who knows how much of that I'll get! If I get too restless, I'll go to the nearest army camp, get a bed roll or some good itchy army blankets, make up a bed of stone in our hotel room and really pour the dreams on. It seems so funny to hear myself talk like that. Now that I recall how allergic I used to be to wool, it is funny. When I first got over, I could sleep on the bare ground or even on the hard floor of the ship. I guess it doesn't make much difference as long as you are tired enough. But I know that having your arms around me and having you near to me, will make all the difference. Ordinarily the transition from bachelorhood to marriage would be a hard one, but when a guy has been away as long as I have and will be away longer, it isn't difficult at all. Just to know that I'll be with you, the person I love so much, will make all of this fade with your first kiss — But I think it's best I don't keep talking like this so early in the morning. This is one of those mornings when a kiss would be like the fan of an angel's wing. I love you.

Speaking of books, and why I am changing the subject but — I have progressed well along the road of *The Apostle*. For lighter reading. I am reading Ring Lardner's *You Know Me, Al!* It's a story of a bush leaguer just breaking into the majors. All it is, is a series of letters written by the busher to his buddy. It really is clever and funny. I can just imagine the kind of yokel this Jack Keefe is.

We saw a damn good show last night. It was *2 Girls and A Sailor*. I guess it is one of the best shows I've seen yet. One thing that we really go for over here is musicals. Dramatic shows have to be really good to be enjoyable here. But just a chance to see Harry James and Xavier Cugat, Lena Horne, Jimmy Durante and a bunch of others is a treat for any GI. Back in civilian life, it was a different story because it was easy enough to go to the Paramount or Strand to see Kaye, Miller, or any of the name bands. There I go again, just babbling along.

Say, Bette, you must pardon my ignorance but what are pralines? As long as they have plenty of pecans in them, I'll like them. The fact that you mentioned pecans, made me positive that those — were something to eat.

Well, Hon, must close. Take it easy, Gal, only 2 more months to another Christmas — as they say in Brooklyn, "Wait 'til Next year." I hope that's the limit.

Give my love to Mother. May God Bless You. Love, Mike.

Following are the October 27-30 entries from the Squadron and Group War Diaries:

> **WD, October 27: 10 planes to Kemble for loads and return. Eight planes were used for local para-drops. One aircraft sustaining damage on landing when right landing gear collapsed. 1 plane XC and return.**
>
> **WD, October 28: 18 plane mission to the continent, 10 of which were loaded the day before at Kemble. One plane returned, 17 completing the mission. Two plane casualty mission to [*Prestwick*] and return. 316th Group Officers held a dance on the post.**
>
> **GWD, October 28: Slight drizzle in the morning, begin to clear and the sun came out for about three hours. Again it clouded and rained all afternoon. All planes returned here to Cottesmore on completion of mission to far shore. In the evening a dance was held at the Junior Officers Club, music by the 316th Troop Carrier Orchestra.**
>
> **WD, October 29: Two XC flights and return. The weather plane was sent to France.**
>
> **GWD, October 29: Very heavy fog lay over the field this morning. Cleared in the afternoon, only to rain in the afternoon and evening. Mission sent to far shore but were unable to land due to weather conditions.**
>
> **WD, October 30: Four planes were used to tow gliders. 11 plane mission to the continent. Six planes to southern England for loads to continent and return. Five men from the parachute department made a free jump, one man is in the hospital with a broken leg. . . . Halloween dance at the American Red Cross.**
>
> **GWD, October 30: Sun shining beautifully this morning and the hum of planes can be heard in preparation for take off. Excellent weather for the newly formed football team which has a good scrimmage today. Little excitement on the field when 21 Enlisted Men (riggers) made free parachute jumps over the field. One broken leg and 2 broken ankles resulted from the jump. Eight plane mission to the far shore carrying mail and ammunition and arrived back early in the afternoon.**

October 31, 1944 [*Tuesday*]

My Darling,

You must forgive me for not writing these last few days but as it is so many things prevented me from doing so. I love you. Gosh, Honey, I'm sorry that you aren't getting my mail. That is, I think, because of the Christmas rush of packages, etc. It is too damn bad that they push us so far to the background. My family has been complaining of the same thing. When I heard last, they hadn't heard from me since D-Day in Holland, which was in the middle of September sometime [*September 17-26*]. I do hope they rectify that condition.

Now to carry on. Friday evening, Dan Smith walked in and he stayed until Sunday evening. Naturally, as long as he was here, I couldn't leave him and go about my business. I took him along with me Saturday and showed him some of the sights. He came at such an inopportune time that I had to borrow money left and right to treat him to drinks at our bar. It wasn't an easy task because most of the outfit was broke. As anxious as I was to see him, I must admit that the visit was a disappointment to me. I felt as if I was forever pretending. In my short time overseas, I have seen and done a few things. Every time I opened my yap about our type of aircraft, he'd boot me about B-24s. Constantly, he reminded me of the dangers of flying — all sorts of stuff that is routine and natural to us. If I felt the way he did, I'd quit and yet all he does or has to do is fly 4 hours a month and get his flying pay time in. The last time I flew only 4 hours in a month was in February 1943. I'd go crazy if that was all I had to do. Besides that he's on detached service from Materiel Training Command at Denver, Colo. Which means that when his 6 months (they may extend it to 9 months) are over, he is sure to be heading back to the States or maybe do a short tour in the Pacific. But Hell, once that is over, he is finished. He doesn't fly into combat. Then he kept talking about home and how much he missed it. Who doesn't? But why keep telling yourself that you do. — If I did that I'd have been in a strait jacket months ago. I know it is rough but what the Hell can you do about it? Don't get me wrong, it was nice to see him but his mode of conversation wasn't what I enjoyed. Whereas with Harry, we can discuss mud and make it gold. To boot I owe ½ of this month's salary. I'm sorry if I seem to be crying on your shoulder, Darling, but I'm afraid it was all a bit of a letdown.

I had a chance to visit Rheims, not so long ago. It is the center of the champagne world. (I didn't have a drink.) But such companies as Piper-Heidsieck, Geo. Mumms, and many more have great big warehouses there. It is a lovely city but the most impressive thing I saw was the world famous cathedral at Rheims. It was too bad that I was unable to go inside but I got a good panoramic view of it. I believe it is done in the Renaissance style with large flying buttresses and gargoyles. (Maybe it's Gothic, I forget my architecture.) All the figures of Saints that are on top of this large, beautiful structure are in gold. All in all, it was a picture well worth remembering.

Gosh, Bette, it seems like ages since I told you how much I love you. If I could reach the fathoms of my heart, and soul, you'd realize how much you mean to me. As I said before, I've seen so much and yet the primary and most innermost thought that passes thru' my brain is, how prettier and nicer all of this would be if I had Bette at my side. Everything I do, I do with you. In my uglier, fanatically stupid moods, you disappear from me because of the mental shame I must endure. Physically there is nothing wrong but when my mind drops into the hellacious depths of misery, I don't want you to be included. You are my most beautiful thoughts. I cannot be justified to share you with my Mr. Hyde. If I could put this into really understandable words, you would know what I mean. As you so aptly and simply put it, it all sums up to the non-complex words of I love you and miss you terribly.

Well, Darling, I say Good Night. I do hope my mail reaches you sooner than it has. I've asked for a day off tomorrow so I can get some things done and catch up with my mail.

Give my love to Mother. Take care of yourself, Darling. May God Bless You. Love, Mike.

The Squadron War Diary entry for October 31 read:

> **Six planes returned from RON on the Continent. Four planes were used to tow gliders. Two gliders were slightly damaged. 1 XC and return. One officer and two EM on rest leave. Show at the new station theatre. Pay call.**

The following from the 316th Group War Diary summarizes the activities for the month of October:

> **The month that has past has been one of routine flights, many of them completed despite the most inclement weather. Only an insignificant few were aborted. The narrative of these flights when reduced to words seems of little consequence; "... A flight of fifty planes flew to Brussels today." Fifty planes to Brussels! That fifty planes flew and landed at Brussels today and returned: is just an incident of this month's flying. Yet thousands of pounds of mail were delivered; millions of pounds of gasoline and ammunition were left there, and perhaps lives of untold men were saved.**

November 1, 1944 [*Wednesday*]

My Darling,

Here ah is again! Got ready to do a little basketball playing and someone had the audacity to push an airplane on the court. So rather than just lazing around, I'd rather dash off this note. We were sitting around over a good bull session and for once the discussion wasn't about women. We were talking about the bright (?) future and its possibilities. To hear most of the fellows talk, I don't feel too badly because at least I think I have a job when I get out of this mess. I have unless Sears changes its manner.

Honestly, though most of the fellows don't feel too enthusiastic. Perhaps the outlook isn't a fun one but remembering the treatment of the last war vet, we'll need some good brain to give us a say in things. I guess it would be a good idea if I join both the VFW [*Veterans of Foreign Wars*] and the [*American*] Legion. There are so many things that the guys think of, it would surprise most people who feel that GIs are merely a bunch of morons or a close resemblance. It is a most comforting thought to know that our futures, as bleak as we paint them, are filled with people like yourself and the wives and fiancees of the other guys. You would realize what all of you mean to us and how big a part of our ideas you take, if you could just sit in on one of these sessions. Personally, I'm as pleased as punch. I think that you and I will fare beautifully.

You'll pardon me a moment, Darling, if I go slightly religious for the moment. St. Paul in his letters writes of marriage in this way. He speaks of the love of the Christ and then goes on, "Even thus ought husbands also love their wives as their own bodies. He who loves his own wife, loves himself. For no one ever hated his own flesh; on the contrary, he nourishes and cherishes it, as Christ also does the Church (because we are members of His body, made from His flesh and from His bones.) For this reason a man shall leave his father and mother, and shall cleave to his wife; and the two shall becomes one flesh. This is a great mystery — I mean in reference to Christ and to the Church. However, let each one of you also love his wife as he loves himself."

It may seem a funny way to say it but that is the way I want my love for you. Those words above express the depth that I seek for you and I. We have a good start but the years will make it more marked. What I have read of Paul, he has done much to make religion a broad minded thing. Listen to what he says of intercourse — "do not deprive each other, except perhaps by consent, for a time, that you may give yourselves to prayer; and return together again lest Satan tempt you because you lack self-control." I don't like to keep harping on religion; I am merely using this as examples of what is perfection. My own words cannot cover such things as aptly as those [that] were spoken. I love you.

Darling, I must rush off. Take care of yourself, Darling. I'll try to dash off another note later on. So Long. May God Bless You. Love, Mike.

November 1, 1944 [*Wednesday*]

Good Evening, Darling,

It is one of those rare, beautiful evenings. The kind of night that drives a man in love to madness. But no sense to stay on that road of thought, I'd probably pass that mode of thought over to you. After I finished my letter this afternoon, I went back to that bull session and quite differently we went over to women. Of course, that isn't the worst subject in the world but — It's a great thing to think that women play such a big part in man's life. Oh, you lovely creature! To go on — I received your letters of the 20th yesterday so I'll see what I can say to them. I do hope that by now you have started to receive my mail. Whenever I get a chance, I write twice a day as I did and am doing today. That I hope will make up for the days that I miss. Unfortunately, when mail is lax as it has been, it is difficult to think of too many things to say.

It is tough to bore yourself to tears, isn't it? The way I counteract that is that I never reread my letters, hence the mistakes, etc. But since you ask me how I stand your "boring" letters, don't you think I have the same privilege to ask you? After all, Darling, it isn't so much what we say but the fact that we are thinking of each other. Lord knows that has been proven by the fact that we write so regularly. If you think that you are boring me, which you don't, just ask questions or talk about anything or everything. Even such questions as your hats. Darling, you know I always liked big ones on your blonde head. Since I am so tall, it doesn't make much difference, the size, I mean. But I think that they are most becoming to you. Personally, I don't care for hats and it wouldn't make any difference to me if you didn't wear one but if you must, a large one, please (and just a dash of sugar). Pardon my rambling but that "just a dash . . ." reminded me of something I tell so often. You know the story of our bottle is one of great memories to us, even if I have never seen the bottle, but whenever we talk about our women, I have never missed telling of the bottle and its significance — minus some facts reserved for you and I. A lot of water has passed under our bridge of time, hasn't it, Bette? And with each passing day my love for you grows stronger and stronger. I keep praying that our patience will not be strained too long. Surely if things keep on course, it can't be too far off. Of course, again we must miss these wonderful holidays that are coming up on us too soon but mayhaps it, this separation, will make us better people. Those oft-repeated phrases must be used; someday we will be sitting under our Christmas tree and laugh about these days. And laugh I will.

You spoke of the book you finished — I just got thru' *The Apostle*. It was a wonderful book. Not so long ago, I could never sit down to such literature because of the type of reading it was. Now I can sit for hours and pour over such things and really concentrate and know what is being said. I just don't read and accept. I read and tear things apart and wonder of the truth and stability of words. I pick things apart, run it parallel to my own thoughts and actions and see how they are allied to the author's or the character of whom he is speaking. Damn good idea, too. One thing I didn't understand in your letter, you were speaking of *Earth and High Heaven*. You said that after reading of those commandos, it would be better to meet me in New York. Since I didn't read the book, I am in a bit of a fog. Some clarification on the subject, if you please!

One thing where you missed the point. You said that it would be nice if I could be sent to Ft. Wayne so that we could take up where we left off. Regardless of where I am sent, we will do just that. After all, Darling, this is just a void. An emptiness that is just a bad dream because we are now sharing nothing. Whatever I have seen or done, I can't help but to remember; but they are not memories with you. When I left you in Ft. Wayne, I didn't say "Good Bye" but "So Long" — Those days were to last until we were together again, where, how, why or when, mean nothing only that we will meet again is important. Do you see what I am trying to say. Darling, we haven't lost anything; we gained a lifetime, a lifetime together. My leaving had changed the whole complexion of so many things. We have had so much time to think that we can never lose because we realize so much more what we missed so much and what we still want so much. My leaving has added a responsibility to both of us that might have been just a useless meaning. We accept each other for what we are and not for the fact that both of us are just around and take each other and our actions for granted. Yes, My Love, we will continue our old life but with more maturity, more depth and more security than before. I love you.

Good night, Bette. You are my love — I'm afraid I've run out of words. Thrown for a loss. Take care of yourself. May God Bless You. Love, Mike.

On November 1, the War Diary recorded, six planes flew cross country to Prestwick and returned, and there was one local navigational flight.

November 2, 1944 [*Thursday*]

Good Morning, Darling.

Just thought I'd dash off a line this AM. There isn't too much to talk about so perhaps when I'm finished you can include this in your boring section. Aha! Great day. Prosperity again — you know I've been paid because I finally got some air mail envelops. Just like every other sucker, the gambling instinct took a few of my pounds. But I'm not too badly off. I've promised myself that I would ease up this month and next month so that I'll have some extra change for myself for Christmas. I always feel as if I'm not too bad off as long as I have the usual dough going home. Hell, Darling, I don't worry about the money angle. I'm sure we can do OK. From what I hear in these parts, they really celebrate Christmas in the right manner.

Gosh, Bette, I don't know what I want to say this morning There are so many suppositions that I could write about but I'm afraid I'll get too much of an enthusiastic pen and run away with myself. I was just thinking of you in Sarasota. I'm afraid I'm kinda' jealous of you. One thing that excites me is that someday I'll be able to do the same thing. Just think, a pair of shorts, a nice balmy breeze, skin kissed by the sun, plenty of exercise, no eating and gangs of lazing about. You know, Darling, one summer, I had my two-week vacation and I didn't feel like going anywhere. So I just spent 2 weeks in the sun, did a little night clubbing in the evenings but the sun the next day always helped to drain the alcohol out of my system. When I got back to work, the gang thought I had gone to Miami. Hell, I was as black as the ace of spades. I always feel lots healthier in the summer. So if I should get home during the winter, don't think badly of my extra weight. I guarantee to shed it during the heat spells. Gad! Bette, it is going to be a wonderful thing to do all these things with you.

You asked me in one letter if I realized how wonderful life will be with me. Not just me but you and I together. The thoughts of it send tingles down my spine. If I don't get too many setbacks that time can't be too far off. It's true that this war is far from over but fortunately for us we haven't made that trifle interfere with us too much. All it has done is kept us apart. Of course, now that seems so big but Hell we can just skip it. There I go again, saying the same things over and over again. You can see that I've been taking life easy. To be honest about it, since the opportunity affords itself, I don't intend to mess up on it. Not exactly sitting back on my laurels but I think I deserve a little freedom of my own. Can't really call it that. I've got gangs of clothes to wash. You know, Darling, when I get home, I think I'll take all the under clothing I have now and just burn it, and then go out and get all new stuff. Gonna go now. But I'm sure I'll be back later in the day. So long for now. I love you and miss you. May God Bless You. Love, Mike.

November 2, 1944 [*Thursday*]

My Dearest,

You must wonder about my excessive enthusiasm but really, Darling, it is most distressing to hear that you aren't getting my mail. Lord knows it isn't because I'm not writing but because something is screwed up somewhere and I don't like it. Most of the fellows have the same complaint. It's not funny. As I said last night, whenever I have the free time, I write twice per day. I like to talk to you, Darling, but I don't like the idea that you don't hear from me. As I again have said before, what the Hell, it's only from a soldier overseas, why worry.

But I can't complain really. I received 3 letters from you today, 18th, 22, 23. Of course, your letters don't arrive in the right succession but I can't bitch as long as I get them. You speak of seeing Mrs. Hooks about that Florida deal and then I won't hear the results of that until your next batch of letters arrive. It all sounds like those continued next week affairs, doesn't it? Obviously your Dr. Bergman is quite a chap. Give him my best and tell him to take good care of you. I need you more that he needs your fees. You are definitely right in your supposition that men cannot always manage when they are away from their women. I'm inclined to believe that the married men are less faithful than the bachelors. But since men and people vary so much it is difficult to pinpoint many things. Ordinarily, men in the circumstances as we are in, cannot possibly do anything except keep busy. As long as a man's hands are busy, the less his mind will revolve.

There are many things in these last few months that could not help but divert our attentions to nothing but our work. I believe that generally speaking the GIs in the States have more opportunity to goof off from their obligations. I've found that many things over here aren't worthwhile. There is not enough sufficient common ground to approach anyone. The customs and mannerisms of foreign people cannot [*possibly*] encourage changes. Whatever changes have occurred to me are due to nervous strain and my being away from you. During my periods of strain, I am totally blank.

Once the let down comes, a good drunk puts me straight. When I have time on my hands as I have now, my thoughts are all of you. (Believe me, Darling, even as in this discussion I cannot help but flatter you — it is all so true!) My other free time is used for reading, cleaning, and whatever recreations I can find. Since I've resolved to abstain from alcohol, I am in much better shape. (Just as you — if I didn't love you, miss you and need you so much, I wouldn't have to take shots — not the needle.)

I received a couple of packages today. One from an old friend, a girl I used to work with. Her fiancee, my old fishing partner, is in Italy. She sent me gangs of hair oil and other toilet articles. Since I never use anything but water on my hair, I donated the oil for common use in my room. We are all very cooperative that way. One of the guys received a bottle of Yardley's Lavender after-shave lotion. Gad! It felt good. All for one and one for all. My brother, Tom, sent me a book, *Out of the Silent Planet*. Since I've already started the book, *The Last Adam*, I'll have to wait to give you a review on that one. Reading has proved a fine pastime for me. But there I go again. Will I never stop repeating myself but I guess after a few years, a guy can't help myself. If I were with you, I'd tell you a million times over how much I love you, so I guess you can't blame me for the repetition.

Your letter of the 22nd had a definite perfume odor. It was great. All this may sound silly but I know that you realize my power of imagination. So I put my nose to the letter, closed my eyes, — Darling, you arms felt so good around me. No. I'm not batty, but a dream can be so near true.

I captured one thought that you mentioned only today. You said, "I thought that the first year you were gone would be the hardest; but, Mike, it certainly wasn't — I suppose it is the knowledge that it is a matter of weeks or months before you'll be home. It is the anxiety of it all — The uncertainty of the certain." That last sentence or phrase was ideal and definitely pinpoint. We both know that someday I'll be home but when — But to get back to your first few lines — every time I hear of some sort of rumor or of some good news, I can't help but anticipate ahead of myself. I can't help but let my imagination run away with my good sense. Each month that passes is another one gone under that bridge. I keep thinking of things that are now pending and I get more and more excited. I know that I've done so much, — how much more can I do to warrant a leave? So many things seen so unfair. The thing that hurts most is that it doesn't bring me to you. We are in love, My Lovely Darling, and for this lifetime that we are in love, we shall always feel this way — even when we are apart but a minute. It is normal for us because we are made so emotionally equal. You see, Darling, our love is so perfect. I'll leave you on those thoughts. Feel like sleeping on them myself. I love you and miss you.

Good night, Bette. Give my love to Mother. May God Bless You. Love, Mike.

There was one six-plane and one two-plane mission to the Continent and return on November 2, according to the Squadron War Diary. Seven planes flew to southern England for loading but were not loaded because no men were available. And four new planes were assigned to the 37th Squadron that day, bringing the total to 24.

The Group War Diary for November 2 read:

> **Missions carried out to the far shore today and returning ships carried casualties back to England. Movie held for the Enlisted Men with Peter Lorre, *The Mask of Dimitries*.**

November 3, 1944 [*Friday*]

Hiya Darling,

I promised I'd be back so here ah is. The poor old censor is going to have a fit, but what the Hell that's his job. You may have noticed that I never commented very much about the coming elections. As I said before, I haven't been able to read much about it. However, my reasons for voting are quite limited I must admit. Now that I have heard [*Norman*] Thomas and Dewey speak, I know that I was best off if I hadn't voted at all. Each day over AFN [*Armed Forces Network*], they have one of [*the*] candidates speak. I haven't heard FDR yet but if I judge from Dewey's speech, I can imagine Thomas has been the only one who spoke with any sense. You said that there was a lot of mud slinging. I am afraid that that was an understatement. What the hell are they campaigning for? Obviously, it is merely to see how deep they can drag each other into the political mire. Surely they can't expect anyone sensible to swallow that junk. We know what has happened. What we want to know is what is to happen or at least what can we expect. We all have our suspicions of Pearl Harbor and definite beliefs of the New Deal's policies, domestic and foreign. We know that we are expected to stay prepared but what are going to be the possibilities for the future; what is going to be done for veterans and their families. No! not to be prophets about the whole thing but what are their ideas and speculations. But, of course, the iron is cast — we'll have to wait for Nov. 7th and 1944, '45, '46 '47 &'48. Just another 4 years out of so many of a lifetime.

"Love is true friendship set on fire!" Very lovely observation. To divert from that and add to what you said below that, Darling, let's look at ourselves. We may not believe in love at first sight but . . . Can you think of any specific incident or moment that gave us an inkling of how our friendship would end up? Do we really know what the word love means? Actually, I mean — Perhaps I've said that wrong — Love covers a million and one things. Ours, we accept as a mutual agreement to so many things. I mean it isn't because you like the way I part my hair, or, I because I like the way you wear your clothes. I believe that we will never know until we are separated finally in death. Those many little things scrambled in the salad of life will be the finished product of love. I can't seem to word this right. To do so, I'd have to write volume upon volume. The four words, "I love you, Darling" are used merely to eliminate those volumes of words, and put them into a simple sentence.

So you see, we will never know what caused that first attraction; maybe it was your height and blonde hair; maybe it was my manner of speech; my smile, my height — who knows. All we know [*is*] that now we are content with each other. That everything we want to do, we want to do together. Regardless of how big or small, we want to do them together. Is that not enough to insure our love? Is it really necessary to remember what was the first thing to bring us together? Did we not accept at the time for then and now that everything was natural and it will be for the rest of our lives? This love of ours, like so many other millions, is a thing deeper than we will ever dare to search. As I said before, the nicest indication was the natural inclination for the both of us to say, "Yes."

We never thought of circumstances and never will because I think from the first night, we both knew, subconsciously, that everything was right. Everything will be natural for us always, My Dearest, because we are made that way. It is not with difficulty that I say this but with joy because with each word, I can recount every memory, every exotic moment, every lovely sacrifice of body and soul. We never questioned each other's faults; we never will, because one will overcome the other. My Dearest, I am so much in love with you that I cannot help but be exalted by the thought of you and I.

The guys think that I am crazy because I write so often and so much, but they don't realize the pleasure I can get from talking to my beloved, to tell her that everything is as it always was and always will be; to assure her that my love grows stronger as the days pass. It is like saying that I feel so close to you. This, the pen, is my only outlet for the accumulation of these many months of emotion; emotions I should have shared physically with you. In the physical sense, they, the emotions, would have been dispersed spiritually to both of us. No need for that nervousness, that slight creeping of impatience but we cannot help but be human there, can we? But all this pent up feeling will let loose, not with someone else, it can't, but with each other on that glorious day when God sees fit to join us again. Whatever recreation we seek and find is merely a slight diversion — only being one will be <u>our</u> pinnacle of happiness. I love you and miss you. — Good night, Darling. May God Bless You. Eternally yours, Mike.

November 3, 1944 [*Friday*]

My Dearest,

   Back again! Luckily, it's a good day for making babies and on days like this, I have nothing to do but think of that wonderful theme. Heard Glenn Miller's "Ole Black Magic." I'm afraid, Darling, that I'm still that sentimentalist. That song brings back memories of hamburgers and malted milks, you and I laughing, dancing and loving. So many things, so many things that bring the odor of perfume and powder to my nostrils — The song in the background and you and I jabbering about everything — the song still further in the background and you and I not caring if the bottom of the world should fall out. The loveliest of all dreams woven together by a song and us.

   Later, the time changes, we have said our "So Long," the "so long" to last how long (?), and I am winging my way across the Atlantic. There we are just a crew of men in a big plane, watching wave after wave pass over an undetermined amount of gallons of water and over the intercom someone decides to sing — we can all hear it, that "Ole Black Magic." — Still later, the monotonous throb of the engines, no more water, different men, different terrain sand dunes and just plain sand passing by at a definite rate of speed, no thoughts and maybe a million different thoughts — someone turns to intercom and decided to sing — "An elevator starts to climb — That Ole Black Magic." [*Bill Baker and the trip to India.*] — Long, long after, England and still that tune goes on — how can anyone forget what it meant to him? My Darling, I love you —

   Now that you ask, Bette, I think that when (?) I come home it will be by boat. I'd like to make it by plane but that isn't for me to decide. At any rate, the change will be well worth it. Who cares how he gets home as long as he does! Of course, anything would seem slow after riding these fat geese all over the world. But they can give me a rubber boat or a pair of water wings and I'll try as hard as Hell!

   Darling, I don't see why the New York State Health Department won't accept your health certificate. As long as it is signed by a Doctor, there is no reason to doubt it. As far as having one, I think that that is one of the greatest improvements of medical precautions. It tends to reduce certain deficiencies. . . . Precaution is a damn good means of preventing further distress. There is more of your letter I'd like to answer but I am reserving it for a later letter. I must dash off a short note of thanks for my packages. Those are obligations I hate to let pass unnoticed.

Well, My Sweet One, I leave you for a while. Not too long, I hope. Give my love to Mother. May God Bless You. Love, Mike.

War Diary entry, November 3:

> **Weather ship sent to continent. All other flying was canceled because of weather.**

Group War Diary entry, November 3:

> **For some time now the group has been interested in forming a camera club for those especially interested in photography as the facilities for developing such film taken by amateurs is poor. The first meeting was held in Group S-2 today and plans are on their way.**

November 4, 1944 [*Saturday*]

Hello Darling,

Back again! You must think that by this time, I am or must be finished saying what I want to say. But as I warned you before, I'm a wind bag from way back when. It was rather noisy in the barracks but most of the fellows have disappeared, thank God! One of the fellows in the outfit is getting married so that accounts for a lot of the peace and quiet.

I just dashed off a few notes to Lucy and Tom. I must have asked Tom a million and one questions about St. Paul, etc. It gives us a good common ground for discussion. Besides he knows more about such things than I'll ever remember. Say, Bette, this is a long way off but when it does happen, I want you to promise to contact my family. A while back, I asked a buddy of mine to contact you by mail and give you some info' about my prospects, etc. I didn't ask him to write to my parents because he is nearer to you than NY. Besides I didn't want to impose on him too much. So if you will, Darling, pass whatever he tells you over to my family. I think you mentioned it to me a while back but I heard "A Fellow on a Furlough." It really is a swell song. The words are swell. Funny how the way a song can tear a guy's insides out and make him feel as melancholy as Hell. Don't mind my rambling on, I'm not even leaving room for paragraphing or punctuation, just talking. You don't mind, do you? It is a swell day and I'm sure you must be wondering why I'm taking life so easy. No reason except that things are quiet all around so I do as the Romans do and resort to my life of leisure. What better way is there to pass life away but to sit here and speak to you?

A few of the married men of the outfit have been fiddling around with plans for their future homes. It's nice feeling but I'd rather sit back and wait. It will probably be a little while before we can build our own home. There will be so many different improvements that I shudder to think of them. Besides, instead of a garage, we'll probably have an airplane hangar. Darling, one request I'd like to make. When I do get home and we finally settle down to housekeeping, please don't try to force any dehydrated food on me. I'll take my potatoes out of the dirt, my beef off the shank of a cow and anything else they try to can. Personally, I've had all the C and K rations I'd like to have for the rest of my life.

Well, Honey, that's all I have to say for now. I hope I can get back later — No promise, just a hope. Give my love to Mother. Take care of yourself. I love you and miss you. May God Bless You. Your Lover, Always, Mike.

The "weather ship" returned on November 4, according to the War Diary. The entry continued by noting one flight to Prestwick hauling casualties, and two local navigational flights.

The Group War Diary entry for that day read:

> **36 aircraft carried personnel of the 82nd Airborne on Mission "Zipper" to the far shore. In the evening the movie *Moonlight and Cactus* with the Andrews Sisters was shown.**

November 5, 1944 [*Sunday*]

Good Evening, Darling,

I am sorry that I didn't write later in the day yesterday, but a matter of happy importance arose, so we had to take the situation in hand. I couldn't write earlier today because I was so busy and I'm afraid I might make this a short note. My eyes feel like a reservoir of tears. I should have taken a shower when I got in this evening but I'm afraid I couldn't survive that either. Fortunately, the Army doesn't permit but one person in a bed. I don't know who would be able to stand me but myself and I am so damn weary I don't give a damn. But it really isn't as bad as I paint the picture.

I received your letter of the 24th and your picture and the score card from the Series. One of the fellows is looking at it now. That picture you sent me is the first one I stole from you. I still have it in my wallet. Darling, I love you so much.

I've already told you what I think of the Florida deal. Go right ahead, Darling, really the change will do you a world of good. You needn't worry. I won't be home by the 15th of Dec. The prospects don't look so good now, so I don't want to try to encourage you. Getting out of KC will do you a lot of good because it won't remind you so much of the many things we did together. You can keep those memories in your mind. In the meantime, you'll get a chance to see something different. It won't hurt you in the least. As a matter of fact, the sun ought to help. A little running around on the beach, if it is possible, will take out some of that excess energy. Don't worry, Bette, I'll find you. As long as I have your address, I won't have a worry.

You said something about taking that Wassermann. But that isn't what I am referring to but to your mention of your 22 years of age. Darling, do you realize that both of us are nearing our next birthday. Your 23rd is on the 19th of March; and mine (24) is on the 28th. (24 years of age, Gad! I am really advancing on the years.) But I am hoping that if things stay as they are, I hope it will be a very, very happy birthday for both of us. I am almost planning a wedding on the same date. But this is really supposition. What I really mean, wouldn't it be nice if we could have it that way? Who knows, the fates play funny tricks sometimes.

Darling, I must really close. I hate to leave in the middle of this but my eyes are leaden. I am going to try to read a little and then I'll pound my ole sack. I love you so very much.

Give my love to Mother. They tell me that the Christmas season is really sunny and warm in Florida. Please do go — if you are waiting for my opinion — that's it.

Good night, Love. May God Bless You. Yours Always, Mike.

War Diary entry, November 5:

> **One 18 plane mission to the continent for the purpose of transporting A/B [*Airborne*] troops and their equipment [*OPERATION ZIPPER*]. Two plane resupply mission to the continent and return. Football game in the afternoon, Cottesmore won 6-0. . . .**

The Group War Diary entry of November 5 read:

> **As the last days of October drew to a close, a football team was formed from members of the Group. Daily practice was held and the team was soon whipped into shape. The team's first game was played today despite the heavy rain and wind during the morning and early afternoon which damaged two gliders. Almost all of the personnel of the field turned out to support the team "Berger's Bouncers" and although the feeling was skeptical regarding the outcome of the game as it was the first game, Berger's Bouncers came through and won 6-0.**

November 6, 1944 [*Monday*]

Good Evening, My Lovely Darling,

Received your letter of the 28th of Oct. And I must say, that is truly good service. But

I still can't understand that my mail is still lacking. I do hope that the next time I hear from you that you will have better info' for me. Well, Darling, I decided to bath this evening. The water felt good until I started to get under it. Gad! Woman, did I freeze? Now, I'm sorry I was so tired last night. But at any rate, it was tonight or never. I kept my word last night. After I finished your letter, I hit the sack and read for about an hour. I was dead to the world by 9:30. I was really enjoying the sleep until some lousy son of a — came in and awakened me early. So it is early this evening and the first opportunity I've had to write to you. I love you or have I said that before?

Two thoughts running parallel, the same strain. Last night, I mentioned one reason why you should go to Fla. Today, your letter mentions that very same reason. So I answered your question before I knew that you were going to ask it. It isn't selfish of you to want some new environment. Lord knows, I know that we covered a lot of KC. We saw and did most of the things that we wanted to do. The new scenes will be enjoyable and the time will pass quickly because of that. We will still have our memories of KC. It will take a lifetime to forget them.

Darling, I don't think it is the shots that are making you blank. I think it is more that you aren't getting any mail. Whatever little I might say, it still gives you something to answer to. As far as your weight goes, I don't think you'll get over 125 for a long time. Not that I'm bragging but I think I'll have a lot to do with your gaining weight. And I will try my damnedest.

Talk about blankness. I guess I must still be tired because I don't feel too talkative tonight. I think it is because of a slight strain. Getting around here is a lot rougher than the desert stuff. Just knocks the living Hell out of a guy. I've changed my way, too. I am not going to touch a drop of liquor until after Christmas. More or less as a sacrifice, to thank That Guy Upstairs for keeping me in good shape for so long. I have been thinking of taking a pass after the 1st of the year and heading for Scotland or Ireland and take a change from this easy life. I can't wait for the holidays to come and go because I feel that this will be my last away from home. Not only for me but for a lot of guys like myself. Yes, Darling, I know it is repetitive but I feel the same way that you do. I don't feel like doing anything unless I do it with you.

I was reading about a poll that was taken at a fighter base over here. About 75% of the guys said that they considered the time overseas and the Army as merely a waiting period. A lesser of two evils, I guess I can put myself in the same class. It would have to be an awfully attractive offer to keep me in this Army and to be part of this life of freedom (?).

Well, Bette, that's it for now. Think I'll do a little more reading and then that dear ole sack. Give my love to Mother.

I love you and miss you. May God Bless you. Ever Yours, Mike.

War Diary, November 6:

One plane returned from RON on the continent. One plane mission

to France. 14 planes to Ramsbury for loads and return. Dance at the American Red Cross.

That same day's Group War Diary read:

> **More aircraft sent out on "Zipper" mission today. In the evening a dance was held at the Red Cross Club for the Enlisted Men, and as many of the members of the orchestra were flying, the music was furnished by the Victrola courtesy of the Red Cross. Guests for the evening were the ATS and WAAFs.**

November 7, 1944 [*Tuesday*]

Good Evening, Darling,

It may sound as gooish as Hell but honestly Bette, I do love you so very much. I had a chance to do a lot of thinking today and the more I think that way, the stronger I realize my love for you. But I'll save that for later in the letter. Still don't seem to be catching up on my rest. Poured into my sack early last night but found that I was restless and warm but these early sackings are leaving me greatly refreshed in the AM. Guess the elections are going on and tomorrow will find us with FDR again in the saddle. We are going to listen to the return as late as our strength will allow us. I don't think that I'll be able to stay up very late. At any rate, tomorrow will be a new leaf in our country's history.

This is what I was dreaming of today. We were floating along and I found that Morpheus was taking a slight hold on me. I rested my head and soon after found myself lost in a whirl of pleasantry. It seemed that we were somewhere off the coast of Canada, and we were heading for LaGuardia [*Airport*]. I don't remember who my pilot was, but whoever it was knew I was from NY so he told me to send a message to the LaG tower and tell them whatever I wanted. It was going to be personal, of course. I was so nervous that I was hardly able to touch my [*transmitting*] key but I got started finally — It was something like this. — "Will you please call Glenmore 2-2289 and tell Miss Lucy Ingrisano that her brother, Mike, is coming home soon." — B (more to follow). Then I went on — "ETA (Estimated Time of Arrival) your station, 1501 (3:01 PM), How does the Statue of Liberty look?" It seems we were going to stay in New York just to refuel and we were heading for somewhere in Pennsylvania. I made my pilot promise that he would "buzz" my home in Brooklyn. And boy! Did he do it. We showed my folks my nose number and all — The next thing I remember was a cab pulling up to 142 Somers Street. I was so grateful that I tearfully fell on my knees and kissed Mother Earth. The next thing I recall, I was shaking uncontrollably while Tom tied the final knot. Then it went on; you and I were walking down Broadway trying to find some service ribbons for me. I had my overseas bars on plus my wings and Presidential Citation but that was all. Then we found whatever I needed. I was pleased as punch because you put the ribbons on my chest. Then we were sitting somewhere having dinner and as much as we wanted privacy, it was impossible, generals, colonels, and all sorts of rank came up to me and kept asking about my experiences. — It ended there. I was awakening by a bump and I was shaking from anxiety. Coming back to reality was a stunning shock but I was happy because I could still dream like that. Believe me, my Bette, all of that didn't take me any longer than 15 minutes.

To get back to what I say is gooey. It isn't really but to some inert person it might be — I don't know who the hell reads these letters of mine but let him endure all this. We keep (We, I mean the gang in my room) discussing so many things. Sure, we are a gang of sentimentalists. I believe we have a good reason to be. It isn't a matter of self-pity. What good American guy doesn't feel the same way. For some men, this life is ideal. As the expression goes, "They found a home in the Army." Personally, I am too eager to see our country go on and I want to be a part of the reason for the increase in morale, happiness, and population back there. Good will is just a two-worded hypocrisy to me. I've seen too much of that "good will" distorted to serve one's purpose. But that hardly tells you what I am trying to say. The core of my words is that all these little things makes me yearn so much for the tenderness of your arms. Whatever comfort I've needed, I know I could never find over here. I've never experimented. I've always found that my thoughts of you could serve the purpose. I've had to resort to prayer a lot of times. Don't misunderstand my purpose in saying that, Dearest. I've cursed my own weaknesses. I've asked help from that Guy Upstairs so often to give me strength to combat my sometimes distorted way of living. Don't mistake my piety as an example for you. I am doing these many things for my own soul. I'll never forget what happened to me one day. I can't put it on paper but you will hear it someday. Oh My Dearest, My Darling, how many ways can I find to tell you how much I love you. So often I repeated but I cannot help myself. If you could only see my heart, you would know how I feel. Unfortunately, I can't mail that pound of flesh to you or I would. I must be content to let my pen do what my body and soul want to. I'll never stop loving you. Don't ever want me to because I won't.

Well, Bette, that's my sugar for tonight. Good night, My Lanky, Luscious, Lovable, Lustrous Blonde. Take care of yourself. May God Bless You. To You, My Love, Mike.

Squadron War Diary entry, November 7:

> **14 plane resupply mission to France, all returning but one. Four plane mail and resupply mission to the continent and return. One plane used to transport A/B troops to France. One officer and two enlisted men returned from rest camp. Show at the station theatre.**

Group War Diary, November 7:

> **Continuation of the "Zipper" mission today. Show in the evening at the Station theatre.**

Squadron War Diary, November 8:

> **The weather plane returned, a RON in France. Three plane resupply and evacuation to the continent and return. 18 planes were used to transport A/B troops and equipment to France. All of them RON. Dance at the NAAFI for EMs, show at the station theatre for officers.**

Group War Diary, November 8:

> **Resupply mission flown into the Paris area and returned with casualties to the United Kingdom. The regular NAAFI Wednesday dance sponsored by Special Service was held with music by the 314th Troop Carrier Orchestra, "Sweet and Low."**

November 9, 1944 [*Thursday*]

Good Evening, Darling,

I was comfortably snoozing in the sack when I received a few of your letters today. I got in early this afternoon and after I ate, the first thing I did was shave and shower and creep into mah sack. I was dead to the world when I was awakened. You must think I'm a dead herring, Bette, but I spent a rather miserable night last night. I could think of a million places I would rather have been than where I was, even Hell would have been warm. I was wet, hungry and cold. I checked my toes this morning and was relieved to find that they weren't blue. I was afraid of frost bite. It took me 2 hours to thaw the poor things out. A couple more like last night and they'll send me to the States in a glass case, frozen stiff. I still haven't recovered so I don't know how good a letter this will be. Oh Well, they tell me that all these things are for one's own good.

I got your letter of the 31st of Oct. and 1st of Nov. I also got your many clippings. One of them by A. I. Goldberg was my outfit. But I am sorry that you sent them now. Don't get me wrong, it was swell of you but I never read so much bull in all my life. There will be a lot of American Mothers who will never know what is going on. I am surprised at the American papers; I thought they had more sense than that. That broadcast that you mentioned happened to be made from one of our planes. I am not going to discuss it any further; the more I talk, the angrier I get. I got a rejection slip from *Stars and Stripes* on the article I wrote to them but they published one that was almost identical. As long as someone sees the light that's all that concerns me. At least I know I'm not the only one with a bitching complex in this man's army.

You know, Bette, speaking of my cousin's marriage, I wondered about it today. So far, I haven't heard a thing about it. Mike is no kid; he is about 27 years old. Oh Hell! I can't think of much but cold.

Your wondering about that Florida deal seem[s] awfully funny to me. At any rate, it seems as if you are determined to go to Fla. I am hoping that you do. At any rate, Darling, please keep me informed. At this stage of the game, it's important because one never knows what will happen. All I hope is that you do what your heart desires. I am not in the least worried about what will happen because no matter what, I won't miss you if I get home, I won't miss you. If I get home, I'll find where you are if I have to tear the 48 states apart. I love you so much, Darling, that each passed day makes me feel better; I am getting closer to you and surer I'll be home to you. Darling, there are so many things I could answer to in your letters but I want to wait until I can concentrate. I believe I have another breathing spell coming up.

Gosh, Bette, I'm afraid my enthusiasm got the better of my judgment. But I think in my letter where I mentioned my plans for our marriage, I overdid myself. I have to be frank because I know that you want me to be. You needn't worry about my nervousness because I realize what the event means. I know that previous circumstances have left a decided distaste in your mouth. I know that I may be forcing something down your throat, not our marriage but the location. But please, Darling, you must bear with me. Whatever I am doing, I am doing for our own good. I promise, Bette, I'll never hurt you nor have you hurt. If only we could discuss this instead of writing about it, I know that our levelheadedness would be the armor to win the battle. Perhaps, I overlook many things. Please tell me of them. I know that I may be denying you certain honors that go with planning such a thing but again we have to see the circumstances. It is so hard to put on paper what I know you want to hear. Again I must say, bear with me; as we have said so often, the actual events are unimportant. All that matters is that we will be together. Gosh, Bette, I feel so tired. I know that you want me to be happy; I want the same for you. We'll have that happiness, — just to be able to tell you what I feel would straighten everything out.

Gosh, Bette, gonna peel off. Take care of yourself. May God Bless You. I love you so very much, so very, very much. Forever Yours, Mike.

On November 9, according to the Squadron War Diary, the 18 planes returned from the previous day's mission in France. Two planes transported casualties from the base to southern England, while another made a cross-country and return trip. The entry concluded: "Show for the EMs at the station theatre. Rest leaves for combat men, five-day furloughs, 12, 24, 48-hour passes still in effect."

The Group War Diary entry for the same day, November 9, read:

Morality lecture was presented to the Enlisted personnel of Headquarters and the Articles of War were read. Movie in the evening, Eddie Bracken in *Hail the Conquering Hero*. One of his best comedies.

November 10, 1944 [*Friday*]

Good Morning, Bette,

It's early morning and I do have a little time for myself. Excuse the pencil. This is the kind of AM I know that you would enjoy. It is cold, crisp and definitely invigorating. I'm sorry that I sounded so down right low down last nite. I hit the sack soon after I finished the letter so I feel extremely refreshed.

You may have noticed in my letter last night that I seemed to be laboring under a strain of thought. I can't help myself at times. For that reason, I was a bit restless. But it is so difficult to put so many emotions into written words. It has been over 14 months since we decided that our friendship was more than that and naturally our minds turned to the best thing, marriage. So it was, a mutual consent to live the rest of this life together. You made me the happiest guy in the world when you showed enough love and respect for me to consent to our marriage. That is all I have been living for and shall continue to live for. That is the prime reason I want to shield and blind myself to everything else and just start from that point. As I was thinking it over, it seemed to me that we talk about some things too much. Therefore, when I told you of my plans, I considered merely convenience and speed. Darling, I hate to waste time. We've wasted 17 months already. Especially now that my time over here seems to be running short, I hate to think that we must alter or try to alter so many things. All I want is you — I love you, Bette, I love you dearly. As I said last night, I don't ever want to hurt you nor shall anyone else. Perhaps, I do sound enthusiastic at times, it can't be helped. The length of our separation has done that. I know that you want to do everything I want to do and believe me, it is the nicest feeling in the world to know that. I am determined to make you realize that whatever I have done or will do will be for our benefit. I am determined to see to that. Perhaps I sound like I am laying down a law; I am, but not to you. I'll never do that; maybe you'll be spanked once in a while, if you need it. But that law is for me, the months of solitary thinking have shown what I must do and how it must be done. Every thought has been for you and I, whatever conventions have been interposed are for the same reasons. I must leave now but I'll continue tonight.

I love you, Bette. Always remember that. I know what the word love means now; on that point I am trying to make our future life as happy as possible. May God Bless You. Your Own, Mike.

November 10, 1944 [*Friday*]

Good Evening, Bette,

Here I am back again! Just about ready to pound my ole sack after I finish this letter. Wrote a long letter to Lucy. Just passing thoughts, things that have haunted me a long time. I hope my letter this morning didn't sound like a blundering idiot. It is hard to say so many things and yet not say anything. Long ago, we promised to live only for the day that we will be together and so it will be. I think that I've been thinking so much lately that I am thinking myself into a quandary of confusion. Over all my thoughts, you stand head and shoulders. Whenever I think I am doing something to hurt you, I want to take everything back and start all over again. Very frankly, Darling, I want you waiting for me always. I am not laboring under any illusions. My love for you is deeper than anything I have ever felt. There I go again, repeating myself. But so many things are on my chest, I don't know where to start. So it is best that I let them go and just speak words of love. But all I keep thinking about is you. I think I am having that period, so it is best that I divert my words elsewhere.

You said that I paid you the highest compliment that any man could pay any woman. I would not want you on any of those hellacious missions. I just want you waiting when all that dreary work is done. Just like any ordinary job, I want to come back to you. Yes, Darling, you came to me when I needed you. You hadn't started to come, yet. I didn't know what life really was then. If you weren't waiting for me when I come back now, I'd give up. Knowing that you are there now is making my hardest moments easier. Every time you say that you'll get to New York no matter how, I know that my light is waiting at the end of the beautiful rainbow. Damn it all, Bette, I love you. It is so much easier to say it that way.

Doing pretty good these days. It has been 2 weeks since I had my last drink. Someone asked me if I wanted some champagne the other day and I refused; that is really going some. I feel a Hell of a lot better for it. In place of all that expensive drinking, I've taken my reading well in hand.

Talk about hot bricks and I don't want anything else. (As long as I am 3,000 miles away why think of anything else!) I took a few minutes to get my dogs warm last night, too and I was in my own sack. Gad! Darling, how will you ever stand me? I gotta get out of that serious mood of mine. Sometimes I think I'm too much of a depressive. As someone once said, when you feel that way, it is best not to write at all. That's a fact, what I really need is to talk to you.

Well, I am going to sign off. The ole eyes are doing tricks. Give my love to Mother. Take care of yourself. I love you and miss you — May God Bless You. Love, Mike.

The War Diary entry for November 10 contained a reminder of the danger of these missions:

> **20 planes were sent on a resupply mission to the continent, all returning but the weather ship. One XC and return. S/Sgt.** [*Staff Sergeant*] **Stanley A. Fischer from missing in action dropped from the rolls as of 17 September '44 to killed in action 17 September 1944.**

The Group War Diary entry for November 10 reported:

> **Aircraft of the group went to the far shore carrying personnel and baggage of the 82nd Airborne and upon arriving over the field they**

were to land on found it to be unserviceable and had to return to base with their load.

November 11, 1944 [*Saturday*]

Good Morning, Darling,

Finally got a day off and to boot we are having a football game this afternoon. Our base team won last Sunday and this is their second game. It has been over 2 years since I saw my last game. It was the game between Green Bay and Brooklyn. Seems like a long time ago.

Look, Woman, you'll have to stay out of my life if I'm going to get any sleep. Hit the sack at 9 last night and read 'til 10 but when I tried to sleep it was 2 AM. Just couldn't get my mind off things. I could see so many things that I had seen before but always you were at my side. I've asked the fellows who were home on leave if it was easy to recapture all the things they knew before — the answer was always negative. No matter how small the changes may be, they are still so noticeable. It seems that the idea is to rebuild a new sort of life. Fortunately, for me, I'll have your help. You may not realize it but you will be such a great help to me. You will probably have to treat me like a naughty child. "Mike, don't do things that way!" "You can't curse and insult people like that, they don't like it!" Honestly, Honey, that may sound silly to you. But it is hard not to form a sort of swaggering indifference toward people and things. These foreigners here haven't taught me anything except the restlessness of some forms of life.

All I can think of now is looking at you adoringly and drinking in every detail I've missed for the last 17 months. Maybe all of you don't know how a guy feels, but I do. Every little detail is so important. If I seem to make an ass out of myself at times, just skip it. If I appear too obvious, scold me, I won't mind. I can't think of anything that will be disagreeable. As long as people leave us alone, I won't get angry. But no one had better get my temper stirred. Once my furlough is over and we are situated near my next base, we can settle down to serious married life. But my first days at home with you will be a thing to remember. Oh well, no use to get too excited about things yet. Of course, I don't expect these next many months to pass too slowly but I try not to let my enthusiasm run away with my imagination. Don't mind me, just rambling along and saying nothing.

Well, Darling, I'll sign off. Got a chance to catch up on some of my correspondence. Take care of yourself. I love you and miss you. May God Bless you. Love, Mike.

War Diary, November 11:

The weather ship returned from the continent. No flying because of bad weather. The base football team played their second game of the season winning 7-0.

Group War Diary, November 11:

Armistice day and no flying because of bad weather, which was a relief to all flying personnel. Berger's Bouncers played their second game today and their backers were less skeptical today than at the first game. The team was victorious. . . . Movie, _Music in Manhattan_ at the station theatre in the evening.

November 12, 1944 [*Sunday*]

Dearest,

Sammy Kaye and another *Sunday Serenade*, one week passed, one week closer to you. I can't think of a better way to [*gauge*] time. I am writing to you this afternoon, Darling, because I think I'll be busy for the rest of the day. I just finished washing clothes, gonna practice basketball later and I don't think I'll have much time after the show tonight to write.

Spent a very enjoyable yesterday afternoon watching our football team win 7-0. Just watching made me hungry to be playing. First game I've seen in 2 years and it had a good background, nice crowd, loudspeaker spurting out losses and gains, etc. Felt as if I was sitting in Ebbetts Field. Heard the ND [*Notre Dame*]-Army game last night, I was never so surprised in my life, 59-0. That doesn't sound like the kind of score one would expect of such a traditional game. Just goes to prove what wartime will do even to our sports. I can't imagine what kind of competition there will be when all the really good players are out of Sam's uniform into their own ball clubs. Seems like this damn mess will never end and see all of us in civilian clothes again.

Nothing much going on. Just sitting back and watching the clock. Feel like I was in a basketball game of life and knowing that I'm winning some of it, just holding the ole apple in my own territory and "freezing" the ball. Dreaming every dream over and over. Keep picturing the day we meet again. All I want is keeping telling you how much I love you, how much I've missed you, how glad I am that God has spared me, to let me return to you, to feel your face and hair to know that it really is you and me — you return all the happiness that you have given me, even in our separation. Don't think badly of me, Darling, I'm not cracking, still smiling and keeping my chin above the water line. Not that I'll ever forget how to do all these things but I don't want to get rusty. I may have changed to some people but I don't think I'll ever change to you, Bette. Whatever this war has done to me, I know it will be forgotten once I have your arms around me again. They are so much security to me.

Well, Darling, those are my sugar notes for today. Take care of yourself. My love to Mother. I love you and miss you. May God Bless You. Love, Mike.

On November 12, according to the War Diary, all flights were cancelled due to weather.

The Group War Diary entry for that day described an Armistice Day service, which was held at a church in the village of Cottesmore, by Chaplain Myron J. Willard. The entry concluded: "Some few resupply missions were flown today."

November 13, 1944 [*Monday*]

Good Evening, My Love,

One of those rather "off" nights, the mail has been poor and there is little to write about that it makes the whole problem difficult. For the second day in a row, I've practiced a little basketball and I feel good. Gosh, Honey, I'm trying my best to get in good shape. I think it'll still take more than a few ball games to accomplish that. I didn't realize that I had gotten so fat, until the Squadron Surgeon mentioned it. Don't fret. I'm not getting too obese but whatever muscles I had trained have softened up from lack of use. It is a natural reaction to laziness. Just can't help myself, Darling, this country is not made for training of any sort. It is too easy to get ill. I'd rather stay slightly plump than disgustingly thin and sick. As a matter of fact, all crew members are forced to take one sulfa tablet a day to counteract cold, etc. Disciplinary action if we don't adhere to the rules. Don't mind my babbling along like this about myself. You see, Bette, we aren't too busy these days and it is tougher when we don't get any mail. Here I go again but I could use 2 weeks of wholesome sunshine and some good active swimming.

It is rougher than hell these days too. Most of the kids that went home a little while back, will often talk of how wonderfully efficient everyone was. I mean once they hit the States, they moved about quickly as Hell so they could get to their homes faster. To hear them talk that way makes everything seem so close and yet so far. All in all, they got a royal screwing. All they had was a leave and they returned over. Most of the guys they might send home now, I guess will go back for reassignment in the states. That's the only way it should be done. What the Hell, most of the kids could be replaced by guys that have been laying on their respective rears since the war began. Personally I'd be glad to sweat out as much service as they want me to but when that time was up, I want to go home for good. I don't like the idea of leaving you once we are together again. A lot of the guys say that the States are so GI that a guy would be glad to go overseas again. My argument to that is this — as long as my wife is nearby, the army has my life only until 5 PM, from that time on, it is mine to do as I please. They could put me on a perpetual KP, take my stripes and flying pay, do a few other obscene things and they still would have plenty to go to tear down my morale. You see, Darling, what I'd take just to be with you, But that's my idea. I'll do that until they give me that HD [*Honorable Discharge*] then I'd be in "civvies" and ready to crack heads. I love you, Darling, that's all that counts.

Well, Hon, that's all for now. Take care of yourself. May God Bless you. Love, Mike.

War Diary entry, November 13:

> **No flying because of weather. 2nd Lt. Peter R. York assigned and joined from the 44th TC Sq., VOCO** [*Verbal Order Commanding Officer*]**, 316th TC GP** [*Troop Carrier Group*]**. Dance for EMs at the American Red Cross.**

Group War Diary entry, November 13:

> **All ships grounded today because of heavy ground fog with the exception of local flight tests. Dance held for the Enlisted Men in the evening at the Red Cross Club, music by the 316th Orchestra.**

November 14, 1944 [*Tuesday*]

Good Evening, Darling,

This, indeed, had been a wonderful day. I went thru' a stiff 2-hour workout this afternoon and when I got back, there were 4 letters from you. Stiff and I'm not kidding. My muscles feel like the knot on a bow tie. But I want to answer your letters. There is so much to say to them. Two of them were dated 3 and 4 of Nov., and the other 2 are 12th and 13th of Oct. So you see, the mail is still uncertain as ever.

I guess I am having some sort of picture trouble but it doesn't worry me except to you. (Major Glenn Miller just came on!) I haven't left the post in such a long time that I haven't had a chance to get a good photograph. But I promise one thing, I am hoping to go on pass, the 1st of the year. Not to London but I think to somewhere in Scotland. I'll try my best to have some made. It may seem strange to hear that I am waiting so long but I have changed my policy to such an extent that I haven't time for passes and the like. And I figure that by next month of Jan., I'll have enough dough to do some sightseeing. The one reason that I am shying from London is that as long as I am still alive, I don't feel like straining my luck too far and take a chance on that place.

Since I received your letters in such an uneven sequence, I became rather flustered and said a lot of wrong things, perhaps. But again I am so glad that you like my plans for our marriage. I knew that you would be just as thrilled as I was when I sat down and wrote about such things. Just planning in that manner brings us so close together, a part of our love that binds me that closer. Naturally, we would have to show some consideration to our best man and maid of honor. We will do whatever is right in that case. As far as the health certificates go, I don't know exactly what the "do" is on that. Since I never planned marriage seriously before, I never ventured into the laws of NY. Darling, I think I'll leave that up to you. Do you suppose that your physician would know about that? However, I am sure that they would accept a recent (recent, at least, at the time I come home) certificate signed by a reliable "doc." I am glad that you mentioned Ted and Louise. I think that it is a good suggestion and I will write to them and ask them. I am sure they will be honored. I've always gotten along with them so well and of all my family they are the most down-to-earth people that I know. I think that it is an excellent idea. As far as Louise's dress and your money problems, I hardly think that that is any bother to us — I am pretty sure that when I get home, we'll have a little dough to carry us a long while. Since you are to be my wife, don't you think I could start accepting the responsibilities a little before hand? Darling, I want to make everything as complete as we can; you can start worrying about our finances once we get going on our own life. As far as corsages go, I think we can manage all of that, if I'm not mistaken the color of orchids would go good with gray. If I am wrong, you can correct me in any way you wish. I think that we may be a little pushed for time, but if you feel as I do, you'll be glad to sacrifice that for our happiness. Darling, since neither (Hey — all this — and I haven't said it once, I love you dearly, My Dearest!) of us knows what the near future will bring, I am sure that we'll adjust ourselves to the times. That "uncertainty of the certain" makes so many plans difficult but I know that we will do well. Yes, we've decided on the double ring ceremony. We will do our best to take care of all details, and right now it seems as if there are so many of them, doesn't it? It makes my head spin in a whirl of happiness. Oh yes, your next question, — I'll answer it as it was told to me by the fellows that went home for leave. They were allowed to send cables. So I doubt if they will change the rules now. When and if I can reach a place for embarking for home, I'll send that cable so that you can make all reservations. One thing I want you to do, if you can, is get a room in the Hotel McAlpine at 34th and 5th Avenue. It is just slightly off the main drag and I've always liked it so. So if you can get any reservations, please remember that name, Darling. You'll have a vague approximation when I get home but you can stay there until I do get home.

Gosh, Bette, these are the most exciting moments of my life. To be able to plan and talk so many things over, it makes everything so easy to take. I'll admit that the time never seems to pass but it has to no matter what may happen. I can't help but feel that our meeting day can't be too many <u>years</u> off. We've survived this time; I'm sure we can keep right on going — and if need be, we will pitch that tent in Central Park. Oh God, I pray that He'll keep on showering me with so many blessings. I love you and miss you, Darling, and each day makes our future so brighter.

Good Night, Bette. May God Bless You. Eternally Yours, Mike.

In the 37th Squadron, there was no flying because of weather on November 14, though the Group War Diary did record some flights that day:

> **Again only a few missions were sent to the far shore because the field closed down early this morning. *Higher and Higher* was shown in the evening starring Frank Sinatra.**

November 15, 1944 [*Wednesday*]

Good Morning, Darling,

It is a lovely day, lovely because the whole world around us is turning white and we don't have to worry about moving an inch. Keep dreaming of a white Christmas. You needn't apologize (blotch — neat, isn't it?) about the way you have been writing. It is almost a normal thing to write about oneself, especially since the mails have been so scarce. After all, Bette, I don't think you need to say "What look at me, don't I always blabber away about myself." If it isn't one thing, it's the other. Like now, I've been smoking my pipe quite a bit — they have cut our rations of cigarettes down to 5 packs a week — since we can't get them and neither can you at home — who is getting all the cigarettes?

Darling, I'm afraid that I'm at a bit of a loss about that rat. I know about those rolls and stuff but when you speak so elaborately about it, I'm afraid I'm at a loss. I judge women's styles in one manner, the way they look to me but I'm afraid I can't say a thing about it when I read of styles. I never did read the society page, you know.

Darling, I guess there are a lot of Smiths in the army, even in the Air Force. I've heard of their outfit. You can see by our outfit numbers that we are rather closely allied. Of course, it isn't easy to run into those guys — so many of the same around that even in this small world, Smiths are hard to find.

Gotta get back to that rat. You said that your new hairdo makes you look shorter. Do you think that that is necessary as long as I'm around? As a couple for size, we are like two peas in a pod. I'll bet our children will all be ½ pints.

I thought I'd feel rough this AM after that strenuous workout, but I guess I can still take it. They are getting ready to start tournament play tonight. We don't play until Friday. So I guess I won't be in bad shape. There I go again talking about myself. But there isn't much to say. Life has become just a routine of nothingness. Thanksgiving isn't too far off, is it? Well here goes another holiday alone — good ole Brooklyn stand by, "Wait 'til next year!"

Well, Bette, gotta peel off for the morning. Take care of Mother, sorry to hear she isn't feeling too well. May God Bless You, Love, Mike.

War Diary entry, November 15:

> **One plane mission to the continent, staying overnight. . . . Dance at NAAFI. Under Sec. II & III, GO [*General Order*] 113, HQs [*Headquarters*] IX TCC, dated 15 Nov. 1944, 144 officers and enlisted men are authorized the air medal, 81 of which was the oak leaf cluster to the air medal.**

Group War Diary entry, November 15:

> **A few aircraft were able to take off during the morning before the field completely closed down. Heavy fog and rain which later turned**

into a snow storm and by late afternoon the entire field was covered by a white blanket. The NAAFI Dance was held this evening with WAAFs and ATS present. Fewer girls are beginning to show up because of the cold truck ride.

November 16, 1944 [*Thursday*]

Good Evening, Darling,

Still nothing to write about. It has been quiet and time just turtles along. Just stoked up the ole pipe — you wouldn't care to join me, would you, Bette? I've seen quite a bit in *S&S* about Noel Coward's *Middle East Diary*. It seems that this English character made a remark about Brooklyn boys being a bunch of cry babies when they were lying around in hospitals as casualties in the desert. Perhaps he doesn't realize it but he has slapped 2 million people in the face. Of course, we have no right to say anything to injure Anglo-American relations but that son of a bitch can go around talking as he pleases. I read that one Representative from New York who is head of the Immigration Committee, said that he will see to it that Coward will be declared *persona non grata*. In other words, we don't want that sort of person in America so that he can take millions out and salt them into English banks. I may sound harsh but unfortunately I can't say as much as I'd like to. My blood is percolating at a rate that would scare anyone. Coward, as a defense, said that he didn't have a copy of the book with him but he doesn't recall any part where he described anyone who came from Brooklyn. That's a pretty bad author who can't recall his own words, surely he must have his heart and soul in his work (?). I could go on like this for a long while. I've been around these people long enough. This is not the only instance. Maybe I'm not very impressive in my words but I'd like to [*be*] given 15 minutes of broadcasting to the people in the States. Perhaps, this hurts morale. I don't know, but if it did then democracy is a very elastic word. Fortunately, for us, as Americans, our primary thought is to get this war over. We want to return to our homes and the people we love. If we were a nation of professional soldiers, we wouldn't give a damn where they sent us nor for how long — I'm not usually a demonstrative person, I mean, I'm not the type that boos heartily at a bad play nor do I toss bottles. But if Coward ever puts his puss on any NY screen, I'll do my damnedest to carry eggs or the such. I didn't think I'd ever feel as I do but when all this bull is jammed past your head, then it's time to blow the lid off. Oh God! That someday all this will be justified. If my hurt were a personal one, I wouldn't bitch but it goes back to my comrades and to those at home that are doing their damnedest to see that our "Allies" are getting everything they need.

Sorry, Darling, just thought I'd let off a little steam. Gonna say "good night," Honey, gotta sleep on that beautiful thought. I love you and miss you so very much despite my nasty temperament.

May God Bless You. Love, Mike.

The November 16 War Diary noted only one return flight from the Continent. The Group War Diary on that day elaborated on the weather conditions:

> **Field closed in early this morning. The Group sent some Enlisted Men to the far shore on DS for communications work. Although they were prepared to leave and anxious to do so, they had to return to their barracks and hope the weather would improve. Some few aircraft were able to return from the far shore and did so with a 400-foot ceiling and ½ mile visibility. The fog was so thick the pilots couldn't see to land. The ground crews tried out the new flare which was fired at the end of the runway and another volley fired down the runway to enable the pilots to land safely.**

November 17, 1944 [*Friday*]

Hi Honey,

Same ole' thing to repeat. No mail but I've read that the guys at the front are getting priority, so I don't mind too much. I'd rather see those kids happy. They need it more because they have a Hell of a harder job than we have.

November 21, 1944 [*Tuesday*]

Hello Darling,

This is the first chance I've had to get back to this letter. I've eaten, shaved and showered, and I was all set to write when I got another scare. I told the guys to shove off; I want to get some rest. So here I am. Everything seemed to go wrong for me. Thank God, I'm back in my own roost. I found 2 old letters from you and a letter from my Sis. Got a bottle of Yardley's Shaving Lotion but the top of the bottle broke and I ended up with enough for at least one shave. Your letters were dated Sept. 25 and Oct. 29. It seems that the September letter was sent to the 316 TC Sq. Well, at least it has gotten here.

I am glad, though I have known it a long time, that we like so many of the same things. I guess you must know very well by now that I am a rabid sports fan. It will be great to sit in the stands with you and watch men participate in something that doesn't necessitate death or pain. I've seen the Rodeo at the [*Madison Square*] Garden once and I promise that we will make it a must.

Darling, I haven't been anywhere nearby where I could get you some "Tabu" but I promise the next time I do, I'll do my damnedest. In Rheims, it looked like they had gallons of the stuff but it seems that all the bottles were empty, just used for an advertisement. I am glad that you put me straight on your tastes. I think perfumes are the best gifts. Since we are doing a bit rougher on our activities, it will be harder for me but I promise to do my best. We never know where we'll be from day to day.

I don't know where that Hill is from but I'll try to find out. If he is any relative of yours, it just goes to prove how small the world is.

Darling, to be honest about it, I wouldn't give you a million for that bottle of Seagram's. I don't intend to drink it alone. That is one bottle I am not eager to tap, unless you have a glass in your hand and I have one in mine. It has been 3 weeks since I touched a drop, haven't even had a glass of beer. It is just as well. I feel all the better for it. I'll probably pitch a good one for the Christmas holidays but I don't even promise that. I've been living such a clean, wholesome life that it almost scares me. I love you.

One reason I don't write to those people in Brussels is that it was just a passing acquaintance. Theirs was an impulse. It is much better that I not try to force the issue. Someday if ever we meet again, they will not be forgotten for their kindness. I don't very often forget a face.

Letters pass between us in such an irregular order that our ideas are sometimes overlapping and in turn seem confusing. I'd like to have Pappy as our best man but as things appear now, we won't be getting home at the same time. I think I'll beat him on that score. I think Ted and Louise are ideal. But as I have said before all these plans are temporary. Who knows we may alter them so much that they will be far different from anything we ever dreamed of. As for the church, we will let that go. You see, Darling, as I said before, our marriage rite will have to be held in the Rectory, not in the Church itself. Everything that we must do, it is best that we do with the least inconvenience. I'm not evading the issue but it is best to wait. Gosh, Honey, we're talking so much that my happiness gets me a bit mixed up on things. The thing I know above everything else is that I love you. Some times each day is like a million torments and when I get a chance to relax, I realize that I have so much to go back to that it all seems so easy.

I received a very nice letter from Chicha in answer to my letter of our (or should I say my) plans. It was a most encouraging answer. It makes me feel as so much of the past is forgotten. All I want to look forward to is that future with you. Discounting so much and remembering everything that made our former life so pleasant. This passing time hasn't been easy to take. Therefore I want to try to make everything as pleasant for you as you want to for me. Our good sense has to leave us the way to pick the mutual alternative. My Darling, if I could just tell you how much I love you.

Must close now. Take care of yourself. Give my love to Mother. Miss you terribly. May God Bless You. Love, Mike.

P.S.: Pappy and I had nothing to do with the champagne deal. Wish we had! M.

There was no flying on November 17 because of weather. The Group War Diary for that day read:

> **Fog again. . . . Venereal Disease picture shown to all personnel throughout the day. 45th Squadron has a party in Leicester in the evening so the regular liberty run was canceled for the evening. Rain**

and wind most of the day although it slackened in the evening. Headquarters enlisted men with aid of the Officers began to make preparations for a Day Room.

Flights resumed the next day, according to the November 18 Squadron War Diary:

> **Five planes with crew chiefs were sent on DS to Saltby. Six planes were sent to the continent with personnel, three were forced back to Cottesmore because of weather. Lt. Col. Fletcher gave a lecture on base and squadron regulations to all the new pilots assigned on the 16th. Lt. McShane also gave them instructions on censorship and mailing regulations. Squadron officers held a dance here on the post, celebrating two years overseas service. USO show was held in the NAAFI hall. Distribution of WD pamphlets No. 21-7 was also made to the new personnel.**

The Group War Diary entry for that day, November 18, read:

> **Field opened once again. Major Milstead and T/Sgt. Welsh of Group S-2 left for the far shore to coordinate public relations matters for the Group. The group of men who have been waiting for so many days to leave on DS to the combat zone were able to leave today.**

Squadron War Diary, November 19:

> **12 planes to southern England for loads and return. Two planes XC and return. One plane XC to Ireland, has not returned. . . .**

Group War Diary, November 19:

> **Church services held this morning by all faiths. Missions sent to far shore on resupply and evacuation.**

Squadron War Diary, November 20:

> **One plane XC and return. Four plane mission to the continent, RON. . . . Show at the theatre.**

Group War Diary, November 20:

> **Little activity on the field today because of the weather, although a few aircraft that had RON'd the night before returned to base. Enlisted Men of the Group held their weekly dance at the Red Cross this evening.**

The next day, November 21, the Squadron War Diary read:

> **12 plane resupply mission to the continent all returning but two, the weather ship and one with a damaged wing tip. Three planes XC two returning one remaining on Burtonwood for modification. Five planes with crew chiefs returned from DS. 14 planes to Kemble for loads and return. . . . Show at the station theatre. Squadron basketball team won their first game, 45-22 [*sic*]. Sixty feet of movie film taken of Sqdn personnel, billets, etc.**

Group War Diary, November 21:

> **Departmental basketball games were started today so that a team could be picked to represent the base in the forthcoming basketball league. Major Milstead and T/Sgt. Welsh returned from far shore today.**

November 22, 1944 [*Wednesday*]

Good Evening, Darling,

I received your letter of the 12th of Nov. We had some not too funny humor going on a minute ago. It's funny because we kid each other so much about certain things. At any rate, here is the story. Last Thursday, three of us, Mac [*Ron MacDougall*], Bill [*Toohey*] and myself went over to the dispensary and had some tests made of our blood. Well the results came back today and they are all negative. Bill knew of it first, so when I walked in, he said, "Mike, Doc wants to see you. Mac's and my tests came out OK. You must have won first prize, 4+." Naturally, that made me feel good, my heart beat like a trip hammer. Then I found out he was kidding. So later, Mac walked in and we said the same to him. To affirm it, we told the medic to come into the room and tell Mac that Doc wanted to see him. The medic looks like death uncovered and very seriously, he went thru' this little speech. You see Mac is married and has a little girl at home. In those few moments, I can imagine how many horrible thoughts must have run thru his mind. To ease the pressure, I uncovered the entire farce. That little *tête-à-tête* passed off.

But I meant to tell you that when I saw Doc late week, I asked him about blood tests and marriage, etc. He didn't know definitely but he said he was sure that any State Health Board would accept any medical statement as long as it is recent, recent, that is, within 3 months of the date of marriage. Since neither of us knows when I'll be home nor the date of our marriage that makes things difficult but I don't believe that you can be too far wrong if you take another blood test around the end of February, that will cover you until May and I'm sure that Spring can't be too late next year.

In reference to that letter of yours, I'll go on to repeat what I said earlier today, I am sure that we'll have at least 2 weeks in Miami. The fellows that went home on leave were sent to Atlantic City but that was because of the time of year. I imagine that during the winter months, Miami would be used. I was stationed in Miami when I first entered the service 2 years ago. It will be interesting to see it again thru different eyes. Eyes that have seen more than they ever anticipated they would. Boy, I'll bet those white sands and hot sun will feel great. Sound like an awful sun fanatic, Don't I? Well, I guess I am. If we ever get down there I'll give you a chance to prove your swimming prowess. Last one in, buys the next round. New York is nice in the spring but it will be a swell change after our leave to head South. You see, Darling, since I am so sure that that will happen, that's why I'd rather spend my whole leave in NY. When all of that is over, I'll send for you as soon as I am permanently located. Next time I see the 48, it is going to be for good, I hope!

I was rather surprised to hear that they celebrated Armistice Day in such a fine fettle. Maybe I'm a sentimentalist but I think that the sorrow that goes with war overshadows the joy of having it ended. A guy can get drunk 364 days out of the year, think of the poor guy who can't be around on that one day. But then again maybe I'm no different from the next guy. I'd probably do the same thing. I wonder how it will feel to be a commando again. Put that red bow on the bottle, Darling, the day I come home we'll paint the town red. Gosh, Honey, just think we are over the hump; the rest of the time we can slide down hill. Are you going to scold me if I throw $10 on the bar and tell the bartender to keep filling them up 'til it's finished? You know married life will cause some changes. A lot of guys thought we were crazy. Gosh, Honey, I love you.

Must close. Take it easy, gal. You start counting the way I am, day by day.

Miss you. May God Bless You. Love, Mike.

November 22, 1944 [*Wednesday*]

Hello Darling,

This is my second attempt to write to you. I didn't like the way my first letter sounded so I am not going to send it. It is best that I put such thoughts on paper, but better that I don't send them out. There isn't much of anything new. There was a big mail call last night but I drew a blank. I did receive one card that you sent me. Clever, indeed, but you only mentioned "Bonnie." I see that you respect the poor mutts that didn't make the grade.

We played our first basketball game last night and it was a pushover. Beat the other team by a slight score of 54-22 [*sic*]. One of the guys on our club scored 23 points, so I guess he alone could have won the game. I scored 4 points, my usual. They used to call me "2-point Ingrisano" back in High School days. Never was much of a point maker — as long as my presence is known, I don't worry about the headlines.

Tomorrow is Thanksgiving Day and I don't feel inclined to do anything but rest. It has been over 2 years since I've been in service and I haven't felt the holiday mood once. Don't think I'll enjoy one again until I am back in the 48. One of the guys that may get a chance to get home for the Christmas holidays, keeps saying to me, "A Very Merry

Christmas to you, Mike!" Makes me so damn mad I want to floor him. He knows how I feel about you and how badly I'd like to see you. You'd think he'd be a bit smarter about the whole thing. So damn sick of pettiness and smallness, I could bust a blood vessel. Honestly, I don't think it is a very funny joke. I keep thinking of so many things, Darling, it scares me to mention them. Usually it is best that I not say anything and so I shan't. You know, Bette, all I keep thinking of is how wonderful it will be to be living a life of ease with you. All I think of is the time when I'll be home. I don't know how much of a furlough I'll get but I do know that it will be that much time of love and life with you. Then we will have at least 2 weeks at Miami or someplace where a guy can get some sun. That's one good thing about the Air Force, they really take care of their own. Keep thinking of all the troubles that bother me all the time and I am happiest when I dismiss all of that and get into the lighter vein of life. I'd be a better guy if I didn't think so much. All that is really important is our love. Nothing else should matter but how the Hell can you tell so many people what you feel.

Well, Honey, gonna sack for a while. Give my love to Mother. Take care of yourself. I love you and miss you. May God Bless You. Love, Mike.

The Squadron War Diary entry for November 22 reported that eight flights were made to southern England to be loaded with supplies. Seven returned, and one continued to the continent, and remained there overnight. The entry concluded: "Dance at the NAAFI. Movie for the officers."

According to that day's Group War Diary entry,

> **No flights were flown to the far shore today because of weather. Some local transition flights were made by the pilots of the group this afternoon. The Wednesday NAAFI dance was held in the evening for the Enlisted Personal [*sic*] with WAAFs, ATS, and civilian girls present. Headquarters Enlisted Men's day room was opened officially this evening at 1800 hours. Although the Club is small, it's very comfortable. Overstuffed chairs, writing desks, reading lamps, card tables and dart board. Colonel Berger and his staff were present and a good time was had by all.**

November 23, 1944 [*Thursday*]

My Darling,

Thanksgiving Day and although I didn't spend it as I had hoped, in leisure, but at any rate your letter of the 14th of Nov. brought me the best news I have had for a long time. Since I haven't heard from Sheila and Tony for a long time, I had no idea what they were thinking of. But their invitation was one of the nicest things that could happen. By the time you receive this, you'll know what swell people they are. Theirs is the first approach to friendliness that you have had yet from my family, isn't it? I know that you will find the attitude entirely different. Most of the fellows have always been welded closely together as brothers. The best part of it is that as an ordinary bunch of guys we always discussed things openly. I'll bet that you'll find Tony very much like me. As Aunt Bette you have to represent me too. Lil Rebel is most fortunate to see you first, at least, she'll know that she isn't getting too horrible a bargain. If she had seen me first, she would ask Sheila and Tony to get another family. Honestly, Darling, forgive me for the childish enthusiasm but I can't help but feel so highly elated by the invitation. I worry so damn much about so many things that the last turn of good fortune makes me feel like a million. Swell, everything seems so rosy and high. Please do tell me everything. This is one time that I am really eager. I love you so very much.

Gosh, Honey, why are you taking that cute mole off your face. But if you feel it will be an improvement, that's OK with me. Bette, I hope you don't go changing all around. Don't mean that figuratively. Cause if you rounded out a bit, I wouldn't mind in the least. You can't change your eyes, Darling. I'll still remember you as a tired, happy girl I left at Fort Wayne. Bette, can't help repeating myself. I love you so very much. Wish to Hell this war was over. I am so eager to get back to you.

I am not going to answer your letter completely tonight. I had a rather hard day today. Though I had my usually good holiday meal, I couldn't enjoy it as much as I wanted to. My mind was a bit preoccupied. (opinion is spelled ion.) Talking about cigarettes, you heard of the shortening of our rations. Fortunately, since we are boys of the blue, they haven't cut out our rations as completely as they have the others. I smoke my pipe often now so that helps to cut down my nervous twitch. Unfortunately, I've been smoking too long to cut it out completely. Haven't had a drink for almost a month. Doing great and feeling better. I'm afraid I was tapping the bottle a little too much after Holland. Right in the groove. I'm living such an angelic life it almost scares me but it is a Hell of a lot healthier. Starting early but I'm trying to shape myself up as much as I can for you. Eager as Hell to be at my very best for you, Darling.

Must close. Try to get off a long note one of these days, if I can get enough time for myself.

Good night, Honey. Take care of yourself. May God Bless you. I love you and miss you — Mike.

Squadron War Diary, November 23:

> **Weather ship returned from RON on the continent. 22 plane mission to the continent with supplies and return. Typical Thanksgiving was celebrated in the afternoon by attending football game at Nottingham Stadium between Cottesmore and North Witham. We won 6-0. A special train was chartered to transport the men to and from the game. Movie at the station theatre.**

Group War Diary, November 23:

> **Thanksgiving Day. Turkey and all the trimmings. Headquarters personnel were recuperating from the opening of the new Day Room and Bar. Berger's Bouncers played another game today at Nottingham . . . and [*were*] victorious with a score of 6-0. Two nurse[*s*] were cheerleaders for Cottesmore. They wore white sweaters with a large "C" on the front and a football on the back, and white flying capes topped the costume off. As yet the team is untied and undefeated. The picture *Marriage Is a Private Affair* was shown on the base.**

November 24, 1944 [*Friday*]

Good Evening, Darling,

Here I am again! First chance to write today. After I had washed some clothes, I had visions of scribbling off a short note but that vision was short lived and out I went. Hope you are enjoying yourself today. I keep thinking of you and the gang in Texas.

The other night after I received your letter asking for some "Tabu," I had a hell of a dream. I was walking thru the streets of Tel-A-Viv [*sic*] in Palestine or someplace like that and every store I passed, I saw millions of bottles of perfume. They had all types and brands. I must have bought gallons and gallons of it. When that thought passed over, I saw myself as a ground soldier, an infantryman. We had just captured a town and I was crawling thru the streets looking for snipers. I was standing behind a store pillar when a Frenchman passed near me and said, "There's a Jerry sniper in back of you." I turned around fast and there was this Jerry clicking and clicking his trigger at me. It seems his clip was empty. I fired from the hip and missed and then realized that that bullet was my last — I was then surrounded by a bunch of Jerries who had their bayonets fixed. I had no other choice but to run but they had already stuck me many times but I did manage to escape. When I came out of that scare, I was sitting straight up in bed, swinging my arms. One of the guys said that someone was yelling during the night. I wouldn't doubt that it was me. Wonder if I'll ever shake off those nightmares.

What makes you think that we were under the influence of bourbon that night? Or any night? I'm surprised at you, Darling. You know full well that we don't drink. Gad! What a horrible thought that is. As I look back, I can hardly remember but once that we showed that we had been drinking. And that one instance was me. Looks like we'll have to be well stocked or stay high and dry. Oh well, can't think of any better way to die! You are right, Bette, our memories are a good part of our present life. Those are the things that bring us together and give us a good meaning of what our love is. How easy it is to be patient as long as we can remember how nicely everything passed and to think how much more wonderful everything will be when we are together again. I do love you so, My Darling.

I've spoken to the guys who had a chance to stay on the continent recently. It seems that most of the better brands of perfumes are difficult to get now. And a lot of the stuff that they had to pay a high price for now is a lot of junk. However, if I get the chance, I'll try my damnedest. As I said before, we don't know from day to day where we'll be.

Well, Darling, I must close now. Give my love to Mother. Take care of yourself. May God Bless You. Love you and miss you terribly. Good Night. Love, Mike.

The Squadron and Group War Diaries for the three days following Thanksgiving were:

> **WD, November 24: 20 planes were sent to southern England for loads and return. . . . The articles of war were read to all personnel.**
>
> **GWD, November 24: All aircraft returned from far shore early. Later in the evening a heavy fog settled on the field. Liberty run sent out in the evening.**
>
> **WD, November 25: 22 planes to the continent with supplies, 19 returning. One plane was forced to RON because of engine trouble. One plane returned from France after being forced to RON because of damaged wing tip. . . .**
>
> **GWD, November 25: All aircraft returned to base after picking up loads for the next day's mission. On the return trip from the continent the weather was excellent until they hit the shore of UK when the ceiling closed down to 100 feet and ¼ mile visibility. The Senior Officers Club gave a party celebrating their second year overseas which was an elaborate affair. The club carried holiday atmosphere with all the holly and evergreen and the gaily colored parachutes. At the Station Theatre *Memphis Belle*.**
>
> **WD, November 26: The following named officers and enlisted men were killed in a mid-air collision over Liege airport, Liege, Belgium: 2nd Lt. Marcel O. Gerdin, 2nd Lt. Eugene H. Simmons, T/Sgt. Floyd H. Webster, S/Sgt. Anthony G. Cimmino. 19 plane mission to the continent. One remaining with a damaged wing tip [*this was "Pappy" Agle's aircraft*].**
>
> **GWD, November 26: Sunday Church services. Attempted snowing again today but turned to rain which lasted a few hours in the afternoon. Cpl. Vang gave a piano concert and Chaplain rendered several vocal selections at the County Theatre in Oakham. The comedy *Palm Beach Story* shown here on the field.**

November 27, 1944 [*Monday*]

Good Afternoon, Darling

It has been 2 days since I wrote to you last and I have a damn good reason for writing now. We are having a squadron anniversary dance this evening and I know that I won't be in shape later in the evening. I have decided to get plastered this night. It has been a month since I touched a drop but I have good reason to blow the old top [*this was in reference to Tony Cimmino's death, which I witnessed at Liege*] and so — making no promises about how I'll feel tomorrow but I don't think I'll be Queen of the May. This is a gala affair. I missed the last one in July. The last one I made was over a year ago. Gad! I'll never forget that one. Really tied on a honey.

Gosh, Honey, things are awfully quiet. I mean mail has been distressing. Aside from that we've been kept busy but that hardly offsets the lack of news. Saw the orders the other day, seems that we finally got that cluster for our air medal. Kinda' takes the bareness off the thing. Personally, I've had all I want. Don't want to get decorated too often or I'll make General "Ike" look like an amateur.

Gosh, Bette, I miss you terribly. In times like these, it gets more and more professed. It is that same ole, nice, warm feeling coming back moment after moment. Of course, I get off the beam once in a while but that's because there are so many different things interposed. All I know whenever I come out of those comas is that I love you more and more each time. Unfortunately, I can't talk the way I want to right now; everyone is flocking around talking about tonight. What can a guy do?

Darling, Gonna close. Sorry for this pitiful note but I'll do better. Let you know how I make out — big head & all. Give Mother my love. Feeling great these days. Take care of yourself. May God Bless You. Love, Mike.

On November 27, the Squadron War Diary reported,

> **No flying because of weather. Squadron Executive Officer, Major Ralph E. Shadwell, Jr. was married in Cottesmore Church. Enlisted personnel held a dance at DeMontfort Hall, Leicester. It was in celebration of 2 years overseas. Another dance at the ARC** [*American Red Cross*]**.**

The Group War Diary for that day noted only:

> **Aircraft landed early in the afternoon. The Red Cross Arrow Club held its dance in the evening.**

November 28, 1944 [*Tuesday*]

Good Evening, Darling,

Yep! I'm sober now. I must admit I wasn't in the best of shape for a long while this morning but I've straightened out a bit. Our party last night was the best we have ever had. There were 6 of us in our gang and we really tied on a toot. Started with a quart of gin and beer chasers. Killed that off and then started on more beer and finally punch that was a "combo" of gin, rum, and few other ingredients. By that time, I didn't really care. When we got back to base, we finished off with chicken soup and candy. Lost one of the guys in the melee. He wandered off and ended up sleeping in a church and got back to base by train this AM. Broke his false teeth; that's about the only casualty we had. I know we had a band but I don't recall how they sounded. The party was held in a large hall which was quite a beautiful place, I think. Our CO and a few of the other Officers were there and they treated us royally. (½ hour intermission to fry some chicken. Mac got a can of chicken so we made a big mess of it and gulped it down!) Well, Darling, I got that drunk out of my system. I can go back to some more sensible living. Our next dance is at the beginning of January, so I'll probably go off on a three day toot. That will last me for a long time.

Darling, you are absolutely ingenious. Every one complaining of lack of cigarettes and here I receive a carton from you. You're marvelous. Thanks for everything. It is swell. Of course the guys kidded the Hell out of me about that soap. They keep insisting you are hinting something. Could it be BO? Then, of course, the paper. Don't I write often enough. The paper is so long that I've doubled it, as you can see! Get just as many words on the paper this way. Darling, I love you.

We got a chance to see *Palm Beach Story* the other nite. It was smashing. Never saw so many characters in one show. I'd like to be in one of those "Ale & Quail" clubs that was featured. One way to get in a few months of heavy drinking. One way to get away from a nagging wife. Don't ever want to do it though. I think it will take me a lifetime to prove to you how much I love you. Guys pinned a new nickname on me, "Noel." Gosh, can't help it if I come from Brooklyn. Mail is still bad, it ceases to be funny now.

I was reading an issue of *Life* magazine today that was used as a special to GIs. I took particular interest in the GI Bill of Rights. There are many good features of it that most GIs will take advantage of. I was particularly interested in the idea of borrowing $2,000 for the purchase of a home, etc. I think it is excellent. Especially since they give us 20 years to pay it back. I'm sure that we ought to be able to take care of that sum in 20 years. Darling, I've been thinking of many things. About this GI Bill. NY offers a chance to get some education. I've been seriously thinking of taking a night course in Journalism at Columbia U[*niversity*]. Of course, the idea is purely that but it would be a good idea for us, both of us, to try to breeze thru something like that. Aside from that idea, I assure you that I am going to try to take complete advantage of the government's offers. Know that I'll have to help pay the taxes eventually; might as well get on the blue side of the ledger.

Well, Honey, must say "good night." I'll be busy tomorrow since my head split so definitely it curtailed my sleep somewhat. Take care of yourself. I love you and miss you more each day. May God Bless You. Love, Mike.

Following are the Squadron and Group War Diary entries for November 28-30, 1944:

WD, November 28: No flying to the continent. Two planes test-hopped. . . . Security and censorship lecture was given to all new personnel by Lt. Roman.

GWD, November 28: Foggy and raining this morning and bad weather continued through out the day. No missions today. Movie *Till We Meet Again*. Headquarters basketball team played the 82nd A/B maintenance team and lost 28-16.

WD, November 29: 18 plane mission to the continent and return. Weather ship made the first flight under prescribed route without landing on the continent. . . . Remaining 24 feet of movie film was taken this afternoon of glider tows and planes landing. This film is for historical records of the squadron. Dance at the NAAFI for EMs of this base.

GWD, November 29: A very beautiful day, unusually so for this time of year. Gasoline and Oil was carried to the far shore. NAAFI dance in the evening.

WD, November 30: 19 plane mission to the continent and return. Show at the station theatre.

GWD, November 30: Pay Day.

Chapter 6

To VARSITY
(December 1, 1944
to February 28, 1945)

*O*N DECEMBER 1944, the Germans staged a last-ditch counter-offensive in the Ardennes (the Battle of the Bulge). Bad weather limited troop carrier planes from delivering much-needed supplies to the embattled U.S. troops trapped by the Germans. By January 1945, the Allies continued their drive into Germany, and the Russians conquered Eastern Germany to the Oder River.

On January 9, 1945, U.S. forces under General Douglas MacArthur invaded the Philippines. By February 4, he entered Manila, and within three weeks completed recovery of the city.

A thousand U.S. Bombers raided Berlin February 3, dropping tons of explosives. British Lancasters raided Dresden February 13 with phosphorous and explosive bombs, creating a firestorm that killed an estimated 135,000.

In the Pacific Theater, the Battle of Iwo Jima was being fought February-March 1945.

Following is the Group War Diary's summary for December 1944:

With the end of December 1944 what remains of our original personnel has completed its second year overseas: The Group has completed its first hundred thousand hours of War flying.

December 1, 1944 [*Friday*]

Hello Darling,

This is the first letter I've written in the last few days. Not only have I been busy but to boot things are so quiet that I thought it best to catch up on sack time rather than write nothing. Got back today to find that the ice had broken and I received one letter from you. It was written on the 15th of Nov. Actually as much as I hate to bitch, but when mail gets so bad, one cannot help himself. But all these words and I haven't even told you how much I love you. I do. Darling, when I don't hear from you, I think more and more of you. My thoughts are the only things that help me to recount so much — To go on —

I heard from Tom and we're still keeping up a discussion of literature. Unfortunately, he's so busy at school that he cannot answer all my questions. But little by little they trickle thru to me. I just finished Quentin Reynolds, *Curtain Rises.* It was interesting because it was about places that I have seen. However, it seems that Reynolds wrote the book merely to hoist himself into a political hullabaloo. In contrast to Pyle's GI itinerary, this R concentrates on the whims and such of men like "Ike," Tedler, Patton, etc. All men who will never be classed in our category until we get back to civilian life. It is good to know of these men's eccentricities but it hardly gets a guy down to the bottom of [*their*] thinking. Another thing that griped me was his consistent mention of those wonderful "C rations." The man's a maniac. Ask any GI who has had them; you have to be pretty hungry and miserable to enjoy them — and so.

In your letter you mentioned the fact that you thought that most English men appeared like "cream puffs." These European males are all almost alike. In the first place they are too interested in being "continental." Their sports are limited; consequently, their choice of activity is poor. It is not strange to see two of these males walking down the street hand in hand. It has always appeared as a disgusting sight to me. Grown up and supposedly intelligent men, acting like a Greenwich Village queer. To the average young American boy, his primary diversion is a good active sport. The Europeans think of sex, etc. It is commonplace and normal — perhaps it is a good thought but everything has its own place. The English, I don't know; it is a rare sight to see a young man out of uniform. To Hell with them all, I'd rather see 22 guys trying to "moider" each other on the gridiron.

Darling, what is the meaning of (10-2 & 4)? Is that meant to be a date of one of my letters? Those few numbers left me guessing as to their meaning.

I have a million and one things to say but I must rush off. Going into Dec. and another month has passed. Thank God. Just can't wait to see the next few pass. Can't wait to hold you in my arms and tell you all the things that have been burning my heart for the last 16 months. Darling, I love you.

Good night, Bette. Give my love to Mother. Take care of yourself. May God Bless you. Love, Mike.

The Squadron (WD) and Group (GWD) War Diary entries for December 1-3, 1944, were:

> **WD, December 1: Seventeen aircraft were dispatched to the continent on resupply and troop movement missions. All planes returned plus one additional aircraft which had been grounded in France** [*actually Belgium*] **since 26 Nov. '44 with a damaged wing tip. . . .**
>
> **GWD, December 1: Aircraft of the group carried out resupply and troop transport missions to the far shore today. Local flights were made checking in new pilots who recently joined the Group.**
>
> **WD, December 2: Eighteen planes were sent to the far shore for resupply and evacuation. Three planes turned back owing to weather conditions. The remaining 15 planes completed the mission. One plane became lost and after flying into enemy territory attracted ground fire. No damage was sustained. A new C-109** [*converted B-24*] **aircraft was assigned to the squadron.**
>
> **GWD, December 2: Some few men of the Group are returning to the states on a rotation program. A plane was dispatched to Cairo, Egypt, and its mission unknown. Aircraft that took off for the far shore returned because of bad weather on the far shore.**
>
> **WD, December 3: Three planes hauled supplies to continent and returned while seventeen planes dispatched on troop movement, RON. The Group football team butted to a scoreless tie under adverse conditions.**
>
> **GWD, December 3: Resupply and air evacuation mission was dispatched to the Continent today and returned safely home. Cloudy during the morning. Early in the afternoon the now famous "Berger's Bouncers" played the Welford Ramblers but neither side were able to score at the half, and the game was called off because of rain. Movie** *Sahara* **in the evening.**

December 4, 1944 [*Monday*]

Hello Darling,

I can't remember if it is Monday, Tuesday or what. See if I can recount the last days. When I got in Saturday, I found 2 letters from you but it was so late that I didn't write. I figured that I'd be able to write Sunday, but they hustled me out. As fortune would have it I didn't get back until today and it isn't early. I had visions of a hot shower and shave but Hell, screwed again. So come what may, I have to write to tell you how much I love you. I hope that when I finish this letter, I'll be able to shower, hot or cold, I will.

Gosh, Darling, I love you so very much. As I've said so often before, I wish the holidays were over. Somehow or other, I can't seem to wait for the time to pass, but so a little more patience. (We are going to have a going away ceremony for another one of our fortunate chaps — can't wait for the day that they do it for me.) All I could see in my dreams last night was you. Yes, Darling, each day makes each moment more wonderful because it brings us that much closer. If I could only express the joy I feel sometimes, it would make everything so easy. I've been so busy lately that I haven't had much chance to do anything but think. That may sound strange but thinking does take little effort especially if you think about the right thing. The right thing to me, Bette, My Darling, is our future. I can't help but feel the most enjoyable tingling in my spine when I think about us.

To boot, I am so far behind in everything. I am far behind in my correspondence and washing. I have gangs of mail to answer, Sheila, Harry, home and lots of others of my friends. I hate to delay but what can I do? Right at this moment, I feel so congested with so many incidentals that I feel inclined to say, the Hell, and just pound the sack but I can't. I want to tell you how comforting and warm your arms were in the cold last night. I felt as if I was sleeping in a dungeon [*on our aircraft in Belgium*] but whenever I really started to feel uncomfortable, I'd think of you and what you mean to me. It made the night short and easy to take. I didn't sleep much but who cares, it wasn't hard to take.

You mentioned something about shrimp in one of your letters. It has been many times that I've leaned back and thought how great it would be to polish off a good shrimp cocktail. It reminds me so much of the night in Ft. Wayne when that was the only thing that we could get for supper. Gosh, Honey, those wonderful days can't be too far off. I keep ticking them off as if they were seconds to the minute.

Well, Darling, I am going to say good night. I've got so much to say and I haven't even started to answer your letters. So you can see that you are in for plenty. So long for now, Honey. Give my love to Mother. Take care of yourself. May God Bless You.

I love you and miss you. Love, Mike.

Squadron War Diary entry, December 4:

> **Four planes were sent to the continent on a resupply mission, all returning along with the 17 planes which had RON from the previous day. One ship taking patients to [*Prestwick*] RON. Twenty-one enlisted men were promoted. . . .**

The Group War Diary entry for that day read:

Personnel and baggage of the 82nd A/B were carried to the far shore. Dance in the evening for the Enlisted Men of the base at the Red Cross Arrow Club.

December 5, 1944 [*Tuesday*]

Good Evening, Darling,

Here I am back again trying to make my few free seconds as enjoyable as I can. After I mailed your letter last night, I proceeded to get stinking. We had to give the kid a good send off and that we did. A couple of the officers were over and as usual we ended singing everything in the books. Polished off 2 quarts of gin and 2 quarts of scotch. Smashing, isn't it? Feeling in the best of spirits and having put everyone else to bed, Pappy [*Agle*] walked in about 11 and said he had some scotch, so Bill [*Toohey*] and I (Bill was the guest of honor, lucky stiff!) went with Pappy and finished the night in good style. He had a ½ finished quart and one of the other officers had some unfinished business and 2 more soldiers did we bury. Pappy says he will write one of these days and he sends his love. Well that's my last blow for a while. I gotta get back to that nice normal swing of life. Darling, did you know that when I get feeling high, I render one of my versions of "Begin the Beguine." It is most unfortunate that so many souls must suffer with me.

This article I am sending you is self-explanatory. Conditions permitting, it is a clear outline of our activities. You can see why I send some horribly putrid letters at times. I just can't help myself. This 434th was my old outfit back in the states, remember? If they think they have an enviable record, they had better start to do some work. He should wait til he's been over a while, the john!

Finally got a letter from Harry after a long while. It is always good to hear from him. He is still taking good care of one of my prized souvenirs, it is an Italian Beretta — that's a small pistol, very handy. Getting Harry's letter adds more to my already overflowing batch of unanswered correspondence. I do hope I get a rest one of these days. Honestly though, Honey, I don't mind too horribly much. It keeps me occupied and it is easier to cross off one more day on my calendar. (Just thought of it — Please save this article for my scrap book. You see, Bette, I've got gangs of stuff to put in my albums. I haven't started work on them because I'd rather do it together with you.) Oh yes, Harry told me that we have another unit citation coming our way, so that means a cluster for my citation. As long as they keep coming, I'll take [*them*]. They actually add points to that day of demobilization. I love you. —

You mentioned something about a camera. Or at least, getting film for one so that we can take some good pictures. Well, Honey, don't get any for my camera. You see, I intend to get a better one because I am so trigger happy that I'd rather have a fast candid camera. Mine is too slow. Don't worry about wedding pictures; we won't forget them. Gotta have a recording of that day.

It has been so long since I thought about some things that I feel lost. Of course, I'll keep sending my mail to your ole address until I get your Miami address. My ole tent mate came from Tampa, Florida. Got a letter from him yesterday. He's at Miami Beach now. Hopes to stay there for a long time. I hope he does. At any rate, I don't know his wife personally, but thru' Max, I know she is a great person. If you should be in Tampa, look her up. The name, Mrs. Sue Gilliam. . . . It is good to know people and if you should need any help, those kinds of acquaintances come in handy. Max is a great guy and he knows you well thru' me. At the rate I'm going, Darling, we'll have friends all over the U.S. As a matter of fact, Max invited you and me to spend a few weeks with Sue and him, when this world gets back to normal.

You mentioned something about periods and stuff but I am not going to say anything in this letter. There will be more and I must try to answer a few more letters before I play ball tonight. Gotta find time for everything.

Good night, Bette, I do love you and miss you more each day. Take care of yourself. Gosh! I miss you. May God Bless You. Love, Mike.

On December 5, the War Diary reported:

> **Twenty planes hauled troops and equipment to the continent, returning the same day. The ship which RON in [*Prestwick*] also returned. T/Sgt. V. J. Immel, T/Sgt. Glenn R. Parrish, Sgt. W. J. Toohey returned . . . to the United States.**

The Group War Diary entry for the same day read:

> **Freight and personnel of the 82nd still being carried to the continent. A few B-24s were assigned to the Group for transition training. A school was started for pilots and crew members at Group Headquarters building today. Movie at the station cinema, *Lady in the Dark*.**

On December 6, according to the Squadron War Diary, 21 planes flew on a troop mission to France, and all returned safely. Squadron Operations Officer Major William E. Childers was returned to the "Zone of the Interior," — the continental United States — and was succeeded by Captain Floyd Miles.

The Group War Diary entry for the same day read:

> **Routine day here in Headquarters. Some few resupply missions flown to the continent. The regular Wednesday night dance at the NAAFI was canceled until a later date.**

December 7, 1944 [*Thursday*]

Hello Darling,

I see that this is the 3rd anniversary of one of America's worst tragedies [*a reference, of course, to Pearl Harbor*]. But so, [*it*] is history and suffer the consequences, we must. Today is my first day of rest in a long time. I pleaded and yelled, and so to quiet me, here I am. I washed clothes til my hands turned blue and then started on my correspondence. I have written 4 letters already and I saved you for last so that I could write as much as I can. Darling, my mind is numb. I looked thru your recent letters so that I could see what you said about [*W. Somerset*] Maugham's *Razor's Edge*. I am reading it now and I wanted to comment parallel to you. However, I didn't find the letter and so. However, I find that the book is one that is impossible to leave. It is well written with an extraordinary idea, I think. But I can't say much more because I don't feel like saying anything but that I love you.

. . . Our minds run on parallel strains. Speaking of that near future, I thoroly agree with you. It is easier to be pleasant than to be disagreeable. All these months that we've spent apart, have been used to think of how many ways we can make each other happy. Our respect, trust and love for each other prevents us from being unkind and selfish. More and more each day, my mind becomes impressed with you. All I've ever asked for was peace; moreso now, because I've seen anything but peace. I dream of the day when we will be together and I've yet to miss a time when I got the same thrill over and over again. Darling, you mean the world to me. As I said before, you came to me when I needed you most. Now I am depending on you to bring back reality to me. To help me to readjust myself to that life over on that side of the ocean. I know that I sound dramatic but no matter how small the change, no matter how much the lacking, it is you who I want to unbend my filthy soul. The stench of war, the stench of army, the stench of too much irresponsible living will be in my nostrils. It will take the sweetness of you, the perfume of your personality to rid me of all that. It may seem strange to hear all this but one cannot help but to feel a barbaric repulsion to all that was so much a part of my life. I want you to renew my faith in what America and Americans always were. To be able to have one cocktail instead of a gallon, to be able to say "please" instead of "— —," to be able to walk to the corner drug store for a soda instead of dreaming of it. All that and more, I want to see again thru your eyes and with you on my arm — And so, My Darling, you see what your love means to me. I love you so much.

Must close. — pardon this "free" business — Give my love to Mother. Take care of yourself. See you later. Miss you terribly. May God Bless You. Love, Mike.

P.S.: I've always thought that my letters end too abruptly. But you must forgive me because I have a million & one things to do, So many things can crop up in a short time, it isn't funny. You must bear with me. You know that my love is not as abrupt as my letter writing. Circumstances are a pain when it comes to us. M.

WD, December 7: Nineteen planes were dispatched upon a resupply mission to the far shore, however owing to adverse weather conditions on the continent all but one returned before reaching the objective. Instrument and transition flights were scheduled. . . .

GWD, December 7: Although the aircraft sent to the far shore had to return again because of a heavy front, some local transition flights were made.

December 8, 1944 [*Friday*]

Hello Darling,

Another day of grace and I do mean it feels good. Saw the picture *Janie* last night. It wasn't bad because it was funny enough to keep going. Personally I think the little gal, whatever her name was, stole the show. The one thing that is most disinteresting about some of these pictures is the false sense of patriotism and GI living that is portrayed. I don't claim to be a veteran, but I've seen enough of this army life. Those "hammy" exclamations like, "Gosh, I may be going over soon, I may not come back." Who the Hell feels like that? I'll bet every guy, and even those that won't come back, never thought of dying. We aren't made that way. Drama is left for the stage. Another thing, our movements are secret; one does not go around blurting, "Well, soldier, we're going." Like Hell — I didn't know where I was actually going until I was on my last leg. And I wasn't traveling with thousands of guys. It's OK to fool the public but if you heard the "guffaws" of a soldier audience, you'd know what I mean.

I finished *Razor's Edge*. I am afraid that in some part, he writes merely for the intellectuals. Strictly out of my class. His revelation of Larry's faith-seeking is something that requires plenty of concentration. I can follow the outer circle but I'm afraid I'm not close enough to scrape the soul of the idea. Whatever I understood of Larry's findings, I disagreed with wholeheartedly. But I understand enough to know that one cannot see the basis of his own religion unless he, too, dwells on that religion of others. M's ending was superb because he explained that it, the story, was a success story. Naturally, he leaves none of his characters unattached from their original courses. His picture of continental sex life leaves me no doubt of the true character of these people who accept sex as normal and routine. Personally, I'll stick to the American depth of sacrifice and love that is attached to the bedroom amour.

I reread some of your letters in which you apologize for your steady discourse of subjects which you feel are most uninteresting to me. No, Darling, you mustn't apologize for that. After all what I must I say then for my varying degrees of consistency, for my seemingly stupid remarks; for my "You must read between the lines to understand," subjects that make sense to me but must be just words to you. Things like that cannot be helped. Darling, whatever we say, big or small, is said with the main thought that we are thinking of each other. Would you rather that we write each other only when we have something to say? No, Isn't it better to let each other know that these words are being passed even if they are in letters? Do you think that we'll be able to spend the next 50+ years absorbed in deep conversation or don't you think that many times silence or simple words will be all the conversation that is necessary? If I know us well enough, I know there won't be many lapses of silence but occasionally it has to be expected, or do you talk in your sleep? I love you.

Gonna peel off. Tell Mother that I'm glad she still thinks I'm the same little man. Sometimes I wish others would feel the same way. So long for now. Take care of yourself. May God Bless You.

I love you and miss you. Mike.

All aircraft were grounded on December 8 due to weather, according to the Squadron War Diary, which also noted:

> **The fifth bronze star to the ETO ribbon was changed from the battle of western Europe to the Normandy campaign.**

The Group War Diary for that day read:

> **All planes were grounded today because of heavy fog. Dance in the evening at the NAAFI with ATS service women from Leicester and special guests for the evening were the ATS from Chillwell, Queen Elizabeth camp.**

On December 9, the Squadron War Diary recorded that 16 planes had flown supplies to the continent, "all returning except six which RON in southern England."

The December 9 Group War Dairy noted:

> **Heavy frost here at Cottesmore this morning. In the afternoon it began to snow but very little remained on the ground. Movie here on the base, *Chip Off the Old Block*.**

December 10, 1944 [*Sunday*]

Good Evening, Darling,

I am sorry that I didn't write last night but due to circumstances beyond my control, it was impossible. When I got back today, the first thing I did after I washed was to sack and I mean it felt good. Went to a show this evening, had a glass of beer after and here I am. Saw some second rate show with Donald O'Connor and Peggy Ryan, and this kid Ann Blyth. Honey, she is lovely. "Ah's in love." Cutest little trick I've seen since I left you. Now that my period of dullness is over, I think of you twice as much. It is the greatest feeling in the world. I must admit that it makes me as eager as Hell to see you but again, I must profess that I can still rely on that patience of ours. But, Gosh, Bette, just to be able to rest my head against that lovely blonde hair of yours and I'd be the happiest guy in the world. As it is, I couldn't love you any more than I do, sometimes I think I've reached my capacity; the only thing that makes me doubt that is that I haven't seen you for such a long time that when I do, I'm afraid my enthusiasm will run away from me. Gosh, it's great to be in love.

Just finished a rather pleasant tale of happy marriage. A book called *Mr. & Mrs. Cugat* by one Rorick. You must have heard of it. It is a swell, light, and entertaining treatise on marriage. I'd say that it was my ideal of what a married couple should be like. Of course, the one thing that hurt was that since I haven't attained Mr. Cugat's financial peak, we couldn't possibly entertain as lavishly as they did. However, the book is handled so expertly that it is not impossible to apply such living to people of the middle class social standing. Don't think we'll be so horribly poverty-stricken that we won't be able to hold our own. The one level that we have with the hero & heroine is that we drink to everything as they do. I enjoyed the book immensely because I've always dreamed of living a fine irresponsible and yet highly responsible life as they did. Keep to the ole saying, "A time and place for everything." The book fits perfectly to normal living. I recommend the book highly.

It is funny but here it is approaching the Christmas holidays — I guess the Army helps to discourage a lot of sentimental dreaming and consequently it is hard to think of any holiday, even those which were always part of our former lives. But the first time I've felt a sprinkling of the Christmas spirit, I walked into the Red Cross and they had the place decked out in fir and holly. It has been so long. Then to boot, I rollicked around in the snow for a while after supper. I felt like someone had dropped me back at least five years. Darling, do you like the ole-fashioned Christmases? You know what I mean, candle light and wine, the strong sweet smell of fir, gangs of presents, a big Christmas tree in the living room, the Yule log — Oh! all kinds of things that made us feel as kids that ole St. Nick would come creeping down the sooty chimney. I'm crazy about that sort of stuff. It seems like only yesterday that I probably asked you the same questions in my letters last year. So much has happened since, and yet deep in my heart, I still cherish all the grandeur and simplicity that comes with the greatest part of the year. It all adds up to anything I want to share with you. I want you nestled in my arms, dreaming of the future, caring for nothing except that we are together. Darling, it's the most wonderful thought in the world. I shan't say a Very Merry Xmas just Merry because it won't be very merry until the Army says, "Mike, go on home; you've done all you need to do — pleasant memories." — <u>Pleasant</u>?

Well, Darling, I say good night and sweet dreams. You don't mind if I go to bed with Bob Hope's book, do you? Give my love to Mother. Take care of yourself, Dear.

May God Bless You. I love you. Love, Mike.

Squadron War Diary, December 10:

> **Five planes dispatched to the continent, four of which delivered their loads and returned to RON in southern England. The fifth ship RON on the continent. The six planes which had RON in southern England from the day before returned. Memorial services were held in the base chapel for the two officers and two enlisted men who were killed in the mid-air collision over Belgium on the 26th Nov. '44.**

The Group War Diary for that day noted only that "Church services were held by all faiths this morning."

On December 11, according to the Squadron War Diary,

> **Sixteen planes hauled supplies to the far shore. All returning except one which RON on the continent with engine trouble. The four ships which RON in southern England picked up loads and returned to Cottesmore. Today a new non-stop weather ship was dispatched to the continent for the first time. Transition training was carried on in the new C-109 while a link trainer [*flight simulator*] was put in operation for the new pilots. Dance at the American Red Cross for Enlisted personnel. Show at the station theatre for officers.**

The December 11 Group War Diary entry read:

> **Aircraft of the group carried British equipment to the far shore and returned with patients. The Enlisted Men's dance was held tonight at the Red Cross. ATS from Chillwell were present.**

December 12, 1944 [*Tuesday*]

Hello Darling,

Here I am again! Not here as often as I'd like to be but nevertheless, I try. Finally, I received a letter from you dated the 29th of Nov. Unfortunately, the time lapse is so great between letters that it is almost impossible to put treads together. The last letter I got, tells me of your visit to Texas. Now I must wait for the full account in another letter. You speak in smattering in this letter but my curiosity is almost beyond control. Happily, I see that you have started to get some of my mail.

I am glad that you are interested enough to read *The Apostle*. However, I must warn you that it is difficult reading. You must endeavor not to lay it down for too long, for if you do, you will not resume reading again. I read it for the basic knowledge and to compare Asch's writing with my learning. Believe me that I must have asked Tom a million questions concerning it. I had to because there was so many things that needed clarification, so many points whose veracity I questioned. I've just been handed Lloyd C. Douglas', *The Robe*. I am going to read it later because I chose Hope's book to give me some entertaining relaxation before I try some deep concentration. I've been told that this book must be read slowly to fully realize its beauty and depth and so —

Thanks for telling me about those pralines. I had no idea what they were. As it is I prefer candy for its taste rather than by name. Another part of my education that needs broadening. Another point upon which I am dense is foods by name. To me it is easier to say Corned Beef and Cabbage than *fromage au gratin* or *lac du jeune filles*. French names are my nemesis. That is why I prefer home cooking to playing my wits against some gushing head waiter who doesn't care if you eat or not.

You are perfectly right when you say that Dan's visit should have been like a short furlough. Where we should have been treading on familiar ground, we discussed a common disgust — I don't prefer that because I see enough planes all day to satisfy my taste for aviation. I can't be impressed any further — but I would much rather have talked about New York, the family, the changes, the liquor and our women. At any rate, I accomplished one thing — he and Gert, his fiancee, were not intending to marry until the end of the war (damn foolishness). I gave him my views and from latest reports from the home front, they've decided to tie the knot as soon as he completes his tour. Do I make a cute Cupid? Hell, Honey, I know how I feel. If I can impress so many people, guess my (our) ideas are pretty strong. Honestly, and we know it only too well, no one but ourselves can refill all our empty, parted moments, so why wait and let more time pass? No one needs to tell us what to do. I'm sure we know full well what our near future plans are — Gosh, Bette, I love you so very much.

I suppose I do know that I was the main subject of conversation. You see, Bette, that adds back to a long time. Sheila and I used to pal out together before I stepped out for Tony. I was the first to know of their pending marriage and I am Rebel's godfather and guardian. If anything should ever happen to Tony and Sheila, I am totally responsible for Lillian's future. But aside from that, I feel proud to add that I am the favorite brother there. And I, in turn, feel a special warmth toward that family circle. I almost accept them all as my own family. It is a close relationship brought about by familiarity and intimacy that is personal beyond some people's comprehension. I hope and pray that you found the same open heartedness that I felt for all the years I've known them.

I am glad that my optimism gave you a fare spell of hopefulness. I don't intend to shatter your dreams because I still feel the same way as I expressed myself in earlier letters. We still have to bide our time a little longer but the months pass easily; they have to. I am tickled silly by the good prospects. Whenever I feel slightly let down, I let my mind wander to you and our closeness and everything seems not too remote. It is the easiest way to keep up shining hope.

Well Darling, I must close. Gonna hit my sack — got some reading to do. Good night. Give my love to Mother. Take care of yourself.

I love you and miss you. May God Bless You. Love, Mike.

On December 12, ten planes were sent on a troop movement and resupply mission, and all returned, according to the Squadron War Diary entry, which concluded with: "The squadron basketball team lost their first game."

The Group War Diary entry the same day recorded the mission, and described the dense fog that made landing difficult.

There were no flights on December 13 or 14, due to bad weather. The Squadron War Diary noted that on both days the newly assigned officers and enlisted men were given a lecture on censorship, security, and prisoner of war procedure by Lieutenant Roman.

All aircraft were still grounded on December 15. That day's Group War Diary entry reported:

> **Again no flights were made. One sure topic of conversation around here is the weather. Preparations being made for Headquarters Enlisted Men's' party on the 23rd of December. NAAFI dance held this evening and the Guest of Honor were Lt. Col. Washburn and Major Sergeant.**

December 16, 1944 [*Saturday*]

Good Evening, Darling,

I must apologize for not writing for the last three days but the Ole Boy has been blank. To be truthful, we started to celebrate our holidays a bit early and we sort of went on a tear. But, please don't worry or get angry with me, just one of those things. We are back to normal so I guess I won't be so lax. Honestly, Darling, the real reason for the stupid action is the lack of mail. If we don't start to get some, there will be a bunch of suicides around here. I know it isn't your fault; it's just some sort of hold up. Damn, it really is disheartening. Bette, you know how alcohol affects me, actually I should never use it to forget because I remember so much. I get so damn lonely for you. You must pardon me if I appear to sound mushy but I do miss you so terribly much. The whole trouble is the opposite effect that damn stuff has on me. I have repeated myself here, haven't I? But ordinarily when I am in complete soberness I realize I must absorb myself in my work. A few drinks help me to relax too perfectly. But don't worry, Darling, still the same guy, love you and waiting for the time to pass. Must make you tired to hear me keep repeating about time and its turtle crawl.

Went before the CO today and received our cluster to the Air Medal. I was rather surprised to see how small it is. It can't be much bigger than this [*small drawing of the oak leaf*]. At any rate, it takes the bareness away from the ribbon. I am not too eager to add any more clusters. Perhaps, next time, I wouldn't be so lucky.

Still doing some reading but I slacked off on that too. I have started *The Robe* and although I find it difficult to lay aside once I start reading, it is impossible to devote all my time to reading. I've had a bit of a head cold that has knocked a little of the life out of me. I'm OK now. This book is the story of the Robe that Christ wore at the time of His crucifixion. It is the story of the men who gambled for that Robe and their life after the event at Calgary. That's as far as I have gone. Really interesting though, because as a matter of curiosity, one cannot help but wonder what people felt at the crucifixion. There are many things that are suppositions of the author but all in all, they make good reading.

Gosh, Honey, although I haven't written for days there is still nothing to say. My mind makes all events incidental and supercilious. Nothing matters but the thought of my future homecoming, whenever that may be. You must forgive my attitude, Bette, but I do promise to make up for all these lapses.

Well, Cheerio, Ole Gal. Take care of yourself. I do love you so much and miss you so. Give my love to Mother.

Good Night. May God Bless You. Love & Kisses, Mike.

WD, December 16: No flying owing to bad weather conditions. At a squadron formation 53 officers and enlisted men were decorated with the Air Medal and 81 officers and enlisted men received an Oak Leaf cluster in lieu of a second air medal, for their participation in the airborne invasion of Holland. The medals were effective as of 15 Nov. '44 under Secs. II and III GO 113, HQs IX TCC. Per par. Sec. 2, GO 125, HQs IX TCC, dtd. 9 Dec. '44, Lt. Woodrow V. Timo and Lt. Edward W. McArthur are authorized the distinguished flying cross for outstanding performance of duty in bringing their aircraft back from the invasion of Holland, however, these medals have not been presented. 2nd Lt. Robert C. Lancaster and PFC William A. Kabaker missing in action in the invasion of Holland on 18 Sept. '44 are reported prisoners of war per Ltr., Subject "Changes in battle casualty status," HQs 52nd TCW, dtd. 15 Dec. '44. Cpl. Hicks was married in Leicester.

GWD, December 16: Mist with heavy fog today although it is much warmer. Again operations are canceled.

December 17, 1944 [*Sunday*]

Hello Darling,

I just heard Sammy Kaye and I forced myself away from a very interesting conversation, nudist colonies. It is a quiet Sunday afternoon but I felt I must write to make up for that horrible missile that I wrote last night. Unfortunately, nothing new has happened except that we've got a new cat, "Erbie." Odd name. Isn't it? But actually since he (or she) is an English product, it is just as well that we keep in the present vogue. Saw a Humphrey Bogart film last night called *Conflict*. It was a clever study of psychology and indeed enjoyable. It's a good thing we have some sort of entertainment around here; it helps the time to pass. To show the type of conversations that filter thru these barracks, last night 2 of the guys were talking about how they air and dry out their sleeping bags. What made it all screwy is that these 2 characters have a habit of letting their kidneys loosen up when they are drunk. Consequently in that state they don't bother to get out of bed; to help this intelligent morsel, they employed cockney accents to their speech and I do mean it was funny. But what a Hell of a topic!

Gosh, Bette, I love you so much. I can't help but think that God has been good to me. It seems like only yesterday that I came overseas. As much as I gripe about the length of a day, week or month, I cannot help but feel that it has passed. Last Christmas I was wallowing around in the mud, making pies with my feet and cursing the wetness and filth of my environment and now a whole year later, I find myself a wiser and a bit older man, who has found happiness in his love for such a fine woman. Believe me, Darling, I have yet to find one time when I could not shrug off some morbid feeling with a mere thought of you. You've shaped an awful lot of sense into me. Think that you could do so much by proxy, what effect would you have on me if we were together all this while? It is going to be great to be together. I can't think of a better way to climax all of this. Gosh, it's wonderful.

So long for now, Darling. Give my love to Mother. Take care of yourself.

I love you and miss you. May God Bless You. Love, Mike.

December 17, 1944 [*Sunday*]

Good Evening, Darling,

It was a lovely day; it was a swell night and I love you deeply. I know that sounds lively as a Lindy Hop but you can't expect a guy to be depressed after he's received 3 letters from the gal he loves. It is a wonderful feeling that written words can give a guy.

You can tell that RAF character that the only reason for those tremendous prices for liquor seems to be part payment for reverse lease-lend. But as it is once these foreigners, not only the English, get one look at an American, they figure we are all walking treasuries. However, I was surprised at the conduct of those men. I do know that they can't dance nor hold their liquor but as a whole, I've felt that they are well-mannered. It is impossible to enjoy their company because they are so totally different from us. The only thing that we have in common is that they speak English. (Or do they?) I've always been able to handle these RAF kids because they are usually so young and I've seen so many of them. At any rate, you can chalk that up to experience. Maybe there will be a day when you'll do that for me.

There will be many days like the one you speak of. The mutual bond between 2 people is usually enough to let silence do the talking. I imagine that there may be many. Just the complete happiness of being together will say the word. Both of us thought that when I left it would be for just a short time, but the Army has ways of doing things differently. However, be patient, Darling. It's rough for both of us but that smile can carry us thru.

It is unfortunate that our mail should pass the way it does. But I see in your latest letter that I am doing much better. 14 letters is a lot and I know exactly how you feel. It seems

rather strange to hear that you are playing the role of cupid but I can see why you are eager
to see that Mother gets married. It would do her a world of good. I can see you going about
planning dates, etc. Cute idea, isn't it?

Now to get down to your visit to Texas. First of all, it's tough that you must have so
much trouble getting everything straightened out. How well I remember your visit to Ft.
Wayne. One good thing about your being late was that I did get some time to sober up.
You must thank my eagerness to see you and my undaunted patience. I wouldn't have left
you if you were 3 days late. It tickles me every time I think of those wonderful days then.
I should have married you then. But spilled milk is lost milk. There will be other years. I
love you.

For a while when I first started to read your letter, I had visions of another NY. That
would have killed me. Unfortunately, I try to picture the better side of people because I'd
much rather that you see them thru that light. I imagine that you and Sheila had a rough
start because it takes a while to get on a common ground. . . . It was natural for her to spill
all the ill-fortunes of family ties. So many of these things can develop over a period of
many years. I've always contended that strange male relatives can get more out of each
other than females. It's no one's fault, women are women. Cynical, aren't I?

You honor me with such a high opinion of my brother, Tony. I think you found just
cause for my liking for him. All my brothers seem to be tops with me. Tony is uppermost
because we never bothered to mince words. His principles (les not als) are high because
he is a man and a good man. You made me feel good when you said that his men idolize
him. He is my idea of the ideal army officer because he's old army and his experience is
practical. His experience was accumulated thru years in China and his wisdom. His
biggest regret is being a 90-day wonder but it is his greatest strength because he has
resigned himself to do a good job. . . . But I am going on to something more important.

Darling, I must scold. (Not rigidly but just a point.) "Sheila expects you to spend 3 or
4 days of your furlough there." Eek! No. Now listen — It has been 18 months since I've
seen you. It will be more by the time I do. In all these months, I've dreamt of our joining.
I've dreamt of all the joy and happiness, the tranquillity of our many moments. Would I
waste weeks to make a trip to Texas and know that you are waiting in NY for me? No.
Sheila may suggest it but she'll never get an affirmative answer. Gosh, Bette, no matter if
the Army gave me a 5-year furlough, I don't want to spend it alone. It is a breach of our
promise to each other. You recall, wherever I go, you are going with me. Only the neces-
sities of the Army can keep us apart. How can I feel that you are selfish for not wanting
me to go? It isn't that you don't want me to go because you want so much to make me
happy but I don't want to. Perhaps when <u>we</u> are stationed somewhere we might take a furlough (Some case!) and go together. Until then, my friends must come to me. That includes most of my relatives. Perhaps I am popular and everyone can cry for my skin but
that skin is going to be chased. You were right when you told her that we'd wait until I am
stationed somewhere. But, Darling, do you mind if I get selfish? Whenever anyone asks
you what we plan or what is going to go on when I get home, — your first words should
be — "We" or "Mike and I plan. . . ." No longer are you to keep thinking that Mike will
do this or that. From now on we will be the "We Kids." Every moment means too much
to us, My Darling. Every second is precious. It will be the beginning of a new life for us.

Whatever obligations we must answer to, will be answered when we are ready. It is a part of a new gained independence that neither of us cares to share with anyone but us. Forgive me for sounding harsh but my words are of the heart because my heart has been empty too long. You are to fill it; how can you if I am in Texas and you in Oshkosh?

Darling, I must close because this will be bulky but I am going to continue in a new letter. It isn't strange, these letters are as if I hadn't seen you for so long. I hunger to speak to you as I want to always. I love you. Mike.

December 17, 1944 [*Sunday*]: part II

Hi Bette,

I call this part II because I cannot possibly stop writing. I must wash and get some sack time but I must also take advantage of my talkative mood. Although when I receive gangs of mail I read yours last; you have first priority when it comes to answering your letters.

Another point that surprised me about Sheila's statement is that she ever thought of it. Tony would not say anything because he realizes the strain, physical and mental that I've been under. He realizes that I will want to crawl into a shell with you. He knows that I will demand little but the desire to be with you. Tony knows because he has felt as I have — that's why Harry and I feel the same way and Dan felt as I did. That's why Doc will feel the same way. Cannot people understand that all of us lost so much that we want to regain with the person who has lost it with us. Tony told you of my going over the hump. I tried to make it sound casual and light. Read between the lines and anyone can see that I wasn't happy over all of it. Sure, it is easy to laugh now — it is one of those musty, horrible sights that is so easy to forget but do we? Do we not see why, in those moments, why we appreciate the comfort of the arms of the person we love, do we not feel the tenderness of those lips, the ecstasy of that embrace. Surely there is fear but not of death but of the fact that we may never have those things again. I must have told you before but I repeat to make my point emphatic — Darling, you rode with me in every one of those nightmarish trips. When my throat was dry and my hands sweaty, even in the cold, my first words were, "Bette, My Darling." I can see you sitting on my wing; you looked in and smiled and I knew I was OK. I never told you that much before because I would have sounded silly and people would think that I was insane. Harry knows of it. But could I put it in a letter to you or my family? They would say it was my imagination. That was why I was so frantic when I heard of your unsuccessful trip to my home. I was afraid that everything was ruined for me by some blundering intruders. I am telling it now because I want you to know how I feel. I wanted to wait and tell it to you and my family. It is on paper now and it can be accepted as a falsehood, but I promise to tell all of you of it. Be I called a liar and a fool, I don't care. I know what I felt. I am sorry, Darling, if I sound dramatic. That is another reason why I was afraid to write. What I said is like someone telling of a miracle. It is hard to believe. It is as if a man with a warped brain was speaking. Unfortunately, no one saw it but me. I have no proof. All the proof I have is that I am sane and mentally healthy — nothing bothers me but missing you. I am being courageous to admit this to you because you may begin to worry about hallucinations. Never have them. Do you wonder why I don't want ever to be separated from you again?

Well, Good night, Darling. Do not worry about me. The guy is sane and he wasn't drunk. I'll clarify it some day. You'll know all the circumstances. Could it be that I love you so much? I know I do. May God Bless You. Mike.

On December 17, all flights were still grounded. The Squadron War Diary noted only that one of the men was married that day.

The Group War Diary for December 17 reported that religious services were held as usual, and that "a courier service has been set up between Cottesmore and Command."

Flights finally resumed on December 18, as the Squadron War Diary reported:

> **Sixteen aircraft were sent to the continent on a troop movement. Three ships RON while the remainder returned. The weather ship carried out its mission.**

The Group War Diary entry, December 18:

> **Aircraft flew glider tow practice in the morning and afternoon and some resupply missions were affected to the far shore. The regular Red Cross Dance for the Enlisted Men was canceled due to shortage of transportation.**

Planes were again grounded on December 19. The Squadron War Diary read:

> **The squadron was taken from an operational status and placed on an intensive 30-day training schedule. It consists of formation flying both day and night, paradrops and glider tows. Two officers and one enlisted man newly assigned . . . were given a lecture on censorship, security and prisoner of war procedure.**

The Group War Diary for December 19 did record some flights that day:

> **Gas Day. The scheduled training program that was to start today was postponed and resupply and troop transport missions were carried to the continent.**

There was no flying on December 20 or 21 due to inclement weather. The Group War Diary on December 20 reported that that evening's dance had to be cancelled, "because transportation was unable to pick up the girls."

On December 21, the only news reported in the Group War Diary was the movie that was shown at the station cinema, *Gentleman from Barberry Coast*.

December 22, 1944 [*Friday*]

Dearest,

You must forgive me for not writing for the last 4 days. Due to uncontrollable circumstances, I haven't been able to do much of anything. When I got back tonight, I found your large card sent from aboard ship plus a few letters. Though I must wash and shave, I must write to you. I damn near came close to not doing anything. I heard from home and they tell me that a buddy of mine who had just flown home, went to see my parents. He gave them as much info' as he could. Before he left, he promised to drop you a line. So you may be hearing soon, if you haven't heard already.

Before I attempt to answer your letters, there are many things I must tell you. First of all, I love you so very much. And so I go on. I have met some very interesting people who may thru the course of years become good friends of ours, but that, too, is most premature. I visited Lille recently and I was able to get some perfume for you. However, I couldn't possibly get any "Tabu" or "Chanel" but I got you a bottle of "Changri-La." Since I know so little about these things, I don't know how good it is but I do know that it cost a bit. It has something else on it, "Comtesse de Jansac" Paris, maybe that's the name of the company, who knows. I am not going to send it until I get your new address. I do hope it gets there in one piece. I think you'll like it because it smells light enough for you. Since I like gardenias, I happened to pick up a bottle of Lucien LeLong "Gardenia" for my Mother and Sis. All this stuff appears to be in such large bottles. I wonder if it is really good. I would have gotten more but I didn't have enough dough. Perhaps, another time. Darling, I do hope you like it.

To go on, my tale may appear as one who has been hobnobbing with rank but actually you'd have to know these men to realize the difference. While I was in Lille, I had the luck to stay at a nice hotel, "The Strausbourg." Since it had a nice bar, I spent my time there. While I was sitting at this bar, 2 English Majors walked in. They were both carrying a good load and at that time so was I. These fellows were both wearing the African Star. That is what really started the friendship because I recognized it and mentioned the fact that I knew a bit about the desert. Right there we started to fight the battle of Africa. First of all, one of them was called "Lofty" because he was at least 2 inches taller than I; the other was called "Short Sam" because he was no bigger than a tear drop. After going thru any number of gyrations, we decided to continue the party after the bar closed at 11:30. So well fortified with 4 bottles of champagne, we headed for my room. We had some K-ration cheese so we could use it for a blotter (soup up the alky). By the way, the champagne cost $6 per and it was well chilled. (Now, you can wonder why I didn't have more money for shopping.) The classic climax for that evening was when Sam drew a line with his foot, called it the "Line." In a rather drunken haze, he kept saying, "The Line, the Line"; but that's all he said. Finally he staggered to a bed and fell into it. We picked him up, put him in his room and he finally ended up in another room. How he did it, no one knows. Since they were on a 48-hour leave, I knew that I hadn't seen the end of them.

Next afternoon, I walked into the bar and again, they were well on their way but this time they had another companion, another major. He had been born in Chile but of English parents, so we had to give him a nickname. It was "Pancho." The evening went by the boards but at 9 o'clock they asked me if I had had dinner. No, I hadn't. So off we went. We had to go to the Royal Hotel and in order to get there, we had to walk a bit. But we took a short cut thru one of the classiest joints in town. Right thru the middle; can you imagine 3 majors, splendidly dressed, and a S/Sgt. in a pair of coveralls, and flying jacket and to boot the orchestra was in the process of playing a piece by Rachmaninoff. If you have enough in you, it doesn't make much difference.

I was embarrassed by the fact that we were dining in an officer's club but they assured me that they'd have it no other way. We walked in and who should we walk into but my officers. You should have seen the eyebrows lift. (Of all, they, my officers, showed themselves to be delicious snobs and I refuse to tell you about it.) I introduced my friends but they chose to eat alone. . . . That is to say, they picked their own table and offered no invitations. So we hurried thru our meal because it was only a necessity or habit that had to be done and off we went back to the bar. When it closed, we grabbed the usual number of bottles and off we went. The rest of the fellows had gone on ahead and Pancho and I followed with the goods. — As we were walking down the hall to our room, we heard a woman's voice say in English, "You are making too much noise. How can I sleep?" With that she turned around and headed for her bedroom. So Pancho and I turned around and followed her to her room, and did our best to persuade her that she should join us — so she did. It seems that she was an English entertainer and she had been ill for the last 4 days and hadn't seen nor spoken to anyone in that time. When we got to the room of rendezvous, we sat her down gently and comfortably and opened the bottles. About this time, Pancho decided to sit down on the floor and thus sitting in that position, Indian style, someone wrapped a towel around his head and threw a blanket over his shoulders and he promptly became "Pascha."

Naturally, he played the role. He took off Betty's shoe and went into an elegy. "From the hills (heels) came" and so on. It was the funniest sight to see, this supposedly reserved, refined Englishman, acting like you and I in our own parlor. Betty took her leave shortly and said that she felt much better because our company was so good a diversion. The party ended up (Oh, I forgot. While Pascha was going thru his act, Betty was sprinkling him with perfume to give the mystic atmosphere, and someone was turning the lights on and off to give the impression of heat lightning) with Lofty dropping a full glass of wine on Pascha's head. After apologies were made, we noted that all the wine was finished and so to bed.

During the course of the evening, I taught [*Short*] Sam how to fly a goose. Actually it was ridiculously funny because he is Royal Army man and knows nothing of planes. Later on as he felt lighter, he'd walk up to one of us and say, "Ah, Messa — I'm Schmidt." (The German craft, Messerschmidt!)

Next morning when I got up, I noted a definite female scent in the room, so I was quite taken aback. I looked all about the room, under the sheets, etc. and was definitely puzzled because no one was around. But it was clarified for me by my buddies who told me of Betty's sprinkling action. I was definitely relieved but non-plussed because I must have been quite tight not to remember it. Sam woke me the next morning and asked me to join them in a shopping tour and then they had to leave because they were driving back to the front and expected to have dinner in Brussels. Before they left, we had a few more drinks and then dinner again at that O. club. When I left them, they were well fortified with 6 bottles of champagne. I promised them that if I could, and if I was in the vicinity of their homes, I would call and assure their families of their health. (I will not mention our time.) I hope that I'll be able to get leave. It will be interesting to visit so many people. I'll let you know if I succeed in my ventures.

Gosh, Darling, I'm sorry if I've bored you. I'm sorry. But the pleasantness of those people was a diversion that I shall never forget. As they told me when they left, it was the best leave they've ever had. They showed me more courtesy than any American officer ever has. Believe me, I shan't forget it.

I'm going to make this a short note because it is getting late and I must wash. I feel "scroungy." But believe me, Darling, I shall try to make up for these last few days. When I get stuck in a big city like that, I miss you so very much because there is so little to do. You must wonder about that because I always mention my good times but they aren't really that good. Eventually, I end up telling everyone about you. Everything would be so perfect if you could be a part of that good life of mine. I love you so very much, My Darling. I have been counting days now and I shall continue to do so until that wonderful day of our joining. I miss you.

Good night, My Love. Take care of yourself. Give my love to Mother.

I love you and miss you, My dearest Blonde. May God Bless You. Love, Mike.

Squadron War Diary, December 22:

Usual garrison duty. No flying, that is to the continent. Two planes returned from the continent where they RON since the 18th of December. A third plane which had RON on the far shore since the 18 December returned to southern England to RON.

Group War Diary, December 22:

Fog still hovering over the field. No liberty run this evening.

December 23, 1944 [*Saturday*]

My Darling,

Just two more days to Christmas and I feel less like a holiday than I have ever. Just can't seem to get any sort of spirit. There is one good reason, a damn good reason for it, guess I love you and miss you so much that nothing will be quite the same until I am with you again. And I know how you feel — I can't help but feel so good — you write to me wherever you are, trains, planes, anywhere — It puts me there right with you. I can't do that. I'll never know from day to day where I'll be or when.

Your card was unique. (Somewhere over Kansas, are you kidding me?) I traveled over the same air lanes but just a bit differently — we went down to about 50 to 100 feet off the ground, chasing rabbits and horses, and at one time we got lost, so Pappy spotted a town and further down we went. On the water tower in that town was Duke, so we knew we were on course — Duke, Texas or Okla. I don't recall. Just like driving up to a gas station. My thoughts, I don't know but if I had to do it over again, I know what they would be. — Can't you guess that they would be the same as yours! I can see from your later letters that your worry about lateness was for naught.

Your concern for me is exciting. But I doubt very much if you can bottle sunshine. I don't like my needs dehydrated. That Arizona sounds good. But for all my yearnings when I get back to the states, I'll probably be stationed somewhere, where the sun will shine all the time and I'll probably start bitching again. Soldiers are never satisfied. As far as the drinking business goes, I think we both fare fairly well on that score. Lord knows, we both have the frames to carry each other home, if need be.

I think that that friend of yours . . . was rather audacious. After all, if you were going for some sort of vacation, you could just as well have gone to Calif. But what the Hell is it her business if you went in the opposite direction?

Your favorite censor seems to be getting along quite blissfully. Though I haven't seen him for a little while. He has invited the bunch of us that came over with him to go to his home for the day after Xmas. I hope nothing comes along to spoil it.

You said that the papers said something about the French and Belgian women being tall, I can't say that they are above normal. It must be those monstrous hats that they wear. At any rate, I daresay these women are quite chic. From my meager observation, I must say that they do have it all over these English femmes.

Well, Bette, I must toddle off. I'll try to get back later. So long for now, Darling. Gosh, Honey, I love you.

Regards to Mother. Take care of yourself. May God Bless You. Love and Kisses, Mike.

There was no flying on December 23, though one plane did return from southern England after being sent to the Continent on the 18th, according to the Squadron War Diary.

The Group War Diary entry for December 23 reported:

> **. . . Headquarters Enlisted Men held their party celebrating their 2nd year overseas tonight in the NAAFI building. Refreshments and dancing.**

The Christmas Eve 1944 Squadron War Diary entry read:

> **Nineteen planes were dispatched on an urgent troop movement.**

They returned to southern England to RON. The courier completed its flight. . . .

Group War Diary entry, December 24:

Christmas Eve. The fog lifted and missions were carried out to the far shore. Chaplain Willard and his choir had a caroling party which helped to lend to the holiday spirit. Those who were able celebrated just to keep up the ole American custom.

December 25, 1944 [*Monday*]

Merry Christmas, Darling,

It is a lovely, frosty, white morning and everything feels so right. I almost missed writing to you this AM but as luck would have it, I am here. I must tell you why I feel so good, so very much unlike my mood of last night. I didn't write last night because earlier in the evening I felt so glum. But after Midnight Mass, it was as if I was totally uplifted from my depths. At Mass last night, there was a tall, lovely blonde sitting in front of me. I didn't get a look at her until Mass was over. But when I did, it was as if I was looking at you. The girl was an American Nurse, so it was all the more appreciable. Though I had a desire to talk to her, it was impossible because she had an escort of rank.

Well, when I got in, it was late, so I retired quickly after I had undressed. The night for me was of incessant dreams, all sorts of queer gyrations, unimportant stuff. But I was awakened early, very early because I was supposed to be on duty today. As is my habit, I fell back into a dreamy slumber and then you appeared. I cannot remember the details but for some reason you were frightened. Every time I arrived at the scene to save you from some dilemma, I was too late. Until finally I caught up to the whole rigmarole — the last scene and the only one I can recapture, you were in my arms in such a tender embrace it was almost real. So often have you comforted me, My Darling, that this one time it was I who was your savior. It was one of the most wonderful things that ever happened to me. This day as every day, I love you.

In one of your letters you mentioned that Tony had told you of my experiences over here. I took the news with mingled emotions. Since it is over, I wanted you to be proud of me but again I never mentioned anything because I don't want to frighten you. You see, My Dear, there will be much time for me to recount my life here but it will be appropriate because we will be safe in each other's arms. If you knew now, you would be in constant fear of my safety. Now that you know, try to accept it lightly — somehow or other, I know that everything will be all right. I hate to burden you with any more. It is hard enough for both of us to be apart, why add to it? I debated about telling you. It would have passed the censors because they are more lenient than ever, and justifiably so — why not, no one else publicizes us, at least, we can make our friends know that we aren't dead weight. But I decided against it for reasons that I told you. In another letter, you hinted that you didn't want me to know how much you worried about me. You've been so good about that. If you were the fretting type of person, it would make every thing so hard for me. Thank God, My Bette, that you are so strong willed and sensible — you are a good soldier.

Another Christmas and it has passed again like the last one. It wasn't hard to take. I feel that our next one will be a much better year. We Brooklynites keep yelling, "Wait til next year!" Surely there is bound to be a year when that is so.

And so, My Darling, I hope that you and your lovely Mother have as nice a day as possible. Give her my love. Tell her that I am with you spiritually — what more can we do?

I love you and miss you. May God Bless You. Love, Mike.

WD, December 25: All aircraft grounded owing to adverse weather conditions. This includes those planes in southern England.

GWD, December 25: Christmas Day. Chaplain Willard gave a Christmas party for the orphans from Oakham with GIs as their Uncles. A real Christmas dinner was served all the personnel on the field who were here with all the trimmings. All detail work was done by the Jewish boys on the base. The aircrews returned early in the evening and were able to enjoy the Christmas meal.

December 26, 1944 [*Tuesday*]

Good Evening, Darling,

I love you. You must forgive me if I make this letter a bit short. I had a bit too much Xmas — I have your perfume packed and ready to go. All I am waiting for is your new address and so I will forward it. You must be in Florida by now but mail has been so poor lately that I haven't had the latest news.

You can see from the menu that I am sending that we had a very good meal for the holiday. And I do mean that I ate and ate plenty. After the meal, I retired for a while and about 4 PM, we opened a bottle of champagne for a toast. After supper, we happened to scrounge a couple of bottles of Black and White Scotch. I must confess that I literally poured myself to bed. I do mean that I felt rough. Fortunately, I didn't have to be on duty. When I got up this morning at 11 AM, I must have poured down 5 gallons of water. Whew! I felt it — I'm sure that I'll recover.

If you recall I told you that all of us had been invited to Nick's home tonight. Unfortunately, those damn circumstances came up again. And so I guess I'll have to wait for some other time. At this rate, I guess I'll never meet the young lady.

We saw some picture tonight, I think it was called, *San Diego, I Love You*. There is a young lady in it called Louise Albritton, don't know if you've ever seen her. She's a tall blonde and a lovely one. She has a body so much like yours. Maybe I'm suffering from hallucinations but people keep popping up who look like you. Some day soon, I hope, I'll see you personally. At any rate, it is pleasant to see people who bring you so close to me. I love you, Darling.

Really, Bette, I'm sorry but I am going to close. In my condition, that sack looks good.

Good night, My Dear. Take care of yourself. I miss you. May God Bless you. Love, Mike.

The December 26 Squadron War Diary entry reported:

> **One of the 19 aircraft dispatched on the 24th returned to this base from southern England due to engine trouble. 17 other aircraft were dispatched to the continent for a second serial and RON in southern England while one ship was grounded at Greenham Common.**

The Group War Diary on that date noted only that "Usual operations were carried out today."

The next day, five aircraft were dispatched to the Continent from southern England, where they remained overnight. The Squadron War Diary entry for December 27 ended: "Twelve ships returned from southern England, one remaining there."

The Group War Diary entry, December 27:

> **Although the weather looked none too good, aircraft flew resupply and evacuation missions over and back. Enlisted Men's dance was called off due to the conditions of the roads.**

December 28, 1944 [*Thursday*]

My Darling,

You must forgive me for missing a day or two and for dashing off some letters that may seem to you listless. But again the ole mail cry. It is even more pitiful now than it has been ever. I haven't received but one of your Dec. letters but I know that you are writing. It is just that the stuff isn't getting here. I do hope you are getting some of my mail, I sent my Mother's perfume out but I can't send yours yet because I haven't gotten that address. Hell! I don't even know if you are in Florida yet.

Another point which I want to write to you about was hats. Strange subject, isn't it? But you misunderstood my statement. I don't like hats for my own personal use but women appear undressed if they don't have a hat on. You look wonderful in those large, wide brimmed affairs. By all means, you must wear one of that type for your wedding. Hats like those look so striking on you — Wonderful is the word. The only thing that I'd ever wear would be a Homburg or Pork Pie. Aside from anything like that I'd let the natures beat

#285 (TL) Dec. 16, 1944

Good-Evening, Darling.

I love you. You must forgive me if I make this letter a bit short, I had a bit of too much Xmas — I have your perfume packed and ready to go. All I am waiting for is your new address and so I will forward it. You must be in Florida by now but mail has been so poor lately that I haven't had the latest news.

You can see from the menu that I am sending that we had a very good meal for the holiday. And I do mean that Pete and I ate plenty. After the meal, I retired for a while and at about 4 P.M. we opened a bottle of champagne for a toast. After supper, we happened to scrounge a couple of bottles of Black and White Scotch. I must confess that I literally poured myself to bed. I do mean that I felt rough. Fortunately, I didn't have to be to duty. When I got up this morning at 11 A.M. I must have poured down 5 gallons of water. Whew! I felt it — I'm sure that I'll recover.

If you recall I told you that all of us had been invited to Nick's home to-night.

-I-

Unfortunately, those damn circumstances came up again. And so I guess I'll have to wait for some other time. At this rate, I guess I'll never meet the young lady.

We saw some picture to-night, I think it was called, "San Diego, I love you" – there is a young lady in it called Louise Albutton, don't know if you've ever seen her. She's a tall blonde and a lovely one. She has a body so much like yours. Maybe I'm suffering from hallucinations but people keep popping up who look like you. Someday soon, I hope, I'll see you personally. At any rate, it is pleasant to see people who bring you so close to me. I love you, Darling.

Really, sweet, I'm sorry but I am going to close. For my condition, that sack looks good.

Good-night, my dear. Take care of yourself. I miss you.

May God Bless You –

Love,
Mike.

their way on my surly, stupid head. All those words and I haven't told you that I love you so very much.

Darling, I've written to you about *The Robe*. It is definitely a "must." I've never before been so moved and impressed by the written word. Douglas makes all his characters move so realistically to the one conception of the people of the time of Christ. I say this not from my standpoint of view as a Catholic but from the standpoint of a reader reading of a Great Man. (It is almost impossible for me to concentrate on what I am saying. They have a program on that is one of those mysterious stories.) How can a guy think? I'll try — (no remarks). I shan't tell you anything about the story because I'd rather that you read the book yourself. It is so much unlike Asch's book because he puts us into the more intelligent class of Jew. Whereas Douglas talks more of people who knew of this Christos (Christ) from afar — from distant lands. It is most interesting and a fine view. *The Robe* as we last see it is given to Peter. I've asked Tom where it has been finally placed. Someone said it is in the Cathedral at Malta. If so, it is most unfortunate that I didn't know; I could have gone to see it when I was on the island.

Well, Honey, that's all for now. Damn mystery story — Give my love to Mother. Take care of yourself. May God Bless You. I love you and miss you. Love, Mike.

The Squadron and Group War Diary entries for December 28-30 are:

WD, December 28: One plane returned from southern England although the weather held our remaining five ships on the continent.

GWD, December 28: No fog although it was very cold. Aircraft returned from the far shore. Movie for the Enlisted Men, *Dragon Seed*.

WD, December 29: The last five ships which were dispatched on the 24th returned to Cottesmore. One ship grounded at Lille since the 10 Dec. also returned. The weather ship completed its mission while 10 aircraft were used locally for transition training.

GWD, December 29: Weather still cold and dry. Missions completed without difficulty. Liberty run this evening. Sunday will be the first trip by the liberty train, which was set up by Special Services. Trucks will carry personnel to the station in Oakham.

WD, December 30: Two one-plane missions were dispatched to the far shore. One was forced back by weather while the other RON on the continent. A twelve plane glider tow formation was scheduled in the afternoon. One glider cut loose at Boothby but landed without damage or injury. . . .

GWD, December 30: Saturday morning inspection made of quarters. Practice for a parade was called but later canceled. Liberty run in the evening.

December 31, 1944 [*Sunday*]

Hello Darling,

I love you. Don't mind my strange handwriting, my hands are so cold that I can hardly hold this pen. It is New Year's Eve and I believe for the first time that the day seems so colorless. So much unlike the many same days I've known before. Not only are we facing the prospect of a dry evening but the unfortunate lack of mail makes everything so disgustingly complete. Darling, I miss you terribly. No one could possibly tell me how rough so many things may be because in these last years since I left you, I've found how many minutes can be empty. These years of experience have changed my whole life for me. — They awakened me to the realization that my life will begin again when we are together. I miss every little thing about you. Little minute things that used to pass unnoticed before are now scrutinized with profound interest by me because they are those little things that give me a fleeting glimpse of you — There is no need to mention what they are because they are so numerous, a song, a picture, a drink, smoke curling from a cigarette — any number of small bits. Darling, I love you — love you so that material life seems like such a vague thing.

I've just finished *Earth and High Heaven*. I can say that my interest was mediocre. I became restless when I read of a problem, a problem brought about by the narrow-mindedness of seemingly intelligent people. The problem of religious or social differences. Whereas such things intersect, as in love, they should be handled merely by the two people concerned. Fortunately, as for the book, it ended as I had hoped it would.

Taking a leaf from all those pages, I cannot help but feel in the eyes of some other people, ours, yours and mine, lives run parallel. I've a feeling that the religious aspect hurt you while you were in New York. I don't blame you for being hurt, if that was the reason. You and I decided that problem long ago. I haven't mentioned it for a long time, nor will I mention it except for a point of view. Problems like that are worked out after marriage, that is, if a problem exists. For us, we are too much in love to bicker about the pettiness of conventions. I might even say that we are a bit crude at times. But in our crudeness. . . . [*Last page missing.*]

WD, December 31: One aircraft was sent to the far shore on an evacuation mission where it RON. One ship which had RON on the continent the previous day returned. The training schedule was continued with a fifteen plane formation and the glider which was cut loose on the 30 Dec. was "snatched" out of its field.

GWD, December 31: Pay Call. Very little activity on the field in the afternoon since it is New Year's Eve and many began celebrating early in the evening. The Officer's Club gave a party and dance. The Enlisted Men of Headquarters celebrated in their day room. And so the New Year was ushered in.

January 1, 1945 [*Monday*]
A New Year

Hello Darling,

Look — [*an arrow pointing to the New Year*] who knows maybe that new one will bring us that new life. I received 3 letters and a card from you yesterday. They did me a world of good, but the more I read, the more I missed you. It got so bad that I felt I needed a drunk, and drunk I got. I won't start to answer your letters 'til later. I just feel like talking for now. I love you dearly, My Dearest — so much that at times like last night, it almost drives me mad — But that's the wrong start for now.

— I got a letter from Tony written right after you had left. They think you are wonderful — think I'm inclined to agree with them there. He says the same thing I've been telling you for years — "Add 20 or 30 lbs. to that frame of hers and — Wow!" See, Bette, I've said it so often before but regardless it doesn't take any of my love away from you. As I told Tony in my answer. "Perhaps some love will help to alter the situation." You said I was capable of it and I shan't let you down. He paid you a very fine compliment when he said at the end of his letter, in a very matter of fact way, "We missed Bette very much last night!" Can't help but love you.

I started off last night with beer, English beer. They do have a few good ales that pack a wallop! After getting well oiled on that, I came back to the barracks to find that Pappy was looking for me and he had a bottle of Scotch. So I took off to find him. (Just finished chomping on a turkey leg — good!) As it was I happened to have 4 bottles of coke in the pockets of my flying jacket. Well, when I got to the Officer's Barracks, I couldn't find him but before I could say "Boo," someone pushed a glass full of Seagram's Special in one hand and a good salami sandwich in the other. I uncorked a bottle of coke and mixed it — Darling, for the first time since I left Ft. Wayne, I tasted bourbon and coke. It made me so homesick for you — felt like crying in my bourbon and coke but I was afraid to dilute it. Finished that slowly because I wanted to enjoy it thoroly. After the good stuff was finished, I was given some gin. (Have you ever heard of such combinations in your life?) Just then Pappy walked in and I do mean he was carrying a load, or vice versa, the load was carrying him. After we finished gushing over each other, a la "Sad Sack," he kept telling me that he had received a card from you. He must have repeated it 50 times. Did you send him a card? (Put that roller down, Babe!) Then someone handed me a glass of champagne and we started to renew old times. We talked for a long time. The last I saw Pappy, he was out cold in someone's bed and I was still talking to a few of the other guys I know. I finally staggered to my sack at 4 AM and died until 10 this morn. My Goodness, Woman, how will you ever stand me? Honestly, Honey, I'm really not too bad but it will seem strange to sit down and just keep ordering bourbon and know that they won't run out and we'll have to drink Scotch, gin, rum, wine or creme de menthe. (That is all in one sitting!) Do you think it will be easy to get me drunk? Ever taste Calvados — don't — it'll knock your moles, teeth and hair out.

Before I close this short note, Darling, (I expect to write again later in the evening) (Still don't know if you are in Fla. Yet the latest letter was dated Dec. 5.) But in one of those, you speak for the first time about a family. It was nice to know that you won't mind a few children. If you feel the same way I do, I don't think you want to start one immediately after I get home. But it is nice to add to future plans — with the Help of God — it will be done.

So long for now, Baby. Take care of yourself — May God Bless You. I love you and miss you. Mike.

January 1, 1945 [*Monday*]

Good Evening, Darling,

Here I am back again. After I had finished writing this afternoon, I reread your letter and my eyes started to do tricks. So I posted the letter and laid down for a while. Gad! I felt horrible. I feel much better this evening. We played a few rubbers of bridge and so — The three letters I received were dated 2, 3, 4 of Dec. At least I know that you were planning to leave for Florida on the 10th or so. Heard part of the Orange Bowl game tonight and could not help but think that maybe you were there. I do hope that we don't have to wait another month for mail again. Wish you could have sent me a spot of bourbon that you sent Tony. It is too risky and it takes a long time. I doubt very much if I'd have anything but broken glass. That Black Gold is good stuff. The first time I ever drank it, I was at a Christmas party in Chicago and they had gangs of it. That is 2 years ago.

You asked me to give some clarification on a point that I said. When I say that whenever I think I have hurt you, I want to start all over again, I mean it in so many little things. It is understood for so long that my thoughts are always of you. My actions are meant to be with you. For an instance, there have been times over here when I've gotten drunk to a point when I am just no good for anything except sleep. A stage of paralysis. It disgusted me because I'd hate to think what you might think about it. You see, Darling, my example is a meager one but it is general. That is just one little point that I can't help but include you. I want to perfect myself for you, where even these little things mean so much. It isn't much more than that. Quite parallel to what you say, it is easier to discuss those things than write about them.

About that health certificate you speak of, I don't know what to say. Actually the only big problem is a Wassermann. That can be done in NY. It won't hurt us to wait a few days, even if I know that both of us are eager. After 2 years, let us say, a few days never hurt anyone. I think you've got a good idea there when you say that it is best for you to get to NY after I do. On the face of previous experiences, I think it would be embarrassing you without me. Besides there are a lot of things I want to straighten out for us. You know, family affairs, that I feel must be looked into. When you do make those reservations, don't set a time limit or any time. We may take a little trip, just you and I — One never knows — I have no ideas as yet and I am not going to disclose any. You asked about those furloughs. I can only quote what has happened to the rest of the fellows that have gone home for good. Those fellows that go home for good are called "Happy Warriors" because they have successfully finished their tours. When they do get home, they are sent thru' a short process which takes a day or two. Then they are given a 21-day (or more) delay in route. (No furlough!) After that, they report to one of the redistribution centers, Miami Beach, Atlantic City, or whatever is close to home. For me, probably, AC. There they go thru' another period of processing. I believe a bit of a rest camp to boot. (I believe they are allowed to have their wives along!) After that they are assigned to an outfit and then they are supposed to be given a furlough — 20 days or so. So you see, Darling, whatever the case, we will have a lot of time together before I get back to soldiering again. With all that time, we can afford to waste a few [*days*] getting our plans set. Once I am finally settled, you will join me. I understand the first 3 grades, Master, Tech, or Staff (me!) are given rations and quarters for their wives. But that too is premature. As resourceful as we are, we can plan and do a lot.

Gosh, Bette, I must say good night. Your old man had a rough night last night. Got a squadron party on tomorrow, wanta get some rest for it. That stuff above is nice to write because it brings me closer to you.

Good Night, My Darling. Give my love to Mother. Take care of yourself. I love you. May God Bless You. Love, Mike.

WD, January 1: Six enlisted men returned from DS, Greenham Common, to this station. No flying because of inclement weather. . . . One plane XC and return. Transition training in C-109.

GWD, January 1: There were a great many blurry eyes this morning after the celebration last night and on into the wee hours of the morning. Turkey dinner today for all personnel and plenty of tomato juice for those who needed it. All aircraft that were out returned in the early afternoon. Field began to close later in the evening.

WD, January 2: No flying because of inclement weather. One plane returned from France. A dance was held at DeMontfort Hall for enlisted men of this squadron.

GWD, January 2: No aircraft out today as the field was still closed in. Movie on the field this evening, *St. Bernadette*.

January 3, 1945 [*Wednesday*]

Good Evening, Darling,

Finally got some mail that gave me some indication of where to write — General Delivery. You will probably be disappointed because there won't be any mail for you but it isn't my fault, Darling. The letters that I got today are dated 12, 13, 15th of Dec. and for the most part you were traveling. Still haven't any letters telling me where you are in

Miami Beach. I do hope that you have someone forwarding your mail for you. You see, Darling, when you told me that you wanted some Tabu, I told my Sis to get some, since it was so difficult for me to get any. In her most recent letter of the 13th of Dec., she tells me that she had the package on its way. It is just a meager Christmas gift from me. I do hope you like it, Darling. I am still holding the bottle I got over here. I can wait until you have a definite address. In the meantime, I'll send my mail to General delivery. Darling, are you going to get settled in that one spot? All in one day, I received your letters sent from KC Hotel President and then the Hotel Lincoln in Ind. It seems that only a few days prior, I got letters from Childress from you. I daresay you are almost more of a traveler that I am. Personally, I'd rather do the kind of traveling in the places that you've been to. If you keep it up long enough, you may get as many hours in the air as I have. Of course, it'll take you a few years.

Our squadron party last night was a success. After you sent me that liquor list from the Hotel President, I'm almost afraid to tell you what we drank last night. We had 3 bottles of horrible gin that cost us $12 per bottle. We had planned to drink one bottle of it on the train and then save 2 bottles for the party. I'm afraid it didn't work out as we planned it. We had only to ride for about an hour but we finished all we had before we got there. We had packed all our stuff into a small traveling bag. Looked like we were heading for a leave rather than a one night stand in town. In it, we had 2 cans of grapefruit juice (mix & chaser), 3 bottles of gin and a few glasses plus a cork screw and mixer [*stirring rod*]. Damn, it was the funniest thing I saw. Well, the music was good and everything was perfect. Wish your were along. I love you.

I'll try to answer some of your letters but I'll start from the beginning. First place, I wonder what happened to those letters between Dec. 5 and Dec. 12. I'm glad that your ex-employers were so good to you. It proves that it pays to stay on the ball and be a good girl. The more you speak of food, the more eager I am to taste some of your cooking. That is on a long time scale. I thought that you knew that I had that small picture of you. As a matter of fact, you must have forgotten because I'm sure I showed it to you back in Ft. Wayne. Sorry, I haven't heard that "Make Believe." It'll get here one of these years.

I am afraid that I misguided you on that leave business. Five days are out of the question but Moe, Don, and I are heading for London, Saturday, for a 48 hour-leave. It will probably be a 48-hour drunk but as long as we get away from the post a while, that's all that counts. Kinda' sick of hanging around. The three of us are looking forward to it. We planned this last May, but D-Day came up and the 2 of them went home for 30 days so this is the first chance we've had to get out together. Glad to see that you are getting most of my mail.

Yes, Darling, it is too bad that Tony and Sheila aren't in New York. It would be nice to have them as our stand-by. I think I've asked Ted and Louise; I don't recall but at any rate, I know they won't mind. I don't think Pappy will be coming home with me. Darling, whatever my buddy writes to you, take it with a grain of salt. Everything that the Army does is subject to change. As a matter of fact, I wouldn't be surprised if they've changed their plans already. I've concluded that it is best to let things ride — just don't plan on anything about my coming until the day that you receive some definite news from me. I hate to sound so damn pessimistic but I'm getting to be such a veteran over here that I feel like a fixture. When we do meet again, it will seem like a dream. It will take a lot of convincing to prove that it isn't. I love you so much, Darling, that waiting is torturous but I've resigned myself again to the fact that nothing is true until it happens. The army's biggest mistake for lowering a man's morale is that they hand out meager tidbits, tease a guy and then take it all away from him. Actually, they are the meanest bastards I know. Like I've said so often before, if they'd set a plan for Troop Carrier and keep it going, it wouldn't be so bad. But they put out that small feeler, just as it gets within reach, they pull it away. I don't give a good damn who reads this but I feel that I've done a good share of my work — The guys that are running this show don't give a damn about anything. Oh Well! It doesn't do me any good to bitch — all I can say is that we've got to be patient. Wait and then make up for every little detail. I love you — All I hope is that when they do decide to send me home, it doesn't happen when you are moving from MB back to KC. With my fingers crossed, I hope that Easter <u>might</u> be our first holiday. That's the first of April, isn't it? Who knows?

Honestly, I shouldn't be distressed by any changes because our love does grow stronger each day. But I do want to put it to actual practice. Funny but time is such a big factor. Can't help but get sick of constantly waiting for my ship to come in. It hurts because I miss you so much. They can't expect us to keep saying that we enjoy life in the ETO. It just doesn't happen. But come what may, Darling, when you left Ft. Wayne, I told you I'd be back — I will.

Well Good Night, Darling. Got that cluster to the Citation or have I said that before? Give my love to Mother. Get some extra sun for me — I love you and miss you. — May God Bless You. Love, Mike.

WD, January 3: Eleven planes flew locally, practicing formation flying and landings. . . . Dance held at the NAAFI for enlisted men of this base.

GWD, January 3: . . . Heavy wind along with a driving rain this morning and early afternoon. Weather conditions again grounded all aircraft. The Enlisted Men's dance was held this evening at the NAAFI.

January 4, 1945 [*Thursday*]

Good Evening, Darling,

Spent a quiet day, waited for mail from you but I can't complain. Can't have things perfect always. Funniest thing that has happened. Don wrote to his folks and asked them to send him some good reading. He didn't request anything definite, so they sent him a stack of pulp magazines, *War Aces*, *Torrid Love Stories*, etc. He is still angry, raising up a storm, "Hell, what do they think I am, a moron?" Typically of good boys, it was natural for us to kid the Hell out of him. — I got a newsletter from my Church — It was the first one I had received and it was enjoyable because I recognized a lot of names of fellows with whom I went to school. Although I had little to do with them socially, it is natural that I keep them in some part of my childhood memories. Sort of makes me feel that the years are passing. You know, Darling, in a very short time both of us will be a year older.

In your letter from the Hotel President, I noticed that you marked off the Drum Room. How can I forget that place? If I recall correctly, that was the night you barked at the bill on the bar, flirted or vice versa, with a naval officer and we ended up with a few civilians, drinking his rye and ended up with a grand finale of a fight. (Need I remind you that it was also the night I passed out on you. I never did figure out what was wrong. — Do you think that you were too much for me that night?)

Darling, you asked me to forget about nightmares. Must have been something I ate. But you've been doing so much flying that I naturally worry about it because last night I dreamt again. When I first started to fly, we carried our own parachutes wherever we went. Well it seems that you and I were going somewhere — The weather was rough and I went forward to speak to the pilot. He told me that our engines were acting up — I don't know if they have 'chutes on those civilian airlines. At any rate, the ship we were on didn't have any, except my personal chute. I took it out of my chute bag and put it on you and explained how to use it. Just then this "civvy" pilot called me up and told me that we'd have to "belly her in." I didn't want to take a chance of having you go down with us, so I asked his permission if you could jump. "But, Mike Darling, I won't jump and leave you." "Bette, you said you'd like to jump, here's your chance." So I kissed you, tore off the door, and pushed you. The last I saw of you, you were floating gently down to earth — I rode the ship down and fortunately we made a good belly landing right where you were. That's all I remember. It wasn't a bad experience at that, was it? I do hope you enjoyed the jump.

Darling, you aren't at all wrong. A good rest back in the States wouldn't hurt me a bit. But I can't convince anyone else but myself about that. Since my ideas of rest are unimportant or unheard, I shan't say anything about it. But I do know that with a good rest with the right people a lot of guys would be ready to fight another day. In a lot of cases, the Army waits until a guy cracks so badly, he isn't worth a tinker's damn for anything. Personally, whenever I feel as if I've really "had" it, I sit back and think as deeply as I can of the days that lie ahead of me. The thoughts, and believe me, nothing else, is of any remedy. If anyone were to tell me that I should be happy in the ETO, there would be a cracked head. I don't mind it terribly if I am busy under the right circumstances but, here in England, it is easier to say than to do. A lot of the times, the odds are too much against you — It would be much harder not to take a setback or disappointment as it was a few months ago. If Troop Carrier changes its plans again, I'm afraid, I'll be a harder person to get along with than I was. However, I shall never crack up too badly; I'd never let the skies nor the men who sit back here have the last laugh on me. The bastards aren't worth "giving in" to. Honey, all I live for is you. — I want you to be proud of me always. I love you so very much — miss you beyond all words. Don't worry about my words, just feel like getting a few things off my chest.

Good night, Bette. Take care of yourself. Give my love to Mother.
May God Bless You. Love, Mike.

The Squadron and Group War Diary entries for the next five days, January 4-8, 1945, read:

> **WD, January 4: Three planes were used this morning for local flying. In the afternoon eighteen planes were used for formation flying.**
>
> **GWD, January 4: Very cold this morning. Pilots started training period today, on local status. High winds again today followed by light snow.**
>
> **WD, January 5: Seven planes were used to ferry gliders back to this base from Southern England. Twelve planes were used this afternoon to tow gliders in group formation. One instrument check. Seventeen planes were scheduled to fly night formation but after a short time in the air they were forced to land because of bad weather. Two enlisted men slightly injured in a jeep accident.**
>
> **GWD, January 5: Crisp and cold this morning with the remaining snow still on the ground. The training was continued today with night flying. Liberty train run made this evening.**
>
> **WD, January 6: Three planes were used locally, one test hopped, one instrument check and one for practicing landings.**
>
> **GWD, January 6: No flights to the far shore. Once again training flights were made.**
>
> **WD, January 7: Eight planes were used in the morning for local transition flying. Eighteen plane squadron formation in the afternoon.**
>
> **GWD, January 7: Church services held this morning. Chaplain Willard held a Vespers service in the evening at the Station Church. Movie, *Going My Way*, Bing Crosby.**
>
> **WD, January 8: Eighteen planes were used in a Group formation in the morning. . . . Dance at the ARC for enlisted men.**
>
> **GWD, January 8: Training program still underway. Began to snow in the morning and by late afternoon the ground was covered. Dance held at the Red Cross and the ATS from Chillwell were the guests of Cottesmore.**

January 9, 1945 [*Tuesday*]

Good Evening, Darling,

You must forgive me for not writing sooner. I mentioned that I had a 48 and I did get back last night but they put me to work immediately and here I am for the first time in 3 days. There are many things I must tell you but first of all, I love you very much and miss you terribly.

The latest news from the home front tells me that my *frere*, Doc, finally got back from the Pacific. Just 3 months short of 3 years. Gad, what a future to look forward to. I can see myself now, going for that long, — they'd ship me back to the U.S. in a box. But believe me that was good news. At least, I know that he is safe and well. Thank God for that. Secondly, Lucy told me that she is undecided about what to do with your package. I think I told you that she had gotten a bottle of "Tabu." She mailed it but obviously it was returned for some reason or other to her. I've told her to hold it until I got your permanent address, and then she should forward it to you. From the way the mail has been rolling, you'll probably receive it in time for your birthday. I hope you don't mind, Darling; at least, you know that I meant well. In Tony's latest letter, he tells me that he received a package [*a bottle of bourbon*] from a Miss Hillman of Kansas City. He was extremely grateful. I can imagine — I wish I was in his shoes.

You see how wonderfully everything has been going. I received your letters of the 6th, 7th, and 10th of Dec. Wonderful, isn't it? And you must wonder why I don't answer ½ of your questions at the right time. Now I know that you are all set to go to Florida, that I should write c/o General Delivery and a multitude of other things that I should have known weeks before. It seems almost pitiful to try to answer anything because you will feel that it is so outdated and have probably forgotten half of your questions. But —

You asked me about a tan. Nothing would suit you better than that. Blondes always look good with a nice, deep, dark complexion. Even though you say that it is difficult for you to get, I'll bet that constant application of sun will finally stick. Plenty of sun, liquids (non alcoholic) and plenty of good food should do you a world of good. — Forgive me, Darling, I envy you —

When I mentioned that show on Noel Coward, I didn't think that you'd take it so harshly. But, at any rate, what you say is very true. I hate to judge by one individual but actually their great failing is class distinction. They are fast to criticize and slow to apologize. However, I've gotten to the stage where it doesn't pay to fret about such people — a listless boring look upon such personalities. The same goes true for others who are so off the path that it is comical to consider them seriously.

I think that I had mentioned that I had received that card, so I won't repeat my answer.

I couldn't help but laugh when I read your account about that fire scare. You sounded like a baby with a new toy. So you like to call firemen! You don't like to chase ambulances, do you? I care for neither, personally; fires don't intrigue me nor do murders, etc. I'll stick to a cold Scotch and Soda and an easy chair. But someone does have to have a diversion occasionally, doesn't one? Sound like the King's own English, don't I?

I am glad that you took that Seagram's along with you. You said that we speak about it a lot. That's true but it is like a symbol — Don't break it — not for what it contains but what it was meant to do and since that wasn't done, for what it is meant to do. That all may sound like a queer mid-point but people are strange, especially people in love. They are so apt to remember little details when they will forget big ones. Actually, do you remember the dance or the events leading up to it? (That is merely an example of anyone.) You said that you not only miss me but that you need me — aside from the physical theme, it is not that either of us is so magnificent but that together we are a pillar of our love — a wall that must be thrown down from both sides to defeat — What I lack, you fill and vice versa —

We are like a gear that needs its opposite to fill in the empty spaces to keep mobile. Yes, Darling, we need each other because our love is meant to be that way. There is always that mutual understanding, that tacit nearness, that overwhelming joy of being together. We are both lost now because we are separated but time and distance is doing that much more to bring us together spiritually. You are in my every prayer, my every thought. I love you very much, My Darling. Yes, My Dear, I went to London but I had to stay drunk practically all the time to shake off that loneliness — Me without you and a body without a soul.

Well, Darling, I must close — My mind is getting sluggish — I am tired. A guy can't do that and keep going. Give my best to Mother. I do hope she likes Miami.

Good night, My Love. Take care of yourself. I am praying for your health — May God Bless You. I love you. Mike.

On January 9, the Squadron War Diary reported:

> **Eight glider pilots were sent to Northwestern England to pick up eight L5s** [*small, two-seat planes called Sentinels made by Stinson*] **to be ferried to this base, thence to France. Three planes were sent to Southern England for loads and return. Eighteen planes were sent to Welford Park, five RON.**

That day's Group War Diary entry read:

> **Early this morning a briefing was called in Group S-2 office for all Glider pilots who are to ferry L5s and L4s to the far shore. Snow is still sticking as the weather is very cold and crisp.**

January 10, 1945 [*Wednesday*]

Hi Bette,

Just finished a long letter to Tony. I'm afraid it lacked my usual pep but I hope it isn't too disappointing to him. I enjoy writing long letters to him. Both of you are the only ones that I really let my hair down to. Occasionally, I let one go at the family or friend but it is a rare thing. Honestly, Darling, very few people mean the same to me now as they did when I came over. Pardon the change of ink. But that is a fact. I am so interested in you and I that a lot of things have become obscure from my mind's view. As I told Tony. All I want is to get home, get married, and live. I love you, Bette.

I guess you must be wondering about that pass of ours. It wasn't very often that we drew a sober breath. We [*went*] to London early, got a room and hit the pubs. We drank Scotch and soda from 3 PM to 9:30 PM with a slight lift for a short meal. It seemed funny but at that rate, we should have been well done in but we were just feeling good. We were heading for the subway [*underground*] when an MP stopped Lil Moe [*Dan Emery*] and asked him for his pass and why he wasn't wearing his cap. So the MP wrote out a ticket for him. In the meantime, Moe kept saying, "I ought to clobber the Son of a — Hell by the time he gets that back to the squadron, I'll be dead." And so on. It was really funny. I kept telling the MP that Moe was worried and so he got drunk — He didn't listen — (When the ticket got back to the outfit, the adjutant asked Moe what had happened and then tore up the ticket.) Sunday, the next day, we started off on some cold lager, got a shine on and headed for the cinema. We saw *30 Seconds Over Tokyo*. It was good but it was strictly an airmen's show. We got to "sweating out" everything that happened. Landings, take-offs, and even crack ups were things that were tortuous to us. Went to a dance at the Red Cross, Sunday night. I was feeling like a wall flower until I decided to dance and the gal I danced with was a college grad. She was really clever and we discussed everything under the sun. She looked like Gert, Dan's fiancee. She invited me to her apartment and we sat around eating ice cream and drinking coffee. For an English girl, she was extraordinary because she was intelligent. She had some excellent illustrations of the old time masters, Da Vinci, Botticelli, El Greco, and so on up to Gaugain [*sic*], Van Gogh (My Boy), etc. It was a most pleasant evening. She was kind enough to listen to my tales of woe; I told her of my loved one. She thought you were very beautiful, who doesn't? The next day, we left early but before we did, we had to fortify ourselves for the long train ride — so we polished off a good number of gins and beer. The train ride wasn't too bad at all. Since we had some time left to our pass, we stopped in Leicester and took in a show (again.) *Snow White and the Seven Dwarfs*. It was wonderful to see it after so many years. I think I appreciated it more this time than I did when I was younger. After the theatre, we started to drink again. When I got back to base that night, I had some mail and thru' a drunken haze, I saw that Lou had returned home or at least was on his way. So you see, My Darling, I did have a good time — a good time in the standards of being alone, without you. People wonder we don't do any sightseeing, etc. It isn't worth it. Everything is so empty without the one you love. A building is a building. It represents no glamorous or venerable background. Been over here too long to be impressed. The only [*thing*] that can impress me is the sight of you. Can you understand that? I am sure you can because things must be the same for you. Sure, it's great to say I've been here, there and everywhere but what do you really elaborate on? — "When Bette and I did" — and so on. Those are the things that one really remembers. The drunkenness is to eliminate any feeling of loneliness and it still isn't a perfect disguise. Gosh, Bette, how else can I tell you that I love you and miss you?

Must go. So long for now, My Darling. The only pass I really want is you and I — alone. Give my love to Mother. Take care of yourself. May God Bless You. Love, Mike.

On January 10, according to the Squadron War Diary, five planes returned from southern England, and there was a dance that evening.

The Group War Diary entry for that day read:

All personnel were restricted to the base today as the AWOL's are being rounded up over the entire United Kingdom.

January 11, 1945 [*Thursday*]

Good Evening, Darling,

I received your first letter from the Cortez. Frankly, Darling, the very thing that seems to worry you is a bit of a problem to both of us. Actually, it is a premature worry but nevertheless, it is best to safeguard against anything that might be a source of time wasting. You've a good idea there when you say that it is best that you let Tony know where you are. He can always be our intermediary. I can always wire him or anything like that. It seems foolish to worry about such things after people have been separated as long as we have. It is best not to lose a trick. Seeing you immediately after I reach home is important. If I have to wait many days, I'd be a nervous wreck. That may be hard to understand for a lot of people but I think it is a mute understanding to both of us. But honestly, Darling, you have a few things on your hands, haven't you? I do hope that you get a place to stay down there. I can realize that things are a bit congested. Darling, I honestly hope that you can stay there because I think the sunshine will do you wonders. Oh God, there are so many reasons. I love you; I need you; I want you and I want you to have all the breaks in the world. Are there many more reasons?

Yes, Dearest, you wonder about all those happy people and their wives strutting around and not caring. You can imagine how we must feel, knowing that there are so many men that can replace us and still we are left holding that well-known candle. But I don't think it pays for me to go thru' that again. — I don't remember the name of the hotel — Yep! I do. The Evans on 10th and Collins. It is quite impressive for a raw rookie to walk into a place like that and know that the Air Force is giving him a good start. After all the joints I've been in since then, I wish I were back. Have a glass of Ballantine's Ale for me! You can say that again — that water. Ah! What a life! After being in England so long, I know how much I miss such things.

You know, Darling, in your letter from Indianapolis, you mentioned something about the type of city KC was compared to the rest of the world. You mentioned the Victorian state of the stores, the lack of cleanliness, and entertainment. Honestly, I'd never looked at in that way. Practically all my stay was spent with you; I didn't really look beyond me. I had no reason to — you attracted all my attention. I still kick myself for shying away and not acting too eager. I'm afraid I can be a bit too conscientious. Gosh, Bette, I've had a year and a half to regret my actions. You also spoke of the fine manner in which your pilot brought that plane in on an icy field. I wish I could tell you more of my experiences. Your pilot has, at least, 5,000 hours in the air. Some of the kids I know will need 10 years to get that and they do a wonderful job. It is amazing. They can do tricks with these kites that made the Air Force sit up and listen. Douglas can well be proud of the airplane that he is making. He'll never go broke if he keeps making them as good as that plane.

We had a hell of a snowball fight today. We employed all sorts of military maneuvers, evasive actions, heavy and light artillery, tanks, mortars, etc. It all boiled down to the point that it was a most enjoyable pastime — believe me, it improves appetites too.

(You know in the letter I had dated yesterday, I had to finish it today. The fellows lured me into a bridge game and bull session.) (Forgot where I had finished. From the second paragraph down was today.) Because of that lack of foresight, I don't recall if I told you that Tony wants to thank a Miss Louise Hillman (guess who?) for her kindness. However, I'll leave that up to him. The thing that makes me feel so wonderful is that you and he get along so well. You don't realize how much of a relief it is to me. You can always rely on him when I can't be contacted too soon. It is also encouraging to me because as yet, my family is cool. I have always depended on Tony more than I have on anyone else. He's a great guy for anything. I shall never forget him for the kindness that he extended to you. Wonderful indeed.

Well, Darling, I must close. 'Fraid the fresh air put the skids on me. Give my love to Mother. Take care of yourself.

I love you and miss you very much. May God Bless You. Love, Mike.

Though the Squadron War Diary reported on January 11 "All planes grounded because of inclement weather," the Group War Diary on that day read:

Field still under restriction. Routine duties carried out . . . training program is again scheduled for today.

January 12, 1945 [*Friday*]

My Dearest,

Just polished off a few beers at the club; If I had stayed there any longer, I would have gotten a bit lit. But honestly, Darling, I'm happy. I received two letters from you and everything seems to be just right. I love you, I love you, I love you. Don't ask me why I feel so exalted. It is just a matter of expectancy. It takes so little to make a guy feel perfect, especially when he is so much in love. You know, Bette, you are wonderful. You must think I'm drunk; I am but from joy. You have felt the same way, a feeling of elevation that can be caused by the least little thing.

The letters that I received from you were dated the 22nd and 24th of Dec. To me, that's good service. At any rate, I am glad that you have gotten a few of my letters. I know very well how it feels to be without mail for a while. I know that feeling of walking on clouds. I feel that way now. But that is because of a special reason. But on other occasions, a letter does more to me than anything I can think of. The mail is a wonderful thing but I am still too much of an idealist, I like the real thing.

Glad you approved of our little party. Actually, I'm not made of iron but I'll bet 2¢ to a dollar that it will take a lot more to make me drunk now than when I left you. I don't like to think of myself as a hard drinker but after pouring all that junk into me, I wouldn't doubt that I'm well fortified against a lot of things. Just changing my winter alcohol to protect me against the cold.

You mentioned something about night flying. It is a novelty at first, isn't it? But it gets both wearisome and worrisome after a while. Personally, I like to see where I'm going. It really isn't too bad especially when what you are going to face is a Hell of a lot more dangerous than just flying. Personally, again, Darling, I'd rather not face too many more dangers before I see you again. Just one of those things.

Now that you've gotten a job, Darling, I guess a lot of your problems are settled. We've discussed it so often that I think that I may have hit on some sort of a solution. Why don't you stay in Miami for a good while. At least I know where you are. You say that you are counting days and months. Neither of us knows when, how or where but I keep counting days and months, too. The system I use is 365 days or 12 months, each one does pass, doesn't it? $35 per month can't be too bad to carry you thru' many months and since you are in Miami, do you think it is much of a task to stay there? Gad! Woman, I do fret over the possibility of missing you. It is a tortuous affair, isn't it? I can gather from your letters that you don't find it a very bad place at all. Physically, it is very healthful. Sunshine, and water never did hurt anyone. A good tan, to me, is the most wonderful color in the world. Especially with your blonde head, it is ideal.

There are so many plans, aren't there, Darling? That GI Bill of Rights is a damn good thing. All I hope is that a lot of these things do go thru'. My urge for more education is taunting. I like to learn and keep it up. Of course, I never expect to be a genius but it never hurts to try to better one's self. I am not totally dissatisfied with my future but it could be improved. What I like most of all is your enthusiasm. Slowly but surely you are teaching me an excellent code of life. "You can't lose." All my life, I've looked for someone who said, "Yes" and kept on meaning it until it is more than a gentle prod. I am not going to be one of those stern, impractical husbands who insists that his wife not work — I believe that it is best to inspect the situation — depending on the outlook, so the course. In everything I've ever said, you've always added, "If that's what you want to do, there's no reason why it can't be done." That's wonderful. I can't help but to love you as much as I do. But, forgive me, if I add a note to that. I don't do anything unless I have your wholehearted consent. Remember, Darling, everything must be 50-50. Gosh, every time I think of you and I as husband and wife, I get such a damn thrill thru' me. It is almost too good to be true.

Good night, Bette. Take care of yourself. I'll take over where you leave off. I love you and miss you. May God Bless You. Love, Mike.

❦❦❦❦

All flights were cancelled for January 12 due to weather. The Group War Diary entry on that day reported:

Much to the relief of all personnel the restriction was lifted today and the Liberty run was made to nearby towns.

January 13, 1945 [*Saturday*]

Dearest Bette,

I sent you that perfume today. I sent it in care of General Delivery. I feel it is just as well, since there is no necessity for me to carry it around with me. It is just as well that I send out whatever I can. The less I have, the less I have to carry whenever I do get home. I do hope it gets to you in one piece and I hope you like it. I don't think I did too badly. Remember I'm a rookie at that sort of stuff.

Nick [*Pappaeliou*] has invited me out to supper this evening. I hope nothing happens to mar the plans because I'd like to meet his wife. I guess it is about time. Something always seems to come up to change everything.

Can't see why (Nick just came in and said it was set for tonight.) you can't get used to that water down there. I'll admit I was always used to batting it around in rough water but hell the beach is like a pool. As a matter of fact, most of it seems to be nothing but a sand bar. It takes a good walk to get into any deep stuff. One thing you can never do is be afraid of the water because if you are, it will beat you every time. I saved Lucy twice before she got used to the idea that it wasn't too rough. Don't worry your pretty head about it though, Darling. I'll try my best to shake your nervousness. Hell, it has been so long since I did any swimming, I wonder if I can still handle myself. When I first got overseas, when I wasn't flying, I was swimming. You remember I got so tan, you couldn't tell me from an Arab. I think that in due time, the oil in your skin will come out so that you will tan beautifully. What a Hell of a thing to worry about, isn't it? Guess it is another one of those things that makes life.

I was reading an article in *Air News* about the 9th AAF. Naturally, they couldn't possibly forget Troop Carrier. And the author knew what he was talking about. One thing he said was, "One thing that a Troop Carrier man hates is to be called ATC." Gal, he wasn't kidding.

Max Gilliam's home is in Tampa. But at present he is stationed in Wisconsin. Susie, his wife and he are so much in love that I know that she is with him. I guess it is too late now but at that time, he was in Miami Beach for only a short while. I know that it would have been enjoyable to speak with him. He and I had some good times in that ole' tent of mine [*in Tunisia*]. Never forget the time that we had to dig a fox hole (slit trench) and then put mosquito netting on our beds. We had a 5 gallon can of wine in the tent. So before we started, we fortified ourselves a bit. We got all the implements, dug about a foot and decided to have a few. We kept a log of all our actions, — e.g., "1301 — had drink," "1305 started to get up — had another drink." By 1500 (3 PM) we were so blind that we never did do any more. Oh well, I guess that's life. Hey, all those words. Darling, I love you very much.

That curl [*lock of hair*] you sent me is wonderful. I've placed it in the portfolio of your large picture. If you can send a little of yourself at a time, I might be able to assemble you and we'd be together. But I don't think it'll be too long before we'll be together.

Honestly, Darling, I may dream a lot but I'd like to give you me for your birthday. Sounds almost impossible now but you know the army, anything can happen. Almost sure that it will be a nice Easter. The more I think of it, the more I like it but my idea in last night's letter sounds good. Since you've got that job, it really can't be too hard to stay in Miami.

Honestly, Darling, must rush off. I want to get dressed and time is passing. Give my love to Mother. Take care of yourself. I love you. May God Bless You. Love, Mike.

The Squadron War Diary recorded one flight on January 13 — a plane was sent to the Continent.

The Group War Diary entry for January 13 was:

> **Glider pilot briefing was postponed today as the weather report was unfavorable on the far shore. Movie at the base cinema, *Dough Girls*. Liberty Run.**

January 14, 1945 [*Sunday*]

Good Evening, Darling,

Got back late today and was just sitting back when I dozed off, not for more than an hour and gad! I felt lousy when I awakened. Too much night life, I guess. I didn't get back from Nick's house until 2 AM and I'm afraid I was packing a bit of a load. His wife is a lovely girl. Rather tall and blonde and get her into the mode of the U.S. and she'll be a doll. Her parents are fine people. It was the first time I ever met English people so intimately and they surprised me by their lack of so-called English reserve, just let your hair down and it isn't so hard. It was a pleasure to put my feet under a table again and once the meal was finished, be able to sit back and relax. He has given me some photos (at least, he had them for me) of the wedding party. Betty, that's her name, is pregnant, but it still will be a few months before I become an uncle. Everyone seems to have a jump on us, Darling. I don't think we need worry though.

In my letter to Chicha this evening, I told her to send your package to the address I am using at present (General Delivery, etc.). I know you will get the package and that's all that worries me. In these days, one doesn't worry about getting things done at the proper time, as long as it is done. Gosh, Darling, I can't help but wish the day will come soon that I'll be able to present things to you personally. I love you so very much.

I received your letter of the 26th of Dec. I can readily understand how you feel. There are so many times when words seem so flat. How can a guy or gal like either of us possibly tell each other how deeply we feel? If we were together, it would be easy. But if it were that easy, we wouldn't be so worried about so many things. Gosh, Darling, I can't seem to say the right thing myself. Better off on a merry-go-round, I'd have a reason to go around in circles.

You are right about Moon over Miami. I must admit that the circumstances are quite different. I was there as a GI. But that wasn't enough to distort my sense of beauty. I couldn't help but see the Moon and actually it wasn't because I wanted to. It was more or less of a forced issue which I didn't mind. If the settings were a bit different, I think that African moon could be a Hell of a lot of competition. But what does all that matter? Our moon and stars and water, all the beauty of the world is wrapped up in our love. It's been said before and it isn't a lie but we could make so much lovely music together. To share each other with anyone would be the craziest thing in the world to do. I sometimes wonder if people really appreciate that. I sit back and plan so many things which I cannot tell you because it isn't allowed (silly thing that but —) but those plans have made my every minute so easy to face. I am the most patient guy in the world but I do lose patience with people who persist in throwing things into my face. I cannot help but go beyond myself to get a bit nasty. My only pleasant moments are those that I share with you and yet my course must be barred by casual remarks that set fireworks off in my head. But there is no sense to burden you with that. We have so much to say to each other, Darling, that I find it hard to control myself at times.

I am glad that you like your job and that you are starting to tan. Yep, I've seen you in white (and no remarks) but a little color, dark color, never hurt anyone.

Well, Darling, gotta get some sack time. Give my love to Mother. Take care of yourself. May God Bless You. I love you and miss you. Love, Mike.

WD, January 14: Twenty two planes were sent to the continent on a resupply mission, all returned but one which was forced to RON because of tire trouble. One other plane returned from France that was sent out on the 13th. Transition training in the C-109 in the afternoon. Eight glider pilots were sent to France ferrying L-4 and L-5 liaison planes.

GWD, January 14: Briefing again called for the Glider Pilots at 0915 hours at Group S-2. Pilots were briefed and began taking off at 1000 hours. Aircraft of the Group effected missions to the far shore and returned. Enlisted Men of Group Headquarters had a movie in their day room, *Double Indemnity*.

WD, January 15: Twenty two planes were dispatched to Southern England to pick up loads, all of them returned to this base. One plane used this afternoon for transition training. Dance at the ARC for enlisted men.

GWD, January 15: Aircraft that flew to the far shore today didn't return this evening. Beautiful weather all day. Monday night dance held at the Red Cross Arrow Club.

January 16, 1945 [*Tuesday*]

Good Evening, Darling,

So sorry for not writing last night. I am in one of those "blah" moods when words come rather hard to me. We have been doing a lot of "bulling" around here. There seems to be so much to talk among ourselves and yet it is impossible to discuss such matters in letters. I do hope that you understand. Unfortunately, I can't clarify it very much. I love you. The mail situation has been rather pitiful and since we haven't been too busy, it is even more difficult to find words. What the Hell am I saying? Sorry, My Love, just struggling along. Lord knows, I'd like to whisper sweet *amour* into your ears but I'm afraid to fall in such a mood, 'fraid I'll get a bit too sentimental. Received a bottle of Seaforth's Shaving Lotion today and the odor was vaguely familiar to me. I wonder if I'm dreaming again. I do know one thing, I had a Hell of a nightmare last night. A Jap stuck his bayonet clean thru' my stomach. I woke up fighting like a maniac. They tell me that sort of thing isn't good for a guy. It must have been the doughnuts and coffee I had.

Gosh, Bette, if I could only say ½ the things I want to say, I could fill endless pages with words. There are so many things I want you to share with me. However, it just isn't being done. I want to tell you how you are included in my every plan, my every counted minute in my very heart. I know it sounds mushy but there are time[*s*] when a guy's chest gets so full of emotion that he has to have some sort of vent for it. In our separation, our only vent has been words. Stars are going to fall, lights are going to flash and the whole world will turn upside down for us, the day that you rush into my arms. But there I go again — must be the music that we have on, it's wonderful!

Just a passing thought but do you recall some of my letters of over a year ago? But then whenever mail was bad and words came hard, I always had something to divert my attention to. I could write always of some scene, something that I had observed. I'm afraid England is not a very awe-inspiring country. I love you, Darling and I am so eager that my inspiration must come from you. Time has done so much to help us grasp our love more firmly. To make it more than something to be cherished but also something to lean on and now as time passes, something to look forward to eagerly. Gosh, Bette, you're wonderful!

Good night, Darling. Forgive me for not sprinkling some more sugar. Give my love to Mother. Take care of yourself. May God Bless You. I miss you — Mike.

There was no flying on January 16 because of inclement weather. The Group War Diary on that day read:

No missions effected to the far shore. Movie, *Gaslight* here at the Cinema. Regular Liberty run this evening.

The January 17 Squadron War Diary reported:

> **Twenty two planes were sent to Southern France [*Bordeaux*] on a supply mission. Two planes RON in France, one because of a flat tire and the other plane was sent to Paris for a new tire.**

That day's Group War Diary entry noted:

> **Cold, gusty wind throughout the day. Aircraft of the Group flew missions to the continent and returned. NAAFI dance held this evening, music by our own band which has some few new members.**

January 18, 1945 [*Thursday*]

Good Evening, Darling,

I received your letter of the 18th of Dec. You had just completed your rather epic journey across the States. I must admit that it took you a long time for an actual 9½ hours of flying. I got you'ah cah'd from Gawga. So you think that drawl is all you can stand, I don't blame you. I don't know if you are a Yankee — we call Missouri the bastard State, neither here nor there. Kansas, if I recall is your birth place [*St. George near Manhattan, Kansas*]. I don't recall what that is. Besides anything South of Brooklyn is rebel. Maybe that's why Noel Coward doesn't like us. So after having received a few letters from you from Miami, I'll answer your first letter from there. If you keep flying long enough, you'll be able to match me, flying phrase for phrase. I can easily see how the weather caused your delay and it appears funny to me. Those men who fly commercially, are old, experienced pilots and they don't leave the ground unless the weather is Cavu. (Ceiling and Visibility Unlimited.) Whereas Army pilots, young kids are allowed to roam the world in the worst muck possible. You said there is nothing that can be done about the weather — there is — first of all, if you are on the ground, you wait. If you are in the air, you sweat. I'll show you my gray hairs someday. Flying is a wonderful thing if you have all the facilities that there are in the States.

I would like to visit the club that you mentioned but I, too, would have to be a guest of the Shriners. Sounded like a rather expensive evening. Hope to Hell someday, we are rich enough to frequent joints like that. One never knows.

No, Darling, I've never been to Tampa. I believe that most American cities are beautiful if they strike the eye in the mood they are supposed to represent. If you had seen Tampa in the rain, I'll bet you wouldn't like it. Just like Pittsburgh, if it is seen at the right moment even thru' the haze, it is a nice city. Of course, one thing that is true of Florida is that it is a beautiful state. I've never seen the Everglades, but I hear they aren't too hot. A flying approach to any city is a Hell of a lot of difference. You can see things in a very favorable light that way.

Yes, My Dear, there is only an ocean separating us, but I wouldn't want to swim it. No matter what, I won't feel close enough to you until I can reach out and have you in my arms. That closeness will be made perfect by what is known as that mental closeness that is so important. Love is a wonderful thing.

Gosh, Bette, I know how much easier it will be for you if I did come down to Miami. But as you suggest, it would mean that although I am in the States, we would still be apart for 2 weeks or so. It is hard to determine anything because we don't know where I'll land or what will happen to me. So many things develop from day to day that it becomes more difficult for me to say anything at all. Lord knows I want to do as many things to please you as you wish to do for me. All I am thinking of is means to cut down wasted time. Believe me, Darling, there will have to be a lot of improvising done to make our plans easier and fuller. As a matter of fact, I don't even think of a definite plan because so often they are subject to change. Remember this, My Darling, we are very much in love, — hence, we want to do the right things at the right time. However, the one hitch of that is that at the present, we are not certain of the right time. The right thing has always been a definite one, marriage. I love you very much, My Dearest One. Our hearts must sensibly control our minds and these two minds are a lot better than one. You said it seems like sunshine is all you have to offer. My sunshine will be to see the light in your eye. My smile will be radiant enough the day we meet again to make the sun look like a piker. I realize only too well that another trip to New York will be twice as tortuous as the first trip but I intend to make it easy, easier than you think. But that again is another plan. Gosh, Honey, I am so tickled by the fact that someday I'll be home that all I want to do is think of that; the time, place and everything else is unimportant. Do you see what I mean? I know you feel what I mean. Therefore, I want you to try to accept it that way. We can find many ways to handle obstacles. We did it before, we'll do it again. You said yourself later in the letter — You know that our love is strong. There is no flaw. Not between you and I. We have had 18 months to iron out a lot of things. Actually we knew what we wanted one day back in April '43. We were sure of it one day back in July '43. And someday in '45, we'll have the fruits of all our great expectations. You mustn't place too much value in other relationships. My Darling, the day and before. That's wrong. Bette, the day we get together, my responsibilities are to you. I know that they sound like hard words to other people but I haven't been sitting around listlessly over here. I've already accepted those responsibilities and I am still 3,000 miles away. I don't know if you received one of my letters but I told you about a lot of things and I wasn't kidding. But one day in June last year [*D-Day*], I knew that I couldn't be wrong. I place a lot of faith in that incident and it will take a lot more than words to change my dreams. And, Darling, you know full well you are my dream. How can we miss? We love each other too much.

Good night, Dream. Take care of yourself. I miss you. May God Bless You. Love, Mike.

All planes were grounded on January 18 due to weather. The Group War Diary noted for the day that the movie *Laura* was shown, and that the train made a Liberty run.

January 19, 1945 [*Friday*]

Hello Darling,

I got in rather late this evening and though I was a bit tired, I had to write. I was most distressed that you aren't getting my mail. That, of course, was due to the fact that I received your change of address so late. Even now, your letters aren't 2 weeks old. It is rather hard to keep apace of things at that rate. I received 3 letters from you today, dated Dec. 28, 30, and Jan. 1st. You see, Dearest, it is just a case of slow moving. At least, from your tone I feel that the novelty of Miami is a comfort for the lack of mail. Darling, I love you so very much. When I am tired like this, I would rather speak of silly things but I find I often fall into a mood of you. If my letter seems sketchy tonight forgive me.

I meant to say something about a sight that appealed to me not so long ago. We were at a rather good altitude. About 8,000 ft., we were over a complete overcast. It looked like the clouds were right down to the ground. The sun was shining over our left wing. And on our right, I saw a perfectly shaped bull's eye, perfectly circular rainbow and right smack in the center was the shadow of our plane. They call it a pilot's eye or light or rainbow, something like that. Even after all this time, it was the first time I had ever seen it. It was impressive, indeed. A little further on, the high mass of clouds dropped abruptly almost like the snow on a mountain side and dropped that way almost to about 2,000 ft. Further on it dissipated to nothing and down below was the greenness of land. All of it made wonderful scenery.

I was glad to see by your letter that you have started to get into the social swing of Miami. I must say that you are a schemer. I knew that you'd try to work Mother into a romance. Sounds almost like an adventure out of Hollywood. I imagine it does her a world of good to get out more often. The leisurely life of such a State encourages a good deal of easy life. What is better than to get out among the people amid such lovely backgrounds?

Darling, you mustn't feel so acutely about our separation. It has been difficult for both of us. I must admit that I like to hear you speak so — your compliments are highly appreciated. We are doing a fine job of patience. There are times when it is harder to face than at others. Both of us have traveled a bit and I have often expressed a similar sentiment to yours. No one can come close to you. We aren't the first people to talk about love and its beauty. Today I was thinking that you and I aren't extraordinary people. All we want is to be together and live a normal married life. Those little things that are so important are the things that we miss so much when we are thrown into the company of people who help us to miss each other all the more. When you spoke of tears, I sat back and looked at your picture for a long while. It is a great comfort because it brings you so much closer to me. My morale soars when I can relax long enough to have you completely in my mind. And to think that compared to what we will have, we had so little before. Actually, in the eyes of most people we are strangers to each other but I feel I know you as well as I know myself. When I speak to anyone of you, I feel as if you are by my side smiling and nodding.

Sometimes you frown when I sound coarse but you love me for it because I am so proud of you. It isn't hard to love, Darling, not a person like you. Even from 3,000 miles away, you are as real to me as you were in Ft. Wayne and KC. Nothing would please me more than to please you again but for always. I love you and miss you so very much. I wish I could go on speaking forever.

Good night, Darling, got a few tough days ahead. Must sleep. My love to Mother. Take care of yourself. May God Bless You. Love always, Mike.

The Squadron and Group War Diaries for January 19-22 told of more problems with weather and a busy flight schedule:

WD, January 19: Twelve planes were sent to France, eight were forced back because of weather; the remaining four RON on the continent. Two planes still out since 17th Jan. '45, another sent out on the 14th still on continent. Five glider pilots returned from ferrying mission that left this base on the 14th of January. Five planes were used in the afternoon for local flying.

GWD, January 19: High wind during the night destroyed at least four of our gliders which were tied down. Because of a bad snow storm, those aircraft returning from the continent had to RON in the southern United Kingdom.

WD, January 20: Eight planes to the continent, all RON. Three planes to France on another mission, two returned because of weather; the other plane completed the mission. One XC and return. Transition training in C-109 in the afternoon.

GWD, January 20: High winds and more snow. Our planes took off for the continent but had to return to base due to the weather conditions over the channel. The movie, *Kismet* was shown on the base this evening. Two showings with both houses full.

WD, January 21: Seven of the eight planes that were sent out on the 20th have returned. Two, one plane missions to France and return. One plane XC and return. Dance at ARC Club for enlisted men.

GWD, January 21: Sunday morning: Usual church services held on base. Departments are preparing for a general inspection by our commanding officer, Colonel Harvey A. Berger. Weather still very cold.

WD, January 22: Two planes were sent out on the 17th returned, another plane that was sent out on the 21st returned. Five other planes returned, four that were sent out on the 19th and one that was sent out on the 14th. Fourteen planes sent to Southern England to pick up loads and return.

GWD, January 22: Barracks, quarters, and Offices were prepared

for inspection this morning by all personnel here at Cottesmore. Colonel Berger and Lt. Col. Washburn inspected.

January 23, 1945 [*Tuesday*]

Hello "Mole,"

So sorry for not having been able to write for the last few days, Darling. It is a relief to be able to relax for a day at least. I don't know what has been wrong but I haven't been able to sleep as well as I'd like to. Must be the clean life I'm living but I think it is more because I'm in love. The mail situation has been poor again; it has been almost a week since I heard from you. Wish to Hell, it would be a bit more consistent.

Well, Darling, time continues to pass. That is one of the best reasons I like to keep busy. What I really am looking forward to is the day when you and I can relax entirely, live a few weeks of total irresponsibility. Just as you once said, a few weeks of rest back in the States would have me as good as new. You know I've told you about many of my nightmares — actually it is a form of warning to you. If I should start to yell and scream and sit upright, just sock me one in the jaw, not too hard. I'm afraid, Darling, that I'm going to be a bit of a task for a while. Gosh, I love you.

I guess the headlines back home on these days must be something to look at. The way those Russians are pushing Jerry around, it seems as if they can't last too long. It would be something to have everything stop suddenly. Maybe I'm prejudiced or something (Just to change the subject!) but one thing really gripes me is the incessant talk about 4-F ball players, etc. Personally, it would break my heart if I thought that baseball was on its last leg. "If they can play ball, they can fight." So what? The country must be in dire straits when they start bitching about one of the things that is a symbol of America. Believe me, I have often thought it would be a great treat to sit in the stands again and yell like a maniac at a bunch of guys beating their brains out. But I guess as an insignificant human, it can't be my privilege to become indignant at the opinions of our so-called numbskull intelligentsia. We were talking about that incident of the President's son's dog. I'll be damned if I'd sidestep for a mutt but if worse came to worse, I'd put that dog on my lap, 130 lbs. and all. It really must be a sad state of affairs when the American people are getting so petty. But why am I torturing you with such nonsensical prattle? (How do you like that for a few bits of words?)

That paratrooper Lt. you were talking about had the right idea. Lord knows how often men thought of the idea of hostesses on our ships. I had that thought a long time ago. We landed in Omaha, Nebraska, and I went in and had a bit of breakfast. When I came out, I watched the airliners land. After one had taxied over and had discharged the passengers, this good looking gal directed a lot of traffic. I couldn't help but marvel at the uniformity of everything. I'll admit we haven't the finesse but we manage to get things done. As a matter of food, well that is a problem. It is not a strange sight to see us cooking some coffee while we are mid-air. The other morning I was stuck in a place [*Belgium*] that was so cold that when I crawled out of my sack and tried to lace my shoes, my fingers damn near froze. I was elected chief cook and we had plenty of 10 in 1 rations which are very good, very complete. We made coffee, cooked bacon and some ham and eggs (canned). We use hard tack and I do mean hard, for bread + jam and butter. By the time we were ready to eat the bacon, it was so cold that the grease froze. But so it is the way, — one must learn to utilize every little detail. I'll admit that it wasn't my idea of utopia but a guy must live. My greatest difficulty is keeping my hands (covered by 2 pairs of gloves) and feet warm. But it is amazing how easy it is to get comfortable in my sack. That ole' sack is a treat and life saver. It is one of the best things that the Army ever issued. I'd like to take it home and give you a shot at it. Don't know how you'd like it. Still like to see if it could hold two. Something would take a Hell of a beating and I'm willing to bet that it would be the sack. — Gosh —

Well, Darling, I hate to close in the middle of a page but I have a few things to attend to. Give my love to Mother. I love you and miss you, Darling. May God Bless You. Love, Mike.

January 23, 1945 [*Tuesday*]

Good Evening, My Love,

Still no mail this evening but it is best that I write again because I hate to stand short. Saw a rather interesting show this evening, *When Hearts Were Young and Gay*. I guess it was sort of a part of the young life of Cornelia Otis Skinner. It was a rather clever affair and I damn near died laughing at one scene where these 2 young gals walked into a rather fashionable English Café wearing enormous fur coats. The damn things started to fall apart and these two gals looked so stupid garmented in this vast store of rabbit. With the main show, they had a short of some gal. In the background was an All-Girl Ork. The sax player rolled and seemed so much at ease that she reminded me of a gal that we saw in London on our last leave.

Mac [*Ron MacDougall*], Beak [*Don Harris*], and I were sitting at the bar drinking some scotch when a Belgian officer and his girl walked in. Since the place was small and she was attractive, it was a normal thing to strike up a conversation. She was drinking scotch too but every so often she would pull a small bottle out of bag and take a sip. Since the three of us were drinking and talking it was natural not to notice her closely only spasmodically. I heard one of her companions ask her about the bottle and she said it was walnut and she used it for flavoring. They were jabbering away and we didn't notice them too closely. But after a while, this gal got rather boisterous and wild. She, then, asked her companion to get her a cab. I noticed too that every so often when I'd say something to her, she was rather curt. The bar maid kept telling us to lay off because she was dangerous. When she left, we realized what was wrong. An extract of any sort like that, Vanilla, Walnut, etc., is used as a narcotic, "smoke." It is habit forming and dangerous. Poor kid, she was well on the road. I pity her boy friend; he must have had a Hell of a job satisfying her that night. I can't help but marvel at the various types of people I've met. Personally, I don't care much for these continental weaknesses. An American must be mentally distorted, a sexual pervert or just loco to go for that sort of stuff. I know that there are such people at home but they aren't usual. Over here, it seems that such people are prominent among the better social class.

Just like the queer I met; I was interested and asked him where he learned his extracurricular activities. I wondered if it was born in him. He said, "No, you see I was a German prisoner for 9 months. It was normal for the men to love each other. What do you Americans do when you have no women?" What a question. I told him that we pursue many other diversions and they don't lean toward the sexual. Since he had a good job and was in the upper middle class, it seemed strange. But he told me that I'd be surprised how many men in his social class were like him. At least, he was honest. It is not a strange sight to see men walking arm in arm, — not as lovers but in the same manner that one of us would throw our arm around a guy's shoulder. They are the damnedest people for handshaking. Just passing "Hello" to them means grabbing each other's hands. Not a firm, honest sincere handshake but a sloppy touch of finger tips. I can't [*do*] it. I have to laugh every time I see it. A young lady can't be introduced unless she throws her hand at you and not to be kissed but shaken.

I guess just to keep in the vogue, I am reading a book about the French system of prostitution. It is called *Houses of the Lost*. I don't recommend it because it doesn't vary in anything but prostitution. It was written by a Frenchman, intended as a means to help abolish the free use of houses of legitimate loving (?). It is a rather raw thing and indeed very revealing. I can't say that I approve of their lax mannerisms. Sexual intercourse, sincere or for pleasure, is something I am old-fashioned about. These women, that he writes about, thought nothing of sleeping with 7 or 8 men per night. It may be a prosperous business but not a highly recommended one.

Seems rather hard to say anything nice, but I've devoted so much of this letter to types. But that hardly stops me from telling you how lovely you are, how much I love you and how deeply I miss you — I do.

Good night, Darling. Take care of yourself. May God Bless You. Love, Mike.

The next five days of Squadron and Group War Diary entries — January 23-27 — read:

> **WD, January 23: No flying because of weather.**
>
> **GWD, January 23: Planes returned from previous mission. Snow still on the ground. Trucks made the run to Oakham to meet Liberty Train. Movie, *Our Hearts Were Young and Gay* played here this evening. The Red Cross is now under new management and a great many changes have been made. Among these is a new snack bar which made a big hit with the Enlisted Men.**
>
> **WD, January 24: Planes grounded because of weather.**
>
> **GWD, January 24: . . . NAAFI dance canceled because no transportation was permitted off the base to pick up the girls.**

WD, January 25: No flying because of weather.

GWD, January 25: . . . Even though weather conditions were bad, liberty run was made this evening.

WD, January 26: Sixteen planes were dispatched to the continent, all of them RON. . . .

GWD, January 26: Fog still persisting. The Red Cross Arrow Club is gaining popularity by leaps and bounds, possibly the success can be contributed to the new snack bar with its varied menu.

WD, January 27: Nine planes sent to the continent on the 26th returned today. Link training for the glider pilots.

GWD, January 27: Mission flown today and some few aircraft returned to home base, while the remaining few RON'd.

January 28, 1945 [*Sunday*]

Dearest:

This is the first time that I've even let so many days pass without writing to you. A few days ago I got a typhoid shot that left me blank. It didn't force me to bed but I felt so listless that I couldn't nor did I feel like doing anything. I started a letter 2 days ago and then tore it up — it was written as badly as I felt. Then I was gone for a few days that it was impossible for me to write. I thought for a while that I would have been still delayed but someone had a change of heart. So here I am. It is Sunday. I love you so very much and the music is soft and low. Another thing that has helped to feel so blah is the fact that I haven't had any mail from you for 10 days or so. Methinks someone is fooling around somewhere. At any rate, it is both a distressing and disturbing situation.

I received a letter from Tom yesterday. He told me of his meeting with brother Lou. It was the first meeting in 3 years. None of us has seen Lou for that long. Tom told me that his wire had gotten home on Xmas Day. Mother, Lucy, and Sally reacted so that it was almost impossible to handle the situation. Mom is still not happy because I am still over here. What more can one say other than that someday I, too, will be home.

About a week ago, I decided to go thru' my stuff and eliminate whatever I could. I got rid of some excess flying clothes and then I started on my personal gear. You must forgive me, Darling, but I burned up most of your letters. You must understand that it is difficult to carry it all over the world. I do know that I had a hell of a lot of them. But before I sorted all of them out, I reread a lot of them. It is amazing to see that we both have been yearning for my return as long as over a year. I guess that is true from the moment I left you. Also, it proves the fact that our waiting is not in vain. What we hoped for last July '43 is still true today only much stronger. It is one of the most wonderful feelings in the world. I hope only that we won't have the same amount of time to wait. In all our waiting we have made and torn apart what seems like millions of plans. You have traveled ½ [*way*] across the States on my request — ½ of our experiments have proved questionable and the other ½ are OK. Even though I regret the first half, I feel that time will alter it to the best for everyone. I think though, Darling, that the distortions of plans prove that that we should fit our future life to suit impulsive actions. I must admit that I am a bit off-balanced by so many ideas. All I do know is that eventually the course that we take will be the right one —

January 29, 1945 [*Monday*]

It seems like years since I stopped. But just as I was really getting used to writing, I was called out. I got back late today and after I finished eating and cleaning, here I am. It is really too bad to be disturbed but since I hadn't written for so long, I wanted so not to waste any more time. One other thing, the time passes quickly and there are hopes always of having some mail waiting. So far the story has been the same for these few weeks. No mail.

It is so difficult to think of things to say without any letters. All I know is that each day that passes increases my love for you. Especially when I don't hear from you. I feel the waiting is so much harder. All I can seem to think of is the day that you and I will be together again. It is a comforting thought, isn't it Bette?

Well, Darling, forgive me for closing so soon. I'm a bit tired and it is about time I got this letter on the way.

Good night, My Love. Give my love to Mother. Take care of yourself. May God Bless You. I love you and miss you. Love, Mike.

✿❧❦✿

WD, January 28: Five planes were dispatched to the continent; they were to stop in southern England and pick up their loads and proceed from there to the continent, all five of them returned because of weather. Nine other planes left this base for the continent, five of them returned to this station; the other four reached their destination but were forced to RON. Seven planes sent to France on the 26th returned today.

GWD, January 28: Sunday morning found us with the remains of another snowfall. Headquarters Enlisted Men enjoyed another movie this evening in their day room, *Carolina Blues*.

WD, January 29: Five planes were dispatched to the continent with supplies, all delivered their loads and returned. Three other planes returned from the continent, two had been sent out on the 28th and the other on the 20th. Ten planes to Southern England, took on loads and returned. Dance at the ARC Club for enlisted men.

GWD, January 29: Much warmer today. Aircraft that had RON'd on the continent returned today, reporting heavy snow storms. American Red Cross Arrow Club dance this evening. Snow and more snow this evening again.

January 30, 1945 [*Tuesday*]

Little Woman of Mine,

   Another day has passed and yet nothing new. No mail, no nuttin' 'til my baby comes home. It is again the 1st of the month, pay day, tomorrow and Moe, "Beak" and I are heading out again for a 48-hour pass. This time we are going North to Leeds. At any rate, it will be a change and someone said we can get plenty to drink. Just like that last pass we had, it's another drunk. You can see that I am cutting down, cutting it down to once per month. I'm in good company, Darling. Beak is married to a gal in Texas and Moe has sort of an inferiority complex. Actually and always, our first and last outlook is liquor. If we were welcomed by a bottle, we'd never move. They are really swell fellows. You must meet them someday. Honestly, Darling, I'll never really enjoy a pass until I spend it with you. But I guess, going out with the fellows is the best alternative. My Darling, I love you so much.

   We saw an excellent show this evening. *Rhapsody in Blue*. The life of George Gershwin. His music will really live in America and the world for longer than we'll ever see. I came to one conclusion while watching the show and that was that a GI audience is one of the most unappreciative in the world. Perhaps, it may be that they don't understand the theme of a man like Gershwin, or that their appreciation of music is boogie-woogie and junk. I don't think that I'll be able to really enjoy a good show until the day I can sit back in a comfortable seat, relax, and have a bit of quiet for concentration. Enuf! of that bitching. One must, though, Bette, — we must see his *Porgy and Bess*. The last time I tried to in NY, it was sold out for 3 weeks in advance. Gosh, there are so many things for us to see.

   You know I was tired last night. Well, I got into the sack about 8:30. Someone handed me a cartoon book of "Hubert" (you recall, "Oh! Frankie"). Bette, I laughed so much that I cried. He is the GIs, GI. Never in my life have I seen so many characters thrown into so many characteristics of army life. Perhaps we aren't as clever but [*we sure*] can appreciate the guy.

   Well, Darling, I am going to close. I've warned you — All I hope is that I have some mail when I get back.

   Good night, My Love. Take care of yourself. I love you and miss you —
   May God Bless You — Love, Mike.

   The Squadron and Group War Diary entries for January 30 to February 2 are:

   WD, January 30: No flying to the continent. Link training for the glider pilots still in progress. Personnel of operations and five crews had their pictures taken for the historical records.

GWD, January 30: Found our deepest snow fall this morning. Large drifts in some places, and in some cases even blocking the streets. The snow crew was called out to clear runways and streets. Movie, *Rhapsody in Blue* at the Station Cinema.

WD, January 31: No flying because of weather. Officers of the 316th TC GP held a President's Birthday Ball at DeMontfort Hall in Leicester. Pay call for all personnel. [*The Resume, a recap of the month's activities, notes some of the flights taken by the squadron.*]

GWD, January 31: Barracks and offices are to be prepared daily for inspection. Pay call this morning at 1030. Started raining this morning and the snow is melting fast.

WD, February 1: Six plane resupply mission to A-93 [*Liege, Belgium*] and return. Ten plane mission to A-79 [*Prosnes, France*], two aircraft RON, one because of engine trouble. A four plane mission to A-40 [*Chartres, France*], returned to home base because of weather. . . .

GWD, February 1: February was ushered in with high wind and rain, and a promise of fair weather, at least a change from snow. Flying schedule improved with the weather. Movie, *Step Lively* with Frank Sinatra at the base cinema. Liberty train was unable to run so trucks substituted.

WD, February 2: One plane returned from the continent sent out the day before. Fifteen planes were sent to Southern England for loads and return. A VD film was shown at the base theater for all personnel. S/Sgt. Les Goldman gave a lecture at the ARC Club on the war situation.

GWD, February 2: Mission sent to far shore and returned. . . .

January 31, 1945 [*Wednesday*] [*letter actually written on February 3, 1945, Saturday*]

Hello Darling,

I returned from my pass today and figured I would have one day of respite. But I give up. You can't argue with rank. So off I went. Not only was I feeling a bit out of sorts but there was no mail. Fortunately, when I got in tonight, I had 4 letters from you. I love you, Darling — Well before I answer, I'll tell you few facts about that drunken orgy of ours. Honestly, Darling, don't you think I'm a Hell of a future husband? We didn't leave the hotel at all. Every afternoon, I'd carry Moe up to his room. When I'd go up to check, he'd be on the floor; put him to bed and let him carry on. Finally, Don and I left the hotel to check train schedules. We took a few pictures. They hope to send them to us as soon as they are ready. Don't know how they'll come out; I was carrying a bit of a load. While we were walking down the street, I saw a pair of RAF souvenir wings. They really looked good, so inquired. I noticed that the price tag had an 11 on it. I figured about 11 shillings. So I told the guy I'd take them. While the fellow went for a box, I threw a £ on the counter. He came back and said 10£s more please. I damn near died. I told him that was a bit beyond my heights and Gad! Did I blush. (Strange, isn't it? But I did.) Finally I ended up buying another pair, not quite as expensive but just as pretty. I'll send them. They are sterling — whereas the others were white gold. How was I to know?

I am glad that you have started to get my mail. I'm sorry that you are still having difficulty with lodgings. I hope it shan't be too long before I'll be able to change your address and name. It is a wonderful thing to think about. I guess it must be the only thing I think of these days. It seems as if the days never pass. Gosh, Bette, there are so many wonderful things to look forward to. Your letters today made me feel as if it has been so long since I last spoke to me. I know you are waiting as patiently as I am and as eagerly. I keep thinking the difference of night and day. The difference of this hellish world and the beauty and peace of you and I. Yes, Darling, you and I doing everything we want to do when we want to do it. No, it can't be too far off and yet it is such a beautiful dream. It seems as if it will never come thru'.

I am going to close — I hope a good night's sleep will shape me up. Good night, Darling. Take care of yourself. May God Bless You. Mike.

   WD, February 3: A Group formation for the presentation of awards was held this afternoon. One, four, five and ten plane mission to France and return.

   GWD, February 3: Aircraft of the group affected missions to the continent. In the afternoon a Group formation was held in front of the base Officers' Club, and presentations were made.

February 4, 1945 [*Sunday*]

Good Evening, Darling,

I can't seem to get over the idea that January is over. Maybe it's because I'm glad that it is over. I knew that mail last night was too good to be true. But, at any rate, there is no reason to bitch. I should be glad that I was lucky to get those.

Now to start to answer. I think you misunderstood [*Van*] Johnson's portrayal of Lawson in *30 Secs*. He didn't show Lawson as a weakling but as a guy that had a lot of things to think about jammed into precious moments. It is hard for a man to admit just what he feels. When we get back, no one says a word and then someone will ask casually, "Were you frightened?" Then there is a very open admission of just what went on. All our tongues are loosened almost simultaneously. But one thing, no one really tells what they were thinking about or who, that is private, something to cherish and nourish. Lawson's ideas were put into a book. There was a reason for that. They had to show people what went on. Of course, it's a grim and tense affair; no on can help that, a dry throat, a tight stomach and wet, sweaty palms in the coldest climate are normal. And so it goes.

Darling, in one of your letters, you closed and forgot to sign it. Is it because you are in love?

I am glad that you agree with me on important subjects. I know that we can discuss things sensibly. That's what makes things about us so easy to comprehend. You are right when you say that I'll never give you cause to be angry with me. I am really an easy person to get along with. I must admit that lately I haven't been too agreeable a person. Maybe it's my fault or not. I guess this being away from you makes me a bit disagreeable. It has been a long time, Darling. As much as I try to keep the face of a relaxed person, a *pagliacci*, there are times when my nerves are a bit bound up. But that is here. Just you and you alone will be able to do so much to rid me of that complex. I know because I wasn't like that before I left you. You made my life that proverbial bowl of cherries. I am not and never will be worried about the religious differences.

You keep mentioning my smile. Well the other day while I was sitting for that picture, the photographer said, "You'll have to smile a little less or your eyes won't be seen. I said, "Go ahead, Brother, the way I feel, no one will see my eyes any how."

Yes, Bette, I guess we will have to wait a little while when I get home. As you said we will be together and there won't be an ocean between us. It will take those few days to straighten out our plans. No matter how often we write of them in our letters, there will still be changes. After so many months, those days won't hurt. It will take me some time to get used to civilization anyway. Gosh, though, Darling, isn't it wonderful to think of it. I love you so very much, so very much that it makes everything so complete. It would be nice to start a family but as you said, it will be best to wait a while. It would probably be very hard on you because Lord alone knows how long it will be before we settle down to some sanity and permanency. I don't think that that is an abnormal train of thought. After what I've seen of the Army and its inconsistency, those thoughts are sensible. Tony is lucky on that score.

Your suppositions about Sheila are correct. You see her mother died when she was quite young. Men make poor mothers so it was difficult for her father to handle Sheila and her 2 sisters. Her grandma was rather old and narrow-minded about the *affaires des femmes*. . . . Tony is what one might call a man of the world. Since he is 10 years older, it was and is normal that I learned and learn so much from him. Dan and Gert are of a different temperament from you and I. . . . Cousin Mike [*Fusco*] and Thelma are doing the same thing. But I think they've both gotten their fingers out and decided that life won't wait. Tom said he was going to NY to perform his first wedding, Mike and Thelma. To the contrary, that's why I like Lucy and Harry. Lucy wanted to wait; Harry said, "No." He's been away too long. Why wait? Can they love each other in a year or if he were to come home tomorrow? It would be the same. . . . We are all old enough to know <u>what</u> life is — Besides, Lucy's as Latin as I am. Those other people don't lack love but they are content to hold hands. . . . I'm glad I found you.

Good night, Darling. I must answer a few more letters. Give my love to Mother. Tell her to see that her daughter gets that Florida sunshine. It doesn't take me long to make up for lost time.

Take care of yourself. May God Bless You. Love Ever, Mike.

According to the February 4 Squadron War Diary:

One aircraft cross country and return. Sixteen plane mission to Southern England to pick up supplies and return. Nine enlisted men transferred into the squadron, formerly infantry. . . . A lecture was given them on security and censorship.

The Group War Diary that same day said:

Sunday morning services were held by all faiths here on the base.

February 5, 1945 [*Monday*]

Good Evening, Darling,

I love you. Kinda thought that lusty mail a few nights ago was too good to last. But there I go again. I hope you don't tire of my continually mentioning that. Sometimes it is my best way to start a letter but it hardly portrays my feelings. I'm feeling rather chipper and sharp this eve. Can't say why except that I must be getting tired of worrying.

That buddy of mine whom I had hoped would eventually write to you, dropped us a note recently. He is stationed somewhere in Calif. He went home on a C-54 and was in NY in 17½ hours. He told us of his visit to my family. Said that he was 2 sheets to the wind when he went to Brooklyn, but after Dad broke out some of his wine, he really finished the job. Perhaps, Buck [*Charlie Krueger*], will have more time now and write to you, if he hasn't done so already.

I was reading an article in *Stars and Stripes* about women's clothes. Didn't realize before that it costs so much to keep a gal dressed. Guy's are lucky that way, an old pair of dungarees, a pair of ole shoes, a sport shirt and no hat, and we can feel like kings. Don't mind me, just pulling your leg. Lovely one at that. Say, Bette, I've been meaning to ask you about the weight situation these days. I imagine all that sunshine and good food ought to help. Are you taking any weight-lifting exercises?

Brr! So you think it was a bit cold in Miami those past weeks. I can very readily sympathize with you. You have heard me lamenting of the cold for the last year or so. It is most uncomfortable, isn't it? Especially since there are none of the comforts of heat. I don't mind you doing your letter writing in bed but I'll give you any odds that you'll not need to worry about heat or letter writing once I hit the States. Not having to send notes across like this will be quite a relief, won't it? If you ever get tired of talking to me, I'll volunteer for overseas duty again, and then you can start writing again. Just you try. If I knew then what I know now, I'd still be an instructor in some base outfit. That's spilled milk, no sense to cry!

I'm the same as you are on the reading situation. I haven't had a chance to get my hands on any good literature for a Hell of a while. The last book I read was *Winter Wheat.* That French slop I told you about was merely a very flirting affair. If I read too much of that stuff, I'd work myself into one of those torrid, sex upheavals. But that I don't. That *Forever Amber* I spoke of is one of those books that is covered with sex acts and their variations. Somewhat of the style of floggers and other acts of sexual perversions. Maybe I'm an old-fashioned American, I prefer mine straight with just sensible variations. But enough of that. At any rate, nothing new to report on the literature angles. Hell, I sound dull, don't I? But one cannot lose contact with the arts and still sound interesting in a discussion like that. That arts business reminds me always of your leanings toward Surrealism. "Midnight in Manhattan" that looks like the traveling DTs. Wonderful for a hangover. I still lean toward a finer symphony of colors and lines. A cow hanging from a tree doesn't impress me in the least. In a French café one day, I saw some landscapes by one of the local painters. His detail was wonderful and his color was perfectly adequate for his portrayals. I saw an El Greco not so long ago and it reminded me of a portrait this fellow [*actually it was a woman in a WPA (Works Progress Administration) artists' project at New York University*] in an art class did of me. I don't mean that the pictures were alike but the shadowing and deep, somber colors were so much alike. But that is neither here nor there. You can notice my slow mood. Here I am speaking of art, but love to me is more important.

Darling, I love you — or have I said that before? There is no change in me except that I do appreciate you so much more. It is amazing how much closer two people can be welded by a separation such as ours. I persist upon mentioning the fact that you will have to teach me how to live again. I mean that only in the renewal of environment. You shall never have to teach me how to love again. That will come easy as long as I'm with you. All I need is to recall how easily such things were for us before. The most wonderful part of it all is that we never waste nor mince words. Sometimes, as I look back on it all, I'm afraid that I appeared a bit gruff. Darling, do you think you'll ever control my enthusiasm, my extreme emotional furor? Or do you want to? Darling, I do need you so. More than you'll ever know. Dear God, that it may not be too long before we are united again. You're wonderful!

Good night, Darling. Take care of yourself. I love you and miss you. May God Bless You. Love, Mike.

WD, February 5: One plane resupply and weather ship was sent to the continent and return. . . . USO show with Al Bernia in *Flying High* was held at the NAAFI Club. Dance at the American Red Cross for the EM.

GWD, February 5: The weather was rainy and foggy this morning so all aircraft were grounded. . . .

February 6, 1945 [*Tuesday*]

Good Morning, Darling,

I received a few more letters from you last night. I didn't write because a few of the guys coaxed me out to a show in town. We saw *Pin-Up Girl*. Just another show but Oh! that Charlie Spivak. He and Sammy Kaye could keep me happy all day long. That sweet trumpet of Spivak's sounds like the sweetness of an angel's voice.

I heard from Max Gilliam and he told me of the note that you had sent him. You see his wife forwarded the letter to him. He is stationed in Wisconsin. Naturally Susie didn't open the letter but Max felt that she would be a bit suspicious. So he sent the note to her and he has told me that he will answer as soon as he can. Poor guy, he has been home 6 months and has had at least 90 days of furloughs. Some guys really get the breaks. But he's swell and deserves every break he can get. I am glad that they do show a bit of consideration for the vets. Hope to Hell they don't stop when I get home.

You spoke of sail boating. I was never much of a hand at it. But I am not at a loss in a boat. We were out fishing one day on the [*Long Island*] Sound. We had a 30-foot, 2 mast affair with auxiliary engine. Rather than dock it nearby, three of us decided to sail it back to its base. It took us 3 hours to travel 17 miles but it was really a thrill. She handled beautifully. We did some damn good navigating and made port just before a storm and darkness hit. I've fiddled a bit around speedboats and I can row as well as the next guy. Gad! Sun and water what a combination!

Gosh, Darling, I'm sorry you misunderstood Lucy's intentions. You see, since it is difficult to have the right sort of finesse from here, I asked her to do a little favor for me. You see, we've never been reluctant to do things for each other, even things as delicate as that. I think I've already explained about the perfume. I've told her to forward it to your address in Miami. But in turn I sent you the bottle that I had gotten here. But when Lucy sent the perfume, she figured it would be a nice touch to send a card. Please forgive the distortion of meaning. It was all like a relayed message, one station to the other, a good old double play. Sorry, Darling, guess I don't do things right, do I?

You know, Bette, we've talked so much of our forthcoming marriage that our plans seem so indefinite. But I think we have it fairly well simplified. Since we've agreed to wait a few days when I get home, I think we can take care of everything then. There is no sense for you to go thru' any additional experiences. It is just as easy to do things together. Don't worry about health certificates until that day. It seems like ever so much trouble for you. Waiting for us then won't be a last minute affair because the important thing is that we love each other. We will be together and planning together will be ever so much nicer. Our letters are so far apart that they lead one into another. Hell, I have been away quite a while and I don't know what changes have arisen due to war time. Besides, I think it a good idea if I court you for a few days. Just don't want to rush you into marriage without telling you how much I love you. Don't think I'm not eager, as eager as ever. Sort of rushing you off your feet period. Gosh, Darling, I love you. Do you think I'll be hard to take?

Well Darling, must close. Gotta' go some place this noon. Give my love to Mother. Take care of yourself. I love you and miss you ever so much. May God Bless you. Your Lover, Mike.

WD, February 6: Fourteen resupply mission to A-79 [*Prosnes, France*] **and return. One plane resupply mission to Y-83** [*Denain/Prouvy, France*] **and return. . . .**

GWD, February 6: Resupply missions carried out to the far shore. Movie on the base *Two Girls and a Sailor* **this evening.**

WD, February 7: Nine planes were dispatched to Southern England for loads and return. Six planes were used for local transition in the afternoon. The C-109 was also up. Four pilots were scheduled for link trainer. Dance at the NAAFI for EM of the base. One EM, assigned on the fourth, confined to the Guard House, AWOL.

GWD, February 7: Aircraft flew to Southern UK this morning to load for a mission to the continent but had to return after loading because of bad weather over the channel. . . .

February 8, 1945 [*Thursday*]

Good Evening, Darling,

The letter I wrote yesterday, I dated the 6th. It was merely because I'd forgotten both day and date. Because it was the eve of the 6th that I headed for that show I spoke of. To go on, — armed with 6 bottles of beer, I headed over to see Pappy last night. We sat around and shot the bull until 11 PM last night. Talked about old times, exchanged a few pictures and he told me that he had written to you but said that he mailed it to Kansas City. It just shows you how long it had been since we'd last seen each other. He didn't even know you were in Miami. You see, Little Woman, you move about so much.

Yes, Bette, in one of my previous letters, I discussed the fact that TC [*Troop Carrier*] does change its plans often. They, the plans, are liable to change at any time. Under the set-up that was recently installed, I'd be counting days, not months. However, like everything I am one of the many. Don't think I've given up hope of anything because I haven't forgotten what we said in Ft. Wayne. Knowing that you'll be waiting for me, no matter how long, is all the assurance I need in this world. But really, Darling, you know as well as I do that at certain periods waiting is harder to take than at other times. I read recently that Rep. Claire Luce has proposed an 18-month tour for everyone overseas; she was vetoed. It hardly seems possible that they'd throw that out. But after seeing Doc do 33 months, I'd never think of any possibilities. As we have said so often before, once we are together, all this time now will seem like nothing. You just keep enjoying those balmy breezes and keep waiting. I only hope that when I am ready to come home, it happens quickly so I don't have to tear my nerves apart waiting for my leave.

Meant to tell you that I had received a note from brother Lou. He spoke of my plans to marry and wished that he could meet you. But he said that as long as that is impossible, he would wait and said that since you are my choice, he is glad of it. Doc has always trusted my judgment. He always treated me with the respect of an older person. Worried continually of my future and was sorry that he couldn't help me feed my previous yearnings for a profession. But that had since passed, he encouraged me in my work and said that I couldn't miss being successful. Although, he is a strange sort of guy, I've never had any cause to argue with him. He said that when I come home, he'll try to get leave and spend some time with us. He has been placed on limited service and will be in the States for the duration. Lucy told me that he was in a few of the beach landings over there and that of all the medics who went in with him, he was the only one that wasn't killed or wounded. He claims it was a miracle — on the face of that, I can't blame him. [*Doctor Lou was with the 116th Medical Detachment, 41st Infantry Division.*]

Yes, Darling, I guess Mother must be a bit tired of hearing of me. So with people over here, I never waste a moment but to tell them of you. It is my favorite subject. I love you very much, Bette. Damn this war, if it must go on, why must it keep us apart so long? Grr!! To quote a phrase.

Nope, I've never been in the Store at Miami. I never left the Beach, do you blame me? I've seen some pictures of it and I believe since it is in a show place of America, to insure sales, the store itself must be a show place.

Darling, I am going to close. I was up at 5 o'clock this AM and in the air before you were turning over for the first snooze. It has been a long day. So Good Night, My Lovely. Give my love to Mother. Take care of yourself. I love you and miss you so — May God Bless You. Love, Mike.

February 8, 1945 [*Thursday*]

Good Evening, Darling,

I hardly know how to start this note. At any rate, another day has passed and it means I am a day closer to you. That's as nice a start as I can think of.

I just finished a book called *Thunder Mountain* — by Pratt. Didn't even notice his name. However, his theme is unique and most interesting. His story centers about one family. What I liked about that was that they were people who didn't mince words, thoughts or impulses. He speaks little of sex, actually, in his theme. But when he does, he makes the scenes as torrid as anyone could live thru'. I must admit that even in the reading, it excited me a bit. But it wasn't enough to take anything out of the original theme which leaned exceedingly toward a modern Shangri-La of isolation. The manner in which the hero, Alex Arrington, almost accomplishes this is both interesting and damn near tragic. I cannot go thru' the theories that are expounded because it would take endless pages. One of the characters, one of Alex's daughters-in-law, is termed a nymphomaniac, a gal that couldn't be satisfied. That factor leads to a lot of complications. The book would be ideal for a motion picture, barring some of the heated behind-closed-doors scenes.

To divert a bit, Darling, did you ever read the Holy Bible. The reason I mention it is that one of the fellows that went home gave it to me and I keep it on the plane. During lull moments, I often pick it up and read a few chapters. Of course, it is the New Testament, the story of the life of Christ. I find it to be most interesting and refreshing. Bruce Barton wrote a book called, *The Man Nobody Knows* and he put a new color to Christ, the Man. It would take years of extensive research to discover just a part of His Life. He was a Great Man. I like to discuss religion in this manner because to me it is hero worship. Just as if one would speak to his baseball heroes or All-Americans. It is hard to ally Christ with material things but even in His divinity one must remember that He stayed among us for 33 years. I believe that believing in the Son of God must come with an understanding of Him. From that it is easy to gain strength that He so bravely gives to us. Believe me there are some things that I like to question and deepen but my primary teachings have given me the chance never to doubt His Powers. I may sound a bit like Tom but I have had a better chance to see Him now than I have ever. I shan't apologize for writing as I am because I know that you are eager always to learn. Like love of woman, love of one's God comes from the heart. My biggest fear is hurting Him because I, in turn, hurt those others whom I love, too. And so I leave those thoughts with you.

I love you, Darling. Day after day I think of us. It has been so long that it seems almost impossible to believe that some day we will be together. I want so to be the perfect husband and lover to you. I dream so often of the many things we will do together someday. Even though I think of our past, it becomes obscure in the new life that is facing us. Just think, Bette, we'll be husband and wife, ready to face whatever we must, as two people, side by side. Does it frighten you? Or do you feel as I do, nothing could stop us once we get started. It is a wonderful feeling which I care not to share with anyone but you. I couldn't help it the other night when I said to Pappy, "Pap, I love her — I wonder if it is possible to love a woman as much as I love Bette." And yet, I know it is possible because I do. Maybe you don't put it in as many words as I do but I know you feel as I do. We are basing our whole life on each other. This is not a lecture on the seriousness of marriage because both of us have our eyes fully open. But just think, Bette, just think how wonderfully happy we will be. Have you ever tried to analyze this love deeply? It can't be done because it ends up as it starts, I love you and need you as much as you love and need me. No questions, no flaws, no interference, and above all, no selfishness. What we do, we do for each other and who else is it right to include? We are selfish only to others because they must be excluded from that wonderful world of ours. I was thinking today about it if it was only possible to see the future — Today I was [*thinking*] leisurely, at 5,000 feet in the air, where would we be and what would we be doing 10 years from now? Ten years to forget all this and 10 years to make life what we have dreamed it would be when we were just kids. My happiness will be to make you happy and keep you as beautiful, as loving for the rest of our lives. What a Utopia! Beautiful, isn't it? That's what I thought while I was thinking of it. — Good night, Dream Girl!

Give my love to Mother. Take care of yourself. Dear God! That time will pass quickly. I love you and miss you. May God Bless You. Love, Mike.

Following are Squadron and Group War Diary entries for February 8-13, 1945:

WD, February 8: Nine plane mission to the continent and return. Six planes used for double glider tow in the morning. Two local transition flights in the afternoon. . . .

GWD, February 8: Aircraft were dispatched on missions today and had to RON as the weather was so bad they couldn't return to the field. Movie, _When Strangers Meet._

WD, February 9: Sixteen planes were dispatched to Southern England for loads thence to the continent. Seven of them were forced to return because of late loading. The remaining nine completed the mission. One plane returned from France sent out on the 1st of February. One plane was used for local training.

GWD, February 9: After completing their missions the planes that had RON'd returned to base. Transition flights are still being flown.

WD, February 10: Seventeen planes were dispatched to the continent on four different missions. Six of them completed their mission, the remaining eleven RON on the continent and in Southern England. Transition training in the C-109 and L-4 in the afternoon. Group inspection in the morning of all departments and living quarters. In the afternoon there was a Group review. . . .

GWD, February 10: Another inspection was made this morning of barracks and offices and found to be satisfactory. In the afternoon a group review was held on the parade grounds.

WD, February 11: Four planes were dispatched to the continent with supplies from Southern England but because of weather conditions, three were forced back to their home base. The other plane RON in Southern England. Three planes returned from France sent out on the 10th. . . . Special showing in the station theater for enlisted men of this base.

GWD, February 11: What few aircraft that were out returned this morning and early afternoon. The enlisted men of Headquarters had a movie, _Strange Affair_ in the day room in the evening.

WD, February 12: All planes were grounded because of inclement weather. Enlisted men of the squadron held a dance in Leicester.

GWD, February 12: Field closed in today by ground fog and no planes were dispatched.

WD, February 13: Seven planes returned from Southern England after RON several nights. They were sent to the continent on the 10 February '45. Six planes were used in the afternoon to tow gliders. One plane XC and return. Show at the station theater.

GWD, February 13: No aircraft were again dispatched but some few returned that had been sent out on missions. Men of the Group donated their blood this morning to the UK Blood Bank. . . .

February 14, 1945 [*Wednesday*]

Good Evening, Darling,

These periodic spasms of mail from me must cause you a bit of consternation. However, it isn't my fault. I've been gone for the last few days and though I was set to write a long letter today, I was called out again. Fortunately, I've got some time tonight, so here I am. I love you, Darling.

I received a V-letter from Sheila and she tells me that Tony has finally gotten a leave. She failed to mention where they were going but it appeared as if they must be heading toward New York or at least to the East Coast. What caused me a bit of unrest was the fact that Sheila said that Tony had volunteered for the Infantry. What the Hell is wrong with him? He has a wife and child and he should be happy to stay as he is. Hell, he should be satisfied with what he has. Sheila said that if his transfer goes thru' then, subsequently, it won't be long after that he'll be on his way overseas. It is a hard decision for him to make and I wouldn't be in his shoes for love or money. But it is his headache and believe me, I am a bit angry with him but it isn't my position to say anything.

When I returned from my slight sojourn, there were five letters awaiting for me from you. I'm afraid there are many times when I make many mistakes. It is because, at times, I make an error in judgment, I refer to your letter of the 3rd of January in which you speak as I want you to, openly, about the subject that seems to be so touchy to so many people in our triangle of affairs. I have written an apology to you already. It is a thing which must be discussed to understand. Letters are useless. However, I want you to know that I understand your meaning. Perhaps, I'm a bit slow at it but I can see it all. As a favor to me, accept the gift this time but I promise you I shan't make the same mistake. I guess the only thing to say is that I'm sorry. At any rate, you must admit the gesture was well-meant and would have been well accepted if the circumstances weren't as they are. I hope that my bottle of perfume will be a form of appeasement. Can't blame a guy for trying, can you Bette? One hit, one error. Still love me?

I know it is a normal thought but I can't help but feel that you seem to think that once I get back, my army life is finished. As much as I hate to think of it, I'm afraid that the Army wants to keep its lease on me for a while. Sometimes I get the feeling that they want to keep me overseas for the duration. I know it does your heart good to know that someday I'll be heading West — it makes me feel wonderful and above everything else, I want to make as many of our plans as possible come true.

I've never seen a Jai Alai game but I have heard that they are one of the [*fastest*] sports there is. They used to play in the Garden but I never did get to one. Actually, up North, it was more of a fad than anything else. There are a lot of things, I lack seeing. Gosh, Bette, all I can think of is the time when we'll be able to do all of that together. Nothing else matters to me — Sometimes I feel as if I can't stand this any more but the time will pass as it has passed already.

A lot of things seem to have happened at home recently. Besides Lou's arrival, Mike and Thelma were married. Now, I guess Tony and Sheila will show up at home one of these days. Mike I's turn ought to come up one of these years.

How very true your words are. If we weren't meant for each other, we would have split cords long ago. I just can't think of life without you. It doesn't seem right to me. I loved you a long time before I said I did. It seemed as if we both knew it, a sort of silent agreement. Filling that empty space was love. I thought it had been filled because I didn't care to change. If you hadn't come along, I'd of been a doomed person. You needn't worry about being perfect for me. You know that feeling when you know that everything is OK, well, that's the way I've felt since I "popped" the question. No one can tell me that there are any mistakes. Each day that brings me closer to you, brings me close not only thru' distance but love. Gosh, Bette, makes a guy feel good to know that someone is waiting. I love you.

Good night, Darling. Take care of yourself. May God Bless You — Miss you terribly. Love, Mike.

On February 14, according to the Squadron War Diary, 14 planes were sent to the continent with supplies, and all returned that day. One plane returned that had been sent out four days earlier. Five planes were used that afternoon for double glider tow, and there was a dance at the NAAFI that evening.

The Group War Diary on the same day, February 14, said:

> **Today was the Group's 3rd anniversary and an excellent meal was served at both the Enlisted Men's mess and Officer's mess. The few originals of the 316th ate dinner with the Commanding Officer, Colonel Harvey A. Berger and his staff.**

February 15, 1945 [*Thursday*]

My Dearest,

Sometimes I wonder if I'll ever exhaust my choice of words. One of these days when it seems like it has been twice as long as it really is since I [*last*] saw you. There are three words I shall never stop saying. I am writing this short note this AM because I may not be able to get a chance to write later in the day. — I love you.

Just for that change of topic, the war does seem to be going remarkably well. The Hun is getting a good kissing from the Air Forces these days — Air Force may not be able to take ground but they sure can make a guy sorry he has it.

You were asking me if I got all the rest I needed after a heavy night of drinking — I'm afraid not — there have been times when I staggered a bit on my way out to my kite. It isn't the most pleasant feeling in the world and many times I promise myself, I'll never do it again. But coinciding with your statement, drinking is a good way of driving out a lot of pent up emotion. You needn't worry I am taking good care of myself — I'll admit I suffer a few days after but plenty of rest after that takes care of a lot of things. Even if I haven't been drinking, I can't honestly say that I've had an honestly heavy night's sleep since last June [*because of the Normandy missions*]. It isn't anything just a form of restlessness that can't be helped. It is the hardest thing to explain because it is a feeling beyond words.

Almost parallel to what I wrote not so long ago, you said the same thing in one of your recent letters. There is really no sense to worry about missing each other, once I get home. I'll turn Hell and high water but I'll find you. The grass won't have a chance to grow under these enormous dogs of mine.

Darling, in a hope, you mentioned Easter. With that you asked me a question; what would I like you to wear? Seems funny for me to answer and I really don't care. You do so nicely without my help. Everything I have ever seen you in looked wonderful — How can I sit back and judge? Easter is somewhere in April, isn't it? It would be nice to think of my being home then but on the face of things, who knows? I'm not giving you a negative answer, just a feeler. O God, I wish I knew — I wish I knew what was in store. At times, the speculations of time and events almost drive me mad. Some of my buddies got good breaks. I am exactly next in line but policies have changed and have a tendency to change more — If I miss the boat this time, it will be hard to take — Yet, I shall be comforted by the fact that you are waiting for me and even time nor this damned Army can beat me down. If I were the inert sort of fellow, I should be content to sit back and wait but I'm made of temperament and will — My nerves are steady until they have been rubbed raw and I explode temporarily. But there I go again, I'm sorry, Darling, I shouldn't fill you full of my troublesome thoughts. What the Hell, a little time, more or less, won't hurt us. It seems to do us a lot of good because each passing day makes our love grow stronger for each other.

Whoa! My Love, all these complimentary words make for conceited young men. If you keep patting me on the back like that, I am liable to start believing it. But again, both of us know what we want, isn't that enough to insure that we will get it? Actually, I don't want too very much out of life — just you and a few other odds and ends.

I am glad to see that you've found a place to stay. However, I'll follow your instructions explicitly. I'll keep sending my mail to the present address. It is just as easy for you to pick up the mail there.

Sorry to hear that you are a bit distressed. Pardon my frankness, but I've always [*known*] that you have always made the decisions for Mother. It isn't too difficult a thing though. Bette, it allows you a form of independence that is helpful. You might as well get used to the idea because with me, it is 50-50. So you'll have to keep up the habit of deciding affairs. However, once my ideas are put together, they will be discussed for a final outcome — Don't let it get you down —

Well, Darling, I must rush off — Give my love to Mother. Take care of yourself. May God Bless You — I adore you and miss you. Mike.

On February 15, all flying was cancelled because of weather. The Group War Diary for that day read:

> **Half of the month gone. Although there has been a great deal of windy weather, it's a vast improvement over last month. Movie, *Bathing Beauty* shown here in the evening.**

February 16, 1945 [*Friday*]

Hello Love,

I didn't go anywhere yesterday but I didn't write because I've got a cold that knocked me down. After I came back from the show last night, I hit the sack at 8 o'clock, was feeling very weary and just a bit feverish but I woke up feeling wonderful this morning. I still have a trace of the cold but I don't feel as logy as I did. Just to show you that it takes a bit to knock the kid down, I went over to the dispensary this AM and gave a pint of blood. Whole blood is a lot better than plasma for those poor kids that get shot up a bit. They need it a Hell of a lot more than I do. I'm not exactly an amateur at the game. I gave 3 transfusions while I was a civilian.

I dispatched a congratulatory note to Cousin Mike this eve. I am glad that he and Thelma went and did it. I must admit that I am jealous of their happiness but someone has to have it. As much as I hate to do it to us, I don't think we will have too much time to wait. We've been so patient, Darling. Thru' out all of this time, I cannot help but to marvel how wonderful you have been. How can a guy not love a gal like you?

We saw *Bathing Beauty* last night. "Red" Skelton was really good. A couple of his scenes caused me to go into a state of hysteria. Esther Williams is a lovely girl. It is a wonder a guy doesn't get crazy when he sees so many gorgeous creatures in one place. I guess it must be mind over matter. They aren't much good to anyone as long as they are on the screen.

Yes, Bette, I did read, *Keys [of] the Kingdom*. I believe it was written by A. J. Cronin. As you said the story was excellent. I say that because Fr. Chisholm's theories of life were as broadminded as anyone could want. A sort of elastic manner of life, enough improvisations to make life enjoyable, and still the epitome of righteousness. We are all guided by the codes of life in some form or other, but there is no necessity to criticize someone who has a lacking somewhere along the line. Fanaticism is the first breach, the worst sin of life. One can believe what he wishes, see the other man's point of view and still believe what he wishes to believe — It seems so democratic and ever so right. I like Cronin's writings very much. We must include many of his books in our library. Daphne du Maurier is another of my favorites. I was thinking about literature the other day. People are so apt to throw any sort of present at people on certain occasions and yet what could be more enjoyable than a book? It has been only since I came overseas that I realized that. As a youngster, I was too preoccupied with sports to consider a book. Now, I realize that many a hard moment has been tided over with the help of a book — (Excuse me, Darling, Deanne Durbin is singing Gounod's "Ave Maria") (She's wonderful. What a wonderful way to pray — Our Blessed Mother, The Virgin Mary, must smile graciously as she hears that song as a tribute to Her. — Of the two versions, Schubert's is my favorite. Perhaps, I'm mushy but shamelessly I must admit that whenever I hear that, the tears flow involuntarily.) To return to what I was saying — Wherever we live, Darling, don't you think it would be a nice idea to have a good selection of books for our private reading? I'll admit that we are rather restless people, but I think of those long winter evenings. Would you like to have me read to you?

In one of your letters, you mentioned moonlight on a beach. What wonderful nights, what ecstasy of joy, what depth of pleasantness, the ideal touch of romance and its many tributaries. I know I sound like I'm going crazy but the feeling is one which cannot be covered with words. I've done a lot of my thinking under such circumstances. One night and a moonlight night, I was sitting on the edge of a pier, hoping that the fish wouldn't bite. (Honestly.) Sitting next to me, ½-filled was a quart of Golden Wedding 3 Star. Just the two of us and my thoughts. I'll admit that that hardly sounds romantic, but Oh those thoughts. I've often wondered about them because they did so much to mold my future life. I had no one to include except my dream girl. It sounds childish but I wasn't a kid. It is hard even to put those thoughts on paper. Even as a youngster I was apt to be restless. It was not strange for me to "peel off" by myself and sit on a bench somewhere, smoke an endless chain of cigarettes and think. (Youngster, I mean after I had graduated from High School and was starting to discover life!) I'll admit [*it*] was a lonely sort of diversion but at times what is more pleasant than loneliness. It isn't or wasn't that I am or was queer but there are so many things that have to be decided. One never answers questions to himself in a crowded room or among any crowd of people. But then there comes a time when a person wants to have someone to share those thoughts, someone to debate the rights and wrongs of life. If you recall how often it was that we used to get philosophical about so many things. How often, we would question events and what leads to them. Even now that we are apart, we do it. Characteristics such as those, My Darling, are a good assurance that we will never want for words. Webster has them all but he hasn't made any restrictions as to who can use them. See how much I need you. I love you, Darling.

Good night, Bette. I pray for us often. Take care of yourself. May God Bless You. Your Lover, Mike.

The Squadron and Group War Diaries sometimes gave conflicting reports, as follows on February 16, 1945:

> **WD, February 16: No flying because of inclement weather. Usual routine duties.**
> **GWD, February 16: Beautiful weather today and our aircraft**

carried out their missions to the continent. Liberty run in the evening.

WD, February 17: Fourteen planes were dispatched to France but after reaching Southern England, thirteen of them returned to home base because of the weather. The other RON. Five planes were used for local transition in the afternoon. One plane test hopped. Two enlisted men AWOL. Show at the station theater.

GWD, February 17: Fog in the morning but by noon it had cleared entirely. Aircraft proceeded to take off for loading point in Southern UK, and upon reaching this point were informed that the weather over the channel was extremely bad. No aircraft reached the far shore. Liberty run. Movie at the base cinema, *The Man of Half Moon Street* with Helen Walker.

WD, February 18: Eleven planes were dispatched to southern England for loads. All RON there. F/O Everett C. Younger, missing on the invasion of Holland is officially listed as a prisoner of war. Show at the station theater.

GWD, February 18: Clear weather this morning with a faint promise of sunshine, and by late afternoon it had cleared completely and seemed almost like spring. Movie at Headquarters Day Room, *The Princess and the Pirate*, starring Bob Hope.

WD, February 19: One plane returned from the continent sent out on the 18th. One other plane was sent to the continent, RON. Three planes were sent to Southern England for loads and returned. Local transition in the C-109. . . . A dance was held at the American Red Cross for the enlisted men.

GWD, February 19: Cloudy early this morning but by noon it turned out to be another beautiful day. All aircraft were able to complete their missions and return to home base by early evening. Dance at the Red Cross Arrow Club.

February 20, 1945 [*Tuesday*]

Good Evening, Darling,

Well, here's your long lost brother [*struck out*] (brother, am I kidding?) boy again! Out again on another one of my long sojourns again (again, 3 times!) and believe me, I'm weary of it all. However, I don't feel as badly as I did — a good wash, shave and supper do well to make a guy feel good. Actually, in all the time I've been gone nothing new has happened, except that I still love you very much — that may not be new but it is as fresh [*as*] ever.

Gosh, Honey, sometimes I think they are overworking me but no matter what I say it is to no avail. I can bitch and moan and find I am still scheduled the next day. I need a haircut so badly that if I were handed a violin and a cup, I'd make a few extra quid for myself. Honestly, Darling, it is distressing because I hate to miss writing to you. It isn't bad enough that mail moves so slowly but when I can't write it makes it all the worse. If there is truly a reward for what I've done, then I shan't be too ungrateful for the passing time. I love you.

On one of my recent trips, I felt I was near enough to Harry to call. I had dreams of a good night's sleep, good food and perhaps a few good drinks. [*Harry was then in France near Chantilly, I believe.*] But alas! Fate was against me. I talked to Harry over the phone but he was just a wee bit too far for me. I decided to try to hitchhike but night was falling and I didn't feel like traveling over strange French territory. So I reversed my field, heading back to my kite, unrolled my sack and hit it. It sure did feel good. It was distressing not to have to have been able to complete my mission.

Darling, again the mail has been bad. It isn't so bad as long as I am away, but it feels swell to have a few letters when I get back. But I guess your complaint must be the same. I've cut down my correspondence to everyone but you but I don't even get enough chance to write to you. I just don't have enough time nor can I say enough how much I love you.

Latest news from the home front tells me that Tony was on his way home. Lucy tells me that Gert had gotten a cablegram from Dan. It seems that he may be on his way home soon. It must be great to do an easy 6-month tour overseas, slap a ribbon on your chest and head for that good ole USA. How do guys manage that? Sometimes I feel as if my number is near the right one. It makes me laugh when I think how Dan bitched because he was overseas. I've done 3 times the service, don't know when it will end and still feel as if I haven't done enough. Oh, Darling, how badly I want to come back to you — All I hope is that when I finish my tour, it will finish my overseas tour for good. I don't want anything again to separate us for any longer time than is necessary. That's why I gripe so much when I can't write to you. It is like not seeing you for a few days. I wrote to Lucy on Sunday. I had intended to write to you Sunday night because my flight had been canceled but at the last moment, they rushed my royal out and so I was so badly delayed. Sorry that I must use so much space on excuses but, Darling, I want you to understand the stupidity of circumstances.

To top it all off, I hear so much of so many people having returned that it seems a bit harder to take. I feel that way only because it seems as it we've been apart so long. Just one of those discouraging moods. Really, Darling, it isn't hard to take but at times, EEK! I know that we will make it all up a thousand fold. Thinking of that future with you is the only thing that keeps me bouncing. I have no patience with people that are uncertain. We are so lucky to have so much determination and strength to know what we want. I met a few old buddies of mine and we got around to the discussion of old times. I could not help but to feel a bit lonely for the many things I left behind, things that made so many memories, gave us so much happiness. It was so pleasant just to walk with you, talk to you, love you. Remember the night, I had dinner with you under candle light. Remember, we went shopping together; you kept asking me what I liked. It seems as if it has been like that so long. "Mike, whatever you want to do is OK with me, just say the word and it is done!" Those are some of the things that I think about. There are many others, personal affairs of ours. So simply, "No, Darling, we can't." It is not a warped brain that is enveloped in such a train of thought but the brain of a guy that loves you so much. My Darling, to be with you again, to be able to live so wonderfully again, it is my peak of happiness. The years are passing, the sands of time merely mix to concrete to cement our love. Yes, you are entering your 23rd year; I, my 24th. Perhaps and most likely, they will pass as the others, alone, alone for both of us but added to each is a wisdom and warmth that will help to warm our future years. Sometimes I feel as if I am cracking, but I help myself by saying — But the other months have passed, how many more you may have to face will and must pass, too, and then you will be with Bette. — "You will be with Bette." — That's enough to sky rocket me into heaven, our heaven. How wonderful — as if the rest of the world didn't matter at all and it doesn't, not where you are concerned. I will never stop being grateful to you for making my life so much easier to take — at the end of it — I shall always have you with me. Just think an eternity of life with you. What other reward could I ask for? I am not going to attempt to apologize for this mood. It is reserved for you because it is my only manner to tell you what is really in my heart. You can see, Darling, that I'll never cease to be your lover. I never want to — If I were poetic, I'd speak of laying roses at your feet, the gold of your hair, the celestial blue of your eyes, the adoring crevices — the dimples of your lovely cheeks but I'm not poetic — My love for you is real, words, — prose or poetry — cannot express its depth. Words may be my present substitute but they will never overshadow my real feelings when the circumstances are altered. I love you, My Darling, and I need you so terribly much. Please, God, that we will be united soon.

Good night, My Darling. Take care of yourself. I love you and miss you. May God Bless You. — Love, Mike.

On February 20, according to the Squadron War Diary,

> **Seven planes were dispatched to the continent on three different missions. One, two plane mission completed. One other two plane mission got as far as Southern England but was forced to return with their loads. One, three plane mission RON in Southern England. Eleven other planes returned sent out on the 18th and 19th. Two planes were used for night landings. Today ends twenty-six months overseas for the ground echelon. Show at the station theater.**

The Group War Diary entry for February 20 read:

> **Bright sun and clear sky again today seems almost too good to be true. All planes returned from the continent late in the evening. Major Milstead and T/Sgt. Andrew Welsh returned from London with the Groups' citations. Four copies for each man.**

The next day, February 21, the Squadron War Diary reported that

Thirteen planes were dispatched to the continent with supplies, all returning. Three planes sent out on the 20th returned. Another C-109 assigned to the squadron bringing the total to two.

There were no Group War Diary entries for February 21-23, 1945.

February 22, 1945 [*Thursday*]

Good Morning, My Love,

Happy George Washington's Birthday to you! Not that it really makes too much difference but I feel as if I must make this letter gay so that you don't think we are two different people, the photo and I. You recall I told you about those pictures that "Snoz" [*Don Harris*] and I had taken. The photographer wasn't kidding when he said that my eyes hardly showed. But if you look at the picture long enough, you will grow to love it. It isn't the best I could do but just imagine if I was sober; mayhaps, it would be worse. Do hope you like it, Darling. I don't send very many pictures so you must be content regardless of the results.

After I had written to you last night, I hit the sack and really poured my soul to Morpheus. Believe me, it felt good. It seemed as if it had been an eternity since I really had a night's sleep. I am standing by now, hoping I will have a day off.

In one of your letters, you mentioned the fact that you'd like to go over to Havana. That doesn't sound like a bad idea. The one thing that remains to be seen is the amount of time I'll have for a furlough. It seems to me that the situation would be a bit difficult because of wartime restrictions. To add, we will wait and see, anything can happen.

Darling, once more I put forth the subject — Lucy has written and said that that package hadn't been picked up but due to the length of your journey, I realize it missed you in KC and Miami. So I've asked her to send it out to you in Miami. If it would make you feel any better, the perfume was paid for by me. I don't ask anyone at home to do any favors unless they are paid by me. Just thought I'd mention it. Please don't feel too badly. Those RAF wings that I spoke of are still not mailed. I was fondling some sort of dream of handing them to you personally but as soon as I get the chance, I'll send them out. You know me though, that could mean weeks or months. Can't blame a guy for dreaming. That's one habit that is hard to break.

Well, Honey, I am going to close. I do hope I'll have a chance to write tonight. Again I pray for the right breaks. Give my love to Mother.

Take care of yourself. May God Bless You — I love you and miss you terribly. Love, Mike.

On February 22, the Squadron War Diary noted a 17-plane resupply mission to France, with all planes remaining overnight. The Diary continued:

> **C-109 was used for local transition in the afternoon. Show at the station theater.**

The next day's entry, for February 23, read:

> **Nine planes returned from the continent sent out on the 22nd. C-109 was up again. Four enlisted men were assigned to the squadron per par. 6, SO # 36, HQs., 316th Troop Carrier Group, dtd. 22 February 1945.**

February 24, 1945 [*Saturday*]

Good Evening, Darling,

Sorry that I missed writing a few days but I've been off again on another of my sojourns. Fortunately, when I returned, there were a few letters from you. Just thought of something which I meant to mention long ago. But since Mac is sitting across from me, he served as a reminder. It seems that every time we tie on a bun, we sit down and write Mac's wife. It is funny because the letters never make any sense. She has received one and another is on the way. I think we've quit drinking but if someone should ever come in with a few stray quarts, I promise that you'll get one of those letters. They don't make any sense but you can always hold it as a testimony of my lax living. Just another hatchet to hold over my head. Lois, Mac's wife, said she got a good kick out of that first one. EEK! What a way to live.

You speak of that book that you read recently. All about these selfish, bossy women. I never have suspected nor thought that you'd ever be such a gal. Darling, you've too much sense for that sort of bunk, Besides, I wouldn't be able to love you if I thought you had that sort of offensive nature. It's OK to beat the Hell out of me but never try to talk me into the ground.

Got near to Harry again but still not close enough. So we went over and gave him a good "buzz" job — I hope he saw it because he knows my crate's number. It pays to be a mediocre sort of linguist. Not so long ago, I was having a drink in a French café. Someone tapped me on the shoulder and started to talk in an Italian dialect. He asked me if I was an Eyetie. After the usual preliminaries, we got thru' a lot of conversation & liquor. It seemed that he was from Milan and had worked in France for 22 years. Our dialects differed a bit but we managed well. Unfortunately, I was broke and couldn't buy him a drink but he didn't make me stand short. He bought me cognac, champagne and wine. The party broke up at 5 AM and I had a good load. I wonder why I meet so many people — do you think that I just naturally attract them? At any rate, these chance acquaintances have done much to make my tours even more interesting. I am most grateful for them.

I can see that the people back home were quite encouraged by the Russian drive. However, such optimism is short-lived. Why do those chair-borne commando bastards at home fill the people's ears with excess optimism? Guys like [*Gabriel*] Heatter and Kaltenborn continually give opinions and points that are known only to them, with no military basis whatsoever. Jerry is tough — ask a guy that has been up against him. Not I but a guy that's sloshed thru' mud, snow and Hell. He'll be beaten the day the last one of them puts his gun down. I know that the people back home need an occasional uplift, but men are still dying. Of course, Heatter's "Hitler is a sad man tonight" bunk sells a lot of Kreml or whatever it is. One of the guys got a letter from his Dad and he said that Kaltenborn had mentioned that within 2 weeks, Jerry would be finished; the letter was written a month ago. Wars are fought on a lot of bloody fields not over a desk at a broadcasting station. Forgive me, Bette, but I cannot help but boil over by such fictitious fantasies.

Tony hasn't changed his mind about the AAF but he is a lot different from fellows who want to stay in the States. He is an idealist who believes in making his principles stick by actions not words. No, he won't lose any rank. Tony was an infantryman in 1932 when he served 3 years in China. His firm belief in doing what he believes is right has always made me admire him all the more. My regret is that in this case, I'm afraid for his safety. His family is a lot to give up. Nevertheless, if Tony didn't do what he intends, it wouldn't be Tony. To those who don't understand him, he may appear eccentric but to me he is as strong and lovable a person as one would ever want to meet. To me, he is the ideal soldier and man. When I went to see him in Texas, it was the first time I had seen him in 18 months. It was the middle of June and very hot. After he and I left the hospital (Sheila was pregnant at the time.), we walked down to the field toward my plane. My sleeves were rolled up a ¼ of the way and I had 2 buttons open on my shirt. He said, "Soldier, roll those sleeves down and button one of those buttons!" Very meekly, I said, "Yes Sir!" That is merely an example but you can see my point. It will be hard on Sheila, harder than you think but you'll not know until I tell you personally. It wouldn't be fair to hear her speak of it in a letter.

Darling, I am going to close. I have a day off tomorrow (I hope). Wanna get some sleep.

Good night, My Love. I love you, miss you, need you very much. Take care of yourself. May God Bless You. Fervently Yours, Mike.

WD, February 24: Eight planes returned from France sent out on the 22nd. One plane XC and return. Two planes to the continent with supplies and return. Four planes were used in the afternoon for towing gliders. . . . An inspection was held by Group.

GWD, February 24: Cold and crisp this morning and our aircraft effected an early take off for the other side. Movie at the base cinema, ***Junior Jive Bombers*.**

February 25, 1945 [*Sunday*]

Hello Darling,

I hope that the letter I wrote last night made some sense. There were a lot of distractions and it was hard to keep my pen to the paper and brain to the subject. Gad! I had one of those crazy fits and for chow, I downed a mess full of raw onions. The odor is almost suffocating. I don't know why I do it; I can't stand the damn things; they used to make me horribly sick. I don't know what effect they'll have on me now.

Lou has written to me a few times. It seems pitiful that we didn't keep up a good correspondence. All the while that he was in the Pacific, we must have written about twice to each other. I know that the letters will have done some good. As it is since he has been home, I've written to him a few times already. The first thing that bothered him was the fact that he owes me $300. Hell, he can pay that whenever he sees fit. There is no sense to worry about it and I've told him so. He is quite happy by my forthcoming marriage to you. He can imagine how I must feel. It will be good to see all my friends again someday. Most of all, you, My Darling. I spend a good many of my moments thinking of all the many things we must do. I love you, Bette.

I was sorry to hear that the mail has been so bad. As it is I hear that a lot of mail has been lost. That is indeed a tragedy. To boot I can imagine that the bad weather in the Northern part of the country (U.S.) has a lot to do with the bad deliveries. Chicha was complaining of the same thing. Another thing, since the first of the year, I haven't been able to write as often as I'd like to. They received the perfume I sent and said it arrived in good shape — Said that I'd packed it so good that there was no reason why it should have broken. I do hope that yours arrives in the same condition. Don't fret about the mail too much. You know that I am OK. Still can't wait until the day that we won't have to exchange letters any more.

You said that you can still blush. Darling, I don't recall if I've ever seen you blush. Of course, the occasion had never arisen. But so far as the blushing bride goes, I still think my knees will be rocking like a 7 come 11. It is a funny reaction. Here we are 2 rather bold people, and yet the thought of a marriage ceremony shakes us. I guess it isn't so funny — that it is normal. I think the one thing that will keep me on the beam is the fact that I'll have my eyes on you all the while that I won't have time to shake. Wonderful to think about it, isn't it, Bette?

I see that you are a bit dissatisfied with your job. There isn't much I can say about that. The one thing, Darling, it is a help when you want to pass time. Time hangs heavy very often. I remember [*pre-D-Day*] a good while ago, all of us were rather restless; we were waiting for something important. Everyone was crazy from inactivity. A good fist fight [*between Toohey and "Sonny" Rice*] helped to relax us but the results weren't what we were looking for. During that spell, time was not only mysterious but endless. It took a good sized invasion to straighten everyone out. (Sammy Kaye just came on; his *Sunday Serenade* is one of my favorite programs. He used to play the cocktail hour in the Casino-in-the-Park [*Central Park*] during the football season. My biggest regret was that most of my afternoons — Saturdays — were occupied with work.) Another thing I want to share with you. Gosh, Bette, it will be great. Just think of the many moments of relaxation —

doing the things that for 20 months have been merely obsessions and someday will all be fulfilled. Wow! How easy to get into a pleasant mood.

Well, Darling, I am going to close. This afternoon is a good opportunity to catch up on my correspondence. —

So long for now, Bette. Take care of yourself. My love to Mother. I love you and miss you — May God Bless You — Yours, Mike.

WD, February 25: Nine planes were used for local formation in the morning and afternoon. One EM confined to the Guard house because of AWOL.

GWD, February 25: Sunday and church services. Today marked the beginning of another training period. Group formation this afternoon — glider tow. Headquarters Enlisted Men were shown *The Conspirators* in their club.

February 26, 1945 [*Monday*]

Hello Darling,

Just thought I'd dash off a few lines as long as I have a few moments to myself. I love you. We hear the latest news from the home front that most of the States have adopted a policy of closing down the bars at midnight. There goes another one of those things that we dream about. Especially since pubs over here close at 10 PM. It was nice to think that once we get home, it would be a pleasure to have a quickie any time that you felt like. But that isn't so important I guess. You and I managed to do OK in KC, and they had a very definite curfew policy, didn't they? Maybe it is because we used to start so early. Gosh, Darling, as I look back, it seems as if the time that we spent together went so quickly. I wish we had it to do all over again. Time would never pass — But I guess there will be other times.

I was reading an editorial in *Life* magazine not so long ago. They contrasted the policies that the Allies have adopted toward defeated Italy. Since the war there has long since passed, it is a normal thing that they should be accepted as a separate state, which has already undergone a process of rehabilitation. They are supposed to have been given a shot of democracy. But according to the editorial, it had a reverse effect. The Italian problem was badly bungled. Of course, I'm not a politician but I've seen a few countries and most of all their respective peoples — I pity the Italian nation and people.

Must be a day of revelation for me but not so long ago, again, someone, a good friend of mine asked me a multitude of questions about you. He wasn't bored although I spent two hours explaining a variety of things. What I mean to say is that when I have a vent for speaking of the choice of my life, it brings you ever so much closer to me. In those thoughts, I bring back everything that has ever meant a thing to us. Not vocally but with each spoken word there is a thought which I book mark and place into my contents of memories. I can feel the changes that have come over me by my very close association with you. Darling, you've changed me in many ways. And with those changes, I have felt a strengthening that I've never had before. You are mine forever, and nothing in this whole wide world can ever reverse that feeling. In the early stages of our companionship, I was cautious because I realized that there was something hanging over my conscience. But as time passed, I realized that I had been wrong for so long, I couldn't possibly see myself doing anything unless it was you that was at my side. It was as I've said before, I'd lost myself to you the day you headed back to Kansas City. It was the last time I saw you. I was so lonely that I didn't know which way to turn. It has been a long time but that vow we made to each other was more than words. I'll be back and you'll be waiting for me. The further the distance became, the more I missed you. At times, the distance was shortened but not as we want it. Our marriage will be only an anti-climax because beyond that we have so many years of happiness. It will be wonderful, Darling, — an eternity of you and I.

Must close, Bette, take care of yourself. May God Bless You. Love, Mike.

P.S.: My love to Mother. Haven't seen "Pappy" for a while. Must be having himself a time just "goofing off." — M.

> **WD, February 26:** One plane was sent to the continent and return. Group formation in the afternoon. Local transition in the C-109. Dance at the American Red Cross for EM.
>
> **GWD, February 26:** Glider tow practice throughout the day and evening. Dance at the Red Cross Arrow Club, with the ATS and WAAFs present. Music by our own 316th band.
>
> **WD, February 27:** Eighteen planes were used in the afternoon in a Group formation. There was also a formation in the evening. Two enlisted men were transferred to the infantry. . . . Seven power pilots were transferred to the 313th TC Group. . . .
>
> **GWD, February 27:** Training flights still continued, with glider tow in the morning and Group formation in the evening. Clear weather, excellent for flying. Movie, *My Pal Wolfe*, at the cinema.

February 28, 1945 [*Wednesday*]

Hello Darling,

Sitting on the threshold of March, I wonder what it has to hold. Each month that comes, I look forward to it eagerly because I hope that it will have a special meaning to me and to us; so far, success has just been flirting. Oh well, I guess there are many more where the last one came from.

I received your letter of the 13th of Feb. I daresay that is making good time but it must have sneaked in somewhere. I don't believe that good mail delivery still exists. If anyone ever knew about it, I'd probably have to return the letter so that they could delay it for a month or so. Why do they call me a skeptic? You spoke of this chap who bore a very close resemblance to me. I hate to think that he has to live under those conditions for so long a time. I couldn't say that he was relative of mine because I am the only gruesome one that I know of. However, there are some relations of my Granddad who settled in Argentina many, many years ago. I've often wondered about them. I've never seen any of them but if I recall correctly, Ma has often told us of the boys. I think there is one down there about the same age as I am. I wouldn't swear to it. I don't even know if they have ever left the Pampas. I think the name is Ingrisano, too. One never knows. Especially with immigrants like my own family, it is not impossible to lose sight of one another.

You asked me if I've ever wondered where our first home would be. You aren't just kidding when you say that we'll never part again. One horse towns don't scare me as long as you are there. The world will be complete. Not only do I think about it but a lot of us talk about it. Everything is supposition but we all would appreciate it if we could get back home together. Most of the fellows are married and we've planned on getting a home for all of us. Uncle Moe is a bachelor and intends to stay one so since we can't leave him out, we figure we ought to get an extra room to pour him into every night. They are nice dreams and help us to pass many hours. I don't think I've ever told you of my penny bank. Well, one of the fellows that went home last year, married and a Lil one is on the way, due sometime about the end of April or 1st of May. Whenever we have any extra pennies in they go and it is called the baby bank. One English penny is worth 2 of ours. I think he has saved close to 3£s — $12. You see, Darling, even among a bunch of men, little things become magnified not only by common wishes but by a close relationship. It is normal because we have been together ever so long. It is not unusual to hear friendly remarks passed. As it is I'll be the only Benedict and believe me, I do get a big part of the remarks. Me and my big blonde are common talk. The companionship shared by all of us has been a big factor of helping us over many rough spots. But I have diverted from the subject, haven't I? You can see how I feel — just to steal a page — Lou and Sally have been together ever since he hit the east. He had to go to WVA for medical reasons and she was with him. He has done quite a bit of traveling along the East Coast and she hasn't left him once. Don't you think I want it the same way? After so long, I don't care to plan unless you are a byword. It will take a short period of readjustment but it won't last too long. You've got a big job on your hands, Young lady, great to think about.

Darling, our birthdays are coming up next month. I don't know what to say to that except that we must continue to sit back and sweat each passing day. Lord knows, I'd like to celebrate it over a bourbon and coke but — I am glad to hear that each passing report on that Seagrams is favorable. I wouldn't care if you put red, white and blue ribbons on it, as long as it doesn't evaporate. Gad! It is going to taste good. Funny that it should mean so much and yet, it shows how little we want and how simple it is that we do want.

Well, Darling, I am going to close. Give my love to Susie [*Mother*]. Tell her to take care

of those colds. Take care of yourself. May God Bless You. I love you and miss you so —
Mike.

**WD, February 28: A Group glider formation was held in the after-
noon while three other planes were up for transition training. There
has been a navigation school set up within the squadron for all glider
personnel who are interested in being a navigator. The purpose being
to lighten the burden for the limited Navigators we already have.**
GWD, February 28: Pay call.

Following is the Group War Diary's "Summary for February":

**The 316th received its seventh battle participation star this month
for the part they played in the German campaign.**
**The Group carried 2,677,045 lbs. of freight, 355 passengers, 1,730
patients, 538 other troops, and flew [*logged*] a total of 5910:10 hours
flying time.**

Chapter 7

VARSITY and
It's Over, Over Here
(March 2 to April 21, 1945)

O N MARCH 24, 1945, Troop Carrier aircraft of the First Allied Airborne Army dropped the British 6th and the U.S. 17th Airborne divisions east of the Rhine in the vicinity of Wesel, Germany. Although the troop carriers suffered extensive damage from ground fire, the troop and supply drops were successful. No further missions were necessary.

As the Allies pushed into Germany, Adolf Hitler committed suicide April 30 in his bunker at the Reich Chancellery in Berlin, as Russian troops converged on the city. Joseph Goebbels, the Reich propaganda minister, also committed suicide. German resistance collapsed, and it surrendered May 7, 1945, effective May 9. President Truman proclaimed May 8, 1945, to be V-E Day.

In the Pacific Theater, the Battle of Okinawa was raging in April 1945.

The 316th Troop Carrier Group War Diary's "March Summary" read:

The month of March started with a vague conviction that the war was approaching its end. By the end of it, that conviction had taken on more obvious aspects.

The 37th Squadron's War Diary entry for March 1 reported:

Eighteen planes were used to transport 43,200 pounds of fuel tanks for the 313 Troop Carrier Group here in the United Kingdom. Eighteen plane formation in the evening.

The Group War Diary for the same day, March 1, noted:

March was ushered in with clear crisp weather and transition and instrument flights still continued during the day and evening. Liberty run this evening and the World Premier of the movie, *My Reputation* was [*shown*] at the base cinema.

March 2, 1945 [*Friday*]

Good Evening, Darling,

It seems like years since I last wrote to you and yet it has been only 2 days. The two days that have passed seem again like an eternity of uselessness. I've done so much and I've accomplished nothing, personally. Fortunately, a few letters from you served as an excellent salve for all my weariness. I am so very proud of you, Darling, and even so much so in love with you. Your letters carried your pictures and I was especially glad. You look lovely, My Dear. I could not help but feel that the Florida weather has done you a world of good. It has removed that peaked look and added so much more radiance. To boot, I believe I can perceive a bit of weight has been added. To certify my conclusions, when I showed your pictures to Pappy, he rather coughingly and cautiously said that it seemed to him that you had added weight in the more appropriate places. I rather coughingly and cautiously was inclined to agree with him. Even the sun squint looks lovely; everything is perfect, so perfect that it would have taken a dozen men to hold me down if I had boisterously shown my approval. After seeing your pictures, mine seem moreso like the rag wheels of Hell. I love you so very much. Might I add that the water, sun, and palm trees look good, too. Pardon my jealousy, Bette.

Not only were your pictures a grand comfort but your letters said everything I wanted to hear. My praise for your understanding and levelheadedness is insurmountable and unequaled by anything. I feel so greatly relieved when I know that you share my sentiments in regard to our problems. My greatest comfort is that I can depend on you to stride with me pace for pace. You said that you trusted my judgment and that you were sure that I'd do right by you. Darling, I had no other intentions. I promised myself that one thing a long time ago. I'm making no mistakes especially when it concerns you and I. And I am depending fully on your help for that. As we've often said before, our love is all that counts. We know the strength of it, what it can be for us, and what it has done for us. There shan't be any recurrences of previous circumstances. I'd rather pop my brains than go thru that torture and discomfort again, let alone allow you to go thru' them. As for the transportation problems, we shan't let that bother us — remember your own words — You've the will, we'll find a way.

The news is being "blatted" out — Our men are doing a wonderful job over there — Pray God that this horror will be over soon.

Yes, My Dear, you make your points very clear — not clear as mud as you say it. When I said that a lot of people would accept us as strangers, I didn't mean it to be a controversial point against us but as a contrast to what people may think. I have never felt that from the first day I met you. Lord knows I've always been ready and willing to reveal myself freely to you as you have been to me. All I know is what I feel and I have experienced. My actions, I am sure spoke for themselves. If circumstances had been different, we would have been happily married long ago. I have never been so confident of anything in my life as I am of us. Whatever anything else there may be, it is unimportant, what counts above everything else is that we know what we want and what we shall have. I have mentioned the fact to Ted and Louise but as I've said before we will have some time to decide whatever must be done. Honestly, Darling, I can't wait but I shan't go into that because I'm afraid I wouldn't be able to stop.

I received your menu from Zissins. It sounds like a good joint in which to let your hair down in. As for the Italian Love Songs, if I'm in voice, I promise to give out with my best to you. I don't think I could fare very well. I couldn't help but marvel at the changes in the prices of liquor since I left. Cordials or liqueurs, if you wish, seem to be frightfully high. It seems pitiful to throw away 65¢ in a shot glass of sugared colored water. I'll admit that I enjoy anisette, or creme de cacao or creme de menthe with my coffee black after an appetizing meal but gad! I noticed that cognac went for 96¢ and yet over here in the most expensive joints, it doesn't go over 60¢. Fortunately, I am glad to see that the stuff that real Americans drink isn't too very high. (Bourbon and coke and a dash of lemon, please!)

I am glad that you accepted my opinion of *The Robe*. Actually, the book speaks for itself. It is impossible to praise such a book too highly because it was wonderful. I hope I haven't steered you wrong.

Well, Darling, I must close. I want to dash off one quick note and then head for the sack. Good night, My Darling. Take care of yourself. May God Bless You. I love you and miss you. Love, Mike.

The Squadron (WD) and Group (GWD) War Diary entries for March 2 read:

> **WD, March 2: Fourteen planes were used locally to drop British Paratroopers. Sixteen planes were used in formation training this afternoon. One plane Cross Country to [*Prestwick*] and return, while another went to the continent. . . .**

**GWD, March 2: Beautiful weather: Aircraft flew practice para-
trooper drop, carrying British troops.**

March 3, 1945 [*Saturday*]

Good Evening, Darling,

I read in *Stars and Stripes* today that a restaurant owner in Miami had reported a loss
of 42 pepper shakers in the last 2 weeks. You aren't getting our household started that way,
are you? That's a Hell of a way to start a letter, isn't it? I received 2 letters from some very
good friends of mine, Mr. & Mrs. Bob Mason, Marie, (Mrs. Mason) mentioned the fact
that she had met you in New York but due to the rush of events at the time, she didn't have
much of a chance to talk to you. Well, at any rate, Bob told me that he had kept up his
record collection since I left and that he had 2,000 by now. He has invited us over; of
course; I had every intention of seeing them anyhow. They were always very close friends
of mine and never shirked a chance to fix me up in some manner or other. I helped Bob
sweat out Marie when she was having her second child, Gary, who was delivered by Lou.
His first baby. There <u>are</u> many reasons for our close relationship because they are part of
the gang. But I had a better in because Bob and I liked our sports so well, and I could always get along with Marie. She's a very frank person and I enjoyed her pleasantness toward me. She would get angry at me often because I'd keep Bob up late playing pinochle,
bowling or having a few snorts. It had been so long since I had heard from them that the
surprise was indeed so very pleasant.

I should have had the morning for myself today but I decided to take a trip with Lil Moe
so I could take some pictures. Besides it gave me a chance to fly in a different type ship
[*C-109, the converted B-24*], and visibility is better. Well, I had an enjoyable "do" of it and
when I hit the ground again and my rear was pushed off into my own kite, and off I was
again. The fact that I hadn't eaten didn't make any difference. I got back rather late this
evening, hence, my night writing. Today was to be a very joyous day for you and I, Darling. But as luck would have it, it is just another uneventful 24 hours ticked off a lovely
life. Patience and love are a wonderful combination. Darling, we have both.

You can tell Mrs. Sambi not to worry about my learning how to dry your hair. Darling,
whenever you want to wash it, we'll make it a stay-in affair. I've always liked the touch of
your hair and I wouldn't mind it the least bit if you used the slower method. I'll just sit
back with you in my arms and stroke it. Gosh, it is wonderful to think of such a fine manner of relaxation. To boot, I don't think you'll have much to worry about those nightmares
of mine. They may be slight recurrences, but I don't think they would be often. I'm in a
lot better shape these days. I was quite shaken after Holland but I've recovered exceedingly since. Pardon my crudeness but I think I'll (we'll) be pretty tired for a while after I
get home. I love you. I had to pause a moment. A guy asked me to help him wrap a package of perfume, "Passion" by Zolazy of Paris. I smell like I've been out on a heavy mug-
ging date after that. Nice accompaniment for letter writing to you, isn't it?

I was a bit puzzled about one thing in your letter. You said that you could save a lot of heartaches if you could say your 2 cents worth. As yet, I'm a bit blind to the whole affair. I don't know if it's in-law trouble or what. However, we have agreed not to force the issue in letters. So it shall be. I am beginning to believe that things are shaping up. There seems to be a bit of bad feeling hanging around but as long as we can discuss it, we'll touch off the solution. Don't get the idea that I intend to do all the talking. But as I've said so often before that's another one of those bridges that we'll cross when we come to it.

I see that you are up on your aircraft. How do you like the majestic look of those C-54s? Aren't they the thing? How I would like to come winging my way back to you in one of those. I was a rookie on planes long ago but I surely can spot them now. I guess it is about time. I've been around them long enough. I wouldn't mind getting a little [*Taylor*] Cub after the war. Sometimes I feel as if I've had all the flying I want and then again I never have enough. Oh! Well, I guess it all fits into the many moods, man against aluminum.

I wish I could give you an optimistic prod about Easter. Since I know nothing and feel less, I cannot say. Under some circumstances, I'd be planting many seeds — but my morale had been given certain deflated signs. Since I am in such a quandary, I feel unsettled, settled, happy, unhappy, any sort of uncertain feeling that at times I am inclined to say — "To Hell with it all!" — sit back and wait. However, I have hopes of seeing you this year and Darling, don't forget this year is already 3 months old! I shouldn't worry, though, Bette, it is as before, wait and plan; someday we won't have to do either. I love you and miss you so terribly much it hurts.

Good night, My Love. May God Bless You — Love, Mike.

WD, March 3: Two missions to France, one, ten plane single glider tow and eight plane double tow. Ten of the gliders were transferred from this organization and the remaining sixteen were picked up at Saltby. One plane to Southern England and return. One other plane was dispatched to [*Prestwick*]. The C-109 was up on local transition. Group inspection of officers and enlisted men's barracks. The air-raid alert was sounded.

GWD, March 3: The Group's aircraft towed gliders over to the continent today and returned safely. Headquarters Enlisted Men had the movie, *To Have and Have Not* in their day room this evening.

WD, March 4: The [*Prestwick*] plane returned, sent over on the third. One XC and return while five other ships were up on local transition. Lt. Robert Roman returned after a three-day course on Prisoner of War in London. Movie at the station theater. . . .

GWD, March 4: In the early hours this morning an alert was sounded here at Cottesmore base "Attack on base." Enemy intruders had tagged on to a returning Lancaster formation. One Lancaster was shot down by the enemy Northwest and just outside the edge of the field, and another about 50 yards just off the Great North Road, ½-mile Northeast of our base. Two of our aircraft were damaged when

one of the invaders dropped a string of anti-personnel bombs. The rest of the night was very uneventful. During the day, our aircraft proceeded to carry out their missions to the far shore and returned early. About 2100 hours the field was again alerted but no intruders appeared in the immediate environs. [*This was the German Operation Gisele.*]

March 5, 1945 [*Monday*]

Hello Baby,

I don't know what this note is going to sound like or how long it will last. This is one of those infrequent "blah" nights. I've kind of come to the conclusion that the early part of the month is when I have my period. I don't have headaches but I do have plenty of heartaches.

I was relaxing a little while ago and I got to thinking about soft beds and clean odors. Do you recall when I went to rest camp last July? Well, I had a bed that was so soft it was pitiful. For the seven days that I was gone, I didn't get a good night's sleep unless I was petrified drunk. It will probably be the same when I hit the glory road. But I promise you I won't get stinking drunk to sleep. I must talk more about that than anything else. But when I get restless and sit by a window waiting for Morpheus, will you be content to sit up in my arms and wait with me? Silly thoughts, but that was what was running through my brain. The scene becomes so vivid that it seems as real as you and I. Another thing, you must be patient with me if I become a shower fiend. It seems as if ever since I came over, I've never really been clean. I know that that too is a crazy feeling but it may be a mania. Just feel as if I could soak for an eternity.

You know, Darling, a man's education in the Army never seems to reach its peak. I guess it must be because so many different guys are thrown together. Did you ever hear of Roy Acuff? He's a radio artist who sings a lot of mountain music. At times, I feel as if I am an authority on that sort of stuff. Before, I'd never think of such guys; music was either sweet swing bands or light classics; but when I start yodeling away I know that I've learned something new. Usually when a few of us carry a load, we hit off a few like, "Does the Spearmint lose its flavor on the bed post over night?" Or "Last Letter," or any number of those things. The education is worth it but again I'd give it all up for just one chance to hold you in my arms. Darling, I love you. You know, Darling, it's a wonderful thing to dream. Kinda' think it leaves me constantly in life. It seems a bit difficult to take the ups and downs over here. Harder so after a long time over here. As long as a guy is in Troop Carrier, he might as well consider himself a roving vagabond. But as soon as he has to bog down to a set place and a constant routine, it's like putting on the old ball and chain. Oh Well, nothing much to think about.

Well Darling, gonna close. I hate to torture you with this horrible epistle. So, Good night, My Love. Take care of yourself.

I love you and miss you terribly much. May God Bless You. Mike.

WD, March 5: Fifteen planes were used to haul 52nd Wing HQs. personnel and organizational equipment to the Far Shore, one plane RON. One plane with additional crew was sent XC to pick up another C-47, both returning. C-109 was up on transition training.

GWD, March 5: Brilliant sun today. The weather has been unusually good the last two weeks. Dance at the Red Cross Club for enlisted men. Very late in the evening, a British [*Oxford*], twin-engine aircraft, crashed just outside the field apparently attempting to land after his gas supply gave out. F/O Kanopka, pilot of the aircraft escaped injury even though the aircraft caught fire immediately after crashing.

March 6, 1945 [*Tuesday*]

Good Evening, Darling,

Here's that monster back again but I do hope that I don't write a horror like the one that I sent last night. Each word was exact and doubly pondered because my thoughts were staggered and uncertain. One of these things that is unexplainable and perhaps doesn't even call for one. I am so dreadfully sorry, Darling. Fortunately, the mails are so slow that they don't reach you at the wrong time. My moods can never be yours, not at this distance, at any rate. See if I can do any better. I was looking for something to read last night when one of the fellows suggested *Martin Eden* by Jack London. Two things were against that choice; one was that I was skeptical of the sort of stuff that this chap would like — our opinions differ. Secondly, I never cared for London's style and stuff. However, I felt that I shouldn't attempt to be narrow-minded to the type of literature to pursue so I had a "go" at it. I don't think I'll continue the book. London's manner is too sketchy and leaves too much to the imagination. With my imagination, his book would have to conform with it; hence, leaving a London-written Ingrisano-thought novel. I'm not too adept at such things so I think the ultimate conclusion would be a horror.

Honestly, Darling, this period of time leaves me reminiscent of another period of my overseas stay. Neither are very healthy but they must be. An anxiety of hopelessness that leaves me nothing but blankness. However, I shan't leave you with a puzzle, or jig-saw of thoughts. I can't supply the fill-ins nor can you surmise, so let it be.

I received a package from my sister today. Gad, she sent me enough writing paper and envelopes to last me for a lifetime. I hope it isn't any sort of ill omen. Hate like Hell to think that I would have to spend so much time over here to use up all that stuff. If I did, I'd write 50 letters a day, 10 pages each. Saw a rather neat picture this evening, *Home in Indiana*. It was used as sort of vehicle to introduce Jeanne Crain, (very cute); Don McAllister (not so) and June Haven (eek! Ah!). It wasn't a bad affair, at least it served us as a time passer.

The other night we saw Bob Hope's *Princess and the Pirate*. Too bad, Hope is so funny, laugh so loud that it is easy to miss half of his cracks. There was another new face in that picture, a lovely blonde who was very lovely. Those pictures may be very good as morale builders but looking at those beautiful women can easily drive a man mad. We had a discussion to day of our favorite subject, women. It was sort of comparison between American and Parisian gals. The reason for the two used was because it was unanimously agreed that they are the loveliest, most chic, best dressed and generally excellently groomed. One argument was that before the war, an American style was a direct copy of the Parisienne — however, since the American gal had to be left on her own due to the war, she has proved a master of ingenuity and originality, that was in reference to style. Again however, the ultimate conclusion was that, in the flesh, as the expression goes, the American girl is unbeatable on all counts. They possess the look and air about them that is unequaled thruout the world. Believe me, these fellows have seen a good choice but to all of us, the American girl is held as a goddess of perfection. You see, My Dear, we are not blind. The cause for the discussion was some pictures that were in *Life* magazine. Some models were flashing some swim suits. I notice in another issue some new style of bedtime wear of the American style called a "Dido." (Why, I don't know unless she, — oh well! Figure it out for yourself!) I don't know if you saw it but it is a sort of diaper-like short that seems not to be complicated to get into. Best of all, pardon my sluttish mind, easy to get out of. Personally, I'll take the usual pale blue nightgown. They hold more sex appeal for me than anything I know of. My mind isn't in the gutter but it certainly is in the sack somewhere.

Well, Darling, I am going to close. I hope this hasn't sounded as bad as last night's epistle. Time still marches on. I love you and I always have only moreso. Keep me over here much longer and I'll "pop" from it. But it can't be too hard to take. Keep smiling, Darling. No frowns, — remember wrinkles.

Good night, my Dear. Words cannot express my love. May God Bless You. Pray for me. Love, Mike.

WD, March 6: One plane returned from the continent, sent out on the 5th. One plane test-hopped. The C-109 was up again. Two planes cross country and return. Show at the station theater for EM of the base.

GWD, March 6: Overcast here this morning. During the early hours bombs were exploding from nearby airdromes and was later reported to be those dropped by the enemy intruders on the 4th.

WD, March 7: Three planes were test-hopped while the C-109 was up on local transition. One plane XC and return. . . .

GWD, March 7: Routine day, flights made as usual. Black out regulations are being strictly enforced here at the base.

March 8, 1945 [*Thursday*]

Good Evening, Darling,

I received a few letters from you. I could not help but to feel that it isn't necessary for you to go thru' any tantrums because you miss one night's writing. Hell! Honey, think of the many days that I've missed and you've been so patient thru' it all. I know how difficult it is to stay on the ball all the time, especially when you don't hear from me. At times, writing comes easily and yet at other times, it is as if one word does not cohere with another and everything seems to be one big jumble. Lord knows I've felt that way many times. Writing becomes difficult and naturally those "blah" moods. Luckily such forms of thought are easily shaken and are not contagious. I cannot help but to be distressed by your lack of mail but the complaint seems to be general from all my correspondents. However, it may be due to the fact that February was a very bad one for me, as far as writing went. It seemed as if I was never in one place long enough to settle for a writing session. There are so many circumstances involved that it is difficult to pinpoint any one of them. I do hope that the next time I hear from you, I'll know that the situation has been altered. It will be a great relief to me. The thing I am waiting for is to hear that you have received the perfume I sent. At least, I shall feel that I have done something.

You spoke of this acquaintance of yours who is a Navy chief and radio operator. With all that service and training plus experience, I'd hate like Hell to be caught in a discussion with him. Technically, I'm no hot-shot. We are trained to do our job as efficiently as is necessary but beyond that I wonder. You can recall how helpful I was when you asked me to repair that little radio of yours. I preferred to talk about anything else but radio. He must have a damn good set to pick up Japan. Quite a thrill to reach out that far, isn't it? Before I go on, I love you very much. The English style of home broadcasting is strange. British Broadcasting Corp. (BBC) has a monopoly on everything. They need never to worry about competition. One need never worry about variety, it just isn't being had. What saves us is that we have a few American stations but they, too, have a limited range and unfortunately have a tendency to fade and gather static. I've picked up New York a few times and in those times, I was either sitting in the Blue Room of the Hotel Edison or in the Hotel Pennsylvania. Very lovely, indeed, but they never lasted long enough. Every time I think of such luxury, I think of the hotel room in Oklahoma City, Hotel Biltmore, I believe, one need do no more than to reach up, turn a switch on the wall and listen to lovely American swing. Of course, that, too, brings back the memories of Pappy and I lounging in that same room and throwing limes at the fans to see how they would ride.

Darling, it has been 7 years since I left high school and I've been away from the States a good while, so I cannot honestly give a pro or con to your statement about the High School girls of today. Those shapes that you spoke of may be caused by those loose fitting sweaters and informal sort of clothes they are wearing. However, if you wish it so, I'll make an investigation. If you want a detailed report, you'll have to let me out of your sight for a while. I dare you. I'm afraid I'm a bit beyond that age. I was weaned (or is that the wrong expression?) on High School girls and after I left H.S., I was shunted off to the business world too quickly to worry about what makes those kids tick. A few of them gave me some good scares. One who impressed me very definitely was quite mature, quite shapely, and quite nuts. Not about anyone but just generally. How I ever escaped that I'll never know. Another thing about those H.S. girls you speak of, I think they will fare well. Once the stringiness gets out of their bones, they'll resort to Turner, Lake, Hepburn or some glamour girl for which to shape or model themselves. I've never been afraid of the future of America's youth but don't get me started on that or I'll go into another one of my infinitesimal blubbers over it.

"Time marches on and leaves a lonely boy, a lonely girl, and slowly marches on!" And so the song goes. I never thought I'd ever be such a clock watcher as I am these days. It takes some of the fullness out of [*life*] and why not? There is some of the fullness gone — you! Oh well, and so we must endure it. I love you — My Darling.

Good night, Bette. Got a little sewing to do. Handy little man, aren't I? Give my love to Mother. Take care of yourself. May God Bless You. Pray for me. Love, Mike.

WD, March 8: Twenty-one planes were used in the afternoon for formation training. Cub training continued for [*glider*] pilots. . . . C-46 assigned to the squadron."

GWD, March 8: Missions were effected today carrying the 52nd Troop Carrier to their new field in France.

WD, March 9: Seventeen planes were used to tow gliders to the continent, seven of which returned, the others RON. A three plane supply mission to France, RON. . . . Another C-46 assigned to the squadron. Also a L-5. This brings the total A/C [*aircraft*] to thirty. 25 C-47s, 2 C-46s, 2 C-109s, and one L-5. Group review for the presentation of awards.

GWD, March 9: Our aircraft today carried the remainder of the 52nd Wing to the far shore. With the leaving of the wing, the rumors are mounting fast and furious. In the afternoon, the group held a review and presented awards. . . . Now that the weather has improved the baseball players are out again. Headquarters Officers played Headquarters Enlisted Men and beat them 7-4. Col. Berger our commanding Officer made a home run to top the score off.

March 10, 1945 [*Saturday*]

Good Evening, Darling,

Here's that man again! Nothing to report on the mail situation yet. We figured it out this evening. We don't receive mail but once every 2 or 3 weeks. That isn't a very good percentage for morale building — As a matter of fact, it stinks. But I shan't complain too bitterly. I do hope you have started to receive some mail. Seems like the situation is normally screwed up on all fronts.

I have been promised Ernie Pyle's *Brave Men* tonight, so I guess I'll have something to sack up with tonight. We saw *To Have and Have Not* the other night. [*Humphrey*] Bogart and [*Lauren*] Bacall were excellent. However, I was a bit disappointed that Hemingway was so unrecognizably distorted. I'll admit that it has been years since I read the book but Hemingway has impressed me always, and it is not easy to forget his writing. However, the picture as a picture was good. Bacall was great. Made me think of a dame that didn't give a damn but she's in love and that's all that counted. I knew that the book would never be used as a theme because it was one of the most sluttish things that he ever wrote. As a matter of fact, it was filthy. I was speaking to a guy that is reading *Forever Amber*. He claims it isn't so hot at all. I can imagine that but it surprises me to think that the American mind has turned to such a rubble of sex. Believe me, I'm no prude, nor would I not read the book if I had the chance. But to place it among the top five, one cannot help but to wonder! I read in the latest reviews that Irving Stone had written another biography, *Immortal Wife*, the life of Presidential Candidate John Fremont. The reviewers claim that it is as good a biography as *Lust for Life*. (Van Gogh's life.) Surely you must recall my discussions on that book. If it is anywhere near that, it must be good. Some day I am going to do some refresher reading to see how the books I once read will impress me now that the years have passed.

Before I go any further, Darling, Happy Birthday. I am sure that next year, we will be together and you'll have to be content to be just plain Mrs. Michael Ingrisano Jr. I've never helped you to celebrate one birthday but when we do, it will be a joint affair. I hope that my love has given you ½ the happiness, and pleasure as yours has given me. I am sure that the year '45 will see us together and with all the dreams that have been a part of us since April '43. We have come a long way, My Dearest, and we have a long way to go, but whatever, they will be the nicest roads and have been, — the nicest roads I have ever traveled. I love you, Bette.

I have read a lot about the picture, *A Song to Remember*. It is only natural that the music would be good. Chopin is so enjoyable, little that I know about his music. They say that [*Merle*] Oberon does a great job as George Sand. It is wonderful what the motion pictures can do to improve one's education. I had no idea that Sand was a part of Chopin's life. So be it, live and learn. Lord knows, we cannot ever stop learning. Hope I never stop.

If I recall correctly, Darling, you never did enjoy the heat too much, did you? I can see that Miami made you a convert. I have a lot of confidence in Old Sol. A taste of it as a steady diet can make anyone a believer in its good healthful powers. Although it has been a long time since I exposed my frame to its rays, I'll never forget the touch of the stuff. Seems to me that it is a panacea for anything. I've never yet seen any time when the sun has done anyone any harm. To add to that, popcorn and beer — what more can one ask for? When I was in Miami, I drank vast amounts of Ballantine's Ale. Pretty powerful stuff — at times I found it a bit too powerful for my capacity. After all the junk that I've drunk, I wonder what good whiskey and beer will do to me.

We read in the *Stars and Stripes* that a bunch of characters in Cleveland, Ohio, went on a strike because they weren't paid for their lunch hour. The same bunch was bitching because they couldn't have their 3 o'clock coffee. Seems to me that there are about

11 million other guys that can bitch, too. But we get paid for 24 hours per day so we aren't supposed to kick. I wonder what that bunch would say if they threw their respectable asses into 1-A and let them share our daily salaries? I guess the home front has to have something to keep up its interest. The war seems to be going fine. Those kids on the Eastern and Western fronts are doing a marvelous job.

Well, Darling, that's all the "griping" from this front. Good night, My Love. Give my love to Mother. Take care of yourself. I love you and miss you. May God Bless You. Love, Mike.

WD, March 10: Ten planes returned from France, sent out the day before while three other returned. One plane XC to Scotland and return [*this may have been my plane, when we went to Edinburgh*]. **One local flight. Group inspection of living quarters and departments. Two more planes were assigned to the Sqdn. Officers of the squadron held a dance in Leicester. Pictures of both the officers and enlisted men were taken.**

GWD, March 10: Saturday morning inspection of quarters and offices. A few missions were carried out the far shore. Enlisted men had the Movies *Animal Kingdom*, *Bowery to Broadway*, **and** *Dark Waters*, **at their club this evening.**

WD, March 11: One plane dispatched to France with 52nd HQs equipment and return. A squadron discussion period was held in the station theater on, "What to do with Germany after the war." It was led by Capt. [*Elias*] **Guterman** [*Communications Officer*]**.**

GWD, March 11: Sunday morning and an overcast sky, regardless our aircraft took off for the other side. Plans being made for Headquarters' Enlisted Men's party to be held a week from today. Movie at the base cinema, *One Body Too Many*. **Our aircraft returned early this evening.**

WD, March 12: One plane was dispatched to the continent and return. In the afternoon there was a squadron formation and in the evening the Group had a night formation. Two planes XC and return. The C-109 and the C-46 were up on local transition. Link trainer and the Cub were also scheduled.

GWD, March 12: Weather a little spicy this morning and sky is still overcast. Headquarters Officers played Headquarters Enlisted Men in the afternoon at soft ball and the Officers won, 6-2. In the evening there was a dance at the Red Cross Club for Enlisted Men. Group formation flown tonight. Rumors are still going strong as to our "Going Home."

March 13, 1945 [*Tuesday*]

My Darling,

Yes! I'm still here. I'm sorry that I've been unable to write for the last few days and to make it worse, I'm afraid I'll have to make this note a bit short. However, I'll try not to bitch about the lack of mail. Some bastard must be screwing up the works. Oh, Well!

I've started to read Pyle's *Brave Men* — as a matter of fact, I'm almost finished. I can't say that I'm not disappointed nor that it isn't enjoyable. Pyle has done a wonderful job to recapture the life of the overseas' soldiers. However, at times, he is apt to probe a bit too technically into some matters. Perhaps the reason I see that is because although I am a soldier, (correction, in the Air Force), it is difficult to comprehend the workings of artillery, infantry, ordinance, etc. I can very well understand everything that he mentions about his tours of various Air Force units. However, the foot soldiers nomenclature of units is far beyond our heads. What I mean is, we have squadrons, groups, wings, commands, etc. but they have corps, divisions, battalions, etc. The differences make it difficult to picture groups of men and their numbers. On the whole, the book isn't bad. Pyle does not paint a pretty picture of war — which is as it should be. The most disappointing feature was his lack of mentioning our branch of the Air Force. I guess I can't help feeling a bit bitter but units like ours do so much and get so little credit. We did a little to help the supply lines of the various fronts. One of the fellows has a clipping out of his home town sheet.

It told of a guy who was a Troop Carrier member of the CBI (China-Burma-India) command. He held the DFC (Distinguished Flying Cross) for 450 hours of flying time, and Air Medal and Clusters for every 150 hours. Hate like Hell to brag, but our guys would be packing a lot of ribbons at that rate. We'd make the guy look sick. I'd even venture to say that our bunch has a better record than any Troop Carrier outfit overseas in any theater. Oh, Well, again, it doesn't pay to cry. Can't help a guy for having a bit of *Esprit de Corps*.

Was walking out to the kite the other day, the weather was rather balmy. I couldn't help but think how wonderful it would be to be with you at that moment. Any moment for that matter but just moreso then. Gosh, Honey, can't help but loving you. You occupy so much of my time. It has been wonderful to have you at my side all the time. I love you and miss you so terribly much.

Gotta go for now. Try to do better if I can later on but I doubt it. I may be gone for a while. Give my love to Mother. Take care of yourself. May God Bless you. Pray for me.

Happy Birthday & Happy Easter, Darling. Love, Mike.

On March 13, according to the Squadron War Diary,

Two one plane missions were dispatched to the continent and return. Fourteen planes were used to ferry gliders to Southern England. They later picked up loads and returned to this base. These planes are to pick up gliders dropped in Southern England after they have been loaded and take them to the continent. This will be done at a later

date. Local transition in the C-109, C-46, and the L-5 in the morning and the afternoon.

The Group War Diary that day reported:

> **Another wonderful day, all our aircraft effected an early take-off. HQs Enlisted Men's party was announced by the committee this morning to be held on Sunday. Movie at the base theatre, *Rhapsody in Blue*. Liberty Run.**

March 14, 1945 [*Wednesday*]

Good Evening, Darling,

Another wonderful day has passed. For some non-understandable reason, the weather has been great. Almost as nice as Spring back home. I guess it's best not to mention it because it is such a surprise, I'm afraid I'd scare it away.

March 15, 1945 [*Thursday*]

Hi Babe,

Sorry, I cut that thing so short but I couldn't keep my eyes open. Rather than make a horrible blotch of things, I thought it would be best if I quit and hit the sack. I wasn't wrong about that weather — Brr —

Darling, I love you. It seems like an eternity since I've heard from you. The last letter I received from you was dated Feb. 17. And it must be well over 3 weeks since I've heard from anyone. It is hard to understand. It is both irritating and bothersome. Talk about lowering of morale, they don't realize what the lack of mail does to everyone. All the fellows appear to be lax and not caring, — really can't help it. It is a feeling of being shut up from the rest of the civilized world. And so it goes, the bad mail situation becomes the gravest and most talked of topic.

Not so long ago, I got a chance to sit up in the cockpit for the first time in a long while. It was a grand day and smooth as silk. Got a chance to tune up on my navigation. I offered the kid that was flying a cigarette and he refused. My regular pilot was sitting between us, so he said, "I guess he's too young to use them." So I asked him how old he was. "Just 20." Of course, my regular pilot will be 21 on the 18 of March — (Old Man). After further inquiry, I found that the kid had gone to H.S. in '40 and graduated in early '44. Naturally I'm no old man but it seemed so strange. I've been out of High School 7 years. I've done much more than spend my youth in the Army and I know that there were presidents other than Roosevelt. The ideas struck me so funny that I became conscious of my gray hairs. If they keep me here much longer, I'll be a granddaddy to myself. O Mores! O Tempera! Wonder what this younger generation is coming to. The one fortunate thing for these young fellows is that they can get back to college, etc. They still won't be old enough to assume any sort of responsibility but after all the money they've made in the Army, $12. a week will be an outrageously puny salary. So be it! God help them.

Well, Darling, that's my thought for this morning. I do hope I have some mail. Try to do better when I get a little time. It is rather limited to me now.

Take care of yourself. May God Bless You. I love you and miss you. Pray for me. Love, Mike.

WD, March 14: Fourteen planes were used to tow fourteen loaded gliders from Greenham Common to the Far Shore. These same planes were loaded with supplies. All returning. The courier plane was also sent to the continent with passengers. Pvt. Arthur W. Weldon was married in Leicester. Dance at the NAAFI hall for the EM. Music by the 316th orchestra.

GWD, March 14: Routine day with flights effected as usual. Dance at the NAAFI this evening and music by our own band.

WD, March 15: Nine planes were used to tow gliders and haul supplies to the continent while the courier plane was dispatched. All returning. Eleven planes were dispatched to Southern England thence to the Continent on a priority mission late in the afternoon. They were forced to remain in southern England. The usual transition was scheduled. . . . One plane test hopped.

GWD, March 15-16: Resupply and evacuation mission carried out to the far shore under excellent conditions.

WD, March 16: Eleven planes sent to Southern England late in the afternoon of the 15th returned with their loads. Ten other planes dispatched to Southern England for loads and return. The usual transition in the afternoon. Show at the station theater for the officers. Enlisted Men's council has been organized on the base.

WD, March 17: Twenty one planes were dispatched to the continent on four different missions, all returning. Two planes returned from XC, sent out two days ago. Local transition. Air raid alert was sounded in the evening. Group inspection of the various departments and living quarters.

GWD, March 17: Saturday morning inspection and Headquarters still held high honors. Four aircraft returned late in the evening from resupply and evacuation missions. Col. Berger, Lt. Col. Kendig, Lt. Col. Lewis, Major Keiser, Major Chiros, and Major Milstead returned from an unknown mission this evening. Movie at the Enlisted Men's Club, *And Now Tomorrow*.

March 18, 1945 [*Sunday*]

Good Morning, Darling,

I returned late last night, felt rather tired, no mail, so when the guys suggested that I help them celebrate St. Patrick's day, what more could a good Irishman do but be open to suggestion. And a foine celebration it was. We had 48 bottles of Indian Pale Ale, a couple of dozen slices of toast and great number of cans of sardines, anchovies, peppers, lobster, etc. Of course, we didn't need a reason to celebrate but it is always best to have a good subject. When all the food and drink were finished, all the guests slowly turned to their sacks and so it was a bit too late to write, altho' I kept insisting that I must write to you. I wasn't lit up, just carrying a slight load but I hadn't had much sleep for the last few nights and I was rather tired. Seemed like an eternity since the last time I had pounded my pillow.

Someone said we would probably get some mail today. That is something to look forward to. I imagine they are right because I received a note from my little cousin, Mickey [*Petruzillo*]. First word I'd had from anyone in a long while. It was cute. He told me all about his marks and school work. The little character will be graduating from grammar school in a year. He tells me he is going to one of our local High Schools and is going to try for the freshman's basketball club. Yep! The years must be passing. You'll be 23 tomorrow. I won't be with you physically, Darling, but you know I wish you the very best — as it is said in Italian, *Per cento anno —* (For the next 100 years.) I love you.

Sort of thought I'd test my nerves a few days ago, [*probably on March 13, see War Diary entry*] so I went up in a Cub [*L-5, Taylor Cub*] with one of the pilots. [*As I recall, it was Jim Madigan, Glider Pilot whom I nicknamed "Slip" after the football coach at St. Mary's College of California. His team used to play Fordham University on a regular basis.*] It was the first time I had ever been in a light craft. It was quite a change, quite a thrill and might even say, a busman's holiday. She lifted off the ground so easily, so quietly that I hardly knew that we were in the air. We looked over the countryside at about 1,000 ft. The cockpit is so small that I had a Hell of a job getting my legs in and then I had a job wrestling into a chute. The pilot told me he was going to show me a 720° degree turn (that is, 2 360° turns). The idea is to make these turns, lose no altitude and come back to the same point from which you start. We started out OK but ½ way thru' she stalled out and we were heading into a spin before he kicked it out. I would not have minded it too much if we had enough altitude, but 1,000 feet isn't a great deal. Since the plane is so small, it is natural to be conscious of gas fumes. I was afraid that a combination of fumes and acrobatics would make me air sick, but I managed to get thru' it. He started to loop it but I vetoed that idea, pulled a few side slips that weren't bad at all. He let me fly for a while. The controls are so light that I had very little idea of judgment; there was a strong wind and I had to keep correcting to keep on course. It was great looking at the scenery and flying at the same time. Finally, we went down and did some hedge-hopping. It's a little different from a goose [*C-47*] but the feeling is the same. You think you are tearing along at an alarming high rate of speed. Gangs of fun. Came in to land, head wind was so strong that when we hit and bounced, we were thrown high into the air. He got it down OK. Guess I can still take it!

Well, Darling, must rush off to church. Hope I get some mail. I'll probably write again tonight. I love you so very much, Darling, and I miss you terribly, terribly much. You're wonderful.

Take care of yourself. May God Bless You. Pray for me. Love, Mike.

WD, March 18: Two planes were sent to the continent with supplies while another was XC here in England, all returning. Local transition. Show at the station theater.

GWD, March 18: Sunday and the usual church services were held for all faiths this morning. Headquarters Enlisted Men's party began early in the afternoon. Guests from Leicester and Chillwell were present for the affair. Buffet supper was served early in the evening. Corsages were given to the ladies as favors, and Col. Berger, Capt. Ness, and Lt. Yarnell were present. Dancing and drinking throughout the evening and a good time was had by all.

March 19, 1945 [*Monday*]

My Dearest,

Happy Birthday! I wish I could be around to help you celebrate. Honestly, Darling, I shouldn't write tonight because I feel as if I am in such a damn ugly mood. As much as I try, it is almost impossible to shake. I have been pretty inactive of late plus lack of mail plus lousy food plus lousy everything. I know I shouldn't speak so but damn it is a feeling of being cut away from the rest of the world. We are like an isolated bunch of men on an isolated island and it stinks. Just to have something to do, I am starting to develop another mustache. When things get that bad, they have reached some Hell of a depth.

I love you, Darling, I love you so very much. I hate to think that you must share this ugly mood with me but I can't help it. The lull is one that leaves a man clinging to the smallest branch and yet there is nothing there, no forward, no retreat. — A void that cannot be filled even by the close companionship of my buddies. It is getting so that we can't even stand ourselves. Darling, I've never bitched this much but I can't help it — someone is screwing up the detail, and he's doing a good job of it.

I've tried to revert my thoughts to the other side of the ocean but I don't succeed very well. Lord knows, Darling, if I had you with me now I wouldn't give a good damn for anything. Just doesn't go like that. America, the States, and everything that goes with that bit of heaven and happiness is as obscure as that pot of gold. If I were alone in my feelings, it would be understandable, but I've got so much company that for once misery has company. These periods of quietude give a man too much chance to think. All I can see is you and I can't help but shudder if my dreams should never be fulfilled — a horrible feeling of fear I've never had before. I've been scared but not so that I feel as if I'll crack. I have no reason to feel like that. One letter from you would solve every puzzle, every bad moment. But since they are not forthcoming, I really feel so all alone and lost. Forgive me, but I lean upon you so much that I cannot help but to feel as I do.

I've been delaying a chance to write because I hope that each night will bring a letter. But if I don't write, you won't get any mail. I know a letter like this isn't worth a damn to you but at least you know, I'm still kicking. Well, I'll spare you any more of this bunk.

Good night, Darling. I love you so very much and I do miss you so very, very much. May God Bless You. Pray for me. Love, Mike.

WD, March 19: All flying to the continent was canceled however there was local transition. . . . Dance at the American Red Cross for the enlisted men of the base.

GWD, March 19: The field was prepared again for inspection this morning as the group was expecting Lt. General Brereton, Commanding General of the 1st Allied Airborne Army. It began to rain though early in the morning and General Brereton's plane didn't arrive. . . .

March 20, 1945 [*Tuesday*]

My Darling,

Forgive me for that horrible missive last night. Just one of those ugly things that happens every so often. (This pen stinks, so if I start cussing every so often — sorry.) I've ruined one page already. But again about last night, I just couldn't seem to pull myself together. Things panned out a bit better today. We spent most of the time laughing at all sorts of foolish things and it was most enjoyable. To boot, we spent a good deal of the afternoon playing ball. It was a pleasant diversion and the first time I had handled the apple since last year. The old guy can still get around. I'll be hitting 24 soon so I can claim a little seniority in the family, can't I? Or will you assert your power in some manner or other? No rolling pins, please. I am allergic to bumps and bruises, especially around the head. This letter will probably be the reverse of last night. I still haven't received any mail but I guess you are as sick of hearing that as I am of saying it.

I love you, Bette, — I love you more than I have ever been able to say. Thruout these long months I've written many words to that effect but never have I really been able to reach the depth of my feeling. Of late, I've left my words to just 3 words but they, too, are insignificant because they are merely scratching the point. Often I have told of what you mean to me; often I have told you how much you have been in my thoughts. I've never forgotten anything that has happened between us. Oftimes, I have gone thru' the transition of soldier away to the man who loved a part of your life and is going to live it as long as you want me to. I know I am getting mushy but I think I rate that little chance to blow my top.

It seems like a long time since I've done that. You know, Darling, the way I feel tonight, I could take that favorite bottle of ours and down it in one gulp and still ask for more. The man must be mad! But honestly, Darling, I wish I were nestled comfortably in your arms right now. It seems like such a long time since I have done that, that I've almost forgotten the thrill of it all. I don't think it will take very much to get back into practice. Gosh, Bette, it is almost impossible to say much more. Just the thought of anything like that drives me mad. If ever we have any children, they are going to have the good sense to join the Navy. At least, they'll get a chance to see home every so often. Oh well, so it must be. I missed the boat but I don't think I'll go thru' life missing the boat. I have you, that gives me everything I've ever wanted out of life. All I need now is to get back to you — I miss you so.

Good night, My Dear. Perhaps tomorrow will bring pleasant tidings on wings of the mail. Take care of yourself. May God Bless You.

Pray for me. I love you. Ever, Mike.

The Group was preparing for a mission to Germany, OPERATION VARSITY, which took place on March 24, 1945. The Squadron and Group War Diaries described the build-up and operation in the March 20-24 War Diary entries:

> **WD, March 20: Two planes returned from the continent after a two night RON. Two other planes were sent out. Local transition. . . .**
>
> **GWD, March 20: Representatives of each office of the group left today for Wethersfield. Aircraft of the Group still effecting missions to the far shore. Movie at the base cinema, *And Now Tomorrow*.**
>
> **WD, March 21: Eighteen plane formation early in the morning. Twenty-two planes and crews plus a skeleton force of administrative officers and enlisted men were sent on TD [*Temporary Duty*] to Wethersfield in Southern England for a tentative mission. C-109 and C-46 flew in the afternoon. Dance at the NAAFI Hall for EM.**
>
> **GWD, March 21: Remaining aircraft, crews, and personnel of the air echelon left for Wethersfield today. The task was at hand for setting up for the unknown.**
>
> **WD, March 22: Four planes with crews from the 314th GP. were on DS [*detached service*] for the purpose of carrying supplies to the Far Shore. One plane returned for supplies for the air echelon now in Southern England. . . . Seven planes, including the four on DS returned from a resupply mission. The four planes on DS were sent back to their own Sqdn.**
>
> **GWD, March 22: General briefing was held for all pilots of the Group at Wethersfield for the coming mission in the Group S-2 office by Major Milstead and Captain Chess.**
>
> **WD, March 23: Three planes were dispatched to the continent and**

return. C-46 was up on local transition. The one C-46 that was attached for storage was officially assigned.

GWD, March 23: At Wethersfield the Squadrons held their briefings throughout the day in preparation for the coming event. Back at Cottesmore, a few C-46s flew resupply to the continent and returned. Weather CAVU [*ceiling and visibility unlimited*]. Liberty run in the evening.

WD, March 24: Twenty-one planes were used to drop ammunition, supplies, and 353 paratroopers of the 6th British A/B [*airborne*] division across the Rhine in the vicinity of Wesel, Germany. All the planes reached the DZ without difficulty with the exception of one and two of his parapacks were lost and the third blossomed out and refused to detach from the plane, thus forcing the pilot to drop from the formation after repeated attempts to pull the chute into the plane. The pilot landed at Eindhoven and turned the troops over to the British authorities. One other plane sustained damage enroute out from the DZ and was also forced down at Eindhoven. It was inadvisable to continue so both crews returned in the one plane. One other plane landed at B-86 [*Helmond, Holland*] with his right engine and hydraulic system shot out. The plane was left there and the crew returned on a plane from the 315th Group. Five planes were undamaged out of the twenty-one. The others were all damaged by German small arms and 88mm. One radio operator was injured by small arms fire. The planes took off from Wethersfield in Southern England and landed here at Cottesmore. While the mission was taking place, the ground echelon came to Cottesmore on the spare plane. Interrogation was carried out here. Four A/C were dispatched to the continent on a resupply mission. The base was on total restriction.

GWD, March 24: Routine day in the rear echelon. 7 aircraft flew missions to the far shore and returned. At Wethersfield it was an early breakfast and last minute briefing before take off and the drop across the Rhine. After the aircraft were off the ground most of the ground echelon returned to Cottesmore to await the return of our planes.

March 25, 1945 [*Sunday*]
[*Day after OPERATION VARSITY*]

Hello You Big, Luscious Blonde,

   I am so dreadfully sorry, Darling, but it has been impossible for me to write to you for the past few days. The mail finally started to come thru' and I got a gang of them from you. I received 3 of them about 3 days ago and believe me, Bette, they came at the most opportune time. I love you, My Dearest, you are a wonderful person. Everything about us has taken on a new perspective, something so gigantic, I can't help but feel so enlightened, so wonderful by the thought of it. I feel I've shaken so much of the childishness in me that I've grown overnight. Listen to the old man, will you? When I got in last night, I was dirty, tired, a growth of beard that would make [*George Bernard*] Shaw look hairless, and I was hungry and thirsty. Without doing anything about anything, I promptly got stinking drunk and for the first time passed out cold in my sack. I feel like a new man today. Feel like I've dropped off the weight of the world.

Darling, in most of your letters, you keep worrying about how I'll like your tan. You know what I think about sunshine and such. I think it is wonderful. But I'll bet you that if I have a week in sunshine like that, I'll make you look pale. I get so black that just my teeth show. It is the greatest feeling in the world and I am glad that you are appreciating such wonderful weather. It'll never hurt you. Throw a little fishing in there and it is perfect. I haven't received your letter telling me of the fishing trip yet but it will be around soon. That Man of War is a new one on me. We have some small stuff that they call Leeches and then, of course, there's that good old sting ray. I'd like to do some of that Florida fishing some day. Darling, I am glad that the weather is doing you so much good. I imagine you must have put on some weight. Fattening up for the slaughter.

I received your card from the Bali. From the scene that you had on top of it, I can imagine that it was one big night. Oh! Big Head! Curfew or not, New York had better watch out when we hit it.

From the latest reports, New York is bustling with activity. (I mean Brooklyn.) Lou gets home; cousin Mike gets married; Tony, Sheila and Reb show up on furlough; and my cousin, Sue, married a sailor. He had been courting her before he joined up. . . . I'm about ready to rest on my laurels and see that part of the world again. Guess a guy can't expect too much. Dan is expected home any time now. I can't see how he does it. I hope I don't keep missing the boat too much. Might as well keep the family with something to celebrate. Personally, all the celebrating I want is to see you. Darling, in all your letters so far, you haven't mentioned a thing about the perfume. Haven't you gotten it yet?

I'm glad you liked *The Robe*. I was sure you would. Douglas did a wonderful job. Your question about Christianity was interesting. It is our state in life, as Christians, to prove the neutralizers. We are supposed to control the oppressors and deflate their ideas of life. If words cannot do that, then it is necessary to do what we are doing. Personally, I'd rather be a pacifist. Wars should be left to the animals not to humans. *The Robe* is one of the books that I intend to read again, too. *Winter Wheat* wasn't too bad but it was light reading and somewhat interesting. Haven't had much time to do any reading these days.

In return to my letter, you spoke of Dan and Gert. I don't think they would enjoy knowing that we are using them as an example. However, so it is, and rightfully so. . . . You speak of Love, My Darling, just as I have believed it to be. It is a thing, — an emotion that is ever present between two people. No matter how grave a situation may be, love must conquer, must comfort. We both know that we are emotionally equal; we proved that a long time ago. The time that we've spent apart has done much to prove that our love is neither elastic nor brittle. It's the real thing. Each passing day has brought us closer not only physically but mentally. We may have more time to wait. March will not be as full as we had hoped it would be. But it will be just another month to add. It hasn't lost anything for us but the time. These 20 months have gained for us something that a life time will never cease us to lose. I love you, Bette. My words must suffice for now but as I have so often said, I want to prove it more that I have ever. I lean on you so much that I do lose myself. These past weeks of silence have proved that. And I am dreadfully sorry that I showed it but the circumstances were a little bit too big for me to take. My mind is more at ease, now — It is going to be wonderful to be together again. We'll make up for everything in every way.

Glad that you heard from "Pappy." I haven't gotten together for a bull session for quite some time but I saw him yesterday. He's in good shape. Getting a little "tubbier." Sheila mentioned in her letter that they hadn't had any answers to her letters to you. She was afraid that you weren't getting her letters. I'll assure her of the fact that you'll write. They must have gotten mail while they were in NY because she wrote from there. I know that you aren't lax about writing; she should know that.

Well, Darling, I am going to close. Give my love to Susie. Don't worry about me, I am OK, well and happy, just waiting. Take care of yourself. May God Bless You. I love you and miss you — Pray for me. — Love, Mike.

WD, March 25: Three planes were sent on a resupply mission to France and return. Local transition in the C-109 and the C-46. Engineering department was busily fixing the combat damage. Show at the station theater. Truck convoy from Wethersfield arrived this morning.

GWD, March 25: All our aircraft had returned from the paradrops over the Rhine but three and the last count of personnel were 2½ crews missing. Lt. Col. [*Mars*] Lewis Commanding Officer of the 45th Squadron is among those missing.

WD, March 26: Three planes were sent to [*Prestwick*] with casualties. All of them returning. Four planes were dispatched to the continent, three of which RON. One other plane XC here in England. Dance at the American Red Cross. Local transition.

GWD, March 26: Monday morning and the mission is still the topic of conversation, although the situation is returning to normal. A number of aircraft flew the routine resupply missions to the far shore today. Liberty run in the evening.

March 27, 1945 [*Tuesday*]

My Darling,

Comes the revelation! Six letters from you and all of them dated for the month of March. I cannot answer all now because there are still a few of your others that are unanswered but a few comments. Now I know that you quit your job. The details are unimportant. I surmise that you are enjoying a bit of a vacation. Good for you, Darling, enjoy every little moment, get all the rest you can because I'll probably drive you to madness and weariness. Secondly, I see that you have your reservations for your return to Kansas City, April 11. Don't be afraid to upset your plans, Darling. I am not getting pessimistic but I don't think that you need fret for a few months. Let time take its course and I know that no matter what, I'll not flub a thing. You can only be two places, either Miami or KC or enroute and you'll know if ever I hit home port. Don't even let those things worry you, Darling, not after all this time because we won't let any little thing disrupt our plans. Gosh, I love you so very much, My Dearest.

So you received my picture. Bette, how can you do it? Let alone you'll have to look at me for a life time and yet you put that damn thing right next to you. Maybe that's why you haven't been sleeping too well lately. You know I hear that insomnia is caused that way. You must love me if you can stand that pan. Surely though, I am glad that you liked the picture. I didn't bother to get a decent frame because it is almost impossible to get anything worth while over here.

Yes, Darling, I do want to court you for a few days. I've told you why already and I am more than sure now. Sorta' get you used to the idea that I'm still the same guy. You say that I've already rushed you off your feet, you haven't seen a thing yet. It will be lots of fun. Play hard to get and Susie [*our private nickname for Bette's mother*] will get her wish; your butt will be as red as your face.

You said something about my being so good that they use me more often. Something about a just reward. I'm afraid I've been in the service just a wee bit too long, Bette. My just reward must have passed me by. I shan't quote any instances of other people's rewards because I'll end up bitching. Don't feel in a bitching mood. Just a wee bit too happy and ever so much in love. All I hope is that whatever I have done and will do will be enough. I want to be at your side ever and watch the war end from the State-side. I realize that the time that we've spent apart will be a hazy dream. I'm not worried about that. All I want is that that time apart ends quickly. I don't think it will be another 20 [*months*].

Bette, you know how drinking affects me. But the solution I have for forgetting is to get blind, to pass out from exhaustion. Everything becomes so blank that there is no need for thought or anything else — just a good sack.

When I have said things, I've said them with the idea that our ideas are coherent. I know that our enthusiasm will be mutual. I know that our control will be nil because it has been such a long time. Not only that but your words are true that we wouldn't be Mike and Bette. We can't help but to be congenial to people. That's normal for us. But as long as we have each other, our congeniality and general behavior will be ideal. Happiness can go a long way to make people's temperament change or stay as it is. There will be no need for nervousness or any other strain of emotion because the two of us together are the most relaxed people in the world. I sound like a song writer, "Me without you, etc." But it is so very true. You're wonderful!

Well, Darling, I am going to close. I was gone yesterday and didn't sleep much. It seems like an eternity since the sack and I have had one nightly *tête-à-tête*.

Good night, Darling. Give my love to Susie. Take care of yourself. May God Bless You. I love you and miss you. Love, Mike.

WD, March 27: Three planes returned from France, sent out on the 26th. One plane was test hopped while the C-109 and C-46 were up on transition training.

GWD, March 27: Overcast sky early this morning but cleared later in the day. Only a few of the aircraft returned from their missions, RON'd in Southern England because of weather. Liberty run this evening.

March 28, 1945 [*Wednesday*]

Hiya, "Fatty,"

Since this is my natal day, 'tis best that I spend a good part of the day with you. Reason, you are so wonderful! Another letter from you; true, it was a wee old but who am I to complain.

I was only kidding you about your singing, My Loved One. I think it is a great thing to have talent. I missed the boat because of poverty and the pursuit of pecuniary values. You'll have to carry that part of the load. When we are entertaining during one of those long winter evenings, you can play that piano and sing while I hustle drinks and keep the other young ladies (ahem!) entertained. If there are any drinks around, I'll be pretty busy with them.

Mac received an answer from his wife, Lois, about one of those drunken orgy letters. She wrote a few pages for me and now, we, you and I have an invite if we are any where in the vicinity. I am glad that she accepted it in the right attitude. She asked me to take care of Mac. Who is going to take care of me?

We had a very interesting discussion about certain types of scheming women. This type that entered the talk was a gal who is divorced and has a child from that marriage. She met a well-educated guy from a fine Eastern family. He is 29, a lawyer, a linguist, etc. He was educated at Yale, Western Reserve, — speaks French, German, Hungarian, and is now scheduled to go to a school to learn conversational Japanese. He is a Civil Affairs Officer. Quite a catch in any ocean. But he is engaged to a gal that goes to Bryn Mawr College. All in all, the affair reeks of money. Now, the first gal admits knowing all that, frankly avows that the engagement will be broken as soon as she pours the coal on. She has chased him all over the States. In all probability, she has no scruples about "shacking" (sleeping) with him. She speaks little of love but more of fortune. He may think he can slide out of her arms but we are willing to bet a year's salary that she causes him a load of trouble — financially or otherwise. The fellow here, who brought up the theme of the discussion, slept with this vixen before her divorce was cleared. All in all, we don't like her, though we don't know her. He claims she is intelligent but our repartee to that is that as smart as she is, she will outsmart herself. Quite a discussion really, it carried on thruout chow and so — Enuf of that. Personally, I don't think she's worth that much trouble.

I received you letter of the 8th of March today. I know that you've quit your job — Soon I'll know of your plans to head back to KC. Great mail service; nothing comes in its proper order. Hell, as long as I get mail! Who cares!

So you thought my statement was clever about wanting a little out of life, "just you and a few other odds and ends." Now, Bette, crawl up out of that gutter. "You" was meant to include the odds and ends that you were thinking of. Those other odds and ends that I spoke of meant little things that I've left back in the States. Little ideas and mannerisms that have become vague, a drunk or snack, whenever it is desired, a walk in familiar landscapes among familiar people, Ebbetts Field, just plain old lounging. Get the idea. And, of course, having you at my side as often as possible. I love you.

You reminded me of Tony. I wrote to him this afternoon. He didn't have a very good stay at home. He said he was awfully glad to see the family, etc. But he said that NY "stank." He has a particular bitch about the civilians there. He painted a not-too-beautiful picture of it all. His advice was to eat well and relax but don't do any thinking. All I want to think about is you. I am sure that you'll arrange the other two items for me. One thing I want you to promise me and that is to keep me out of trouble. I am not afraid of the civvies, only of the MP's. I don't want anyone to bother me with inane, foolish remarks or any bickering. But that remains to be seen. I know that Tony can take care of himself. The only thing I don't like is the work that the infantry does. Oh well! I know how he is and his high principles and ideals.

I was glad to hear that you understand my ideas about my army life. I don't want to scare you with the horrid aspects but we will have to travel light for a while. We are lucky that we adjust ourselves easily. Just give us a hole in the wall and that is probably all we'll have. But it will have to suffice as home as long as we are in the Army. No home will be permanent as long as we are army people but once we get out, we'll be ready to settle wherever it may be. I say "we" because you will be in the Army as well as I am when we get married — *Compris*?

Well, Darling, good night for now. Tell Susie that I won't beat you up because of a mere sunburn, as long as you don't eat crackers in bed —

I love you, My Dearest. May God Bless You — Love, Mike.

March 28, 1945 [*Wednesday*]

Hiya Chocolate Drop,

They may call me "Big Nig" but if you keep it up, we'll be the "Gold Dust" Twins. Here's your old man back again, trying to smile thru a false mask and mustache and enduring whatever must be. Twenty-four years old and I feel like a heel of 70 winters (quote Longfellow.) Seriously, Darling, don't feel as bad as I sound. I don't have a care in the world — all I know is that I love you; I am safe, well and happy (reasonably so!) and still patient as ever. The only puzzle I have is that I don't know whether to send this to KC or Fla. In any event, I guess it will be forwarded so I shan't worry.

I reread all the letters that I received so far for the month of March. My conclusions are that you've quit your job, you are enjoying a vacation, getting tan, being as patient as I am, returning to Kansas City and you still love me. Of all those items, due to the lack of a few letters, the one thing I am certain of is that you still love me. Of all those items, that is the only one that is truly important to me besides the facts that you are happy and healthy and are enjoying life. I can see that your nervousness is coming back but you will have a chance to quell that with a change of climate and cities. By the time you are settled in Kansas City again, I hope I can be of some help to you. And so it must go, — we are in love, time is passing, and our hope buds as do the flowers at this time of the year. I am glad that you remembered my fondness for gardenias and that you wore them in your hair. I can see that you are learning, My Dear. You'll know all my habits in due time. By the way, Bette, how do you like that song, "Easter Sunday"? My only sensation of Easter is thru' our religious ceremonies. I miss the fragrance and beauty of this time of year that announces the birth of a new world. Christ showed us many things in His death. He gives us the opening of the New Year, symbolic of a New Life. It's a grand thought and a wonderful outlook for the future. He must have been a brilliant Fellow.

I didn't realize that our thoughts of the Bible were so allied. It is a good story, isn't it? You spoke of waywardness due to lack of understanding. That is true because we do not have Him at our sides physically at all times. (People must see to believe! Not all of us but most of us at many times.) But we do follow His examples in our subconscious minds. Whatever wrong we do, we do in moments when our physical powers overcome one decent restraint of emotion. When the furor has subsided, then the pain of sin is felt. We learn thru these errors, not fully, of course, but in our repentance, we can more easily visualize the many false courses that we have assumed. I could go on like this for hours, Dearest, but your words show me that you understand the basis of the Man and His teachings. It is important because that realization for both of us makes many pictures clearer and the future easier to plan and so on.

I will start my spelling lessons as quickly as you wish. Line forms on the right. I think I'll let you keep writing even after I get home, so I can correct your papers when I get home at night. Analyze, interruption, etc. But I think I've made you too conscious of your habit, Darling, I'm sorry. But I do these things just to help; don't think too badly of me. (Oh, yes, limousine!)

Why do you worry about expenses? I know I'm not a millionaire nor even a thousandaire but when we go broke we can start over again. We've worried so much about meeting each other that we will not only be nervous wrecks but two watch watchers. Let us wait and let nature or whatever it may be take its course. OK? Another thing, you mentioned Thelma and Mike [*Fusco*] to stand up with us. That, too, we can let wait. I know it is good to mention such things but, we will have a little time to straighten out all these affairs. Easily and inch by inch each little detail will formulate and place itself as it should be.

I didn't know that you did much singing. You must serenade me to sleep one of those nights. How about a little of that Lullaby? If I get enough practice, maybe we can do a few duets. I know some hill-billy songs —

Darling, I must close. I hope my few paltry words have brought you some smiles.

Cheerio, Ole Gal! Give my love to Susie. I love you and miss you. May God Bless You. Mike.

> **WD, March 28: Two planes XC and return. The usual local transition in the C-109 and C-46. Lt. Jack A. Murrell, missing since the Holland invasion on the 18th Sept. '44, returned to the squadron on a 10 days TD after escaping. He is to be returned to the States. . . . Lt. Lawrence Rankin was married at the Cottesmore church. . . .**
>
> **GWD, March 28: Overcast sky and showers in the afternoon. Aircraft from yesterday's missions returned, and those that left today returned early in the afternoon. Dance at the NAAFI with ATS girls and Civilians from Leicester. T/Sgt. Baker's appointment came through today for 2nd Lt., and he celebrated with the Enlisted Men in the evening at their club.**

On March 29, 18 Squadron planes were sent to southern England for loading, and returned that day. The Squadron War Diary continued, "The C-109 and C-46 were up again. . . ."

The Group War Diary on that day noted:

> **Beautiful weather. Aircraft out on resupply missions and returned by 2000 hours today. Movie at the base cinema, *Keys [of] the Kingdom*.**

March 30, 1945 [*Friday*]

Howya All Sugar,

Sorry I didn't write last night but I got in rather late and I went to the second show — when I got back to the barracks, lights were out and I had no alternative but to sack. The reason I went to the cinema was that they were showing, *Keys [of] the Kingdom*. I didn't want to miss it. It was excellent; it has been a long time since I have been deeply affected by any sort of movie. Since I read the book, it made everything doubly enjoyable. Wisdom is a rare virtue and one to note closely and duplicate just as closely.

I got in late again this evening, had a long haul and it couldn't be helped. Since it is Good Friday and Easter is so near, I went to church this evening to be spiritually prepared for the wonderful day. Hence, I am writing at a rather late hour but I don't intend to let another day pass without writing to you.

Please forgive me, Darling, but when you received no cable from me, you must have thought, "Just like Mike, doesn't realize how much I worry about him and he doesn't do anything about it!" But your letter requesting me to cable didn't arrive until yesterday. Hence I knew it was no sense to do a thing because your late letters tell me of your receipt of my letters. It is obvious that the famine of mail has been prominent across the ocean. You will receive those morbid letters of mine and wonder. So it must be. The mail passes so slowly at those times that we are both lost. Our worries are mutual; when I don't hear from you, I think all sorts of things. Accidents do happen and you do have a fancy for falling, don't you? Thank God, the situation has been altered and we are both satisfied. I love you so, My Dearest.

So you caught that first fish. Are you sure it isn't a grouper? We have a few of them up North and they are a close family of the fighting bulldog, the blackfish. I don't want to go thru a big discussion because if I do you'll never hear the end of it. Just one of those things that makes me so very talkative! (Ahem! Just like clothes and perfumes!)

No, Bette, I never went to the Howdy Club in New York. Personally, I cannot feel proud of my sex when I watch such antics. It embarrasses me. One night I was riding the subway in New York and one of those characters walked in. He was perfect, lipstick to a waving handkerchief. Fortunately, the train wasn't very crowded but directly across from me sat a few young ladies. They noticed my discomfort and put me at ease with the remark, "Oh! It's OK. We see him every night." I smiled politely and stuck my nose into the newspaper I had. It is educational, I'll admit but only for an occasional diet. On a whole, it is pitiful. I much rather prefer normalcy, although I'm neither prudish nor narrow-minded. So it must be!

Hey, Lady, don't get so excited — it was only a bottle of perfume. The wrappings were meant to be so, so you could get an idea of our literature. The *NY Times* just happened to be on hand and so I used it. But I'm pleased as punch that you enjoyed the gift so thoroughly. I worried so that I'd make a "dud" of it. If I had had more money, I would have spent more time at it. The atmosphere of the salon was ideal [*in Lille*]. The young ladies were all cute and very chic, and French. They treated me wonderfully. [*To help me make the selection, they asked me all sorts of questions about Bette's hair, skin tones, moods. Then they suggested the type of perfume best suited to that description.*] Then, too, during that same stay I was sitting all alone at the Strasbourg Bar and I was talking to Thoni. She didn't understand a thing that I said but I showed her your pictures and kept talking about you — some French, mostly English. She kept saying, *Tres Jolie.* Of course, I know that. I guess the new world atmosphere made me miss you all the more. It would have been so much nicer shopping with you. Lille holds some of my fondest memories.

It is most unfortunate, My Darling, that I can't inject any optimism into your letters these days. It is because so many of my hopes fell thru' so beautifully. I had as many hopes for March as you did. Now I don't dare pin my hopes on any set date. The Army is teaching me that lesson day after day. So it is best that we just continue to wait. It isn't too hard, look how easily the last year and a half have gone by. We deserve so much and yet so far we have gotten so little of our time. What little we had we have made the best of it, so much so that our memories have carried us along so wonderfully and we will continue to be as we are; we both know that each day puts a stronger link in our chain of love. Almost six months to the day, Dan arrived home. He and Gert are waiting 2 weeks, can you imagine it? True, I'm bitching but gad! . . . Oh well! It can't be too bad. I can't go much over two years, at least, I hope not. Keep smiling. I am. — Time is not that hard to conquer. At least, I am still safe and healthy — above all extremely happy. I have you — What more can I ask?

Good night, Darling. Give my love to Susie. Take care of yourself.

May God Bless You. Pray for me.

I love you and miss you terribly; Yours Eternally, Mike.

The March 30 Squadron War Diary entry described another mission to Germany:

> **Twenty planes were dispatched to the continent with supplies, three of which hauled gas into Germany for General Patton's Third Army. All of the planes returned. Local transition in the C-109 and C-46. Show at the station theater.**

We landed at an obscure base in Germany. The perimeter was lined with explosives. American infantrymen had been through just shortly before we got there. There were dead German soldiers in the tower. As we taxied up behind other planes, General Maxwell Taylor was in a Jeep directing and expediting the unloading of Patton's much-needed gasoline. We were pulled off to the side to receive cargo to return to England. It was then that I saw the tower occupants. The cargo was a V-2 bomb. Apparently the first one to be captured by the Allied. We ferried it back to a base near London. On our arrival, we were told to vacate the aircraft because this item was highly classified. I had sat on the damn thing and looked at all the particulars while we were in flight back to England. If I had known, I could have sold this classified material to those dead Germans!

The Group War Diary for March 30 noted only:

> **Very windy today just a little rough for flying. All aircraft of the group returned to home base early.**

March 31, 1945 [*Saturday*]

Hello Southern Fried,

Here's that character back again. I've been doing a lot of skipping around these days. It seems that the days are infinitesimally long and the nights are painfully short. Sorry if I blew my top for a few pages last night. There are such times when it is difficult to control my temper. I never was like that before. Temper was an unknown quantity in my nature — whatever occasional outbursts I had, I dismissed easily with a smile. Guess my nerves aren't what they used to be. Guess I couldn't help blowing my top.

Guess (again!) looks like Ole Gabe Heatter was not only a bit wet but he was soaking. With these tremendous drives going on now, I can imagine what our grandstand generals and pleasant 4-Fers must be saying. From the look of things back there, the war must be over. I never did like commentators. I think my love for them has decreased more.

I chalked up a new country not so long ago. Got a chance to see Germany. I think the country really makes England and France look sick. I can't imagine why Hitler was looking for *lebensraum* or something like it. If he had concentrated on his own land, he really would have stayed at the top of the world heap. His land, that part of it which I saw, was rolling hills and beautiful green, flourishing wooded areas. It looked so fertile that it seemed pitiful that it should be so shell-torn and crated and battered. "Hitler is a sad man these days." He deserves all of it and more — Too bad!

It seems a rather queer way to carry a memory but I guess bourbon and coke stains are as good as any. Well do I remember the gray chiffon dress (of course, I couldn't tell if it was chiffon or cotton — I'll learn!) I wouldn't try to remove them if I were you; perhaps they are a symbol of my consistency. The first night that I told you and how often have I yearned to repeat those little words into your ears. I am to blame for wasting so many of our precious moments and I've had a long time to regret such willful waste. I am so sorry that it took so long to grow up. Guess I didn't realize that life was not a toy. I've played with it many times since but now I realize it must not be left to pass. Oh! My Darling, how many times will I prove my love for you. The thrill of the thought chases little mice up and down my spine. Surely we did much and it has carried us far. Things happened as they did, not only because they did happen but because we helped them along. Just a slight push but hard enough to prove that we are Bette and Mike, the two people who realize the beauty and strength of their love and intend to fight for it — Yes, My Dearest, you can sleep in my arms. Well do we know the emptiness of that unresponsive pillow. Well do we know the many tears that uncontrollably fell on that pillow. Yes, My Darling, we have many years of fullness ahead of us. I cannot tell you what I feel in my heart because I haven't the ability to express it. Words are empty tonight. They do not seem big enough to uncover the emotion that I feel. I love you so much, My Dearest, that tonight is one time when our separation seems unbearable. But it is best that I not incite a furor within myself. Believe me, Bette —

Good night, Sugar Plum. Give my love to Susie. I still have gangs of your letters to answer. Slowly but surely, I'll get them all done. Take care of yourself.

May God Bless You. Pray for me. Miss you terribly. Ever and Ever, Mike.

WD, March 31: Sixteen planes were dispatched to Southern England for their loads and return while one plane was sent to France on a courier run. Pay call.

GWD, March 31: . . . Barracks and Offices were inspected by Lt. Col. [*Bertie*] David. Still a very high wind out today.

So ends both war diaries. Since the Group was preparing in late April to head home to the States, the histories for April which might have been written in May were not recorded, as far as I know.

April 1, 1945 [*Sunday*]
<u>Easter Sunday</u>

Hello Darling,

It is rather a quiet Sunday afternoon. Our only acclaim toward Easter is the fact that it is Sunday. Very few of the guys are around — Most of them are writing as I am. Mac is in his sack and he's reading — Hemingway's *To Have and Have Not*. His wife just sent it to him. I intend to read it when he finishes it. It has been nearly 5 years since I read it. You know what I think of H. so I don't think I'll miss anything by rereading one of his works. I have gangs of correspondence to answer but I hardly feel in the mood to talk to so many people. I'd rather spend my time with you. Leisure time at that, day off and I'm sitting around in a pair of OD pants, a "T" shirt and suspenders. Just like "Jiggs" [*in the comic strip*].

You mentioned in one of your letters that you had been to see the Miami Orchestra. True, that it was composed of old men but surely that wasn't why you didn't enjoy the concert. I believe you are a listener like me, the program must be composed of your favorites before you really like it. After I had written last nite, I heard a radio program of music from Disney's *Fantasia*. — "Nutcracker Suite" and "Ave Maria." It was truly wonderful. I was in a melancholy mood anyway, and that did more to improve my condition. It doesn't hurt though because people realize more about life when they allow themselves a chance to think. I love you —

I couldn't help but to feel awed by the prices you quoted concerning liquor. If bourbon and coke cost as high as a $1.00 a throw, I'd have to be a millionaire to get both of us lit. I don't blame people for taking their parties indoors. It seems to be the sanest and cheapest thing to do. Lord, Woman, do you recall how we could throw $10 on the bar, pick up change (not much!) and still walk away feeling high. I don't enjoy liquor that much and yet I'll spend $16 for a bottle of rot gut over here. But we expect it here but surely not at home. Looks like Papa Mike will have to bring home a case, so that we can entertain our friends at home. Oh, well, I'd rather do that at home, wouldn't you? But I'm sure we'll find an angle for that.

Darling, you are very much like Chicha on one score. She was speaking of Dan's early return and in turn she compared my time and Harry's time to Dan's. She realizes that she must continue to live as an army wife but she said she'll never be able to understand how they do some things. I'm in the service and I still don't understand their way. I just keep hoping that the Army doesn't forget that I don't live over here.

Mac and I were having a discussion one day with which I disagreed wholeheartedly. He said that there wasn't one letter which he received from his wife which didn't include something mushy in it. Not mushy so much as it spoke words of love. I told him that it wasn't easy to think of so many different things to say. After all in a world of so many pent up emotions, people had to alleviate that condition by words. It was their only way out. You've heard me say that so often. It is our duty and manner to understand when, why and how these things are said. After all, how else can we speak to each other? Do you believe I'm right?

Well, Sweet One, must close for now. Give my love to Susie. Take care of yourself. Happy Easter. I miss you so — May God Bless You. — Eternally, Mike.

The following is from the unpublished history of the 52nd Troop Carrier Wing, *At Home and Abroad (Mostly Abroad) with the 52nd Troop Carrier Wing*: *May 1943-May 1945*, p. 38:

> Once again the 52nd TC Wing reverted to its work horse status and ran its freight missions deeper and deeper into Germany. Easter, 1 April, came and went and the wild rumors that peace would be declared turned out to be nothing more than rumors.
>
> We were grieved this month of April [*actually April 3*] to learn that Col. Harvey A. Berger, former Wing A-5 officer, subsequently Group Commander of the 316th TC GP. was officially reported dead as a result of enemy action while in flight in an advanced area of Germany in an A/C loaded with 114 cans of gasoline. The loss of Col. Berger is impossible to put into words, but all who knew him feel it keenly.

April 4, 1945 [*Wednesday*]

Hi Sugar Plum:

Finished all our green ink, so you must now be content with this morbid, lifeless color. I've been going like a bat out of Hell, thank God. I got back early enough to wash up decently; I was starting to feel "scroungy." All showered and shaved, I feel good. To make everything complete, mail is coming thru' beautifully, and quickly. I've got so many of your letters to answer that I hardly know where to start. First of all I want to tell you that I love you very much.

You spoke of our plans for our library. For a while I think it is best to store everything away. We will have to travel lightly for a while. I hardly know what to plan any more. It seems so easy to put everything off for the last minute. It seems so difficult for me to offer any suggestions any more. How vague so many things appear. All I know definitely, truthfully, honestly, decently and all the "lys" you can think of — is you and you and I. Besides that all material angles are blurred and so apt to reconstruction and change. We will see in due time.

Darling, since you are heading back to KC and it will be a good while before I get back, you'll probably lose all of that tan. I'd like to see that cute home plate design you have. Why didn't you find some secluded spot and strip. You needn't worry then, you'd have a complete tan. Besides, the way you talk — Susie can laugh every time you undress — I shan't say any more but pardon my drooling.

Bette, I think I have a vague idea of how you were dressed when I saw you last. (All things considered.) I think you were wearing a sort of white or tan sort of heavy dress — I wouldn't swear to it. We were both so tired. I remember you were sitting on your suit case and I was playing with your hair. It looked like we had given each other a hard time — hard but wonderful. Honestly, Darling, if we get that close to each other, I don't care if you do a Lady Godiva on me. Anything, My Dearest, as long as you are in it. It will probably be warm enough, you could even wear a pair of shorts. Lewd, aren't I?

Looks like Washington and I are running a close race. Unfortunately, I hate to outdo the guy. To ease your mind a bit, I shaved off that mustache. I still have a Hell of a job trimming Lil' Moe's for him. Bette, do you intend to go back to Mastin's when you get back to KC? No reason for asking, just wondering. Just imagined that you'd want to keep busy until the "Ingrisano" comes roaring in. Damn, I wish they'd send me home so we could arrive to some definite conclusion — So it must be!

I'm afraid I've never read Tarkington. There are many authors who I've missed. You mentioned that you'd like to read *Brave Men*. I don't call it a must but Pyle does recapture a lot that is common to us. However, it might be difficult for you to catch some of his themes and ideas. Personally, I'd rather you stick to the fiction — why distort your ideas of war and its outlying reasons and effects.

Darling, you amaze me more and more each day. I never cease to learn more and more about you. I know that your manner of dress always fascinated me but I didn't know that you knew so much of the technicalities. Above all, I didn't know that you did any modeling. These Germain gowns sound like something but the prices you quote sound a bit out of our line, don't you think? Regardless of what styles, I've always been a stickler for simplicity. I'll let you handle that end of the family.

Ah! Yes, those good old HS days. Personally, I never went around taking figures on pregnancy. As a matter of fact, our gang never had any sort of scandal — that couldn't be handled. I've seen a few rather trying and close affairs — I shan't say more on that score. As for the difference of maturity, I don't know. Since I've always been a part of big city life, it was difficult to pinpoint any thing of that sort. One had to be a sort of "hot rock" to keep up with the various changes. The depression took a good chunk out of my social life. I never had any dough. Cigarette money was scarce — had to play gigolo for a while to exist. Horrible, isn't it?

Gosh, Bette, I can't go on any more. I'm really getting pretty tired. The old eyes and the head are tired. I'm really sorry, Dear. Getting old. Give my love to Susie. Morpheus, let me feel thy sting!

Good night, Bette. Take care of yourself. I love you and miss you terribly. May God Bless You. Pray for me. Ever Yours, Mike.

52nd Wing History, p. 38: "There were no troop carrier combat operations in April though one was planned, code name EFFECTIVE designed to assist the 12th Army Group across the upper Rhine. This operation was scrubbed within an hour of the receipt of the field order." Thank God.

April 5, 1945 [*Thursday*]

Hello Lovely One,

I've been writing all afternoon; I'm sure I'm due for a writer's cramp soon. Must have smoked a pack of cigarettes. Answered little Stinky's [*Mickey Petruzillo*] letter and a few others. The kid is growing up; it is a pleasure to hear from the little brat. Threatens to kick my brains out when I get home but I told him that you have already asked for the exclusive rights for that privilege. News of the gang, Lil Moe [*Dan Emery*] has a birthday coming up on the 13th of the month and he has started to celebrate already. He's been at it 3 days now but I suspect he'll quit soon. He and John went out on a bicycle sortie while I was gone and when I got back, John had a fractured elbow. Seems that the bike got a bit too drunk for him. Moe fell off his a million times but has no visible bruises. You'll have to pardon me, Dearest, for not mentioning name[*s*] but it can't be done. You'll have to be content with nicknames. At any rate, you can see that the guys still live, though I sometimes wonder how. To eliminate any thoughts you may have, I am not joining Moe in his celebration. I celebrated my birthday a bit royally so I've decided to shape up a bit. I've got one of those unusual holidays and I've done as much as I can. Letter writing, except for a tired hand, is the most relaxing. I love you —

Had a Hell of a dream last night. By some fancy, Moe, John and I were at a sort of conference. One of us was to be picked by FDR, [*Winston*] Churchill and [*Joseph*] Stalin to represent the 3 nations in an interview with the Pope. I was selected and the other two were to be my men-in-waiting. But before we left, we had to go before the Big 3 and get a final OK. We had to join a big pilgrimage that was going to Moscow. Of course, we were the big shots of the parade. So they decked us out in formal afternoon dress but instead of top hats, we were given soft hats with a long feather on the left side — somewhat of a Tyrolean style; they were light gray color. Finally, the procession started. We had a long way to go. We were a bit late and so the line was well ahead of us. After 20 miles we still did not catch up — so John said, "The Hell with this, I'm going back for a drink!" After a little more distance, Moe did the same thing. So I started to run so that I could join the procession; when I got there I asked someone if this was the line to Moscow. He said, "No, we are going to Berlin; your line started on that last big road." The last I recall, I was still running. Thank God, I woke up — when I did I was covered head to foot with sweat. Someone had forgotten to open my window after I had fallen asleep. — Gad! I was dry, tired, and sweaty. Next time I have a dream like that, I'm going to fly! Who's Crazy?

I wonder what causes things like that. It couldn't have been something I ate — I hardly had much supper. To beat it all, I was so tired, I should have died but I was most restless. I always do hate the beginning of the month. It seems that I am always at my worst. Someday, I'm going to go thru an intense study of such a variety of moods. By that time, I shall [*have*] forgotten all of that rot and not care.

Gosh, Darling, I wrote that last page so quickly that when I stopped short I realized that I had raced thru so many ideas. Just like applying the brakes. Gosh, Bette, you know I love you so very much. Nope, I just didn't think of that. Just wanted to say that much earlier but my other idea captivated me so. So it must be and I am going to close. I still haven't finished answering your letters. Give me time, I'll get down to all of it.

Good-bye for now. Give my love to Susie. Take care of yourself — you Lovely Blonde — Miss you so — May God Bless You. Eternally yours, Mike.

April 5, 1945 [*Thursday*]

Hello Darling,

Right after I finished writing to you, I sort of rested in my sack but my ole brain was working double time. I closed my eyes and relived a thousand years with you. Not all of my thoughts were of the past, many of them wafted me clearly thru the future years. It is amazing how many different things that can pass thru a man's brain, especially when there is nothing else to occupy the cells; the music is inspiring and the weather is wonderful. I could even visualize you sitting among the white clouds and blue sky. I was thrilled and chilled — heated and frozen, inert and potent — so much and yet so little and you were the bottom of it all. You know, Darling, the days get long here — we will have daylight for many hours yet and it is 8:PM. The days are long and lonely and at times almost unbearable. Longer nights are easier to take because darkness can more easily cloak yearning; for Morpheus comes more eagerly. But long daylight lifts the veils and unbuttons one's sight and with sight comes the opening to intense thought. Can you see what I am trying to say? I miss you, Bette, Darling, miss you and need you more than you'll ever know. True your words when you say that our desires will never be satisfied until we are together again.

I was especially warmed by your statement of "purring like a kitten." It will be a content feeling for you and I. You hit the nail on the head, I didn't think anyone would grasp how I felt. Relaxation and above all slowing up are important. I couldn't ask for better company to help me along the road.

That shopping spree that you speak of sounds wonderful but you make me sound almost sissified. Believe me, though, I do miss a lot of things. I'll probably seem like a baby in a toy shop. Sometimes wonder if I won't make an ass of myself.

Say cut it out, Bette, you make me sound like a hero beyond reproach. Least of all, I care little what people say but I cannot help but to be short-tempered with people that refuse to see simple fact. Oh well, it is just as well not to worry about it. Above all, I like your statement that you'll wait if I'm gone for years. I don't think it will be that bad but it is great to hear. If it is that many years, you'll have to accept me in a strait jacket.

Well, Dan and Gert finally did it. They were married on the 25th of March. Fr. Tom officiated. I should send them a congratulatory message. . . . Lou and Sally celebrated their 3rd anniversary on the 28th of March, the same day I celebrated my 24th anniversary.

I am sorry that my letter fell so flat this afternoon. I couldn't explain the reaction very easily and I know I did a messy job of it. But I did feel that melancholy mood coming over me and I didn't want you to notice it. However, I can't conceal such things from you so you notice I told you about it in my very first paragraphs. Darling, you are so much a part of me that I can't exclude hardly a word. Many times, I will revert from form and leave it to myself but actually such instances are rare. But I'll bet that letter sounded a bit queer. Let alone the dream sounded fantastic but the rest of my tone sounded too flat. I knew that right after I had written the letter. I had to make up for it, so you lucky person, I showed up again tonight. Now, I can close.

Good night, Darling, miss you and love you terribly. (Almost horribly!)

Cheerio, Ole gal. May God Bless You. Writ by hand — Yours, Mike.

April 6, 1945 [*Friday*]

Good Evening, Darling,

I had meant to write earlier in the evening but Mac and I got into a Hell of an interesting conversation and it is past 10 PM now. We were talking of that far distant future—the day all of us will be in civvy clothes again. He kinda figures I've got a good deal at Sears [*my pre-war employer*]. I figure the same thing but time will tell. So you see you must be content with a short missile this evening.

I am extremely cheered by the fine mail service that we are getting now. One can almost expect some sort of mail every night. Shades of the good old days. The time period is excellent, too. I've received letters from you as late as the 28th of March. It sorta brings a guy closer to people. I love you.

Tony asked me to look up a buddy of his that is over here now. I found his outfit but not him. It seems that he had a little misfortune and his plane was shot down and he was forced to bail out. He is OK but I guess the experience sort of shook him up. He is at rest camp now. Perhaps, some day soon, our paths will cross — Tony says he's a Hell of a fine Joe, — that's good enough for me.

I got my mitts on a copy of the March edition of *Reader's Digest*. I spent most of last evening reading it from cover to cover. It was enjoyable but I found it most unfortunate when I was rustled out of bed at 6 AM. The extra sleep would have come in handy. But I guess I can sacrifice a little sleep for a touch of education. The articles in that magazine are not only condensed but in their condensation, they add a touch of reading that is unequaled in any sort of literature.

I haven't seen *A Tree* [**Grows in Brooklyn**] but I can very readily imagine that it could not quite equal the book. No human can enact the power of the written word. Even the written word must be accepted in the same mood that the author meant it to be — no person is like unto another. The picture may touch the surface and do a good job of portraying a sort of character but it cannot fully uncover a person's soul. Just as love cannot be put into words, actions or personalities, it must be a consolidation of the three plus many other minute details that are not easily seen but are ever present. Wow! There I go again. Think I'll ever be an author?

Say, Sissy, so you need oil to tan. I don't know about baby oil or of olive oil and iodine.

I always figured that as soon as you wash off the oil, the sun benefits leave, too. Personally, of course, just black me, I depend on the natural skin oils to soot me up. I'm just a plain ole nigger anyhow — The sun never bothers me, only changes my complexion —

Sorry, My Dear, but I must close. Have another one of those early jobs, so I think I'll "peel" off. Give my love to Susie. Take care of yourself. I love you and miss you — May God Bless You. Yours, Mike.

April 9, 1945 [*Monday*]

My Darling,

You must forgive me for not writing but I have been as busy as Hell. First of all, I had an excellent chance to see Harry and I wasted no time whatever. It was imperative that I see him because there were so many things to talk about and I wanted to get a few things done. It was necessary for me to hitch a ride and in all I did very well and covered about 40 kilos in about an hour. It was worth the trouble. I got to his place about 7 PM and the first thing was to wash., etc. I felt like a bum. I was carrying a 3-day growth of beard, my coveralls were lousy and I was in dire need of a shower. After we were fed, he showed me the place. There was nothing lower than a Capt. there; I hobnobbed with rank but since it didn't bother me, I didn't care. It was a beautiful place that was formerly owned by the Rothschilds. Herman Goering used it as a retreat whenever he was in the vicinity. The chateau was beautiful and the surrounding grounds not only were enormous but wonderfully free. In the rear of this spacious lawn was a 60' by 35' swimming pool. The entire set up was one that enabled me to breathe freely as a free man. We sat up and talked until 5 AM. We'd sip cognac and water and talk. I had about 2 hours rest, had breakfast, and Harry drove me back to the field that I was stopping at. He's a great guy, Bette, and Oh so much in love. In part, I felt sorry for him because, in his eagerness to please my sister, he has to bypass a lot of his pleasures. What I mean is that he wants to comply with all of Lucy's wishes, — their plans are mostly hers. I must talk to her and tell her that she is wrong. The conversation made me realize that you and I are mutually happy because we have planned or wish to plan together. It is hard to understand but I shan't say a word until I can see Lucy personally. . . .

Yes, Darling, we made more history. I got another crack at combat [*OPERATION VARSITY, March 24, 1945*]. It wasn't as easy as we had hoped but it is always best to accept the worst at a time like that. I got off fairly easy but even so, I was afraid as I usually am. I may appear to be a hero, but when Jerry tries to give me presents, I don't accept them smilingly. Just a bit reluctantly, I'm afraid.

Bette, I love you. You'll have to be content with short letters for a while. I find that my time these days is as limited as gold. Lord knows, I do want to write infinitely. It isn't that I feel blah but I feel so wonderfully happy that words do not have the force nor the power to express myself. All I do is pray and my prayers are slowly but most surely being answered. I've come thru everything without a scratch. Although my nerves are edgy, they are settling to normalcy. It takes very little to do that. But so it must be.

This month, the 1st to be exact, was the anniversary of our meeting. It has been wonderful, My Dear. Each day apart has meant so much to us. Our patience has held so wonderfully, I know it cannot be too long before we will reap the fruits of our love. God has
been good to us. I know that He will continue to be so. I've always remembered that New
York is pretty in the Spring. As it is, I take each season of the year and dream how wonderful it would be to spend each of them with you. We had Spring in KC and Summer in
Ft. Wayne, just think what it will be to have 365 days, every Spring, every Summer, every
Fall, and every Winter together for the rest of our lives. You are my most wonderful dream
come true; you have made everything so easy for me. Please God, that I can repay you for
all this happiness. I've often said it, Bette, Spring will be a little late this year, but late or
early, our hearts will forever feel the blossom time of the year. What beautiful music we
will make together. I love you.

There I go again. 'Tis best that I say good night. I am sending this to your KC address
because by that time you will be home again.

Give Susie, my love and thank her for taking such good care of you. Lord knows, I'd
like that job myself.

Good night, Sweet Princess. Take care of yourself. May God Bless You. Your Patient
Lover. Mike.

April 10, 1945 [*Tuesday*]

[*On April 10, 1945, a V-Mail form letter was sent*]

From: S/Sgt. M. N. Ingrisano 12129759
316 TCG-37 TCS
APO 133 c/o PM, New York.

TO: Miss Bette L. Hill
4908 Brookside Blvd
Kansas City (2) Missouri
April 10th 1945

Effective immediately and until further notice please do not send any more mail to me
at the address given below. I will advise you promptly when mail should be resumed and
will give you my proper address. I cannot do so now for military reasons.

[*signed*]: Michael N. Ingrisano Jr.
S/Sgt. Michael N. Ingrisano-12129759
37 Troop Carrier Squadron
316 Troop Carrier Group
A.P.O. No. 133 c/o Postmaster
New York, New York

52nd TC Wing History, p. 38: "At the moment all groups of the 52nd TC Wing, the 61st, 313th, 314th, 315th, 349th [*Troop Carrier Groups*] were stationed in France, with the exception of the veteran 316th TC GP, now at Cottesmore awaiting transportation to the Zone of the Interior."

April 13, 1945 [*Friday*]

My Darling,

    I must beg your forgiveness for not having written for the last few days but I've been so damn busy I haven't been able to do anything. I miss you so when I don't write. I hate any circumstances that keep me from doing so. And I still have some of your March mail to answer. So I'll see what kind of job I can do, I love you.

    In your letter of the 25th, you mentioned that we were making history again and yet in your letter of the 23rd, you mention that the newspapers are writing of another possible airborne invasion. It is bad enough to have Jerry waiting for us but when people start to telegraph our punches, then glory! I can't understand why censorship doesn't cause some sort of restriction on what people say in the papers. Enough people are losing their lives these days without helping them along. But I guess wars are won in NY and Los Angeles, etc. behind some big desks. Yes, we made history — some of us are fortunate enough to talk about it.

    You mentioned something about clarifying some of the mysteries in *To Have and Have Not*. I've already mentioned in one of my previous letters that the picture and book are totally unlike that one would never notice any relationship except for the title and author. In the book, Harry Morgan is 43 years old, has a wife 45 and 3 female children. He is minus an arm and as ornery a bastard as you'd ever want to meet. As I said before that book was one of Hemingway's dirtiest. Perhaps it's the money angle but I can't see why he allowed so much distortion. Fortunately, for the picture, the actors and actresses did a most creditable job for their parts but I am sure Hays would not have liked the original story. "Slim" isn't even in the book unless one terms her as one of the many whores who intermittently pops in and out. So be it!

    Darling, why do you worry so about your freckles and mole. I think both of them are cute. I know that the mole is attractive. The freckles, I don't know but surely anything looks good on you. You can count about 6 freckles on each of my shoulders. They came from sun blisters when I was about 10 years old. But hell that hardly bothers me. Life, love and the pursuit of happiness. Ah, Yes, so very important.

    Wow! Thanks for the great big kiss. That lipstick looks edible. As a matter of fact, a guy could get ideas awfully easy. Tell Susie she must learn to keep her feet dry. I've seen the self same thing happen often. It may appear tragic but it is funny, isn't it?

    I see by your letter of the 23rd that you tried one of my stunts. Creme de Menthe is a dangerous royale. Personally, I'd rather use it merely for a mix or for an opening for a heavy session. It really isn't awful green stuff. But mix it with bourbon and egad, what a result or need I tell you any more. Unfortunately, I wasn't at hand to ease your aching tummy — There are a few questions in your letter of the 23rd which I shan't answer. Length of service is indeterminable. One spends as much time as is warranted of him. Once it is over, then he thinks little of what has gone on before. We, as people, forget easily because we are of such stature. We are like that because everything is made that much easier for us. We do everything with our hearts and as hard as we know how. Waste, destruction and death are easily overcome by happiness, love and contentment. Why not? Life is too short to let the minor things worry us.

Darling, I must close. Getting a bit tired. Do not worry about me. I am doing fine. Time still marches on. Surely it hasn't forgotten us — we must deserve something for all this past time. Give my love to Susie. Take care of yourself. I love you and miss you terribly. May God Bless You — Love, Mike.

April 16, 1945 [*Monday*]

Hello Darling,

Read recently of that plane crash at Morgantown, PA [*or was it West Virginia?*]. It frightens the Hell out of me knowing that you are flying from place to place around the States. I know that it is a safe practice but accidents do happen and they do scare me. I sweat a lot more for other people. Don't have the time for myself, just a little too busy and can't help but feel that I am that unimportant.

The weather is so beautiful it fits perfectly with my mood — Not like this ink but an elation so great that I cannot find the words to explain it. I love you, My Dearest, I love you so very much.

The mail is coming in, in a sort of static manner but I don't mind it too much. I find it so hard to find time to write these days that I cannot in turn expect much attention.

Yes, Bette, Easter was our only holiday together but really we have lived everyone of them together, regardless of the distance. If I recall correctly, I was a bit naughty that day. As it was, we couldn't help but to stay on the right side of the track or am I thinking of another day? At any rate, the show was good.

Glad to hear that you met an old buddy. But I suppose altho' you both bemoaned the fact that you are still spinsters, you have one jump on her. It won't be long after I hit home that you can desert the ranks. I couldn't think of so much beauty being wasted. It will be great working together. There really isn't too much to be accomplished because in each other we have our happiness and love; but materially speaking, I haven't a fright in the world. We will accomplish a lot on that score together. The world will be a nice playground.

Guess I made a mistake — I thought we met on the 1st. Forgive me, Bette, I must be getting vague or sumpin'.

I was rather surprised to hear that the servicemen are taking a beating in Miami. That's one reason I'm glad that New York is so big. It is hard to keep tabs on anyone there. I shan't get nasty but I don't think you and I need worry about curfews and such.

The thing that makes me feel rather content is your manner of discussing "in law" problems. Tho' it is all a ticklish position for all concerned, I worry very little. I have so much faith in us that I need not worry. I realize that my first duties are to you. Believe me, I know it only too well. As I have often said, I've woven my whole life about you; need I look to either side when my goal is you in my eyes. Be assured, My Dear, that my love is not a divided one. What an ass of a man I'd be if I allowed myself to be pushed about like a chess piece. I love you and I will always.

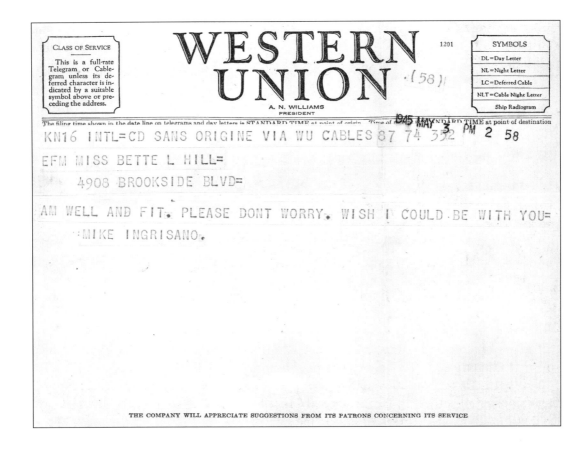

Good night, Bette. Take care of yourself. Give my love to Susie. I miss you so. May God Bless You. — Love, Mike.

April 21, 1945 [*Tuesday*]

Good Evening, My Darling

You must forgive me for not writing for such a long while. I warned you in my previous letters that my letters would be rather scarce. I can see from your latest letters that you are now comfortably settled in KC again. Above all, I am glad that you were able to rectify all the complications that had set in. It frightens me to think that it would necessitate a tracer to scare you down. As long as you are in KC, it will be easy to contact you. Funny that both of us fret so much about such things. Gosh, Darling, I guess we aren't to blame. It has been so long that I know that neither of us wants to waste any time apart. I love you so very much.

I received the letter you sent from St. Louis. There are other letters that I have to answer but I hardly know where to start. First of all you mentioned about Mother not being able to make our wedding. Surely, there is a solution. In the face of all the circumstances,

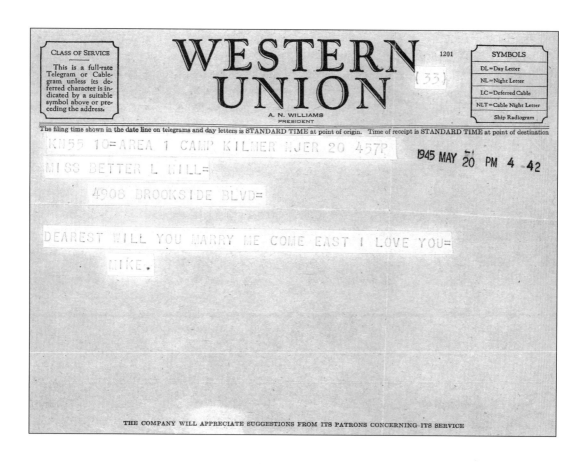

Darling, since you are the only one she has and I will be taking you away from Susie, don't you think I ought to finance the traveling expenses, etc.? After all, I've done so little and you have done so much for me. I am sure that although I don't know how much I have at home, I can certainly lay out the money. It will be no trouble to wire money to you. I realize that you have expended a lot and the stuff doesn't grow on trees. After all, Darling, you mustn't be afraid to ask me for any sort of small favors. It wouldn't be right not to have Susie East for the big day. Hell! I wouldn't think of it any other way. Don't let it worry you; we can arrange anything. Everything is tentative and Hell I don't know what to say but regardless, I'll send money as soon as I can, which immediately after [*I get to the States*]. Don't let those little things bother you. If you keep that up that golden hair will turn to silver.

Honey, I must close. I have to get up at 5:00 AM tomorrow, so I do want to get some sleep. I'll try to do a bit better on this letter writing. Don't worry about me. I am perfectly healthy and extremely happy. I do love you so very much and miss you so. Give my love to Susie and tell her she must come to our wedding.

Take care of yourself. May God Bless You. Love, Mike.

I do believe that this early rising was for my last overseas flight in my aircraft, serial 43-48293, 25F. We turned these planes over to the next users. I cannot recall if it was to the British or a U.S. troop carrier squadron.

52nd Wing History, pp. 38-39: "This was the month [*April 1945*] too the entire world had occasion to mourn the sudden death of the President of the United States. Not long afterwards, on the 29th, the assassination of Mussolini was announced as well as the questionable heroic death, 1 May, of Hitler."

KN16 INTL = CD SANS ORIGINE VIA WU CABLES 87 74 352
EFM MISS BETTE L. HILL =
 4908 BROOKSIDE BLVD =

AM WELL AND FIT. PLEASE DONT WORRY. WISH I COULD BE WITH YOU= MIKE INGRISANO.

Received in Kansas City, Missouri, at 2:58 PM on May 3, 1945.

The 37th Squadron Morning Report for May 10, 1945, records that "Personnel departed Rutland, England, enroute to the Z.I." I recall our train passing through cheering crowds in London, still joyful over the end of war in Europe. In Southampton we boarded the liberty ship USS *General J. R. Brooke* bound for New York and the Statue of Liberty. On May 20, the Morning Report stated: "Perosnnel arrived in Zone of Interior, United States, for Furlough, Rest & Recuperation. Health and Morale Excellent."

KN55 10 = AREA 1 CAMP KILMER NJER 20 457p
MISS BETTE L. HILL
 4908 BROOKSIDE BLVD =

DEAREST WILL YOU MARRY ME COME EAST I LOVE YOU = MIKE.

Received in Kansas City, Missouri, at 4:42 PM on May 20, 1945.

Epilogue

*B*ETTE AND I were married on May 30, 1945, Decoration Day then, before the altar at Our Lady of Lourdes Church in Brooklyn, New York. We were married by my brother, Father Tom, O. Carm. (Carmelite Order). Our best man was another brother, Captain (Doctor) Lou Ingrisano; and his wife, Sally Koch, was the maid-of-honor. Our small wedding party was held at the Astor Hotel Roof, with Sammy Kaye and his orchestra entertaining the patrons.

Despite the oft-written wishes to celebrate our marriage with a glorious honeymoon, we settled for a one-room apartment in Fayetteville, North Carolina, where what was left of the 316th Troop Carrier Group was stationed at nearby Pope Field. Most of us had enough points (credited for overseas service) to merit immediate discharge.

But the war was still going on in the Pacific Theater. The thinking, I believe, was that the invasion of the mainland of Japan would have been a paper copy of the invasion of France in June 1944. Troop Carrier planes carrying airborne troops would drop before the seaborne troops to ensure a foothold on the beaches. We were practicing with the 82nd Airborne Division much as we had prior to the Sicily, France, and Holland invasions — that is, when we were not dropping these troopers for War Bond Drives.

Fortunately for all of us, the atom bombs — dropped on Hiroshima August 6 and Nagasaki August 9 — negated the possibility of a slaughter of American troops in an invasion of Japan. On August 14, 1945, Japan surrendered. I was on a cross-country flight, and happened to be in Memphis, Tennessee, on that memorable day. I was discharged at Fort Bragg, Fayetteville, on September 3, 1945, three years to the date on which I had enlisted at the recruiting office at Whitehall Street in New York City.

In our letters, Bette and I had often discussed our future plans. Where to live? How to support ourselves and our future family? What would be our long-range plans?

Where to live? The years I had spent in my little radio compartment aboard my planes seemed to have infused in my psyche a shred of claustrophobia. But I did not want to return to the "big city" where I had spent my life. Bette still lived in a small apartment in Kansas City, Missouri. So we decided that that would provide enough open spaces for me to rid myself of the "abnormal fear of being in an enclosed or narrow space."

How to support ourselves and our future family? I was working for Sears, Roebuck and Company in New York City when I enlisted. During my service, I was kept on the roles as an active employee. So when I moved to Kansas City, I applied for employment with Sears. I was told, however, that all their positions locally were reserved for their service-men-employees.

This decision virtually dictated/formed our destiny. In October 1945, I was accepted and enrolled, under the GI Bill of Rights, at Rockhurst College (now University), where I began, after the semester had already started, my studies for a Bachelor of Science degree in English. (To attain a Bachelor of Arts, then, one needed formal training in one of the classical languages. I had had Latin in high school and decided not to continue along that route.)

My classes were on an accelerated basis which would have, if I succeeded, gotten me a degree in three years. Since the GI Bill paid all tuition, it took care of my education; but the living allotment was, I believe, about $120 per month. So I got a job as a salesman at a local liquor store. I worked every night from 7:00 p.m. to 10:00 p.m. On Saturdays, since I was taking classes, I worked from 1:00 p.m. to midnight. Bette, in turn, with her mother, worked at home designing and sewing clothes. Civilian married life, school and work demands, as well as a limited budget tamed my wartime drinking habits. With an added resolve to buy a book for every bottle, drinking reverted to normal social bounds without having to add an extra room for the library. Bette and I did not quit smoking until 1969, but we managed it together, "cold turkey."

Incidentally, we never had the good fortune of building a family.

What about long-range planning? Before I enrolled at Rockhurst, I had had an interview with the sports editor at the *Kansas City Star*. He advised me to get an education and then come back to his office. During one summer break at Rockhurst, Bette and I took off for Chicago, where I had written for an interview at the Medill School of Journalism at Northwestern University. The interview was short and chilling! We did manage to visit with one of my old crew chiefs, Ed Tuman, and his family — a friendship we maintained over the years. While some would be closer than others, to this day there are strong bonds among all the surviving veterans of the 316th Troop Carrier Group. And I still correspond with the British widow of "Short Sam" — Major Arthur Hughes, — a friendship begun that weekend in Lille, France, in 1944.

I received my BS in 1948. I had decided that I would go into teaching in higher education. So, I had applied and been accepted at the State University of Iowa in Iowa City. We left for Iowa City without taking the time to attend the baccalaureate service. While I resumed my studies, Bette got a job at a local store selling and buying dresses. I received my Master of Arts degree in Language and Literature in August 1949. My thesis was on F. Scott Fitzgerald.

I then continued my education by entering the doctoral program at the University of Kansas. I had heard that that institution had not, at that time, granted a Ph.D. in English for many years. I was given a teaching assistantship in the English Department for which I was paid $1,200 per year. Bette got a job at the Student Union as a cashier and general assistant.

My schedule was teaching basic English to college freshman and to engineering students, and a course of teaching "English for Foreign Students." This was a relatively new field in that period. According to the staff, of all the new teaching assistants, I was best suited for this class because I was a hyphenated-American (my parents had both been born in Italy). I continued to teach that course for the three years I was at Kansas.

While still concentrating on studies in literature, I also took tutored classes in history from Dr. James C. Malin. I was also asked by the Greek organization on the campus to be their advisor. As a hyphenated-American, a World War II veteran, a pacifist, and harboring no biases (the African-American fraternity and the Jewish fraternity both accepted my advice, and in the former case asked Bette and me to chaperone their dances), I ran into problems with the department's chairman. After three years, my teaching assistantship was cancelled.

We left Lawrence, Kansas, for Washington, D.C., where I enrolled in the Georgetown University School of Foreign Service. My GI Bill had run out so I had to finance my education. Six weeks into the course, the advisor at Georgetown told me that I was wasting my time, and since I already had two degrees, I should apply directly to the State Department. Bette and I were both interviewed for a possible position as a cultural attaché in Thailand or India (I had taught students from these lands at Kansas, and it was determined that Bette would also be of help in the foreign community).

I waited but never heard from State, and I lost my tuition at Georgetown because I had spent six weeks there. In the meantime while waiting for State, I took a job as a day laborer.

The mystery of my unacceptability was eventually solved by a woman at a personnel agency in D.C. After reviewing my resume and making a few phone calls, she found that my career, any career, was being hampered by a "black ball" from the University of Kansas. Fortunately, she told me about it. After three years of digging ditches, and with the help of confirming letters from colleagues at the University, I was able to eradicate any stains from my previous records. Throughout all of this, Bette continued to work. As a team we managed to live respectably.

We finally settled in Virginia where I eventually went into public affairs in private industry, and then with the U.S. Customs Services as a public affairs officer, manager, and historian. I retired in 1988.

Just before she died in 1985, Bette had advised me to not quit my job, not sell the house, and to remarry. Her mother, who had lived with us, had died in 1984 from the same type of cancer which proved fatal for Bette.

I have taken her advice on all counts. In 1986, I married Nancy Helen Day. Having worked half a career for the government, she happily took up "homemaking" as an unpaid early retirement. Nancy and I were married in Purcellville, Virginia, to accommodate my aging mother. As they had 40 years earlier, Father Tom married us, and Dr. Lou was our best man. Nancy's sister, Kathie Latham, was our maid-of-honor.

Nancy, a native of Buffalo, New York, is the great-granddaughter of Gustave Dey, who immigrated from Konigsburg, Prussia, sometime in the early 1850s. Gus Dey joined the U.S. Army in 1854, and served honorably until 1865. When I retired in 1988, with my background in history and an interest in the Civil War, I researched Dey's military career. The result of this research was my first book entitled, *An Artilleryman's War: Gus Dey and the 2nd United States Artillery* (Shippensburg: White Mane Publishing Company, 1998). I continue to write, and I have reviewed books for a Civil War newspaper for the past seven years.

There are not enough words to express my gratitude to those who have believed in me, nor can I find enough words to thank God for all the gifts He has bestowed upon me, including sparing my life in World War II. And so I end as I began. And nothing is said — but silent prayers of gratitude and of love.

Index

by Paula S. LaCoe